Human Sexuality

The Search for Understanding

Human Sexuality

The Search for Understanding

David Knox
East Carolina University

West Publishing Company
St. Paul   *New York*   *Los Angeles*   *San Francisco*

Production credits: Copyediting Elaine Linden
Design Janet Bollow
Composition Carlisle Graphics
Position Drawings Heather Preston
Two-color artwork Barbara Hack Barnett
Four-color artwork Marsha Dohrmann
Part and chapter opening art © 1983 Eleanor Dickinson
Cover: *Picking Flowers;* Auguste Renoir; National Gallery of Art, Washington; Ailsa Mellon Bruce Collection 1970

Library of Congress Cataloging in Publication Data

Knox, David, 1943–
   Human sexuality.
   Bibliography: p.
   Includes index.
   1. Sex. I. Title.
HQ21.K64   1984   306.7   83-16711
ISBN 0-314-77999-X

Photo Credits

5 Stock, Boston: Peter Vandermark. **9** Stock, Boston: Owen Franken. **17** Stock, Boston: Hazel Hankin. **45** Reuter Photos/FPG. **47** Stock, Boston: Richard Sobol. **61** Stock, Boston: Robert V. Eckert, Jr. **61** Stock, Boston: Jean-Claude Lejeune. **61** Aster and Bill Magee/FPG. **115** Courtesy Body By Soloflex. **121** Stock, Boston: Charles Gatewood. **121** Stock, Boston: Peter Menzel. **129** Stock, Boston: Ellis Herwig. **147** Bradley Green. **149** The News World/FPG. **170** William Touhi/FPG. **172** Stock, Boston: David A. Krathwohl. **178** Stock, Boston: Frank Siteman. **178** Stock, Boston: Peter Vandermark. **178** Stock, Boston: Peter Vandermark. **212** Stock, Boston: Hazel Hankin. **217** Stock, Boston: Jean Boughton. **237** Stock, Boston: Barbara Alper. **247** Stock, Boston: Christopher S. Johnson. **273** Stock, Boston: Jeff Albertson. **273** Stock, Boston: Charles Kennard. **274** Carolyn A. McKeone/FPG. **299** Stock, Boston: Gregg Mancuso. **305** Stock, Boston: Peter Vandermark. **311** Stock, Boston: Mike Mazzaschi. **324** Photograph by Scott F. Johnson. **325** Courtesy Dr. William E. Hartman. **327** Photo by Ella Mazel. **334** Stock, Boston: Bohdan Hrynewych. **344** American Medical Systems, Inc. **358–364, 367** Center for Disease Control, Atlanta. **391** Carolyn A. McKeone/FPG. **402** Stock, Boston: Charles Kennard. **405** Stock, Boston: Donald Dietz. **411, 412** Bradley Green. **420** Stock, Boston: Ellis Herwig. **423–425, 427** Bradley Green. **442** Jeffrey Grosscup. **447** Jeffrey Grosscup. **454** Stock, Boston: R.S. Spring-Daytona. **461** Stock, Boston: Charles Gatewood. **476** Stock, Boston: Jerry Howard. **482** Stock, Boston: Cary Wolinsky. **487** F. Lezus/FPG. **515** Douglas Baton. **537** Stock, Boston: Jim Harrison. **544** Stock, Boston: Lincoln Russell. **547** Stock, Boston: Elizabeth Hamlin. **550** Robert Spence. **557** Stock, Boston: Peter Menzel. **559** Stock, Boston: John Coletti; Judy S. Gelles.

To Frances, one of the last great ladies,
and to our children,
Lisa and Dave.

Contents in Brief

Contents

ix

Chapter Eight   *Orgasm*   *229*

Preface

Human sexuality, fascinating and complex, permeates our lives and our society. It colors our perceptions, self-concepts, and relationships with others. It provides the basis for our deepest attachments; it inspires poets; it is used to sell products. And it conspires with violence and anquish.

From prehistory to the present, men and women have sought to understand their sexuality. Yet its very power and importance have hindered this pursuit. Only in recent years has sexuality become an accepted area of serious scientific inquiry. The insights gained through this inquiry can help us achieve a better understanding of ourselves.

The book's purpose is twofold: to convey the current status of the inquiry into human sexuality and to provide the basis for a personal search for understanding. To achieve the first goal, we must become aware of the latest in physiological, psychological, and sociological research, and understand how the disciplines intertwine to explain sexual behavior. To achieve the second, we must become more aware of ourselves as sexual beings. And we must place our sexuality within the context of the core of human experience—obtaining self-knowledge, communicating and bonding with others, and procreating.

The book's organization reflects its goals. Part I provides the rationale and basis for the study of human sexuality. It explores the concepts of gender and examines the physiological basis of sexuality. In doing so, it offers a base from which to explore sexuality's broader dimensions.

Part II expands upon this base. It explores the social expression of sexuality, including our sexual ethics and attitudes; examines its individual expression; discusses the reasons for and consequences of its interpersonal expression; and explains its physical expression.

Enhancement of these expressions is the focus of Part III. This section examines the role of love, the purpose of fantasy, the meanings of sexual fulfillment, and the bases for its achievement. It presents sexual facts and dispels sexual myths. It explores sexual problems and their amelioration, and it discusses sexual health.

Part IV examines sexual variations. It first places "normality" within the context of society and time. It then discusses the incidence and consequences—individual and societal—of several variations—celibacy, homosexuality and bisexuality. It also explores the darker side of sexuality, discussing abuses such as rape, incest, sexual harassment and prostitution.

Part V places sexuality within the context of procreation. It explores the social influences on and personal reasons for having children, and examines the prevention of conception through contraception. Finally, it examines the consequences of parenting—its effect on each partner in the marriage and on the relationship itself.

Two general themes run throughout the text. The first is a theoretical framework based on social scripts and operant conditioning. This theme recognizes that while human sexuality has a physiological basis, its expression is primarily the result of learning. The second is a focus on personal decision making. This theme grows out of a recognition of the personal significance of sexual decisions. Few decisions have more effect on our lives than, for example, the decision to initiate a sexual relationship with a new partner, to use or not use contraceptives, or to avoid being victimized by such behavior as sexual harassment.

Yet our need to make educated, thoughtful decisions about such matters coincides with an abundance of sexual information that can confuse or mislead. As a result, few skills are more important to enhanced well-being than the ability to evaluate the worthiness and significance of this information.

To help readers acquire such skills, *Research Cautions* appear throughout the book. Research studies provide the basis for this text. But the *Research Cautions* feature acknowledges that most studies have one or more inherent limitations—an unrepresentative sample, no control group, or vaguely defined terminology. Still others may use a questionable research methodology. To alert the reader to these limitations and provide a foundation for understanding future research reports in the popular press, a logo appears in the margin next to the research cited. This feature is one of several designed to aid readers in effective decision making by helping them transfer objective knowledge into personal understanding.

Other important features include:

- *Self-Assessment Inventories.* Throughout the text, "My Sexuality" boxes provide opportunities for readers to assess their sexual attitudes and values. Readers seeking greater personal understanding can benefit from the sexual autobiography outline provided in Appendix C.
- *Reflections.* Throughout the text, case histories, examples and surveys, reflecting a variety of sexual preferences and orientations, summarize and personalize objective data.
- *Issues in Debate and Future Directions.* This feature acknowledges that to understand the study of human sexuality is to understand that profession-

als don't speak with one voice. They disagree on a multitude of issues. Special setions at the end of each chapter examine thirty-nine such controversial issues. An exploration of trends in sexual values and behaviors concludes these sections.

- *Illustrations and Photographs.* Special attention is paid to photos and illustrations to achieve utmost clarity. Four-color representations in the anatomy and sexual health sections enhance the readers' comprehension of physiological illustrations.

Acknowledgments

Although writing is often viewed as a singular effort, in truth, an author incurs a considerable debt. Some of this debt, such as that owed to the numerous researchers on whose work this book is based, is general. But much of it is of a more personal nature.

I am indebted to Bruce King, a physiological psychologist in the Department of Psychology at the University of New Orleans. He provided invaluable aid by writing Chapter Three on Basic Anatomy and ensuring the accuracy of the physiological material throughout the other chapters.

I am also indebted to a number of faculty who reviewed and commented extensively on the manuscript. Their suggestions substantially improved the final result. These reviewers include:

Spurgeon Cole
Joseph Colistro
Margaret Freese
Richard Hartley
Maggie Hayes
George Janzen
Betty Morrow

Marilyn Myerson, to whom I am especially grateful for an exceptionally detailed review.

Gary Woodruff, the editor, provided superb direction throughout the book's development. The competence and good nature of Lenore Franzen transformed the manuscript into a reality. She was ably assisted by Elaine Linden, whose copyediting clearly improved my writing. A special thanks to the artists who were involved in this project and who greatly enhanced the text. Finally, I would like to thank Jean McCoombs for her attention to detail in securing permissions.

While these individuals have helped immeasurably, final responsibility for the book's content remains mine.

Human Sexuality

The Search for Understanding

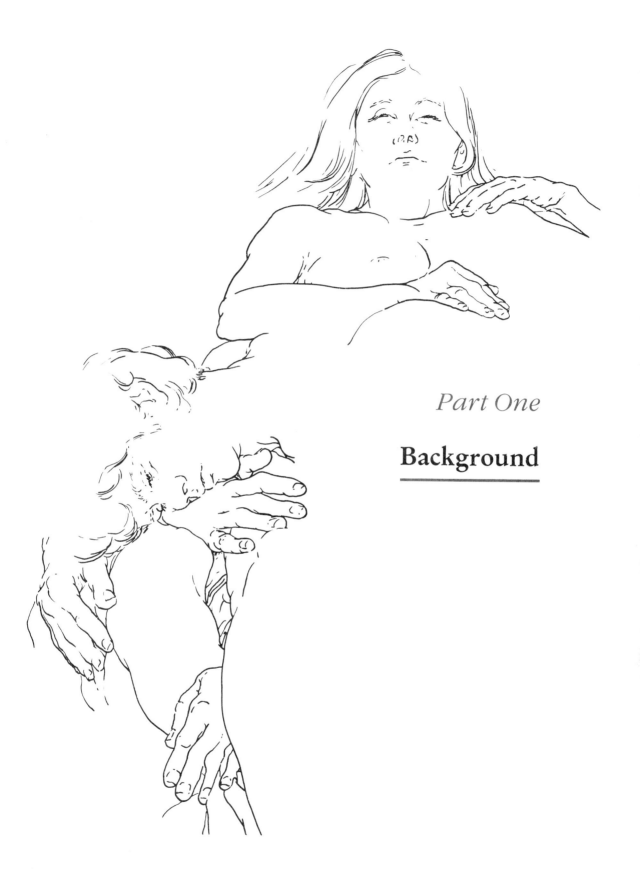

Part One

Background

Chapter One

Human Sexuality:
An Introduction

There may be some things better
than sex, and some things
worse, but there is nothing
exactly like it.

W. C. FIELDS

Chapter One

In your daily life you may occupy several social roles—student, daughter or son, sibling, spouse, employee, lover, or parent. These social roles are aspects of yourself that influence who you are and the interactions you have with others. But beyond these roles you are a sexual person with a unique, ongoing existence. You can choose not to be an employee—to stop work—but you cannot choose to stop being sexual. Your sexuality is always a part of you.

In this chapter we examine the meanings of **human sexuality** and the benefits we might derive from learning more about it. We also look at two perspectives for understanding our sexuality; these form the theoretical basis for this book. The chapter ends with a review of research issues, which may sensitize us to the mixed but improving quality of sex research in the 1980s.

What Is Human Sexuality?

A definition of human sexuality must include a number of facets, including relationships, anatomy, behaviors, thoughts and feelings, values, and variability.

Relationships

A major theme of this book is that sexuality is a part of human relationships. Such relationships may occur in the context of a variety of life styles (single-hood, living together, marriage) and sexual orientations (heterosexual, homosexual, bisexual). While we focus on heterosexual relationships, the same principles apply to homosexual and bisexual relationships.

Your sexuality affects your relationships directly in your choice of a partner or partners and in your commitment to unwritten agreements to be sexually exclusive or not with a partner. One person said, "Being faithful is easy for me and I tend to stay in one relationship for a long time." But another

4

While being at the beach may emphasize your sexual self, your sexuality is always evident.

said, "I've found I can't be monogamous with anyone . . . I'm always on the lookout for someone new . . . I really prefer it this way." The nature and stability of your relationships will be influenced by your sexual choices.

Anatomy

Human sexuality also has to do with the way you look, your anatomy, not just your genitals, but your hair, skin, eyes, lips, and limbs. It is your entire physical makeup—the package with "you" inside. When someone says, "I like your body," they like the package in which you are encased.

Behaviors

You express your sexuality by the way you move your body—at work or at play or even at rest. Much of this is unconscious. A man striding along the beach or a woman reaching for a tennis ball sparkles with sexuality. But sexuality also includes an array of conscious behaviors including talking, touching, caressing, kissing, masturbating and sexual intercourse.

Thoughts and Feelings

Behavior, which is often equated with sexuality, is only *one* aspect of sexuality. Human sexuality is, to a large degree, the thoughts you have about yourself and others. How do you view yourself—what is your self-concept? One woman described herself, "I am quiet, compassionate, and sensuous." Concerns about being fat, bald, or flat-chested are other thoughts many people have about themselves.

Other thoughts relevant to human sexuality are sometimes about feminine–masculine stereotypes. When you compare yourself with others, how do you fit the culturally approved concept of femininity or masculinity? Also, what thoughts do you have about others? What men or women do you find attractive and desirable, and why? What aspects of people do you find repulsive and aversive?

Your thoughts are connected to feelings. Having considered how you view yourself, how do you feel about yourself? How much do you like yourself? One graduate student said, "I like myself very much and couldn't have made a better me."

Thoughts and feelings may be erotic and sensual, and both of these may be independent of sexual behavior. One woman said, "There's no partner in my life now—at least *you* can't see him. But I continue to enjoy my past lover and can feel him with my mind."

Values

Human sexuality is also about values. What you feel comfortable doing or not doing will, in part, reflect your values. Whereas some people have the value that being married is the only condition under which sexual intercourse is appropriate, others have the value that being in love is the necessary condition. Still others may not require love but feelings of affection. Such conditions suggest that a value system is operative in all sexual expressions. (A person's thoughts also are affected by values, since he or she may feel guilty when certain thoughts occur and not others.)

Variability

Human sexuality is highly variable. All people (young and old, handicapped and able, fat and thin, black and white, Hispanic and Asian, and so on) are sexual beings just as we are. Their behavioral expressions and the thoughts and feelings associated with them will vary from person to person and in the same person over time.

Why Study Human Sexuality?

Since you are enrolled in a course on human sexuality, you will be investing an academic term in the systematic study of this subject. What are some of the potential benefits of such study?

Define Meanings and Feelings about Sex

Sex means different things to different people (Table 1.1). These meanings reflect both definitions and feelings about sex. One of the goals of this book is to encourage you to consider what sex means to you and how the expression of your sexuality affects your life and interpersonal relationships.

Answer Questions about Human Sexuality

Most of us have some questions about human sexuality (Am I normal? Do other people have intercourse—or masturbate— as much—or as little—as I do? Are other people's sexual fantasies like mine?) In this book we try to an-

---

Table 1.1 How 50 People Who Have Not Had a Course in Human Sexuality Define and Feel about Sex

Sex Is:

The ultimate expression of one's love for another

What happens when two people love each other

Love shown through intercourse

Emotional and physical release

Intercourse between two people without any emotional feelings

Fellatio

Cunnilingus

Means of reproduction

Emotional bond, intimacy

Companionship

Everything that leads to intercourse

Lust, romance, fun

My Feelings about Sex Are:

It is a beautiful experience shared between two lovers.

It is like a fall day spent with a great friend.

Sex is not worth getting upset over.

My feelings about sex depend on who I'm with, when, and why.

It is natural.

It is dangerous (herpes, pregnancy).

You shouldn't do it all the time to keep a relationship going.

It can be being loved or being screwed.

It is the best thing that you can do on this earth.

It is great if you love the person and awful if you don't.

I wish I had waited until I was married to experience it with just one instead of several.

It is a closeness I share with one special person.

swer some of these concerns. We also examine sexual issues on which there is currently little agreement, for example, whether a woman ejaculates, the degree to which sexual desire has a biological versus a social origin, and the degree to which having a lot of sexual partners correlates with personal adjustment or maladjustment.

Reduce the Chance of Unwanted Pregnancy and Contracting Sexually Transmitted Diseases

While information alone does not make people use contraceptives, it furnishes a basis for discussion of sexual issues with sexual partners, peers, and parents. Such discussion often helps people feel less anxious and more comfortable about sex (Serdahely, 1982), and the more comfortable individuals feel about discussing sex, the more likely they are to bring up the issue of contraception early in a sexual relationship. "When you've had a class in human sexuality," said one partner, "and learned how to bring up discussing contraceptives, it's not as awkward as you may think."

Knowledge about sexually transmitted diseases (STDs, including genital herpes) and being able to discuss them may also increase the chances that their presence may be detected and that a contagious person will avoid sexual contact. Such action will reduce the spread of sexually transmitted diseases.

Improve Yourself as a Sexual Partner

While a general understanding of the psychological, physiological, and sociological aspects of human sexuality is the primary goal of this book, much of the information will be applicable to you and your sexuality. For example, Part 3, Enhancement, includes a discussion of the negative effects of anxiety on sexual performance. Such anxiety may result when there is pressure to perform sexually. In men this translates into the expectation to get and keep an erection; in women, to have an orgasm. But the self-imposed demand to stay erect and to have an orgasm sometimes ensures that the man will not get an erection and that the woman will not climax. Informed sexual partners try to keep performance demands out of their sexual relationship. The more you know about sexuality, the greater your chance of dealing with it effectively when something is not satisfactory.

Increase Comfort in Seeing a Sex Therapist

It is not unusual for sexual partners to have some type of sexual problem in their relationship. While not all sexual problems suggest the need for sex therapy, it is wise to consider such therapy as an alternative to hoping that a problem will go away.

A course in human sexuality is one of the few places we are encouraged to learn accurate information about our sexuality.

Most of us are reluctant to contact a therapist about anything, least of all about sex. We have been socialized to see a dentist for an aching tooth and a physician for a broken arm but to see a sex therapist is to suggest that we have something to be embarrassed about. The stigma associated with sex therapy arises from our deepest fears about ourselves and our partners.

The alternative to keeping a sexual problem hidden and hoping it will go away is to seek help in resolving it. Certified sex therapists have been trained to help us sort out what is wrong and what to do about it (see Chapter 11). Another goal of this book is to encourage you to get beyond the negative implications of sex therapy and to seek help if you need it.

Effects of Taking a Course in Human Sexuality

While there are several potential benefits of studying human sexuality, what are some of the effects actually reported by those who have taken such a course? Although your reactions may be entirely different, students enrolled in one course noted the following effects (Gunderson & McCary, 1980).*

---

*Gunderson, M. P., and McCary, J. L. Effects of sex education on sex information and sexual guilt, attitudes and behaviors, *Family Relations,* (July 1980): 375–379. Copyright © 1980 by the National Council on Family Relations. Reprinted by permission.

1. *Increased sex information.* There was considerable gain in learning more accurate information about human sexuality.
2. *Reduced guilt.* Students reported less guilt and less anxiety about their own and others' sexuality after completing the course.
3. *Encouraged liberal attitudes.* The course had a liberalizing effect on the sexual attitudes of the students. This was particularly true for female and nonmarried students. Sex education helped them to become more comfortable with, and more tolerant and open minded toward, individuals and sexual practices that differed from their own.
4. *Reduced double standard.* Students were more likely to reject the double standard prescribing different behavior for men and women, for example, women must abstain from intercourse before marriage.
5. *Increased masturbation.* College females became more free of their fears, inhibitions, and reluctance to engage in such sexual behaviors as masturbation or oral-genital sex.
6. *Stabilized traditional values.* The course did not cause rejection of the traditional values of sex-with-love, monogamy, and fidelity.

Another researcher (Kilmann et al., 1983) noted that when 48 couples took a short-term sex education class, they reported less anxiety during sexual activity and in thinking about sexual activity.

If these are mostly positive consequences (depending on your point of view, they may also be negative), what are the potential negative effects of taking a course in human sexuality? While some people may view themselves as "normal" after they learn that other people also masturbate, engage in oral sex, and use vibrators, others may feel they are not normal because they do not engage in these behaviors. However, if the potential exists for exacerbating fears, such a course may also allay them. The issue of what is normal sexual behavior will be addressed in detail in Chapter 13, but it is important to note here that many concerns about being normal are socially induced, for example, through magazine articles like "Penis Size—Do You Measure Up?" and "Orgasm—Are You Getting Your Share?" A human sexuality class is one of the few places that the anxieties about being normal can be openly addressed and reduced.

An extension of the concern about being normal is the possibility of feeling pressure to act in so-called normal ways. If intercourse, oral sex, or whatever is what you view others as doing, you may feel compelled to do likewise. Of this dilemma, one person said, "I didn't want to be the only one of my group who hadn't had intercourse, so I picked somebody up in a bar and got it over with." As we noted, there is tremendous variability in human sexual experience, and people have a wide range of sexual values, interests, and behaviors. No matter what you think, feel, and do sexually, there are others who think, feel, and behave in similar ways.

The important issue is that you develop a good feeling about your own sexuality. The goal of your taking a course in human sexuality is not to encourage you to enjoy all forms of sexual expression at any time with anyone, but to provide a forum for you to discover your own values and to feel comfortable with them.

Finally, a potential negative effect of taking a human sexuality course is that it might create a gap in understanding between you and your parents. Parents usually regard education as important but they sometimes are not pleased at its content. At the same time, students in such courses may become aware of their own lack of sexual information. Inevitably, students discuss in class what their parents told them about sex. More often than not, their response is "nothing." While some students understand that their parents were simply repeating the pattern of their own sex education (nothing), others develop feelings of mild resentment. These feelings usually dissipate with the resolve to break the cycle of sexual ignorance in rearing one's own children.

The Language of Sex

Just as there is a language for football ("end run," "trap play," "pass"), swimming ("back stroke," "tread water," "dog paddle"), and computers ("terminal," "64K," and "disk drive"), there is a language for sex. Whether a formal or informal sex term is used depends on the gender of the person talking, the topic, and the interpersonal context in which the interaction takes place (Simkins & Rinck, 1982). Women tend to use formal words and men informal words when talking to others of their gender. When lovers talk to each other, both genders tend to use formal words when referring to the vagina, but both women and men tend to use informal words when talking about intercourse.

The words we use reflect our social and cultural attitudes toward sex. Words like "intercourse," "masturbation," and "fellatio" are clinical words usually spoken in a serious, no nonsense context. But the informal words for these same phenomena ("screw," "jack off," and "blow job") have a negative connotation. Where are the warm, human, loving words for these sexual expressions? Why does our society designate very limited contexts in which such references may occur? Society is sending us at least two messages by treating sexual words in this manner: (1) sex is private and the less said the better, and (2) sex is vulgar. The fact that most of us tend to talk about sex only in private and to view some aspects of sexuality in negative terms reflects the impact of society on our sexual socialization.

Theoretical Frameworks

Sexual scripts and operant learning are two interlocking theoretical frameworks. They view sexuality as learned social behavior and provide the basis for the understanding of human sexuality presented in this book.

Social-Script View of Human Sexuality

The **social-script** view of human sexuality suggests that what you do (or don't do) sexually is based on what your society and culture has taught you to do (Gagnon, 1977; Gagnon & Simon, 1973). Feeling the need for sexual expression is not the result of a blocked biological drive seeking orgasmic release but a result of having learned to define an internal state in sexual ways.

From the social-script perspective, the most erogenous zone of your body is your mind. It is your mind that selects from the environment those cues that stimulate sexual thoughts and behavior. For example, you and another adult in an otherwise empty classroom may or may not interact sexually depending on the social script (shared interpretations and expected behaviors of a social situation) each of you brings into the room. If you come into the classroom to catch up on some studying, you will likely not consider the presence of an opposite-gender person as creating a potential sexual situation. However, if the other person engages in a series of behaviors (looks up from studying, smiles, moves closer, and initiates touching), you might define the situation in sexual terms. In the absence of such cues from the other person, each of you will assume that your script is to study quietly, and both of you will act accordingly.

So, how we perceive a situation, the meanings we attribute to it, and the behaviors we engage in depend on learned social scripts. These define situations, name actors, and plot behaviors (Gagnon & Simon, 1973). In the preceding example, if the person already in the room was someone with whom you were emotionally involved, the situation would have been defined immediately as a meeting of two lovers, making some form of sexual expression appropriate and expected.

Scripts have two dimensions—external and internal. The external portion refers to shared meanings or sexual understandings of two actors, as in the example of you and another person in an empty classroom. Your words and gestures (the external dimension of a sexual script) cue each other as to the appropriate and expected behaviors.

The internal dimension of sexual scripts refers to physiological changes occurring within you as a result of attaching sexual meanings to environmental stimuli. Viewing a centerfold or watching a love scene or feeling the touch of your partner's lips may trigger physiological arousal (erection for the man and vaginal lubrication for the woman). These are reactions to items or events in the culture that you have learned to regard as sexual. To paraphrase Shakespeare, nothing is either sexual or nonsexual but thinking makes it so. If you define rubbing your partner's elbow as sexual, it is. Otherwise, you are just scratching someone's elbow.

Different cultures designate different stimuli as sexually arousing. Although our society imbues the female breast with considerable erotic potential, other societies attach no sexual significance to it. In those societies, the sight or touch of a woman's breasts will not produce an erection or physiological response since no sexual meaning is attached to the breast. Gagnon (1983) observed ". . . no one will be a satisfactory sexual member of a cul-

Sexual Script

What . . . are the components of a sexual script?

Who one does sex with is defined. The range of "whos" emerges from the social order itself. Most people do sexual things with a restricted number and kinds of other people, usually members of the opposite sex who are about the same age. There are limits set by blood relation, by marital status, and more distantly but nevertheless powerfully by race, ethnicity, religion, and social class. There are certain categories of people with whom sex is or is not allowable. And there are people one fantasizes doing sexual things with, some of whom are on the "approved list" and some who are not.

What one does sexually is also important. Of the whole range of sexual acts that people can perform, most are classified as right or wrong, appropriate or inappropriate. The thought of hugging and kissing is fairly comfortable to most people, if they can specify with whom. Vaginal intercourse seems all right to most experienced heterosexuals, and it is part of the usual marital sexual script. Oral sex and anal sex fit into a script in more complex ways, requiring careful specification of when they occur and with whom, and requiring a complex set of reasons. What is to be done and the order of doing it are learned in fragmentary ways from a variety of social sources.

When is sex appropriate? In the United States, among married couples with children, it is usually after the children have

gone to bed or are out of the house. That is, sex is for private times, when no one is likely to knock on the door, and when others do not have to be cared for. In societies whose members generally believe in sexual privacy, but where there is no privacy, people may have intercourse in irregular places (automobiles) and at irregular times (two in the afternoon).

"When" can be construed in a number of ways—the day, the week, the year, or a person's age. Most societies tend to see sex as more or less appropriate at one age, one phase of the human life cycle (e.g., reproductive adulthood), than at another. . . .

Where does the society approve of doing sexual things? As with "when," the notion of privacy is very important here, at least in U.S. society and the societies, present and past, most closely linked to it. These are societies where the bedroom door is closed. When Sigmund Freud concluded that it would be terrible for a child to see his parents having intercourse, he was quite possibly making the mistake of thinking that all of history had been like middle class, nineteenth century Vienna: a door on every bedroom and no more than two people to a room. For most of human history, however, most families have slept in the same room, hut, cave, or tent, and when there were beds, in the same bed. . . . Notions about the importance— even the necessity—of privacy represent a cultural adaptation that is relatively recent.

Why, finally, do people have sex? That is, not "why" do human beings have the ability to reproduce or put organs together, but what are the culturally appropriate explanations for doing sexual things that people learn? How do individuals explain,
(Continued)

both to themselves and others, why they do approved and disapproved sexual things?

The why of sex is its rhetoric. Sex is for: having children; pleasure; lust; fun; passion; love; variety; intimacy; rebellion; degradation; expressing human potential/ nature/instincts/needs; exploitation; relaxation; reducing tension; achievement; service. Whatever reasons people offer for doing anything else they use for sex. Some reasons are approved, some disapproved; some we share with others, some we conceal; we may tell others one thing, and tell ourselves another. We acquire the whys in the same ways we acquire our sexual techniques and sexual preferences. They fit into our scripts, they are substitutable and revisable. "I do it because I love her/him." "I was carried away by passion." "I was being used." "I was just horny at the time." "I feel emotionally closer to the people I have sex with."

"Why" raises the most complicated and perplexing questions of all: questions about which societies and individuals are the most ambivalent; questions that carry with them the greatest potential for confusion, detachment, and alienation as well as clarity, attachment, and innovation.*

*From *Human Sexualities* by John H. Gagnon. Copyright © 1977, pp. 7–9, Scott, Foresman and Company. Reprinted by permission.

ture without acquiring at least a partial version of the relevant intrapsychic and interpersonal scripts and cultural scenarios" (p. 40).

In developing sexual meanings, children are dependent on others for definitions of what is sexual. Young children stroking their genitals are not masturbating in the same sense that a 15-year-old would be. The latter has developed a script about sexual organs, learned ways of producing different sexual feelings, and interprets these feelings as sexual and pleasurable. Unlike young children, adults have developed sexual scripts which, like blueprints, specify the whos, whats, whens, wheres, and whys for given types of sexual activity (see pages 13–14).

Operant-Learning View of Human Sexuality

We have seen that social scripts detail how we interpret environmental stimuli in sexual terms and how we act on those interpretations. The operant view of human sexuality explains how specific sexual behaviors are learned.

An analysis of the principles of **operant learning** will help to explain why some individuals delight in masturbation, oral sex, and intercourse, while others abhor these behaviors as disgusting and immoral. Operant-learning theory states that the consequences of a behavior affect the chance that the behavior will recur. These consequences may be described in four rules of learning: positive reinforcement, negative reinforcement, punishment, and extinction. In addition, the concepts of shaping and modeling help to explain sexual behavior.

Positive Reinforcement

Positive reinforcement results when something favorable happens after a behavior. Positive reinforcement includes mental, physical, and interpersonal experiences. Describing her sexual experiences with her live-in partner, one woman remarked, "I really enjoy making love with him." The statement not only reflects her mental enjoyment of a physical pleasure, it implies that the relationship with her partner is a significant factor affecting her enjoyment. Since making love was regarded as a positive experience, it is predictable that this woman will make love again.

Negative Reinforcement

A behavior that is associated with the termination of something negative will increase the chance that the behavior will recur. This is called negative reinforcement. One man observed about his masturbating, "I'm nervous and upset a lot of the time. Masturbation feels good and relaxes me. My usual pattern is to masturbate during my shower and then go to bed. I usually get a good night's sleep that way." This man's masturbating relieves feelings of nervousness (unpleasant situation), thereby serving as a negative reinforcer and increasing the chance that masturbation will be used as a relaxing agent in the future. Intercourse similarly may be negatively reinforcing.

The principle of negative reinforcement may also help to explain a person's decision to have intercourse for the first time. "I wanted to get it over with (lose my virginity) so I got drunk and let it happen." This statement implies that the stigma associated with virginity (unpleasant situation) would stop after having intercourse (negative reinforcer).

Punishment

Unlike either type of reinforcement, punishment is defined as something negative that happens after a behavior and reduces the chance that the behavior will occur in the future. A student stated that he was impotent the first time he attempted intercourse and he had not gotten "the nerve to try it again." One woman revealed that her partner called her a slut after having intercourse with her. "It will be a long time before I do that again," she remarked.

Extinction

While reinforcement (positive or negative) and punishment account for how most sexual behaviors are learned, extinction may also have an influence. Extinction means that when a behavior is no longer reinforced, it will stop. For example, you will no longer make sexual advances to a partner if you feel that she or he does not want you to. Hence, since your partner will not reinforce you for such advances, they will be extinguished.

Shaping

Shaping refers to the systematic rewarding of small units of behavior that lead to the eventual goal. If a stranger approaches you and says, "Let's go to my house and have intercourse," you are likely to be suspicious and withdraw from the interaction. Under these conditions the gap between first meeting and suggested first intercourse is so great there is little possibility you will respond as requested. However, the gap can be closed through shaping. Suppose a friend introduces you to this same person in the snack bar of the college union. After enjoying a brief conversation, the person asks if you would like to go to a campus jazz concert Saturday night. Since you are pleased with his or her appearance and manner, you agree to go. This may be the first stage in the shaping process toward intercourse.

Several weeks or months go by during which you develop an exclusive relationship with this person. You visit your respective parents, study, and party together. One evening while walking back to the car from a movie, your partner says, "Let's go back to my place and drink some wine." The implication of the statement is clear to the two of you—intercourse will follow the wine. Your agreement to do so suggests that you have been "shaped" into having intercourse with this person by saying yes to attending concerts, visiting parents, and so on. All of these rewarding experiences have made it easier to say yes to intercourse.

The shaping process is subtle. The distance from meeting in the college union and saying yes to a concert date is similar to the distance between saying yes to wine after several months of dating and having intercourse.

Modeling

While modeling is not an operant-learning term, it is a principle that helps to explain sexual behavior. Modeling refers to learning through observation. For example, watching a couple kiss in a movie enhances the desire to engage in this behavior with one's own partner. If your closest friend describes to you the delights of intercourse or going to the beach spring break, the probabilities are increased that you will engage in these same behaviors.

Parents may greatly influence the degree to which their offspring are affectionate with their partners. If you grew up in a home in which you observed your parents kiss, hug, and be affectionate toward each other, you are more likely to feel comfortable displaying affection in your own relationships. But if they never openly displayed affection, you did not have a consistent model for this behavior and are less likely to engage in it.

In summary, we learn sexual behaviors through the consequences of those behaviors, shaping by our partners, and modeling from our peers and adults who are important in our lives. All this learning occurs in the broader context of acquiring scripts that dictate appropriate sexual expression in our society. While the operant-learning and social-script frameworks emphasize environmental influences on sexual behavior, they interact with biological factors. The impact of these factors is discussed in Chapter 2.

Much of our learning about sexuality is a result of observing parental models.

Other Perspectives of Human Sexuality

There are several other perspectives for viewing human sexuality that, with the two just discussed, help to provide an integrated overview of human sexuality. Aspects of each of these perspectives are discussed throughout the text.

The *historical perspective* looks at sexual attitudes and behaviors as they have changed over time since the beginning of recorded history more than 5000 years ago. It may also focus on human sexuality expressed in American society from the colonial period until the present. We learn, for example, that premarital sex was common for both men and women during part of the Puritan era.

The *cross-cultural perspective* considers sexual practices in other societies. Among the people of Inis Beag off the coast of Ireland, premarital intercourse is very rare (Messinger, 1972). But among the Mangaians in the South Pacific, parents encourage their teenage daughters to have sexual experiences with several men (Marshall, 1972).

The *cross-species perspective* examines sexual behaviors of animals. For example, it has been reported that baboon males use their hands and tongues to stimulate the female prior to intercourse. Female chimpanzees grasp the semierect or erect penis of the male and pull it rhythmically (Ford & Beach, 1951). Also, various animals have been observed engaging in homosexual behavior (Gadpaille, 1980).

The *legal perspective* explains what our legal system defines as appropriate and inappropriate sexual behaviors. In some states premarital intercourse (fornication), fellatio, and cunnilingus are against the law.

Finally, the *religious perspective* classifies what values various religious groups promote as guidelines for sexual expression. Intercourse between married people is often viewed as the only ethical and moral sexual behavior, while premarital or extramarital intercourse, masturbation, and homosexuality are viewed as immoral.

Sex Research

This book is based on a comprehensive review of studies in the area of human sexuality that have been reported in professional journals.

Suppose you want to find the latest research available on a particular sex-related topic. The following journals specialize in sex research, and some may be available in your library. (See Appendix D for a list of journal addresses.)

Journal of Sex Research
Archives of Sexual Behavior
Journal of Sex Education and Therapy

Journal of Sex and Marital Therapy

Journal of Social Work and Human Sexuality

Sexuality and Disability

Journal of Homosexuality

Medical Aspects of Human Sexuality

Sexually Transmitted Diseases

While not specific to sex research, the following journals frequently include information on sex-related topics.

Family Relations

Journal of Marriage and the Family

Alternative Lifestyles

While not journals, the following publications report the latest information in the field of human sexuality.

Sexuality Today

SEICUS Report

Emphasis Subscriber Service

The articles in these publications reflect various sex research ethics, methods of data gathering, and types of data analysis. After examining each of these issues, we suggest some cautions to keep in mind when reading the material on sex research presented in this book.

While we should be cautious about the validity of any research, professional journals provide a scientific basis for information about human sexuality.

Ethics of Sex Research

Sex researchers are obligated to follow two basic ethical guidelines in gathering their data: informed consent and protection from harm. Informed consent means that the subjects have a right to know before they participate the purpose of the research and what will be expected of them. Should they not wish to participate, for whatever reason, they should not be coerced to do so. For example, it would be unethical for a teacher to threaten a student with a lower grade if the student did not want to complete a sex history questionnaire.

Protection from harm obligates investigators to minimize the risk of exposing their subjects to either physical or psychological harm. While the risk of physical harm may be minimal or easily avoided, psychological damage may be more extensive and more subtle. Asking rape victims to describe their rape event can reopen painful memories that have been repressed or forgotten. An interviewer must be especially sensitive and caring in such a situation.

Beyond ensuring that their subjects do not incur physical or psychological harm as a result of participating in sex research, investigators must guarantee anonymity. Under no conditions should the identity of a respondent be identified to those not associated with the research project.

Methods of Data Collection

Sex researchers use five basic ways of collecting data: **participant observation**, **direct observation**, **surveys**, **case studies**, and **experiments**.

Participant Observation

As the term implies, participant observation means becoming involved in the phenomenon being studied. Sociologists have used this procedure to gather information about group sex (Bartell, 1972), nude beaches (Douglas, Rasmussen, & Flanagan, 1977) and male strip shows (Petersen & Dressel, 1982). A more highly publicized (and less professional) use of this technique was made by journalist Gay Talese, who reported his findings in *Thy Neighbor's Wife* (1980). Among his experiences, Talese lived as a nudist at Sandstone, a sexual community in Los Angeles, and had sexual relations with women in massage parlors. While professional sex researchers rarely engage in this type of participant observation, the method is productive. If you wanted to study commune life or singles' bars, one of the best ways to do so would be to join a commune or go to singles' bars regularly.

Direct Observation

An alternative to participating in the activity being studied is to directly observe others engaging in the behavior. Various researchers and therapists, including Masters and Johnson, have observed couples engaging in intercourse, masturbation, and oral sex. Usually, observers use a one-way mirror.

While we can gain valuable information from observing exactly how people behave in sexual situations, we must also ask, are those people who permit others to observe them engaging in sexual behavior similar to those who have sex behind closed doors? If not, we only know about the sexual behavior of those we can observe and are left to assume or guess about the others.

Surveys

Another way to collect data is to interview people who have experienced what you are studying. Rather than join a sex commune, you could interview commune members or give a questionnaire to each member of the commune. Either survey method, interview or questionnaire, would give you considerable detailed information without requiring direct involvement or observation.

"My latest survey shows that people don't believe in surveys."*

Case Studies

Unlike surveys, which gather information from a large number of people, a case study focuses on one individual. The book and subsequent movie *Three Faces of Eve* was based on a case study of a woman who had multiple personalities. By studying her case in detail, psychologists were able to learn more about the nature and dynamics of so-called split personalities.

Similarly, much of what we know about transsexuals, rapists, and incest victims is a result of case studies on some of these individuals. The problem with the case study method is that we cannot assume that what we find out from one subject is representative of other subjects of the same category. Conducting a case study on a transsexual does not tell us how other transsexuals behave, think, and feel. Nevertheless, case studies do give us details surveys often miss.

Experiment

Still another way to collect data is to conduct an experiment. Suppose you wanted to know the relationship between reading erotic literature and reported desire for sexual intercourse. After identifying a population, say 100 people, with similar characteristics (female, age 26, married, no children, full-time job, Protestant, with a current desire for intercourse twice a week, and husband out of town), you would divide the population into two groups—an experimental and a control group. You would then ask the 50 experimentals to read 20 pages of *The Sensuous Woman* each night for 10 days. This is the group that does something you are monitoring for effect.

The other 50 women—the control group—would be asked not to read anything at night for 10 days. Finally, instruct the subjects in each group to record the frequency with which they desired to have intercourse each day. If after 10 days, the women who read the erotic literature significantly increased their desire for intercourse in contrast to the control group, you would conclude that reading erotic literature was probably related to increasing the desire for intercourse.

The difficulty of finding enough people (so you can have two groups) with similar characteristics (so the people in the experimental group will be similar to those in the control group) and of getting them to participate in sex research are two reasons why most sex research is not experimental. While such research is excellent, there is too little of it reported in the various sex research journals.

Levels of Data Analysis

The purpose of data collection in sex research is to enable us to make accurate statements about behavior. There are three levels of data analysis that allow us to make such statements: **descriptive**, **correlational**, and **causative**.

Descriptive

Most of the research in this book is descriptive—the data have been collected via interviews and questionnaires in an attempt to describe human sexuality. Descriptive research may be both qualitative and quantitative. The qualitative aspect conveys attitudes and feelings about sexual issues, while the quantitative gives numbers—what percentage of respondents feel a certain way or engage in a specific behavior.

Correlational

Beyond describing what is, research often attempts to see if certain variables are related. For example, is there a relationship between church attendance (factor A) and number of sexual partners (factor B)? The degree to which factor A is correlated with factor B is statistically determined and expressed in one of three ways: an inverse relationship (as church attendance increases, the number of sexual partners decreases); a positive relationship (as church attendance increases, the number of sexual partners increases); and no relationship (going to church has nothing to do with the number of sexual partners).

Causative

To suggest that factor A causes factor B is a much stronger statement than to say the two factors are correlated. Causation is also determined statistically and requires that factor A come before factor B. For example, when heat (factor A) precedes water boiling (factor B), there is the strong probability that A caused B. In human sexuality, if a person contracts genital herpes shortly after sexual contact with another person, such time sequencing might suggest that the sexual contact caused the outbreak of herpes. But another condition must be met. It must be demonstrated that in the absence of A, B will not occur. Since genital herpes could be contracted from someone else, it is difficult to say that a particular person caused an individual to get genital herpes. Because these criteria for proving causation are rarely met, causation statements in sex research are rare.

Some Cautions about Research

Sex research focuses on what is, rather than on what we believe or want to be true. For instance, while we may believe that husbands and wives have intercourse only with their spouses, the data show that half of the husbands and 20 to 40 percent of the wives in the United States have intercourse with someone other than their partner at least once during their marriage. But although sex research attempts to be value free, the facts provided by social scientists are not necessarily reliable. As you read the various data and conclusions from the studies referred to in this book, it is important to be aware of various research limitations.

Sampling

Most information about human sexuality is based on samples—studying a relatively small number of individuals and assuming those studied are similar to a larger group encompassing many people not studied. For example, suppose you want to know what percentage of unmarried seniors (US) on your campus have had intercourse. While the most accurate way to get this information is to get an anonymous yes or no response from every US, doing so is not practical. To save yourself time, you could ask a few USs to complete your questionnaire and assume that the rest of the USs who did not complete your questionnaire would say yes or no in the same proportion as those who did. To decide who those few USs would be, you could put the names of every US on your campus on separate note cards, stir these cards in your bathtub, put on a blindfold, and draw 100 cards. Since each US would have an equal chance of having his or her card drawn from the tub, you would have what is known as a random sample. After administering the questionnaires to this sample and adding up the yeses and nos, you would have a fairly accurate idea of the percentage of USs on your campus who had had intercourse.

Because of the trouble and expense of obtaining **random samples**, most researchers study those to whom they have convenient access. This often means students in their classes. The result is an overabundance of research on **"convenience" samples** who are white, Protestant, middle-class college students. Since today's college students comprise only about 5 percent of all American adults, their attitudes, feelings, and behaviors cannot be assumed to be similar to those of a noncollege population.

While the human sexuality data presented in this book includes that obtained from young unmarried college students, it also includes that of people representing different ages, marital statuses, life styles, religions, social classes, and societies.

Control Groups

Just as most samples are not representative, most sex research is not experimental, as it does not use control groups. The value of a control group is that, for certain questions, it allows you to be more certain in your conclusions than if you do not have a control group. In our earlier example, we could not conclude that erotic reading influences reported desire for intercourse, (which was true in the experimental group), if those in the control group also reported an increased desire for intercourse even though they did not read the erotic literature. Hence, it is essential to include a control group in sex research when we want to know the effect one factor has on another.

Terminology

In addition to being alert to potential shortcomings in sampling and control groups, you should consider how the phenomenon being researched is defined. For example, if you were studying students on your campus who were living together, how would you define *living together*? How many people, of what gender, spending what amount of time, in what place, engaging in what behaviors will constitute your definition? Researchers of living together have used more than 20 definitions.

What about other terms? What is meant by sexual fulfillment, sexual adjustment, or sexual compatibility? Before accepting that most people are sexually fulfilled or sexually compatible, be alert to the definition used by the researcher. Exactly what is the researcher trying to measure?

Researcher Bias

Even when the sample is random and the terms are carefully defined, two researchers can examine the same data and arrive at different conclusions. In your study of living together, suppose you find that a quarter of the students on your campus are living together. In discussing your findings, would you emphasize that fact or the fact that the majority of the students (75 percent) were not living together? You can focus on either aspect of the data to make the point you want to make. Many researchers tend to focus on selected aspects of the data they are reporting.

Also, the answer a sex researcher gets is related to the question she or he asks. In one *New York Times*/CBS News poll, 30 percent of the respondents answered yes when asked, "Do you think there should be an amendment to the Constitution prohibiting abortions, or shouldn't there be such an amendment?" But when the same people were asked, "Do you believe there should be an amendment to the Constitution protecting the life of the unborn child?" one-half answered yes.

Time Lag

There is typically a two-year lag between the time a research study is completed and its appearance in a professional journal. Since textbooks are based on these journals and take from three to five years from writing to publication, by the time you read the results of a study, other studies may have been conducted that reveal different findings.

Beginning in 1965 and at five-year intervals through 1980, unmarried female students at a large, state-supported university were asked if they had experienced intercourse. In 1965, 29 percent reported having had intercourse. But the percentages changed every five years (1970, 37 percent; 1975, 57 percent; 1980, 64 percent) (Robinson & Jedlicka, 1982). You would want to make sure that you read the most recent findings, while being aware that they still may not reflect current reality.

Deception

While all studies may have problems of sampling, lack of control groups, terminology, researcher bias, and time lag, there is another problem specific to social science research—particularly sex research. That is deception. Sex is a very private behavior, and we have been socialized not to reveal to strangers the intimate details of our sex lives. Therefore we are prone to distort, omit, or exaggerate information to cover up what we feel is no one else's business. This means the researcher sometimes gets inaccurate information. One researcher contends that when 23-year-old Margaret Mead interviewed Samoans about their sexual behavior reported in *Coming of Age in Samoa*, (reported in 1928), her respondents told her lies to tease her (Freeman, 1983). Sex researchers who rely on interviews and questionnaires only know what people say they do, not what they actually do.

An unintended and probably more frequent form of deception is inaccurate recall. Sometimes researchers ask respondents to recall details of sexual thoughts or behaviors that occurred years ago. Since time tends to blur some memories, respondents may not relate what actually happened but only what they think happened.

In addition to deception on the part of the person being surveyed, outright deception on the part of the investigator is not unknown. In response to pressures to publish or from a desire for prestige and recognition, some researchers have doctored their data (Bobys, 1983). For example, the late British psychologist Cyril Burt, winner of the Thorndike Award given by the American Psychological Association, was renowned for his research designed to test the relative importance of heredity and environment on a person's development. He studied identical twins who had been raised in separate environments since birth and presented data that seemed to indicate clearly that heredity was more important. Five years after Burt's death, it was discovered that he had altered his data. In addition, there were suspicions that his "coauthors" never existed and that the investigations were never conducted (Hearnshaw, 1979). While such research fraud is rare, it "reduces public respect for the findings of scientific research" (Bobys, 1983, p. 47).

In view of the research problems outlined here, one might ask, Why bother to report the findings? The research picture is not as bleak as it may seem at first. A number of studies have been conducted on random samples that provide, as accurately as possible, a picture of what is currently happening. In addition, even though the bulk of studies is not based on national random samples, some information is better than no information. When enough nonrandom studies are conducted in one area, consistent findings may give us information that approximates the information we would get from a large random sample. The alternative to gathering data is guessing, and this is unacceptable.

Some Major Research Studies

Some of the more important studies on human sexuality are described in the following pages. These studies and their researchers reflect a great deal about what we know regarding human sexuality.

The Kinsey Studies

Alfred C. Kinsey and his colleagues conducted the most comprehensive study of reported sexual behavior ever published, personally interviewing more than 18,000 people. While no study has duplicated the scope of the material presented in *Sexual Behavior in the Human Male* (1948) and *Sexual Behavior in the Human Female* (1953), some reservations should be kept in mind about the data. These concerns include the nonrepresentativeness of the subjects, Kinsey's biological focus, respondent reliance on recall, and respondent tendency to distort answers.

Kinsey only studied those individuals who were willing to talk about the intimate details of their sexual lives. The use of volunteer subjects raises the question, Do those people who did not volunteer to participate in the study have different frequencies and types of sexual behaviors from those who did volunteer for the study? We do not know and we cannot make any assumption either way.

In addition to studying only selected groups,* Kinsey, an entomologist by training, focused on the biological aspects of sexual behavior to the neglect of emotional factors. Although we know how often the subjects reported having had intercourse, we do not know the meanings they attributed to that sexual experience. One respondent observed, "How often I have inter-

*Examples of the groups sampled by Kinsey included church congregations, clinical groups, college classes, sororities, fraternities, PTA groups, prisoners, women's clubs, etc. Most of these groups represented white, urban, Protestant, college-educated people from the northeastern quarter of the country. Kinsey's findings are most likely to be valid for this type of person (Reiss, 1976).

Research Cautions

As a reminder to be cautious about the conclusions of a particular study, the symbol [?] is used in the margin throughout the book to indicate one or more research weaknesses. The word below the question mark specifies the specific concern. A list of symbols and their meanings follows.

 The sample is a convenience sample (not random) and represents *only* how those responding think, feel, or behave; or the sample is too small to make generalizing the findings beyond the sample warranted.

 The study did not include a control group, so we can make only speculative conclusions.

 The terminology used in the study was not clearly defined.

 The study is biased toward a particular conclusion because of the way the data have been presented to the reader.

 The information contained in the study may not reflect current patterns.

 The data may be distorted because of the respondent's or researcher's dishonesty or because the respondent was asked to recall events that occurred long ago.

 This symbol indicates that more than one of these problems is a concern in the research cited.

course with my partner is very much related to how I am feeling about our relationship." Since emotional variables of this type were not studied, the Kinsey data told us almost nothing about why certain patterns were observed or why one subject's behavior differed from another's.

Another weakness of the Kinsey studies was their reliance on the respondents' recall. The question, "How many persons have you had intercourse with?" required respondents to remember accurately events that occurred up to 40 years earlier. For some people who could not recall exactly the number of partners they had, there may have been a need to distort—either to exaggerate or to understate the number to appear normal. Such distortion may have affected the accuracy of Kinsey's measurements. However, in spite of these concerns, the Kinsey volumes on male and female sexuality are still regarded by most sex researchers as two of the best ever published.

The Masters and Johnson Studies

Two of the best-known names in contemporary sex research are Masters and Johnson. Also a married couple, William Masters and Virginia Johnson are co-directors of the Masters and Johnson Institute in St. Louis, Missouri. Their publications *Human Sexual Response* (1966) and *Human Sexual Inadequacy* (1970) were on the nonfiction best-seller list of the *New York Times* within four weeks after their respective releases. The first book was a result of 12 years of research in which 694 participants experienced more than 10,000 orgasms under laboratory conditions. The sequel focused on the treatment of sexual problems such as lack of orgasm, impotence, and premature ejaculation. The purpose of conducting this research was to examine the physiological reactions to sexual stimulation.

Their most recent research, *Homosexuality in Perspective* (1979), reports interviews with and observations of 176 homosexual men and women in both committed and casual relationships. Masters and Johnson focused on the sexual behaviors and fantasy patterns of these homosexuals and offered sexual therapy to those who requested it. In some cases, they assisted homosexuals in becoming heterosexuals. While some of the Masters and Johnson research has been criticized (see Chapter 11) they remain two of the most respected sex researchers and therapists in the United States today, and their work constitutes some of the best research available on human sexual response.

The Hunt Study

Although neither a sex researcher, physician, or therapist, Morton Hunt, a freelance writer, attempted to update the Kinsey studies with the publication of *Sexual Behavior in the 1970's* (1974). The book was based on data collected by the Research Guild, Inc., of Chicago. In 1972 the Guild gathered 2,026 questionnaires which had been completed in 24 American cities. While providing some indication of current trends in sexual behavior, "this study is not, strictly speaking, a replication of the Kinsey surveys, for it is much less detailed, it used a different sampling procedure and a self-administered questionnaire, and these questions were worded differently from Kinsey's" (Hunt, 1974, p. 18).

Commenting on the inadequacies of the Hunt research, Reiss (1976) observed:

> The sampling procedure in this study was the poorest of the major studies of the 1970's . . . The research organization that was hired used the telephone to approach a selected sample of people eighteen and over in twenty-four cities around the country. The telephone approach for a study on sexual attitudes and behavior is probably a very poor choice. Many people do not know if such a call is authentic; others who might be persuaded by a face-to-face contact with an interviewer will not be so persuaded by a phone call. On such a sensitive topic it makes sense to use more personal approaches. The refusal rate was over 80 percent. (p.177)

The Zelnik and Kantner Studies

While the Kinsey, Masters and Johnson, and Hunt studies focused on both male and female sexuality, the early Zelnik and Kantner research concerned itself only with premarital female sexuality. In 1971 and 1976 Zelnik and Kantner (1977) studied a national sample of women 15 through 19 years of age living in households and in college dormitories in the continental United States. Their sampled population included women of all marital statuses and races. In 1979 they studied the sexual and contraceptive behavior of teenagers, both women and men, living in metropolitan areas (1980). Their data were collected through personal interviews and are among the best available. Zelnik and Shah (1983) have continued research into the sexual behavior of teenagers.

Popular Books

Because sex sells, books for the nonprofessional are popular publishing ventures (*Dr. Ruth's Guide to Good Sex,* Westheimer, 1983). The authors and their publishers are more concerned with sales than scientific methodology. These books are often mass marketed to the public, which is led to believe they are buying *the* survey on female and male sexuality. Sherre Hite has written two of these money-making sex books, which have been heavily criticized by professional sex researchers.

The Hite Report (1977), presented as "a nationwide study of female sexuality," was based on only 3,019 of an initial 100,000 questionnaires. This 3 percent return rate is hardly sufficient to allow for any meaningful generalizations. But despite severe methodological shortcomings, the Hite study did make a contribution to sex research literature, as many of the women who completed questionnaires furnished a wealth of anecdote and personal insights into their sex lives—the kind of information that was not available from earlier studies. One woman said, "I wish men would be more sensitive rather than acting like a big penis, having an orgasm and that's all" (p. 7).

In her more recent book, *The Hite Report on Male Sexuality* (1981), the author gives information on the sex lives of more than 7,000 men aged 13 to 97. While the number of respondents is impressive, it represents only 6 percent of the 119,000 questionnaires distributed. Since most of the respondents answered questionnaires in *Penthouse* and *Houston Breakthrough* (a feminist newspaper), we cannot assume that those not responding have sex lives similar to those who did. Nevertheless, the book reflects in vivid detail what the men felt about masturbation, petting, intercourse, and the sexual interests of women.

Magazine Surveys

Magazine publishers also make money from selling sex. Some ask their readers to complete questionnaires from which they develop articles that appear in different issues. While the information in these articles reflects only the sexual attitudes and experiences of the readers of that particular magazine, the results are sometimes insightful because of the large number of respondents.

Redbook

In 1974 and 1975 *Redbook Magazine* published a series of articles on married female sexuality based on the responses of 100,000 women to a 75-item questionnaire. This was one of the largest samples of women ever to provide information about their sexual behavior. Questions on the importance of sex, what makes for a good sex life, and how sexual satisfaction is related to religion, orgasm, and the woman's assertiveness were included in the survey (Tavris & Sadd, 1977). In 1980 *Redbook* published a study on sexual relationships based on data from 6,000 men and 20,000 women (Sarrel & Sarrel, 1980).

Cosmopolitan

Not to be outdone by *Redbook*, *Cosmopolitan* magazine published a study in 1980 based on a survey of 106,000 of its readers. From this group the researchers selected 15,000 women to represent the "Cosmopolitan girl"—women 18 to 34 living in large cities (more than one million population) and employed. Age at first intercourse, number of lovers, and masturbation were among the topics explored. A paperback version of the study was published in 1982 (Wolfe).

Playboy

Based on a survey of about 80,000 readers, *Playboy* published several installments of "The Playboy Readers' Sex Survey" in 1983. Eighty percent of the respondents were men; 20 percent, women. Acknowledging that the sample was not randomly selected and was not a cross-section of the U.S. population, the authors stated that those who completed the survey met only two requirements: "They are readers of *Playboy* and they are interested in sex" (Petersen et al., 1983a, p. 108). The researchers tabulated all questionnaires that had been completed legibly and that were mailed on time. The result was 2,000 pages of computer printout detailing responses on a wide variety of topics in human sexuality, including bisexuality and sadomasochism.

Ladies Home Journal

Focusing on relatively young (average age was 35) married (80 percent), employed (68 percent), educated (70 percent attended college), religious (71 percent viewed themselves as religious) women who had good household incomes ($20,00 to $40,000 a year) the LHJ survey represented the sexual attitudes and behaviors of 83,000 respondents (Frank & Enos, 1983).

While data from these magazine surveys are referred to in the following chapters, it should be kept in mind that the samples reflect the readership of the magazine only and are not representative of all people. Our best information about human sexuality continues to come from research conducted by professionals like Kinsey, Masters and Johnson, and Zelnik and Kantner.

Summary

Human sexuality is a broad concept that emphasizes relationships, anatomy, behaviors, thoughts and feelings, values, and variability. While human sexuality is often thought of as behavior, this is only one aspect.

In addition to examining its psychological, sociological, and physiological facets, the goals of studying human sexuality include defining meanings, answering questions, and enchancing one's own sexuality. Those who have taken such a course report that they increased their knowledge about sexuality and became more tolerant of a variety of sexual behaviors for themselves and others. They also became more comfortable and had more positive feelings about their own bodies.

While there are numerous ways to view human sexuality, two theoretical frameworks emphasized in this book are social scripts and operant-learning theory. The social-script framework suggests that sexual behavior and interaction is doing and saying things that are defined as sexual. Lovers play their roles by acting out the sexual scenes scripted for them by society. Operant-learning theory suggests that lovers are rewarded or punished for their sexual behaviors, which influences their subsequent engaging in those behaviors.

The systematic study of human sexuality involves reading what sex researchers have discovered. But the reader should be careful to keep in mind cautions about sampling, control groups, terminology, time lag, researcher bias, and deception when evaluating the research.

Key Terms

human sexuality

social script

operant learning

participant observation

direct observation

survey research

case study research

experimental research

descriptive analysis

correlational analysis

causal analysis

random sample

convenience sample

sex science*

sexology*

sexosophy*

*These terms are discussed in the "Issues in Debate" section that follows.

and Future Directions

Sexology focuses on the content of the investigation. But these are not clear-cut distinctions. Sexologists are also concerned about methodology just as sexual scientists may study sexual values.

Still another term related to the study of human sexuality is **sexosophy**. This new concept, suggested by Dr. John Money (1982), encompasses the "philosophy, principles, and knowledge that people have about their own personally experienced erotosexuality and that of other people, singly, and collectively" (p. 365). Sexosophy emphasizes that human sexual behavior occurs in the context of different values that each sexual partner brings to the other, which will influence the perceptions and behaviors of their interaction.

Sexual Science: Is It Respected?

Rodney Dangerfield, the New York comic, said, "I don't get no respect." The same can sometimes be said of the study of human sexuality. "The public perception of sexology is utterly distorted by popular pseudoscientific 'sex reports,' therapy fads, and various moral crusades. The mass media, lacking any reliable guideposts, lean toward sensationalism. In short, the study of sex is still widely regarded as suspect, frivolous or, at best, unnecessary" (Haeberle, 1983, p. 156).

One of the reasons for society's dismissal of the study of human sexuality is the lack of historical tradition. Such study had its beginnings in Germany and Austria at the turn of the century, and journals, sexological organizations, books, firms, institutes, and international congresses reflected the growth of the discipline. But Hitler's virulent anti-

Sex

Altho
a rose
sweet,
call the
science
past pre
Study of
in 1906 by the Berlin dermatologist Iwan Bloch, who emphasized that the sexual sciences should have the same exactitude and objectivity as the natural sciences, such as chemistry (Reiss, 1982). Bloch's term was *Sexualwissenschaft,* literally translated as "**sex science**."

An alternative term to describe the study of human sexuality is **sexology**. "Sexology is defined as that body of knowledge that comprises the science of sex, or more precisely, of the differentiation and dimorphism of sex and of the erotosexual pairbonding of partners" (Money, 1982, p. 364). This definition focuses on how an embryo develops female or male external and internal sex organs and the emotions and cognitions involved in the interaction of partners.

The terms sexual science and sexology do not compete with each other but emphasize different aspects of the same phenomena. Sexual science is concerned with how information is obtained—with representative samples, statistical tests, and terminology.

Semitism—the overwhelming majority of sexological pioneers were Jews—and his hatred of all human sciences sealed the doom of this early work. Under Nazi rule "no further congresses could be held, the sexological journals ceased publication, and great sexological works were burned, the sexological societies disbanded, and the sexological institutes were closed . . . As a result, sexology, as we know it, is a rootless, ill-defined, and ill-understood enterprise, a science without a historical consciousness and without a sound theoretical foundation. Furthermore, having no recognized tradition, it appears to many outsiders as an illegitimate academic upstart" (Haeberle, 1982, p. 306).

But studying human sexuality is becoming increasingly respectable. Many German and Austrian sexologists who were not killed or imprisoned escaped to other countries and continued their work. In the last 25 years there have been significant and unprecedented advances in sexual research (Reiss, 1982). In addition to the numerous professional journals devoted solely or in part to sexology (see Appendix A), various organizations provide a forum for research and dialogue. These organizations include the following: American Association of Sex Educators, Counselors, and Therapists, Society for Sex Therapy and Research, Association of Sexologists, Sex Information and Education Council of the U.S., and Society for the Scientific Study of Sex.

Furthermore, some graduate programs offer degrees in human sexuality. Doctoral programs are available in the Department of Education at the University of Pennsylvania, in the Departments of Health Education at New York and Purdue Universities, and in San Francisco at the Institute for Advanced Study in Human Sexuality. The result of these journals, organizations, and graduate training programs in human sexuality is to lend renewed credibility to its study.

Future Directions

The future of sex research will likely include more emphasis on theory, on explaining what is, than on the accumulation of facts. In the past, sex research has tended to focus on numbers (how often intercourse occurs, in what positions, with how many partners) without considering a theoretical framework for such data. But now that many of the numbers on what people do sexually are available, the next step is to give more attention to what the numbers mean.

Sexual information, particularly the "why we do what we do sexually" variety, will continue to be disseminated in popular magazines and books. Such media, coupled with television (programs like *Donahue*), will increase the acceptability of human sexuality in both talk and behavior. One behavioral expression of this freedom will be economic. People will spend more money on sex—on cable TV sex shows, sexually explicit videotape cassettes, sex devices (vibrators, lotions), sex magazines and books, and erotically appealing clothes (like those sold by Frederick's of Hollywood).

The new air of openness in purchasing these products can be seen in a variation of the traditional Tupperware party. A woman invites several friends to her house for a demonstration of sexual products by a sales representative. Among the offerings are vibrators, erotic negligees, panties, and bras, lotions, oils, and candy bikinis. The hostess receives a gift whose value is based on the total sales of the evening.

Chapter Two

Gender Roles

*Male and female personalities
are socially produced.*
MARGARET MEAD

Chapter Two

Human sexuality expresses itself in who we are as women and men, not just anatomically but also psychologically and socially. In this chapter we are concerned with how we develop into women and men and the consequences of this development. First, we define some terms.

Terminology

Psychologists, sociologists, and health educators often have different definitions and connotations for the terms gender, gender identity, and gender role. We will use these terms in the following way.

Gender

Gender refers to the biological distinction of being female or male. The primary sex characteristics that differentiate women and men include external genitalia (vulva and penis), gonads (ovaries and testes), sex chromosomes (XX and XY) and hormones (estrogen, progesterone, and testosterone). Secondary sex characteristics like the female's larger breasts and the male's beard are additional distinctions.

Gender Identity

In contrast to the biological gender distinction, **gender identity** is the psychological state of viewing one's self as a girl or boy and later as a woman or man. Such an identity is learned and is the reflection of society's conceptions of masculinity and femininity. A person's gender identity is usually formed at about age 3.

Gender Role

Gender role, also known as **sex role**, refers to the socially accepted characteristics and behaviors typically associated with a person's gender identity. In our society the traditional concept of being female includes being emotional, dependent, and family oriented, while the traditional concept of being male includes being nonemotional, independent, and career oriented. Books like *Real Men Don't Eat Quiche* and *Real Women Don't Change Tires* emphasize the gender-role confusion and change our society is currently undergoing.

Whether gender-role behaviors are primarily a function of biological or social influences is a continuing controversy (see Issues in Debate section at end of chapter). Most researchers acknowledge that biological and social factors interact to produce these behaviors. While children are born female and male, they learn culturally defined feminine or masculine characteristics. In the remainder of this chapter, we examine the biological beginnings of women and men and review the ways in which they are socialized.

Biological Beginnings

While all human life begins with a zygote—a fertilized egg—all zygotes are not alike. They carry different chromosomes and hormones that stimulate variations in our biological development.

An individual is born with a certain biased predisposition to interact with the world in certain ways.

MILTON DIAMOND

Chromosomes

Chromosomes are threadlike structures located within the nucleus of every cell in a person's body (Figure 2.1). Each cell contains 23 pairs of chromosomes, a total of 46 chromosomes per cell. One of these 23 pairs of chromosomes is referred to as sex chromosomes because they determine whether an individual will be female or male. There are two types of sex chromosomes, called X and Y because they differ in appearance. Females have two X chromosomes, while males have one X and one Y chromosome. The basic units of heredity, called **genes**, make up the chromosomes. These genes not only determine such physical characteristics as eye color, hair color, and body type, but also predispositions for characteristics like baldness, color blindness, and free bleeding (hemophilia).

When the egg and sperm meet in the Fallopian tube (Figure 2.2), each contains only half the normal number of chromosomes (one from each of the 23 pairs). The union of sperm and egg results in a single cell called a zygote, which has the normal 46 chromosomes. The egg will always have an X chromosome, but the sperm will have either an X or Y chromosome. Since the sex chromosome in the egg is always X (the female chromosome), the sex

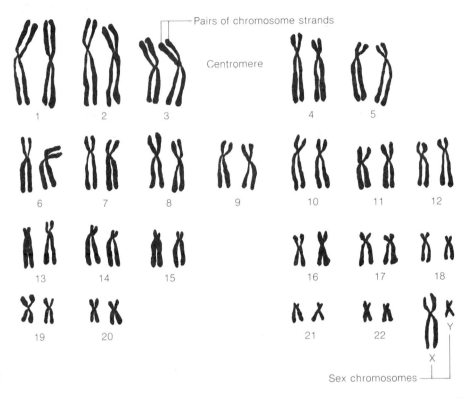

**Figure 2.1
Chromosome Pairs.**
Twenty-three
chromosome pairs
are within each cell
of a person's body.

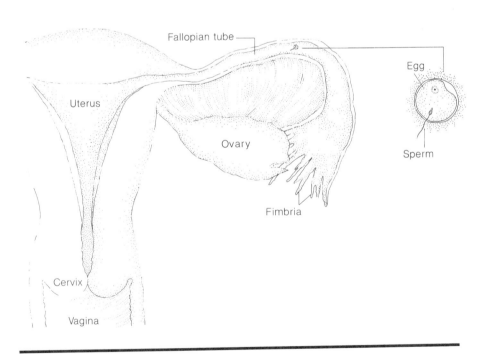

**Figure 2.2
Fertilization.**
Fertilization occurs
when a sperm
penetrates an egg in
a Fallopian tube.

chromosome in the sperm will determine the gender of a child. If the sperm contains an X chromosome, the match with the female chromosome will be XX, and the child will be genetically a female. If the sperm contains a Y chromosome (the male chromosome), the match with the female chromosome will be XY, and the child will be genetically male. The important thing to remember is that an individual's genetic sex is determined at the moment of conception. As we shall see, however, whether one is anatomically a male or female depends additionally on the influence of hormones. Genes determine anatomical sex only indirectly by influencing hormone production.

Hormones

Male and female embryos are indistinguishable from one another during the first several weeks of intrauterine life. In both, two primitive gonads and two paired duct systems form about the fifth or sixth week of development. While the reproductive system of the male (epididymus, vas deferens, ejaculatory duct) develops from the Wolffian ducts and the female reproductive system (Fallopian tubes, uterus, vagina) from the Müllerian ducts, both are present in the developing embryo at this stage (Figure 2.3). If the embryo is genetically a male (XY), a chemical substance controlled by the Y chromosome stimulates the primitive gonads to develop into testes. The testes, in turn, begin secreting the male hormone testosterone, which stimulates the development of the male reproductive and external sexual organs. The testes also secrete a second substance, called Müllerian duct-inhibiting substance, which causes the potential female ducts to degenerate or become blind tubules. Thus development of male anatomical structures depends on the presence of male hormones at a critical stage of development.

The development of a female requires that no (or very little) male hormone be present. Without the controlling substance from the Y chromosome, the primitive gonads will develop into ovaries and the Müllerian duct system into Fallopian tubes, uterus, and vagina; and without testosterone the Wolffian duct system will degenerate or become blind tubules. Animal studies have shown that if the primitive gonads are removed prior to differentiation into testes or ovaries, the organism will always develop anatomically into a female, regardless of genetic composition.

Although the infant's gonads (testes and ovaries) produce the sex hormones (testosterone, estrogen, and so on), these hormones are regulated by the pituitary gland, which is located at the base of the brain about 2 inches behind the eyes. The pituitary releases hormones into the blood that determine the amount of testosterone released by the testes and the amounts of estrogen and progesterone released by the ovaries. Production of sex hormones in males is relatively constant, while production of female hormones is cyclic (see Chapter 3). Does this mean the pituitary glands of males and females are different? In animal studies the pituitaries of male and female organisms have been transplanted, yet production of sex hormones remains

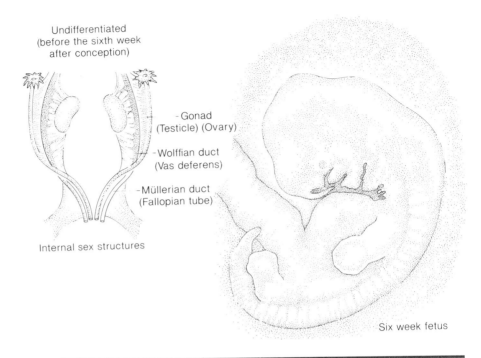

Undifferentiated
(before the sixth week
after conception)

- Gonad
(Testicle) (Ovary)

- Wolffian duct
(Vas deferens)

- Müllerian duct
(Fallopian tube)

Internal sex structures

Six week fetus

**Figure 2.3a
Gonads, Duct
Systems, and
Embryo Before Six
Weeks,
Undifferentiated.**

cyclic in females and constant in males. The release of pituitary hormones, as it turns out, is controlled by additional hormones (also called releasing factors) from a part of the brain just above the pituitary called the hypothalamus. It is the hypothalamus that differs in males and females in both the connections between cells and the size of various groups of cells. The presence of male sex hormones before birth not only stimulates the development of the male reproductive system, but also apparently stimulates the development of a male hypothalamus (McEwen, 1981). A female hypothalamus develops in the absence of male sex hormones.

At puberty the hormones released by the testes and ovaries are necessary for the development of **secondary sex characteristics**. Higher levels of testosterone account for the growth of facial hair in males and pubic and underarm hair in both males and females. Breast development, on the other hand, results from increasing levels of estrogen.

Biological Accidents

Several factors must be present for a person to be biologically female or male.

1. Chromosomes: XX for female; XY for male.
2. Gonads: ovaries for female; testes for male.

Differentiated internal sex structures
(12 weeks after conception)

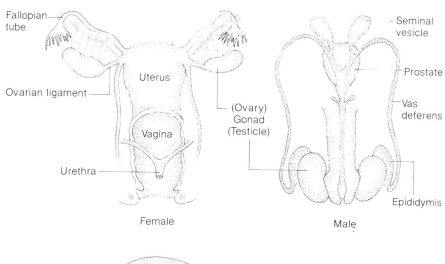

Female

Male

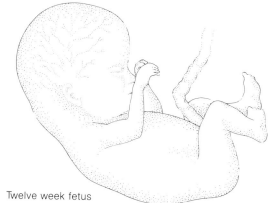

Twelve week fetus

Differentiated external sexual structures

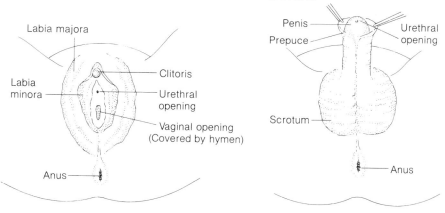

**Figure 2.3b
Gonads, Duct
Systems and
Embryo at Twelve
Weeks, Showing
Differentiated
Internal and
External Sexual
Structures.**

3. Hormones: greater proportion of estrogen and progesterone than testosterone in the female; greater proportion of testosterone than estrogen and progesterone in the male.
4. Internal sex organs: Fallopian tubes, uterus, and vagina for female; epididymus, vas deferens, and seminal vesicles for male.
5. External genitals: vulva for females; penis and scrotum for male.

The biological events necessary to produce a person with all five of these characteristics are complex. A useful analogy is the preparation of say, a Hollandaise sauce. If an ingredient is left out or added at the wrong time, the outcome will be entirely different. So it is with the developing embryo. Chromosomes and hormones must be present in exactly the right amount at the right time.

Chromosomal Abnormalities

For every sex chromosome from the mother (X), there must be a corresponding sex chromosome from the father (X or Y) for normal sexual development to occur. Abnormalities result when there are too many or too few chromosomes. Two of the most common of these abnormalities are **Klinefelter's syndrome** and Turner's syndrome.

Klinefelter's syndrome occurs in men and results from the presence of an extra X chromosome (XXY). This happens in 1 out of 500 male births. The result is abnormal testicular development, infertility, low interest in sex (low libido), and, in some cases, mental retardation.

Turner's syndrome occurs in women and results from the absence of an X chromosome (XO). This syndrome occurs in 1 out of 2,500 female births. It is characterized by abnormal ovarian development, failure to menstruate, and infertility. In addition, these individuals are quite short and have poor breast development.

Hormonal Abnormalities

Too much or too little of the wrong kind of hormones also can cause abnormal sexual development.

A few people are born with both ovarian and testicular tissue. These individuals, called **hermaphrodites**, often have one ovary and one testicle, feminine breasts, and a vaginal opening beneath the penis. They are generally genetic females (XX), and while their internal reproductive systems are usually mixed and incomplete as well, many hermaphrodites menstruate. Individuals born hermaphrodite may be reared as either males or females, depending largely on their appearance. The condition is extremely rare; there have been only 60 known cases in this century. Much more common is a condition known as pseudohermaphrodism, which is found in both females (androgenital syndrome) and males (testicular feminization syndrome).

Androgenital Syndrome

You will recall that for the female fetus to develop normally, it must avoid un-usually high doses of androgen (male hormones). Male hormones, however, are produced not only by the testes but also by the adrenal glands. Exposure to high levels of androgen can result from a malfunction of the mother's ad-renal glands or from the mother's ingestion of synthetic hormones like, for example, progestin that have an androgen effect on the fetus (in the 1950s progestin was often prescribed for pregnant women to prevent premature delivery). Sometimes a genetic defect causes the adrenal glands of the fetus to produce excessive amounts of androgens. The result of either factor is what is called the **androgenital syndrome**. Excessive androgen causes the clitoris to greatly enlarge and the labia majora often to fuse together to resem-ble a scrotum, resulting in ambiguous-looking genitals. The genetic and ana-tomical female may be mistaken for, and raised as, a male for the first few years of life. With corrective surgery and hormonal therapy (cortisone to counteract the effects of androgen and female hormones to promote the de-velopment of breasts), a prenatally androgenized woman can have a life not unlike other females. "She will grow up like other girls, can marry and have children, and is not more likely to become a lesbian than is a girl who was not overexposed to synthetic progestin or androgen prenatally" (Money & Tucker, 1975, p. 58).

Sometimes the androgen in the developing infant has a more profound ef-fect, so that the clitoris of the infant female is the size of a penis and her labia look like a scrotum although there are no testes inside. Since the physician and parents may not be aware of the chromosomal makeup (XX) and because the genitals look like those of a male, the infant will be reared as a male. With the help of surgery to remove female internal organs (ovaries and uterus) and hormones, despite the XX chromosomes, the male-reared individual can be-come a man not noticeably different from other men. One such 24-year-old man was described as follows: "nothing in his appearance, manner, gestures, or conversation betrays the fact that genetically and gonadally he was born female" (Money & Tucker, 1975, p. 59).

Testicular Feminization Syndrome (TFS)

Another hormonal fetal abnormality is the lack of development of male geni-tals in the body of a person who is genetically a male (who has XY chromo-somes). In TFS, also known as androgen-insensitivity syndrome, the external tissues of the fetus should turn into male genitals when androgen is pro-duced by the testes. But for some reason, even though normal amounts of androgen are produced, the tissues do not respond to the male hormones and female external genitals are formed—labia, clitoris, and vaginal opening. The production of Müllerian duct-inhibiting substance is not impaired, so the Fallopian tubes and uterus do not develop and the vagina is quite short. Hence, while the newborn infant has the external genital appearance of a fe-male (and is therefore reared as a female), the infant has testes embedded in the abdomen. These individuals are called male pseudohermaphrodites.

Parents are usually unaware of this hormonal abnormality until they realize at midadolescence that their daughter has not menstruated. She cannot since she has no uterus. Surgery can be undertaken to remove the testes and increase the depth of the vagina. Since most TFS individuals are reared as females, they develop normal gender identity.

Transsexuals

Transsexuals have the genitals of one gender but the self-concept of the other. "I am a woman trapped in a man's body" (or the reverse) reflects the feeling of a transsexual. The transsexual thinks of himself or herself as belonging to the opposite gender, tries to live in the social role of that gender, and may seek surgery to alter the genitals to conform with the self-concept. It has been reported that between 10,000 and 20,000 men and women (80 percent are men) feel that their sexual organs are different from their "real" self (Restak, 1979). James/Jan Morris, George/Christine Jorgensen, and Walter/Susan Cannon have gone public with their transsexuality. Of the latter, a friend said, "A tall, balding, broad-shouldered man, Cannon did not affect qualities of womanliness or softness. He was a woman in a man's body wearing women's clothes (Latham & Grenadier, 1982, p. 69).

Transsexual, Homosexual, Transvestite

The transsexual does not have the self-concept of a homosexual. Both may be attracted to their own biological gender (for different reasons), but only the transsexual considers sex reassignment surgery. Whereas a homosexual male is attracted to other males, the transsexual male is attracted to other men because he sees himself as a woman. Likewise, the transsexual woman is attracted to other women because she sees herself as a man.

Another important distinction is between transvestite and transsexual. Transvestites dress in the clothing of the opposite gender for sexual pleasure. But they retain their anatomical sexual orientation and would be horrified at the thought of surgery to change their genitals. Hence a male transvestite has a penis, enjoys dressing up as a woman, but wants to keep his penis. A male transsexual has a penis, but sees himself as a woman, and wants to have his genitals changed so he can dress as the woman he feels himself to be.

In a study of 39 transsexuals who had undergone sex-change operations, the researchers observed a tendency toward narcissism. "Narcissism is, in our opinion, one of the most conspicuous characteristics in these persons. The transsexual is inclined to refer all incidents to him/herself and often invests little interest in surrounding persons. This results in a certain emotional stereotype, an intrapsychic rigidity" (Sorensen & Hertoft, 1982, p. 135).

Sample
Control

Transsexual Surgery

Most physicians are very cautious about performing surgery to alter a person's genitals. According to Prince (1978), only about 5 to 10 percent of transsexuals seeking surgery are good candidates for the procedure. A physician's profile of such a candidate includes the following:

> [a] male who views his penis as an abnormal growth, capable of giving him no pleasure whatever, who thinks, and has always thought, of himself as a female person, who comes into the office dressed as a woman and who is so thoroughly feminine in his carriage, bearing and outlook that secretaries, receptionists and the man on the street believe, without reservation that "this is a woman" (Morgan, 1978, p. 274).

Procedures

Sex reassignment takes time (one to two years) and money ($10,000 or more over the two-year span). Although a urologist will normally perform the actual surgery, a number of other professionals are usually involved. A psychiatrist or psychologist provides intensive presurgery therapy to assess the appropriateness of the transsexual's motivation for wanting the operation and to help the person adjust to the new sex identity. This may take a year or longer. During this time the patient usually begins to cross-dress and take hormones monitored by an endocrinologist. If the counseling and hormonal therapy are successful, the surgery is performed. A gynecologist and plastic surgeon may be asked to assist the urologist with the surgery.

Results

The consequences of having transsexual surgery are mixed. Physically, the male-to-female transsexual can have an orgasm when having intercourse; and while the female-to-male transsexual can also have an orgasm, a true erection and penetration are not possible. Also, most transsexuals do not have physical complications following surgery, but others complain of infection, bleeding, and what they regard as the unacceptable appearance of their new genitals (Jayaram, Stuteville, & Bush, 1978).

George Edwin Turtle, a Naval Officer for 37 years, became Georgina Carol Turtle following transsexual surgery.

Psychologically, patients differ in how they evaluate their anatomical transformation. Their responses range from feeling that surgery saved their lives to wanting to commit suicide. Of her positive experience, the writer Jan Morris (1975), a male-to-female transsexual, said, "But I do not for a moment regret the act of change. I could see no other way, and it has made me happy" (p. 186).

Some physicians are skeptical about such reactions and are divided about the advisability of transsexual surgery. In summarizing a follow-up study of surgery for 25 male-to-female transsexuals, Hastings & Markland (1978), noted that, while recognizing the problems one physician said, "It is the alternative that is sobering. In the light of present knowledge, there is no known approach to the treatment of transsexualism other than the surgical route. Nothing else holds promise" (p. 335). Another physician observed that not one of the 130 transsexuals on which he had operated regretted the operation (Eicher, 1983).

In direct contradiction to this view, after performing more than 100 sex-change operations, the team at John Hopkin's University Medical Center decided against performing subsequent transsexual surgery. This decision was based on a study that compared transsexuals who had received surgery and those who received counseling or therapy (Meyer & Reter, 1979). The results showed no difference in the sexual activity, family relationships, and adaptations to daily routine (job, social life) of the two groups. These medical professionals viewed surgery as pacifying the transsexual by giving him or her hope that things would be different, but the basic problem was psychological and remained after the surgery had been completed. Other professionals disagree and suggest that in some cases the basic problem is not psychological but chromosomal and hormonal. Still others believe the issue is sociocultural as our society does not acknowledge or approve of such gender-role confusion, which forces the person to seek surgery.

To conclude this section on biological beginnings, it is clear that some biological differences resulting from chromosomes and hormones help to ensure different life experiences. Only women have the capacity to experience menstruation, pregnancy, and childbirth. Only men will experience penile erection and the ejaculation of semen. But socialization experiences also have a significant impact on who we are and what we become. We now examine these socialization influences.

Socialization Influences

We learn to engage in behavior that is socially defined as appropriate for our gender role. After examining the importance of environmental influences, we look at how parents, teachers, and peers influence us toward gender specific behavior.

Significance of the Environment

The vast majority of psychological and social characteristics designated as feminine or masculine in any given culture are not innate. Rather, they are learned from the material and interpersonal environment in which we grow up. Gender-role prescriptions in our culture not only signal the color of the blanket in which an infant is to be wrapped, but they also dictate appropriate toys (doll or football), clothes (panties or briefs), and work roles (baby sitter or paper boy) for children. Gender roles also tell us whether to be aggressive or passive in interpersonal and sexual interaction.

That women's sexual aggressiveness or passivity is learned behavior is illustrated by a study of females attending male strip shows. In such a situation where women receive peer support for sexual aggressiveness, their passivity seems to disappear. After attending a male strip show weekly for eight months, Peterson and Dressel (1982) summarized their observations.

> A primary feature of the club is that it provides the opportunity for women to be assertive in sexual transactions with males. This takes several forms. Members of the audience initiate expressions of sexual interest, and they emulate male-typed courting behaviors by bringing gifts to, or doing favors for, their favorite dancers, as well as by propositioning strippers of their choice. This display of assertiveness by members of the audience is described by strippers as frequently being excessive, with women often becoming verbally and physically aggressive and sometimes engaging in behavior that dancers describe as lewd (pp. 203–204).

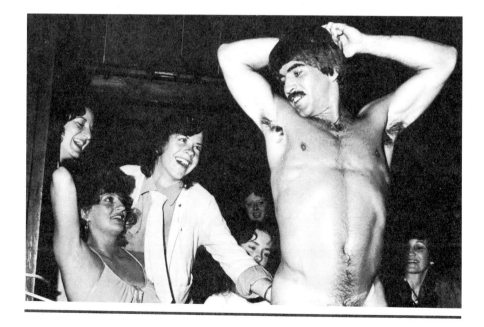

The aggressive behavior of women at male strip shows rebuts the idea that female sexual passivity is innate.

Theories of Gender-Role Learning

Although most theorists agree that the environment has a profound effect on our gender-role development, they do not agree on the specific processes. There are three main explanations of how female and male gender roles are acquired.

Identification Theory

Identification results when the child takes on the demeanor, mannerisms, and attitudes of the same-gender parent. A child who identifies with her or his parent acts like that parent.

Sigmund Freud, the father of psychoanalysis, said that children identify with the same-gender parent out of fear (1925, 1933). This fear may be one of two kinds: fear of loss of love or fear of retaliation. The first type, which results in both girls and boys identifying with their mother, is caused by their deep dependence on her for love and nurturance. Fearful that she may withdraw her love, young children try to become like her to please her and to ensure the continuance of her love.

About age 4 the child's identification with the mother begins to change, but in different ways for boys and girls. Boys experience what Freud calls the Oedipal complex. Based on the legend of the Greek youth Oedipus who unknowingly killed his father and married his mother, the Oedipal complex involves the young boy's awakening sexual feelings for his mother as he becomes aware he has a penis and his mother does not. He unconsciously feels that if his father knew of the intense love feelings he has for his mother, the father would castrate him (which may be what happened to his mother and sister since they have no penis). The boy resolves the Oedipal struggle—feeling love for father but wanting to kill him because he is a competitor for mother's love—by becoming like his father, by identifying with him. In this way the boy can keep his penis and take pride in being like his father. According to Freud, the successful resolution of this Oedipal situation marks the beginning of a boy's appropriate gender-role acquisition.

While her brother is experiencing the Oedipal complex, the girl goes through her own identification process known as the Electra complex. Around age 4 she recognizes that she has no penis, wishes she did (penis envy), and feels her mother is responsible for its absence. To retaliate, she takes her love away from her mother and begins to focus on her father as a love object. But her desire for a penis is gradually transformed into the need for a baby, and to get a baby from her father she recognizes that she must be more like her mother. So she identifies again with her mother. Her goal now is to be a woman like her mother and to be a mother herself. According to Freud, such gender-role identification is characteristic of a mature female.

While Freud's identification theories make interesting stories, there is little scientific support for their validity as explanations for gender-role acquisitions. Most 3- and 4-year-olds do not know the difference between males and females on the basis of their genitals. Also, it is likely that girls have status envy rather than penis envy. They may view the male role as offering more rewards "but the envy originates from the power associated with the male role not with the penis" (Brooks-Gunn & Mathews, 1979, p. 104).

Nevertheless, although verification for Freud's identification theories is weak, his belief in the biological basis of gender-role differences has had significant impact. His dictum "biology is destiny" is still influential in research on gender differences.

In contrast to the negative identification theories suggested by Freud, positive identification theories hold that the child identifies with the parents out of love and good feelings. Since the parents are associated with praise and the elimination of discomfort, the child identifies with the parent as a way of maintaining the feeling of closeness with the parent. In addition, it ". . . is believed that there is a strong emotional tie existing in this relationship (with same sex parent) which does not exist in the child's other relationships with adults or children. This unique emotional bond is the stimulus which activates the child's motive to identify with or imitate the parent" (Frieze et al., 1978, p. 102). Evidence for this positive identification theory is also lacking. Parents of either gender are also punitive, which raises the question of why the child would want to identify with a punishing parent.

Social Learning Theory

Gender-role acquisition also can be explained from a social-learning perspective. Derived from the school of behavioral psychology, the social-learning perspective emphasizes that when gender-appropriate behaviors are rewarded and gender-inappropriate behaviors are punished, a child learns the behaviors appropriate to her or his gender. For example, two young brothers enjoyed playing "lady." Each of them would put on a dress, wear high heeled shoes, and carry a pocketbook. Their father came home early one day and angrily demanded that they "take those clothes off and never put them on again. Those things are for women," he said. The boys were punished for playing "lady," but rewarded with their father's approval for playing "cowboys," complete with plastic guns and "Bang! You're dead!" dialogue.

Reward and punishment alone are not sufficient to account for the way children learn gender roles. There are too many gender rules to learn that require the use of other mechanisms (for example, modeling).

The concept of modeling is important in understanding gender-role acquisition from a social-learning perspective. In modeling the child observes another's behavior and imitates that behavior. Bill, an 8-year-old boy, helped his younger sister repair her tricycle. The Saturday before this event, Bill had observed his father putting spark plugs in their Oldsmobile. His father was the "fix-it man" in their home, and Bill, modeling after him, was the fix-it man in his father's absence.

But the impact of modeling on the development of gender role behavior is controversial. For example, although a modeling perspective implies that children will tend to imitate the parent of the same gender, children are usually reared by women in all cultures. Yet this persistent female model does

Activities are less gender-specific for today's children.

not seem to interfere with the male's developing the appropriate behavior for his gender. One explanation suggests he learns early that males have more status and privileges in our society and he therefore devalues the feminine and emphasizes the masculine aspects of himself. Some research has found that grade-school boys are more likely to reject opposite-gender behavior than are girls (Bussey & Perry, 1982).

Women also do not strictly model their mothers' behavior. While women who work outside the home usually have mothers who did likewise (Stevens & Boyd, 1980), their mothers may also be traditional homemakers (Haber, 1980).

Cognitive Developmental Theory

A cognitive developmental theory of gender-role acquisition suggests that the mental maturity of the child is a prerequisite to acquisition (Kohlberg, 1966, 1969). Although 2-year-olds can label themselves and each other as "girl" or "boy," they have superficial criteria for doing so. People who wear long hair are girls and those who never wear dresses are boys. Two-year-olds believe they can change their gender by altering their hair or changing clothes.

Not until age 6 or 7 does the child view gender as permanent (Kohlberg, 1969). In Kohlberg's view this cognitive understanding is not a result of rewards and punishments for appropriate, gender-role behaviors. Rather, it involves the development of a specific mental ability to grasp the idea that certain basic characteristics of people do not change even though their hair style might. Once children learn that gender is permanent, they seek to become competent and proper members of their gender group. For example, a child standing on the edge of a school playground may observe one group of children jumping rope while another group is playing football. Her or his self-concept ("I am a girl" or "I am a boy") connects with the observed gender-appropriate behavior and she or he joins one of the two groups. Once in the group, the child seeks to develop the behaviors appropriate to her or his gender.

In reviewing the identification, social-learning, and cognitive-developmental perspectives of how individuals become women and men, it is clear that no one explanation is adequate. Depending on the social situation, the age of the child, and the attitudes of the child's parents, each process is influential at different times, in different ways, and to different degrees. Young children will, at times, identify with their parents, be rewarded or punished for gender-appropriate or -inappropriate behaviors, and cognitively choose to develop gender-appropriate behaviors. Table 2.1 describes central acquisition tasks for females and males at different levels and stages throughout the life cycle.

Sources of Socialization

The preceding discussion has implied that different social environments are created for females and males. Since parents, teachers, peers, and the mass media make up our social environment, what are the effects of each? Researchers have suggested the following answers.

Table 2.1   Gender-Role Socialization Across Time

Level of Sex Role	Stage	Central Acquisition Tasks		Sources of Influence (in order of importance)
		Females	*Males*	
Level I: Learning of appropriate child sex roles	Infancy (0–2 years)	(1) Discrimination of males and females	(1) Same	(1) Parents
		(2) Correct categorization of self	(2) Same	(2) Siblings
				(3) Other adults (e.g., grandparents)
	Preschool (2–6 years)	(1) Learning content of sex roles	(1) Same, but more stringent	(1) Parents and nursery teacher
		(2) Acquiring gender constancy	(2) Same	(2) Siblings
				(3) Peers
				(4) Media
	Grade school (6–12 years)	(1) Elaboration of child sex-role content	(1) Same	(1) Same-sex peers
		(2) Development of strong same-sex friendships	(2) Same	(2) Television
				(3) Books
				(4) Teachers
				(5) Parents

(continued)

Table 2.1   Gender-Role Socialization Across Time (Continued)

Level of Sex Role	Stage	Central Acquisition Tasks		Sources of Influence (in order of importance)
		Females	*Males*	
Level II: Preparation for adult sex roles	Early adolescence (12–15 years)	(1) Adjusting to menstruation	(1) Adjusting to ability to ejaculate (early maturing)	(1) Biological factors
		(2) Adjusting to sexual body changes (primary and secondary)	(2) Same for early-maturing boys; less intense	(2) Same-sex peers
		(3) Adjusting to sexual feelings	(3) Same for early-maturing boys; more intense	(3) Television (4) Books (5) Teachers (6) Parents
		(4) Concern with physical attractiveness	(4) Less concern	
	Late adolescence (15–19 years)	(1) Dating	(1) Same	(1) Peers (same- and opposite-sex)
		(2) Concern with physical attractiveness	(2) Less concern	(2) Media
		(3) Adjusting to sexual behavior	(3) Same	(3) Parents
		(4) Courtship (for some)	(4) Same	
		(5) Decreased academic interest	(5) Increased academic interest	
		(6) Conflicts about combining vocation with marriage	(6) Development of vocational interest— no conflict	
Level III: Development of adult sex roles	Young adulthood (20–35 years)	(1) Finding marriage partner	(1) Same	(1) Peers
		(2) Establishing marriage relationship	(2) Same	(2) Spouse
		(3) Pursuing occupation (some)	(3) Pursuing occupation (all)	(3) Same-sex parent
		(4) Pregnancy	(4) Fathering	
		(5) Childbirth	(5) —	
		(6) Breastfeeding (some)		
		(7) Child care (primary responsibility)	(7) Child care (secondary responsibility)	
	Middle adulthood (35–50 years)	(1) Developing and/or re-evaluation marriage relationship	(1) Same	(1) Spouse
		(2) Adjusting to children leaving home (more intense)	(2) Same, less intense	(2) Peers (3) Media
		(3) Adjusting to feelings of loss of youth	(3) Same	
		(4) Developing vocational interests if have not previously	(4) Contemplation of career change	
	Late adulthood	(1) Adjusting to menopause	(1) Adjusting to declining sexual potency	(1) Spouse
		(2) Adjusting to one's own and/or spouse's retirement	(2) Adjusting to retirement	(2) Peers (3) Children (4) Media
		(3) Adjusting to aging	(3) Same	
		(4) Grandparenting	(4) Same	

Parents

The description parents give of their newborn infant depends on the gender of their baby. In one study (Rubin, Provenzano, & Luria, 1974) 30 first-time parents, 15 parents of girls and 15 parents of boys, were asked within 24 hours of their baby's birth to "describe your baby as you would to a close friend or relative." Although hospital records listing the weight, length, and Apgar scores* of the babies showed no significant differences, the parents described their daughters as little, beautiful, delicate and weak, and, in contrast, their sons as firmer, more alert, stronger, and better coordinated.

Beyond these differential reactions to newborns, there are differences in the way parents rear their daughters and sons. Parents tend to give their daughters dolls and their sons baseballs or footballs. They are also more protective of their daughters out of fear they will be sexually molested, although such protectiveness often encourages girls to be less active in exploring their environment. Daughters are more socialized to be family oriented, to be aware of who is having what birthday, and to "want" the family to be together for various holidays. Finally, daughters are often expected to provide more care for ailing family members and relatives than their brothers.

Parents from different social classes also tend to encourage different gender-role views. Middle-class children have less traditional and more blended gender-role definitions compared with working-class children. For example, a middle-class child might feel that both men and women could be gentle, whereas the working-class child would more likely view gentleness as characteristic of women only (Romer & Cherry, 1980).

Teachers

While parents have the earliest and most pervasive influence on their children, teachers are a major influence outside the home. In a study of preschool teachers' interaction with children in their classroom (Serbin & O'Leary, 1975), the researchers observed that the teachers rewarded the boys for being aggressive (by showing attention when they were rowdy), rewarded girls for being dependent (by showing attention when they were near), and gave more individual instruction to boys. The 15 teachers who were being observed were unaware they were treating the genders differently.

Peers

While parents and preschool teachers are important socialization influences in the life of a young child, peers become the dominant influence beginning with grade school and continuing through adolescence. The individual looks to her/his peers to discover "the" appropriate language, dress, and interests. Notice in your own peer group how you "talk the same language,"

---

*A physician's rating of the infant's heart rate (is it normal?), breathing (is it regular?), color (blue to pink), muscle tone (healthy infants are active and move about), and reflex irritability (healthy babies will cough when an object is inserted into their noses).

wear similar clothes, and have interests appropriate for your gender and age. Parents often recognize the significance of peer group influence and encourage their children to have the "right friends."

Media

Television plays a significant role in gender socialization. It has been estimated that the typical child and teenager spends more time in front of the television screen than in school. What the child views often presents a male bias and emphasizes stereotyped roles. In a three-year study of television commercials during the Christmas holiday season, researchers found that boys were significantly more likely to be in such commercials than girls (Feldstein & Feldstein, 1982). In another study of children who watch television (McGhee & Frueh, 1980), boys and girls in grades 1, 3, 5, and 7 were classified as heavy TV viewers (25 or more hours per week) or light TV viewers (10 or fewer hours per week) before they took the Sex Stereotype Measure Instrument. Results showed that those who were heavy TV viewers had more stereotyped gender-role perceptions than light viewers; for example, that men were competitive, persistent, not easily hurt, and "rough" whereas women were noncompetitive, lacking drive, sensitive, and "gentle." Similar sex-role stereotyping is also true of adults who watch a lot of television (Ross, Anderson, & Wisocki, 1982).

Children and adults are even confronted with the same stereotypes in the museum. In a study of gender-role imagery in modern Western art, O'Kelly (1980) found that men frequently are depicted doing something, whereas women are more often at rest; "they are merely like plates or fruits painted for shape, texture, and color" (p. 105). Women also are more often seen nude in seductive poses.

Consequences of Becoming a Woman

A combination of biological factors and feminine gender-role socialization produces a woman. While most women take pride in being a woman, there are various consequences associated with living in this gender role.

Self-Concept

In some cases, women may have less confidence in themselves than men. In one study (McMahan, 1982) 49 men and 62 women were presented with nine cognitive tests (object categories, word endings, and the like) and asked beforehand how they would expect their performance to compare with that of others taking the same tests. The women were much more likely to predict they would perform more poorly than others.

Women may also have lower self-esteem than men. When 925 females and 928 males took the Rosenberg and Simmons' Self-esteem Scale (items included "How happy are you with the kind of person you are?" and "Are more of the things about you good, bad, or are they about the same?"), women scored significantly lower than men (Hoelter, 1983). Research also suggests that some women envy men. In a nationwide sample of 3,000 adult women (Roper Organization, 1980), 4 in 10 felt there were more advantages in being a man. Fewer than 1 in 10 felt that there were more advantages in being a woman.

Disenchantment with being a woman may be related to sexism—which has been defined as the systematic persecution, domination, and degradation of women based on the supposed inferiority of women and the supposed superiority of men—or to traditional gender roles (Seidenberg, 1974). It has also been found that women's self-acceptance is, in part, tied to their physical attractiveness. "The demand to be fashionable, to alter one's body or face, takes its toll on women who constantly feel the need to keep up this front and never to appear as their real, perhaps unacceptable selves" (Whitehurst, 1977, p. 7). But self-acceptance may be increasing. "I am a woman," declared one woman. "I am tired of being called a person." The women's movement, employment outside the home, and greater assertiveness on the part of women may be related to an improved self-image.

Marriage: A Personal Trap?

Because the role of wife is closely related to adult feminine identity in our society, many women feel enormous pressure to get married (more than 90 percent of women marry). But the consequences of socializing women for marriage to the exclusion of other options is often negative.

There is abundant evidence that although marriage is often "good" for men, it is more often "bad" for women (Bernard, 1972). About their marriage, more wives than husbands report frustration, dissatisfaction, problems, unhappiness, and a desire to divorce. About their mental health, more married women than married men feel they are about to have a nervous breakdown, experience more psychological and physical anxiety, and more often blame themselves for their own lack of adjustment (Mugford & Lally, 1981; Rubenstein, 1982).

The changed relationship with her partner upon marriage and her role as housewife are key aspects contributing to the poorer mental health reported by wives. Prior to marriage the woman is catered to by the man. He tells her how nice she looks, takes her to dinner, movies, and other entertainments, and gives her his undivided attention. She is led to believe that his world revolves around her. After marriage she discovers that his world revolves around his work. She becomes the caterer.

But increasingly, wives are leaving the home and entering the work force (more than 50 percent now work outside the home), and doing so seems to have positive results. In a *Psychology Today* survey, employed wives reported feeling less anxious than nonemployed wives (28 percent to 46 percent)

and less lonely (26 percent to 44 percent) (Shaver & Freedman, 1976). Employed wives also report happier marriages than nonemployed wives (Simpson & England, 1981).

Motherhood: A Short Venture

Whether a married woman is employed outside the home or not, she is likely to have children (9 out of 10 women do). Her role as mother tends to take priority over other roles. Her children come first in making decisions about the rest of her life. In a study of over 140,000 mothers, 92 percent said that they were satisfied with the way their children were turning out (Keating, 1983).

But, in perspective, the role of being an active mother is relatively brief. A woman who marries in her early twenties will have children who leave home when she is about 50. Since she can expect to live to be 80 or more, she will have more than a quarter of a century in which her mother role is not primary. The relatively short-term nature of the mother role emphasizes the need for developing other roles, and employment is a primary alternative.

Marriage and Motherhood: Achievement Barriers?

Being a wife and mother may limit a woman's achievements in areas like education and employment.

Education

Women now constitute more than half of all entering college students. While they make better grades than men, they earn fewer degrees at every level. Whether the explanation is that women choose motherhood over long-term career preparation, or women lack educated female models, or they believe there are not enough professional opportunities open to them, the result is the same—women tend to have other priorities than earning academic degrees.

One woman mused about education and her life. "It seems to me that women in general don't look ahead and ask, 'What will I be doing in ten years?' For example, even though I had talent in graduate school and worked for my master's, it never occurred to me to go ahead to a Ph.D. Once I married, I looked forward to having a family. In some ways, I'm glad that I didn't have the pressure of a career while my family was young. I loved that period and made the most of it" (Frankel & Rathvon, 1980, p. 91).

This picture may be changing. As external barriers to professional schools (law, medicine, business) are removed and dual career marriages increase, more academic degrees, will be awarded to women.

Employment

Marriage and motherhood may also interfere with a woman's economic potential. The fact that fewer women earn academic degrees than men and 50 percent drop out of the labor force during their children's preschool years (compared with almost zero percent for men) has implications for the jobs women have and the money they earn. Two researchers observed that women tend to select jobs on the basis of how enjoyable they might be rather than for their income-producing value (Kenkel & Gage, 1983). This may be accounted for by women's lack of job skills and work experience as well as their expectation that work will be interrupted by child-rearing.

Women are also discriminated against in employment. They are given lower positions than men with equivalent qualifications and experience resistance when they seek jobs traditionally held by men (Riemer & Bridwell, 1982). The facts that women earn fewer academic degrees, work in lower-status jobs, and experience barriers to jobs traditionally held by men translate into a lower lifetime income than men achieve. On the average, a man who completes four years of college and works full time will earn $1,190,000 from age 18 to age 64. A college-educated woman who works full time will earn $846,000 (or about 70 percent) between the same ages (Census Bureau, 1983).

With the 50 percent chance of divorce, the likelihood of being a widow for at least 10 years, and the almost certain loss of her parenting role midway through her life, a woman without education and employment skills is often left high and dry. One mother said, "The only thing I want my daughter to remember is to become economically independent doing something she enjoys as a first priority. That way if her husband divorces her or dies and her kids are gone, she will still have something left."

Marriage, Motherhood, Job: Who Has the Best of Everything?

Some women view divorce as happening to someone else and death of their husband as "too far off to worry about." For these women and others, the traditional gender roles of wife and mother offer more rewards than drawbacks. In contrast to many working mothers, full-time homemakers can more freely control and plan their own work and be their own bosses. They are more likely than employed women to see their children's first steps and hear their first words than women who must depend on reports from a babysitter or child-care worker about their child's achievements. Women who enjoy the homemaker role find greater fulfillment in caring for those they most love than in working in a more impersonal setting toward more impersonal goals. They do not see the traditional role as an achievement barrier because they define achievement as providing a good home life for their families and rearing their children successfully.

While many women might prefer to stay at home with their children, especially when they are young, the 50 percent divorce rate has created a number of female-headed households in which the woman is the sole wage earner. In addition, in couple households inflation and high interest rates may require that the wife work outside the home to provide the standard of living desired by the couple or simply to make ends meet. Many are found to work in jobs they do not enjoy.

Most wives who are employed outside the home are personally happy (Gilbert et al., 1981). Among the benefits wives derive from such employment include increased interaction with a variety of individuals, a broader base for recognition, improved economic conditions for self and family, and greater equality between self and spouse. But sometimes the aggressiveness needed to compete successfully in the employment arena is not viewed as positively when expressed by a woman as by a man. On the job, as elsewhere, different standards of behavior may be applied to men and women.

> A business man is aggressive:
>   a business woman is pushy.
> A business man is good on details;
>   she's picky.
> He loses his temper because he's so involved with his job;
>   she's bitchy.
> He follows through;
>   she doesn't know when to quit.
> He stands firm;
>   she's hard.
> His judgments are
>   her prejudices.
> He is a man of the world;
>   she's been around.
> He drinks because of the excess job pressure;
>   she's a lush.
> He isn't afraid to say what he thinks;
>   she's mouthy.
> He exercises authority diligently;
>   she's power-mad.
> He's close-mouthed;
>   she's secretive.
> He climbed the ladder of success;
>   she's slept her way to the top.
> He's a stern task master;
>   she's hard to work for.*

Consequences of Becoming a Man

The role of men in our society has its own difficulties and rewards. We now look at some of these.

*Anonymous poem reprinted in Margrit Eichler's *The Double Standard*. New York: St. Martin's Press, 1980, pp. 15–16.

The Job Requirement

A recent career advertisement in a national magazine showed a young wife looking at her husband while leaning on his shoulder. The man-to-man caption read, "One day, it suddenly strikes home that we're going to be working for a living the rest of our lives." Just as the woman is more often channeled into the roles of wife and mother, the man is tracked into the world of gainful employment to provide primary support for his wife and children. He has little choice. He must work—his wife, children, parents, in-laws, and peers expect it. A college senior responded to this observation by saying, "Baloney! I'm not getting caught in the work trap. I'm going to paint houses now and then—just enough to keep me going—and enjoy life." Three years after graduation he reported, "I'm married now and stuck in a crummy job. I want to get into graduate school so I can get a good job."

A man's responsibility to earn an income and society's tendency to equate income with success have implications for his self-esteem. The assumption is that the man who makes $50,000 annually is more of a man than the one who makes $5,000. Ultimately a man must turn his brain into gold.

The personal, social, and cultural pressure to make money may also interfere with a man's development of other roles and skills. Also, some men have never learned how to cook, wash clothes, or take care of a house. As a result they feel dependent on a woman for these domestic needs. Some men stay married and others remarry because they feel at a loss to take care of themselves. One divorced man said, "I can't deal with cooking and clothes. I need a woman to look out for me."

The Identity-Equals-Job Syndrome

Ask a man who he is and he will tell you what he does. His identity lies in his work. It is the principal means by which he confirms his masculinity. In studies of unemployment during the Great Depression, job loss was regarded as a greater shock to men than to women, although the loss of income affected both.

The identification of self with job becomes problematic when it forces human concerns into a low priority. For example, one father told his 5-year-old daughter who had asked him to play with her, "Don't bother Daddy. I'm busy. Please leave the study." Later that afternoon when he came into the child's room to play with her, she said, "Don't bother me. I'm busy. Please leave my room."

For most men fatherhood is a secondary role, and, as we know, role socialization begins early. When 20 middle-class male children were asked what they wanted to be when they grew up, athlete, fire fighter, and police officer headed the list. "Father" was not on anyone's list (Zuckerman & Sayre, 1982).

Emotional Stereotypes

Some men feel caught between society's expectations that they be competitive, aggressive, independent, and unemotional and what they may feel like being (more open, caring, emotional). Men are expected to show less emotion than women (to cry in public is still taboo for men), and there is abundant evidence that men are less able to express love, happiness, and sadness (Balswick, 1980). The words "I love you," "I'm happy," or "I'm depressed" do not come easy for some men.

When men do display their emotions, they often do so in a more "forceful," "dominating," "boastful," and "authoritarian" way than women, who are more likely to be gentle in their speech (Kramarae, 1981).

Pleck (1981) suggests that parents put too much emphasis on trying to ensure that their sons fit the cultural stereotypes of masculinity. Addressing parental concerns about situations in which the father is away because of divorce or career, he argues that "boys can grow up perfectly well without a strong 'masculine identity' and may be better off without it" (p. 69).

Adapting to Changing Relationships

There is a new equality in relationships between women and men. Modern women, in contrast to traditional women, are more likely to disagree with their partners, challenge their reasons, and suggest alternative explantations and preferences. Acquiescence, submission, and apology are words that less often describe women in today's heterosexual relationships.

But there may be a lag between the relationships women want and relationships men are socialized to accept. In one study (Wilson & Knox, 1981) the women viewed themselves as equal and sought egalitarian relationships. However, the men viewed themselves as traditional and less inclined toward egalitarian relationships.

The egalitarian issue also expresses itself in education. The question has changed from "Where will you work to put me through school?" to "How will we finance our educations?" or "Do you want to finish your education before I finish mine?"

Because of women's increasing desire for education, career involvement, and economic independence, men today can expect women to be less interested in early marriage than formerly.

Also, when women do marry, they are likely to expect more from their partners in sharing child-care and housekeeping reponsibilities than changing a diaper and setting the table. Some feel that liberation for men is not only their freedom to cry but also their willingness to share domestic work.

Finally, women have begun to assert their own sexual needs. Prior to the influence of Masters and Johnson, men could be concerned solely with their own sexual pleasure. Today a man, after ejaculation, may look into the eyes of his frustrated partner who says, "I didn't have an orgasm." He can no longer be the great lover by satisfying only himself.

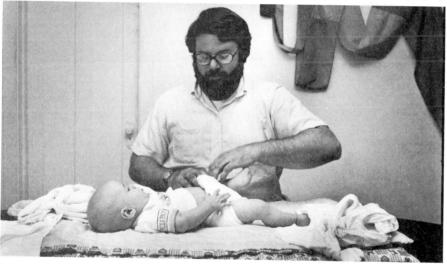

Gender roles are
changing.

Although there have been women's groups for years, some men's groups recently have been formed to assist men in various areas of adjustment. Increasingly, counselors are being trained to conduct such groups. The Male Awareness Leadership Education (MALE) Program in Minneapolis, Minnesota, an eight-week course for professionals, covering such topics as "machismo," "male fears," and "violence." Such groups provide a forum for men to discuss an array of issues which few other opportunities provide.

Women and Men: Some Psychological Differences

Beyond the biological differences between the genders and the way they have been socialized, some evidence suggests there are psychological differences, both cognitive (such as verbal or mathematical skills) and personality (such characteristics as dependence–independence). However, in discussing these differences it should be kept in mind that they are group or average differences. While women as a group may have greater verbal skills than men, the winner of the National Spelling Bee may be a man.

Cognitive Differences

Women and men have somewhat different cognitive skills. These include the following.

Verbal Ability

Although the sexes do not differ in intelligence and creativity, they do differ in verbal ability (Flake-Hobson, Skeen, & Robinson, 1980). Although there are few differences during childhood, around age 11 females begin to excel in creative writing, reading comprehension, and spelling. Greater language skills in girls have been attributed to mothers talking more to their daughters than to their sons (Cherry & Lewis, 1976) and to brain differences (discussed below).

Math Ability

Females are more skillful with words, but males are sharper with numbers. Beginning about age 13, boys evidence superior math ability and score higher on the math aptitude section of college entrance exams. The math gap continues into adulthood (Brooks-Gunn & Matthews, 1979). Greater math ability in boys has been attributed to their being encouraged by counselors, teachers, parents, and persons to excel in math. Girls are not given this same encouragement (Fox, 1981). Although studies disagree about the extent to which females and males vary on math and verbal ability, some suggest that different brain organization may account for any variations. For example, it is known that the left hemisphere (the left side of the brain) tends to influence language ability and the right hemisphere (the right side of the brain) tends to influence spatial–math abilities. We emphasize the phrase "tends to influence" as either side of the brain can influence language or spatial math abilities. But the fact that women score significantly higher than men on verbal tests and men score higher on spatial–math tests suggests that brain differences may be operative. Still, the overall score differences are small and do not suggest that men cannot develop good language skills or that women cannot be math teachers. Indeed there are tremendous social and cultural forces beyond the innate ones which impact language and math skills.

Personality Differences

Psychological differences between the sexes on cognitive abilities are relatively easy to measure. But when psychological differences in personality are compared, the measurement becomes more difficult and the interpretations more elusive. Some of these presumed personality differences between the genders include the following.

Fear and Anxiety

Women are stereotyped as being fearful of everything from mice to ferris wheels, and men are often regarded as being brave about everything from snakes to cliffhanging. Two researchers reviewed 26 studies that assessed sex differences on fear and anxiety. Whereas nine studies revealed no differences, the remaining ones found that females were more fearful and anxious than males (Maccoby & Jacklin, 1974). But these findings may be misleading. Not only may females be more willing to admit such feelings than males, but also their socialization involves considerable fear induction by parents who warn their daughters about strange men, lonely places, and other situations associated with the possibility of sexual molestation.

Some researchers have suggested that women fear success in the male-dominated career world. Such fear is not innate but acquired. It may be due to women assuming a new role, say, that of an engineering student, or to their fear of obligating themselves to too many roles—worker, wife, and mother (Bremer & Wittig, 1980).

Dependency

If some women have been socialized to be fearful, others have been taught to be dependent, in need of the protection of others. Traditionally, many women have been brought up to be dependent on men throughout their lives—first on their fathers, then on their husbands, and finally on their sons. But studies on dependency have been inconsistent in their findings (Maccoby & Jacklin, 1974).

When being independent is defined as the ability to terminate a love relationship and to adjust well to its end, women excel. In a study of 103 couples who had ended their relationships, the women were more likely to initiate the termination and to be less depressed, lonely, and unhappy afterward (Hill, Rubin & Peplau, 1976).

Nurturance

Defined as the tendency to help others, nurturance also seems related to the social context. One researcher analyzed data collected in six different cultures (Kenya, India, Okinawa, the Philippines, Mexico, and the New England region of the United States) on 134 children aged 3 to 11 (Whiting & Edwards, 1973). While no gender differences in nurturance were observed through age 6, the 7- to 11-year-old females offered help and gave more emotional support to others than did males. But this gender difference was related to the tasks assigned to the young in the respective societies. For example, in the East African culture of Kenya in which males baby sat and had other domestic duties, males differed little from the females on nurturance.

After reviewing this and other studies on nurturance, Tavris and Offir (1977) remarked:

> . . . though caring for children, home, and spouse is traditionally the woman's job, protecting them is the man's: he is expected to buy life insurance, investigate night noises in the basement, and go down with the ship if the lifeboats are full. There is no doubt which parent usually spends more time with the children, but we cannot conclude with any confidence at this point that one sex is inherently the more nurturant. (p. 53)

Cross-Cultural Stereotypes

To what degree are women and men in different countries viewed as having different psychological characteristics? Williams and Best (1982) conducted a study in which students in 25 countries were presented with 300 adjectives and asked to describe whether each was more frequently associated with women or men. Results showed that in all countries women were viewed as dependent, affectionate, fearful, and sentimental, and men were viewed as independent, dominant, adventurous, and forceful.

The researchers explained their findings by observing that most societies assign child care to women, who can nurse the infant, and hunting and defense to men. Once these gender-role assignments have been made, it is functional to view women as innately dependent, affectionate, and sentimental. Likewise, if men are to be hunters and warriors, it is comforting to believe that they are independent and forceful.

Attribution of Gender Differences

Deaux (1976) emphasized that the evaluation of a person's performance varies in relation to whether a woman or man is being evaluated. In a series of studies Deaux observed that successful performance by a woman is explained by statements like "she was lucky," "the task was easy," or "she cheated," in contrast to successful performance by a man, which is viewed as a result of his ability. The implication of the negative attribution of success to women and positive attribution of success to men emerges in the employment line. Employers, who believe that success (that is, profits) is based on ability and competence rather than luck, might be biased against hiring a woman whose success may be based on that more ephemeral substance.

Summary

The term gender refers to the biological distinction of being male or female. In contrast, a person's gender identity is her or his self-concept of being a girl and later a woman or a boy and later a man. Gender roles are the socially accepted characteristics and behaviors associated with a person's gender identity. In our society the traditional role of women is to be emotional, dependent, and home oriented, whereas the traditional male role is to be unemotional, independent, and career oriented. Today these stereotypes are breaking down under the impact of changes in family structure and job participation.

Gender-role behaviors of women and men are a result of the combined effect of biological inheritance and environment. Biological inheritance includes chromosomes, genes, and hormones, resulting in sexual differentiation. Only women menstruate, get pregnant, give birth, and nurse their infants. Only males get penile erections and ejaculate semen.

But biological inheritance is overlaid with environmental influences. There are several explanations of how children learn appropriate gender-role behaviors: identification, social-learning, and cognitive-developmental. Identification theory suggests that children either out of fear or love, take on the role of the same-sex parent. The social-learning perspective states that children learn their roles by being rewarded for gender-appropriate behaviors and punished for inappropriate (opposite-gender behaviors). In the cognitive-developmental view of gender-role learning, children first reach the stage where they understand that their gender is permanent and then actively seek to acquire masculine or feminine characteristics. While biology via chromosomes, genes, and hormones predisposes people to behave in certain ways, society (represented by parents, teachers, peers, and mass media) guides the person's behavior into culturally approved-channels; for example, girls playing with dolls and boys playing with cars and trucks.

Being socialized as a woman or man has consequences for the person. Women sometimes have less confidence in themselves than men because of pervasive sexism and the cultural demand that they always be young, trim, and beautiful. Marriage is sometimes a trap since wives discover that husbands are often more interested in work than family. Women also get less education and earn less income than males. Those who do not develop an interest other than their husbands and children may feel a void when those roles terminate.

Men, on the other hand, feel an imperative to earn money and are looked down on by society if they do not. They are also less emotionally expressive and sometimes place human relationships below their work. Adapting to more assertive, egalitarian-oriented women is becoming increasingly more important to men.

The psychological differences between the genders include greater verbal ability by women and greater math ability by men. Differential reinforcement patterns and innate brain differences may be operative in accounting for these differences. From a cross-cultural perspective, most societies regard women as affectionate and men as aggressive. These perspectives may be due to the assignment of child care to women and nondomestic activities to men.

Key Terms

gender
gender identity
gender role (or sex role)
primary sex characteristics
secondary sex characteristics
chromosomes
gene
Klinefelter's syndrome
hermaphrodite

androgenital syndrome
testicular feminization syndrome
transsexual
identification theory
social learning theory
cognitive developmental theory
sexism
monozygotic twins*
androgynous*

*These terms are discussed in the "Issues in Debate" section that follows.

Issues in Debate and Future Directions

Each of us began life as a zygote, a fertilized egg. Yet whether we become a woman or a man depends on an array of biological factors and socialization influences. The importance of "nature" versus "nurture" continues to be debated heatedly among scientists. Here we examine both sides of the heredity versus environment issue; then we look at the future of gender roles in our society.

Are Gender Role Behaviors Innate?

Those on the "nature" side of the nature–nurture controversy strongly contend that it is our biological inheritance that programs us to be who we are. As we have seen in this chapter, women and men have different chromosomes, genes, and hormones. Not only do these factors result in biological differences (women typically weigh less, are shorter, have lower blood pressures, and die later than men), but also they influence an individual's sexual preference and his or her psychological makeup.

Studies of identical twins who were reared apart emphasize the impact of heredity. Also known as **monozygotic twins,** identical twins develop from a single fertilized egg that divides to produce two embryos. These embryos develop into individuals that, from a genetic viewpoint, are identical. If these individuals are exposed to different environments in their infancy and childhood, yet show striking similarities as adults, heredity is the suggested cause.

A team of researchers at the University of Minnesota (Bouchard et al., 1980) have studied 15 such pairs of twins, asking each twin about 15,000 questions. The researchers observed a striking tendency for the twins to show very similar physical and psychological characteristics. If one stuttered, had a phobia, had headaches, was shy, anxious, or depressed, or had a particular interest, the other tended to have the same characteristic.

Additional evidence for biological determinism has been suggested by a study in the Dominican Republic (Imperato-McGinley et al., 1974). Due to a genetic endocrine problem, a large number of males were born who at first appeared to be females, having a vaginal pouch instead of a scrotum and a clitoris instead of a penis. The parents, unaware that anything was unusual, reared the biological males as females.

But at puberty a spontaneous hormonal change caused the development of a penis in these individuals and a change in their psychological orientation. These males who had been reared as females began to view themselves as males and to develop a sexual interest in females. Other researchers feel strongly that sexual identity is innate. Dr. Milton Diamond (1982), a specialist in sexual and gender identities, says that each individual has an inherent male or female nervous system that biases the development of that person's sexual identity and partner choice.

Are Gender Role Behaviors Learned?

In contrast to the belief that we are biologically programmed to become who we are, other researchers state just as emphatically that we learn to be who we are. While the fact that women and men have different biological makeups which result in different body sizes and reproductive outcomes (only women become pregnant) is acknowledged, this group completely rejects the idea that various personality traits and social behaviors are also innate.

We have examined some of the evidence that we are products of our experiences via modeling, identification, and social learning. Further evidence for the impact of learning experiences on the development of gender-role characteristics comes from a study at the University of Arizona (Ridley et al., 1982). Twenty-six couples were assigned to a problem-solving skills training program after taking the Bem Sex Role Inventory (BSRI), designed to assess the degree to which each person viewed herself or himself as masculine or feminine.

The training consisted of meeting in small groups for three hours weekly for eight weeks with an instructor who outlined various problem-solving skills, modeled the skills, and gave feedback to the couples who practiced the skills. A specific aspect of the training sessions was teaching the participants how to disclose themselves to each other and to express their own feelings. After completing the training, the participants took the BSRI again. Results showed that both men and women scored higher on femininity following the training. Similar changes were not observed in the control group of this experiment.

This study indicates that empathy and self-disclosure, two traits typically associated with women, can be learned. They are not innate traits but are acquired through social and cultural exposure to various learning situations. The fact that males typically show less empathy and are less self-disclosing than females is a consequence of their socialization, not their heredity. "Our biological legacy is the ability to choose how we would like to live" (Weisstein, 1982, p. 85).

The fact that the nature–nurture, heredity–environment controversy continues underscores the fact that *both* innate and learning influences interact to produce who we are, what we think, and how we behave.

Future Directions

Although we continue to recognize that a person's biological heritage has a significant impact on her or his development, our society is becoming less rigid in its gender-role socialization. As a result there will be fewer roles closed to women, more **androgynous** people (those with both feminine and masculine characteristics), and more assertive females and expressive males. In the past 10 years, a number of social barriers to women's participation in formerly all-male activities have been removed. No longer are women barred from being Supreme Court justices, West Point Cadets, or astronauts. Girls now play baseball on Little League teams.

As each gender begins to fill a wider range of roles, the trend toward androgyny will increase. For example, men will feel more free to be gentle and to express their emotions, while women will more often be assertive and competitive. Part of this change will result from women's greater participation in work outside the home and men's greater involvement in child care. Developing more of the qualities of the opposite gender is often viewed as developing the best of both worlds, feminine and masculine, and may also be associated with good mental health (Burchardt & Serbin, 1982). Androgynous people are flexible and easy going.

Chapter Three

Sexual Anatomy and Physiology

*What did your body say to mine
deep in velvet night's delight?*

WILLIAM ROSE BENÉT

Chapter Three

People enrolled in a human sexuality course often ask why they must study sexual anatomy. Many people are sexually experienced without having learned the correct terminology for the female and male reproductive systems. But we have found that students taking a course such as this may have erroneous ideas about sexuality because they lack an understanding of anatomical structure and function; for example, some believe that a sexually inexperienced female must have a hymen and bleed during first intercourse or that the ability to satisfy a woman sexually is related to penis size or that couples can become "locked" during intercourse.

Although a knowledge of basic anatomy would dispel these and other myths, would it make us better lovers? Well, maybe. Many people are so inhibited about their sexuality that they have never examined their own genitals. Such behavior is discouraged or even punished by many parents. By becoming more aware of our own body and that of our sexual partner through studying sexual anatomy, we might also become less inhibited about exploring our sexuality. The meaning of *intercourse* is "communication" (*Webster's New World Dictionary*). It is difficult to communicate about anything, including our bodies, without some basic knowledge.

Female External Anatomy

The external female genitalia are collectively known as the **vulva** (VUHL-vuh), a Latin term meaning "covering." The vulva consists of the mons veneris, the labia, the clitoris, and the vaginal and urethral openings (Figure 3.1). A less preferable term for these structures is pudendum (pyoo-DEN-dum), derived from the Latin word *pudendus* meaning "something to be ashamed of." This term reflects the ambivalent feelings that many females have toward their genitalia. A woman's judgment about her overall physical appearance often affects her feelings about her sexual anatomy. Like faces, the female genitalia differ in size, shape, and color, resulting in considerable variability in appearance (Figure 3.2).

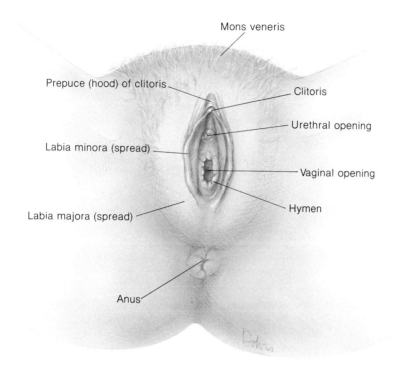

Mons veneris

Prepuce (hood) of clitoris

Clitoris

Urethral opening

Labia minora (spread)

Vaginal opening

Labia majora (spread)

Hymen

Anus

Figure 3.1
External Female
Genitalia

The Mons Veneris

The soft cushion of fatty tissue overlaying the pubic bone is called the **mons veneris** (mahns vuh-NAIR-ihs), Latin for "mound of Venus," the Roman goddess of love. Also known as the mons pubis, this area becomes covered with hair at puberty. The pubic hair varies in color and texture depending on genetic factors. The mons has numerous nerve endings and many women find that gentle stimulation of this area is highly pleasurable. In addition, the mons acts as a cushion to protect the pubic region during intercourse. The pubic hair also serves to trap secretions that occur during sexual arousal, the odor of which is often found to be erotically stimulating (Hassett, 1978).

The Labia

In the sexually unstimulated state, the urethral and vaginal openings are protected by the **labia majora** (LAY-bee-uh muh-JOR-uh), "major lips," two elongated folds of fatty tissue that extend from the mons to the **perineum**,

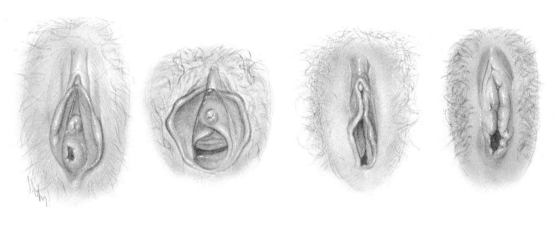

**Figure 3.2
Variations in the
Vulva**

(pair-uh-NEE-uhm), the sensitive area of skin between the opening of the vagina and the anus. The labia majora usually meet in the middle in women who have not given birth, but often remain apart in those who have borne children. The skin on the outer surfaces of the labia majora is darker than the surrounding areas and covered by pubic hair, whereas the inner surfaces are hairless and lighter in color.

Located between the labia majora are two additional hairless folds of skin called the **labia minora** (muh-NOR-uh), "minor lips," which also cover the urethral and vaginal openings and join at the top to form the prepuce or hood of the clitoris. It is not uncommon for the labia minora to protrude beyond the labia majora. In fact, in some societies such as the Hottentots of Africa this is considered desirable and the women purposely attempt to elongate their minor lips by pulling on them. The pinkish labia minora, which have numerous nerve endings making them very sensitive to tactile stimulation, also have a rich supply of small blood vessels. During sexual stimulation the labia minora become engorged with blood, causing them to swell and change in color. With prolonged stimulation the inner surfaces of the labia minora receive a few drops of fluid from the small **Bartholin's** (BAR-toh-lihnz) **glands**, which are located at the base of the minor lips. However, the small amount of fluid does not make a significant contribution to vaginal lubrication and the function of the glands remains unknown. Unfortunately, the Bartholin's glands are sometimes the site of infection or cysts, and any swelling or local irritation should be examined by a physician.

The Clitoris

The **clitoris** (KLIHT-uh-ruhs) is the most sensitive area of the female genitalia (Figure 3.3). It has no direct reproductive function and is apparently the only structure whose sole purpose is to focus sexual sensations and erotic

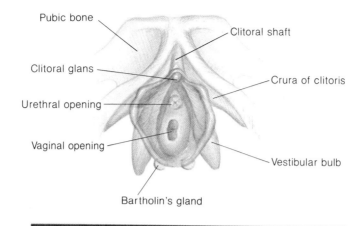

Pubic bone

Clitoral shaft

Clitoral glans

Crura of clitoris

Urethral opening

Vaginal opening

Vestibular bulb

Bartholin's gland

**Figure 3.3
Anatomy of the
Clitoris**

pleasure. It develops embryologically from the same tissue as the penis and has as many or more nerve endings as the much larger penis. In a sexually unaroused woman, the only visible part of the clitoris is the glans, which looks like a small, shiny button located just below the clitoral hood. The size of the clitoral glans, which is about ¼ inch in diameter and ¼ to 1 inch in length, is not related to the subjective experience of pleasure. Nor is female responsiveness related to the distance between the vaginal opening and the clitoral glans, as some people mistakenly believe. Hidden from view by the clitoral hood is the shaft of the clitoris, which divides into two much larger structures called crura (CROO-ruh), which are attached to the pubic bone. The body of the clitoris consists of spongy tissue, which fills with blood during sexual arousal, resulting in a doubling or tripling in size. Like the penis, stimulation of any part of the body may result in erection of the clitoris. With sufficient sexual arousal, however, the glans of the clitoris disappears beneath the clitoral hood.

Surgical removal of the clitoris, or **clitoridectomy**, is a common ritualized practice in many Middle Eastern and African countries. Today, half of all young girls in Egypt have their clitoris removed to keep the girl a virgin and the woman faithful (Khattab, 1983). In the past clitoridectomy was performed in the United States and European countries ostensibly to prevent masturbation. As many as 75 million women worldwide may have had their clitoris crudely mutilated or removed.

The Vaginal Opening

The area between the labia minora is called the **vestibule**. This includes the urethral opening and the vaginal opening, or introitus (ihn-TROH-ih-tuhs), neither of which are visible unless the labia minora are parted. Like the anus and other bodily orifices, the vaginal opening is surrounded by a ring of sphincter muscles (the bulbocavernosus muscles). Although the vaginal entrance can expand to accommodate the passage of a baby at childbirth, under conditions of tension these muscles involuntarily contract, making it difficult to insert an object, including a tampon, into the vagina. On the other hand, women learn to voluntarily contract these muscles to increase sensation during intercourse. Also contributing to the tightness of fit are the vestibular bulbs, which are located underneath the bulbocavernosus muscles on both sides of the vaginal opening. These swell with blood during sexual arousal and help the vagina to grip the penis. The vaginal opening has numerous nerve endings and is very sensitive to stimulation.

Human females are typically born with a thin membrane called the **hymen** partially covering the opening to the vagina (see Figure 3.4). It has no known physiological function. The appearance of the hymen varies from a single opening (annular hymen) to two (septate hymen) or more openings (cribiform hymen). In rare instances the hymen may have no opening (imperforate hymen), but this may be corrected by a simple surgical incision at the time of first menstruation. The opening of the hymen is usually large enough to allow insertion of a finger or tampon.

Probably no other body part has caused as much grief to so many women as the hymen, which has been regarded throughout history as proof of virginity. A newly wed woman who was thought to be without a hymen was often returned to her parents, disgraced by exile, or even tortured and killed. It has been a common practice in many societies to parade a bloody bedsheet after the wedding night as proof of the bride's virginity. The anxieties caused by the absence of a hymen persist even today, and in Japan and other countries sexually experienced women may have a plastic surgeon reconstruct a hymen prior to marriage. Yet the hymen is really a poor indicator of virtue. Some women are born without a hymen or with incomplete hymens, while in others the hymen is accidentally ruptured by vigorous physical activity or insertion of a tampon. In some women the hymen may not tear but only stretch during sexual intercourse. Even most doctors cannot easily determine whether a female is a virgin.

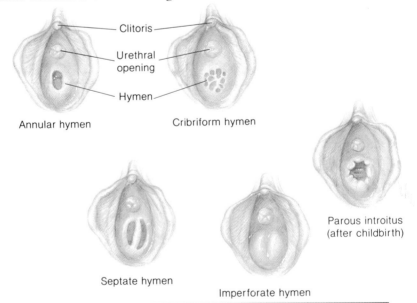

**Figure 3.4
Variations in the
Hymen**

The Urethral Opening

The female's urinary system, (unlike the male's), is not related to the reproductive system; there are separate openings for coitus and urination. Urine passes from the body through the very small urethral opening, which is located below the clitoris and above the vaginal opening. A short tube, the urethra, connects the bladder where urine collects with the urethral opening. Small glands called **Skene's glands** are located just inside the urethral opening and develop from the same embryonic tissue as the male prostate gland. These glands are the source of the fluid that some women emit from the urethra during orgasm (Perry & Whipple, 1981).

Because of the shorter length of the female urethra and the close proximity of the anus to the vestibular area, women are more susceptible than men to **cystitis**, a bladder inflammation. The most common sympton is frequent urination accompanied by a burning sensation; there also may be a discharge of blood or pus. A gynecologist should be consulted if a woman experiences any of these symptoms. A common cause of cystitis is the transmission of bacteria that live in the intestines to the urethral opening. After a bowel movement a woman should avoid wiping herself from the anus toward the vulva, and anal intercourse should never be followed by vaginal intercourse. Vigorous intercourse, particularly in sexually inexperienced women, can also cause irritation of the urethral wall, but this "honeymoon cystitis" is less serious than that caused by bacterial infection.

Female Internal Anatomy

The internal female sex organs include the vagina, uterus, and the paired Fallopian tubes and ovaries (Figures 3.5 and 3.6). These are often referred to collectively as the female reproductive system. For fertilization to take place, sperm must travel a path through the vagina and uterus and into the Fallopian tube containing a mature egg from one of the two ovaries.

The Vagina

The **vagina** (vuh-JIGH-nuh) is a 3- to 5-inch muscular tube located behind the bladder and in front of the rectum pointing at a 45° angle toward the small of the back. In addition to receiving the penis during intercourse, the vagina functions as a passageway for menstrual flow and as the birth canal. The walls of the vagina are normally collapsed. Thus the vagina is actually a potential space, which can expand by as much as 2 inches in both length and diameter during intercourse.

The walls of the vagina have three layers, the inner layer having a soft, pliable, mucosal surface similar to that of the mouth. Vaginal lubrication begins

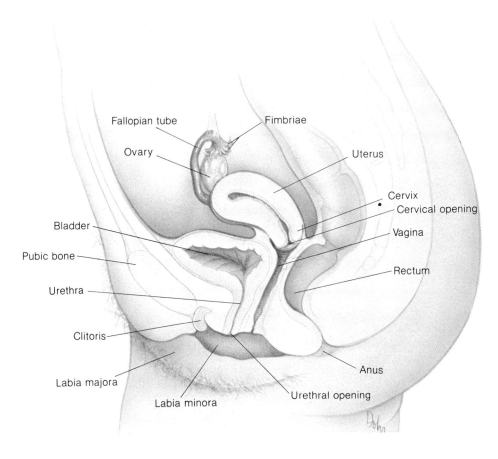

Fallopian tube   Fimbriae

Ovary   Uterus

Cervix

Cervical opening

Bladder   Vagina

Pubic bone

Rectum

Urethra

Clitoris

Anus

Labia majora

Urethral opening

Labia minora

**Figure 3.5
Internal Female
Sexual and
Reproductive
Organs, Sagittal
View**

within a minute after sexual arousal. The vaginal walls become engorged
with blood and the consequent pressure causes the mucous lining to secrete
drops of fluid. The vaginal walls are very thin before puberty, but thicken
and become highly vascularized during puberty as a result of increasing hormone levels. Lower levels of female hormones after menopause cause the
walls again to become thinner and less richly supplied with blood, decreasing the amount of lubrication during sexual arousal. In some cases, vaginal
lubrication may be so impaired after menopause that a lubricant may be required for intercourse.

Unlike the vaginal opening, the walls of the inner two-thirds of the vagina
have few nerve endings and are thus relatively insensitive to touch. In fact,
some women cannot detect the presence of a vaginal probe under laboratory
conditions, but it is uncertain whether the vaginal walls are so insensitive
during normal sexual arousal. Other factors may contribute to subjective
feelings of pleasure during intercourse. The vagina is surrounded by the **pubococcygeal muscles**, which are more richly supplied with nerves, and
during intercourse they involuntarily or voluntarily contract sometimes in-

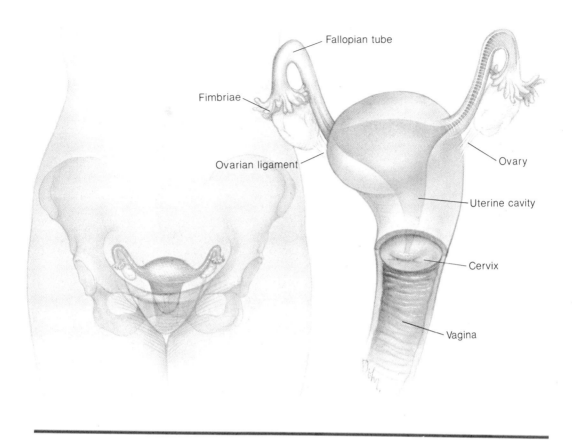

creasing sensation for the woman and her partner. In addition, it appears that many women have an extremely sensitive area, called the **Grafenberg spot**, in the anterior wall of the vagina about 1 or 2 inches into the opening. The spot swells during stimulation, and although a woman's initial response may be a need to urinate, continued stimulation generally leads to orgasm (Perry & Whipple, 1981).

The vagina is a self-cleansing organ. The bacteria that are found naturally in the vagina help to destroy other potentially harmful bacteria. In addition, secretions from the vaginal walls help maintain its normally acidic environment. The secretions have a musky odor that advertisers of feminine hygiene products have sought to characterize as offensive. However, in many nonhuman mammalian species the chemical secretions of the vagina act as sexual attractants and, as we noted, many men find the normally musky odor of the human vagina to be sexually arousing (Hassett, 1978). The use of feminine hygiene sprays, as well as excessive douching, may not only mask these odors but also cause irritation, allergic reactions, and, in some cases, vaginal infection by altering the normal chemical balance of the vagina (see Chapter 12).

Some women fear that an erect penis may be too large for their vagina and cause pain or injury during intercourse; extreme anxiety can cause severe in-

**Figure 3.6
Internal Female
Sexual and
Reproductive
Organs, Front View**

voluntary contractions of the pelvic muscles, preventing intercourse. However, as we have noted, the vagina expands during sexual arousal and is capable of accommodating a penis of virtually any diameter. Stories that a couple can become locked together, which are based on observations of dogs during coitus (the penis of a dog expands into a knot), are unfounded. If a penis should prove to be too long for full penetration by the male, which seldom occurs, simple adjustments can be made in the position of intercourse. Most of the so-called problems of vaginal size are caused by psychological factors.

Other women may be concerned that their vagina is too large for their partner's penis, leading to decreased sensitivity for her and her partner. This problem, which may occur after childbirth, can be largely offset by the woman learning to voluntarily contract the pubococcygeal muscles surrounding the vagina as well as the sphincter muscles surrounding the vaginal opening through Kegel exercises (discussed in Chapter 11).

The Uterus

The **uterus** (YOOT-uh-ruhs), or womb, resembles a small, inverted pear which in women who have not given birth measures about 3 inches long and 3 inches wide at the top. It is here that the fertilized ovum develops into a fetus. No other organ is capable of expanding as much as the uterus does during pregnancy. Held in the pelvic cavity by ligaments, the uterus is generally perpendicular to the vagina. However, in 1 in every 10 women the uterus tilts backward, which poses no serious problems but may cause discomfort in some positions during intercourse.

The broad rounded part of the uterus is the **fundus**, and the narrower portion, which projects into the vagina, is the **cervix**. The cervix feels like a small slippery bump at the back of the vagina. The opening of the cervix, through which sperm and menstrual flow pass, is normally much too small for a penis or finger to be inserted, but at childbirth it dilates to about 4 inches to allow passage of the baby. Secretory glands located in the cervical canal produce mucus that differs in consistency at different stages of the menstrual cycle.

The uterus consists of three layers. The inner layer, endometrium, where the fertilized ovum normally implants, is rich in blood vessels and glands. It is surrounded by a layer of strong muscles, the myometrium, which contracts during childbirth aiding delivery. The external cover of the uterus is called the perimetrium. The uterus has no surface nerve endings, and thus stimulation of the cervix or uterus during sexual intercourse does not contribute to actual feelings of pleasure.

The Fallopian Tubes

The **Fallopian tubes** (fuh-LOH-pee-uhn) or oviducts, extend about 4 inches laterally from either side of the uterus to the ovaries. It is in the Fallopian tubes that fertilization normally occurs. The tubes transport the ovum, or egg, from the ovary to the uterus, but the tubes do not make direct contact with the ovaries. The funnel-shaped ovarian end of the tube, or infundibulum, is in close proximity to the ovary and has fingerlike projections called fimbria, which are thought to aid in picking up the egg from the abdominal cavity. However, there are cases in which women who are missing an ovary on one side and a Fallopian tube on the other side have become pregnant, suggesting some sort of chemical attractant of the ovum for the tube.

Passage of the egg through the tube, which takes about three days, is aided by the sweeping motion of hairlike structures, or cilia, on the inside of the tubes. Occasionally, a fertilized egg becomes implanted outside the uterus, called an ectopic pregnancy. The most common type of ectopic pregnancy occurs within a Fallopian tube and poses a serious health threat unless surgically treated.

Tying off the Fallopian tubes, so that egg and sperm cannot meet, is the most common type of sterilization procedure in females. The tubes can also be blocked by inflammation and serious infections can result in permanent scarring and even sterility.

The Ovaries

The **ovaries** (OH-vuhr-eez), which are attached by ligaments on both sides of the uterus, are the female gonads corresponding to the testes in the male. These almond-shaped structures have the two functions of producing ova and the female hormones **estrogen** and **progesterone**. At birth the ovaries have about 400,000 immature ova, each contained in a thin capsule to form a follicle. Some of the follicles begin to mature at puberty, but only about 400 mature ova will be released in a woman's lifetime.

Menstruation

Sometime around the age of 12 or 13 in females, a part of the brain called the hypothalamus signals the pituitary gland at the base of the brain to begin releasing **follicle-stimulating hormone (FSH)** into the bloodstream. It is not known what causes the pituitary gland to release FSH at this time, but the hormone stimulates a follicle to develop and release a mature egg from the ovary. If the egg is fertilized, it will normally implant itself in the endometrium of the uterus, which has become thick and engorged with blood vessels in preparation for implantation. If the egg is not fertilized, the thickened tissue of the uterus is sloughed off. This flow of blood, mucus, and dead tissue cells from the uterus is called **menstruation** and the time of first menstruation is the **menarche**. Except during pregnancy, this process will repeat itself at roughly monthly intervals until the menopause. Although the average menstrual cycle is 28 days in length, cycles may vary between 15 and 45 days in different women and there are a few women whose cycles are so consistent that they can accurately predict the day when menstruation will begin. Some feelings about menstruation follow:

What women say . . .

I'm tired of going through it (cramps, headaches, backaches) every month. I'm also very irritable and emotional.

It doesn't bother me.

I hate it.

It is part of being female.

I dread it coming but am always glad its here.

It's a pain and bother.

It's inconvenient.

Yucko!

I get depressed.

It doesn't change my moods or alter my sex behavior.

If they take tampons off the market I'm going to stop having mine. It's already enough of a pain without having to use rags.

I wish there was a way to turn it off until I am ready to have children.

I wish men had to go through it.

It is a curse; sometimes I wonder if being able to have a baby is worth all the trouble.

It makes me feel good to know that I am a woman and can have a baby.

What men say . . .

It means my partner isn't pregnant.

I'm glad I don't have to go through it.

My partner gets edgy.

It's a good and healthy thing for a woman; it cleans the inner body.

Women deserve some understanding from the male.

It's natural.

It's one of the benefits of being a male.

It means my partner won't have sex so I don't like it.

Phases of the Menstrual Cycle

The menstrual cycle can be divided into four phases (Figure 3.7): preovulatory (also known as the follicular or proliferative phase), ovulatory, postovulatory (also known as the secretory or luteal phase), and menstrual. The preovulatory phase begins with the release of FSH from the pituitary, stimulating the growth of a follicle in the ovary. As the follicle grows, it secretes increasing amounts of estrogen, which causes growth of the endometrium of the uterus and an increase in the cervical mucus to provide a hospitable environment for sperm. Estrogen also signals the pituitary to inhibit further releases of FSH and to begin secreting **luteinizing hormone** (LH). When the levels of estrogen reach some critical point, there is a great surge in blood levels of LH followed within 36 hours by ovulation. During ovulation the follicle moves to the periphery of the ovary and expels the ovum into the abdominal cavity. Ovulation occurs about 14 days before the start of menstruation regardless of the length of the cycle.

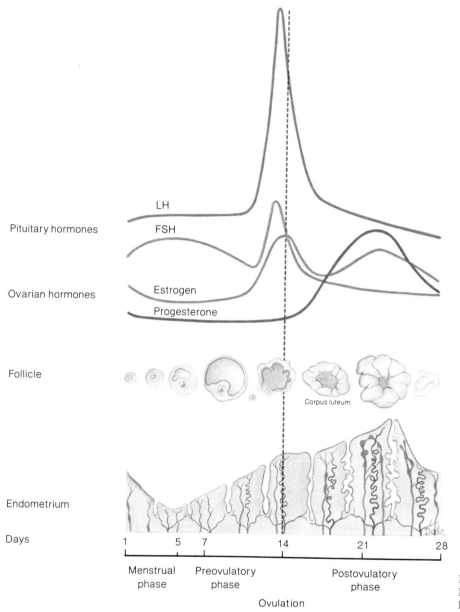

Pituitary hormones

LH

FSH

Ovarian hormones

Estrogen

Progesterone

Follicle

Corpus luteum

Endometrium

Days

| 1 | 5 | 7 | 14 | 21 | 28 |

Menstrual phase

Preovulatory phase

Postovulatory phase

Ovulation

Figure 3.7
Four Phases of the Menstrual Cycle

In the postovulatory phase, the remaining cells of the follicle in the ovary (now called the corpus luteum) continue to secrete estrogen and another female hormone, progesterone. These hormones cause the endometrium to thicken further and build up nutrients should the egg be fertilized and implant in the uterine wall. If fertilization occurs, the lining of the uterus is maintained during pregnancy by continuous secretion of estrogen and progesterone from the corpus luteum. If fertilization does not occur, the corpus luteum disintegrates, resulting in decreasing levels of the two hormones maintaining the endometrium and in menstruation. Menstruation lasts from three to seven days. With the decrease in estrogen levels, the pituitary again begins to secrete FSH and the cycle starts over again.

During menstruation the endometrial matter is sloughed off in small shreds or larger pieces. The total blood loss during menstruation is only about 4 to 6 tablespoons. A smaller amount of blood does not mean as old folklore suggests that blood is accumulating elsewhere in the body, later to poison the female.

Problems of the Menstrual Cycle

Although most adolescent women have regular periods, irregularity, or **oligogmenorrhea** is not unusual. The intervals may range from every three weeks to every six weeks. Some women have periods only once a year. If periods have not stabilized by age 17 or so, a gynecologist should be consulted. Spotting or bleeding between periods also suggests the need for a checkup.

A missed period may or may not imply pregnancy. Anxiety over work or the relationship with a partner or the fear of being pregnant can cause a woman to miss her period. Training for competitive athletics may also be a cause.

Amenorrhea is the absence of menstruation for three or more months when the woman is not pregnant, through menopause, or breast feeding. A pituitary or ovarian tumor or a metabolic disease are possible causes of amenorrhea; hence a physician should be consulted. Excessive or prolonged menstruation, or **menorrhagia** may suggest other problems. These include uterine infection as well as tumors.

Many women experience painful menstruation, or **dysmenorrhea**, symptoms of which can include spasmodic pelvic cramping and bloating, headaches, and backaches. In addition, the woman often feels tense, irritable, nauseous, and depressed. As the result of the hormone changes, some women retain excess body fluids and experience painful swelling of the breasts (mastalgia) during menstruation. Dysmenorrhea is caused by prostaglandins, chemicals in the menstrual flow that cause spasms of the uterus, and can be relieved by prostaglandin inhibitors. Masters and Johnson (1966) reported that orgasms provided relief from painful menstruation by speeding up the menstrual flow, thus eliminating the prostaglandins. Many women who experience dysmenorrhea report less intense symptoms after taking birth control pills, which contain estrogen and progesterone and disrupt the normal hormone changes of the menstrual cycle. Some women complain of lower abdominal pains during ovulation *(Mittlelschmerz)*, but the cause has not yet been determined.

Painful menstruation can also be caused by endometrial tissue growing outside the uterus, for example, in the Fallopian tube or abdominal cavity, a

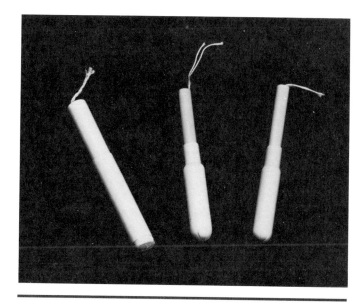

Regular and
superabsorbent
tampons.

condition known as endometriosis. These tissues deteriorate during menstruation, just as the lining of the uterus normally does, and a painful infection can result when the tissue cannot be expelled. Treatment ranges from aspirin to hysterectomy (Lanson, 1983).

A recent, serious problem is **toxic shock syndrome** (**TSS**), which has been linked to the use of superabsorbent tampons to absorb the menstrual fluid. The onset of the syndrome is rapid, with high fever, vomiting, diarrhea, abdominal pain, and rapid drop in blood pressure. Once the body is in shock, coma and death can result. The cause is unknown, but the syndrome may be produced by toxins from the bacteria *Staphylococcus aureus*. One theory suggests that the larger tampons might collect a lot of blood and provide a favorable environment for the bacteria. Women with weak immunity systems are particularly vulnerable. It has been suggested that women who want to continue to use tampons should avoid the superabsorbent variety and should change the tampon every six to eight hours.

Attitudes Toward Menstruation

In many societies throughout history, menstruating women were thought to have special powers and to be unclean. They have been blamed for such things as crop failure and driving dogs mad. They have also been feared as a source of contamination of their sexual partner. The Bible warns men against having intercourse with a menstruating woman. "And if a woman have an issue, and her issue in her flesh be blood, she shall be put apart seven days; and whoever toucheth her shall be unclean" (Leviticus 15:19). In some societies menstruating women have been quarantined to prevent contamination (DeLaney, Lupton, & Toth, 1977). One survey found that even today the vast majority of people in the United States over 55 have never had intercourse during menstruation (Paige, 1978). Younger people have apparently become more enlightened to the fact that menstruation is a normal physiological response that does not indicate uncleanliness, for the same study indicates that only 28 percent of people under 35 had never had intercourse during menstruation.

The Breasts

The breasts are not part of the reproductive system but are a secondary sex characteristic like pubic hair. They are considered part of the female's sexual anatomy in most Western societies. The breasts of females develop at puberty in response to increasing levels of estrogen. The hormone has a similar effect if injected in males.

The breast of an adult female consists of 15 to 20 mammary, or milk-producing, glands, each of which is connected to the nipple by a separate duct (Figure 3.8). The soft consistency and size of the breasts are due to fatty tissue that is loosely packed between the glands. It is common for one breast to be slightly larger than the other. The nipple is made up of smooth muscle fibers and has numerous nerve endings making it sensitive to touch. The nipples are kept lubricated during breastfeeding by secretions of oils from the **areola** (uh-ree-OH-lah), the darkened area around the nipple. This area becomes permanently darker after pregnancy.

In the United States and many other countries, women's breasts are considered to be highly erotic by men and sometimes by women. Unfortunately, a lot of men equate the size of the breasts with their erotic value and may not take the time to stimulate the breasts of small-breasted partners. There is no relation, however, between the size (or shape) and sensitivity of the breasts. Many women, small and large breasted, enjoy having their breasts stimulated, and a few are capable of achieving orgasm from this means of arousal. However, others derive no particular pleasure from breast stimulation. Some women who feel sexually unattractive because of their small breast size attempt to enlarge their breasts. However, lotions, mechanical devices, and so-called breast augmentation exercises are not effective, and injection of liquid silicone, which was once popular, has been found to result in medical complications. Today breast enlargement can be safely and permanently achieved by surgically implanting soft silicone-filled pouches in the breast tissue. A few women are troubled by having breasts that are too large (mammary hyperplasia); this can be alleviated by surgically removing some excess breast tissue.

Some females have nipples that are pushed inward, but this is generally not a health problem even for women who wish to nurse. Still other individuals, including males, may have extra nipples, but this also does not pose any health problem.

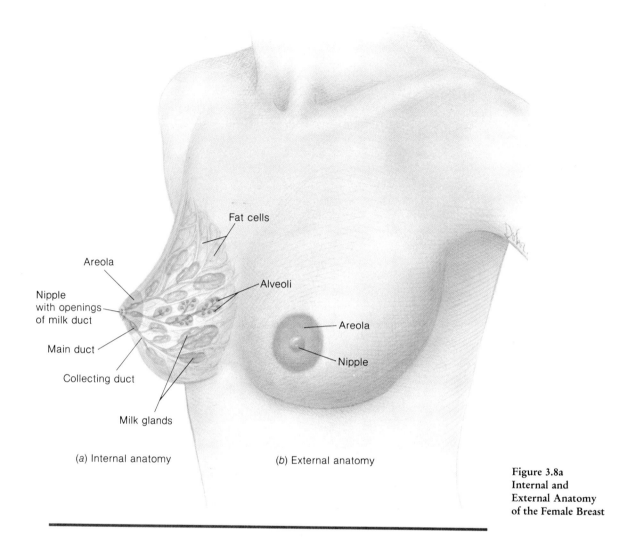

Fat cells

Areola

Alveoli

Nipple with openings of milk duct

Areola

Main duct

Nipple

Collecting duct

Milk glands

(a) Internal anatomy

(b) External anatomy

**Figure 3.8a
Internal and
External Anatomy
of the Female Breast**

Male External Anatomy

Although they differ greatly in appearance, many structures of the male and female genitals develop from the same embryonic tissue, for example, the penis and the clitoris. But whereas females find it difficult to view their genitals except by use of a mirror, which many are reluctant to do, male genitalia are easily visible. Males also touch and hold their genitals when urinating. Most males, therefore, are very much aware of the appearance of their own penis and scrotum. Like the vulva, male genitalia differ in appearance and no single example can be labeled "normal" (Figure 3.9).

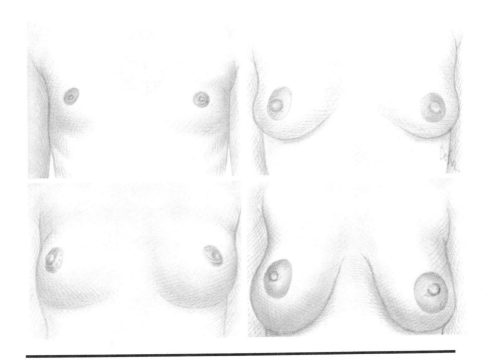

**Figure 3.8b
Variations in the
Female Breast**

The Penis

The **penis** (PEE-nihs) is the primary male sexual organ which, in the una-roused state, is soft and hangs between the legs. When sexually stimulated, the penis enlarges, hardens, and becomes erect, enabling penetration of the vagina. The penis functions not only to deposit sperm in the female's vagina but also as a passageway from the bladder to eliminate urine.

The visible, free-hanging portion of the penis consists of the body, or shaft, and the smooth rounded glans at the tip. Like the glans of the female clitoris, the glans of the penis has numerous nerve endings. The penis is especially sensitive to touch on the raised rim, or corona, and on the frenulum, the thin strip of skin on the underside, which connects the glans with the body. The body of the penis is not nearly as sensitive as the glans. The urethral opening, or meatus, through which urine is expelled from the body, is normally located at the tip of the glans. Occasionally, the urethral opening is located at the side of the glans, a minor anatomical defect that may prevent depositing the sperm at the cervical opening; this can be surgically corrected.

Unlike the penises of some other mammalian species, the human penis has no bone. Nor is the penis a muscle that the male can contract to cause erections. In cross-section the penis can be seen to consist of three parallel cylinders of tissue containing many cavities, two corpora cavernosa (cavernous bodies) and a corpus spongiosum (spongy body) through which the urethra passes (Figure 3.10). Each is bound in its own fibrous sheath. The spongy body can be felt on the underside when the penis is erect. The penis has nu-

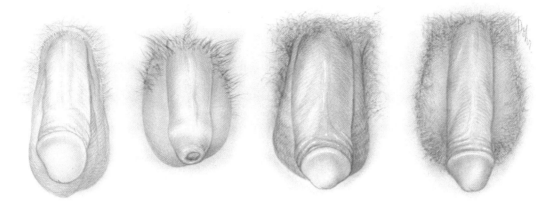

Figure 3.9
Variations in
External Male
Genitalia

merous blood vessels and when stimulated the arteries dilate and blood enters faster than it can leave. The cavities of the cavernous and spongy bodies fill with blood and pressure against the fibrous membranes cause the penis to become erect. Like the clitoris, the penis is attached to the pubic bone by the inner tips of the cavernous bodies, called crura. The root of the penis is made up of the crura and the inner end of the spongy body, which is expanded to form the bulb. Two muscles surround the root of the penis and aid in ejaculation and urination. Voluntary contractions of these muscles result in a slight jerking of the erect penis. It has been suggested that strengthening this response by exercise can enhance ejaculatory control (Zilbergeld, 1978).

The glans of the penis is actually the expanded front end of the spongy body. The skin of the penis, which is extremely loose to enable expansion during erection, folds over most of the glans. This **foreskin**, or prepuce, is fixed at the border between the glans and body of the penis. Small glands beneath the foreskin secrete small amounts of oils that have no known physiological function. These oily secretions can become mixed with sweat and bacteria to form smegma, a cheesy substance similar to that which can build up under the clitoral hood in females.

The surgical procedure in which the foreskin is pulled forward and cut off is known as **circumcision**, and approximately 80 percent of the males in the United States have been circumcized. Circumcision was performed by the Egyptians as early as 4000 B.C. and was an early religious rite for members of the Jewish and Moslem faiths. To Jewish people, circumcision symbolizes the covenant with God made by Abraham. In some societies circumcision is performed, often very crudely without anesthesia, as a puberty rite to symbolize the passage into manhood. In the United States the procedure is generally done within the first few days after birth. Among non-Jewish people, circumcision first became popular in the United States during the 19th century as a means of preventing masturbation. But research by Masters and Johnson (1966) indicates that there is no difference in excitability in men with circumcized and uncircumcized penises.

Today the primary reason for performing circumcision is to ensure proper hygiene. The smegma that can build up under the foreskin is a potential breeding ground for infection. But circumcision is a rather drastic procedure merely to ensure proper hygiene, which, as the Academy of Pediatrics suggests, can just as easily be accomplished by pulling back the foreskin and cleaning the glans during normal bathing. However, circumcision is indicated when the foreskin will not retract.

The Scrotum

The **scrotum** (SCROH-tuhm) is the sac located below the penis that contains the testicles. Beneath the skin is a thin layer of muscle fibers that contract when it is cold, helping to draw the testicles closer to the body. In hot environments the muscle fibers relax and the testicles are suspended further away from the body. Sweat is produced by the numerous glands in the skin of the scrotum. These responses help to regulate the temperature of the testicles. Sperm can only be produced at a temperature several degrees lower than normal body temperature and any variation can result in sterility.

Male Internal Anatomy

The male internal organs, often referred to as the reproductive system, include the testicles where sperm is produced, a duct system to transport the sperm out of the body, and some additional structures that produce the seminal fluid in which the sperm is mixed before ejaculation (Figure 3.10).

The Testes

The paired **testes**, or testicles, are the male gonads and develop from the same embryonic tissue as the female gonads, the ovaries. The translation of the Latin *testes* is "witness." In biblical times it was the custom when giving witness to hold the testicles of the person to whom one was making an oath (hence "testifying"). The Romans adopted this custom, except that they held their own testes while testifying.

The two oval-shaped testicles are suspended in the scrotum by the spermatic cord and enclosed within a fibrous sheath. The testes are undescended in about 2 percent of male births, a condition called **cryptorchidism**, but in most cases the testicles descend within a few months. It is normal for the left testicle to hang lower than the right one in right-handed men and the reverse in left-handed men. However, the two testicles should be about the same size and if one is noticeably larger, a physician should be consulted. The testes are

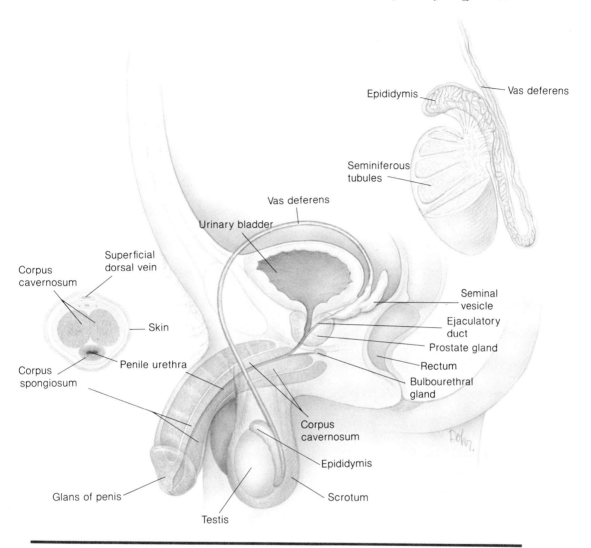

very sensitive to pressure; whereas some men find gentle touching or squeezing of the scrotum to be sexually arousing, others may wish to avoid this type of stimulation.

The function of the testes, complementary to that of the ovaries, is to produce **spermatozoa** and male hormones. Billions of sperm are produced each month in the seminiferous tubules, and the male hormone testosterone is produced in the interstitial or Leydig's cells, which are located between the seminiferous tubules.

It is particularly hazardous for a male to contract a case of the mumps, a viral infection that often causes swelling of the testicles. The sheath in which the testes are enclosed does not readily expand and the resulting pressure can cause destruction of the seminiferous tubules and sterility.

Figure 3.10
Internal Male Sexual Organs, Sagittal View, Showing the Cross Section of the Penis

The Duct System

The several hundred seminiferous (sehm-uh-NIHF-er-uhs) tubules come together to form a tube in each testicle called the **epididymus** (ehp-uh-DIHD-uh-muhz), the first part of the duct system that transports sperm. The epididymus, which can be felt on the top of each testicle, is a C-shaped, highly convoluted tube, which if uncoiled would measure about 20 feet in length. The sperm spend from two to six weeks traveling through the epididymus as they mature and are reabsorbed by the body if ejaculation does not occur.

The sperm leave the scrotum through the second part of the duct system, the **vas deferens** (vas DEF-uh-renz), or ductus deferens. These 14 to 16 inch paired ducts transport the sperm from the epididymus up and over the bladder to the prostate gland. The sperm is forced upward through the vas by rhythmic, wavelike contractions of the smooth muscle fiber wall and are stored prior to ejaculation in the expanded end of the vas called the ampulla. The scrotal portion of the vas is located near the surface of the skin, and thus cutting the vas for sterilization purposes can be easily done under local anesthesia (see Chapter 17).

Rhythmic contractions during ejaculation force the sperm into the paired ejaculatory ducts that run through the prostate gland. The entire length of this portion of the duct system is less than 1 inch. It is here that the sperm mix with seminal fluid to form semen.

The final portion of the duct system is the urethra, which is about 8 inches long and is divided into prostatic, membranous, and penile portions. In the prostatic portion the previously paired duct system joins together to form the final common pathway. The male urethra transports urine from the bladder as well as semen. The urethral sphincter muscles surround the membranous portion of the urethra, enabling voluntary control of urination. The penile portion of the urethra runs through the corpus spongiosum and the urethral opening is at the top of the glans. As in women, transmission of bacteria to the urethral opening can result in inflammation of the urethra and bladder (urethritis). The most common symptoms are frequent urination accompanied by a burning sensation and discharge. The man should consult a urologist if these symptons appear.

The Seminal Vesicles and Prostate Gland

The **seminal vesicles** resemble two small sacs about 2 inches in length located behind the bladder. They are mistakenly called vesicles because it was once believed that they were storage areas for semen. The seminal vesicles, however, secrete their own fluids, which empty into the ejaculatory duct to mix with sperm and fluids from the prostate gland. Substances secreted from the seminal vesicles include fructose and prostaglandins. Sperm that reach the ejaculatory duct as a result of both muscular contractions of the epididymus and vas and the sweeping motion of hairlike cilia on their inner walls are made active by fructose. Prostaglandins induce contractions of the uterus, aiding movement of the sperm within the female.

Most of the seminal fluid comes from the **prostate gland**, a chestnut sized structure located below the bladder and in front of the rectum. In the prostate the ejaculatory ducts join the initial portion of the urethra from the bladder to form a single common passageway for urine and semen. The prostate enlarges at puberty as the result of increasing hormone levels. It normally shrinks as males get older, but in some cases it becomes larger and constricts the urethra, interfering with urination. Surgical removal of the prostate may be required. The prostate is also a common site of infection, resulting in an inflamed condition called prostatitis. Major symptoms are painful ejaculation or defecation. The condition can be treated with antibiotics. Some men develop prostate cancer. Among males the frequency of prostate cancer is second only to lung cancer and the risk increases with age. All males should have their prostate checked annually, a procedure in which the physician inserts a finger in the rectum and palpates the prostate to check for any abnormalities.

The structures of the prostate give the whitish seminal fluid its characteristic odor. In addition to sugars, prostaglandins, and bases (sperm can not live in acidic environments), seminal fluid has recently been reported to contain a potent antibiotic, which probably serves to protect both the vagina and male reproductive system from infection. About one teaspoonful of **semen**, consisting of sperm and seminal fluid from the prostate gland and seminal vesicles, is expelled from the urethra during ejaculation. Although a normal ejaculation contains several hundred million sperm, most of the volume consists of seminal fluid.

A small amount of clear, sticky fluid is also secreted into the urethra before ejaculation by the two pea-sized **Cowper's**, or bulbourethal, **glands** located below the prostate. This can often be noticed on the tip of the penis during sexual arousal. The quantity of this alkaline fluid is too small to serve as a lubricant, and it probably acts to neutralize the natural acidic environment of the urethra. It may contain stray sperm, however, making withdrawal of the penis from the vagina (before ejaculation) a risky method of birth control.

Summary

Many people have erroneous ideas about human sexuality because they lack an understanding of anatomical structure and function. The goal of studying sexual anatomy is to dispel such ideas and permit sexual partners to talk more knowledgably about their sexuality.

The external female genitalia are known as the vulva. The vulva consists of the mons veneris, the major and minor labia, the clitoris, and the vaginal and urethral openings. The clitoris is the most sensitive part of the vulva. It contains numerous nerve endings and its only purpose is erotic pleasure. Most women require stimulation of the clitoris for orgasm.

The hymen may partially cover the opening to the vagina, but some women are born without a hymen or with incomplete ones and in other women the hymen may be accidentally ruptured during physical activity or insertion of a tampon. In all cases, it is a very unreliable indicator of virginity.

Internal female sex organs include the vagina, uterus, Fallopian tubes, and ovaries. Menstruation occurs when the uterus has prepared to receive a fertilized egg but does not. The thickened dead tissue, blood, and mucus sloughs off and drains from the body. Use of superabsorbent tampons should be avoided because of their association with toxic shock syndrome. The female breasts are a secondary sex characteristic whose function is to produce milk.

Male external anatomy consists of the penis and scrotum. When sexually stimulated, the penis enlarges, hardens, and becomes erect, enabling penetration of the vagina. The functions of the penis are to deposit sperm in the vagina and to act as a passageway from the bladder to eliminate urine.

The scrotum is the sac below the penis that contains the testicles. The scrotum constricts to keep the testicles close to the body in cold temperatures and relaxes to keep the testicles away from the body in warm temperatures. Sperm can only be produced at several degrees lower than normal body temperature and any variation can result in sterility.

Male internal anatomy includes the testes, seminal vesicles, and prostate gland. The testes produce sperm and male hormones. The duct system transports the sperm to the seminal vesicles and prostate gland where the sperm are mixed with other fluids and transported out of the body. The urethra joins the duct system to transport urine from the bladder.

Key Terms

vulva	menstruation
mons veneris	menarche
labia majora	luteinizing hormone (LH)
perineum	oligogmenorrhea
labia minora	amenorrhea
Bartholin's glands	menorrhagia
clitoris	dysmenorrhea
clitoridectomy	toxic shock syndrome (TSS)
vestibule	areola
hymen	penis
Skene's glands	foreskin
cystitis	circumcision
vagina	scrotum

pubococcygeal muscles
Grafenberg spot
uterus
fundus
cervix
Fallopian tubes
ovaries
estrogen
progesterone
follicle-stimulating hormone (FSH)

testes
cryptorchidism
spermatozoa
epididymus
vas deferens
seminal vesicles
prostate gland
semen
Cowper's glands

Issues in Debate and Future Directions

The importance of penis size and the degree to which sexual desires have a biological or social origin are continuing controversies in human sexuality. We examine these issues in this section.

Does Penis Size Matter?

Few of us originally learn about sexual matters from accurate sources. For both males and females, the first knowledge of sexual anatomy and behavior often comes in the form of dirty jokes, "locker room" conversation, passages from erotic literature, and peeks at magazine centerfolds. More recently, the invention of video recorders has made it easy for people to view pornographic movies in the privacy of their own home. Most of these sources of sexual knowledge place an emphasis on penis size. Male centerfolds and erotic movie stars are generally individuals with a greater than average anatomical endowment, and writers often describe the penis as if it had special powers. The penis of the gamekeeper in D.H. Lawrence's *Lady Chatterly's Lover* was even given a name of its own (John Henry) by the infatuated heroine. It is not surprising, therefore, that many males have a great deal of anxiety about the size of their penis, for all of these sources leave the impression that a large penis is more attractive, more virile, and better able to sexually satisfy a woman.

Penises differ in size and shape like any other bodily structure. The average size of an unstimulated flaccid penis is just under 4 inches in length and just over 1 inch in diameter, but there is considerable variation. However, according to Masters and Johnson (1966), the increase in size during stimulation is proportionately greater in penises that are small in the flaccid condition than in ones that are large in the flaccid condition, obscuring some of the difference. The average size of the penis in the erect state is about 6 inches in length and 1.5 inches in diameter. Contrary to popular belief, there is no relation between skeletal size and penis size or race and penis size. The vast majority of men have a penis that when erect measures between 5 and 7 inches in length, and the range of values beyond this is very limited. But many men are so convinced that the ability to please a woman sexually is related to penis size that even those with a normal-sized penis may wish it was larger. As one sex researcher stated, " . . . about the only thing most penises have in common is that they are the wrong size and shape as far as their owners are concerned" and "it is not much of an exaggeration to say that penises in fantasyland come in only three sizes—large, gigantic, and so big you can barely get through the front door" (Zilbergeld, 1978, p. 26).

Knowledge of basic anatomy and normal physiological responses should put to rest many of the myths concerning the relation of penis size and sexual responsiveness in females. The vagina, it should be recalled, is a potential space. Its walls are collapsed in the sexually unstimulated state. During sexual arousal and intercourse, the walls of the inner two-thirds of the vagina expand, not to a predetermined size, but just enough to accommodate the male's penis whatever its size. The inner two-thirds of the vagina also has very few nerve endings and is relatively insensitive to touch, minimizing the importance of penis length. Most of the pleasurable sensations experienced by females during intercourse are the result of the penis indirectly stimulating the clitoris by pulling the clitoral hood back and forth over the glans of the clitoris. On the basis of these physiological facts, Masters and Johnson have concluded that the belief that males with a large penis are more effective partners in intercourse has no basis. Other research is inconsistent. In one study (Zilbergeld, 1978), women were asked what things were important to them during intercourse. Not one mentioned penis size. But when 15,000 women in the *Playboy* study were asked, "Does penis size matter?" 20 percent said "yes." (Petersen et al. 1983a). Whether penis size matters seems to be an issue of perception. If a person thinks it matters, it does. As Shakespeare said, "There is nothing either good or bad, but thinking makes it so."

Does Sexual Behavior Have a Biological or Social Origin?

Hormones are necessary for the development of secondary sex characteristics in both females and males (for example, breast development and beard growth). But do hormones produce sexual behavior or is such behavior learned?

The best evidence for the possible role of hormones comes from studies of individuals who have had their ovaries or testes surgically removed. Removal of a woman's ovaries (a major source of estrogen and progesterone) has not been found to reduce her sexual desire (Waxenberg, 1969). However, even with her ovaries removed, a woman's adrenal glands may still produce small amounts of estrogen and progesterone. After these glands have been removed by adrenalectomy, women report a marked reduction in sexual desire. Hence, the absence of estrogen and progesterone in a woman's body seems to have a negative influence on her sexual activity. On the other hand, women administered testosterone for medical reasons have been reported to display increased sexual desire (Willson, Beecham, & Carrington, 1975). Also, a study of healthy couples found higher frequencies of intercourse and greater gratification in those couples in which the female had high levels of testosterone (Persky et al., 1978). In view of these findings, there *may* be a hormonal basis for sexual behavior in women.

Studies suggesting the effects of hormones on male sexual behavior are less clear. European studies have found that surgical removal of the testicles in sex offenders greatly reduced sexual desire in about two-thirds of the men (Bremer, 1959). The problem with castration studies is that the decrease in sexual desire may have been a result of the psychological reaction to the surgery. However, reduced sexual desire has also been reported by men with low testosterone levels (Segraves, Schoenberg, & Ivanoff, 1983). But when men have high levels of androgen, there is no corresponding increase in sexual activity (Brown et al., 1978; Schwartz et al., 1980). Also, when men who have difficulty getting an erection are given high levels of testosterone, they do not regain their erectile potency (Segraves et al., 1983).

Whereas these studies would suggest that behavior in men is decreased by the absence of testosterone or unaffected by the presence of high levels of androgen, other studies have found that males castrated before puberty may enjoy regular sexual intercourse (Money & Alexander, 1967). There are also numerous stories of eunuchs assigned as harem guards who were sexually active with the women. Hence, research is contradictory as to whether there is a hormonal basis for male sexual behavior.

Even if hormones play a role, the expression of sexual feelings depends on social situations. Two researchers emphasized that although infants and preadolescent children are capable of orgasm and sexual behavior, the full expression of their sexuality awaits the signal from peers that such feelings are to be sought and enjoyed (Gagnon & Simon, 1973).

Future Directions

While the sexual anatomy of women and men will remain basically unchanged, the feelings they have about their bodies is likely to become more positive. This trend will be a result of more nudity via magazines, movies, and television. While only "beautiful bodies" are permitted media exposure, and there is the risk of feeling negative by comparison, the idea that one's body is a positive part of one's self may supersede the potential negative. In addition, women are being socialized to view their genitals as sources of potential pleasure rather than places to clean (for example, due to menstruation).

Chapter Four

Sexual Ethics and Society

Noah, you're so full of what's
right you can't see what's good.

N. RICHARD NASH, THE RAINMAKER

Chapter Four

Our sexual behavior is guided by our ideas of what is right and wrong, appropriate and inappropriate. Think about the following situations.

- Two people are slow dancing to romantic music at a party. Although they met only two hours ago, they feel a strong attraction to each other. Each is wondering how much sex is appropriate when they go back to one of their apartments later that evening. How much sex in a new relationship is appropriate?
- A woman is married to a man whose career requires that he be away from home for extended periods of time. While she loves her husband, she is lonely, bored, and sexually frustrated in his absence. She has been asked out by a colleague at work whose wife also travels. He, too, is in love with his wife but needs female companionship. They are ambivalent about whether to see each other when their spouses are away. Should they see each other?
- A couple have decided to live together but they know their respective parents would disapprove. If they tell their parents, the parents are likely to withdraw their financial support and each will be forced to drop out of school. Should they tell?
- While Mary was away for a weekend visiting her parents, the man with whom she is living had intercourse with an old girlfriend. He says he is sorry and promises never to be unfaithful again. Should she take him back?

The individuals in each of these situations will make a decision based on their personal value system. While we may not have experienced these particular encounters, we have confronted others that require examining our own values. These values represent our ethics and the priorities we give them help us make decisions.

In this chapter we look at how our ethics guide sexual behavior and the religious origin of these codes of moral conduct. Since these codes affect and are affected by the society in which we live, we examine the degree to which we are a liberal and a conservative society. We end with a discussion of sex education to illustrate how our society socializes us in reference to sex.

Sexual Ethics

Our sexual ethics become visible when we choose one course of action over another. This choice may be based on our feeling of what is right and wrong, moral and immoral, or a perception that one course of action will have more positive consequences than another. Sometimes a combination of factors affects our choice. A single woman who felt she was drifting into a love relationship with a married coworker stated: "Although I felt strongly about him, I thought it was wrong and immoral for me to get involved with him. He also had three kids and the hurt it would cause them and his wife wouldn't be worth my getting involved with him so I decided not to date him."

There are several ethical views that may offer guidelines for people making decisions about their sexuality. These include legalism, situationism, hedonism, and asceticism.

Legalism

A legalistic view of sexual ethics involves making decisions by adherence to a strict set of laws or codes of moral conduct. In the example of the single woman and her married coworker, part of her reasoning was legalistic—it is "wrong" to become involved with a married person.

The official creeds of the Protestant, Catholic, and Jewish religions reflect a legalistic view of sexual ethics. Intercourse between a man and a woman is viewed as a gift from God to be expressed in marriage only, and violations are regarded as sins against God, self, and community. The person who adopts a legal set of sexual ethics has no anxiety or confusion about what is appropriate, right, or moral. "I never wonder when I'm out with my fiancée if we're going to have intercourse or not—we won't," said a devoutly religious man.

Situation Ethics

One of the most prevalent forms of contemporary sexual ethics is situation ethics. Made popular by Joseph Fletcher in his book, *Situation Ethics* (1966), this perspective suggests that sexual decisions should be made in the context of the particular situation. Genuine love and good will should be the core motive for each decision and the prediction of positive consequences a basic guideline. The situationist believes that to make all decisions on the basis of rules is to miss the point of human love and to do more harm than good. While the legalist would say it is morally right for married people to have intercourse and morally wrong for the unmarried to do so, the situationist would say "it depends" and would ask: "Suppose the married people do not love each other and intercourse is an abusive, exploitative act. Also suppose that the unmarried people love each other and their intercourse experience is an expression of mutual concern and respect. Which couple is being more moral?"

It is sometimes difficult to make sexual decisions on a case-by-case basis. "I don't know what's right anymore" reflects the uncertainty that a situation ethics view may bring. Once a person decides that mutual love is the context that justifies intercourse, how often and how soon should the person fall in love? Can love develop after two hours of conversation or dancing? How does one know that his or her own love feelings and that of the partner are genuine? The freedom that situation ethics brings to sexual decision making requires responsibility, maturity, and judgment.

Hedonism

A third ethical perspective suggests that one need not be concerned with moral or contextual issues but with pleasure. "If it feels good, do it" emphasizes the hedonistic ethic that sexual desire is an appropriate appetite and its expression is legitimate. Like hunger and thirst, the sexual urge need not be subject to moral constraints. Too much has been made, says the hedonist, of the sexual act. It should be regarded as one of many pleasures we are capable of experiencing.

Asceticism

The ascetic believes that giving into what he or she considers animal lusts is crass and calls us to rise above the pursuit of sensual pleasure into a life of self-discipline and self-denial. The spiritual life is the highest good and self-denial helps us achieve it. Monks, nuns, and other celibates have adopted the sexual ethic of asceticism.

Religious Roots of American Sexual Ethics

Although we live in a pluralistic society in which people pursue different ethical ideals, the roots of our ethical philosophies are religious in nature. The Jewish and Christian influences have been the most prominent.

Jewish Heritage

Many of our feelings about sex can be traced to the laws and customs of Judaism. The Old Testament, written between 800 and 200 B.C., reflects the society of the Jewish people at that time and should be viewed in its historical context. The Jews were a small, persecuted group. Their goal was to increase their numbers as rapidly as possible and to minimize defections. Keeping in mind this need to solidify their position as a group and a nation, they developed the following sexual norms.

Marriage Is Good

Marriage was a way to encourage the birthing of new members into the Jewish faith and to control their upbringing in this communal faith. Males were permitted to marry at 15; females even younger. Eighteen was considered the maximum age a male could remain single before he would have to explain to the elders of the community why he was still unmarried. Conversely, singlehood was unnatural and immoral. Even widows and widowers were encouraged to remarry as soon as possible. In the case of a widow, her husband's brother was expected to marry her. Jewish men could have up to four wives.

Children Are Expected

Once married, the couple were expected to "be fruitful and multiply." Sexual intercourse was encouraged. During the first year of marriage the husband was exempt from military service so as to be with his wife. "When a man hath taken a new wife, he shall not go out to war, neither shall he be charged with any business: but he shall be free at home one year, and shall cheer up his wife which he hath taken" (Deuteronomy 24:5). Also, taking a new wife did not exempt the husband from having intercourse with his first wife. "If he take him another wife; her food, her raiment, and her duty of marriage, shall he not diminish" (Exodus 21:10). "Duty of marriage" in this context refers to the obligation of a husband to keep his wife sexually satisfied and pregnant.

Adultery Is Wrong

To ensure that the children born into a marriage were the biological offspring of the married couple, the couple was restricted to having intercourse with each other. Keeping sex within marriage would also reduce divorce, community strife, and the number of abandoned children. Hence for both religious and social reasons, the Jewish society did not tolerate adultery. "And the man that committeth adultery with another man's wife, even he that committeth adultery with his neighbor's wife, the adulterer and the adulteress shall surely be put to death"(Leviticus 20:10).

Other Sexual Admonitions

Homosexuality, bestiality, and masturbation were also forbidden as they did not involve marriage or procreation. As in many other societies, incest was prohibited. (This issue is dealt with in detail in Chapter 15.) Transvestism was also disapproved of because it was a pagan practice and, as such, a threat to the community.

Judaism has had a major impact on our view of sexual ethics. Our feelings about marriage (more than 90 percent of us marry), children (more than 90 percent of us have children), and sex in marriage (most Americans regard infidelity as something to be ashamed of) began with the ancient Hebrews. But Christianity also has strongly influenced our views of sexuality.

Christian Heritage

Jesus Christ was a Jew who claimed to be the Messiah, the son of God. Only some Jews believed him but those and others who did came to be called Christians. They split from the traditional Jewish faith and developed their own. Just as Judaism was based on the teachings of Moses in the Old Testament, Christianity was based on the teachings of Jesus (and the subsequent interpretations by others) in the New Testament.

Jesus

Most of Jesus' teachings were about salvation and living an honorable life. He said very little about sex, although in one instance he equated thoughts about having intercourse with the act itself. "But I say unto you that whosoever looketh on a woman to lust after her hath committed adultery with her already in his heart" (Matthew 5:28). The notion that one should be pure of thought as well as deed is still prevalent.

St. Paul

After the death of Jesus, his followers continued to preach the message of Christianity. Among these was St. Paul, who added his own interpretations of sexuality. He felt that abstinence and singlehood were virtuous and desirable. Marriage should be resorted to only if the person could not control his or her sexual desires. "It is better to marry than to burn" (Corinthians 7:8–9) meant that you would go to hell if you had intercourse and were not married, so marriage was better than hell if you could not control yourself. So St. Paul contributed two ideas to the developing system of sexual ethics: (1) intercourse is the expression of shameful desires that should be avoided, and (2) marriage is for weaklings who have given in to their passions.

The writings of St. Paul should be viewed in their historical context. He and others of his day believed that the return of Christ was imminent. Sex and marriage were seen as unnecessary uses of a person's time when there was so much to do in preparation for Christ's return (recruit new members) and so little time.

St. Augustine

Around A.D. 386 at the age of 32, Augustine read the writings of St. Paul. Before this time he had lived a promiscuous life, fathering an illegitimate son, living with his son's mother, becoming engaged to another woman, and being unfaithful to his fiancée. Frustrated with his inability to control his sexual desires, he converted to Christianity, broke off his engagement, stopped his affairs, and never married.

His own writings, particularly *The City of God*, reflect a very negative view of sex and sexuality. He felt that sexual desires, emotions and passions, expressed through sexual intercourse, were sinful. Even in marriage, while intercourse was necessary to propogate children, the act itself was tainted with shame. This shame, according to St. Augustine, was a result of the lust Adam and Eve felt for each other, their disobedience to God by engaging in sexual intercourse, and their expulsion from the Garden of Eden. The need for infant baptism grew out of the belief that children were conceived in an impure act (original sin) and must be cleansed of this sin.

St. Augustine rose to be bishop in the Roman Catholic Church and his views became widespread. Today the doctrine of original sin, as well as the sacrament of infant baptism, is still recognized by the Catholic and Protestant religions.

Other Influential Religious Leaders

St. Thomas Aquinas is another important religious writer whose thinking influenced the code of sexual ethics in Western culture. A thirteenth-century Roman Catholic, Aquinas specified in *Summa Theologica* that any sexual act that did not lead specifically to procreation was sinful and against the will of God. Masturbation, bestiality, homosexuality headed the list. Even sexual caresses were sinful if engaged in solely for pleasure. Also, face-to-face intercourse was the only acceptable position for intercourse.

Martin Luther and John Calvin in their break from the Roman Catholic Church adopted a more positive view of sexuality. According to Luther, marriage was a good and honorable relationship and not second to singlehood. He also regarded sexual desires as normal appetites much like hunger and thirst. Calvin, too, saw sex, at least in marriage, as holy, honorable, and desirable.

The Puritans

The Puritans who settled along the coast of New England in the seventeenth century were radical Protestants who had seceded from the Church of England. We can trace many of our sexual values to their beliefs and social norms.

The Puritans wanted their members to get married and stay married. Religious values (avoiding temptation), social values (being a member of a close-knit community), and economic values (working hard for material reward) helped to emphasize the importance of the marital relationship. The Puritan woman had little choice of an adult role other than wife and mother. Only in marriage could she achieve the status accorded to an adult woman. Men were taught that their best chance for survival was to find a wife to satisfy their needs for clothing, food, companionship, and sex.

The Puritans approved of sex only within marriage. Like St. Paul, they viewed sex as a passion to conquer or control and marriage as the only safe place for its expression. Rigid codes of dress helped to discourage sexual thoughts.

Any discussion of sex among the Puritans would not be complete without reference to bundling, also called tarrying. Not unique to the Puritans, bundling was a courtship custom in which the would-be groom slept in the girl's bed in her parents' home. But there were rules to restrict sexual contact. Both partners had to be fully clothed, and a wooden bar was placed between them. In addition, the young girl might be encased in a type of long laundry bag up to her armpits, her clothes might be sewn together at strategic points, and her parents might be sleeping in the same room.

The justifications for bundling were convenience and economics. Aside from meeting at church, bundling was one of the few opportunities a couple had to get together to talk and learn about each other. Since daylight hours were consumed by heavy work demands, night became the time for courtship. But how did bed become the courtship arena? New England winters were cold. Firewood, oil for lamps, and candles were in short supply. By talking in bed, the young couple could come to know each other without wasting valuable sources of energy.

Although bundling flourished in the middle of the eighteenth century, it provoked a great deal of controversy. "Jonathan Edwards attacked it on the pulpit, and other ministers, who had allowed it to go unnoticed, joined in its suppression" (Calhoun, 1960, p. 71). By about 1800 the custom had virtually disappeared.

The Victorians

Another influence that lingers in our society is the Victorian. The Victorian era, which took its name from the English queen Alexandrina Victoria, who reigned from 1837 to 1901, is popularly viewed as a time of prudery and propriety in sexual behavior. However, there was a great disparity between expressed middle-class morality and actual practices. In his study of this era, Wendell Johnson (1979) wrote:

> What were the Victorians actually doing? One might reply, "Just about everything." Free love, adultery, male homosexuality and (in spite of the Queen's disbelief) lesbianism, nymphetism, sadism, and masochism, exhibitionism—the Victorians practiced them all . . . the number of whores per acre in mid-Victorian London and the consumption of pornography . . . would put today's Times Square to shame. (p.11)

But the official view of sexuality during the Victorian era was that sexual behavior and the discussion of it should be suppressed. This reflected a larger social belief at the time, which was to avoid anything that was unpleasant. Some of the prevailing notions were as follows.

Marital Sexuality

Sex was a passion that should be channeled into marriage. But uncontrollable sexual desires were only characteristic of men. Women were thought to be asexual and nonorgasmic. William Hammond, the surgeon general of the United States Army during the 1860s, wrote that it was doubtful that women experienced the slightest degree of pleasure in even one-tenth of the occasions of sexual intercourse.

Prudishness

Skirts to the ankle, and discreet references to anything sexual became the norm. Women were not pregnant, they were "in an interesting way." Ladies delicately nibbled their "bosom of chicken."

Female Types

There were good women and bad women in Victorian society. The latter were whores or women who practiced no social graces in expressing their sexuality. Women who were not whores but who did enjoy sexual feelings were in conflict. Some felt degraded, even insane. "If I love sex I must be a whore" was an inescapable conclusion. Some women even had clitoridectomies (surgical removal of the clitoris) performed to eliminate the "cause" of their sexual feelings.

Contemporary Religious Ethics

What is the position of religion today on the appropriateness of various sexual behaviors? We live in a pluralistic society with numerous religious denominations, churches, and sects, which have different philosophies about and foundations for sexual ethics. While conservative Protestant churches and the Roman Catholic Church take the position that intercourse before marriage is wrong, some liberal religious groups such as the Unitarians believe there are conditions under which it is morally legitimate for two unmarried people to have intercourse.

In addition, individual leaders within a religious group may have views that are contrary to the group's official position. For example, a priest counseling a distraught couple with nine children might recommend they consider using the pill to prevent subsequent pregnancies. One writer on sexuality and the Roman Catholic Church said that the question is no longer whether people go to bed or not, when, and with whom. Instead, people should be concerned with achieving wholeness and intimacy for themselves, others, and the universe (Ohanneson, 1983).

Keeping in mind that ideas about sexual ethics will differ by religious groups and, to some extent, their leaders, there is basic agreement on three sexual issues.

1. Sexual behavior has a spiritual dimension and should not be viewed as an act devoid of moral implications. A person's self-concept, relationship to divinity, and to the larger community are all affected by his or her sexual decisions, the latter especially when sexual union results in illegitimate offspring.

2. The highest moral approval is attached to sexual intercourse in marriage. This implies that both premarital and extramarital intercourse are wrong.

3. Homosexual behavior is wrong.

While there is general agreement on these three issues, there is vigorous debate on two others—contraception and abortion as options to control family size.

Personal Sexual Ethics

In spite of official religious pronouncements on sexual ethics, we must ultimately decide what ethics we will adopt as guidelines for our own sexual behavior. Mary Calderone (1980), president of SIECUS (Sex Information and Education Council of the United States), said that "what we need now is a sexual morality of *use* rather than of crippling *denial*. But, to be successful and ethical in our use of sexuality, each of us is required to be *knowledgeable* about it, *understanding* of its potential for good or destruction, and *awed* and *respectful* of its profound and almost limitless ability to capacitate human energies" (p. 465). Like alcohol or electricity, according to this situational ethics perspective, sex itself is neither good nor bad. It is the way in which it is used that determines its moral value. Sex that exploits (ego enhancement), demeans (rape), or has negative consequences (unwanted pregnancy) is bad. Sex that enhances positive feelings about self and partner is good.

Such a value position—that sex is okay if the consequences are okay—should not be translated into pressure to engage in sexual behavior. People have their own values and time frames, and responsible sexual ethics not only acknowledge but requires individuals to follow the moral values they feel are right for them. In the Boston Women's Health Book Collective's *Our Bodies, Ourselves* (1976) this sentiment is expressed as follows:

> The sexual revolution—liberated orgastic women, groupies, communal lovemaking, homosexuality—has made us feel that we must be able to have sex with impunity, without anxiety, under any conditions and with anyone, or we're uptight freaks. These alienating, inhuman expectations are no less destructive or degrading than the Victorian puritanism we all so proudly rejected. (p. 6)

Deciding About Intercourse

Your personal sexual ethics are called into play in your sexual decision making. In each new relationship, some issues to consider in deciding whether to have intercourse include the following.

Personal Consequences

Your reaction to intercourse will depend on your motivations (as well as your partner's), your religious beliefs, and the degree of involvement with your partner. First, it is unrealistic to expect the relationship to improve automatically following intercourse. Second, if you are strongly influenced by religious values, your reaction to violating religious teachings may be intense. Finally, the greater the degree of emotional involvement with your partner, the less likely you will feel guilty about the experience.

Partner Consequences

Since a basic moral principle of life is to do no harm to others, it may be important to consider the effect of intercourse on your partner. While intercourse may be a pleasurable experience with positive consequences for you, your partner may react differently. What are your partner's feelings about intercourse and his or her ability to handle the experience? If you suspect that your partner will not feel good about it or be able psychologically to handle it, then you might reconsider whether intercourse would be appropriate with this person.

One man reported that, after having intercourse with a woman he had just met, he awakened to the sound of her uncontrollable sobbing as she sat in the lotus position on the end of the bed. She was guilty and depressed. He said of the event, "If I had known how she was going to respond, we wouldn't have had intercourse."

Relationship Consequences

As we will discuss in Chapter 7, whether couples have intercourse does not seem to affect whether they stay together. Those who have intercourse are as likely to stay together as those who do not. "Remained the same" was the most frequently chosen description of the effect intercourse had on the relationship of 234 respondents (Ratcliff & Knox, 1982).

Contraception

Another potential consequence of intercourse is pregnancy. Once a couple decides to have intercourse, a separate decision must be made as to whether intercourse should result in pregnancy.

If the couple want to avoid a pregnancy, they must choose and effectively use a contraceptive method. But many do not. In one study, although 78 percent of the men and 65 percent of the women had had intercourse, 56 percent reported that they had not used contraceptives (Diederen & Rorer, 1982). Pregnancy is a common consequence. More than one-third of those who have intercourse before marriage get pregnant before they turn 19 (Zelnik et al., 1979). Those who use contraception tend to have close relationships with their partners and to plan intercourse.

Sexually Transmitted Diseases

Avoiding sexually transmitted diseases (STDs) is an important consideration in deciding whether to have intercourse. The result of increasing numbers of people having more frequent intercourse with more partners has been the rapid spread of the bacteria and viruses responsible for numerous varieties of STDs. For some, the fear of contracting herpes is a deterrent to having intercourse with someone they do not know. "A close friend got herpes on a one-night deal and has been plagued by it ever since," said one person. "Intercourse isn't worth getting herpes so I've decided to be very careful about who I sleep with."

Values Clarification

There are several exercises you can perform to help clarify some of your own sexual ethics. One is a self-administered questionnaire, of which the following is an example. Select one ending for each of the following statements and consider why you chose that answer. You may wish to think of additional statements about sexual behavior that similarly include a range of choices.

For me, it is most important that a sexual experience:

1. Be morally correct.
2. Be fun and pleasurable.
3. Increase the love feelings with my partner.
4. Improve my self-concept.
5. Result in an orgasm.

The worst thing that I could find out about my sexual partner is that she or he:

1. Has herpes.
2. Is sterile.
3. Is homosexual.
4. Is unfaithful to me.
5. Has had intercourse with 50 people before me.

In a sexual relationship, I would prefer that:

1. Sex be more meaningful to me than to my partner.
2. Sex be more meaningful to my partner than to me.
3. Sex mean the same thing to both of us.

4. We are both married.
5. My partner is completely uninhibited.

If I am feeling the need for sexual release, I would rather:

1. Masturbate.
2. Have intercourse.
3. Have my partner perform oral sex.
4. Engage in vigorous physical activity.
5. Have a sex dream.

Another way of clarifying sexual values is to think of the degree to which you regard various sexual issues as acceptable. What category on the continuum below best reflects your sexual values about sex without love, abortion, group sex, oral-genital sex, anal sex, masturbation, intercourse, homosexuality for others, homosexuality for self, extramarital sex, and virginity at marriage.

Acceptable   Does Not Matter   Unacceptable

An important dimension of values clarification is becoming aware that you may have different standards for yourself and others. For example, there is a distinction between "I would never have an abortion" and "I believe every woman should be able to choose whether to have an abortion." Most people separate their values and choices from those they feel others "should" have.

Still another exercise in values clarification is to develop an answer to a moral dilemma. For example, Katherine is involved in a mutual love relationship and plans to marry Bob in June, two months away. One evening Katherine and Bob's conversation drifts onto the topic of abortions. Bob states that "an abortion means the girl is promiscuous and irresponsible," and he is highly critical of a mutual friend who had had an abortion. Unknown to Bob, Katherine had an abortion two years before she met him. Should she tell him?

The goal in examining this and other moral dilemmas like those presented at the beginning of this chapter is to explore our own sexual ethics. These ethics are influenced by the society in which we live. Our society is pluralistic; both liberal and conservative elements coexist. In the remainder of the chapter, we explore the ways in which our society is sexually permissive, look at some of the conservative views of sexual behavior, and examine the controversial issue of sex education in the home and school.

American Society: A Liberal View

Sociologist Pitirim Sorokin (1956) described the sensate society, which seeks to titillate the senses to their maximum potential. An experience like watching strobe lights flicker on an array of rock concert artists and listening to their amplified voices and blaring guitars feeds our visual and auditory senses to the hilt.

Orgasm, and the erotic feelings that lead to it, is another sensation our society seeks to market. The first law of advertising is "sex sells." Our attention is regularly grabbed by references to sex in advertising (such as McDonald's slogan in the early 1980s, "We do it all for you"). Seminudity is used as a visual appeal in countless ads in every magazine, on billboards, in movies, and on television.

We continually promote new media stars to personify our ideas of feminine and masculine sex. Female sex symbols like Marilyn Monroe, Raquel Welch, Bo Derek, Linda Evans, Audrey Landers, and Nastassia Kinski are not to be outdone by male sex symbols such as Clark Gable, Burt Reynolds, Robert Redford, Tom Selleck, Richard Gere, and John Travolta. With our female sex stars we even focus on certain aspects of their anatomy—the back and legs of Betty Grable, the breasts of Marilyn Monroe and Jane Mansfield, and the total body (10) of Bo Derek.

In a sensate, sex-advertised, sex-symbol society, every member is affected by the pervasiveness of sex. From sex grafitti to the grinding hips on "American Bandstand" to the sensuous perfume commercials on television, we are reminded daily that we live in a sexually permissive society. Some of the effects of this sexual permissiveness are described in the following pages.

Sexual Openness

Society's increased willingness to tolerate and even encourage openness about sex has positive and negative aspects. Colleges and universities provide a responsible forum for open discussions of sexuality. The course in which you are enrolled is a forum for learning and talking about sex. Some universities sponsor conferences on sexuality, contraception, and sexually transmitted diseases. The result is a more systematic examination of human sexuality and a more informed public.

But such university sponsored discussions on sexuality occur in the context of a societywide openness about sex. A sex media blitz is on. We are bombarded with stimuli from magazines (even *Sports Illustrated* emphasizes its annual swimsuit issue), television (soap operas, late night cable TV), and music (with sexually explicit lyrics and a radio station in Chicago with the call leters WSEX).

Books and movies also emphasize sex. Sex researchers Abramson and Mechanic (1983) analyzed best selling novels and high demand films in regard to their sexual content and messages. They concluded,

. . . performance standards are exceedingly high; sex appears to be the sole province of the young; contraceptives are unheard of; orgasm is either exceptional or taboo (in major motion pictures); sex is rarely couched within the context of a longstanding, intimate relationship (married or otherwise); sex is often void of foreplay or erotic elaboration, and so on. (p. 203)

Sexual themes permeate the advertisement industry.

To unlock your body's potential, we proudly offer Soloflex. Twenty-four traditional iron pumping exercises, each correct in form and balance. All on a simple machine that fits in a corner of your home.
For a free Soloflex brochure, call anytime 1·800·453·9000.

SOLOFLEX, HILLSBORO, OREGON 97123   ©1983 SOLOFLEX

Sex as Recreation

Sex for the purpose of having children has been replaced largely by an emphasis on sex as recreation. But sex for recreation (nonprocreative sex) is still preferred in the context of a love relationship. Analyzing the important place of sex in our impersonal society, Petras (1978) observed, "Sexuality represents one form of the search for intrinsic meanings and gratifications—one aspect of an ideology of seeking out nonmaterialistic goals and rewards" (p. 30). Sexual sharing, in this view, allows a person to retreat from the impersonal and often alienating world to find rewards within a mutual caring relationship.

Less Virginity

While some people remain virgins until marriage, most do not. In a random sample of students at a large university and nonstudents 18–23 years of age residing in a city of 170,000, "only 5 percent of the men and 11 to 13 percent of the women endorsed premarital abstinence from intercourse" (DeLameter & MacCorquodale, 1979, p. 90).

Also, in each successive decade a higher percentage of premarital intercourse is reported for women. At one university in 1958, 1968, and 1978, 30, 39, and 76 percent of the engaged females reported having had intercourse (Bell & Coughey, 1980). Other studies suggest that both men and women are having varied sexual experiences at earlier ages and with more partners (Petersen et al., 1983a; Robinson & Jedlicka, 1982).

Despite these trends, there are some individuals for whom virginity is important. One person said, "I have been taught that sex outside of marriage is wrong and I feel that it is. Besides, I think that waiting till you're married to have intercourse makes it special for you and your partner and gives the two of you a special beginning." Those who prefer to be virgins at marriage prefer partners who are also virgins. Likewise, those who are sexually experienced also prefer mates who have had intercourse (Istvan & Griffitt, 1980).

People who have decided to remain virgins until marriage sometimes fear "being left out, of missing something, of being ridiculed, of losing a desirable girlfriend or boyfriend, or of being a 'sexual cripple'" (Lee, 1980). But the ultimate liberation for both women and men is the freedom to choose what one does sexually with one's own body.

The Slow Death of the Double Standard

The double standard suggests there are different standards for sexual behavior for men and women. The double standard is weakening at both the high school (Lance, 1979) and university level (King, Balswick, & Robinson, 1977). As Reiss (1976) stated:

The basic change during the past centuries has been from an orthodox double standard ethic of premarital sexuality which allowed males to copulate but which condemned their partners as "bad" women to a more modified version of the double standard wherein women are allowed to have premarital coitus but not with quite the abandon that men are. Of course, this is an oversimplification, and with over 220 million Americans there are many variations in standards. There are those who are fully equalitarian in a permissive direction and also those who are equalitarian in a restrictive direction and there still are those who are orthodox double standard. But the overall shift is toward less dominance of the sexual scene by males. (pp. 190–191)

But while the double standard may be weakening, it has not disappeared. It is apparent in all aspects of relations between men and women. "There are double standards everywhere," observed one woman. "It's very hard for me to ask a guy to go out with me because of the expectation that he should ask me out." Sexually, the man is still expected to be aggressive and initiate sex while the woman is expected to be passive. Many women fear a negative response from men if they are sexually aggressive. "One man I dated jokingly called me a 'sexy slut' when I reached for his zipper," said one woman. "I know he was joking and we both laughed but I don't like the implication of what he said."

Liberal Obscenity Laws

While some people in our society enjoy looking at pictures of nude bodies and sexually explicit scenes, others regard them as offensive and obscene. But the availability of "adult" magazines and movies suggests that we have a relatively liberal view of what is pornographic or obscene.

For a group of citizens to close down an adult book store or movie theater, they must prove that the materials sold are obscene. There are three criteria for obscenity. First, the dominant theme of the material must appear to a *prurient* (literally, "to itch") interest in sex. Such interest implies that the material is sexually arousing in a lewd way. Second, the material must be patently *offensive* to the community. In general, a community can dictate what its standards are regarding the sale, display, and distribution of sexual materials. Thus, the local community of Cincinnati, Ohio, could ban *Hustler* magazine and jail its publisher while *Hustler* remained on the newsstands in most other parts of the country.

The third criteria for obscenity is that the sexual material must have no *redeeming social value*. If the material can be viewed as entertaining or educational, a case can be made for its social value, and a small degree of social value can outweigh prurience and offensiveness. For example, in one community, some citizens wanted to close the movie theater that featured X-rated films on the grounds that the films were both prurient and offensive. But a local sex therapist testified as an expert witness that some couples could profit from viewing the films in question as an aid to overcoming sexual dysfunction. The judge ruled that because the film had therapeutic value, it had more than sufficient social value to justify its availability to the public.

Control of Pornography

Pornography comes from the Greek words *porne* ("prostitute") and *grapheim* ("to write") and originally meant "stories of prostitutes." Today the term refers to any photograph, movie, book, and so on that is designed to arouse or excite a person sexually. But there is disagreement about what is pornographic and what is merely erotic. "What turns me on is erotic: what turns you on is pornographic" (Shea, 1980).

Attempts to control pornography have been sporadic. In the 1930s and mid-forties, John O'Hara's *Appointment in Samarra* and Ernest Hemingway's *For Whom The Bell Tolls* were banned in various places for "the public good." The underlying assumption of censorship is that sex via pornography is bad for the public's moral health.

To gain more perspective on the pornography issue, a United States commission was set up in 1967 to study pornography. The commission made several recommendations. First, it recommended that federal, state, and local legislation prohibiting the sale, exhibition, and distribution of sexual material to adults be repealed. The commission could find no evidence that explicit sexual material played a significant role in causing individual or social harm. On the contrary, it found that erotic materials were sought as entertainment and information and that exposure to such materials seemed to enhance sexual communication. More important, the commission felt that adult obscenity laws impinge on the right of free speech and communication and that the government should not try to legislate individual moral behavior.

But the right of adults to have access to sexually explicit materials should not be extended to young people (under the age of 17 or 18 depending on the state). The commission recommended that the states adopt laws to prohibit the distribution and sale of sexual materials (specifically X-rated films) to young people. However, parents should be free to make their own decisions about the suitability of sexually explicit materials for their children.

Aware of the federal government's reluctance to become involved in restricting pornography, citizens in various communities have launched campaigns to register their disapproval. Some angry citizens have protested that "smut" is not just being made available, it is being thrust upon them.

(Continued)

Dispersing, zoning, and picketing are three ways local communities may try to control pornography. Detroit, Michigan, for example, has chosen the technique of dispersal, passing laws requiring that adult bookstores, theaters, massage parlors, and the like be at least 1,000 feet from a similar establishment, 500 feet from a church, and, if in a residential area, have the consent of 51 percent of the people who live there. The goal in dispersing pornography establishments is to scatter them so that people will be discouraged from patronizing them.

An opposite tactic is zoning, in which all the X-rated movie houses, bookstores, and the like are concentrated in a small area. Boston's Combat Zone is an attempt at this. But the results have been unfavorable since such zoning results in a concentration of the criminal element, which increases the danger to customers (a Harvard football player was stabbed there in the 70s).

Still another way to control pornography is picketing, which was tried in Fremont, California. Here pickets appeared in front of pornography establishments and wrote the license plate number of the alleged customer's car on their picket signs. While this did discourage patronage, it took a considerable effort on the part of the pickets.

Occasionally, the federal government becomes involved in curbing the pornography industry. In the early eighties the FBI conducted a "sting" operation known as MIPORN. Undercover agents posed as pornography dealers in a fake business they set up in Miami called Gold Coast Specialties. Over a 2½ year period they cultivated business relationships with some of the major producers and distributors of pornography, which resulted in the indictment of 54 key individuals. But the government's interest in the pornography business is not necessarily because of its concern with morality. In addition, it is the pirating and distribution of major motion pictures, often done by those in pornography, that costs legitimate business about $700 million each year (on which no taxes are paid).

Child pornography, also known as, "kiddie porn," "child porn," and "chicken porn," consists mainly of photos and films depicting children masturbating, performing fellatio (oral sex upon the male), and having intercourse with adults. In an attempt to prevent such exploitation of children by adults, Congress has passed legislation providing a maximum penalty of 15 years in prison and a fine of $15,000 for trafficking in child pornography (Geiser, 1979).

Reasons for the New Sexual Liberality

Changing sexual ideologies, the women's movement, the gay liberation movement, young people's perception of liberal adult sexuality, and contraception are influences that have combined to create a more liberal American society.

Changing Sexual Ideologies

Sexual behavior is one form of social behavior. Every society develops an ideology, a way of viewing or interpreting the social behavior of its members. Our society has at least three such ideologies: religious, scientific, and secular.

Religious (Sacred) Ideology

The central mission of Judeo-Christian religion as it relates to sexual behavior has been to subordinate the urges of the individual to society's goals. Marriage is a means by which this is accomplished. The result is a social and legal bond between two hetrosexual adults who will produce, nurture, and socialize children so that our society will continue.

To help control sexual behavior, many religions set up a dichotomy between body and mind. As traditionally interpreted, the mind housed the spirit and the body was the place of physical desire (Petras, 1978). It became the job of the mind to monitor and control sexual impulses. By implication, the body was corrupt. Unlike other animals who copulate instinctively, humans were expected to think and act on the basis of "higher" values and ideals.

Religious ideology teaches that various sexual orientations (heterosexual, homosexual, bisexual), sexual behaviors (masturbation, intercourse, oral sex) and sexual life styles (cohabitation, singlehood, marriage) are morally right or wrong. Heterosexual penile–vaginal intercourse, according to most religions, is morally correct, just as homosexual fellatio is sinful.

Scientific Ideology

Religious interpretations of sexuality have gradually given way to a scientific ideology. "Since the turn of this century, there has been a general change in our way of thinking about the world. We are less likely to look to religion to explain the unknown, but are more likely to look to science" (Petras, 1978, pp. 76–77). Sigmund Freud, Havelock Ellis, and Hendrick van de Velde were three early-twentieth-century scientists who were instrumental in shifting society's ideas about sex from a sacred to a scientific perspective.

Sigmund Freud (1885–1939) is responsible for a number of concepts about sexuality. In addition to the Oedipus complex and Electra complex and their role in the formation of gender identity, which we discussed earlier, other

We live in a pluralistic society with both liberal and conservative elements.

important concepts are libido, sublimation, and the anal, oral, phallic, and genital stages of psychosexual development.

Libido refers to sex drive. A person with no libido is said to lack an interest in sex. A person with an active libido is sometimes said to be "horny." Sublimation means the redirection of sexual energy to a more appropriate goal. For example, a worker may be sexually attracted to his or her employer. But since the direct expression of that sexual interest is inappropriate, the sexual energy may be redirected into working harder and performing well on the job.

Freud also suggested that human sexuality evolves through predictable developmental stages (oral, anal, phallic, and genital), each psychological stage being linked to a change in the body. For example, the oral stage begins at birth and lasts through the first year. During this period the child receives primary satisfaction through stimulation of the lips and mouth. During the anal stage (about age 2), the child focuses on elimination. The phallic stage involves an emphasis on the genitals and self-pleasure (masturbation). The genital stage occurs near the end of adolescence. At this time sexual emphasis shifts from self-pleasure through masturbation to interpersonal sexual pleasure.

Sexual problems, according to Freud, are the result of not making the successful transition from one stage to the next. While Freud's theory lacks supporting data, it has had a profound impact on the way sexual development is viewed.

Havelock Ellis (1859–1939) emphasized that sexual behavior was learned social behavior, that "deviant" sexual behavior was merely that which society labeled as abnormal, and that an enjoyable sex life (a desirable goal) was not something that just happened but had to be achieved. About the sex education of children, Ellis (1931) wrote, "no doubt is any longer possible as to the absolute necessity of taking a deliberate and active part in this sexual initiation, instead of leaving it to chance revelation of ignorant and perhaps vicious companions or servants" (p. 43).

Theodore Hendrik van de Velde (1873–1937) was a Dutch gynecologist, who, in 1926, published a guide to sex, *Ideal Marriage*, which became a best seller. Like Ellis, van de Velde believed that sexual response was not automatic. He prescribed specific sexual techniques whereby his patients—and readers—could translate their emotional commitments into delightful orgasms. He also emphasized that sex is an interpersonal experience and considered lack of orgasm and impotence a couple's problem rather than the wife's or husband's problem.

Beyond these contributions, the works of Kinsey and Masters and Johnson have added scientific credibility to the study of sexuality and have influenced the continued drift from a sacred to a scientific ideology. But, although the balance has shifted, both ideologies continue to function in our society.

Secular Ideology

The secular (worldly) ideology does not compete with the religious and scientific ideologies but focuses them on the need for relevant, here-and-now, "how does it affect me" applications. Some religions have responded by issuing new translations of the Bible, which help to ensure relevance. Scientific sex research has also responded by developing treatment procedures for a variety of sexual dysfunctions and making these techniques available to the layperson through the popular paperback books.

While fundamentalist religious groups have not modified their ideology, they are becoming increasingly isolated. As scientific and secular ideologies continue to interact, fewer people in our society are internalizing a rigid set of values for sexual orientations, behaviors, and life styles. The result is a more permissive and liberal society.

To determine your score on the Sexual Attitude Scale on pp. 124–125, reverse the scores for statements 21 and 22 in the following way: $1 = 5$, $2 = 4$, $4 = 2$, $5 = 1$. For example, if you wrote 1 for statement 21 ("There should be no laws prohibiting sexual acts between consenting adults"), change that number to 5 for scoring purposes. Reverse score statement 22 similarly.

Add the numbers you assigned to each of the 25 statements. Your score may range from a low of 25 (strongly disagreed with all items: $1 \times 25 = 25$) to a high of 125 (strongly agreed with all items: $5 \times 25 = 125$). If you scored between 25 and 50, you might be regarded as a high-grade liberal, between 50 and 75, a low-grade liberal. If you scored between 100 and 125, you might be regarded as a high-grade conservative; between 75 and 100, a low-grade conservative.

In this scale a liberal is one who feels that the expression of human sexuality should be open, free, and unrestrained. A conservative is one who feels that sexual expression should be considerably constrained and closely regulated. When 689 students (primarily seniors and graduate students) took the Sexual Attitude Scale, both genders tended to score from borderline low to high-grade liberal (Nurius & Hudson, 1982).

The Women's Movement

The National Organization for Women (NOW) has a membership of more than 220,000 people. A basic theme of the women's movement, of which NOW is perhaps the best-known representative, has been the equalization of rights and privileges for women and men. In the area of sexual behavior, the movement has attacked the double standard that allows men the privilege of enjoying sex outside marriage without being stigmatized. Traditionally, women have had to carefully monitor their sexual behavior to have the chance for marriage and a relatively secure economic future. Men were under no such constraint. The women's movement has challenged the double-standard assumption that a bride must be a virgin. At the same time, the movement has encouraged women to be economically independent, with the result that fewer women feel that marriage—and premarital virginity—is essential for economic security.

My Sexuality

How Liberal or Conservative Am I?
The Sexual Attitude Scale

This questionnaire is designed to measure the way you feel about sexual behavior. It is not a test, so there are no right or wrong answers. Answer each item as carefully and accurately as you can by placing a number beside each one as follows:

1. Strongly disagree
2. Disagree
3. Neither agree nor disagree (undecided)
4. Agree
5. Strongly agree

	SD	D	U	A	SA
1. I think there is too much sexual freedom given to adults these days.	1	2	3	4	5
2. I think that the increased sexual freedom seen in the past several years has done much to undermine the American family.	1	2	3	4	5
3. I think that young people have been given too much information about sex.	1	2	3	4	5
4. Sex education should be restricted to the home.	1	2	3	4	5
5. Older people do not need to have sex.	1	2	3	4	5
6. Sex education should be given only when people are ready for marriage.	1	2	3	4	5
7. Premarital sex may be a sign of a decaying social order.	1	2	3	4	5
8. Extramarital sex is never excusable.	1	2	3	4	5

(Continued)

	SD	D	U	A	SA
9. I think there is too much sexual freedom given to teenagers these days.	1	2	3	4	5
10. I think there is not enough sexual restraint among young people.	1	2	3	4	5
11. I think people indulge in sex too much.	1	2	3	4	5
12. I think the only proper way to have sex is through intercourse.	1	2	3	4	5
13. I think sex should be reserved for marriage.	1	2	3	4	5
14. Sex should be only for the young.	1	2	3	4	5
15. Too much social approval has been given to homosexuals.	1	2	3	4	5
16. Sex should be devoted to the business of procreation.	1	2	3	4	5
17. People should not masturbate.	1	2	3	4	5
18. Heavy sexual petting should be discouraged.	1	2	3	4	5
19. People should not discuss their sexual affairs or business with others.	1	2	3	4	5
20. Severely handicapped (physically and mentally) people should not have sex.	1	2	3	4	5
21. There should be no laws prohibiting sexual acts between consenting adults.	1	2	3	4	5
22. What two consenting adults do together sexually is their own business.	1	2	3	4	5
23. There is too much sex on television.	1	2	3	4	5
24. Movies today are too sexually explicit.	1	2	3	4	5
25. Pornography should be totally banned from our bookstores.	1	2	3	4	5

The Gay Liberation Movement

While the women's movement has been the most prominent social movement in the past few years, the gay liberation movement has increased the visibility of alternative sexual norms and life styles. Carrying banners that read, "Out of the closet" and "Better blatant than latent," male homosexuals and lesbians have marched in San Francisco and in New York City's Greenwich Village seeking an end to discrimination on the basis of sexual preference. In addition to public demonstrations, there are currently more than 600 homosexual organizations and publications in the United States that have helped raise people's consciousness as well as offer support to their members.

Although homosexuals still receive little social support and often encounter hostility from heterosexuals, public awareness of the homosexual's social world, values, and difficulties has encouraged some rethinking of both homosexual and heterosexual values. The result has been a more liberal society that recognizes the existence of alternative sexual norms and behaviors.

Young People's Perception of Liberal Adult Sexuality

"My parents have been divorced since I was 7" remarked a high school junior. "Since then my dad has been involved with numerous women, another marriage, and another divorce. Now he's 'dating' again. My mom doesn't live with her boyfriend, but she might as well. He stays at our house late on weekends, and I'm sure they are having sex."

In some families liberal attitudes about sex will be learned from parents. Even children from traditional homes are likely to be exposed to the permissive sexual attitudes of other adults, of friends, and of the media. They need only to go to the nearest drugstore or newsstand to see *High Society*, *Playboy*, *Penthouse*, and *Playgirl*, magazines featuring adult sexual behavior in close-up color photography. The basic value suggested by these sexually oriented magazines is that sex is available and enjoyable and that there are few limits that need to be observed.

Contraception

Heterosexual partners may now conveniently separate their lovemaking from their baby making. The almost 100 percent effective birth control pill permits a couple to include sex in their relationship without worrying about pregnancy. Although the controversy regarding the potential hazards of the pill continues, most people prefer the pill to other methods of contraception. If a woman is unable to take the pill because of a family history of blood clots or other relevant health problems, the couple may opt for other methods, such as an intrauterine device (IUD), diaphragm, sponge, or condom.

But regardless of the contraceptive chosen, the result is a new freedom from fear of pregnancy. (See Chapter 16 for a more detailed discussion of family planning.)

American Society: A Moral Majority View

While sex in our society is pervasive and the limits of what is acceptable seem to be expanding, the conservative religious element that has come to be known as the Moral Majority has mounted a vigorous opposition to permissive sexual values. But what percentage of Americans support the so-called moral majority, who are they, and what is their impact on our society?

Moral Majority or Minority?

The Moral Majority, which takes its name from the loosely organized group founded by Reverend Jerry Falwell in 1979, does not represent the majority of Americans, in spite of the group's claim to the contrary. In a 1981 Gallup poll, 8 percent of a national sample said they supported the Moral Majority. This represents about 12 to 13 million Americans.

A study conducted by the Connecticut Mutual Life Insurance Company (1981) throws some light on the characteristics of those people making up the "moral majority."

In this study religious ultraconservatism was measured by agreement that the following 10 activities were morally wrong: adultery, use of hard drugs, homosexuality, intercourse before the age of 16, lesbianism, pornographic movies, abortion, smoking marijuana, living with someone of the opposite gender without being married, and intercourse between two single people. Of 1,610 randomly selected individuals, those most likely to feel that the activities were wrong had similar background characteristics. These characteristics included:

1. *Age.* The older the person, the more likely that person was to take a conservative stand on all 10 moral issues.
2. *Region.* Southerners were three times as likely to describe all activities as morally wrong. Those in the Northeast and Midwest were between the extremes.
3. *Race.* Whites were more likely than blacks to describe all 10 actions as morally wrong.
4. *Gender.* Women were more conservative than men on these issues.
5. *Income.* Those with lower incomes, ($12,000–$25,000), were twice as likely to feel the actions were morally wrong as those with incomes above $25,000.

6. *Education.* Those with less than high school educations were twice as likely as those with college educations to condemn all 10 actions.
7. *Residence.* Those living in small cities or rural areas were twice as likely to object to the actions as those living in large cities or urban areas.*

Impact of the Moral Majority

While the Moral Majority represents only a minority of Americans, it has become an influential force in our society, a "powerful lobbying group of Christian fundamentalists dedicated to electing their own political candidates" (Negri, 1981, p. 4). The movement has identified a number of trends contributing to the country's moral decay: escalating divorce, the prohibition of school prayer, abortion on demand, pornography, homosexuality, drug use, and sex education in the public schools. Falwell said that "America is the last launching pad for world evangelism—and if it falls to Communism as a result of its own moral decay—that will mean the end of Christianity" (FitzGerald, 1981, p. 108).

In 1980 the Moral Majority and their conservative allies helped unseat several prominent liberal U.S. senators as well as numerous local officials and elect conservative candidates in their place. With the cooperation of a conservative administration, this group has introduced several pieces of legislation into Congress for the following purposes.

1. *Eliminate abortion.* The "human life" bill defines life as beginning at conception, making all abortions a criminal offense.
2. *Encourage chastity.* The Adolescent Family Life Act is a $30 million program to teach teenagers "self-discipline and chastity" and to discourage the use of birth control. The bill's definition of promiscuity is "a person under 21 having intercourse out of wedlock."
3. *Restrict sex education.* Schools getting federal funds would be required to obtain parental approval of content and course material before providing sex education courses.

Although at the time of this writing the fate of these proposals is not yet known, they testify to the current strength of the ultraconservative movement.

The future of this movement is uncertain. There is some suggestion that it will continue to swell. One researcher observed, "Parents are increasingly uncomfortable with the sweeping permissiveness their own pursuit of new options has created (Yankelovich, 1981, p. 6). As a result they may desire a more conservative society. How these desires will affect public policy remains to be seen.

*Source: *The Connecticut Mutual Life Report on American Values in the '80s: The Impact of Belief.* Copyright © 1981 Connecticut Mutual Life Insurance Company, Hartford, Connecticut.

Sexual themes that permeate our society are used not only in sexually explicit magazines but those designed for a wider audience as well.

Sex Education

Sex education is more than learning about heterosexual intercourse through formal classroom course work. Sex education "covers a highly complex and extremely subtle blend of biologic, psychologic, social, and interpersonal aspects of the total meaning of being either a man or a woman. In addition, sex education is the process of helping men, women and children to accept, gladly and positively, all of these aspects of themselves and to learn to take full responsibility for their use" (Schiller, 1980, p. 467). Informal and formal sources of sex education include peers, parents, and teachers.

Peers as Sex Educators

During adolescence peers are the most common source of information about sex (Davis & Harris, 1982). But such information is often erroneous, misleading, and perpetuates misconceptions. Unfortunately, many of these faulty ideas about sexuality stay embedded in the person's belief and attitude system.

Parents as Sex Educators

Whether intentionally or not, parents are our primary sex education teachers (Gordon, 1982). When we were children, whether they let us observe their nudity, how they reacted to our touching our genitals or using sexual language, and whether they were affectionate with us or each other were all les-

The SIECUS/NYU* Principles Basic To Education for Sexuality

The principles that follow were first set down by SIECUS staff in 1976, then commented on at length and approved with changes by the SIECUS Board of Directors in 1977. The board again considered them in 1978, with further refinement.

In the summer of 1979 a group of sex educators generously came at their own expense to Uppsala, Sweden, to attend a SIECUS/New York University Colloquium. They were invited for the specific purpose of couching the principles in language that might be less technical and therefore more readily translatable for other languages, cultures, and levels of education. The versions they finally agreed upon were once again submitted to the SIECUS Board, whose relatively few comments are herewith integrated.

The purposes to which SIECUS proposes to put these principles are, first, to provide a position base broad enough to be acceptable to health workers everywhere, and second, to enlist official support for the document by organizations in the health field throughout the United States and elsewhere in the world.

*Sex Information and Education Council of the United States/New York University.

Definition

The SIECUS concept of *sexuality* refers to the totality of being a person. It includes all of those aspects of the human being that relate specifically to being boy or girl, woman or man, and is an entity subject to life-long dynamic change. Sexuality reflects our human character, not solely our genital nature. As a function of the total personality it is concerned with the biological, psychological, sociological, spiritual, and cultural variables of life which, by their effects on personality development and interpersonal relations, can in turn affect social structure.

The Principles

1. Human sexual functioning begins in the uterus and, in one or all of its many aspects, will continue throughout the life cycle of all human beings.
2. Sexuality is a vital and basic human function. It manifests itself in every dimension of being a person. Therefore, as a part of every human being, its existence cannot be questioned or subjected to moral judgment. However, because sexual *behavior* and *attitudes* vary in different cultures, these may become appropriate subjects for debate and moral judgment.
3. Sexuality is learned as the result of a process that should not be left to chance or ignorance. The sexual learning process actually begins with the intimate relationships between the infant and the parents or parent-figures, e.g., with clinging, skin and face stroking, hugging, rocking,

(Continued)

kissing, and the crucial elements of eye and voice contact with the infant. These constitute only a small part of what leads to the establishment of gender *identity* before the age of three. With relation to acquiring positive attitudes about one's gender *role*, this learning process continues throughout life. It is important that the informal process of sex education within the family be supported by planned, enlightened learning opportunities offering information at appropriate times in the growing period.

4. The developing child's sexuality is continually and inevitably influenced by daily contacts with persons of all ages and especially by contacts with peers, the family, religion, school and the media.

5. In many cultures, for both boys and girls reproductive maturity precedes by some years emotional and social readiness for parenting. Puberty, with the arrival of reproductive capacity, can be made of especial significance for enhancing the sexual learning process.

6. While the reproductive and pleasurable aspect of genital sexual expression may occur together, it is possible for humans to separate each from the other. The development of values recognizing and acting upon this fact can facilitate acceptance of family planning in order to allow individuals to enjoy their sexual lives in a socially responsible manner.

7. Sexual self-pleasuring or masturbation is today medically accepted as a natural and nonharmful part of sexual behavior for individuals of all ages and both sexes. It can help girls, boys, women, and men to develop an affirmative sense of body autonomy. It is a source of enjoyment and can provide an intense experience of the self as well as preparation for experiencing an *other*. Many persons, however, do not express their sexuality in this way and this also is an individual choice.

8. In providing healthy perspectives on sexual practices and attitudes for children, the aim should be to facilitate a child's capacity and right to explore, enjoy, and integrate sexuality into his or her developing self-concept. Thus the most constructive response to, for example, masturbation, nudity, and rehearsal sex play, would be to teach children to understand them as personal rights that are subject to responsibility for the rights of others and to appropriate degrees of privacy within the family and the community. It should be recognized that such experiences can contribute positively to their future sexual health.

9. Children of all ages have the capacity to establish caring, loving relationships with people of all ages. These relationships should be seen as important elements in the development of their sexuality, and some can even continue throughout life.

10. The expression of sexual orientation is a fundamental human right. Preference for sexual partners and sexual relationships (sexual orientation) is one important component of an individual's sexual identity, which thus

(Continued)

includes gender identity, gender role, sexual orientation, and recognition of the self as a sexually functioning person. The examination and understanding of these components can lead to an understanding by a person of the degree to which he or she is heterosexual, bisexual, or homosexual.

11. The manner in which sexual orientation occurs is not known, but it appears that it is established early in life. The majority of individuals have some elements of both homosexuality and heterosexuality in their makeup which may or may not be identified or expressed by the individual throughout his or her life.

12. All human beings, regardless of sexual orientation, may be subject to personal difficulties which are not necessarily related to that orientation. Social structures or attitudes which lead to repression of sexuality in general, and homosexuality and bisexuality specifically, may cause individual and interpersonal difficulties.

13. The sexual orientation of any person, whether child, adolescent, or adult, cannot be changed solely by exposure to other orientations. Occasional and/or situational sexual experiences are not necessarily indicative of a person's sexual orientation.

14. Sex education can be formal or informal. Everyone receives sex education in one way or another. All persons are informal sex educators whether or not they are aware of it. Formal sex education should be planned and implemented with careful attention to developmental needs, appropriateness to community settings and values, and respect for individual differences.

15. Sensitive sex education can be a positive force in promoting physical, mental, and social health. It should be geared to the three levels of learning—affective, cognitive, and operative—and should begin as early as possible.

16. Television and other mass media have an important and widespread impact on the community. Their vast potential for informal and formal sex education should be put to productive use.

17. Rational understanding and acceptance of the wide range of possible expressions of sexuality constitute one goal of education for sexuality. Where sexual fulfillment is limited by life circumstances, or restrictive lifestyles such as aging or disability, alternative ways of meeting the need for such fulfillment should be encouraged and facilitated by society. However, when sexual expression infringes on the freedom of choice of other persons, management must then be consistent with basic human rights.

18. All health, social science, religious, teaching, and counseling professionals should receive education in human sexuality.

19. It is the right of every individual to live in an environment of freely available information, knowledge, and wisdom about sexuality, so as to be enabled to realize his or her human potential.

sons in human sexuality. In adolescence they continued to teach us about sex by encouraging or discouraging the discussion of sexual issues.

Most parents feel it is their responsibility to provide sex education for their children. But feeling such responsibility does not always translate into talking about sexuality with their children. Many parents are reluctant to talk with their children about sex. More than half (55 percent) of the parents in one study said they do not volunteer information to their children about sex, preferring to wait until their children ask for information (Wyatt & Stewart-Newman, 1982). When young people are asked to describe the degree to which their parents are effective sex educators, only 20 percent say they are "adequate" (Gordon & Dickman, 1981).

A basic reason parents sometimes are reluctant to talk about sex with their children is that their own parents avoided the issue. Examine the modeling effect in reference to your own life. By watching your parents brush their teeth and telling you how to brush your own, you know how to brush your teeth and can easily pass this on to your children. But if similar modeling through talking about sex did not occur, you may not have acquired this skill. In such a circumstance, if you have your own children, it would be easy for you to do what your parents did—nothing.

Many parents feel uncomfortable when talking about sex with their children. Sex is an emotionally charged subject and it may elicit a number of feelings—anxiety, guilt, shame, and delight. To talk about sex is to imply a person's own sexuality. Because parents feel a surge of mixed emotions when discussing sex with their offspring, they may choose to eliminate the discomfort by avoiding the discussion entirely. When a married daughter announced to her parents that she was pregnant, her mother stumbled through a brief congratulatory remark and her father got up and left the room. While he was proud to know that he was soon to be a grandfather, he couldn't tolerate the idea of discussing pregnancy with his daughter.

Parents also may have certain fears about the effect of sex education on their children. One of the most common fears is that information about sex will lead to sexual experimentation. A discussion of reproduction inevitably involves a penis in a vagina. Will a child try this act him- or herself? The parent may think, "If they don't know about it, they can't do it" and try to keep such information from their children. A related fear is that the child will interpret such a discussion as encouragement or license to experiment sexually.

Regardless of the reasons parents do not provide systematic sex education, most offspring wish they would. Two-thirds of the men and three-fourths of the women in one study said that "parents should be primarily responsible" for their children's sex education (Bennett & Dickinson, 1980). Most sex educators agree. Van Emde Boas (1980) has suggested the following "10 Commandments for Parents Providing Sex Education."

1. Thou shalt not separate sex education from any other education, but realize that sex education starts in the cradle.
2. Thou shalt realize that skin and hands are our most important sex organs.

3. Thou shalt neither curb spontaneous sex expressions of the child, nor ever stimulate it artificially.
4. Thou shalt answer every question of the child according to truth, wherever possible immediately but always according to the emotional and spiritual level of the child; never answer more than was asked for.
5. Thou shalt realize that a living example carries more weight than words.
6. Thou shalt realize that sex information at school can never be anything but an addition to sex education in the family.
7. Thou shalt realize that overstressing of the biological aspects of sexuality must lead to underestimating of the emotional and relational aspects.
8. Thou shalt teach that sexual exploitation of another human being is equally as reprehensible as any other form of exploitation.
9. Thou shalt teach your children that the stem "co" in coitus means "together": being together, belonging together, becoming one and thus presupposes an intimate relationship.
10. The Pill: rather a year too early than one night too late.*

Sol Gordon's Parent Training Program

To help parents overcome their fears about sex education and to help them improve their skills as sex educators for their children, Sol Gordon, Ph.D. (1977) of the Institute for Family Research and Education developed a training program in Syracuse, New York. Stressing that ignorance, not information, stimulates inappropriate sexual behavior and that responsible parents give their children the full range of information on which they can make informed decisions, Dr. Gordon and his colleagues examined the concerns parents have about discussing sex with their children.

One concern is that parents believe they must know a great deal about sex to be able to give their children sex education. One parent said she was not sure about the details of fertilization and she was afraid her children might ask her something she did not know. While this is a common concern, parents might ease the pressure on themselves by recognizing that it is okay not to know everything (Will Rogers said we are all experts on some subjects and real dumb on others). Indeed, most parents know enough to contribute positively to almost any discussion of sex, and when they feel inadequate in their knowledge, they can simply say, "I don't know . . . but I will find out." Such a statement gets the parent off the hook, keeps the subject of sex open between parent and child, and stimulates the search for accurate information.

Another concern parents have is the feeling that you can tell a child too much, for example, that telling a young child about intercourse may be too deep and involved for the child. Of course, information should be appropriate to the child's level of maturity. But in reality, parents cannot harm their children by giving them information about sex; on the contrary, it is ignorance that can hurt them. When the words, descriptions, or explanations about sex go beyond the child's interests and ability to understand, the child

*Source: From Med C. Van Emde Boas, *Journal of Sex Education and Sex Therapy*, 1980, 6, 1, p. 19. Reprinted by permission of American Association of Sex Educators, Counselors, and Therapists, Washington, D.C.

will simply get bored and shut off the dialogue. Parents often assume that the child wants an hour's lecture when she or he asks, "Where did I come from?" But even the answer, "You grew in a special place inside Mommy called the uterus" may be more than the child is interested in. One child asked the question simply to verify that she came from inside her mother rather than from inside the doctor's black bag. While the "uterus" was more than she was interested in, she was not harmed by this information.

Parents may also feel they must wait until a child asks before they offer information. But the child is always asking. In fact, information about genitalia and intercourse are the most frequently expressed sexual interests of preadolescents (Gilbert & Bailis, 1980). For example, when a parent goes to the bathroom, the child may want to go and see what goes on in there. Likewise, parents who take a shower have experienced children waiting to take a peek behind the shower curtain. Such behaviors are demonstrations of their interest. Seizing the teachable moment, a parent might begin giving names to various body parts—"This is my penis," "This is my vulva"—in the same manner that he or she labels the parts of a car when a child wants to see what is under the hood: "This is the battery," "This is the air filter," "This is the radiator." Even if parents do not see teachable-moment occasions to talk about sex they can bring up the subject. Just as parents involve their children in conversations about table manners, appropriate dress and other concerns without waiting for the child to ask, so might parents take the initiative in the discussion of sex.

Topics Parents Find Difficult

Even if parents are willing to provide sex education for their children and have overcome their hesitancy about doing so, there are several topics some parents find particularly difficult to discuss. These include masturbation, nudity, obscenity, and playing doctor.*

1. *Masturbation.* While, intellectually, parents know that masturbation does not cause blindness, insanity, or any of the horrors other generations were confronted with, they often have mixed feelings about it. But it is normal and healthy for children to masturbate; the only way it is "bad" is for children to be told that it is. Such parental admonitions do not stop children from masturbating, but they do produce guilt and anxiety, which produces more masturbation to relieve the anxiety, which only results in more guilt. Making children feel guilty about masturbation also encourages them to feel anxious about sex in general. The alternative is to tell children that masturbating is acceptable and enjoyable but should be done in private.

2. *Nudity.* Some parents wonder about whether it is appropriate to undress in front of their children. Doing so may help their children to feel more comfortable about nudity and to develop positive feelings about their own bodies. Parents who never allow their young children to see them nude are

*The following four items are based on information provided by Sol Gordon, Ph.D. Director, Institute for Family Research & Education, 1983.

teaching them that being nude around others is not acceptable. This may have unfortunate consequences for a person's adult sexual life, as in the case of one woman who never allowed her husband to see her nude—they had intercourse under the sheets in the dark. She said that her parents "made a big thing" out of not being nude.

3. *"Dirty" words.* Children hear slang words for sexual parts and functions from their peers and bring them home. Parents might respond to the use of such words by explaining what they mean and telling their children the more appropriate term. Such a response conveys to children that their parents are people with whom they can share what they know—even when it is sexual.

4. *Playing doctor.* It is not unusual for parents to discover that their children play doctor (alternately looking at, and sometimes touching, each other's genitals) with their siblings or with other children. Parents may feel caught between their disapproval of this activity and their desire not to give the impression that sex is dirty and that it is wrong to touch and look at the bodies of others their same age. One solution is to communicate a mild enough form of disapproval to stop the behavior without traumatizing the children by telling them they have done something terrible.

Parents and Teenagers

Both parents and their teenage children are interested in the issue of premarital intercourse (Gilbert & Bailis, 1980; Lewis & Lewis, 1981). A major fear of parents is potential pregnancy. A daughter's pregnancy may mean a shattered family image ("The Jones girl got pregnant"), a threatened reputation ("She is sexually promiscuous"), and a questionable beginning for a marriage ("They got married because she was pregnant"). The consequences of an unwanted pregnancy for their son may be less dramatic because he does not carry the baby. However, a major concern is that he could be forced into a marriage that would not have occurred were it not for the pregnancy.

Such worries may cause parents considerable anxiety and unhappiness, and they may feel frustrated in their inability to control their children's sexual behavior. As already mentioned, parents rarely know how to communicate effectively with their offspring about sex. While some use fear tactics that emphasize the dangers of sexually transmitted diseases and an unwanted pregnancy, others communicate only vague expectations about sexual behavior. These expectations are usually in the form of "Don't be out too late," "Who else will be there?" or "What time will you be back?"

But the most effective influence parents have on their teenagers' sexual behavior may be their relationship with them. At least this seems true of the mother–daughter relationship. In one study (Inazu & Fox, 1980), the researchers concluded that the strongest predictor of the daughter's sexual experience was a good relationship with her mother: the better the relationship, the less likely she was to have had sex. Also, the greater the rapport between parent and adolescent, the more likely that sexual issues will be discussed (Bennett & Dickinson, 1980).

It is not unusual for parents to assume that their children, particularly their daughters, will not have intercourse before marriage, that "immorality" and "permissiveness" are behaviors of other youth. An engaged woman said, "I have been having intercourse with my boyfriend since we met three years ago. Mother *must* know because she is aware of our having spent some time at the family's beach house when she and Daddy were on vacation. But, when we went to pick out my wedding dress last week there was never a discussion of whether or not it would be white. I think she is incapable of thinking that I would have intercourse before I was married."

Teachers as Sex Educators

Society increasingly has looked to the schools to provide formal sex education to supplement the informal sources of peers and parents.

What Schools Provide

Since 1960, in an effort to reduce sexual ignorance, several prestigious national panels have recommended that the federal government take a leadership role in encouraging sex education in the secondary schools. Yet, because education is financed and administered almost entirely through state and local school boards, only limited initiatives are possible on the federal level. Throughout the United States, only eight states (Hawaii, Kentucky, Maryland, Michigan, Missouri, North Dakota, Delaware, New Jersey) and the District of Columbia require some sort of sex or family life education in their public school systems. Although not mandated in all states, 36 percent of U.S. public high schools offer a sex education course (Orr, 1982).

Where they exist, sex education programs differ widely in content and presentation. There are four basic types:

1. *Facts.* This type of course emphasizes the anatomy and physiology of men and women: reproductive organs, physical maturation, menstruation, and the like. One person who had been exposed to this model observed, "The course tells you what you've got and how to use it."
2. *Consequences.* Sexually transmitted diseases, unwanted pregnancy, unachieved educational goals, and potential medical complications are investigated as potential negative consequences of unprotected intercourse, as well as the economic strain on a marriage forced by a premarital pregnancy.
3. *Morality.* This model emphasizes responsible sexual behavior involving the use of contraception and avoiding the exploitation of one's partner. While alternative value systems are explored, a basic theme suggests that the best sex is that which enhances the relationship and the self-concepts of the partners.

Sex Education Curriculum

Kindergarten

(1) Know sex differences between girls' and boys' bodies. (2) Give direction toward male or female role in adult life. (3) Learn correct names for body parts and terms concerned with elimination.
(4) Understand that a human baby develops inside the body of the mother in the uterus.
(5) Understand that a baby gets its milk from the mother's breast by nursing.
(6) Appreciate that there are good body feelings. (7) Learn to recognize signs of love and devotion within the family.
(8) Develop the idea of continuity of living things—incubate hen's eggs.

First Grade

(1) Understand that the egg cell is basic to new life. (2) Learn that some animals hatch from eggs and others develop inside the body of the mother until birth.
(3) Appreciate the wonder of the human body. (4) Develop a sense of responsibility for one's own body. (5) Appreciate the

efforts of mother and father for family members. (6) Recognize the influence of emotions on body health.

Second Grade

(1) Learn that different animals need different amounts of time to get ready to be born. (2) Understand that the egg cell does not develop into a baby by itself (role of father). (3) Understand the process of internal fertilization. (4) Learn that some animals are born alive through a special opening in the mother's body.
(5) Recognize that growing up brings responsibility. (6) Appreciate importance of mutual love and consideration in family.
(7) Understand that the composition of family does not necessarily determine happiness of the family.

Third Grade

(1) Know that growing up means more than just getting bigger. (2) Appreciate the amazing structure and function of major body organs. (3) Develop an increasing sense of responsibility to self, peer group, and family. (4) Understand that each person's unique heredity is determined at

(Continued)

the moment of fertilization. (5) Understand the function of gonads and the process of menstruation in the human reproductive cycle. (6) Study life cycles of various animals, including humans.

Fourth Through Sixth Grade

(1) Learn that certain glands regulate each person's unique pattern of body growth and development. (2) Appreciate wonders of circulatory, respiratory, and digestive systems and realize that their functional potential is influenced by habits being developed. (3) Understand the importance of protecting vital body parts from injury, e.g., during sports. (4) Appreciate the miracle of reproduction and maternal care among various animals, including humans. (5) Learn to evaluate responsible and irresponsible behavior in peer and family group relationships. (6) Understand that menstruation occurs as a natural part of a girl's growing up. (7) Understand that seminal emissions occur as a natural part of a boy's growing up. (8) Learn that although nature readies our bodies for reproduction at puberty, several more years are needed to prepare for marriage and the responsibility of parenthood. (9) Understand one's

emotions—feelings of love, anger, aggression— and how anxiety and guilt affect relationships between family members and friends.

Junior High School

The junior high school curriculum goes into greater depth than the sixth-grade course of study on the reproductive system and body changes and their influence on interests, attitudes, and feelings. The curriculum can deal with customs, values, and standards in dating and in boy–girl relationships. Emphasis can be laid here on the developing aspects of maleness and femaleness and the various creative roles young people play. Because for many young people this is a time of sexual experimentation, the curriculum needs to deal with venereal disease, pregnancy that is unwanted, and the economic, social, legal, and psychologic factors involved in carrying on the responsibilities of adulthood.*

*From: Patricia Schiller's "New Advances in Sex Education" in *Medical Sexology* edited by R. Forleo and W. Pasini. Reprinted by permission of John Wright. PSG Incorporated. Copyright © PSG Publishing Company, 1980. pp. 470–471.

4. *Student oriented*. This model involves the active participation of students in the development and execution of "sex seminars" on campus.

In spite of the different approaches to sex education, the content of such courses is often minimal. Even in the school districts of states that mandate sex education, 6 in 10 do not cover contraception and 4 in 10 omit discussions of human reproduction and ethical standards (Gordon & Dickman, 1980). The outline suggested by Schiller (1980) for kindergarten through junior high school is an example of a thorough sex education curriculum.

Problems Sex Education Teachers Experience

Sample

Three-fourths of approximately 100 secondary teachers reported they had problems teaching sex education (Herold & Benson, 1978). Lack of training was a major problem. Only 2 in 5 reported they had taken a credit course in human sexuality. Since sex education is often taught as part of a course in biology, home economics, or health education, many of these teachers did not feel adequate to handle some of the questions students asked and more than 70 percent said they would sign up for a workshop on teaching sex education if it were offered. Teachers who do get such training report an increase in sexual knowledge and the development of more liberal attitudes (Smith et al., 1982).

Student shyness or embarrassment was another concern mentioned by these teachers. While most said that their students do become comfortable enough to talk about sex, about 20 percent said that their students were very hesitant to risk letting others know how they feel about sex.

Teaching values was a problem for some teachers. Should they just present facts or should they also teach values. If they were to teach values, which ones? While most (9 in 10) felt they should teach about birth control, only 1 in 10 felt that discouraging premarital intercourse was a goal (Herold & Benson, 1978).

But the goals of sex education may be conceived of too narrowly. Two sex researchers (Dunn & Ryan, 1982b) noted that unless school systems have a firmer rationale for sex education than dealing with the teenage pregnancy problem, sex education programs have little to recommend their inclusion in schools. "Human beings are sexual just as they are mental and social. Sexual problems should not need to exist in order to educate about sexuality anymore than an epidemic of rickets or pellagra is necessary to educate about nutrition" (p. 613).

Summary

Sexual ethics are moral guidelines for appropriate behavior. Our ethics have a religious base beginning with the laws set down by Moses to govern the ancient Hebrews. Subsequent religious influences include the teachings of Jesus, St. Paul, St. Augustine, St. Thomas Aquinas, and others. The result has been different views of sex ("it is a sin"; "it is a gift from God") over time. Current sexual ethics include traditional viewpoints and a situation ethics perspective. More often people are considering the individual, personal, and social consequences of their sexual decisions.

There are both liberal and conservative elements in our society's attitude toward sexuality. On the one hand is an increased openness about sexual matters, especially in the media, changing standards of sexual behavior for women, and liberal obscenity laws. Some of the causes of the new sexual liberality are the increased influences of scientific and secular ideologies, the women's and gay liberation movements, and the availability of safe and effective contraception. On the other hand is the reaction of the "moral majority" to increased liberalization, especially their efforts against abortion, gay rights, and sex education.

Peers, parents, and teachers provide the major sources of sex education in our society. While the most common source of sex education during adolescence is from peers, much of the information is inaccurate. Parents often feel anxious about providing sex education for their children because of the lack of good parental sex education models. Some teachers also feel inadequate as sex educators because of the lack of training to teach such courses. However, most feel adamant about the need for such sex education in the public school system. The result of such sex education from uninformed peers, anxious parents, and inadequately trained teachers in our society is a great deal of sexual ignorance.

Key Terms

sexual ethics
legalism
situationism
hedonism
asceticism
bundling
double standard

pornography
sacred ideology
scientific ideology
secular ideology
Moral Majority
sex education

Issues in Debate and Future Directions

Whether students should take sex education classes in the public schools is a hotly debated issue in many communities. After examining both sides of the debate, we look at future directions in sex education.

Sex Education: Home versus School

Parents' attitudes toward sex education in the public schools vary. Some feel that sex is an important area of life and that both parents and the school have some responsibility for sex education. Where sex education programs do exist, parents are given the option of asking that their children not be exposed. But less than 5 percent of parents exercise this option (Gordon & Dickman, 1981). Other parents are vehemently opposed to the school providing sex education for their children, believing that sex is a subject that is best taught (or not taught) in the private domain of the home. For some, the anger is high. They feel that sex education is obscene pornography designed to indoctrinate youth into promiscuity (Allen 1972). Others say that sex education is designed to "ensconce the principle of sexual liberation" (Shornack & Shornack, 1982, p. 542). The John Birch Society has attacked sex education as a "Communist Conspiracy."

The Mel Gablers Educational Research Analysts Newsletter is published by a husband and wife team from Longview, Texas. They review and rate human sexuality textbooks so that parents will be aware what their children are reading. The Gablers feel that many sex education courses are filled with pornography and are designed to change students' values.

Many teachers feel such charges are inappropriate. One such teacher, when told by a parent that "sex education belongs in the home," replied, "I also believe it belongs in the home. By the way, I would love to know where you are in the process of conversation with your children. What are you talking about together? What feelings and attitudes about themselves are your children exhibiting right now?," and so on (Tatum, 1980).

What are the consequences of sex education in the home and the school? As already discussed, many parents provide little sex information for their children, convey that sex is a topic to be avoided, and, in general, display anxiety and discomfort about sex. In a study comparing the sex education of children in the United States and Sweden, the researchers concluded that U.S. children are socially precocious and sexually ignorant (Goldman & Goldman, 1982).

While these may be negative consequences of the usual home sex education, the positive consequences permit the parents to feel good about being in control of the sex education of their children. Such pro-sex-education-in-the-home parents tend to hold a traditional view of the family (being married and having children is better than being single, divorced, or childless), women's roles (a woman's place is in the home), and sex before marriage (it is wrong) (Mahoney, 1979).

There is some evidence that children benefit from more formal sex education in the classroom. A study of sex education in the public schools (Kirby, Alter, & Scales, 1979), found that such a course increases students' knowledge about sexuality and makes them more tolerant of the sexual behaviors of others. But it does not seem to alter their personal values or increase the amount of sexual behavior (petting and intercourse) they engage in (Zelnik & Kim, 1982).

Regarding the long-term effect of formal sex education courses, it is often suggested that such courses will result in fewer unwanted pregnancies, less venereal disease, fewer sexual problems (lack of orgasm, impotence, premature ejaculation), and the development of more satisfying interpersonal relationships. But as yet there is no evidence for these claims (Voss, 1980).

Dr. Carol Cassell (1983), president of the American Association of Sex Educators, Counselors, and Therapists, emphasized that the sex education controversy is good.

> I would like to give us the same challenge Dorothy Broderick gave to those librarians, "I would like to see National Library Week get off its butt and design posters that read, 'This library has something offensive to everyone,' or 'If you aren't offended by something we own, please complain.'" Can we do the same for our sex education classes? We need to put a perspective in the 'Great Debate': values about sexuality differ and controversy is the 'American Way'. (pp. 106–107)

After studying sex education programs in 23 U.S. communities, 9 state departments of education, and 5 federal agencies and conducting a survey of 104 professional sex educators, Scales (1982) concluded that (1) controversy cannot be avoided, only managed; (2) support for sex education is high and widespread; (3) supporters can influence those who oppose sex education though effective community involvement; (4) supporters do not have the only valid opinions about sex education; and (5) sex education is not value-free; supporters should express clearly the moral values that underlie their programs.

Some communities have tried to resolve the controversy between parents and the school by seeking cooperation between the two groups. The Marin Country Day School in Corte Madera,

California, for example, offers a five-week sex education course for fifth graders. Concurrent with the course is a program for the parents, which informs them of the student program content, allows them to experience the exercises their children will be exposed to, and builds confidence and skills in discussing sex-related matters with their children at home (Evans, 1980). Other communities offer specific parent education programs in sexuality for the parents of school children (Dean & Hrnyak, 1982).

Future Directions

The trend toward using a situation ethics decision-making perspective in contrast to a rigid legalistic one will continue. Individuals will rely more on their own judgment than authorative dictums of official religious leaders and creeds.

Meanwhile, Protestant churches will increasingly view sex in positive terms as God's good gift, recognize that sexual pleasure is good, affirm that masturbation is an appropriate expression, and provide sex education through the church. These special programs will focus on the enhancement of both individual and couple sexuality.

Proponents of the Moral Majority will remain a minority (Falwell's television following peaked in 1982). While their influence will continue to be expressed through occasional conservative legislation and television (such as the Coalition for Better Television), the majority of Americans will continue to support a sexual choice position—that a wide range of sexual behavior and attitudes should be regarded as legal and appropriate (Reiss, 1982).

The debate on whether sex education should be taught in the public schools undoubtedly will continue. Those approving will contend that it exposes children to a significant aspect of their lives that cannot be ignored. Those disapproving will view it as an intrusion of the government through the school system into the private family domain.

Where sex education courses are offered, an increasing number of seminars for parents will be offered at the same time. Teachers will come to recognize parents as valuable allies in helping children learn about their sexuality rather than viewing them as roadblocks to sex education progress. A resource for those interested in setting up public school sex education courses for children and youth is *Winning: The Battle for Sex Education* (Dickman, 1982).

Chapter Five

Individual Sexuality

Masturbation—it's sex with someone I love.

WOODY ALLEN

Chapter Five

Although we are born and live in social groups, we are individuals first; and although some aspects of our sexuality are interpersonal, other aspects are individual. These include the feelings we have about our bodies and the feelings we have about masturbation. The bulk of this chapter focuses on masturbation, but we begin with a brief comment on how we view our bodies.

Body Image

The feelings we have about our sexuality are influenced by what we see in the mirror and the image other people reflect to us about ourselves. When we look closely at ourselves in the mirror, we form an impression (positive or negative) about how we look. Most of us are satisfied with what we see. In a survey of 2,000 *Psychology Today* readers, 90 percent of both women and men were satisfied with their face and three-fourths of the women and 85 percent of the men were satisfied with their overall body appearance (Berscheid et at., 1973).

Our society places great emphasis on physical appearance. We give prizes to the most beautiful people (Miss America, Mr. World) and have derogatory labels for those who are not beautiful. Most of us want to look young, trim, and physically attractive forever.

Capitalizing on our need to look more like the cultural ideal, the cosmetic industry sells us the perception of a more attractive self. Their basic product is a younger, sexier appearance, not makeup in a bottle. Some people turn from cosmetics to surgery like face lifts, breast enlargements, and hair transplants to improve their physical appearance.

Attitudes Toward Masturbation

Beyond the way we feel about ourselves is the degree to which we feel comfortable producing physical pleasure in ourselves by ourselves. **Masturba-**

Most people are concerned about their body image.

tion is defined as stimulating one's own body with the goal of experiencing pleasurable sexual sensations. Other terms for masturbation include autoeroticism, self-pleasuring, and sex without a partner. Three older, more pejorative terms for masturbation are self-pollution, self-abuse, and solitary vice. The negative connotations associated with these terms are a result of various myths about masturbation. Table 5.1 lists some of the myths and truths about masturbation.

As these myths suggest, masturbation traditionally has had a "bad press." It is almost as though religion, medicine, and psychotherapy have conspired to give masturbation a bad name.

Religion

While the Jewish and Catholic religions have been most severe in their stand against masturbation, Protestants have not been very positive. Ancient Jews considered masturbation a sin so grave that it deserved the death penalty. Catholics regarded masturbation as a mortal sin which, if not given up, would result in eternal damnation. Although Protestants felt that neither death nor eternal hellfire were appropriate consequences for masturbation, hell on earth was. The basis for these indictments was that masturbation is **nonprocreative sex**, and any sexual act that cannot produce offspring is wrong.

Table 5.1 **Myths and Truths About Masturbation**

Myths	Truths
1. Masturbation causes insanity, headaches, epilepsy, acne, blindness, nosebleeds, "masturbator's heart," tenderness of the breasts, warts, nymphomania, undesirable odor, uninhibited sexuality, and hair on the palms.	1. There is no evidence that masturbation impairs physical or mental health.
	2. Masturbation is a natural function. People in most cultures masturbate.
2. It is an abnormal, unnatural act.	3. Many people masturbate throughout their lives. Many sexually active people with available partners masturbate as an additional gratification.
3. It is immature.	
4. It is practiced mostly by simple-minded people.	4. Masturbation is a good way to create your own orgasm.
5. It is a substitute for intercourse.	5. Intercourse and masturbation can be viewed as complementary sexual experiences, not as mutually exclusive.
6. It is antisocial.	
	6. Masturbation is a good way to learn about your own sexual responses so you can communicate them to a partner.

From *SAR Guide For a Better Sex Life* by National Sex Forum Staff. Table on Masturbation. Reprinted by Permission, National Sex Forum, San Francisco.

Medicine

The medical community reinforced religion's prohibition of masturbation by bringing "scientific validity" to bear on their description of the hazards of masturbation. In 1758 Samuel Tissot, a French physician, published a book in which he implied that the loss of too much semen, whether by intercourse or masturbation, was injurious to the body and would cause pimples, tumors, insanity, and early death (Tissot, 1766).

Adding to the medical bias against masturbation was Sylvester Graham, an American. In 1834, he wrote that an ounce of semen was equal to the loss of several ounces of blood. Graham believed that every time a man ejaculated, he ran the risk of contracting a disease of the nervous system. His solution was Graham crackers, which would help the individual control the release of sexual energy (Graham, 1848).

By the mid-nineteenth century, Tissot's theories had made their way into medical textbooks and journals. With no data, physicians added to the list of disorders resulting from masturbation—pimples, falling hair, weak eyes, and suicidal tendencies.

Although it has been clearly demonstrated that there is no scientific basis for these ideas, some physicians still feel negatively about masturbation. A board-certified obstetrician-gynecologist was overheard telling an audience of several hundred, "If I ever came home and found my wife masturbating, I'd sure set her straight" (Myers, 1981, p. 85).

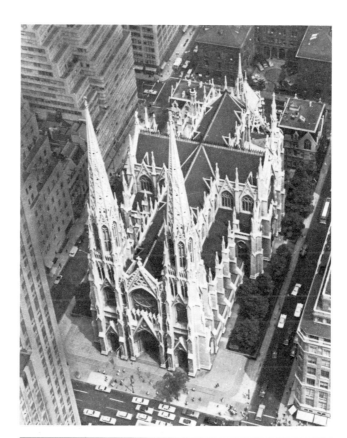

Religion has been influential in the development of a society wide negative view of masturbation.

Psychotherapy

In the early twentieth century, psychotherapy joined religion and medicine to convince people of the negative effects of masturbation. Psychotherapists, led by Freud, suggested that masturbation was an infantile form of sexual gratification. People who masturbated "to excess" could fixate on themselves as a sexual object and would not be able to relate to others in a sexually mature way. The message was clear: if you want to be a good sexual partner in marriage, don't masturbate; and if you do masturbate, don't do it too often.

The result of religion, medicine, and psychotherapy taking aim at masturbation was devastating. Those who masturbated felt the shame and guilt they were supposed to feel. The burden of these feelings was particularly heavy since there was no one with whom to share the guilt. In the case of a premarital pregnancy, responsibility could be shared. But with masturbation, the "crime" had been committed alone.

Benefits of Masturbation

Shame, guilt, and anxiety continue to be common feelings associated with masturbation in our society, but new attitudes are emerging. Although the attitudes of some religious leaders are still negative, most physicians and therapists are clearly positive about the experience. Masturbation is not only approved but recommended. Specific benefits of masturbation include the following:

1. *Self-knowledge.* Masturbation gives you immediate feedback for what you enjoy during sexual stimulation. You can tell another what turns you on sexually by exploring your own feelings, rhythms, and responses in private.

2. *More likely orgasm.* Ninety-two percent of a sample of more than 1,000 women said they achieved orgasm most of the time when they masturbated, but only 30 percent achieved orgasm regularly when they had intercourse (Hite, 1976). (Men almost always climax during both masturbation and intercourse.)

3. *Pressure off partner.* When one partner in a relationship does not want to have intercourse or other sexual involvement, masturbation is a way of experiencing sexual pleasure without obligating the partner.

4. *No partner necessary.* Masturbation provides a way to enjoy sexual feelings if no partner is available.

5. *Unique experience.* A person's own fantasies make masturbation a unique sexual experience, different from petting, intercourse, mutual stimulation of the genitals, and other sexual behaviors.

6. *Avoid extrapartner entanglements.* Sexual tensions can be released by one's self without risking sexual involvement with a partner external to the relationship.

Masturbation can also be valuable in helping a woman improve her **body image** and her perception of herself as a woman. One woman spoke of how this happened for her.

● I laid there for a few minutes and thought, okay, here goes. And then when I touched myself it was almost an earth-shaking feeling because I felt that this was down there and even though my husband has given me a lot of reinforcement and I enjoy oral sex I still couldn't believe men really enjoy that [a woman's genitals] because I thought it was an ugly thing. And even though I have tried to tell myself that it's not, I still thought what a strange fascination you have in that, and he would always describe me as being soft and warm and I thought, ah, that's really dumb, soft and warm.

The moment I touched myself I almost laughed. I almost started laughing out loud because I am soft and warm, I really am. I'm a very interesting thing to touch and I thought I am an erotic, feeling thing and before this I had thought it was just a mess of anything. It wasn't very attractive; it wasn't very interesting. And now I was proud of myself. *It was the first time I can ever remember being proud of my* *genitals* and being proud of myself as a woman and enjoying it and thinking that it is fantastic being a woman. Never before have I felt this way.* ●

Betty Dodson in her book *Liberating Masturbation* (1974) writes, "Masturbation is a meditation on self-love. Since so many of us are afflicted with self-loathing, bad body images, shame about body functions, and confusion about sex and pleasure, I recommend an intense love affair with yourself" (p. 43). In her workshops on masturbation, she notes that "our first sex is with ourselves. This is our base for learning to become erotic human beings . . ." (Riisna, 1983, p. 68). Both *Liberating Masturbation* and *I Am My Own Lover* (Blank & Cottrell, 1978) are explicit guides to female masturbation.

Correlates of Masturbation

Frequency of masturbation tends to be associated with several factors: gender, education, religion, locus of control, and marital status.

Gender

Men have higher masturbation rates than women. Not only do a higher percentage of males than females masturbate, they do so more often. The median number of times per year for the more than 65,000 males in the *Playboy* survey was 140; for the slightly less than 15,000 responding females, the number was 44 (Petersen et al., 1983b). Other, more sophisticated research studies with varying samples have also found fewer women masturbating less often. The explanations for higher masturbatory rates among men include greater genital availability (a male's penis is easy to touch or rub—a woman's genitals are more hidden), the greater need for release of periodic seminal buildup, and the greater socialization of males to view sexuality as release than relationship.

Education

The more education a person has, the more often that person is likely to masturbate. Kinsey (1948) noted that college males masturbated twice as often as those who did not go beyond grade school. A similar relationship between education and frequency of masturbation is true of females but it is less dramatic.

What might account for higher masturbation rates among the more educated? Intercourse begins earlier and is more frequent for those who have

*Reprinted with the permission of the publisher from "Masturbation and Body Integration in the Post-orgasmic Female" by Richard H. Waltner, *Journal of Sex Education and Therapy*, 1981, 7, 2, p. 42. American Association of Sex Educators, Counselors and Therapists.

less education. Masturbation may become viewed as unnecessary if intercourse is available. Also, less education may mean less talk about masturbation. If masturbation is not discussed or read about, then there may be less inclination to practice it.

Religion

Masturbation rates are also lower among those who attend church or synagogue and who regard themselves as devout. This is not surprising in view of the traditional negative attitude of religion toward masturbation.

Locus of Control

Psychologists define **locus of control** as the degree to which an individual views outcomes (events and rewards) as depending upon his or her own abilities (internal control), or, alternatively, as determined by chance, fate, or other people (external control). For example, if your locus of control were internal and you were at the county fair, you might feel that winning a prize would be due to your skill and not to luck. But if your locus of control were external, you might feel that no matter how skilled you were, you would not win because forces beyond you would dictate the outcome. In one study (Catania & White, 1982) 30 elderly persons (average age 68.5) completed a scale that revealed the degree to which they tended to be internally or externally controlled. They also indicated how frequently they masturbated. Results showed that those who felt in control of their lives (internally controlled) had higher masturbatory frequencies than those who felt out of control (externally controlled). The researchers concluded that "internal control in a sexual context may reflect a person's perceptions of self-regulation with regard to his/her body and sexuality. For persons with a chronic illness, masturbation may then represent a means of acquiring psychological control over a body 'out of control'" (p. 243).

Marital Status

Unmarried, separated, divorced, and widowed individuals are more likely to masturbate than those who are married or who are living with someone. While those who are married or have a regular sexual partner also have a private masturbatory life, their frequency of masturbation is lower.

Masturbation in Marriage

It is assumed that single people masturbate because, among other reasons, no regular sexual partner is available to them. It is also sometimes assumed

that married people do not masturbate because they sleep next to a sex partner every night. The question "Why would a married person masturbate?"
implies "They don't *need* to." But, as we shall see, people with partners often
have two sexual lives—one with their partners and one without them.

Wives Who Masturbate

In the *Redbook* study of 100,000 married women, two-thirds said they had
masturbated since marriage (Tavris & Sadd, 1977). Two in 10 wives in another study did so more than once a week (Petersen et al., 1983b). Many
women masturbate in bed after their husbands have fallen asleep (Hessellund, 1976). Others masturbate in the bathroom. But regardless of where, 70
percent of the husbands are unaware that their wives masturbate (Gross-
Kopf, 1983).

Most wives say they masturbate because their husbands are away and not
available for intercourse. "My husband is in the Navy," said one wife. "And
they keep him away six months at a time. I don't believe in fooling around so
I masturbate."

Other wives report masturbating for the unique experience it provides
even though they have intercourse at other times. "Intercourse is great but
so is masturbation."

Still others masturbate to relieve tension and relax. One woman said she
felt "uptight" at certain times and masturbation was a way of relaxing. "I
would rather masturbate than take a tranquilizer," she said.

For a smaller percentage of wives, masturbation is used as a substitute for
unsatisfactory intercourse with their husbands. These wives say they do not
like their husbands, intercourse is aversive, or "my husband rejects me." Regarding the latter, one woman said she "needed sex" more than her husband
and masturbation was a way of taking care of herself "between the times we
have intercourse."

In the *Redbook* study (Tavris & Sadd, 1977), the more often a wife masturbated, the less likely she regarded sex with her husband as good.

> For example, of the women who rate their sex lives as very good, only 10 percent
> masturbate often, compared to 36 percent of those whose sex lives are very poor.
> While many of these wives occasionally masturbate for the pleasure of that activity
> or as a way of sexual experiment, those who do so often are compensating for bad
> sex with their husbands, and they don't find masturbation especially gratifying. (p.
> 95)

Husbands Who Masturbate

Husbands also masturbate, and they do so more frequently than wives. In
the *Playboy* study (Petersen et al., 1983b), 43 percent of the husbands, in
contrast to 22 percent of the wives, reported masturbating more than once a
week. Secrecy is still the norm, since most wives are not aware that their husbands masturbate.

The motives of husbands who masturbate are somewhat different from the motives of wives. Husbands tend to masturbate as a supplement to intercourse rather than as a substitute for it. "I've been masturbating as long as I can remember," stated one husband, "and while intercourse with my wife is great, I also enjoy masturbating."

Other husbands masturbate because their wives are not sexually available to them. "My wife is asexual," expressed one husband. "She says she's just not interested in sex and doesn't want me to bother her. I'm not into having affairs or going to bars to pick up women so I masturbate."

Still other husbands say they masturbate to avoid having intercourse. "I'm impotent with my wife because she always belittles the size of my penis," one husband said. "So I masturbate and avoid the hassle. I wish things were different but I'd rather masturbate than go through the failure and humiliation."

Effects on Marriage

The effects of masturbation on the marriage relationship are speculative, as no study has focused on this aspect of masturbation. Masturbation may have positive effects on the marriage. For some couples, viewing each other masturbate is a "turn on" and adds another dimension to the couple's sex life. Also, differences in desire for intercourse can be reduced by one partner masturbating, as we have seen in the example of the wife who masturbated because she "needed more sex" than her husband.

Masturbation may also have negative consequences for the marriage. Some husbands or wives may regard their spouse's masturbation as rejection. One husband felt that his wife's masturbating meant he was not a good sexual partner and he could not satisfy her. Although his wife protested that she also enjoyed intercourse, the husband did not believe her and insisted that she "really" liked masturbation better than sex with him.

Another way masturbation may hurt a couple's marriage is by the guilt it produces. In general, most husbands have a positive attitude about masturbation and wives are more likely to view it as wrong, unnatural, or repelling (Hessellund, 1976). Those spouses who have negative feelings about masturbation may unconsciously displace these feelings onto their partners. One husband felt ashamed that he was compelled to masturbate because his spouse was not interested in having intercourse. His frustration, combined with his guilt and shame about masturbating, created very negative feelings toward his wife.

Female Masturbation

Having examined masturbation in marriage, let us look more closely at masturbation among women and men in general. We begin by viewing the rates, reasons, and techniques of female masturbation.

Incidence

Between 65 and 89 percent of women report masturbating sometime (Hite, 1977; Wolfe, 1982). As already noted, masturbation rates are higher among more educated and less religiously devout women. Relationship status also seems to correlate with female masturbation rates. Women who are single, married, divorced, and living with a partner masturbate an average of 10, 5, 7, and 7 times a month respectively (Petersen, 1983a). One woman said,

> I masturbate both when I have a steady boyfriend and when I don't. Masturbation gives me unlimited satisfaction and I see no reason to give it up. I have orgasms both with my partner and as a result of masturbation (Wolfe, 1982, p. 124).

Motivations

Pleasurable sensations and physical release are the most frequent reasons women masturbate. Exploring their own body, getting to sleep and relieving boredom and menstrual cramps are other motivations. It is not unusual for a number of motives to be involved when masturbating. One woman in her thirties said, "Masturbation is important to relieve tension, to indulge in fantasies, plus, I feel I owe it to myself, as a belated form of self-love" (Hite, 1977, pp. 76-77).

Techniques

While no two women masturbate in exactly the same way, masturbatory techniques of more than 4,000 women include the following (Hite, 1977; Kinsey, 1953; Masters & Johnson, 1979b).

Lying on Back

Most women masturbate most of the time by lying on their back and stimulating the clitoral-vulval area with their hand. They may stimulate the clitoris directly and may accompany this by vaginal insertion. In one study (Clifford, 1978b), women stated that their most effective masturbatory technique for achieving climax was to lay on their back, use several fingers, and stroke around and on the clitoris.

One woman recalled her experience:

● Usually I lie on my back, my legs apart. I almost always have my panties on, as rubbing the clitoris itself directly is just annoying. I use one hand, two fingers together, rubbing up and down in short, quick strokes right over my clitoris. As I get closer to climax, my legs tend to spread apart and my pelvis tilts up more. I don't move around too much, but sometimes during climax I roll from side to side. (Hite, 1977, p. 81) ●

Lying on Stomach

Some women prefer to lie on their stomach when masturbating. While they may use their hands to stimulate the clitoral vulval area, they also may press and thrust the vaginal area against some object—the bed, a pillow, or bedding. One woman said she would wad up the blanket on her bed into a ball and lie on her stomach on top of it so that it exerted pressure on her vulval area. She would then move her hips in a circular motion until she climaxed.

Thigh Pressure

A variation of the preceding masturbatory styles is for the woman to cross her legs and squeeze them together tightly, thereby exerting pressure on her vaginal area. Her clitoris and labia respond to the sensation of muscular tension and pleasurable sexual feelings. Some women stimulate their genitals with their hand at the same time they are exerting thigh pressure.

Water Massage

Rather than hand, object, or thigh pressure, some women use water. The woman turns the faucet of the tub or shower to a strong warm flow. She then lies on her back with her legs up on the wall and her clitoral-vulval area positioned under the rushing water, or she may stand and let the water from the shower stream over her clitoral area. Hose attachments enable a woman to lie in the tub, hold the massage attachment in her hand, and direct the flow of water onto the clitoral area.

Vibrator

Deceptive

Vibrators, known as *the* sex toy, are gaining increased visibility and acceptance. Half of the 15,000 plus women in the *Playboy* survey reported having used a vibrator (Lowe et al., 1983). Sex therapists also encourage women to use a vibrator to help achieve an orgasm. In their book *Becoming Orgasmic*, Heiman, LoPiccolo, and LoPiccolo (1976) state:

> Vibrators are wonderful for massaging your body in order to help you relax and to soothe sore muscles. And they can also provide very pleasurable sensations on your genitals. This isn't surprising when you think about it. When you stimulate your genitals with your finger(s), you rub, stroke, and massage. This is what vibrators do at a faster rate, more steadily, and more intensely than most people can achieve with hand stimulation. Some women need this quality of genital stimulation, especially when they are learning to have orgasms. (p. 107)

While most women do not use a vibrator, those who do seem to enjoy it. Only 3 percent of 100,000 women in *Redbook's* survey of married women reported that such sexual devices were not pleasurable (Tavris & Sadd, 1977). One woman said of her vibrator, "I'm responsible for packing our suitcases when we go on vacation. And I always pack the vibrator first. Like American Express traveler's checks, I wouldn't leave home without it."

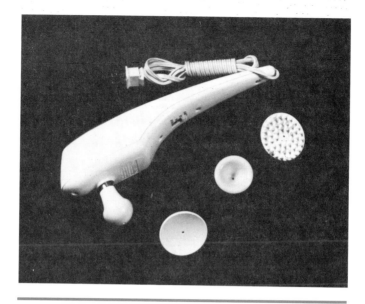

A number of vibrators are available, including penis-shaped, battery operated models. The vibrator shown here comes with several attachments.

Vaginal Insertion

Less than 2 percent of women masturbate exclusively by inserting an object into their vagina (Hite, 1977). Those who use this technique usually insert a finger or fingers just inside the vaginal opening to transfer vaginal lubrication to the clitoral area. Rarely do women make deep insertions into their vagina.

Breast Stimulation

Some women derive pleasure from stimulating their breasts. The woman might rub her breasts with her hands or press them against a pillow or some object. In most cases, she stimulates her breasts simultaneously with genital manipulation. Only rarely is breast stimulation sufficient to cause an orgasm.

Many women use combinations of these masturbatory techniques. They may begin on their back, then shift to other positions. Although they most often use their hand, they also may use a vibrator or other sexual devices (oils, feathers, objects to insert in vagina). Sexual fantasies frequently accompany masturbation. Sixty percent of the women in one study said they masturbated to a sexual fantasy (Wolfe, 1982). Sexual fantasies are discussed in more detail in Chapter 9.

Effects of Female Masturbation

Most women have an orgasm when they masturbate (92 percent in Hite's 1977 study), and most experience an orgasm within 5 minutes (Kinsey, 1953). Those who take longer may deliberately do so to prolong the pleasure they experience during masturbation.

Masturbating to orgasm before marriage seems to have a positive effect on having an orgasm during intercourse after marriage. Forty-four percent of the women in Kinsey's (1953) study who had not had an orgasm before marriage failed to have a climax during their first year of marriage. But of those who had experienced orgasm before marriage, only 13 percent had not had an orgasm during intercourse their first year of marriage.

These figures emphasize that sexuality is learned. Although everyone has the physiological capacity to respond orgasmically to stimulation, unless the person actively engages in the necessary sexual stimulation to produce the orgasmic response, no sexual learning will occur. Masturbation allows a person to discover and awaken his or her own sexual responsiveness. A person can learn such responsiveness at age 30, but the earlier a person begins, the more experience he or she has at having orgasm as desired.

Most women enjoy the physical effects of masturbation, but the psychological effects are often negative. Women may feel they are doing something they should not do or should not have to do. This suggests that if these women had a partner and the right kind of relationship, they would rather be having intercourse. But other women do not feel guilty or ashamed of their masturbation. Rather, they enjoy both the physical and psychological payoffs (one woman said, "My head feels clearer after I climax"). Some prefer masturbation as the way they most enjoy sex.

Male Masturbation

Masturbation is much more prevalent among males. More than 90 percent of all men have masturbated at some time (Hunt, 1974; Kinsey, 1948). Most males begin masturbating between the ages of 10 and 13 (Miller & Lief, 1976). Males learn how to masturbate through self-discovery (60 percent), from a friend (34 percent), a book (4 percent) or a film (2 percent) (Hite, 1981). Some men do not remember the source of their learning about masturbation. One man said, "I don't remember how I found out about masturbation—I just always have."

Frequency

More than 60 percent of the 65,000 men in the *Playboy* survey reported masturbating between one and "a few times a week" (Petersen et al., 1983b). But some men never masturbate. Kinsey (1948) suggested that a low sex drive, dependency on nocturnal emissions, and the regular availability of a sexual partner may account for this. Another explanation may be that these men have strong religious beliefs against masturbation.

Techniques

Observations, interviews, and completed questionnaires of nearly 17,000 men reveal how males masturbate (Hite, 1981; Kinsey, 1948; Masters & Johnson, 1979b; Shanor, 1978). Compared with women, men have a narrow range of masturbatory techniques. Most frequently, the man lies on his back and strokes, rubs, and caresses the shaft and glans of his penis until it becomes hard. Once erection occurs, he increases the pressure and speed of the stroking pattern. He places pressure on the shaft with occasional pressure on the head of the penis.

One man described his experience:

● I take my right hand and get a rhythm motion going up and down—moving the loose skin and touching the fringe area around the head. Sometimes I put lotion on my hand to lessen the friction. I start out slowly and go faster and faster. I can feel my penis swell in my hand—then the sperm comes exploding out. (Shanor, 1978, p. 36.) ●

Variations of this technique include putting the penis between the thighs and rubbing them together, using two hands (the other usually stimulates the scrotum), or using an electric vibrator.

Masters and Johnson (1979b) reported that 20 percent of men stand when they masturbate. They may stand in the shower or in front of the sink in the bathroom and ejaculate. A few men sit or lie face down. In the latter position, the penis is stimulated by the friction between the person's abdomen and the bed or whatever he is lying on.

The time from erection to ejaculation is usually between 1 and 2 minutes. While some men are capable of bringing themselves to a climax within 10 seconds, others intentionally delay ejaculation for an hour or more. Masturbation may occur with another person who also masturbates or who just observes. Some men masturbate while talking on the phone. One man said that he calls his lover when he is out of town and asks her to tell him "sexy stories" while he masturbates. For those who do not have personal phone lovers, an array of adult magazines provides pictures and phone numbers of individuals (called fantasy phone mates) who promise to "get you off over the phone" for a fee.

Most males masturbate when they are alone, and being discovered may be embarrassing. One man described his experience of masturbating in the bathroom when the woman he was living with "walked in on me unexpectedly and there I was with my hand on my erect penis. I turned twelve different shades of purple and hastily concocted the weirdest story about having a sore spot on my penis which I was trying to examine" (Zilbergeld, 1978).

Effects of Male Masturbation

How do men feel about masturbating? Of the responses of 7,000 men, Hite (1981) wrote:

Most men felt guilty and inadequate about masturbating, at the very same time that they enjoyed it tremendously (many had their strongest orgasms, physically, during masturbation), and seemed to have a great sense of freedom and fun while doing it. Most men seemed to feel freer to stimulate themselves in ways they liked, and to experiment . . . Almost no men told anyone else that they did this. (p. 487)

Mutual Masturbation

Although both women and men have their own private masturbatory lives, they may also enjoy masturbation as a couple activity. This involves each person masturbating her- or himself while the partner does the same to self or just watches. This scenario may serve a number of purposes. For some couples it is very arousing; it is a way to learn what kind of stimulation each partner likes; it may be enjoyable in its own right; and it is an alternative when there is a reason not to touch the other (for example, if a woman has a vaginal infection that would make intercourse painful for her). Since masturbation is a behavior people typically engage in when they are alone, it may take time before the partners feel comfortable about mutual masturbation.

Summary

Masturbation is self-stimulation that results in sexual sensation. Traditionally, religion, medicine, and psychotherapy have considered masturbation as bad and harmful. However, attitudes toward masturbation are changing. Although religious leaders may still express disapproval, most physicians and therapists are clearly positive. Masturbation is not only approved but recommended. Masturbation provides self-knowledge about what is sexually stimulating, is easier for the woman to orgasm than by intercourse, and does not require a partner.

In marriage about the same percentage (two-thirds) of husbands and wives masturbate, but husbands do so more frequently. Masturbation occurs in marriage for the same reason it occurs outside of marriage—it is an enjoyable experience and a part of each spouse's private life. The effects of masturbation on the marriage relationship are speculative as no study has focused on this aspect of masturbation. It can have positive or negative effects on the marriage depending on the attitudes and perceptions of the partners.

Between 65 and 89 percent of women report having masturbated. Masturbation rates are higher or lower depending on education, religion, locus of control, and marital status. Pleasurable sensations and physical release are the most frequent reasons women masturbate. Females typically manipulate the clitoral-vulval area while lying on their back. But there are numerous variations and combinations, using thigh pressure, water massage, vibrator, breast stimulation, and vaginal insertion. Most women have an orgasm when they masturbate.

Masturbation is much more prevalent among men, and most begin between the ages of 10 and 13. Compared with women, men have a narrow range of masturbatory techniques. Most frequently, the man lies on his back and strokes his penis until it becomes hard. He increases the pressure and speed of the stroking until he ejaculates. The time from erection to ejaculation is usually between 1 and 2 minutes. This technique is used by most men most of the time, but some men report variations.

Masturbation may also be mutual, with the partners masturbating in front of each other. Some partners report that they are sexually aroused by watching their partner masturbate.

Key Terms

masturbation
nonprocreative sex
body image

vibrator
mutual masturbation
locus of control

Issues in Debate and Future Directions

Whether masturbation should be encouraged by therapists and the advisability of using the vibrator to obtain an orgasm are issues over which there is disagreement. After reviewing these issues, we look at trends in masturbation.

Is Masturbation Always Therapeutic?

In this chapter we have stated that masturbation has a number of benefits. It is a means of gaining knowledge about one's own sexuality, of increasing the chance for orgasm, and of avoiding extrapartner entanglements. Many sex therapists routinely encourage masturbation in those clients who report little interest in sex and who reach orgasm infrequently or not at all.

But not all therapists agree with this viewpoint. Dr. Thomas Szasz (1980), a psychiatrist, notes that some clients who feel very uncomfortable about masturbating are, nevertheless, browbeaten into masturbating. In the hope of therapeutic success, therapists induce them into something they do not want to do. Dr. Szasz feels that therapists should recognize that opting not to masturbate is an acceptable alternative.

> Masturbation—like any sexual activity uninjurious to others—is a matter of private, personal conduct. It expresses and reflects, as does all behavior, the individual's medical and moral convictions about the nature of human sexuality and its proper role in her or his own life. The fact that a particular act is unpleasant or bad does not make it a disease; nor does the fact that it is pleasant or good make it a treatment. (p. 69)

Are Vibrators Always Beneficial?

Sex therapists are also likely to recommend the vibrator to a woman who has difficulty achieving an orgasm. But even without such direction, many women (and men) use vibrators when they masturbate. One-half of the women and one-third of the men in the *Playboy* survey reported having used a vibrator (Petersen et al; 1983a). Some women even have names for their vibrator.

● My husband travels. He is gone all week, and comes home just on weekends. I don't mind. My life is great. I work in the daytime, take college classes in the evening, and go to bed at night with Victor—my vibrator. (Wolfe, 1982, p. 121) ●

But a person should observe both physical and psychological caution in using a vibrator. A vibrator should never be used near water since it may produce a deadly shock. Also, some people report a feeling of pain or a sensation that is too intense when the vibrator is placed directly on the clitoris or head of the penis. To avoid this, the vibrator should not be in direct contact with these areas. A piece of material such as a thin towel placed between the clitoris or penis and the vibrator will eliminate these unpleasant sensations.

Virginia Johnson also recommends caution in using the vibrator (Masters & Johnson, 1976).

She suggests that if a woman uses intense mechanical stimulation over a long period of time, she may lose her appreciation of the various stages of buildup and may diminish her ultimate joy. In other words, since the vibrator will usually produce an orgasm quickly, it may short circuit erotic fantasies, slow buildup, and eventual release so that some of the emotional and cognitive aspects of orgasm are lost. Of course, these admonitions are also appropriate to men.

A final caveat is for a person who uses the vibrator to be sensitive to a partner's feelings about such use. Some partners encourage the use of a vibrator, but others may be threatened by them. One man said that his fiancée had gotten "hooked" on her vibrator and "I think she prefers it to me." The vibrator should be integrated with caution into an existing sexual relationship.

Future Directions

Masturbation among women will increase; there is likely to be somewhat more open discussion of masturbation and some lessening of negative attitudes and feelings associated with masturbation. A classic joke about masturbation is that "most research shows that over 90 percent of men masturbate and this means that the other 10 percent are liars." That most men masturbate has been a known fact (at least by other men), but the incidence of female masturbation has been more hidden. Adolescent males joke about masturbation and have their own vocabulary to describe the act. But, in the past, females rarely talked about masturbation with each other. This pattern is slowly changing. While it is rare for a woman to talk with her mother about masturbation, it does occur.

● I didn't masturbate until I was a grown woman and then, strangely enough, it was my mother who first put the idea in my mind. I was complaining about my husband, and she said that her answer to an impatient husband was her finger. So we discussed masturbation. She said she'd been reading that women need sex biologically, just like men do, and that if you couldn't get it in a love relationship, at least you could—and should—satisfy yourself. I tried it. I liked it. You're never too old to change. Who said life begins at 40? (Wolfe, 1982, p. 111) ●

One effect of the increased willingness of women to talk about masturbation is the closing of the frequency gap between women and men. Eighty-nine percent of the 106,000 respondents to the *Cosmopolitan* survey (Wolfe, 1982) reported having masturbated. While the *Cosmo* reader does not represent all women, a high frequency among this group is not without significance.

As masturbation is increasingly enjoyed by both women and men, it is likely to be a more frequent topic of discussion in the media, particularly television. For example, on a segment of "The Tonight Show" Johnny Carson discussed masturbation with a sex therapist.

But because negative feelings about masturbation like embarrassment and shame have become entrenched through years of socialization, discussion of masturbation will not come easily. Nevertheless, feelings are learned; and just as most of us have learned a negative set of feelings about masturbation, with more open discussion, we might also learn to regard masturbation as a positive, healthy, and fulfilling expression of our sexuality.

Chapter Six

Interpersonal Sexuality

The best way to hold a man is in
your arms.

MAE WEST

Chapter Six

Most human sexual expression occurs in the context of an interpersonal relationship. **Petting** is the term that traditionally has been used to describe interpersonal physical stimulation that does not include intercourse. (While the term may seem out of date, no new one has replaced it.) One psychiatrist observed, and most professionals agree, that couples who equate sexual satisfaction solely with intercourse and orgasm deprive themselves of the erotic pleasures of touching and caressing (Procci, 1981). The noncoital behaviors discussed in this chapter are viewed as pleasurable and desirable in themselves.

Petting is a common interpersonal sexual behavior. Ninety-eight percent of the women in one survey reported that they had experienced petting (Huk, 1979). Although few had petted before age 13, most had done so by age 18. In another study (Rubinson et al., 1981), men reported participating more frequently in a variety of petting behaviors than women.

Contents of Petting

Like all sexual behaviors, petting occurs in an environmental context. It is affected by the life style and interpersonal relationship of the partners, the place where it occurs, and the drugs, sights, sounds, and scents that may stimulate it.

Life Style

We can identify several life styles in which interpersonal sexual experiences occur; singlehood, including the never married, separated, divorced, and widowed; marriage; and communal living.

Singlehood

At any one time, about 38 percent of men and 44 percent of women in the United States 15 years old and over are living a single life style.* Most (29 percent men, 22 percent women) of these singles have never married; and although most will eventually marry, about 10 percent will remain single by choice or lack of opportunity. Those choosing to remain single point to the freedom to have a variety of sexual experiences as an advantage of singlehood (Stein, 1981). Increasing numbers are choosing the single life style.

In addition to the never married are the separated (2 percent men, 3 percent women) and divorced (5 percent men, 7 percent women). They, too, are only in the single life style temporarily since 80 percent of the divorced remarry. People who get divorced are not necessarily disenchanted with marriage. They are disenchanted with their mate, separate, and find another. The availability of a sexual companion with whom one shares a stable emotional relationship is one of the major attractions of marriage. "I can find someone to screw," said one man, "but I want to do it with someone I love and am committed in marriage to."

Widows (12 percent) and widowers (3 percent) also live the single life style, but they are single by fate, not by choice. Widowhood, for some, is the most devastating of all life crises. The loss may be both emotional and sexual. "Sometimes I lie awake at night," said one widow, "and look at where he used to sleep. While I miss him as someone to talk to, I also miss him as someone I enjoyed having sex with."

In 1980 about 1.5 million of the never married, separated, divorced, and widowed were living together with someone of the opposite gender to whom they were not married, an increase of 247 percent from 1970. Many of these cohabiting couples are college students. One researcher estimated that one-fourth of all college students in the United States will live in a cohabitation arrangement at least once by the time they graduate (Macklin, 1978). The sexual problems they experience (differing degrees or periods of sexual interest, lack of orgasm, impotence) are similar to the problems experienced by married couples. Some cohabitants also mention jealousy and mistrust. "Since we're not married, I have a greater fear that my partner will sleep with someone else," said one live-in companion.

Marriage

Marriage is the life style sought by most Americans. Although more than 90 percent of Americans eventually marry, about 63 percent of men and 60 percent of women are married at any one time. Marital sex is the only completely socially and legally approved sex in our society. "There is something 'right' about having sex with someone you are married to," said one spouse, reflecting the way most of us have been socialized to feel about marital sexuality.

But the marital relationships in which the sexual interaction occurs are not all alike. They differ by degree of intimacy, some spouses sharing their lives

*The source of the statistics in the discussion of singlehood and marriage is as follows: U. S. Bureau of the Census, Marital Status and Living Arrangements (March 1980); Current Population Reports, Series P-20, No. 365 (Washington, D.C.: U.S. Government Printing Office, 1981).

completely and others never talking to each other. One wife said, "I've been sitting at the dinner table with him for 20 years and all he ever says is 'pass the butter.'"

Communal Living

In 1977, about 250,000 individuals lived in communes (Zablocki). Twin Oaks in Louisa, Virginia, and The Farm in Summertown, Tennessee, are among the older successful communes. Types of communes include rural, urban, spiritual, drug, and ideological communes. An example of the latter is Twin Oaks, which was founded on the principles of behavioral psychology as expounded by B. F. Skinner. Sharing life with an array of others and cutting expenses by group living are two of the major motivations for living in a commune.

Whereas some communes encourage their members regularly to change sexual partners with other commune members, other communes require their members to have sex only with those who are not members of the commune to reduce sexual jealousy in the group. Still other communes encourage monogamy or celibacy or sex only for procreation.

Life styles and living arrangements are not restricted to any sexual orientation. Singles, marrieds, and communards may be heterosexual, homosexual, or bisexual. Homosexuality and bisexuality are discussed in detail in Chapter 14.

Interpersonal Relationship

Regardless of life style, the emotional relationship with a person influences the degree to which sexual behavior is viewed as appropriate. This is true of more women than men. When 334 undergraduates were asked after how many dates it was appropriate for kissing, petting, and intercourse to take place, women were much more likely to say a greater number of dates than men (Table 6.1). The most frequent problem these women said they had on dates was the man making unwanted sexual advances (Knox & Wilson, 1983).

While more than three-fourths of the women felt that petting should be delayed until after the fourth date, only one-third of the men felt that way. Rather, almost one-third of the men felt that petting should occur on or before the *first* date. Sometimes these men force their preferences. One-third of a random sample of men at the same university said they had made a "forceful or offensive attempt for petting" (Wilson, Faison, & Britton, 1983).

Since how much sex occurs how soon ultimately depends on the nature of the relationship and not on the number of dates, these students were asked to specify the relationship conditions under which kissing, petting, and intercourse would be appropriate. The conditions included "feeling no particular affection," "feeling affection but not love," "being in love," "en-

Sample

Table 6.1 Percentage of 227 Women and 107 Men University Students Indicating Appropriateness of Various Sexual Behaviors by Number of Dates

Sexual Behaviors	Number of Dates						
	0	1	2	3	4	5	6 or more
Kissing	W = 14%	W = 55%	W = 73%	W = 6%			
	M = 14	M = 69	M = 14	M = 1			
Petting	W = 3	W = 4	W = 5	W = 9	W = 3%	W = 15%	W = 58%
	M = 12	M = 19	M = 13	M = 7	M = 11	M = 15	M = 22
Intercourse	W = 8	W = 4	W = 1	W = 1	W = 1	W = 8	W = 69
	M = 8	M = 11	M = 9	M = 8	M = 2	M = 10	M = 52

D. Knox, and K. Wilson, Dating behaviors of university students, *Family Relations*, 1981, *30* (2), p. 256. Copyright © 1981 by the National Council on Family Relations. Reprinted by permission.

gaged," or "married." The results indicated that the more emotionally involved a person was in a relationship, the more likely increasing levels of intimacy were regarded as appropriate. Again, this was significantly more true for women than men. For example, intercourse with no particular affection was approved of by about 1 percent of the women but 10 percent of the men. Other research also has indicated that women are more concerned about the emotional context of a sexual relationship (DeLamater & MacCorquodale, 1979; Ratcliff & Knox, 1982).

Why? Why are men more willing than women for increasing levels of sexual intimacy to occur within a shorter number of dates and with less concern for a deep emotional relationship?

The answer does not appear to be hormonal. High testosterone levels in males do not correlate predictably with frequency of sexual activity (Bancroft, 1983). Rather, a social learning explanation seems more plausible. Men have been socialized to be sexually aggressive. "Get all you can, as soon as you can, from whomever you can, as often as you can" is the theme the adolescent male absorbs from his male peers. The message is clear—don't wait for sex to happen, go after it. And men do. They have significantly higher rates of sexual activity than women in terms of masturbation and intercourse (premarital and extramarital). They also report more sexual partners and are more likely to go out of their way for sex—buying pornography or hiring a prostitute.

In contrast, women masturbate less and report fewer intercourse partners before marriage and extramaritally. Buying pornography and hiring a male prostitute are very rare among women. Their socialization has been primarily in terms of sex in the context of a relationship. They have been socialized to be the gate keeper of sex—to slow the man down, to pace his access to her sexually in exchange for increasing his commitment to their relationship. Women have been taught to act like they like sex in order to get love (in contrast, men have been taught to act like they like love in order to get sex).

Interpersonal relationships are the context for much human sexuality.

Place

Most people pet in private, but some pet in public. Lovers kissing and pressing their bodies together can be observed at the beach, in movie lines, or on street corners. More than 30 percent of 80,000 respondents in one study reported that they had had sex in public (Petersen et al., 1983a).

On the bed in a partner's apartment or house is the most frequent place for petting. The floor is an enjoyable place reported by respondents of the *Cosmopolitan* sex survey (Wolfe, 1982). "My lover and I often start caressing each other while we're watching television on his couch," said one woman. "After that, there's something incredible about just sinking down onto the floor and going on with the fun, right there, instead of spoiling the spontaneity by having to trek to the bedroom (p. 46).

The couch, shower, and outdoors are other favored places for petting as well as intercourse. The beach and woods are typical of the latter. "We camp a lot," said one traveler, "and sex on an air mattress isn't bad." Married couples may find sex away from home more enjoyable; a new place away from the demands of children and the telephone often helps to enhance sexual involvement.

Duration

The amount of time couples spend in petting depends on whether it is viewed as a prelude to intercourse or as an end in itself. Men are usually more goal directed in sex (desiring climax soon), while women are more process oriented (enjoying the activities that lead to orgasm). The orgasm orientation of men is related to early masturbatory patterns that emphasize orgasm attainment, as there is no partner whose needs must be considered.

It is generally assumed that the male does not need as much petting to become aroused as the female. But more than 90 percent of 100,000 women said that 15 minutes or less was long enough for them to become sexually aroused (Tavris & Sadd, 1977). More than 70 percent were aroused within 10 minutes.

For couples who do not plan intercourse, petting may continue for hours. Orgasm may or may not occur depending on the various petting behaviors the couple engage in. In general, the longer a couple pets, the greater the chance they will reach orgasm.

Recreational Drugs

Drugs that are not used for medical purposes under the supervision of a physician have been referred to as recreational drugs. Although, in most cases, their harmful effects outweigh their benefits, some couples use recreational drugs. Fifty percent of more than 65,000 men and 60 percent of almost 15,000 women reported that they had used drugs during sex (Petersen et al., 1983a).

Although not commonly thought of as a drug, alcohol is the most frequent drug taken by Americans. Half of 334 respondents in one survey (Knox & Wilson, 1981) reported that they drank alcohol on their last date. Some people mix alcohol and sex to reduce anxiety, guilt, inhibitions, and fears about performance. Alcohol is a depressant that sedates the brain and slows reflexes. Under the influence of alcohol a person may feel more relaxed and less anxious about a sexual encounter. One woman said:

● In my experiences with alcohol, I have concluded that it definitely causes me to become sexually aroused. If I have a few beers or mixed drinks at a party, I loosen up and find it easy to approach people I otherwise would hesitate to talk to, and for some reason I desire physical closeness. Obviously, other people who have been drinking feel the same way and this often results in two relatively unfamiliar people going home together. ●

Alcohol may help a person become aroused through a lowering of inhibitions, but too much can slow the physiological processes and deaden the

Alcohol is the drug that is used most frequently in reference to sexual behavior.

senses. In Shakespeare's phrase, "alcohol provokes the desire but not the performance." This results in a reduced chance that the woman will climax and greatly increases the probability of impotence in men (Malatesta et al., 1982).

Marijuana is also used during sexual arousal, but the reactions to marijuana are less predictable than to alcohol. While some report a short-term enhancing effect, others report that it makes them sleepy. In men, chronic use may decrease the sex drive since marijuana may lower testosterone levels.

Other drugs used during sexual arousal include barbiturates, amphetamines, cocaine, and amyl nitrate. Barbiturates have an effect similar to alcohol as they blunt anxiety and reduce inhibitions. But because barbiturates are primarily sedatives that depress the central nervous system, at higher doses the effect is loss of sexual ability. As with most sleeping pills, which contain barbiturates, the desire for sleep replaces the desire for sex.

Amphetamines, such as pep pills and diet pills, are "uppers" that stimulate the central nervous system. The effect of such drugs is to overcome fatigue and to give a feeling of alertness and energy. Prolonged use of amphetamines may make orgasm difficult for the male although he can still have an erection. For females, menstrual difficulties have been associated with the use of amphetamines.

One percent of 25,000 respondents said they had used cocaine in the last 24 hours (Rubenstein, 1982). Cocaine is sniffed into the nostrils or injected into the vein. The latter results in an erection that may last for 24 hours or longer. Even when this does not occur users report that cocaine increases their sensory awareness and enhances their enjoyment of the sexual experience. However, high doses may result in impotence.

Amyl nitrate is used most frequently by young men, who inhale it at the ap proach of orgasm with the goal of enhancing orgasm. The person feels a "rush" along with an altered state of consciousness, a loss of inhibition, a tingling sensation in the head and body, and a sensation of faintness. But there are negative side effects. Six in 10 amyl nitrate users said they had experienced negative effects, including nasal irritation, nausea, loss of erection, coughing, and dizziness (Lowry, 1979). Table 6.2 lists the effects of some drugs on sexual functioning.

Table 6.2 How Some Drugs Affect Sexual Functioning

| | Phase of Sexual Response Affected | | |
Drug	Desire	Excitement	Orgasm
Alcohol	Increased in low doses; decreased in high doses	With low doses excitement may be prolonged due to decreased sensitivity; impotence with high chronic intake	Delayed in high doses
Marijuana	Some report increased desire; others report no effect; still others report decreased desire depending on partner and situation	Mixed reactions	Enhanced orgasm is reported by some; may be due to perception of prolonged orgasm
Amphetamines	Increased at low doses; decreased at high doses	Decreased in chronic doses	May be enhanced; but high doses may interfere with orgasm, more so in females
Cocaine	Reported to be enhanced	Reported to be enhanced; high doses may cause impotence	May be enhanced; high doses may interfere with orgasm, more so in females
LSD	Mixed effects reported; depends on partner and situation	None	No physiological effect, but perception of the experience is altered

From Helen S. Kaplan, *Disorders of Sexual Desire* New York: Brunner/Mazel, 1979, pp. 203–211. Reprinted with permission.

Prescription Drugs

Various prescription drugs, like those taken to lower blood pressure, reduce anxiety, and improve psychological functioning, may have a negative effect on sexual functioning. Psychiatric drugs reported to cause erectile dysfunction (impotence) include Tofranil, Vivactil, Pertofran, Anafranil, Elavil, Parnate, Actomol, Nardil, Eskalith, Prolixin, and Mellaril. Those reported to impair or delay ejaculation include Librium, Haldol, Stelazine, Mellaril, Elavil and Tofranil. Those reported to delay female orgasm include Nardil and impipramine (Segraves, 1981).

Aphrodisiacs

"Power is the ultimate aphrodisiac."
HENRY KISSINGER

The term aphrodisiac refers to any substance that increases sexual desire. One of the more prevalent myths of human sexuality is that there are specific drugs or foods that have this effect. In reality, there is no drug or food that reliably increases a person's sexual desire. Where such sexual interest does increase, it is often the result of a self-fulfilling prophecy. If the person thinks a substance will have a desire-inducing effect, it will.

Nevertheless, the trade in aphrodisiacs has a long history, from the Chinese belief in the sex-enhancing power of a ground-up rhinoceros horn (the origin of the word "horny") to beliefs in the efficacy of other foods and spices like the following:

Oysters	Turtle Soup
Crabs	Pepper
Tomatoes	Paprika
Eggs	Nutmeg
Carrots	Ginger
Celery	Saffron

In contrast to aphrodisiacs, anaphrodisiacs are those substances thought to decrease sexual desire. Potassium nitrate (saltpeter) is sometimes regarded as an anaphrodisiac, yet it contains nothing to diminish sexual desire. Depo-Provera (medroxyprogesterone acetate or MPA) is a synthetic progestinic hormone and has been associated with decreased libido (sex drive). This hormone, as well as tranquilizers like Mellaril, have been used in the treatment of sex offenders (Chapter 13).

Sights, Sounds, and Scents

The sights, sounds, and scents sexual partners immerse themselves in are also part of the context of petting. Sights like pictures, plants, mirrors, and the colors of fabrics and painted surfaces; the sounds of music; the scents of flowers or burning incense all help to create a pleasant environment for lovemaking. "I fixed up my room with flowers, a stained glass window, and our favorite music because I wanted the first time that we made love to be a memorable one," said one lover.

Who Initiates Sexual Involvement?

Since men traditionally have been socialized to be sexually aggressive and women to be passive, it is not surprising that most sexual experiences are initiated by men (Hite, 1981). There are at least four negative consequences of this expectation: (1) men are under pressure always to want sex; (2) women are under pressure always to be receptive; (3) women who initiate sex are regarded as morally loose, castrating, or suffering from "penis envy"; and (4) men who do not initiate sex very often are viewed as unmanly (James, 1980).

But gender roles are changing and women are initiating lovemaking more often. More than 95 percent of the 83,000 respondents to the *Ladies' Home Journal* sex survey reported that they sometimes initiate sex with their partners (Frank & Enos, 1983).

How do women and men encourage their partners to become sexually intimate? In a study of approximately 300 undergraduates, both genders said they are open about their sexual desires and expectations (Knox & Wilson, 1981). "I get the sex issue up front," expressed one respondent. "I simply say that I want to make love." A quarter of the men and a third of the women encouraged sexual intimacy in this way. Other ways included "creating an atmosphere (music, candles, incense)," "expressing love," "moving closer," and "hinting." Women were more likely to use the latter two methods than men.

Table 6.3 defines 10 strategies used to influence the partner toward a sexual encounter. Males are more likely to use these strategies than females (LaPlante et al., 1980).

Touching

Regardless of who approaches whom, lovemaking begins with **touching**. Our skin contains about 900,000 sensory receptors and represents our external nervous system (Montagu & Matson, 1979). It is a primary organ of sexual pleasure. Many regard touching as the most significant aspect of sex. The 3,000 women in Hite's (1977) study stated repeatedly that touching, holding, caressing, being close to, lying next to, and pressing bodies together was more important to them than intercourse or orgasm. Such physical closeness gives a feeling of emotional closeness that is satisfying whether or not intercourse or orgasm follow. "Long, gentle passionate encounters, with much touching and enthusiasm, give me a feeling of being loved all over and are all

Table 6.3 Ten Strategies for Influencing Sexual Encounters

Strategy	Definition
Reward	Giving gifts, providing services, and flattering the date in exchange for compliance.
Coercion	Punishing or threatening to punish noncompliance by withdrawing resources or services or by sharing negative feelings.
Logic	Using rational, but not moral, arguments to convince the date to have or avoid sexual intercourse.
Information	Telling the date whether or not sex was desired in a straightforward or direct manner.
Manipulation	Hinting at sexual intentions by subtly altering one's appearance, the setting, or the topic of conversation.
Body Language	Using facial expression, posture, physical distance, and relatively subtle gestures to communicate one's sexual intentions.
Deception	A strategy for having or avoiding sex which relies on giving the date false information.
Moralizing	Telling the date that it is the influencing agent's legitimate or socially sanctioned right to have or avoid sexual intercourse.
Relationship conceptualizing	Influencing a date by talking about the relationship and indicating concern for the date's feelings.
Seduction	A definite, step-by-step plan for getting a date to have sexual intercourse, especially a plan which focused on sexually stimulating the date.

*Reprinted with permission of the publisher from N. B. McCormick's "Come ons and Put offs: Unmarried Students' Strategies for Having and Avoiding Sexual Intercourse. *Psychology of Women Quarterly,* 1979, 4, 194–211. Copyright © Human Sciences Press, New York.

I need most of the time," expressed one woman (p. 556). Masters and Johnson (1976) echo the feeling of most women: "It is important to avoid the fundamental error of believing that touch is a means to an end. It is not. *Touch is an end in itself.* It is a primary form of communication, a silent voice that avoids the pitfall of words while expressing the feelings of the moment" (p. 253).

While women delight in the experience of touching (and, often get less touching than they want) they may feel that men do not share their enthusiasm. Most feel that men "provide" foreplay only as a means of priming them for intercourse and many resent it. Their suspicions are mostly accurate. The large majority of Hite's (1981) 7,000 men said that physical affection should always lead to intercourse and orgasm.

But other men do enjoy intimate embraces with their partners without intercourse following. "I like to snuggle and cuddle," said one man. "It feels very good to be physically close to the person I love. And I don't want to have intercourse all the time either. In fact, she wants it more than I do."

Kissing

There are different types of **kissing**. In one style of kissing, the partners gently touch their lips together for a short time with their mouths closed. In another, there is considerable pressure and movement for a prolonged time when the closed mouths meet. In still another, the partners kiss with their mouths open, using gentle or light pressure and variations in movement and time. Kinsey referred to the latter as deep kissing (also known as soul kissing, tongue kissing, or French kissing).

One woman described a good kiss:

● Variably soft and hard, but never rough. Tender touching of the lips, gentle parting—not too wide—playful archery and tactile explorations with the tongues. Letting emotions control the intensity of the contact—sucking, licking, and kissing. ●

Kissing may or may not have emotional or erotic connotations. A goodnight kiss may be perfunctory or may symbolize in the mind of each partner the ultimate sense of caring and belonging. It may also mean different things to each partner.

Kissing is a common experience. More than 98 percent of the respondents in one study (Diederen & Rorer, 1982), both male and female, reported having experienced kissing. Indeed, it is rare that individuals in their twenties have not kissed or been kissed. But, for both men and women, how often this behavior is engaged in varies by education level, with more education associated with more frequent kissing. For example, Kinsey (1948) observed that 88 percent of the males with little education (less than 8 years) reported lip kissing (as opposed to tongue kissing) on a frequent basis as compared with 98 percent of those with more education (13 years and over). The less-educated males viewed kissing as "dirty, filthy, and a source of disease," while the college-educated males regarded kissing as erotic play. A more recent study (Pietropinto & Simenauer, 1977) concluded that educational background still affects how males view kissing.

Breast Stimulation

In a random sample of college students, 92 percent of the males and 93 percent of the females reported experience in breast stimulation (DeLamater & MacCorquodale, 1979). "Touching and sucking" the female breasts was the most pleasurable petting activity reported by 22 percent of more than 4,000 males (Pietropinto & Simenauer, 1977).

"A kiss is not just a kiss." There are many varieties, motivations, and emotions associated with kissing.

In our society the female breasts are charged with erotic potential. A billion-dollar pornographic industry encourages the male to view the female's breast in erotic terms. *Playboy, Penthouse,* and an array of adult magazines feature women with unusually large breasts in seductive erotic poses.

Not all women share men's erotic feelings about breasts.

They rarely manually stimulate their own breasts and seem to neglect the breasts of their male partners. The latter may be unfortunate as male breasts have the same potential for erotic stimulation as female breasts. For some males breast stimulation by their partners is particularly important.

Penile Stimulation

Caressing the penis is another form of petting. This may be done by the woman caressing her partner's penis with her hand(s) or with her mouth or rubbing it inside her vaginal lips.

Manual Stimulation

Eighty-six percent of the female respondents in one study reported that they had manually caressed, manipulated, or stimulated the penis of a male (Diederen & Rorer, 1982). Being in love or feeling strong affection was the condition under which most of these women were most comfortable engaging in this behavior.

Usually, **manual stimulation** of the penis occurs at the request of the man who takes his partner's hand and moves it to his genitals. But some males use body language. "I usually have to move her hand to my penis," said one male. Once manual caressing begins it may result in ejaculation, or be a prelude to oral stimulation, intercourse, or both. Sometimes the woman becomes aroused by observing her partner's erection and ejaculation as a result of her manual stimulation.

Whether a woman manually caresses her partner's penis is related to whether she has had intercourse. Kinsey (1953) observed that those women who had had intercourse were three times as likely to report manual caressing of the penis. As with other petting behaviors, penile stimulation is influenced by age and, to some degree, education. Women in their twenties are much more likely to have stimulated their partner's penis than women in their forties, and the more educated a woman, the more likely she is to manually stimulate her partner.

Fellatio

One of the most intimate forms of petting is **fellatio**, or oral stimulation of the male's genitals by his partner. The term comes from the Latin word *fel-*

lare meaning to "suck." While fellatio most often refers to the woman's putting her partner's penis in her mouth and sucking it, fellatio may also include licking the shaft and glans, frenulum, and scrotum. Women vary the depth to which they take the penis in their mouth. Some direct the penis down their throat as if to swallow it. Others take only the head of the penis in their mouth while alternating sucking and blowing motions. The woman's hands also may caress the scrotum and perineum during fellatio. Feilatio may be enjoyed as foreplay, afterplay, or as an end in itself. If fellatio results in orgasm, the semen may be swallowed without harm if the partner desires to do so.

Between 60 and 95 percent of men and women report that their petting sometimes involves fellatio (Bell & Coughey, 1980; DeLamater & MacCorquodale, 1979; Petersen et al., 1983a). Some women regard fellatio as a more intimate form of sexual expression than intercourse, something they do with a person they are in love with (Diederen & Rorer, 1982; Young, 1980). "I'd have intercourse with a guy any day before I would go down on him," said one woman. "Fellatio means that you are involved with the guy. Otherwise I feel used." But fellatio does not always take place in a love context. It is the preferred sexual activity in early sexual encounters for women who want to avoid the possibility of pregnancy or who believe in saving intercourse for marriage. Prostitutes also may prefer fellatio as a means of reducing the risk of contracting a sexually transmitted disease.

In spite of the reported high incidence of fellatio, it remains a relatively taboo subject for open discussion. In many states legal statutes prohibit fellatio as a "crime against nature." "Nature" in this case refers to reproduction and the "crime" is sex that does not produce babies.

People engage in fellatio for a number of reasons. Pleasure is a central one. Next to kissing and hugging, oral sex was reported as the most pleasurable form of petting by more than 4,000 males (Pietropinto & Simenauer, 1977). Since the mouth is warm, moist, muscular, and capable of various motions, pressures, and rhythms, it is not surprising that men find the experience delightful. But it is the interpretation of the experience, as well as the physical sensations, that produce the pleasure. One man said that his partner fellating him meant that she really loved him and enjoyed his body. "It means total acceptance to me," he said.

Dominance may be another reason for the enjoyment of fellatio. A common theme in pornographic movies is forcing the woman to perform fellatio. In this context the act implies sexual submission, which may give the male an ego boost. Aware of this motive, some women refuse to fellate their partners. One woman said that her partner viewed her as a prostitute when she fellated him, that she did not like such a perception, and that she had stopped doing so.

Variety is another motive for fellatio. Some lovers complain that penis-in-vagina intercourse is sometimes boring. Fellatio adds another dimension to a couple's sexual relationship. The greater the range of sexual behaviors a couple has to share, the less likely they are to define their sexual relationship as routine and uninteresting.

Beyond these motives, fellatio may be used as a means of avoiding intercourse. Unmarried couples who feel that intercourse outside marriage is wrong may view oral sex, including fellatio, as an acceptable alternative. Although there may be clear social and religious prohibitions against premarital intercourse, little or nothing is said about oral sex. So any activity that is not intercourse may carry only limited guilt.

Fellatio is regarded as an enjoyable petting experience by most men and some women. In one study (Petersen et al., 1983b), 7 in 10 wives reported that they enjoyed giving oral sex.

Vaginal Lip Stimulation

Rubbing the penis inside the vaginal lips is another method of stimulating the penis. **Vaginal lip stimulation** usually occurs just before penetration, but it may also be done as a substitute for intercourse. "I love it when she grabs my penis and rubs it up and down her vaginal lips," said one male. While no percentages are available, some couples do this as a means of technically avoiding intercourse. "As long as there isn't actual penetration, we still haven't had intercourse," remarked one female.

Clitoral Stimulation

"Please take me clitorally" is the message most women would like their lovers to act on. Again and again, the women in Hite's (1977) study, when asked how men made love to them, said their partners spent too little time (sometimes none at all) stimulating their clitoris and that they had to have such stimulation to derive maximum pleasure from the sexual experience. The clitoris may be stimulated by hand, mouth, or the penis.

Manual Stimulation

About 85 percent of men and women report that the man stimulating the woman's clitoris and genital area with his hand is part of their petting repertoire (DeLamater & MacCorquodale, 1979). Such stimulation may be to ready the woman for intercourse or as an end in itself, and the style of stimulation may vary. Some partners rub the mons veneris area, putting indirect pressure on the clitoris. Others may apply direct clitoral pressure. Still others may insert one or several fingers into the vagina, with gentle or rapid thrusting, at the same time they stimulate the clitoris.

Not all women enjoy the insertion of the man's fingers in their vagina during petting. Some women permit it because their partners want to do it, and often the man wants to do it because he assumes that the woman wants something in her vagina. But the key to sexual pleasure for many women is pressure on and around their clitoris, not necessarily insertion.

Cunnilingus

Cunnilingus translated from the Latin means "he who licks the vulva." Specifically, cunnilingus is stimulating the clitoris, labia, and vaginal opening of the woman by her partner's tongue and lips. As noted earlier, the clitoris is an extremely sensitive organ. The technique many women enjoy is gentle teasing by the tongue, with stronger, more rhythmic sucking movements when orgasm approaches. While the partner's mouth is caressing and licking the clitoral shaft and glans, some women prefer additional stimulation by finger or vibrator in the vagina or anus.

Sixty percent of college women and men report participating in cunnilingus (DeLamater & MacCorquodale, 1979). Nonstudents of the same age (18–24) report a slightly higher rate of participation (about 70 percent). But married women have the highest rates of all. In the *Redbook* study of 100,000 married women (Tavris & Sadd, 1977), 93 percent reported that their husbands had performed cunnilingus and about 80 percent did so "often" or "occasionally."

To what degree do women enjoy cunnilingus? There is an old joke about two women discussing sex. One asks the other, "What do you call a guy who likes girls?" The answer "Heterosexual." A second question, "What do you call a guy who likes guys?" The answer "Homosexual." Final question, "What do you call a guy who kisses you here" (pointing to her vaginal area)? The reply, "If you can catch your breath, you call him precious." Most women enjoy cunnilingus. In a study of women aged 27 to 49 in established sexual relationships, heterosexual cunnilingus was their preferred sexual activity (Kahn, 1983).

The moist, warm, mobile tongue on their clitoris feels very good to most women. Those who find it unpleasant or repulsive view their vaginal area as dirty and oral sex as obscene and unnatural. One woman said that her partner's mouth was for eating, drinking, speaking and kissing those he loved—not for using on her genitals.

Contributing to the negative feelings that some women have about cunnilingus is the belief that their partners could not possibly enjoy it. "When he's doing that to me," said one woman, "I just know it doesn't taste good and probably smells awful. While I thoroughly enjoy the physical experience of cunnilingus, I'm distracted by the thought of how unpleasant it must be for him to do it."

How do men feel about cunnilingus? Nine in 10 husbands in one study (Petersen et al., 1983b) said they enjoy giving oral sex to their wives. In another study of 4,000 men (Pietropinto & Simenauer, 1977), less than 3 percent said cunnilingus was boring or unpleasant. Indeed, some men perform cunnilingus because they want to rather than because their partners ask them to. Their enjoyment in cunnilingus may spring from doing something forbidden or from their enhanced self-image as a good lover. "I feel better about myself when my partner enjoys me sexually and my going down on her is something that she really gets off on," expressed one man.

Some couples engage in cunnilingus and fellatio simultaneously. The phrase "69" has been used to identify the respective positions of the couple engaging in mutual oral–genital stimulation. Sixty-nine may be enjoyed as a prelude to intercourse or as an end in itself. However, some people find it difficult to be a skillful giver and an appreciative receiver at the same time.

Penile Stimulation

In addition to stimulating the clitoral-vulval area by hand and mouth, some women rub their partner's penis inside their vaginal lips. The penis may be rubbed in a circular motion, or up and down the vaginal lips, or directly on the clitoris. Such stimulation may precede penetration or be just for itself. As suggested earlier, premarital couples who wish to avoid intercourse for moral reasons may enjoy such stimulation, yet stop short of intercourse to maintain their virginity. This has been referred to as "technical virginity," measured in millimeters!

Other Petting Behaviors

Another means of experiencing intense physical stimulation without having intercourse is **genital apposition**, or pressing the genitals close together while clothed or unclothed. The couple lie together, entwine their legs, and "grind." An orgasm may or may not result. About three-fourths of college students report having engaged in genital apposition, and they do so about a quarter of the time they are with their partner (DeLamater & MacCorquodale, 1979).

Fewer people have experienced **anal stimulation**, which involves manual or oral stimulation (rimming) of the anus and surrounding area. These areas are particularly sensitive and some couples routinely stimulate each other there during petting. About 35 percent of the 80,000 plus respondents in the *Playboy* study (Petersen et al., 1983a) reported having engaged in oral anal contact. The percentages were higher for anal intercourse: 6 in 10 women and almost 5 in 10 men reported having engaged in this behavior. In *Anal Pleasure and Health* (Morin, 1981), the author details the history of the anal taboo and suggests ways for those interested in anal sex to relax, desensitize their fears, and discover potential pleasures.

Fellatio, cunnilingus, manual stimulation, vaginal lip stimulation of the penis, penile stimulation of the vaginal area, genital apposition, and anal stimulation are behavioral forms of petting. But petting may also be verbal. Some lovers stimulate each other by telling sex stories, using sex talk, or sharing fantasies. One woman said that she calls her partner at his office and tells him how hot she is and that she wants "some good sex" after a bottle of wine that night.

While such talk may precede sexual activity, it may also be a part of the petting sequence. "I like for my partner to talk dirty to me. It terribly excites me," remarked one man. Some partners share their fantasies as a way of stimulating their lover. One couple described how, before making love, they would tell each other about a stranger they saw that day who they would like to make love to. In telling the story they would turn the stranger into the partner.

Other couples use sexual devices in petting. More than 75 percent of the women and 65 percent of the men in the *Playboy* study (Peterson et al., 1983a) said they used such devices for sexual stimulation in their lovemaking. The most frequently used devices were erotic books, sexy underwear, and vibrators. Erotic movies and oils were also used but less frequently. In all cases, women reported using these devices more than men.

Effects of Petting

Petting usually results in erection for the male and lubrication for the female. Lubrication is important in preparing the woman for comfortable insertion of the penis if intercourse is to follow. But independent of intercourse, petting sometimes results in orgasm. Two-thirds of the single men and half of the single women less than age 25 in Hunt's (1974) study reported that they had petted to orgasm. These orgasms may occur during deep kissing, genital apposition, or manual or oral stimulation. But when prolonged petting does not result in orgasm, people may experience discomfort and frustration as a result of the neuromuscular tensions that have been built up during erotic arousal. Half of the females in Kinsey's (1953) sample reported that they were nervously upset, disturbed in their thinking, and incapable of concentrating on some occasions after prolonged petting. One-quarter reported pains in the groin, the feeling also reported by males who are erotically aroused and who fail to reach orgasm. Women used physical exercise, masturbation, or intercourse to reduce these feelings of discomfort.

Women who pet to orgasm before marriage seem to report more orgasmic frequency in marriage. Among the women in Kinsey's sample, 90 percent of those who had experienced an orgasm during premarital petting also reported experiencing a climax during their first year of marriage. Only 35 percent of those who did not have an orgasm before marriage reported having had a climax the first year of marriage. This suggests that premarital petting may contribute to later enjoyment of marital sex.

Petting gives many women their first orgasmic experience. Whereas most men experience their first orgasm through masturbation, petting is the primary means for numerous women (a quarter of Kinsey's sample). "It is petting rather than the home, classroom, or religious instruction, lectures or books, classes in biology, sociology, or philosophy, or actual coitus, that provides most females with their first real understanding of a heterosexual experience" (Kinsey, 1970, p. 264).

Another potential effect of petting is guilt. One man in the Hunt (1974) study recalled:

● When I started going steady with Amy, we began to pet, and after a while it would get quite heavy, and then we'd both get frightened and guilty and make a pact to see each other but not touch each other. But that would collapse and we'd go further than ever. We'd even stay in bed all night, and masturbate each other to orgasm—and still we had some kind of conviction that it would be wrong to have real intercourse. At times we'd be ready to do it—and, at the very point of trying it, suddenly the vision of what we were doing would come down on us, and we'd stop and feel all torn up. (p. 141) ●

Some lovers do not have guilt feelings about petting. Eighty percent of the university women in one study (Huk, 1979) said they never felt guilty about engaging in oral-genital sex. "Why should I feel guilty?" asked one woman. "What I do with my partner is my own business."

Petting in Other Societies

The degree to which men and women engage in petting behavior differs from society to society. In some societies (such as the Lepcha and Kwoma), couples almost never pet before intercourse but proceed directly to the act. But in other societies (like the Ponape), petting may be extended for hours. Grooming is one form of petting (for example, among the Trobrianders), which consists of each partner licking lice from the hair and wood ticks from the body of the other. This may go on for hours and penetration may or may not follow.

Stimulation of the woman's breast, although common in Western and other societies, is not universal. Some (like the Kurtatchi and Kwakiutl) seem to attribute no erotic significance to a woman's breasts. In these societies the breast is like the woman's elbow—it is not a socially identified erotic zone. But among the Alorese, for example, a woman's breasts are viewed as the key to sexual arousal and intercourse. When her breasts are "pulled," she is supposed to find the man who does so irresistible. How the woman's breasts are stimulated also varies. Manual stimulation is more prevalent than oral stimulation, but whether the touch is teasing or squeezing, nibbling or biting, is influenced by the society in which it occurs.

Like breast stimulation, the style and acceptability of kissing also varies by society. Styles include sucking the lips and tongue of the partner so that saliva flows from one mouth to the other (the Trukese and Kwakiutl), kissing the mouth and nose at the same time (the Lapps), and simply placing the lips near the partner's face while inhaling (the Tinguian). In some societies kissing is unknown, as among the Balinese and Thonga. When the Thonga first observed Europeans kissing, they viewed it as eating each other's saliva and dirt (Ford & Beach, 1951).

Genital stimulation by hand or mouth varies, too. Men may be forbidden to stimulate the woman's genital region, as are the Tikopia, or encouraged to do so, like the Ponape. Also, the pattern of stimulation may be unique. The Ponapean man is reported to place a fish in the woman's vulva and to lick it out before intercourse. Manual play of the genital area is a more common occurrence with the man using his finger to stretch the vaginal opening prior to penetration.

Summary

Petting is a frequent sexual behavior involving any sexual contact that does not include intercourse. Like all sexual behaviors, petting occurs in a social and environmental context. It is affected by the life style and interpersonal relationship of the partners, the place where it occurs, and the drugs, sights, sounds, and scents that may stimulate it.

Many regard touching as the most significant aspect of sex. It is a primary form of communication. There are different types of kissing and kissing may or may not have emotional or erotic connotations. Regardless of the way individuals label the kissing experience, it is a common experience.

Petting may also involve breast stimulation, penis stimulation, and stimulation of the clitoris. Breast stimulation may be manual or oral. The woman may caress her partner's penis with her hand(s), with her mouth, or rub his penis inside her vaginal lips. Fellatio means oral stimulation of the male's genitals by his partner. Stimulation of the clitoris may be by hand, mouth, or the penis. The term cunnilingus means oral contact with the female genitals.

Genital apposition, pressing the genitals close together while clothed or unclothed, and anal stimulation are other petting behaviors. But petting may also be verbal. Some lovers stimulate each other by telling sex stories, using sex talk, or sharing fantasies. Other couples use sexual devices in their petting.

There are both positive and negative effects of petting. It usually provides the female with her first orgasmic experience. Also, women who pet to orgasm before marriage seem to report more orgasmic frequency in marriage. But when prolonged petting does not result in orgasm, discomfort and frustration may result. Some couples feel guilty about petting.

The degree to which men and women engage in petting behavior differs from society to society. In some societies there is virtually no petting before intercourse. But in other societies, petting may be extended for hours. Breast stimulation, the style and acceptability of kissing, and genital stimulation by hand or mouth all vary.

Key Terms

petting
touching
kissing
manual stimulation
fellatio

vaginal lip stimulation
cunnilingus
genital apposition
anal stimulation

Issues in Debate and Future Directions

The impact of sexual permissiveness on emotional health and why men have more sexual partners than women are two controversial issues in interpersonal sexuality. After discussing these issues, we note several trends in interpersonal sexuality.

Does Sexual Permissiveness Promote Adjustment or Maladjustment?

With delayed marriage, more liberal sexual norms, and the demise of the double standard, more people are having intercourse with more partners than in previous years. The median number (half the respondents had more, half had less than this number) of partners reported by 65,396 males in one study was 16; the median for 14,928 females in the same study was 8 (Petersen et al., 1983a). These medians are more than double those of the Hunt study reported in 1974. But what is the effect of having a number of sexual partners on a person's emotional health? Does having intercourse with an array of partners result in low feelings of self-esteem, depression, and despair or improved self-esteem, contentment, and emotional well-being?

One researcher (Scarf, 1980) suggested that promiscuity, or seeking out many sexual partners, often occurs when a person is emotionally vulnerable such as just after a divorce or the ending of a significant emotional relationship. The bodies of the sexual partners are used as a means to heal the pain of loneliness and despair. "The enhanced activity and the gamesmanship help to stave off those frightening and even potentially overwhelming feelings. Feelings of sadness and of anxiety—fears that one will experience oneself as totally abandoned and alone" (pp. 83–84).

But not all new sexual experiences are begun under conditions of despair. Many are a product of two people feeling good about themselves and each other; sexual expression becomes an extension of their enjoyment. Although they present little data to support their conclusion, the *Playboy* researchers conclude; "For both men and women, experience contributes to a good self-image" (Petersen et al., 1983a p. 244).

In a more refined study, two researchers (Diederen & Rorer, 1982) asked 188 women and 203 men what they believed about the relationship between sexual liberality and emotional adjustment. Most stated either that there was no relationship or that they did not know what the relationship was. Both genders tended to act in accordance with their beliefs. Those who believed that sexual conservatism is associated with better adjustment tended to act more conservatively, and those who believed sexual liberality leads to better adjustment tended to act liberally.

Why Do Men Tend to Have More Sexual Partners Than Women?

As the figures from the Petersen et al., and Hunt studies suggest, men usually have more sexual partners than women. The same pattern holds for marriage, where husbands have more extramarital partners than wives. Fifty percent of the wives in the *Redbook* study (Tavris & Sadd, 1977) reported having only one extramarital partner compared with an average of seven partners for the husbands in the Yablonsky (1979) study.

Symons (1979), an anthropologist, suggests an evolutionary reason for men having more desire for sexual variety than women. The male who achieved the greatest reproductive success—who had the most surviving progeny—would be the one who impregnated the greatest number of females. On the other hand, reproductive success for the female depended on mating with the most fit male. She did not need a variety of partners. Her reproductive goals could be accomplished by inciting male–male competition to eliminate the weaker males. She would then mate with the strongest, most fit male to ensure that her offspring would have the best possible chance of survival.

Symons also believes that "women do not generally seem to experience a pervasive autonomous sexual desire for men to whom they are not married" (p. 238). Women seem to want the man they know or with whom they have developed an affectional relationship. Men are more likely to want *a* woman and to be less concerned about a deep emotional relationship.

The counter to Symons' argument is that men and women do not seek sexual partners mainly for reproductive reasons. While Symons' point may be valid for the survival of early homo sapiens, it has no bearing today. Men have more sexual partners than women because of opportunity, social expectations, and social consequences. Regarding opportunity, men have always been under less social control than women. "Where are you going and when will you be back?" are words more frequently said to adolescent females than males. Also, the fact that virtually all husbands but only half of American wives are in the work force suggests greater opportunity for men to meet available women.

Men are also expected to have a number of sexual partners to prove their virility to their peers. Gagnon (1977) has observed that much of male sexuality is homosocial—its purpose is to impress the male's same-gender peers. Women are not rewarded by their female peers

for having intercourse with a large number of men.

The negative social consequences of having multiple partners traditionally have been less for men than women. The number of sexual partners a male had did not effect his marriageability. But women were socialized to have a limited number of sexual partners before marriage for fear they would be labeled promiscuous, reducing their chances for marriage.

The facts that women are entering the work force in record numbers, are becoming economically independent, are delaying marriage and parenthood, and are less constrained in making decisions about their sexuality will increase their potential to have multiple sexual partners. These changes have begun. The readers of *Cosmopolitan* are typically liberal, urban, career-oriented women. When 106,000 of them responded to a survey that included the number of sexual partners they had had, 10 percent reported having had one lover; 28 percent between 2 and 5 lovers; 25 percent between 11 and 25 lovers; and 15 percent had 25 or more lovers (Wolfe, 1982).

Future Directions

Trends in interpersonal sexuality include more lovers enjoying petting as a pleasure for itself. Although intercourse and orgasm will remain the dominant goal of sexual activity for most couples, an increasing number are discovering the pleasure of extended lovemaking without intercourse. "All we do is screw,"said one lover. "I'd like for us to get back to straight hugging, kissing, and playing with each other's face and body."

Couples increasingly will experiment with different forms of sexual behavior and the use of sex gadgets. Mutual manual and oral stimulation will be enjoyed as a natural part of sexual sharing. The availability of vibrators in local drug stores and national department stores like Sears and J. C. Penney and their being publicized in national magazines such as *McCall's* and *Family Circle* will increase their acceptability.

These behaviors will also be experienced with a greater number of partners. As mentioned earlier, as the age at marriage continues to rise, more people will be sexually available for a longer period of time. Also, since single relationships are less stable than marriage relationships, there is a greater turnover of partners. The result is a series of sexual relationships.

Chapter Seven

Sexual Intercourse

Sexual intercourse is not just a
skill to be mastered, an activity
to exercise the body, or a game
to be played.

WILLIAM H. MASTERS AND
VIRGINIA E. JOHNSON

Chapter Seven

Sexual intercourse, or coitus, refers to the sexual union of a man's penis and a woman's vagina. It is the event most people think of when the phrase "having sex" is used. But sexual intercourse is also a means of communication that occurs for various reasons and in different interpersonal contexts—before marriage, during marriage, outside marriage, and after marriage. Of course, intercourse may also occur independently of marriage.

Sexual Intercourse as Communication

Intercourse is more than two bodies in motion. Each partner brings to the intercourse experience a motive (pleasure, reconciliation, procreation, duty); a psychological state (love, hostility, boredom, excitement); and a physical state (tense, exhausted, relaxed, turned on). The combination of these motives and states may change from one sexual encounter to the next. Tonight one partner may feel aroused and seek intercourse mainly for physical pleasure. But the other partner may feel tired and only have intercourse out of a sense of duty. Tomorrow night both may feel relaxed and loving and have intercourse as a means of expressing their feelings for each other.

The verbal and nonverbal communication preceding intercourse may also serve as a relationship barometer. "I can tell how we're doing," said one woman, "by whether or not we have intercourse and how he approaches me when we do. Sometimes he just rolls over when the lights are out and starts to rub my back. Other times he plays with my face and kisses me while we talk and waits till I reach for him. Still other times we each stay on our side of the bed so that our legs don't even touch."

Intercourse is also a time to communicate a sense of emotional connectedness with one's partner. One of Hite's (1981) respondents said:

● Even more important than orgasm is being able to wrap your arms and legs and whatever else around another human being. It makes you feel less alone, more alive. There's just nothing like it. (p. 342) ●

Writers on sexuality have paid little attention to the communication of lovers after intercourse. Yet one psychiatrist observed that this time "reveals more about the basic relationship between the partners than any other preceding sexual activity. The instinctual, biological, and sensual phases of this sexual process give way to the more social and circumstantial aspects of the engagement" (Crain, 1978, p. 80). Whereas some partners may curl up in each other's arms and relax in silent companionship, others may avoid touching each other and withdraw as soon as possible. Indeed, there are a number of different behaviors people engage in after intercourse. These include talking, holding each other, drifting off to sleep, giggling, crying, eating, drinking, smoking, taking a shower, or leaving the room or the home. Lovers may use some of these activities as a prelude to renewed intercourse.

Motivations for Intercourse

People initiate intercourse for a number of reasons. These may be positive or negative, ranging from the desire for intimacy to the desire for revenge.

Express Emotional Intimacy

In our relatively impersonal society, sexual intercourse may help a person feel emotionally connected to another. The physical closeness of intercourse may signify a more general closeness between the people sharing a relationship. "Though the rim of the penis or the head of the clitoris may provide the most intense stimulation because they are such sensitive nerve packages, these organs are connected to bodies which belong to persons" (Mazur, 1973, pp. 45–46).

The goal of intercourse for intimacy is "closeness, full body contact, cuddling, and affectionate exchange. The closeness is comforting and feels natural; the person is at home with the intimacy" (Mosher, 1980, p. 29).

● We usually start out with long French kisses while hugging each other tightly so that our bodies are pressed against each other. This generates a feeling of warmth and security between us. Then we engage in broad body caressing, which is the starting point of the actual stimulation. My husband fondles my breasts, often sucking on them. This doesn't arouse me greatly but brings on a feeling of satisfaction, as that of a mother breast-feeding a child . . . About five minutes after orgasm, I feel very peaceful and satisfied. I like to hug my husband tightly and hold him still inside of me, symbolic of the feelings I have for our oneness and unity, and just lay in each other's arms, eking out every ounce of satisfaction from the act. (Fisher, 1973, pp. 208–209) ●

Have Fun

Intercourse may be regarded solely as a pleasurable, sensual experience. A noted marriage counselor described this motive as play, sport (Neubeck, 1974). In studies on sensation seeking and sexual behavior, the evidence suggests that those individuals who have a strong drive to excite their senses are more likely to have intercourse with a greater number of partners (Zuckerman, 1979).

Enhance Ego

Although a couple may engage in intercourse primarily for fun, one (or both) of the partners may be attempting to boost his or her own ego, even at the expense of the partner. As mentioned in Chapter 6, men traditionally have been socialized to take pride in seducing women and in discussing their conquests with their peers. In one study (Carns, 1973), 30 percent of the men told a friend they had had intercourse within a few hours after it occurred. This contrasted with 14 percent of the women who did so. Men tend to talk about the number of sexual encounters, and women about their feelings of emotional involvement. Hence, men may be more motivated than women to have intercourse to enhance their status among their peers.

Other people may have intercourse to compensate for feelings of inadequacy in other areas. Finding that someone is interested in having intercourse may supply an insecure person with confirmation of his or her own worth.

Reduce Negative Feelings

Related to ego enhancement as a motive for sexual intercourse is the need to be physically close with someone to help allay feelings of despair, grief, and depression, especially after losing a mate. Sexual intercourse can produce a kind of a 'high.' That sense of aliveness, of 'making things happen,' serves to combat—admittedly not completely and not for long—those feelings of abandonment, of emptiness, of helplessness, of being half a person (the remaining portion of what was formerly a couple, a unit) (Scarf, 1980, p. 84).

Relieve Peer Pressure

Peer pressure can influence an individual to have intercourse. It is a subtle motivating factor for first intercourse experiences. One woman said:

● I lived with a group of women last year and was influenced by peer pressure to have my first intercourse experience. I was the only virgin among them and they teased me a lot. They couldn't understand it—I had plenty of dates and partied like crazy . . . staying out all night, yet I still had not had intercourse.

But, alas, the kidding got to me. Last spring I took this guy back to my room (the other women said I could have the place for the night). It was our first date although he had been asking me out for three months. We had intercourse. I laughed the whole time and decided intercourse was no big deal.

I have no regrets or guilt about having intercourse but I do feel bad for using a nice guy because he fell in love after that and wanted to get married! Uck! ●

Improve Relationship

Some couples have intercourse in the hope that it will improve their relationship. It is impossible to predict the specific effect having intercourse will have on a relationship. One partner reported, "Intercourse for us was the best thing that ever happened. Since we began having sex over a year ago we have felt more emotionally involved with each other. It's really magic." But another said, "It was a mistake for us to have intercourse. I thought it would draw us closer together but it hasn't. My partner has been avoiding me lately and things are not the same. I'm sorry it happened." In one study of more than 200 respondents (Ratcliff & Knox, 1982), 30 percent said the effect of their last intercourse was to improve their relationship, 8 percent said things got worse, and 62 percent said their relationship remained the same.

Relieve Partner Pressure

Sometimes only one partner is interested in moving the relationship toward intercourse. "I put pressure on him by telling him how frustrated I was. We joked about it a lot, but I believe it did influence him to have intercourse with me. He felt sorry for me."

Sometimes the partner's influence is so subtle it is not perceived as pressure. Rather, one partner may feel the need to please the other. "I knew it would make him happy so I made love with him," stated one woman.

Ensure Marriage

Another kind of pressure is the tactic of using intercourse in the hope of pregnancy to force the issue of marriage on an undecided or unenthusiastic partner. "Some men are pressured to get married," one woman commented. "I saw it happen with my friend and her boyfriend. They had been dating for five years, but they didn't talk about marriage until she got pregnant."

Rebel

Some people have intercourse to rebel against religion, their parents, or a previous partner. A student said, "After I took a course in the sociology of religion, I felt angry. I had been protecting my virginity because of religious scruples. It turns out that every culture feels differently about sex and uses religion to control sexual behavior. I don't want to be made to feel guilty any longer about something I have wanted to do for a long time."

Other people rebel against parents. "I'm tired of being told 'no.' It's all I've heard since I was 12. I'm a college sophomore and I'm on my own now. If I want to have intercourse, my parents can't stop me."

Still other individuals may rebel against a previous partner as a motive for intercourse. "After Steve dropped me I felt terrible. I felt truly alone for the first time in my life. When Gary came along, we had intercourse the first time we went out. I was on the rebound and I guess I thought it was a way of getting back at Steve for having hurt me."

Rebellion is a questionable motive for having intercourse because the "real" reason is in reference to something else (religion) or someone else (parents, a previous partner). Such external motivations suggest that the sexual partner is being used to help settle a previous issue.

Take Revenge

Whereas intercourse as a rebellious act uses the sex partner to direct hostility toward others, intercourse for revenge is a direct attack against the partner. "When I found out that she had gone to the drive-in with her old boyfriend, I decided to break off with her. But I wanted to pay her back so I came on real strong about marriage and we had intercourse. When I left her that evening, I left her for good." Clearly, in a case like this intercourse is used to vent anger, and deception and exploitation are the means.

The motives for intercourse just discussed are not exhaustive. Others include conceiving a baby, passion, relief from tension or boredom, duty, and reconciliation. Also, motives are often mixed. Rarely is an intercourse experience just for intimacy or passion or fun; it includes a combination of motives.

In one study (Ratcliff & Knox, 1982), 234 undergraduates (54 percent female, 46 percent male) were asked to describe the motive for their most recent intercourse experience. Emotional intimacy was the predominant motive for a majority of the respondents engaging in intercourse. "Love" and "fun" were the second and third most often reported motivations. Negative motives such as exploitation, revenge, and rebellion were rare. Whereas women were more likely to report intimacy and fun as motivations, men were more likely to report relief from sexual tension.

Intercourse Positions

There are five basic positions of intercourse. These are presented in order of frequency with which they are used by couples in the United States. With the exception of rear entry, all of the positions are face to face. Whereas some couples may use some or all of the positions, others may use only one. The older a couple, the less likely they are to vary coital position.

Man-on-Top Position

Also referred to as the missionary position because the Polynesians observed that the British missionaries had intercourse with the man on top, it is the most frequently used position during intercourse. The woman reclines on her back, bends her knees, and spreads her legs. The man positions himself between her legs supporting himself on his elbows and knees. The man or woman may guide his penis into her vagina.

This position may be preferred because of the belief that this is the way most people have intercourse and, therefore, it is "normal." In addition, it permits maximum male thrusting and facilitates kissing and caressing.

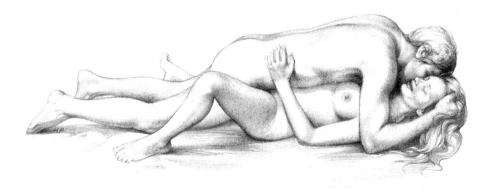

But there are disadvantages to the missionary position. Some women experience pain from the deep penetration. Unless such a woman closes her legs after penetration, she is likely to feel the penis thrusting against her cervix. The man-above position also makes clitoral contact difficult. Although a woman can move her buttocks in circular fashion to achieve some clitoral friction, some women find it almost impossible to achieve clitoral stimulation in this position except by hand (theirs or their partner's).

Woman-on-Top Position

The second most frequent position couples use during intercourse is the woman on top. She may either lie lengthwise so that her legs are between her partner's or kneel on top with her knees on either side of him. The primary advantage of this position is that it permits maximum freedom for the woman to move so as to ensure clitoral stimulation. Many women report that they have an orgasm most often in this position. "I like to be on top," wrote one woman, "because I can better control the amount of friction in the right places." In addition, both partners may have their hands free and either the man or woman may stimulate her clitoris during intercourse.

Some women report drawbacks to the woman-above position. Some feel too shy in this position and do not enjoy "being on display." Others complain that the penis keeps falling out since the woman may lift too high before the downward stroke on the penis. Still others say there is a "lot of work when you're on top" and prefer the more passive role.

Side-to-Side Position

A relaxing position for both partners is the side-to-side position. The partners lie on their sides, with one leg touching the bed. The top legs are lifted and positioned to accomodate easy entry of the penis. Neither partner has the strain of "doing all the work," and the partners have relative freedom to move their body as they wish to achieve the desired place of contact and rhythm of movement.

Rear-entry Position

The rear-entry position is achieved with the woman lying on her side with her back to her partner. She may also support herself on her knees and hands as though to crawl or she may lie on her stomach and tilt her buttocks upward. The man enters her vagina from behind. His hands are free to caress her breasts and legs or stimulate her clitoris as she desires. While clitoral stimulation is a major advantage of this position, there are disadvantages. These include a tendency for the penis to slip out and the loss of face-to-face contact.

Sitting Position

In the sitting position the man sits on a chair or edge of the bed with his partner sitting across his thighs. She can lower herself onto his erect penis or insert his penis after she is sitting. She may be facing him or her back may be turned to him. The face-to-face sitting position involves maximum freedom of the hands to hug the partner and stimulate the breasts.

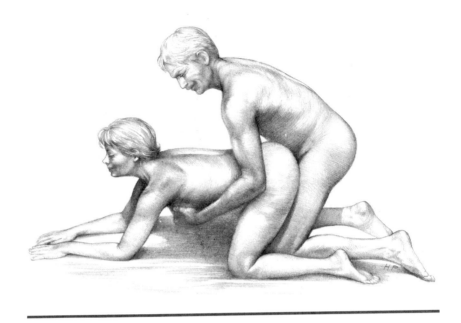

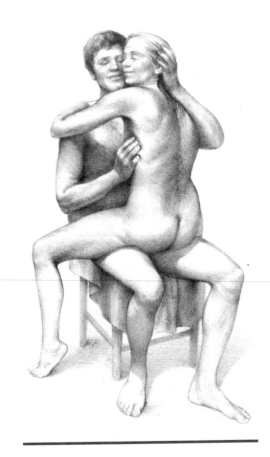

In the standing position the woman raises one leg or the man picks her up and places her onto his erect penis. She puts her legs around his waist and her arms around his neck while he is holding her. Both must be well coordinated and in good physical condition.

Variations

There are innumerable variations to these five positions. For example, in the man-above position, the woman's legs may be closed or open, bent or straight, over his shoulders or around his back. The partners may face each other or face in opposite directions. Increasingly, couples are willing to explore a variety of intercourse positions.

Premarital Intercourse

Intercourse occurs in a variety of social contexts. **Premarital intercourse** is one of them.

First Intercourse Experience

Because people attach a great deal of emotional, social, and psychological significance to intercourse, the first experience is likely to be memorable. Some confusion, anxiety, and frustration about the when, who, and how of first intercourse is typical. The following statements reflect such feelings: "I'd like to get it over with"; "My closest friend has intercourse regularly; I wonder when I'll be doing it"; "I feel that I should already have had intercourse by now, but I haven't." Compounding these personal concerns are those about the partner (Will my partner respect me?) and consequences (What is the chance that I'll get herpes?).

Huk (1979) asked a random sample of women at one university about their first intercourse experience. Most (78 percent) did not discuss the possibility of having intercourse with their partner or "preplan" the event (only 9 percent used contraception). "It just happened" was a typical description. But although first intercourse was not planned, it occurred with someone for whom they had feelings of love and affection. More than 60 percent said they were in love with the partner. Men are more likely to have their first intercourse experience with a casual acquaintance (Lewin, 1982).

But apparently a love relationship was not enough to make the first experience an enjoyable one. Only a quarter of the women described their experience as "satisfying and pleasurable." They were more likely to say that the experience was painful (40 percent) or frightening (22 percent). Also, more than half said they had guilt feelings following the first experience. But the guilt usually is not long lasting. In another study of 355 sexually active women (Herold & Goodwin, 1981), 41 percent reported guilt over their first experience. When asked about their last experience, only 8 percent said they felt guilty. It also appears that sex guilt reduces but does not stop sexual behaviors (Brown & Pollack, 1982).

In summary, the first intercourse experience for these college women was mostly negative in terms of pain, fear, and guilt. Only a few (9 percent) reported that they had an orgasm their first time. However, these reactions did not stop them from having intercourse since almost 80 percent had intercourse again with the same partner.

One woman reported her first intercourse experience as follows.

● When I had my first sexual experience, I was scared to death. I didn't know how to act or even what to do. I was not on any type of birth control and with my luck I knew I would get pregnant my first time. I felt very guilty since I had been taught that premarital sex was wrong and that a guy would lose respect for a girl once she made love to him. To make matters worse my boyfriend thought I was on birth control and became upset when he found out I wasn't. Now, a year later, I don't regret my experience and I think having sex has strengthened our relationship. ●

Men, in general, report that they experienced a combination of surprise, relief, and pleasure at first intercourse. They were surprised that their partner accepted their advances, relieved that they could perform intercourse, and pleasured at the experience of the act. The basic feeling was "Today, I am a man" (Auerbach, 1980).

A forty-year-old man described his first intercourse experience.

● I was 15 years old and my partner was 16. I had two fears. The first was my fear of impregnating her during our first time. The second was of "parking" in dark and desolate areas. Therefore, once we decided to have intercourse, we spent a boring evening waiting for my parents to go to sleep so we could move to the station wagon in the driveway.

After near hyperventilation in an attempt to fog the windows (to prevent others from seeing in), we commenced to prepare for the long-awaited event. In recognition of my first fear, I wore four prophylactics. She, out of fear, was not lubricating well, and needless to say, I couldn't feel anything through the four layers of latex.

We were able to climax, which I attribute solely to sheer emotional excitement, yet both of us were later able to admit that the experience was disappointing. We knew it could only get better. ●

Facts about Premarital Intercourse

The following paragraphs describe who has premarital intercourse, the percentage of such intercourse for different groups, and the number of premarital partners.

Who Has Premarital Intercourse?

Some people are more likely to have intercourse than others. Among college students, the factors most likely to influence intercourse before marriage include the following.

- *Gender.* Men are more likely to have premarital intercourse than women. In a random sample of college students, 75 percent of the men and 60 percent of the women reported having had intercourse (DeLamater & MacCorquodale, 1979). But this discrepancy between men and women is disappearing (Keller, Elliott, & Gunberg, 1982).
- *School level.* Each year in school increases the percentage of students who have intercourse. In one study 35 percent of both men and women freshman had experienced intercourse, but 75 percent of the senior men and 68 percent of the senior women had done so (Rockwell, Ellinwood, & O'Hare, 1977).
- *Emotional relationship.* Those who are involved in a reciprocal love relationship are more likely to have intercourse. Love is viewed as justifying intercourse (Knox & Wilson, 1981).
- *Religious affiliation.* Protestant college women have a higher incidence of intercourse than either Catholic or Jewish women (Bell & Coughey, 1980).
- *Church attendance.* The less often a college student attends church or synagogue, the more likely that person is to have had intercourse (DeLamater & MacCorquodale, 1979; Diederen & Rorer, 1982).
- *Drugs.* College students who use drugs are more likely to have had intercourse. In one study 67 percent of the women who had had intercourse had used marijuana more than once. Among those who had not, only 21 percent had smoked marijuana more than once (Jessor & Jessor, 1975).
- *Race.* Black men and women are more likely to have premarital intercourse than white men and women (Zelnik & Kantner, 1977).*

Age at Premarital Intercourse

In a nationwide study of the first intercourse experience of women and men (Zelnik & Shah, 1983), the mean age for women was 16.2; the mean age for men was 15.7. The sexual partners of the women at first intercourse were about three years older. The sexual partners of the men were about six months older.

*These characteristics do not imply causation. Females, freshmen, Catholics, frequent church attenders, nondrug users, and whites, or a person with all of these characteristics, may also have intercourse before marriage.

Percentage Having Premarital Intercourse

What percentage of college and noncollege men and women have intercourse before marriage? In a random sample of both groups, ages 18–23, two researchers (DeLamater & MacCorquodale, 1979) revealed that three-fourths of the men had had intercourse. Women were slightly less likely to report having had intercourse—60 percent of college women and 72 percent of nonstudent women.

In general, most people have intercourse before marriage and men are more likely to do so earlier than women. Both genders believe that others are more sexually active than themselves (Rubinson et al., 1981).

Number of Premarital Partners

Most people have from one to five premarital partners (one-half to two-thirds of the experiences are with one, two, or three partners). About 15 percent of men and 30 percent of women have had intercourse with only one partner (Barrett, 1980; DeLamater & MacCorquodale, 1979). These data indicate that men are more likely to have a variety of sexual partners than women, a fact that Kinsey noted more than 30 years ago.

Effects of Premarital Intercourse

A possible effect of premarital intercourse (as with any intercourse) is pregnancy. Three in 10 white women aged 15–19 and almost 5 in 10 black women in the same age group who had premarital intercourse reported that they became pregnant (Zelnik & Kanter, 1980). In most cases, the pregnancy was a surprise.

Does premarital intercourse affect the stability of the couple's relationship? Apparently not. The sexual behavior of 5,000 sophomores and juniors at four colleges in Boston who had ongoing sexual relationships was studied (Hill et al., 1976). In a two-year follow-up, the researchers found that those who had had intercourse were no more likely to have broken up than those who had not had intercourse. In another study (Ratcliff & Knox, 1982), less than 2 percent of 234 respondents said their relationship terminated as a result of their last intercourse.

To summarize what we know about premarital intercourse, most people (men more than women) have intercourse before marriage. They do so with relatively few partners and in the context of an affectionate, love relationship. Having intercourse does not seem to affect whether a couple stays together.

Marital Intercourse

Intercourse after marriage is different from intercourse before marriage. Since more than 90 percent of Americans marry, marriage is the social context for most intercourse experiences.

What Is Special about Marital Intercourse?

Marital intercourse is special in terms of its social legitimacy, declining frequency over the course of the marriage, and varying importance to the partners.

Social Legitimacy

In our society marital intercourse is the most legitimate form of sexual behavior. Homosexual, premarital, and extramarital intercourse do not enjoy society's approval, although attitudes and also laws are changing. It is not only okay to have intercourse when married, it is expected. People assume that married couples make love, and if they do not, something is "wrong."

Declining Frequency

Marital intercourse is also characterized by declining frequency. The longer most spouses are married, the less interest they have in intercourse (Mancini & Orthner, 1978). While married couples in their twenties have intercourse about three times a week, those around 40 do so about once a week (Trussell & Westoff, 1980).

A traditional wedding prank is based on awareness of this decline in frequency. Someones gives the bride and groom a half-gallon jar on their wedding day with the following instructions taped on it: "Every time you have intercourse during your first year of marriage, put a penny in this jar. Then, beginning with your second year, take a penny out every time you have intercourse. It will take you five years to empty this jar, which you will fill in one."

For some couples it does not take long for the frequency of intercourse to decline. Twenty-one couples kept a record of how often they made love throughout the first year of their marriage (James, 1981). The first month they had intercourse a median of 17.5 times; a year later the median had dropped to 8.5 among the couples where the wife was not pregnant. In another study, those who had been married one year reported having intercourse an average of 15 times per month. Those who had been married six years reported that their frequency had dropped to about six times per month (Greenblat, 1983).

The advent of children helps to reduce the frequency of marital intercourse. In general, couples with children make love less frequently than couples without children (James, 1981). Taking care of children, particularly young children, is an exhausting chore. A spouse, more often the wife, who is up all night with a colicky infant and then spends much of the day in the pediatrician's waiting room may not feel up to having sex that evening. Rather, she may prefer to read as a reward for dealing with the demands of children all day (Mancini & Orthner, 1978).

The career/jobs of the respective spouses may also decrease the frequency of marital intercourse. One of the wives in the Greenblat study (1983) experienced this effect.

● Exhaustion is a very big problem. I never thought it could happen. When I'm working and running my business, it is totally absorbing and it takes me a long time to decompress at night, by which time Jerry is usually sound asleep! And I guess Jerry, unlike when we first got married, has a lot of responsibility in his position—so it's work that's taking its toll in our sex life! (p. 296) ●

"I have steak and sex the same way—very rare."

RODNEY DANGERFIELD

Psychological and sociological factors also may help to account for the gradual decline of intercourse in marriage, for example, loss of peer interest, loss of reproductive capacity, and boredom. Before marriage, and particularly among males, the sexual self-image may depend on peer group approval, based on the number of sexual conquests. But, as Gagnon (1977) noted, married men can only "count their wives once. The wedding night is it as far as peer group approval is concerned" (p. 210).

For spouses who feel that conceiving children is the major justification for intercourse, loss of reproductive capacity may end all interest in sex. "What good is sex to me now? My children are grown, and all I want now is to have grandchildren."Also, because marital sex happens with the same partner, usually in the same way, year after year, both spouses may become bored. The popularity of sex manuals and of magazine columns that offer advice on sexual relations suggests that there is a sizable group of those wanting to recapture the sexual excitement of earlier years.

After conducting in-depth interviews with 80 spouses regarding the frequency of intercourse in their respective marriages, Greenblat concluded that from the first year on "almost everything—children, jobs, commuting, housework, financial worries—that happens to a couple conspires to *reduce* the degree of sexual interaction and almost nothing leads to increasing it" (p. 294).

Varying Importance

How important is intercourse to married couples? The range is very wide. Whether for physiological or psychological reasons, some couples have "sexless marriages" (Cuber, 1969). For them, sex is not a meaningful event. Yet they may love each other deeply and delight in the companionship they share.

Other couples regard sex as the only positive aspect of their relationship. One husband said that he and his wife had decided to separate, "and since we both knew that I would be moving out on Friday we had intercourse twice a day that week." A year after the separation, he said, "Sex with us was the best there is. I don't miss the fights we had, but I do miss the sex."

Between the extremes of "sex is nothing" and "sex is everything" is "sex is good but not everything." Gagnon (1977) has observed that if the average couple spends about 50 hours a year having intercourse, they will also spend about 1,000 hours in front of the television and 2,000 hours at work (40 hours a week for 50 weeks). While sexual involvement may have been a dominant theme before marriage, it diminishes in importance after marriage.

Speaking before the International Academy of Sex Research, Schmidt (1982) said:

> There is the illusion that a couple's relationship can be continuously and permanently compatible with the intensive sexuality experienced in the early days of falling in love. This is impossible because the closeness that comes from living together, sleeping, eating, and spending leisure time together, and bringing up children together cannot additionally cope with sexual symbiosis. (p. 95)

Influences on Marital Intercourse

The women's movement, contraception, and the mass media have had their influences on marital intercourse, as well as on intercourse in other social contexts. Traditionally, the wife's role was to satisfy her husband without regard for her own sexual needs. Although some married women, particularly older ones, still have such a view, the perspective is changing. The women's movement has sensitized women to seek the same sexual satisfactions enjoyed by men. This translates into making their preferences known and expecting that their sexual needs will be taken into account in terms of foreplay, positions, and frequency.

The development of reliable and safe contraception, which allows women to separate lovemaking from baby making, has also contributed to women feeling more free in sexual intercourse. Finally, the mass media—magazines, television, and radio—regularly feature dialogue on sexual issues, increasing people's awareness and the potential for communication about sexuality. Couples may sit in their living room and watch programs on pregnancy, sexually transmitted diseases, homosexuality, impotence, and sexual apathy.

Extramarital Intercourse

The terms "playing around," "cheating," and "getting some on the side" all refer to the same phenomenon—having intercourse with someone other than one's own spouse. Although it is difficult to know how many spouses have **extramarital intercourse** (there is a tendency to be dishonest about this very private aspect of one's life), various studies suggest that about 50 percent of husbands and between 20 and 40 percent of wives have at least one such encounter (Frank & Enos, 1983; Hassett, 1981; Petersen et al., 1983b). All such encounters are not alike. The nature of the event, the participants, their motives, and the consequences for themselves and their marriages vary tremendously.

Deceptive

Who Has Extramarital Intercourse?

The factors most likely to influence extramarital intercourse include the following:

- *Gender.* The incidence of husbands who have extramarital intercourse is at least 10 percent higher than wives. Reasons why women are less likely to have an affair include more limited opportunities and social constraints. Most affairs are the result of interaction in the work environment—businessmen have affairs with secretaries, pilots with flight attendants, physicians with nurses, and teachers with colleagues and students. Although married women are joining the work force in increasing numbers, about half of them still spend most of their time at home. Since an affair is dependent on knowing someone to have an affair with, the wife's contacts and opportunities are more limited.

    But even though they may have the opportunity, society is less kind to wives who have affairs than husbands. The terms slut and whore are available for the wife who has an affair, but no comparable term is used for the husband who does the same.
- *Sexual Experience.* Having had intercourse before marriage is also characteristic of those who have intercourse outside of marriage (Thompson, 1983). Not only do most premaritally sexually experienced people have more than one sexual partner, but they also learn how to break norms. Both behaviors are involved in extramarital affairs.
- *Marriage quality.* Spouses who report low marital satisfaction, infrequent intercourse, and poor quality of intercourse are more susceptible to extramarital involvements (Thompson, 1983).
- *Peer influence.* Having a close married friend who has been sexually involved in an extramarital relationship is also related to an individual becoming involved in an affair (Atwater, 1979; 1982). The greater the similarity between the friends, the greater the influence.
- *Social class.* Social class also helps to identify lovers. When defined in terms of income, occupation, and education, those at the lower end of the social-class scale are more likely to report involvement with extramarital partners (Edwards, 1973). Since blacks are more likely to have lower incomes, less prestigious jobs, and less education than whites, it is not surprising that they also report higher rates of intercourse outside of marriage.
- *Length of Marriage.* How long a person has been married is also related to having an affair. Although some spouses report having had extramarital intercourse during their honeymoon, most report that several years of married life go by before their first experience. In the *Redbook* study of 100,000 wives (Tavris & Sadd, 1977), 40 percent of those over 40 in contrast to 20 percent of those under 25 reported that they had been involved in extramarital intercourse. This age–extramarital intercourse relationship is also true of men (Petersen et al., 1983b).

- *Divorce.* Spouses who have been married previously are more prone to having an extramarital relationship, possibly because they are more experienced in breaking social constraints.

Types of Extramarital Encounters

Intercourse outside of marriage may be a brief encounter or a full-blown affair.

The Brief Encounter

The lyrics to the song "Strangers in the Night" describe two people exchanging glances who end up having intercourse "before the night is through." While the partners may see each other again, more often their sexual encounter is a "one-night stand." The typical script is to meet in a bar at a convention when away from home, have a few drinks and enough dialogue to establish that the partner is acceptable. After a while one partner suggests that they go up to one of their rooms for another drink. Going to the room often implies that intercourse will occur. After intercourse they may part or sleep together until morning. In one study (Spanier & Margolis, 1983), 28 percent of the men and 5 percent of the women said their last extramarital encounter was a one-night stand.

A variation of the one-night stand is intercourse with a prostitute or call girl. Most often the man who is away from home on a business trip will ask the bell captain at his hotel to send up a woman; or he may walk the streets until he spots a prostitute and negotiate directly with her. Sometimes he need not walk the streets but only have a drink in the hotel lobby where he may be approached by a prostitute. Regardless of how they get together, the agenda is understood and accepted by each—intercourse for money with no relationship and no follow-up.

The Affair

An affair implies a relationship with the partner beyond the sexual involvement. There are several combinations of pairs.

- *Married Man–Single Woman.* More than half of the married men in one study who were having an affair reported that the other person was a single woman (Yablonsky, 1979). The married man and single woman most often work together. The person most likely to be in a managerial position is the married male. The person assigned to work with him in a supportive role is often a single woman. Since people are most likely to have an affair with the person with whom they spend the most time in the work environment, the married man–single woman combination most frequently emerges.

Sample

This combination is particularly stressful for the single woman. She must adapt to his schedule, which means spending Saturday nights and holidays alone. She is told not to call him at home and is encouraged to keep her time free so that when he is free they can spend time together. Because she is often emotionally committed to the married man, she does not seek other relationships. "I don't mind playing third fiddle to his wife and children as long as he takes me out of the case and plays me some time," said one woman.

- *Married Man–Married Woman.* The married man–married woman is the second most frequent combination of extramarital partners. Unlike the partners in the married man–single woman combination, each understands the commitment the other has to his and her own spouse and the emotional ties to children. As long as the partners stay committed to their marriages, the affair is viewed as a loving or fun relationship with no future. When one partner becomes more involved than the other, the affair or their respective marriages may be threatened.

- *Married Woman–Single Man.* One single man said the best women were older married women because "they know more about sex." But because society traditionally has encouraged women to select men older than themselves and men to select women younger than themselves, this combination is less common.

These combinations are typical, but the single person of an extramarital pair also may be divorced or a prostitute. Also, while the married man usually wants to stay married, there are occasions in which he wants to leave his wife and marry the single woman. This may not always be the desire of the husband's lover. Fearing that their love relationship would be destroyed by marriage, one single woman said to her lover who was planning to leave his wife, "Don't do it. If you leave her and marry me, instead of being what you want, I'll be what you've got."

Intense reciprocal emotional feelings characterize most affairs. Such feelings are more a function of the conditions under which the relationship exists than any magical matching of the partners involved. For one thing, the time together is very limited. Like teenagers in love who are restricted by parents, adult lovers are restricted by their spouses and other family responsibilities. Such limited access to each other makes the time they spend together very special.

The words they say and the things they do when they are together also make for memorable experiences. Phrases like "I miss not being with you," "I think about you all the time," and "I love you" are typical. The things they do together are what couples in courtship do—dine out together, talk about the intimate details of their lives, and please each other in bed. The time the couple has together is also exclusive. The distractions of children running throughout the house and business interruptions are nonexistent or minimal.

● Married woman (early 30s) looking for discreet playmate (attached or un-) for adventurous romping and total fulfillment. NO STRINGS. ●

Someone to have an affair with does not seem to be a problem. The preceding ad placed in a national magazine received more than 2,000 responses (Foxman, 1982).

Motives for Extramarital Involvements

There are a number of reasons why spouses seek intercourse with someone other than their mate. Some of these reasons are discussed here.

Variety

One of the characteristics of marital sex is the tendency for it to become boring and monotonous. Before marriage the partners cannot seem to get enough of each other. But with constant availability, the attractiveness and excitement of intercourse seems to wane. Intercourse before marriage can be thought of as eating one corner of a Hershey chocolate bar—the desire for more is always there. Marriage is like having boxes of Hershey chocolate bars available all the time.

The **Coolidge Effect** helps to explain the need for sexual variety.

● One day the President and Mrs. Coolidge were visiting a government farm. Soon after their arrival they were taken off on separate tours. When Mrs. Coolidge passed the chicken pens she paused to ask the man in charge if the rooster copulates more than once each day. "Dozens of times" was the reply. "Please tell that to the President," Mrs. Coolidge requested. When the President passed the pens and was told about the rooster, he asked "Same hen every time?" "Oh no, Mr. President, a different one each time." The President nodded slowly, then said, "Tell that to Mrs. Coolidge."* ●

Men seem more motivated by the need for variety than women. In the *Redbook* study (Tavris & Sadd, 1977), 50 percent of the wives reported having extramarital sex with only one partner, compared with an average of seven partners for the husbands in the Yablonsky (1977) study. Although men

*From Chapter 4 "Sexual Behavior: Hard Times with the Coolidge Effect" by Gordon Bermant in *Psychological Research: The Inside Story* edited by Michael H. Siegel and H. Philip Zeigler. Copyright © 1976 by Michael H. Siegel and H. Philip Zeigler. Reprinted by permission of Harper and Row, Publishers, Inc.

The work environment often involves married people of the opposite gender spending a lot of time together. Some affairs grow out of such social structure and interpersonal interaction.

typically have more opportunity and fewer social constraints, the desire for variety is difficult to overlook.

Nevertheless, some women do seek extramarital sexual partners for reasons of variety.

● I began to realize that I had made a mistake by not having sex before marriage. It suddenly hit me that I—who was only 28—would die having had sex with only one man! I decided that was not what I wanted to do with my body, and after that the idea of having sex with another man became something possible, even desirable. (Atwater, 1979, p. 48) ●

Women need not necessarily be emotionally involved with the men with whom they have extramarital sex. Only 4 in 40 women who had had an affair described themselves as being "in love" with their first extramarital partner (Atwater, 1979).

Friendship

Some people view intercourse outside the marriage as a natural consequence of a developing relationship. "It's not that I'm crazy about sex; it's just that I enjoy relationships with other women and sex is only a part of that" is an expression that typifies this feeling. Such relationships usually develop when people work together. They share the same world 8 to 10 hours a day and over a period of time may develop good feelings for each other that eventually leads to a sexual relationship. Sometimes professors and students become friends and an affair follows (see "Academic Affairs").

Aging

A frequent motive for intercourse outside of marriage is the desire to reexperience the world of youth. Our society promotes the idea that it is good to be young and bad to be old. Sexual attractiveness is equated with youth, and having an affair may confirm to an older partner that he or she is still sexually desirable. Also, people may try to recapture the love, excitement, adventure, and romance associated with youth by having an affair. For some, it is viewed as the last opportunity to be young again.

One 47-year-old woman said she felt that life was passing her by and that "before long, it will all be over. To be in love is the most magical feeling I have ever experienced and I want to have that feeling once more before I end up in a nursing home somewhere."

Peer Influence

The desire to have an affair may be instigated by friends who have affairs and tell of the positive aspects. One man said that his coworker seemed to be "having all the fun" with various women. Since he had married his high school sweetheart and had never experienced any women other than his wife, he felt now was the time. His friend introduced him to a woman over lunch and later offered him the key to his apartment. The more people an individual knows who engage in a behavior like extramarital sex, the more likely he or she is to follow suit.

Apathetic or Uncooperative Spouse

Some people have affairs because their spouse is a poor lover. "He doesn't like sex and never has," remarked one wife. "And it frustrates me beyond description to have intercourse with him when I know it's just a duty to him. So I've found someone who likes sex and likes it with me."

Although a spouse's lack of interest in intercourse is often a reason for an affair, some go outside the marriage because their spouse will not engage in other sexual behaviors they need and enjoy. This seems more of a problem for men than women. Wives generally engage in more sexual variety (like oral sex) with their husbands than with their extramarital partners (Tavris & Sadd, 1977). In contrast, husbands report much greater sexual variation with their lovers. Almost three-quarters of the 700 husbands in the Yablonsky (1979) study said that sex with their extramarital partners was different than with their wives. Activities like fellatio and anal intercourse and sexual positions like rear entry and standing occurred more often with the extramarital partner. In many cases, these behaviors were engaged in only with extramarital partners.

Academic Affairs

Anecdotes about campus sex between college students and faculty members take two basic forms. In the first, a male professor is told by a female student that she will "do anything" for an A. The professor gives her an F, but later he is struck by the fact that despite severe limitations of intellect, the young lady is still in school. He looks up her record and finds that it is a perfect C average—eight As and eight Fs.

The second tells of the male professor who informs his female students that "there is more than one way to get an A in this class." In this one, the professor is commonly portrayed as a lecherous old coot who forces himself on defenseless women.

If any broad conclusions can be drawn from a small study I have just completed, student/faculty affairs do not all have such simple plots. I studied 25 cases of people who had had recent affairs on seven campuses in the Denver area. The majority of the students, three-quarters of them undergraduates, had been taking courses from the professors they were involved with, but I concluded that the students rarely needed to trade sex for grades; virtually all were doing well academically before the affairs started. As for the

question of who seduces whom, evidence refuted the second stereotype: although the circumstances were sometimes ambiguous, most often the students, not the professors, seem to have made the initial overtures.

Through word of mouth, I found 38 informants, most of them graduate students and faculty members. They provided the names of 111 people they knew had been involved in at least one such affair recently. I picked as diverse a sample as I could from the initial roster and asked (usually through the informants) 31 people to participate in confidential, in-depth interviews structured around a list of open-ended questions. Of those, 25 agreed—11 students and 14 professors.

For 84 percent of the 111 cases my informants had identified, relationships occurred between male teachers and female students. This pattern may predominate in part because women held fewer faculty positions than men did at the campuses my sample came from. Since these days the average undergraduate is older than in the past, the student and faculty lovers were not very far apart in age. The median age of the students I interviewed (male and female) was 27; the median age of the 11 male professors was 35; of the three female professors, 33.

Sexual involvement in these affairs usually moved from a situation in which the professor initially noticed and

(Continued)

respected the student's abilities to a period in which the two became friends. They then began to date and spend considerable time in each other's company. This phase was followed by a period, varying in length from a few months to several years, in which they were lovers. Virtually all of the liaisons were based on respect and friendship, according to the accounts I got.

The student's records revealed a median grade average of 3.7 out of a possible 4, and though some rationalizing may have been going on, nine of the 14 faculty members said they felt their student lovers were their intellectual equal. Though hardly typical, one female graduate student startled her professor/lover by getting one of her papers published in a journal that had previously rejected several of his.

Who made the first move? Only one female student said that a professor had been the one to broach the idea of sex. Five of the 11 male professors reported that the student had taken the initiative in their affairs, although only two of the eight female students said they had made the first move. Still, large portions of both groups—five professors and five female students—said the idea of intercourse had, for them, arisen mutually.

In 72 percent of the interviews, the respondents denied that any kind of favoritism involving grades had been part of the affair. In three cases, however, students got As when their cumulative test scores or reports from graders showed they had actually earned only Bs. When bias in grading did appear to be a problem, it occurred after the relationship had ended and was thus less likely to be a *quid* pro *quo* for sexual favors. Grading punishments were not usual; after a breakup, just being near each other often proved painful enough.

More commonly the professors bestowed on their student lovers academic favors other than high grades. With their influence, contacts, and glowing letters of recommendation, the professors helped the students get choice jobs, teaching and research assistantships, and entrance into highly selective graduate-degree programs. But those examples of the academic spoils system are not unique to sexual liaisons; students who develop nonsexual friendships with professors also receive such help.

The relationships varied in length from one-night encounters to marriages (for two), with an average length of three to four months. Without exception, professors and students said they thought that, in general, student/faculty sexual relationships were not a good idea. But three-quarters of them said they would become involved again under similar circumstances.

Source: From Dick Skeen, "Academic Affairs" in *Psychology Today Magazine*. Copyright © 1981. Ziff-Davis Publishing Company. Reprinted by permission.

Unhappy Marriage

It is commonly believed that people who have affairs are not happy in their marriage. But this is more likely to be true of wives than husbands. Although husbands are more likely to have an affair than wives, they usually are not "dissatisfied with the quality of their marriage or their sex life with their wife" (Yablonsky, 1979, p. 15). Rather, men seem to seek extramarital relationships as an additional life experience. This is generally not true of wives. Only 6 percent of the wives in the *Redbook* study who had been involved in an extramarital relationship reported being happy in their marriage (Tavris & Sadd, 1977). Most wives "appear to seek extramarital sex when they experience some deficit—sexual, emotional, or, perhaps, economic—in their marriage, or perceive another man as being superior to (not merely different from) their husbands (Symons, 1979, p. 238). While trapped in a bad marriage, they may not want a divorce. "So they turn to an affair or a series of them as a means of treading water, keeping the marriage afloat for the time being until their children grow up or they [the wives] earn a degree, etc." (Schaefer, 1981).

Poor Self-Concept

A bad marriage is likely to be a relationship in which the husband or wife does not feel loved by the spouse. One spouse may criticize, ignore, or reject the other sexually. As a means of surviving this psychological assault, the person may become involved in an affair to build her or his feelings of self-worth. In contrast to the rejecting or hostile spouse, the lover will communicate immense enjoyment in being with the wife or husband.

Encouragement from Spouse

"My wife does a bird imitation—she watches me like a hawk."

LAWRENCE PETER

Some spouses unknowingly influence their partners to become involved in an extramarital relationship by accusing them of such a relationship. This becomes a self-fulfilling prophecy. Such accusations are usually made by wives who have learned not to trust men. For example, the former husband of one wife was a traveling salesman who had had a string of extramarital encounters and had lied about all of them. But his wife caught him on two occasions and found evidence of other relationships. She felt she could no longer trust him. Eventually, they divorced. But with her new husband, she still had the old feelings. Although he had never given her reason to doubt him, she, nevertheless, was suspicious of his behavior, often making comments like "Where have you been?" "Are you seeing one of the women at the office?" and "I don't feel I can trust you out of my sight." The effect of this mistrust was to encourage her husband to do what she was accusing him of doing. After all, he thought, since he was being punished for having an illusory affair, he might as well have a real one.

An unhappy marriage may force one or both of the partners to seek an extramarital relationship.

Absence from Spouse

Circumstances have more to do with some extramarital relationships than specific motives. One factor that predisposes a person to an extramarital encounter is the prolonged absence from the spouse, which may make the partner particularly vulnerable to other involvements. Wives whose husbands are away for military service report that the loneliness can become unbearable. Some husbands who are away say that it is difficult to be faithful. "You've almost got to be a saint to get through two years of not having intercourse if you're going to be faithful to your spouse," one air force captain said. "Most of the guys I'm stationed with don't even try." Some spouses do not need prolonged separation to become extramaritally involved. An overnight trip or a weekend away is enough to encourage the behavior.

Weis and Slosnerick (1981) studied attitudes toward extramarital involvement when the spouse is away. They asked 321 undergraduate students the degree to which they felt each of several behaviors would be appropriate if their own spouse were out of town and the spouse of a friend were out of town. Each behavior was rated on a 5-point scale. Assigning a value of 1 meant total rejection of the idea; assigning a value of 5 meant total acceptance. The numbers to the right of each event represent the average score given by the 321 students for the appropriateness of that event.

Event	Score
Spending an evening or evenings with him/her in his/her living room	3.7
Going to the movies together	3.6
Going out to dinner at a secluded place	2.9
Dancing with him/her to the stereo	2.6
Spending a couple of days with him/her at a secluded cabin near a beautiful lake where no one would find out	1.7
Harmless necking or petting	1.6
Becoming sexually involved	1.5

While most did not approve of extramarital sexual involvement, they did approve of a variety of nonsexual extramarital behaviors.*

The Other Woman–Other Man

Where the other person is a prostitute or the sexual encounter is a one-night stand, there may be few concerns about consequences. Each forgets the other within a short time. But where the other person is involved emotionally, there may be pain at not being able to achieve more access to and commitment from the married spouse. The degree of pain experienced by the other person depends on the degree to which that person is emotionally involved with the married lover. A study of 26 "other women" (Richardson, 1979) revealed that while some wanted their man to leave his wife, others asked him not to and terminated the relationship when he did. One said, "He was going to tell his wife that night. I freaked. I panicked. I told him not to. I loved him but suddenly I saw white picket fences and the PTA. If I married him—if I married anyone—I would lose my life style" (p. 406).

Rarely does the extramarital relationship result in marriage to the other person. In a study of 108 affairs, Humphrey and Strong (1978) found that while 30 percent of affairs resulted in divorce for the married spouse, less than 4 percent of the spouses planned to marry those with whom they had had the affair. Lovers who do marry often discover that their relationship changes. When a couple has unlimited access to each other, and in the context of children and responsibilities, the emotional impact of the relationship often subsides. "When I left my spouse and moved in with my lover we stopped having fun" is a common description of what happens.

Swinging

In the traditional extramarital affair, one or both of the spouses has intercourse with someone outside the marriage without the partner's knowledge.

*Source: D. L. Weis and M. Slosnerick, Attitudes toward sexual and nonsexual involvements among a sample of college students, *Journal of Marriage and the Family*, May 1981, p. 352. Copyright © 1981 by the National Council on Family Relations. Reprinted by permission.

Swinging is another form of extramarital intercourse in which the spouses of one marriage or pair-bonded relationship have sexual relations with the spouses or partners of another relationship. Swinging is different from an affair in that the former implies no deception (both partners know of the extramarital encounter) and involves the participation of both partners. But swingers may differ in the degree of emotional relationship they consider appropriate with the other partners. "Recreational" swingers believe that neither partner should become emotionally involved with the other individuals or couples they meet. In contrast, "relational" swingers may build and maintain close and affectionate relationships with those with whom they swing, usually as a foursome. There are also "utopian" swingers, sometimes members of a commune, who feel that loving others may include sexual sharing and should not be viewed as threatening to the primary partner.

Our focus in this section is on recreational swingers. In practice, this means a husband and wife who meet another couple to trade sexual partners. The husband will have intercourse with the woman of the other couple and the wife will have intercourse with the man of the other couple. Neither is to establish an emotional relationship with the other partners. In some cases, only one spouse of a swinging pair will actually engage in intercourse with someone else. An example is a wife whose husband had a debilitating illness. He encouraged her to find sexual partners who would come to their home where the pair would then make love. Although some husbands like to observe their wives have sex with others, this husband preferred to drink coffee and watch TV while his wife and the other man were in the bedroom.

Who Swings?

Swinging is rare. Less than 5 percent of married men and women report that they have been involved in swinging, and most of these have done so on only one occasion (Murstein, 1978). While the stereotypes suggest that swingers are sexual freaks, political radicals, or nonconformists, a consistent profile emerges from the various studies that have been conducted. Swingers are typically "a middle-class, middle-aged American couple, with children, who have been married 10 to 20 years and live in an urban or suburban area, and who, in most aspects of their life style, political activity, and behavior are conservative, stable, and conventional" (Spanier, 1979, p. 15). However, one study of 16 female and 14 male swingers (Duckworth & Levitt, 1982), revealed that "there are also clear indications that some swingers tend to be psychologically not normal, including some who appear to be seriously emotionally disturbed, some who may be substance abusers, and some who have serious sexual problems."* The basis for these observations was scores of the swingers on the Minnesota Multiphasic Personality Inventory (MMPI), which is widely used by psychologists to diagnose psychopathology.

*Reprinted with the permission of Jane Duckworth from "A Personality Analysis of a 'Swinger' Club" by Jane Duckworth and Eugene E. Levitt. 1982.

The reason spouses give for swinging is that they are bored with both the sexual and nonsexual aspects of their marriage. Rather than cheat on each other, they view swinging as a way to bring excitement into their relationship—an excitement they can share without either partner feeling dishonest or betrayed. The husband usually initiates the couple's involvement into swinging. It is not uncommon that he soon wants to drop out and the wife wants to continue.

Becoming Involved in Swinging

There are a number of ways couples may become involved in swinging. One way is by responding to an advertisement in one of several magazines, like *Select* or *Adam*, that cater to swingers. Some ads designed to attract potential swingers read as follows.

● Broad-minded responsible couple, he 29, she 23, seeking other couples or single men and women for adult fun. Photography buffs, many varied interests. Photo and phone will insure prompt reply. Will send same.

Lovely, stacked swinger, 27, divorced twice because the boys couldn't keep up. Like everything with everybody. French culture a special liking. All attractive men and good looking bi-gals write. I want fun, not money.

Love intimate relationships with extra-special pairs or singles built upon sincere and sensuous friendship. We're twentyish, attractive, considerate, and aim to please. Not far out but not afraid to explore (B&D included). ●

Some of these advertisements include special terminology, such as B&D (bondage and discipline), French culture (cunnilingus and fellatio), Roman culture (orgies), Greek culture (anal intercourse), TV (Transvestite), S&M (sadomasochism) and A-C D-C (bisexual), dominatrix (dominant woman partner), and English culture (bondage, spanking, and sadomasochism).

The publishers of some swinger magazines also sell memberships in organizations or clubs for swingers. There are about 300 swing clubs and publications in the United States (Singer, 1982). These organizations sponsor parties, which are often held in hotel suites complete with buffet dinner and a band. Such parties provide an opportunity for swingers to get together, exchange phone numbers, and set up future meetings or, in some cases, a get-together that evening.

Swingers may meet other couples in bars that cater to swingers, particularly in large urban centers. But the way most swingers meet is through their own networks. Just as video game players know other players, coupon users know other users, and golfers know other golfers, so swingers know other swingers. Once a couple become involved in swinging, they soon learn about others in the same life style or how to make contact with them, passing information and phone numbers to others through mutual consent.

Swinging not only involves finding others to have sex with but also it means developing a new way of looking at sex, love, and marriage. Since one of the rules of swinging is not to get emotionally involved with one's sex partner, the woman especially must learn to separate sex and love. This is difficult for some women as most have been socialized to have sex only in the context of an affectionate or love relationship. Meanwhile, the husband must also give up the traditional idea that his wife is his exclusive sexual property and overcome his feelings of jealousy when she is having intercourse with another man.

What Swingers Do

Once a couple arrange a sexual encounter with another, one of two agendas may be followed. They may have an open or a closed party. An open party implies that after eating, dancing, and drinking in the early evening, all of the couples will take their clothes off (the host usually disrobes as the cue) and stay in one room where the sexual encounters take place.

In a closed party the spouses go to separate bedrooms with someone else's spouse and agree to meet back in the same room. The sexual behaviors in the closed party include fellatio, cunnilingus, and intercourse. These same behaviors also occur in the open party except the women may provide cunnilingus for each other. Fellatio among men is rare, as is anal intercourse (Bartell, 1972).

Sexually Open Relationships

Couples who swing have **sexually open relationships**—the spouses know of and approve of their partner having intercourse with others— but not all spouses in sexually open relationships are swingers. Some spouses do not like the swinging environment. Rather, they prefer to establish a relationship with someone independent of the swingers network. They still have intercourse with someone who is not their mate, and their spouse is aware of their sexual encounters. But the spouse does not go with them and they do not market themselves as a couple. They simply agree not to limit their sex lives to each other, at least for a while. Of 38 individuals who reported that they were involved in sexually open relationships, only one still had a sexually open marriage two years later. The others returned to monogamous relationships with their spouses (Watson, 1981).

"I haven't known any open marriages, though quite a few have been ajar."

BOB HOPE

Sample

Effects of Swinging–Sexually Open Relationships

Spouses report both positive and negative effects from swinging–sexually open relationships. Most of the spouses in 50 sexually open marriages reported that their extramarital relationships were satisfying—both emotionally and sexually (Buunk, 1980). Many swingers point to an improved marriage relationship. Before swinging their marriage was dull; they did few things together and sex was humdrum. Swinging gave them an activity to share. Writing ads, answering correspondence, getting dressed up, meeting new people were things they enjoyed doing together, and being with a new sexual partner was exciting and also enhanced their martial enjoyment. In a comparison of 100 swingers and 100 nonswingers, the marital adjustment for both groups was the same (Gilmartin, 1974). In a similar study comparing 130 couples in sexually open marriages with 130 couples in sexually exclusive marriages, the author concluded, "Sexually open marriages are not more poorly adjusted than sexually exclusive marriages (Rubin, 1982, p. 107). Furthermore, in a study of 17 sexually open marriages, 65 percent reported increased satisfaction with their marriage (Knapp, 1976).

But there is a less positive side to swinging. Couples who dropped out of swinging said the jealousy and guilt were more than they could cope with (Denfeld, 1974). "I thought I could be mature and open about it," one spouse said. "But when I saw my spouse walk naked into another room with a stranger, I felt sick." Others say they dropped out of swinging because it was too boring or they were disappointed with it.

Postmarital Intercourse

Postmarital intercourse by the divorced and widowed is the last type of intercourse situation that we consider in this chapter. First, we look at the situation of the formerly married.

Intercourse among the Divorced

About two and a half million people get divorced every year (U.S. Department of Health and Human Services, 1983). Most will have intercourse within one year of being separated from their spouse. The meanings of intercourse for the separated or divorced vary. For many, intercourse is a way to reestablish, indeed repair, their crippled self-esteem. Divorce is often a shattering emotional experience. The loss of a lover, the disruption of daily routine, and the awareness of a new and negative label "divorced person" all converge on the individual. Questions like "What did I do wrong?" "Am I a failure?" and "Is there anybody out there to love me again?" loom in the mind of the divorced. One way to feel loved, at least temporarily, is through sex. Being held by another and being told that one feels good provides some evidence that one is desirable. Since divorced people may be particularly vulnerable, intercourse is a life raft they may reach for. "In most cases the test results [of intercourse] are positive, and this is not only reassuring but positively transforming: those who feel 'dead below the waist,' 'unmanly,' 'unwomanly,' or 'utterly worthless,' are suddenly alive, proud, confident, able to like themselves again" (Hunt & Hunt, 1977, p. 146).

While some use intercourse to mend their self-esteem, others use it to test their sexual adequacy. The divorced person may have been told by the former spouse that he or she was an inept lover. One man said that his wife used to make fun of him because he was occasionally impotent. Intercourse with a new partner who did not belittle him reassured him of his sexual adequacy so that impotence ceased to be a problem. A woman described how her husband would sneer at her weight and say that no man would ever want her because she was so fat. But she found men who thought her attractive and for whom her weight was not a problem. Other divorced men and women say that what their spouses did not like, their new partners view as turn-ons. The result is a renewed sense of sexual adequacy and desirability.

Beyond these motives for intercourse, many divorced people simply enjoy the sexual freedom their divorce state offers. Freed from the guilt that spouses experience when having extramarital intercourse, the divorced are free to have intercourse with whomever they choose. Most choose to do so with a variety of partners. In the *Playboy* survey, divorced men and women reported having an average of 30 and 22 sexual partners; respectively. These averages were higher than those averages among singles, marrieds, remarrieds, and live-ins (Petersen et al., 1983b).

Sample Deceptive

Before getting remarried, most divorced people seem to go through predictable stages of sexual expression. The initial impact of the separation is followed by a variable period of emotional pain. It is during this time that the divorced look to intercourse for intimacy to soothe some of the pain, although this is rarely achieved.

This looking-for-intimacy-through-intercourse stage overlaps with the feeling-of-freedom stage and the divorced person's desire to explore a wider range of sexual partners and behaviors than marriage provided. "I was a virgin at marriage and was married for 12 years. I've never had sex with anyone but my spouse so I'm curious to know what other people are like sexually," one divorced person said.

But the divorced person soon tires of one-night stands, casual sex, and seeking intimacy through intercourse. One man said that he had been through 22 partners since his divorce a year ago. He likened his situation to that of a person in a revolving door that is in motion but isn't going anywhere. "I want to get in a relationship with someone who cares about me and vice versa." The pattern is typical. Most divorced people initially use sex to restore their ailing self-esteem and to explore sexual parameters. But they soon drift toward sex within the context of an affectionate love relationship (Patton & Wallace, 1979). Within five years, 80 percent have remarried.

Intercourse among the Widowed

The 12 million widowed in the United States are different from the divorced in their sexual behavior. In general, widowed men and women have intercourse less frequently than those who are divorced. A major reason is the lack of an available partner (Starr & Weiner, 1982). But others have intercourse less frequently because they feel that they are "cheating" on the deceased. "It's a guilty feeling I get," expressed one widower, "that I shouldn't want to get involved with someone else and that I shouldn't enjoy it."

Social expectations also do not support sexual expression among the widowed. They are considered "too old" for sex. In the *Playboy* survey of sexual behavior no mention was made of sexuality among the widowed. The lack of an available sexual partner, personal feelings of "cheating" on the deceased, and an unsupportive social context seem to conspire against the widowed. When a group of widows (ages 67 to 78) were asked how they coped with their sexual feelings when they had no partner, they responded,

- Only by keeping busy. Keep occupied with various activities and friends.
- Do physical exercise. Have many interests, hobbies.
- We just have to accept it and interest ourselves in other things.
- By turning to music or other arts, painting, dancing is excellent . . . using nurturant qualities, loving pets, the elderly, shut-ins. Reading, hiking . . . lots more.
- My mind controls my sex desires. (Starr & Weiner, 1982, pp. 165-167)

Other widows, particularly young widows, enjoy active sex lives with a new partner. "Just because your spouse is gone doesn't mean you're dead," said one 43-year-old widow. "I figure I've got half my life left and I'm not about to give up sex yet."

Widowers have more access to sexual partners because there is an abundance of widows competing for a small number of men at later ages. And since our society supports male agressiveness, widowers are more likely to initiate contacts than widows.

Summary

Sexual intercourse is a method of communication. People initiate intercourse for a number of reasons. These motivations most frequently include the desire to feel emotionally close, to express love, and to have sensual fun with one's partner.

Intercourse also occurs in different interpersonal contexts: before marriage, during marriage, outside marriage, and after marriage. Premarital intercourse is significant because it represents first intercourse for most people and it does not have the legitimacy of marital intercourse. Most people who have premarital intercourse do so with relatively few partners and in the context of an affectionate love relationship. The effect of premarital intercourse on the couple's relationship is minimal.

Since more than 90 percent of people in the United States marry, marriage is the social context for most intercourse experiences. Marital intercourse is the most socially approved form of sex. The women's movement, contraception, and the mass media have combined to make spouses feel more free in intercourse. But its frequency also declines with the length of the marriage.

Various studies suggest that about 50 percent of husbands and between 20 and 40 percent of wives have extramarital sex. But the nature of the event, the participants, their motives, and the consequences for themselves and their marriages vary tremendously.

Swinging is another form of extramarital intercourse. Unlike the traditional affair, the partner knows and participates in the encounters with the spouse. Although husbands often pressure their wives to become involved in swinging, it is frequently the wives who want to continue when the husbands want to stop. For most couples swinging represents a temporary phase in their relationship.

Intercourse among the divorced and widowed are two types of postmarital intercourse. The divorced typically have very active sex lives that include a number of sexual partners. But the period of casual sex among the divorced usually dissipates and they drift into monogamous relationships. Eighty percent remarry.

The widowed are usually more socially isolated and have more difficulty finding sexual partners than the divorced. Widows more than widowers often resign themselves to diverting their interest with hobbies and other interests.

Key Terms

sexual intercourse
premarital intercourse
marital intercourse
extramarital intercourse

Coolidge Effect
swinging
sexually open relationships
postmarital intercourse

Issues in Debate and Future Directions

One of the more controversial issues in human sexuality is the degree to which extramarital sexual intercourse in the traditional relationship has positive or negative consequences for the spouses and their marriage. This debate and a forecast of extramarital sexual behavior follow.

Extramarital Sex: Does It Strengthen or Destroy a Marriage?

Since having intercourse outside the marriage affects the respective spouses and their marriage, we examine each in detail.

Effect on Spouse Having Affair
Guilt, fear of discovery, the anxiety of managing two relationships, cost, and risk of getting a sexually transmitted disease are among the potential negative consequences of extramarital intercourse for the spouse having the affair. Guilt over the dishonesty and deceit head the list. Some feel it is wrong to have intercourse with someone other than their spouse. For some, depression follows an encounter, since it is viewed as a negative aspect of self: "I am someone who will cheat on my spouse." But such feelings are also related to the frequency of occurrence. Those who have a string of extramarital encounters seem less bothered by guilt. Sixty percent of 40 women who had had extramarital intercourse went on to have additional experiences with other partners (Atwater, 1979).

Some spouses experience positive consequences from their extramarital involvements. These may include improved self-esteem, a break from the routine of marriage, and renewed sexual vigor or energy. Repeatedly, spouses who have affairs say they feel good in the new relationship. "I felt wanted, loved, desired, and sexually attractive," mused one wife. "And every time I was with him I felt I was someone special." In contrast to the spouse who has become familiar and inattentive, the lover is new and exciting—and makes the partner feel this way, too.

Because the relationship with the lover is new, the sexual experience may be interpreted as superior. Husbands often say they experience a sense of renewed potency with a new partner (the Coolidge Effect?). Although wives are less likely to have an orgasm in their extramarital encounter than in their marriage (Tavris & Sadd, 1977), the sexual experience may be viewed as better.

Effect on Partner Discovering Affair
"How could you do this to me?" reflects the pain and disillusionment of the partner who finds out about the spouse's affair. This reaction has the sanction of society. Extramarital intercourse is still called adultery. Like conspiring with a thief to rob their home, the adulterer is seen as conspiring with another to invade the privacy of the marriage. Also, as we noted earlier, the partner may develop a deep sense of distrust, which often lingers in the marriage long after the affair is over. One woman said that whenever her husband was late or away on a business trip she had visions of him being involved with another woman. "I just don't trust him anymore," she said.

But sometimes knowledge of the spouse's affair can have a positive effect. The partners may become sensitive to the fact that they have a problem in their marriage. While most will try to resolve their marriage problems on their own, some will seek marriage therapy. "For us," one spouse said, "the affair helped us to look at our marriage and to make it a place we both want to be." The thesis of the book *Beyond Affairs* (Vaughn & Vaughn, 1980) is that couples need not view the discovery of an affair as the end of their marriage but as a new beginning.

Another potential positive effect if the partner finds out is that the partner may become more sensitive to the needs of the spouse and more motivated to satisfy them. The partner may realize that if spouses are not satisfied at home, they will go elsewhere. One husband said that his wife had an affair because he was too busy with his work and did not spend time with her. Her affair taught him that she had alternatives—other men who would love her emotionally and sexually—and so to ensure that he did not lose her, he became intent on satisfying her.

Effect on Marriage   Whether extramarital sex strengthens or destroys the marriage relationship may also be related to which spouse has the affair. In a study of 51 husbands and 57 wives (Humphrey & Strong, 1978) not married to each other, who sought counseling because of their respective involvement in an extramarital sexual relationship, the researchers observed:

> The primary difference seems to be that wives' participation in an extramarital relationship is associated with more serious questioning of their desire to remain in their current marriage. The wives express a strong interest in clarifying their own needs, exploring the unhappiness in their present marriage, and deciding whether or not to dissolve their present marriage. Husbands who have participated in an extramarital relationship, by contrast, appear to be concerned more with working through uncomfortable feelings of guilt, anxiety, or depression and with returning the marriage to its former state. They seem less likely to become involved with serious questioning of the viability of their present marriages. (p. 2)

Of the marriages represented in this study, about 30 percent ended in divorce over the extramarital issue. In another study (Spanier & Margolis, 1983), 7 in 10 of the spouses said that outside sex was a result, not a cause, of marital problems. Husbands are much less forgiving of wives who have extramarital encounters than the reverse. Only 1 in 10 husbands compared with 8 in 10 wives is likely to overlook or forgive the extramarital relationship of their partner (Sexual Survey No. 43, 1981).

One researcher (Britton, 1982) observed that extramarital affairs tend to have the least negative consequences for a person's marriage under the following circumstances.

1. The spouses have a solid marriage relationship. The one who has the affair has a strong emotional commitment to the mate. The lover is viewed as short term only, not as a potential replacement for the mate.
2. The spouses compartmentalize easily. The one who has the affair can keep the lover and the mate separated in time, place, and thought. Memories of the experiences with the lover are not allowed to blend into the relationship with the spouse so that behavior is adversely affected.
3. The spouses avoid disclosure. Disclosure is like a rattlesnake in the relationship, which strikes the spouse and introduces a deadly venom. Few spouses can tolerate the information that their partner had or is having a sexual relationship with someone else.
4. The spouses limit contacts. Frequent contacts with one or more lovers take the energy away from the marriage and increase the chance of getting caught.
5. The spouses seek recreation only. Sexual experiences that are for spontaneous recreation do the least damage. Those that are carefully orchestrated for emotional impact take time and energy away from the mate.*

Future Directions

Regarding the future of extramarital encounters, the proportion of married women having affairs will increase. As more wives join the labor force (now about 55 percent), they will have increasingly frequent contact with more men. Also, since women are having fewer babies, they will be less homebound. The result will be more freedom and opportunity to become involved in extramarital encounters.

Some evidence suggests that this trend has begun. In a survey of sexual behavior among *Cosmopolitan* readers (Wolfe, 1982), 40 percent of the responding wives reported an affair. But among the wives who were over 35 years of age, 60 percent reported such involvement.

*Source: Tim Britton, Lenoir Community College, Kinston, North Carolina, Personal communication, 1982. Reprinted by permission.

Chapter Eight

Orgasm

This explosive discharge of neuromuscular tensions at the peak of sexual response is what we identify as orgasm.

ALFRED C. KINSEY, *SEXUAL BEHAVIOR IN THE HUMAN FEMALE*

Chapter Eight

Orgasm is a mind-altering, ecstatic, transcendent experience that takes us to a place where time stops. At least, that is the stereotypical idea of the orgasmic experience. Although most people have had an orgasm (Table 8.1), it is not a predictable happening that feels the same to all people. Indeed, the most reliable fact about orgasm is that it is a highly variable experience.

In this chapter we examine the various attitudes people have toward orgasm, the sources of orgasm, and the sexual response cycle of which orgasm is a part. In addition, we explore several related issues such as the existence of the G spot, multiple orgasms, faking orgasm, and what happens after orgasm.

Although this chapter focuses on orgasm, we recognize that orgasm is only one aspect of sexual experience. Many people have been taught that orgasm is the goal of sexual interaction. But this preoccupation may interfere with our ability to appreciate and enjoy other good sexual feelings. It is with this idea, that orgasm is not the end all of sexual involvement, that we begin.

Table 8.1 Percentage of Females and Males Experiencing Orgasm Under Different Conditions[a]

Condition	Women[b]	Men
Orgasm while masturbating	90%	Almost 100%
Orgasm from dreaming	40%	80%
Orgasm regularly during intercourse	30%	Almost 100%
Orgasm during first intercourse experience	10%	Almost 100%
Orgasm from breast stimulation	5%	None
Never experienced orgasm (usually have never masturbated)	5–10%	Almost none
Multiple orgasms	50%	5%
Multiple ejaculations	No data	20%

[a]Percentages are derived from research presented elsewhere in this chapter. The exception is source for "Orgasm during first intercourse experience," found in Huk (1979).

[b]While most research has been conducted on white women, black women have similar orgasmic percentages (Fisher, 1980).

Attitudes Toward Orgasm

People differ in the way they view their orgasmic experiences. Some of these attitudes are described here.

Orgasm as an Emotional Bond

"When my partner and I find ourselves floating after orgasm, we feel an emotional closeness that is very fulfilling," reported one person. "And while we don't need an orgasm to feel close, it brings us even closer." This person's experience illustrates one of the more common attitudes about orgasm. The emotional bonding capability of orgasm is seen as giving the partners a special feeling about each other and their relationship.

Orgasm as Release of Sexual Tension

Some people view orgasm primarily as a physiological release that makes them feel good. "After several days of no orgasm, I feel tense and anxious. Orgasm helps me to relax and puts me in a good frame of mind," said one lover. "Getting my rocks off" is a common phrase used by men that refers to this view of orgasm as release. But women also may view it as release. "No pill in my cabinet is as good as the one I take in bed," noted one woman. "It puts me to sleep—sound asleep."

Orgasm as Fun

Orgasm to others is for fun, like a ride on the water log at an amusement park. "My reason for seeking orgasm is simple," said one respondent. It is the most fun thing I do. Nothing else is even close." Since much of life is spent engaging in routine activity, orgasm is an exciting break from the ordinary.

Orgasm as Procreation

Some husbands anxious to father a child look at orgasm in terms of its procreation potential. "I've wanted a child all my life and now Judy and I are going to try and conceive one," stated a husband. The ejaculation that deposits semen near the woman's uterus is seen as symbolic of procreation. While a woman's orgasm has nothing to do with her capacity to get pregnant, she may view her partner's orgasm as the event that will impregnate her and start her on the way toward motherhood.

Orgasm as a Goal

Some view orgasm as the goal of sexual interaction. "If I don't climax" said one man, "there's no reason to start anything." Others disagree. "Orgasm as a goal, as an objective, or even as a barometer of a good sexual encounter is placing too much emphasis on physical feelings" said one woman. "It's the relationship I have with my partner that's important. If it's a good one, an orgasm is nice, but not essential." The latter perspective places the orgasmic event in the context of the larger relationship and ensures that the relationship is not dependent on it. In one study of 42 couples (Waterman & Chiauzzi, 1982), both men and women reported higher levels of sexual pleasure when orgasm did *not* occur. The idea of sex without orgasm is not new. For 2,000 years the Chinese have recognized that greater sexual energy is produced when one or both partners withhold orgasm (Gross, 1981).

Sources of Orgasm

Just as people view orgasm differently, they achieve it in different ways. Two primary ways are physical and cognitive.

Physical Sources of Orgasm

The primary physical source of orgasm for men is the penis; for women the primary sources are the clitoris, the vagina, and the breasts.

Penile Orgasm

Male orgasm most often occurs in response to manual, oral, or vaginal stimulation of the penis. Manual stimulation may be by a partner or by masturbation. Both methods of stimulation are capable of inducing intense orgasms.

But orgasm resulting from fellatio and intercourse may also be intense. One man compared the two experiences.

● An orgasm from fellatio is much more strenuous because as your lover's mouth is sucking on your penis while you're coming it feels like your soul is pumping right out. This is a great feeling, but I enjoy an orgasm from intercourse more. The orgasm is much more relaxed because it is your own muscles pumping the semen out. Orgasm from fellatio confuses me because at times I don't know if the semen is coming out because the partner is sucking it out or my own muscles are pumping it out. ●

Clitoral Orgasm

As noted in Chapter 3, the clitoris exists solely for the purpose of sexual pleasure. It has no eliminative or reproductive function. Stimulating the clitoris is
the most reliable way for a woman to achieve an orgasm. In one study (Clifford, 1978b), 100 percent of the women reported that they had achieved an
orgasm by stimulating their clitoris. A similar observation was made by Masters and Johnson (1979b). They reported that a woman failed to experience
an orgasm less than 1 percent of the time if she was getting stimulation of her
clitoral area through masturbation, cunnilingus, or manual stimulation by
the partner.

Some women feel that something is wrong with them if they do not orgasm through intercourse alone. This idea is a heritage from Sigmund Freud,
who suggested that orgasm by clitoral stimulation was a sign of immature
psychosexual development. Clitorally orgasmic women, Freud said, were
not truly feminine women. Rather, they were rebelling against their "place"
in society by refusing to have an orgasm through vaginal stimulation (Freud,
1965). Although this idea has been discredited, many writers promoted it in
marriage manuals throughout the forties, fifties, and early sixties. Today responsible writers and professionals encourage women to view clitoral orgasms in positive terms. "There is nothing magic about a 'Look, mom, no
hands!' orgasm that automatically makes it better, more appropriate, more
proper, or more 'mature'" (Bragonier & Bragonier, 1979, p. 11). "The need
for direct stimulation of the clitoris to attain orgasm during sexual relations is
normal" (Wilcox & Hager, 1980, p. 165). One woman reflected on her orgasmic experience as follows.

● In having an orgasm through masturbation, I must first be mentally "psyched" to
have one. I have to want or need one. I "strive" for it—it doesn't just happen. At
this stage I fantasize or, more commonly, "relive" past sexual experiences
(generally those involving oral sex). Within two to three minutes, I lubricate and I
begin to massage and stimulate my entire vaginal (and sometimes anal) region.
My mind focuses on what my fingers are doing and the sensations (tingling,
pressure) and the feelings (warm, wet). My back arches and my legs and feet
stiffen. Often tingles run up and down my spine and my nipples become erect.

My finger eventually rubs only the right (the most sensitive) side of my clitoris. I
generally massage my breasts with my other hand. As I near climax, my
breathing quickens, my leg and buttock muscles tighten, and I rub my clitoris
harder and faster. At the moment of climax I feel a "pop" or an intense burst of
"pleasurable pain." My clitoris tingles and my entire mons region throbs.
Lubricant flows from my vagina. The area is then too sensitive to touch for two or
three minutes. If I desire another orgasm at this point, it takes considerably less
time than the first (two or three minutes for the second versus 10 to 20 for the
first). Often the second orgasm is more intense than the first.

After the orgasm it takes about five minutes for my breathing to return to
normal. Orgasms can either be relaxing or energizing depending upon my mood

and the time of day or night. Either way, orgasms provide an incredible release of tension.

With a partner, the physical sensations of orgasm are similar. However, it takes longer for me to climax (20 to 30 minutes) since his tongue or fingers move more slowly and he applies less pressure than I do. I don't fantasize when I am with a partner. If I am having trouble becoming aroused (which happens if I'm with someone I'm not particularly attracted to), I concentrate on the physical sensations rather than the man doing the act. ●

In a study of 138 women (Myers et al., 1983), orgasmic responsivity was found to be positively correlated with the level of noncoital heterosexual satisfaction, gratification from masturbation, and comfort with heterosexual contact. In other words, those women who were stimulated by means other than intercourse (manually or orally) and who felt comfortable with their partners were the most likely to orgasm.

Vaginal Orgasm

Although most women can climax through direct clitoral stimulation, only about 30 percent can do so regularly during intercourse alone (Frank & Enos, 1983; Wolfe, 1982). Those who do climax during intercourse often position themselves (usually on top of the man) so that their clitoris receives stimulation by rubbing against the man's pubic area.

There is some controversy about clitoral versus vaginal orgasms. In the recent past sex educators and therapists have told women that their clitoris is the only receptor sensitive to erotic pleasure and is the source of orgasm. In contrast, the vagina has been described as devoid of orgasmic potential. Kinsey et al. (1970), after finding that most women were insensitive to touch in their vaginal walls concluded, "it (vagina) is of minimum importance in contributing to the erotic responses of the female" (p. 592).

But Dr. Carol Ellison (1980) disagrees with Kinsey, who assumed that a light touch from a probe in an unaroused vagina is similar to the thrusting of a penis in the vagina of a woman who is highly aroused. She cites LeMon Clark, who in 1970 noted that moving the cervix moves the uterus and the broad ligaments, both of which are covered with the peritoneum (the abdominal cavity), some of the most sensitive tissue in the body. The peritoneum provides a much broader base for sensation in the lower abdominal area than does mere stimulation of the clitoris alone.

Ellison surveyed 70 women who reported climaxing at least half of the time during intercourse without direct clitoral stimulation. Seven in 10 of these women reported sensation beyond the outer one-third of their vaginas (where Kinsey said feeling was almost nonexistent) and half reported that deep internal sensations were one of their triggers to orgasm.

Several of the women commented as follows.

● My orgasms have always come from intercourse. I was 38 before I even heard of a clitoral orgasm, and then I felt like a freak. (a 50-year-old woman)

When the women's movement came along with all the talk about the clitoris, I began to think something was wrong with me. (a 40-year-old woman)

Last year when I took a human sexuality course, I was too embarrassed to speak up and say I don't turn on by being manually stimulated. I don't even particularly like it. (a 30-year-old woman)* ●

Still other women report that their orgasms are triggered by stimulation of the front wall of their vagina—the area just inside the vagina (Hoch, 1980). This area also has been referred to as the **Grafenberg spot** after Ernest Grafenberg, the gynecologist who first reported it. But not all researchers have been able consistently to find such a spot. In one study, (Goldberg et al., 1983), two female gynecologists examined 11 women to ascertain the presence of the G spot. "Both gynecologists claimed to be able to locate a sensitive area in 4 of the 11 women. The area seemed to be located in the 11 P.M. to 1 A.M. region of the vagina, ranged in diameter from 2 to 4 centimeters, and consistently swelled when continuously palpated. The drawings of the gynecologists revealed congruence in that they tended to agree on the shape, size, and location of the area in the four women" (p. 34). No such sensitive area was identified in the other 7 women.

Hoch (1983) finds no evidence for the existence of the G spot and advises against the use of the term.

The "G spot" does *not* exist as such, and the potential professional use of this term would be not only incorrect, but also misleading . . . The *entire* extent of the anterior wall of the vagina (rather than *one* specific spot), as well as the more deeply situated tissues, *including* the urinary bladder and urethral region, are extremely sensitive, being richly endowed with nerve endings . . . The female orgasm results from successful stimulation of the "sensory arm of the female orgasmic reflex" consisting of clitoral *and* anterior wall simultaneous stimulation (same innervation) or the separate stimulation of either one of these sensory components. (p. 166)

For the woman who is interested in exploring the location of her own so called G spot, Doctors John Perry and Beverly Whipple offer the following instructions on how to find it.

Every woman has one, but most of us just don't know it. Where is it, you ask? First off, the Grafenberg spot is located just under the bladder, near the urethra, about halfway between the backside of the pubic bone and the front edge of the cervix, about one inch beneath the vaginal surface. It varies in size from smaller

*Reprinted with permission of the author, Dr. Carol Rinkleib Ellison, from *A critique of the clitoral model of female sexuality*. Presented at the Annual Meeting of the American Psychological Association, 1980.

than a dime to larger than a half dollar, although in most women it is about the size of a nickel.

How do you find it? Unless you can easily contort yourself into a pretzel, you'll find it easier to locate it on somebody else first (if you're a male, it's essential!).

1. The best position to initially find the spot is with the woman lying on her back, knees apart and partly elevated.
2. Place one or two fingers in the vagina, palm up.
3. Locate the backside of the pubic bone, directly behind the clitoris.
4. Slide your finger back into the vagina to locate the cervix (that's the end of the uterus which sticks into the vagina and feels like the glans of an erect penis).
5. Halfway between these two points, on the upper wall of the vagina, begin to press with a gentle but firm pressure.
6. When you've hit the spot, the woman will immediately know it. The first sensation is one of a need to urinate, but that is quickly replaced by feelings of pleasure.
7. At this point, the spot begins to swell in size and its shape becomes much more definable.
8. After a few minutes of stroking the spot, the woman's level of sexual arousal becomes unmistakable.

Once you are able to recognize the spot, you can stimulate your own Grafenberg spot with a small vibrator which is inserted within the vagina. Also note that if the woman is utilizing a diaphragm for contraception, it will be difficult to locate the spot since it is obscured by the rim of the diaphragm. Many women report that the diaphragm interferes with vaginal stimulation during intercourse by making it more difficult for the penis to reach the Grafenberg spot.*

Although there are no physiological distinctions between orgasms originating in the clitoris and vagina, women often report that there are differences in the way each feels. When 100 women were asked, "Is there a difference between clitoral and vaginal orgasms?" half said "yes" and one-fourth said they were "unsure." Only one in four said there were no differences (Clifford, 1978a). Clitoral orgasms are usually described as being more intense, stronger, sharper, and localized. In contrast, vaginal orgasms are more diffuse and are associated with a more generalized emotional satisfaction.

Women differ in which type of orgasm they prefer. Clifford's respondents had a preference for orgasm during intercourse because of the emotional feelings they experienced. Hite's respondents (1977) described it as a vaginal ache—a desire to be filled. But Fisher (1973) studied female orgasms in hundreds of women over a 10-year period and concluded that most (6 in 10) preferred orgasm from masturbation because it produced a higher state of excitement.

Orgasm from Breast Stimulation

Stimulation of the woman's breasts may also result in orgasm. Although the occurrence is rare, women have reported that breast feeding their babies has induced orgasm (Masters & Johnson, 1966). Breast play alone resulted in or-

*Created by Health Technology, Inc. 50 Lawn Avenue, Portland, Maine 04103 © 1981 Forum International. Reprinted with the permission of John Perry.

gasm for two women being stimulated by their lesbian lovers (Masters & Johnson, 1979). Orgasm resulting from self-stimulation or from a heterosexual partner is also possible. "I get very excited," said one woman, "when my lover runs his tongue around my nipples and sucks them—sometimes I climax."

Not all women derive pleasure from breast stimulation. One said, "Men I've gone out with used to pinch and squeeze my breasts and I hated it. I wonder how they would like it if I did that to their penis" (Ayalah & Weinstock, 1979, p. 71).

Whether orgasm occurs through clitoral, vaginal, or breast stimulation, many women report the importance of their partner's patience, understanding, and willingness to experiment to achieve a satisfactory orgasmic experience. For this, communication between the partners must be open, clear, and honest.

Cognitive Sources of Orgasm

Our thoughts, in the form of dreams and statements about our love feelings, may result in orgasm. (Fantasies, which also may lead to orgasm, are discussed in Chapter 9.)

Dreams

Both men and women may have an orgasm during a dream. In the Kinsey studies approximately 80 percent of the males and 40 percent of the females reported that they had experienced orgasm while dreaming. While it has been known that men experience cyclic episodes of arousal (such as erec-

Both genders may orgasm while dreaming.

tion) during REM (dream) sleep, more recently it has been confirmed that women manifest similar episodes throughout the night of sexual excitation and arousal (such as vaginal vascular engorgement) during this same sleep stage (Fisher et al., 1983). The term used to describe male orgasm during sleep is **nocturnal emission** or "wet dream." The term for the corresponding female experience is nocturnal orgasm.

Orgasms from dreams occur infrequently. Of all the orgasms men and women experience, those from dreams account for only a small percentage (2–8 percent for males, 2–3 percent for females). Those who do have orgasms while dreaming have them less than five times a year.

Most of the dreams are about something that has already been experienced. But other dreams are of the wish fulfillment type, for example, dreaming of erotic encounters with celebrities (Wolfe, 1982).

Love

Feelings of love are expressed in thoughts like "I love you," "I've never felt this way before," "Loving you makes me feel so good." When these thoughts occur in the context of physical stimulation with the loved partner, there is a heightened sense of arousal leading to orgasm. One researcher noted, "Orgasm can be reached with minimal sexual stimulation and deep involvement" (Mosher, 1980, p. 32). Of the 15,000 women in the *Playboy* survey, those most likely to have an orgasm had been in relationships lasting more than four years (Cook et al., 1983b). When a person is deeply in love, each touch of the partner is imbued with such emotional significance that erotic responses are easily triggered. "When her lips barely touch mine, as though she is teasing them, I go absolutely wild," said one man of his fiancée. "I don't get to see her often because we live in different states but when I'm with her, even the slightest touch arouses me."

Interaction of Physical and Cognitive Sources

Both physical and cognitive sources are usually involved in orgasm. Not only do the bodies of the respective partners respond physiologically to each other, their minds must label such interaction and responsiveness in positive terms. Phrases such as "I love to touch him," "I feel like gold the way she touches me," and "This feels terrific," reflect the importance of cognitive processes. Without such positive labeling, the physical stimulation will take on a neutral or aversive meaning. Orgasm is a complex response to different stimuli: both physical and cognitive elements are important in different ways at different times.

Cultural Attitudes Toward Orgasm

In addition to the physiological capacity for orgasm (the body) and the cognitive elements that help stimulate the senses (the thoughts), cultural attitudes toward orgasm also influence people's orgasmic experience. Every society decides what aspects of life it chooses to give visibility and support to. In our society sex is regarded as an appropriate interest and orgasm an appropriate goal. Magazine articles within arms' reach at supermarket checkout lines alert us to new techniques for a better sex life.

Other societies may or may not encourage sexual expression. Among the Mundugumor, a New Guinea tribe, women are expected to have orgasms and men are trained in ways to stimulate women to achieve them. But among the Arapesh, another New Guinea tribe, the concept of orgasm is nonexistent with the result that few women ever experience it (Mead, 1967).

Phases of Sexual Response

Orgasm is only one phase in the sexual response cycle. The cycle is made up of several phases: transition, desire, which may be thought of as prephases, excitement, plateau, orgasm, and resolution (Kaplan, 1979; Knoepfler, 1981; Masters & Johnson, 1966).

Transition Prephase

Before any sexual behavior is likely, the partners must make the transition from nonsexual to sexual roles. Much as we use the door and entrance hall of a building to provide a transition from outside to inside, so we use various means to help us make a transition from a nonsexual to a sexual state. One author has noted some of the means partners use to make the transition: "a relaxed meal or a small amount of alcohol will facilitate transition. Nonsexual physical touching, such as massage, is a very potent transition agent for many. The use of hot water, principally moving hot water such as is found in hot tubs and jacuzzis, will promote transition for many people" (Knoepfler, 1981, p. 16). Such a transition is followed by the desire prephase.

Desire Prephase

When individuals become aroused, they have entered the next prephase of the sexual response cycle. Feeling the desire for sexual involvement is a result of socialization and a complex interplay of social, psychological, and physiological factors.

The attitudes people have toward sex are a function of their socialization—what they were taught by parents and peers, their experiences, and the level of their exposure to sexual phenomena through books, movies, and the like. As we have noted, the initial (parental) socialization of women tends to be more conservative than of men. Women are supervised more closely and taught to regard their sexuality more seriously. Male socialization, on the other hand, tends to be directed toward sexual involvement with women.

The result of different socialization for women and men is predictable: women are more conservative sexually. They report less sex urge, are less easily aroused, masturbate less, have intercourse less often and with fewer partners than men (Mercer & Kohn, 1979). When more than 200 university students were asked how often they had the urge to have intercourse, 4 in 10 of the men said "daily" or "more than daily" in contrast to 1 in 10 of the women.

Beyond socialization, social context also affects sexual desire. You rarely think about your sexual needs in the middle of a final exam. But after a glass of wine and music in your or your partner's home on Friday night, your sexual desires are more likely to emerge; the context permits sexual expression.

Psychological factors are also at work. If you have decided that you want to break up with your partner—say you discovered your partner had intercourse with someone else while you were out of town—even though the context permits intercourse, your sexual desire may be muted because you feel hurt and betrayed.

Finally, physiological factors stimulate sexual desire. Unlike the bases of our needs for food, water, and sleep, the physiological bases for sex desire remain somewhat of a mystery. What is known suggests that both the brain and hormones are involved (Kaplan, 1979). The brain has specific nerve centers that, when activated, make us conscious of our need for sexual expression. These neural centers that activate sexual seeking are closely connected to pleasure centers which have been identified in the brains of mammals. Laboratory experiments with rats have shown that when these centers are stimulated with electricity, they induce intense pleasure so that the animal continues to choose stimulation over food, water, or other reinforcers.

It is not known to what degree hormones are responsible for activating the sex centers of our brains. Pheromones, odor signals that attract sex partners, have been identified in insects and some mammals.* When the female hamster is receptive, she emits a vaginal odor (dimethyl disulfide) that attracts and excites the male hamster. The odor is so powerful that he will mount whatever contains the fluid. If his olfactory bulbs are removed, making him unable to detect the odor, he loses all interest in mating (Hopson, 1979).

The data for human pheromones is slight and contradictory (Hassett, 1978). However, what some people report privately suggests that there may be a link between scent signals and sexual attraction. One woman said that she likes to edge close to her partner when he is sleeping because of the way he smells. "He has an odor that smells 'right' to me. And he's the only one that smells that way to me," she said.

Sexual desire is the result of complex interactions between physiology and social context as perceived by the individual. When we experience sexual arousal, it suggests that we are perceiving a socially appropriate partner in a socially appropriate context and that our hormones and other chemicals are feeding the correct sexual circuits in our brains to take us to the next phase of the sexual response cycle.

*Scent signals also mark off territory. For example, dogs often stop at vertical objects and sniff. These "scent posts" convey messages such as whether another dog is in the area (Hopson, 1979).

Excitement Phase*

Assuming the person has made the transition from a nonsexual to a sexual mode and is with someone who arouses her or him the excitement phase of the sexual response cycle begins. The word orgasm comes from the Greek *orgao* which means "I am excited." In women, the excitement phase begins with vasocongestion, which means that blood flows into the vaginal region and swells the labia and surrounding tissues. The clitoris also enlarges and the nipples become erect. The breasts may enlarge. But the most frequent, obvious, and accurate indicator of sexual excitement in women is vaginal lubrication, which appears to be a result of lubricating droplets coming from the vaginal walls (Figure 8.1).

Erection is the primary response during the excitement phase of the sexual response cycle in men. Erection, which may occur within 60 seconds of stimulation, is a result of blood flowing into the penis at a rapid rate with only a small amount flowing back. The trapped blood inflates the penis, which is transformed from a soft to a hard state. During erection the man's nipples also may become erect and his testes move closer to his body as the spermatic cords tighten and become shorter.

"In both men and women, the physical changes of the excitement phase are neither constant nor always ascending" (Kolodny, Masters, & Johnson,

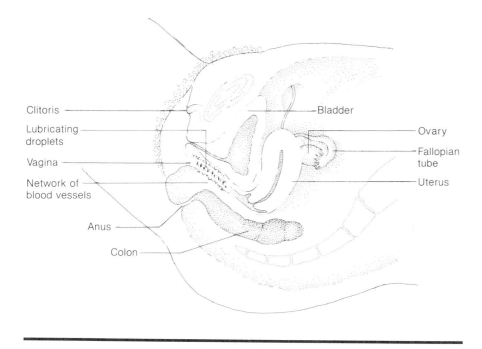

Clitoris

Lubricating droplets

Vagina

Network of blood vessels

Anus

Colon

Bladder

Ovary

Fallopian tube

Uterus

**Figure 8.1
Excitement Phase:
Vaginal Lubrication**
The first evidence of the vaginal barrel's physiologic response to sexual stimulation is the presence of droplets of lubrication from the walls of the vagina. They form a smooth, glistening coating for the entire vaginal barrel.

Source: *Human Sexual Response* by William H. Masters and Virginia E. Johnson, Boston: Little, Brown and Company, 1966. Copyright by Masters and Johnson, 1966. p. 70.

*Discussion of the excitement, plateau, orgasm, and resolution phases of the sexual response cycle and of the alternative sexual response cycles is based on *Human Sexual Response* by William H. Masters and Virginia E. Johnson. Copyright © Little, Brown, and Company, 1966. Reprinted by permission of Little, Brown and Company.

1979, p. 11). Vaginal lubrication may be minimal or have ceased and erection may be at varying levels of firmness. Continued sexual excitement is dependent on a stable environment with minimal distractions. For example, if someone knocks on the door and calls out to you while you are making love with your partner, sexual excitement can disappear.

Plateau Phase

If stimulation is uninterrupted, the sexually excited person moves to the next phase of the sexual response cycle. In the plateau phase in women, the lower third of the vagina becomes smaller while the upper two-thirds expands. If the sexual contact is through intercourse, the constriction of the lower third results in the vagina gripping the penis tighter. This **orgasmic platform** is illustrated in Figure 8.2. At the same time, the clitoris withdraws behind a fold of skin known as the clitoral hood, which provides insulation for the extremely sensitive glans of the clitoris. Direct clitoral stimulation would be painful at this time since the glans has a tremendous concentration of nerve endings in a relatively small area. Even though the clitoris is under the hood, it continues to respond to stimulation as long as the area surrounding the clitoris (mons) is stimulated.

Male reactions during the plateau phase include a slight increase in the diameter of the penis, a considerable increase in the size of the testes (from 50 to 100 percent), and, in some men, a color change to deep red-purple on the head (glans) of the penis.

Figure 8.2
Plateau Phase:
Orgasmic Platform
During the plateau phase, the lower third of the vaginal barrel narrows as a result of localized vasocongestion. The width and length of the vaginal barrel also increase slightly during this phase.

Source: *Human Sexual Response* by William H. Masters and Virginia E. Johnson, Boston: Little, Brown and Company, 1966. Copyright by Masters and Johnson, 1966. p. 76.

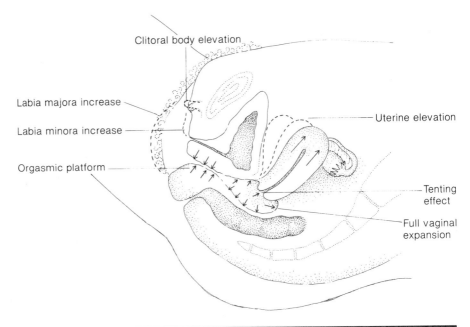

Clitoral body elevation

Labia majora increase

Labia minora increase

Orgasmic platform

Uterine elevation

Tenting effect

Full vaginal expansion

Some changes during the plateau phase are common to men and women: muscle contractions and spasms (**myotonia**), heavy breathing (**hyperventilation**), heart rate increase (**tachycardia**) and blood pressure elevation. Also both women and men may experience a **sex flush**. This looks like a measles like rash on parts of the chest, neck, face, and forehead; it sometimes suggests a high level of sexual tension.

Orgasm Phase

Orgasm is a genital reflex, which has both a sensory (stimulus) and a motor (response) component. A good analogy is the knee jerk response. Just as your lower leg shoots forward when your knee is tapped by a physician's hammer, you will have an orgasm when your genitals get the appropriate stimulation. In females the clitoris receives the sensory information and sends it to the vaginal muscles. In males the nerve endings on the head of the penis receive the stimulation and send a message to the muscles at the base of the penis. All orgasms involve the reflex model.

In women the orgasmic experience involves "simultaneous rhythmic contractions of the uterus, the orgasmic platform (outer third of the vagina), and the rectal sphincter, beginning at 0.8-second intervals and then diminishing in intensity, duration, and regularity" (Kolodny et al., 1979, p. 15). An average of 18 contractions lasting a total of 36 seconds was observed in 11 women (aged 24 to 33) who masturbated to orgasm (Bohlen, Held, & Sanderson, 1982).

Orgasm in men occurs in two stages. First there is a buildup of fluid from the prostate, seminal vesicles, and vas deferens in the prostatic urethra (the area behind the base of the penis and above the testes). Once this pool of semen collects, the man enters a stage of ejaculatory inevitability. He knows he is going to ejaculate and cannot control the process. The penile muscles contract two to three times at 0.8-second intervals and propel the ejaculate from the penis. Thereafter, the contractions may continue but at longer intervals. The more time since the last ejaculation, the greater the number of contractions. The average time of an orgasm for a male is about 25 seconds (Bohlen et al., 1980).

As mentioned earlier, some male orgasms occur in the form of nocturnal emissions, or wet dreams. The typical male begins to experience nocturnal emissions at age 13 to 14 as a reponse to an erotic dream. The male wakes up to find his underclothes, leg, and bed sheet wet with semen. Unless he has been told that wet dreams occur, are normal, and signify the capacity to reproduce, he may think something is wrong with him. Not all males have nocturnal emissions. Those who regularly reach orgasm through masturbation or intercourse may never experience them.

In both men and women there is an increase in heavy breathing (sometimes reaching 40 breaths per minute), heart rate (from 110 to 180 beats per minute), and blood pressure (systolic pressure may elevate 30–80 mm and diastolic pressure by 20–40 mm).

What an Orgasm Feels Like

One Woman's Experience

The slow buildup begins as soon as he comes into sight—tightness around the outer muscles of my vagina and the wetness of lubrication. As his smell reaches my senses, my vaginal muscles again quiver in recognition of his sexual attractiveness.

Once the touching and kissing begins, the whole area of my vagina pushes outward in slow rhythmic motions. It feels swollen and sensitive. This pleasure gradually heightens and turns from an outward pushing to an inner craving felt far inside my body. The area of intense sensitivity and extreme constriction is now focused on the inner lips directly around the opening of my vagina. Breathing becomes quicker and the deep inhaling brings a slow moving projection of my breasts with larger, erect nipples. My body and thoughts swell with sensual feelings.

As the pleasure increases it feels as if I *need* a penis thrust up inside of me to satisfy the now tremendous craving. The wetness now flows outward, moistening my pubic hair and inner thighs as if to attract and envelop his penis. With no penetration, the inner cavity continues to lust for his penis. The hollowness of my vagina aches and I begin a conscious pulling motion as I inhale more sporadically. A mixture of pulling-in and pushing-out gestures with my vagina begin to predominate as my pelvic area rotates back and forth. Tongue kissing (gently sucking and encompassing my partner's tongue) at this point increases my arousal and desire for intercourse.

My shallow breathing is now interspersed with soft sighs of anxiousness, pleasure, and impending orgasm. A confusion takes over my senses so I become totally controlled by my physical response. My thinking processes become fogged and absorbed into physical ecstasy. I am vaguely aware of the sweat covering my body from the warmth generated by physical closeness with my lover.

Just before I orgasm, the inner craving rushes back to a concentrated feeling in my clitoral area and the muscles around my vaginal opening become even more profoundly tense. This tension is reflected in the rest of my body as my arms and legs stiffen and my fingers press rigidly into my partner's skin as if to ground myself before the explosion.

(Continued)

Then it hits—the vaginal muscles wildly contract—a vibrating sense of extreme pleasure as the tension throbs to relief. It is a sensation which absolutely cannot be expressed in words. The pulsating of my vagina is heavy and the thrill is carried throughout my body with involuntary shaking and thrusting of the pelvis and limbs. Breathing becomes gasping and the sighs are now louder expressions of pleasure—calling my partner's name, telling him of the pleasure he gives, and "I love you's." My head has totally floated away—I can't think and don't want to—I just enjoy!

After a few seconds I am exhausted, my legs and arms are shaky as if the blood is still flying through them. I just die, resting on my partner for a short while in order to recover and get some air. Small tremors continue to explode in my vagina and no energy is left in the rest of me.

Recovering a bit, I now experience the joy my heart is pouring out. Opening my eyes I hold my partner gently. Love feelings abound and a few tears of happiness appear in the corner of my eyes. I can't stop smiling!

My energy level is up again and I want the friction and burning warmth of my partner inside of me. It is not an orgasmic craving but a need for friction against my vaginal wall. The more he thrusts the more I want, as if one is feeding the other.

One Man's Experience

The rough edges melt away—life flows through uninterrupted—every cell is hot. My muscles tingle and the fluid boils in my belly. There is a sensation of fullness and weightlessness—sharing my very life, savoring all the juices, all the passion, rising above what's been—creating what is. Naturally, each touch of her fingers on the smoothness of my skin stirs life in my inner being—the feeling swells, it spreads, it concentrates and when it erupts to join her, all of my life force is propelled outward. For an instant, I am breathless, suspended . . .

Another Man's Experience

Prior to ejaculation warm sensations begin to build whether it be through foreplay or actual intercourse itself. The buildup gives a very warm and gentle feeling throughout my body. The buildup wants to explode. When ejaculation occurs, it is like the body is being massaged with the perfect touch from the inside out. There is warmth but there is coolness in the tingling sensations that make the five to seven seconds what it really is . . . outrageous!!

The orgasm experience is usually one of intense pleasure. Both men and women describe their experience in basically the same way. In one study (Vance & Wagner, 1976), 48 descriptions (24 male, 24 female) of orgasm were submitted to a panel of judges, who were asked to determine if the descriptions were written by a man or woman. The judges were unable to make accurate identifications.

"Good," "enjoyable," "ecstatic," "wonderful," "great," and "fantastic" are words often used to describe orgasm. One person said, "It is like champagne bubbles splashing through my veins." Another said, "It's like coming to the top and going over the edge—like hang gliding." Others describe the experience as an explosion—"after which I go limp as if I'm floating." Many experience a temporary loss of consciousness. This is a result of the heavy breathing, which increases to three times the normal rate at orgasm and reduces the flow of blood to the brain. Others report feeling warm in their brain and genitals. The "heating up" of the genitals has been measured by thermography (infrared photography) (Seeley et al., 1980). In some, muscle tension is evident. "My leg muscles flex and my whole body shakes for a few seconds," said one person.

Not all orgasms are of the "champagne splashing through my veins," "loss of consciousness," or "red hot" variety. Some orgasms are so subtle that the person is not aware they have had one until after it is over. Because so much has been written about the glories of orgasm, some people may feel disappointed because their experience is different from their expectation. One woman said, "The big deal about orgasms is for the birds. I can have a so-called orgasm with my vibrator in a few minutes—or even a few seconds—with no good feelings at all" (Myers, 1976, p. 285). The accompanying boxes describe the orgasmic experiences of a woman and a man. They are *not* to be regarded as typical or ideal.

So orgasms are different for different people. The experience varies by number, partner, mood, manner of stimulation, importance, and intensity.

Resolution Phase

During this phase the body returns to its preexcitement condition. In women "the orgasmic platform disappears as the muscular contractions of orgasm pump blood away from these tissues. The uterus moves back into the true pelvis, the vagina begins to shorten in both width and length, and the clitoris returns to its normal anatomic position" (Kolodny et al., 1979, p. 17). In men there is the loss of erection, the testes decrease in size and descend into the scrotum. In both sexes the breathing, heart rate, and blood pressure return to normal. A thin layer of perspiration may appear over the entire body.

Some prefer to avoid additional stimulation at this time. "My clitoris feels very sensitive—almost burns—and I don't want it touched after I orgasm," said one woman. Other women say their clitoris tickles when touched after orgasm. Men often want to lie still and avoid stimulation on the head of their penis.

The resolution stage of the sexual response cycle is often a relaxing, joyful time.

Alternative Sexual Response Cycles

The excitement, plateau, orgasm, and resolution phases of the sexual response cycle are not isolated. They overlap and the orgasm phase is sometimes skipped. Also, women and men may exhibit different patterns. A discussion of how these patterns vary follows.

In Women

A woman may travel through the sexual response cycle in one of three ways. These are illustrated in Figure 8.3. The most usual pattern (C) is a progression from excitement through plateau to orgasm to resolution, passing through all phases and returning to none for a second time. Experientially, the woman gets excited, enjoys a climax, and cuddles in her partner's arms after one orgasm. If she is masturbating, she relaxes and savors the experience.

In pattern A the woman goes from excitement to plateau to orgasm to another or several orgasms and then to resolution. The interval between orgasms varies. In some cases, it is only a few seconds. In effect, the woman gets excited, climbs through the plateau phase and bounces from orgasm to orgasm while briefly touching the plateau phase between orgasms. Multiple orgasms are discussed in greater detail later in this chapter. A third pattern (B) is movement through the sequence of phases of the sexual response cycle

Figure 8.3
Female Alternative Sexual Response Cycles
The female may experience one of three patterns in her response to sexual stimulation: Pattern C, the typical response, involves moving from excitement, to plateau, to orgasm (one), to resolution. Pattern B involves becoming excited, stabilizing at the plateau phase, and moving toward resolution. Pattern A involves having an orgasm, returning to the plateau phase, and then back to another orgasm. This latter pattern may be repeated again and is referred to as multiple orgasm.

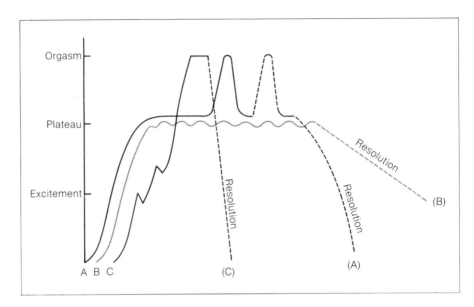

Source: *Human Sexual Response* by William H. Masters and Virginia E. Johnson, Boston: Little, Brown and Company, 1966. Copyright by Masters and Johnson, 1966. p. 5.

but skipping the orgasm phase. The woman gets excited, climbs to the plateau phase, but does not go over the edge to orgasm. Insufficient stimulation, distraction, or lack of interest in the partner (if one is involved) are among the reasons for not reaching orgasm (other reasons are discussed in Chapter 11). The woman moves from the plateau phase directly to the resolution phase.

In Men

Men progress through the sexual response cycle in a somewhat different pattern (Figure 8.4). Once sexual excitement begins, there is essentially only one pattern—excitement through plateau to orgasm. After orgasm most men experience a **refractory period** during which sexual tension is reduced to a low level. During the refractory period, the penis usually becomes flaccid and further stimulation (particularly on the glans of the penis) is not immediately desired.

The desire and ability to have another erection and begin stimulation again depends upon age, fatigue, and amount of alcohol in the male's system. In general, the older, more tired, less sober individual will be less interested in renewed sexual stimulation than the younger, rested, sober male. The typical refractory period lasts from a few minutes to several days, but some men

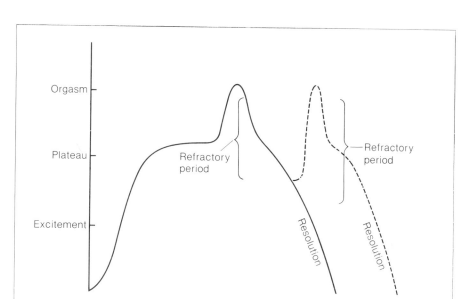

Source: *Human Sexual Response* by William H. Masters and Virginia E. Johnson, Boston: Little, Brown and Company, 1966. Copyright by Masters and Johnson, 1966. p. 5.

Figure 8.4
The Male Alternative Sexual Response Cycle
The male typically experiences the pattern indicated by the solid line in his response to sexual stimulation. He becomes excited and moves through the plateau, orgasm, and resolution phases of the sexual response cycle. The pattern indicated by the dotted line describes the pattern whereby, after a brief refractory period during which the male does not want additional stimulation, he enters the cycle at the plateau phase and has another orgasm, which is followed by another refractory period and resolution.

maintain an erection after orgasm and seem to skip the refractory period. Although this is rare, it does occur.

When the sexual response cycles of women and men are compared, there are two essential differences: (1) whereas the man usually climaxes once, the woman may do so not at all or several times; and (2) when the woman does experience several climaxes, she is capable of doing so with only seconds between climaxes. In contrast, the man usually needs a longer refractory period before he is capable of additional orgasms.

Multiple Orgasm

Defined as the ability to have several orgasms in succession with no refractory period and no break in stimulation, multiple orgasms occur in both women and men. Multiple orgasms are different from sequential orgasms. The latter refers to several orgasms but with significant periods of rest in between. The lover who gets excited, has an orgasm, rests, and gets excited again to have another orgasm is not regarded as being multiorgasmic. Only those who have a series of orgasms in response to continuous stimulation are said to have multiple orgasms.

Female Multiple Orgasm

● Sure, I've had them. It just depends on the partner. I tell you one thing, I don't have them as often as I'd like to.

It usually takes me by surprise. The first level of arousal doesn't drop completely and it moves back up, kind of like if you drew a line. It scares you sometimes because you think you might keep on and never stop. ●

Although it is known that women are capable of multiple orgasms, less is known about what percentage have how many orgasms how often. In the *Cosmopolitan* survey of 106,000 readers (Wolfe, 1982) 67 percent reported having had multiple orgasms on occasion. Ten percent always have them and 23 percent never have them. Multiple orgasms occurred from two to five times during a lovemaking session. In another study (Bohlen et al., 1982), a 36-year-old unmarried woman who was monitored in a laboratory while she masturbated had 7 orgasms in 16 minutes.

These figures are very different from those given by other researchers. Clifford (1978a) and Masters and Johnson (1966) reported that between 10 and 30 percent of heterosexual women were multiorgasmic. But among committed lesbian couples, half were multiorgasmic (Masters & Johnson, 1979). One researcher reported that some women have 20 to 30 or more orgasms in an hour of lovemaking (Jensen, 1978). Finally, women who have multiple orgasms report longer durations of intercourse (Swieczkowski & Walker, 1978). These figures may be confusing, but they emphasize the wide range of orgasmic experience by women. They suggest that women may have the natural capacity to be multiorgasmic but that social learning inhibits that expressiveness.

Is more better? Not necessarily, wrote one woman. "I'd just as soon have one body-shattering, mind-obliterating orgasm than a dozen little ones" (Wolfe, 1982). But other women feel differently. One woman said that more *was* better and that she liked to lie in bed for hours and be teased from orgasm to orgasm. "When I get to the other side of several orgasms I'm literally exhausted." Four of 100 women in one study (Clifford, 1978b) said they required more than one orgasm for satisfaction.

Male Multiple Orgasm

● It's very rare for me. It seems like the longer I put the climax off, the better the chances that it [multiple orgasm] will happen. The ejaculation is always stronger.

It feels like it's lifting you straight up and it's a wild sensation. ●

Most men have only one orgasm each sexual encounter, but there are exceptions. In one study (Robbins & Jensen, 1977), 13 men reported having between 3 and 10 orgasms per lovemaking session. This occurred in four out of five intercourse experiences. One man had 30 orgasms 15 to 60 seconds apart in one intercourse session lasting one hour. Although only the last of these orgasms was accompanied by ejaculation, the previous orgasms had all the other physiological signs—increased heart rate, breathing, and anal contractions. Men who have multiple orgasms seem to exercise a conscious or unconscious control of their ejaculate. It is not known how common the multiorgasmic experience is among heterosexual males. In their study of about 100 male homosexuals, Masters and Johnson (1979) reported that none were multiorgasmic.

Although multiorgasmic men usually ejaculate only on their last orgasm, some have multiple ejaculations. After ejaculating at orgasm, there is a short refractory period followed by additional stimulation and another orgasm. Some men have four or more ejaculations in an hour. "My penis stays mostly erect after the first ejaculation," said one man, "and if I continue thrusting into my partner I start climbing again and have another ejaculation. By the third one I'm about dead." About 20 percent of young adolescents are capable of a series of ejaculations and their capability decreases with age. Among men in their fifties, only about 3 or 4 percent are multiejaculatory (Pomeroy, 1976). But there are exceptions. "Write this down," said one 47-year-old man who had just returned from his honeymoon with his new wife. "I had 17 ejaculations in 24 hours."

Having the capacity for multiple orgasms or ejaculations does not always imply the use of that capacity. On any particular lovemaking occasion, a man may have one orgasm with one ejaculation or several orgasms and one ejaculation or several ejaculations each accompanied by an orgasm. Likewise, a woman may have none, one, or several orgasms. The pattern is not important. It is important, however, that people avoid trying to meet a performance standard.

To what degree is each successive orgasm pleasurable? Most are pleasurable. "I've never had a bad orgasm" is a classic Woody Allen line. Multiorgasmic men say that the orgasm accompanied by ejaculation on their last of several orgasms is the most intense. "It's like all that fluid has been building up and is waiting to break the dam. And when it does, I really feel it," said one man.

After Orgasm

Just as partners differ in their orgasmic experiences, they have different feelings and preferences during the postorgasm phase of their lovemaking. Some lovers feel loving; they want to cuddle, be close, and savor the emotional and physical feelings of being together. "It's a time we feel like our souls are sharing each other," recalled one lover. Other lovers drift off into sleep. Still others feel energized. Some feel vulnerable. One man said, "Sometimes I feel like crying, like being a little boy again, and being held by my mother or someone else who will love and protect me" (Shanor, 1978, p. 26). Some want to break the sexual embrace immediately and do something else—smoke, eat, take a shower, watch TV, or read.

When the partners differ over the agenda there may be hurt feelings. "I like to just lie there and hold her close to me but she can't wait to get out of the bed and take a shower. It really unnerves me how she can break out of the sexual trance so quickly and makes me wonder if she enjoys me sexually at all," said one man. But his partner said, "I just like to break contact and get up after my orgasm. It doesn't mean I don't love him. I do love him—intensely."

But getting up soon after climax may be an indication of emotional distance. This is particularly true of sexual partners who are using each other or where money is involved. In the former case, one woman said she always felt guilty after she climaxed with a man whom she picked up for sex and did not care about. "I hate myself and the quicker I get out of there the better." About his experience with a prostitute, one man said, "It wasn't erotic or fun like I thought it would be. It was business and I felt sick the moment I ejaculated—I wanted to get out of there."

Rather than withdrawing from the sexual situation, some partners want to begin another round of intercourse or sexual stimulation. Such preferences are highly variable. There are women and men who feel that a sexual encounter is not satisfactory unless they have had several orgasms during several hours of lovemaking. Others may sometimes prefer renewed lovemaking, sometimes not.

No Orgasm

About 10 percent of women report never having had an orgasm (Frank & Enos, 1983; Wolfe, 1982). Rather than anything being "wrong" with them, these women have not experienced the conditions under which an orgasm is likely to occur. Essentially, they have never been sexually awakened—they have never been in love, have never petted to arousal, and have never masturbated. Many have been warned repeatedly about the dangers of sexual involvement, making them fearful and unreceptive to sexual stimulation. Given the right conditions (and this also includes patience), almost everyone who is physically healthy can experience an orgasm.

How do women feel who have never climaxed? Most would like to do so. One of Hite's (1977) respondents said, "How would you like to be colorblind and keep reading about rainbows and butterflies?" (p. 205)

For women who are orgasmic most of the time but not always, the reaction to no orgasm varies. Some women feel terrible, start to cry, get a headache, and experience general bodily discomfort when they have achieved a high state of sexual arousal but do not climax. "I have to *work* to have an orgasm," said one woman, "and it's very frustrating and aversive to me when I don't have one." Others feel less negative. "Sometimes I don't climax. And it's no big deal when I don't," said another woman. "I enjoy being held tightly with him inside of me; that's the best part of intercourse for me."

Men are more likely to climax during sexual stimulation, but sometimes they do not. They report considerable discomfort, similar to a muscle cramp, if they reach a high level of excitation with no climax (Pomeroy, 1976).

Faking Orgasm

Since our society, particularly the media, encourages the idea that every good lover should have an orgasm during each sexual encounter, it is not unusual that some orgasms are faked—by both women and men.

Orgasm Faking by Women

● Mike and I have been together for two years and I have faked only one time with him. Before I met him, I did it a lot. The guy would just keep on and on and I knew I wasn't gonna come, so I faked it [orgasm] so I wouldn't hurt his ego. ●

Two-thirds of 14,928 women in the *Playboy* study (Petersen et al., 1983b) reported having faked orgasm. In a more intensive study (Davidson & Hoffman, 1980), 10 percent of 235 female respondents reported that they "frequently" or "very frequently" faked an orgasm during intercourse. One in four said that they did so "occasionally."* The most frequent reason they gave for faking orgasm was to please the partner or to avoid disappointing or hurting him. As one woman said, "I love him and want him to enjoy making love with me. My having a climax is a big thing to him, so I try to 'come through' for him. Sometimes I have an orgasm anyway, so he never really knows that I'm faking the other times."

Other women regarded intercourse as an ordeal and faked climax to get it over with. One woman said her husband lasts for hours and likes to continue long after she is ready to stop. "So, I just breathe heavy, groan a little, and then try to make him be still. Sometimes it works."

*From "Sexual Fantasies and Sexual Satisfaction: An Empirical Analysis of Erotic Thoughts" by J. Kenneth Davidson, Sr. (University of Wisconsin—Eau Claire) and Linda E. Hoffman (University of Notre Dame), 1980. Used by permission.

Only a few (5 percent) said they faked orgasm because they were "sup-posed to have one." Most women do not climax all the time and resent the expectation that they should.

How do women fake orgasm? Two women described their experience.

● I usually breathe heavily and clutch at him. Then I gradually slow down my moving and end with the statement "that was good."

I arch my back and tense everything. Then I tell him he was real good. ●

"Did you come?" is a question that infuriates many women. Some feel frus-trated trying to answer. If they did not have an orgasm, they may not want to hurt their partner's feelings by being honest. But if they try to protect their partner's feelings, they are introducing dishonesty into the relationship. "I never know what to say in that situation," said one woman, "so I just hug my partner tightly and mumble something about how great it feels."

A woman may not be sure what information her partner is really seeking. Is he asking for feedback on the level of sexual pleasure she experienced or his skill as a lover or her feelings about him and their relationship? Suppose she says she did not have an orgasm. Will he accept her answer without getting angry?

To avoid ambiguity the man should ask exactly what he wants to know and not hide his real question in another question. If he wants to know if his partner loves him, he should ask. If he asks about her orgasm but interprets her answer as a reflection of her feelings for him, he may not be getting the right information. If he wants to know if she had an orgasm because he wants her to experience sexual pleasure, he might ask if there is anything he can do for her that would give her more pleasure (James, 1979).

There are other problems with the question "Did you climax?" Some women view it as a demand that they have an orgasm. "Sometimes I feel like I am expected to scream like a Comanche Indian to prove that I'm climaxing. I really resent that my partner looks on sex as a stage performance," expressed one woman. Other women feel that the question is a signal that the man is bored and wants to get it over with (Wise, 1979). "Sometimes I take a long time to climax and I know he gets tired manipulating my clitoris. But rather than wait it out, he'll pop that question and break my concentration. Some-times I let my anger fly and tell him that I could have a climax if he would stop asking me that question."

Orgasm Faking by Men*

● When I'm really tired and want to get the thing over with, I will thrust forward, tense my back and leg muscles, grimace, and say something like "aah". My partner never knows the difference.

---

*Appreciation is expressed to Renee Foster for her assistance in developing this section.

Sure I've faked it [orgasm]. I just did it to make the girl think everything was fine. ●

———————————————————————

Yes, men fake orgasm, too. Thirty percent of 65,000 males reported having done so (Petersen et al., 1983b). Although their reasons include not wanting to hurt their partner's ego ("She likes to know that she pleases me"), they also want to protect their own ego (Friedman, 1978). Our society places a heavy burden of expectation on the man to climax every time he has intercourse. A man who loses his erection shortly after penetration may fake an orgasm so that his partner will not know his penis has become flaccid; or, after a prolonged period of intercourse the man may not be able to bring himself to climax, so he may fake it. He no longer has to keep trying and his partner will have the perception (he hopes) that she pleased him.

Men most often fake orgasm after they have already achieved one climax and are attempting to achieve additional ones (Shanor, 1978). Since the capability of having successive orgasms diminishes as the man gets older, he might find himself wanting additional orgasms only to discover that he cannot. So rather than deal with the "why" with his partner, he fakes it.

Summary

The interpretation of the experience of orgasm varies from person to person. People may view the orgasmic experience as an emotional bond, as a physiological release, as fun, as procreation, or as a goal in itself. Orgasm results from both physical and cognitive experiences. Oral, manual, or vaginal stimulation of the penis are the principle sources of physical stimulation that produce orgasm in men. The physical sources of orgasm for women are more varied and include stimulation of the clitoris, vagina, and breasts. Our thoughts, in the form of dreams and statements about our love feelings, may also result in orgasm. Orgasm is a complex response usually involving both physical and cognitive elements.

The sexual response cycle is made up of several phases: transition and desire, which are prephases, excitement, plateau, orgasm, and resolution. Specific physiological changes occur during each phase of the sexual response cycle, but these phases overlap and some phases are sometimes skipped. Whereas women may travel through the sexual response cycle in one of three ways, men have essentially one pattern—through plateau to orgasm.

Multiple orgasms, several orgasms in succession with no refractory period and no break in stimulation, occur in both women and men. Studies emphasize the wide range of orgasmic experiences by women and suggest that women may have the natural capacity to be multiorgasmic but that social learning may inhibit that expressiveness. Men usually have only one orgasm, but some men have the capacity for multiple orgasms, with or without multiple ejaculations.

Lovers have various feelings during the postorgasm phase of their love-making. Some feel loving; others feel sleepy; still others feel energized. They may want to cuddle and be close, drift off to sleep, break the sexual embrace immediately and do something else, or begin another round of intercourse or sexual stimulation. Partners may differ over the postlovemaking agenda.

Since our society encourages the idea that everyone should have an orgasm during each sexual encounter, it is not unusual that some orgasms are faked—by both women and men. In one study the most frequent reason women gave for faking orgasm was to please the partner or to avoid disappointing him. Others said they faked climax to get the ordeal over with. Although men's reasons for faking orgasm include not wanting to hurt their partners' egos, they also want to protect their own egos, since our society places a heavy burden of expectation on the man to climax every time he has intercourse.

Key Terms

clitoral orgasm
vaginal orgasm
Grafenberg spot
transition prephase
desire prephase
excitement phase
plateau phase
orgasm phase
resolution phase

pheromone
orgasmic platform
myotonia
hyperventilation
tachycardia
sex flush
refractory period
nocturnal emission

Issues in Debate and Future Directions

Faking orgasm, female ejaculations, and the benefits of Kegel exercises are among the controversies regarding orgasm. After examining these issues we look at various orgasmic trends.

Should Orgasm Be Faked?

Although both women and men fake orgasms from time to time, whether they should do so on a regular basis might be viewed in terms of the consequences. The advantages of faking orgasm seem to be that the partner is spared feelings of self-doubt about his or her capabilities as a lover. If a man does not know that his partner never has a climax, he can live under the illusion that she does and that he is a good lover. But such illusions may be costly in terms of the discontent or frustration of the partner doing the faking. One woman said that she had been faking orgasms for so long with her partner that she just couldn't tell him now that what she really needed was cunnilingus to help her climax. "He would know I have been lying to him and it would kill him—and me," she said. In effect, she had boxed herself in. If she did not tell him, she would continue to be dissatisfied; if she did, he would accuse her of being dishonest and feel his masculinity threatened.

One perspective that might resolve the "whether I should or shouldn't fake it" issue is an educational one. If both partners knew that lovers do not always climax every time they have intercourse and that failing to climax does not necessarily mean lack of love or sexual arousal, there would be less pressure on each partner to perform—and to lie. In addition, accepting the partner's response whatever it might be would help to ensure a pleasurable sexual experience whether or not an orgasm occurred. To require that each sexual encounter end in orgasm may result in frustration for both partners. A more realistic goal is to enjoy each other without being concerned about who has an orgasm. In one study of 42 couples (Waterman & Chiauzzi, 1982), each partner said that her or his own sexual enjoyment was unrelated to whether their partner had an orgasm.

This perspective does not suggest that partners should complacently accept recurring sexual problems, and consistent lack of orgasm may be such a problem. Rather than fake orgasm and introduce dishonesty into the relationship, an alternative is to recognize lack of orgasm as a problem to work on. Open communication was the key for one couple. "She told me it was her clitoris and not the back of her vagina that needed to be stimulated," said one man. "She even told me where and how on her clitoris it felt best. I did what she said, and she hasn't had to fake it anymore."

Not all couples are able to solve their sexual problems themselves. Some seek sex therapy. Chapter 11 discusses the major sexual problems and how to resolve them.

Do Women Ejaculate When They Climax?

Previously, it was thought that only males ejaculate, but today a new controversy has arisen about the possibility of female ejaculation. The reaction of one board-certified

(continued)

obstetrician-gynecologist emphasizes the confusion.

I first learned about female ejaculation at an American Association for Sex Educators, Counselors, and Therapists meeting. The presentation was full of foreign-sounding phrases like Grafenberg spot and female ejaculation.

"Bull," I said. "I spend half of my waking hours examining, cutting apart, putting together, removing, or rearranging female reproductive organs. There is no prostate and women don't ejaculate."

After the presentation, I, along with two other physicians and a registered nurse (all sex therapists), challenged the presenters. "Show us," we said. And they did.

Strange as it sounds, the whole group went up to a room in the hotel and had the opportunity of examining one of the subjects about whom the paper was written. The vulva and vagina were normal with no abnormal masses or spots. The urethra was normal. Everything was normal. She then had her partner stimulate her by inserting two fingers into the vagina and stroking along the urethra lengthwise. To our amazement, the area began to swell. It eventually became a firm 1 X 2 cm oval area distinctly different from the rest of the vagina. In a few moments the subject seemed to perform a Valsalva maneuver (bearing down as if starting to defecate) and seconds later several ccs of milky fluid shot out of the urethra. The material was clearly not urine. In fact, if the chemical analyses described in the paper are correct, its composition was closest to prostatic fluid.*

The source of the fluid, which has also been described as "watered-down fat-free milk," is from the Skene glands just inside the urethral opening. About 10 percent of women emit such a fluid from the urethra during orgasm (Perry & Whipple, 1981). These women also seem to experience a refractory period (a time of relaxation) after ejaculation similar to that experienced by men (Belzer, 1981). Another researcher has presented evidence for the physiological existence of the female prostate and ejaculation (Heath, 1983).

Other research has failed to confirm the existence of a unique female ejaculate. In a study that examined the ejaculate of six women (Goldberg et al., 1983), the biochemical analysis revealed that it was similar to urine.

Do Kegel Exercises for Women Improve Orgasmic Potential?

The muscles running between the legs from front to back, which control bladder and bowel discharge, are known as the pubococcygeal muscles. Kegel's vaginal exercises (named after Dr. Arnold Kegel) involve becoming aware of these muscles and tensing them regularly to increase their strength. Since the muscles also control urine flow, the woman can familiarize herself with them while urinating by stopping and starting the flow. After this is done a couple of times, she will become aware of these muscles and can tense them anytime, anywhere. Some women perform Kegel exercises up to 300 times a day in which they contract these muscles, hold them for 3 to 4 seconds, and then relax. The presumed result of these exercises is the ability of the woman to grip her partner's penis tighter, providing greater stimulation of the nerve endings in the vaginal walls.

Based on Kegel's observation that his patients reported improved sexual satisfaction as a result of strengthening their pubococcygeal muscles, sex therapists have advocated the use of these exercises for women who have difficulty achieving an orgasm. But data to support the relationship between Kegel's exercises and orgasmic potential are lacking. To test the relationship, two researchers compared vaginal pressure readings from a perineometer (an instrument inserted into the vagina) of 92 women and their estimates on the probability that they would have an orgasm in various types of sexual episodes (intercourse, cunnilingus, masturbation, and so on). There was no significant relationship between strength of vaginal muscles and the reported ability to climax (Freese & Levitt, in press).

Future Directions

Orgasmic trends of the future include more orgasmic women, more women experiencing orgasm during intercourse, and fewer faked orgasms by both women and men. Women will become more orgasmic partly as a result of continued media education about female sexuality through magazines, books, movies, and television. These sources of sexualization telegraph the message that sex for women is no longer a duty but a pleasure and orgasm is part of the pleasure. This new education also stresses the importance of communication with one's sexual partner and encourages women to tell their partners precisely the place, pressure, and rhythm of stimulation they need to climax.

As women are able to articulate their need of clitoral stimulation to climax, they will have orgasm during intercourse more often. Also, with women getting the clitoral stimulation during intercourse to bring them to climax, there will be fewer faked orgasms. Open communication will also encourage a woman's partner to be more open about his orgasm or lack of it.

*Source: Adapted from "A Note on Female Ejaculation" by Martin Weisberg in *The Journal of Sex Research*, 1981, 17, 1, p. 90. Reprinted by permission of the Society for the Scientific Study of Sex.

Chapter Nine

Love and Sexual Fantasies

The word sex, when coupled
with the word love, makes the
most exciting phrase in our
language. For sexual love is a
powerful force that makes life
worth living.

ELEANOR HAMILTON, *SEX, WITH LOVE*

Chapter Nine

We now shift our focus from physical sexual interaction to the minds of the partners. Sexual encounters include an array of love feelings and fantasies. In this chapter we examine each in detail.

Love

Since love is one of the primary emotions of interpersonal sexuality we look at its origins, definitions, importance, development, and to what degree a love feeling is romantic or realistic. In addition, we examine jealousy as well as the similarities and differences between love and sex.

Origins of Love

Psychologists and philosophers (as well as biologists and poets) have tried to explain the origin of love. Sigmund Freud (1960), the Viennese psychoanalyst, stated that love was a mental feeling of tenderness and affection, which resulted from blocked biological sexual desires and needs. He referred to love as **aim-inhibited sex**, noting, "Love with an inhibited aim was originally full sensual love and, in man's unconscious mind, is still so" (p. 96). Freud equated love with sexual desire, which, when not expressed through intercourse or other sexual behavior became an emotion, a feeling called love.

Taking the opposite view, Dr. Ian Suttie wrote in *The Origins of Love and Hate* (1952) that love was a positive instinctive feeling based on the need for companionship with others. Love, therefore, was social rather than sexual and derived from a person's self-preservative instincts. He wrote, "The specific origin of love, in time, was at the moment the infant recognized the existence of others (p. 20).

Theodore Reik (1949), who once studied with Freud, thought that love was neither sexual nor social but psychic. He believed that "the origin of love belongs to the ego-drives (p. 65)." By this he meant that love sprang from a state of dissatisfaction with self and was a vain urge to reach one's "ego-ideal." Love, therefore, was the projection of one's ideal image of one's self onto another person.

Sociologist Joseph Folsom (1948) focused on the conditioning or learning aspect of love, stating that whatever object was frequently perceived while needs were being reduced or satisfied became an object of desire. In addition, he noted, "We tend to repeat that which was satisfying or that which immediately accompanied a satisfying experience" (p. 156). From this viewpoint, if a man and woman spend enough enjoyable time together, love will result.

A philosophical explanation of love has been suggested by theologian Paul Tillich (1960), who conceived of love as a drive toward the unity of the separated. He wrote, "Reunion presupposes separation of that which belongs essentially together" (p. 25). His belief in the spiritual and physical union that makes up love refers to the ancient myth that men and women were once two halves of the same body. Although split, each half has continued to look for the other half.

Definitions of Love

Because love feelings are personal and the individual alone has access to what he or she experiences, the definitions of love are varied. Some classic definitions of love include the following.

> When the satisfaction or the security of another person becomes as significant to one as is one's own security, then the state of love exists (Sullivan, 1947).

> Love is an active power in man; a power which breaks through the walls which separate man from his fellow men . . . In love the paradox occurs that two beings become one yet remain two (Fromm, 1956).

> Love is the passionate and abiding desire on the part of two or more people to produce together the conditions under which each can be and spontaneously express his real self; to produce together an intellectual soil and an emotional climate in which each can flourish, far superior to what either could achieve alone (Magoun, 1948).

> Love is that intense feeling of two people for each other which involves bodily, emotional, and intellectual identification; which is of such a nature as to cause each willingly to forego his personality demands and aspirations in favor of the other; which gains its satisfaction through creating a personal and social identity in those involved (Koos, 1953).

> Love is a dialectic, which means that the bond of love is not just shared identity—which is an impossible goal—but the taut line of opposed desires between the ideal of an eternal merger of souls and our cultivated urge to prove ourselves as free and autonomous individuals. No matter how much we're in love, there is always a large

"They do not love that do not show their love."

SHAKESPEARE

and nonnegotiable part of ourselves that is not defined by the love-world, nor do we want it to be (Solomon, 1981).

Cherubino in Mozart's *Marriage of Figaro* asked, "What is this thing, love?"

> Cherubino was still a beardless adolescent and did not know the answer, but he took it for granted that there was one. So have most other people, and many of them have tried to give it, but the most noteworthy feature about all their answers is how thoroughly they disagree. Sometimes, it seems, they cannot be referring to the same phenomenon, or even to related ones. After a while one wonders whether there is something wrong with the question itself, or whether perhaps it employs a word of no fixed meaning and can have no fixed answer (Hunt, 1959, p. 3).

Importance of Love

Although people may disagree about the definition of love, there is little disagreement about its importance. Dr. Robert Coutts in *Love and Intimacy* (1973) wrote:

> I've come to realize that the most compelling aspect of my life has been my search for intimacy. It seems that all my life I've needed intimacy—to feel close to people, to feel included, to feel understood, and to feel wanted! I've come to realize that the possession of intimacy has been the source of both my moments of greatest happiness and well-being and of greatest pain and misgivings. (p. 11)

Coutts expressed one of our most basic needs—to feel connected to others.

"Having someone wonder where you are when you don't come home at night is a very old human need."

MARGARET MEAD

The consequences of unfulfilled love needs may be physical or emotional, often both. A specialist in psychosomatic disease reported that being lonely and unloved often leads to heart disease and premature death for the single, widowed, and divorced (Lynch, 1977). Also, in a study on love and health (Kemper & Bologh, 1981), the respondents who had recently ended a love relationship had the most negative health status. The authors concluded, "A relationship of long duration that is going well appears to have a positive effect on one's health status (p. 86)." In a nationwide study on happiness, the researcher concluded that the presence of a love relationship was essential for many people if they were to be happy (Freedman, 1978).

Peele and Brodsky (1976) have suggested that love is addictive. Like a drug, love produces a feeling of euphoria that we learn to enjoy and depend on. Once we get accustomed to the euphoria of love we need to be with our partner to feel the heightened sense of contentment and happiness. Withdrawal symptoms—depression, unhappiness, even somatic complaints—begin when the love relationship breaks. According to these writers, the person suffering from a broken love relationship goes through withdrawal in much the same way as an addict who has given up heroin.

Although love may be important for our emotional and physical well-being, we all differ in our need for emotional relationships. For some of us, our support system of friends satisfies our need for connectedness. An intense one-on-one love relationship may not be necessary or desirable. "I don't like the obligations that creep into a love relationship," said one man. "I have a lot of friends and enjoy being with them, but I don't need to be 'deeply in love' with a particular person to be happy or productive in my work." Other people may feel inordinately depressed if not in a love relationship and only feel content in such a situation.

Conditions of Love

Love develops under predictable social, psychological, physiological and cognitive conditions.

Social Conditions

Our society provides a basic context for love feelings to develop by emphasizing the importance of love. Through popular music, movies, television, and novels, the message is clear: love is an experience to pursue.

Peer influence is also important in creating the conditions for love to develop in that many of our peers establish love relationships and pair off. Their doing so makes love relationships normative and encourages us to seek the same experience.

Our society also links love and marriage together. Couples who are about to get married are expected to be in love. If they are not in love they would be ashamed to admit it. The fact that over ninety percent of Americans marry suggests that there are few who escape the love feelings that are supposed to accompany courtship and marriage.

Psychological Conditions

There are two important psychological conditions for the potential lover: a positive self-concept and the ability to self-disclose.

Positive Self-concept   The way you feel about yourself is your self-concept. A positive self-concept is one in which you like yourself and enjoy being who you are. A person who has achieved genuine self-acceptance can say:

> This is all that I am; I am no more and no less. I am sometimes wise and sometimes foolish. I am sometimes brave and sometimes cowardly. I am caring and uncaring; selfish and unselfish. I am moral and immoral. I am sometimes the best and sometimes the worst. I am all these things. I do not approve of everything I am, but that doesn't prevent me from recognizing and accepting myself for what I am. (Coutts, 1973, p. 169)

A positive self-concept is important since once you accept yourself, you can believe that others are capable of doing so, too. In contrast, a negative self-concept has devastating consequences for the individual and those people with whom he or she becomes involved. Individuals who cannot accept themselves tend to reject others.

The way we feel about ourselves and our ability to relate intimately to others have been learned. Our first potential love relationships were with our parents or the person who cared for us in infancy. As babies we were helpless. When we were hungry, cold, or wet, we cried until someone came to take care of us. Our parents became associated with reducing our discomfort. When we saw them, we knew that everything would be okay.

If we were well cared for as infants, we were helped to establish a good self-concept by being taught two things: (1) we were somebody that someone else cared about and (2) other people were good because they did things that made us feel good. When people learn as young children to love and trust those around them, they can generalize this lesson to others and eventually establish adult love relationships.

Self-disclosure   In addition to feeling good about yourself, it is helpful to disclose your feelings to others if you want to love and be loved.

> One who does not disclose himself (herself) truthfully and fully can never love another person nor can he (she) be loved by the other person. Effective loving calls for knowledge of the object. How can I love a person whom I do not know? How can the person love me if he (she) does not know me? (Jourard, 1964)

It is not easy for people to let others know who they are, what they feel, or what they think. People often fear that, if others really knew them, they might be rejected as a friend or lover. To guard against this possibility, they may protect themselves and their relationships by allowing only limited access to their thoughts and feelings.

Trust is the condition under which people are willing to disclose themselves. To feel comfortable about letting someone else inside their head, they must feel that whatever feelings or information they share will not be judged and will be kept safe with that person. If trust is betrayed, a person may become bitterly resentful and vow never to disclose her- or himself again. One woman said, "After I told my partner that I had had a homosexual experience, he told me that he was shocked and didn't know that I was 'one of them.' He refused to see me again." (How much a person should disclose is discussed in the Issues in Debate section at the end of this chapter).

Physiological and Cognitive Conditions

After the social and psychological conditions of love are set, the physiological and cognitive components of love become important. The individual must be physiologically aroused and interpret this stirred-up state in emotional terms (Schachter, 1964; Walster & Walster, 1978). For example, Carol was beginning her first year at a midwestern university. Being three states away from home in an unfamiliar university environment, she felt lonely and bored. During registration she met a good-looking junior. They exchanged pleasant glances and small talk and planned to go out together that night around 8:00. Carol became anxious when Brad had not shown up by 8:45.

When he finally arrived at 9:00, they went to a concert, drank some beer, and played the video games at a local pub. Carol had a terrific time.

Two days went by before Carol heard from Brad again. He called to ask if she wanted to go home with him for the weekend. By the end of that weekend, Carol felt she was in love. Her loneliness, fun when they were together, frustration (she never knew when Brad would call or come by), and sexual arousal (they petted but had not yet had intercourse) were enough to induce an agitated, stirred-up state. Since both her roommates were "in love," Carol identified herself as being in the same condition.

> "The magic of first love is our ignorance that it can never end."
>
> DISRAELI

Romantic and Realistic Love

Since Carol had known Brad for only a short time, the love she felt for him was probably **romantic love** (sometimes referred to as **infatuation**). It is characterized by such beliefs as love at first sight, there is only one true love, and love is the most important reason for getting married. The utlimate, almost obsessional form of romantic love has been called **limerence** (Tennov, 1979). Symptoms include drastic mood swings, palpitations of the heart, and intrusive thinking about the partner.

> "I don't want realism, I want magic."
>
> TENNESSEE WILLIAMS,
> *A STREETCAR NAMED DESIRE*

In contrast to romantic love is **realistic love**, or **conjugal love**, which tends to be characteristic of people who have been in love with each other for several years. Partners who know all about each other, yet still love each other, are said to have a realistic view of love.

The Love Attitudes Inventory on page 270 measures the tendency to be romantic or realistic. You might want to take the inventory and sum up your numbered responses in a total score. Since 1 (strongly agree) is the most romantic response and 5 (strongly disagree) is the most realistic response, the lower your total score (30 is the lowest possible score), the more romantic you are, and the higher your score (150 is the highest possible score), the more realistic you are about love. A score of 90 places you at the midpoint on the scale of romantic–realistic love.

Using the Love Attitudes Inventory, several studies have been conducted to find out the degree to which various categories of people are romantic or realistic. When 100 unmarried men and 100 unmarried women college students completed the inventory, the results revealed that men were more romantic than women and that freshman were more romantic than seniors (Knox & Sporakowski, 1968). Similar results were found almost 15 years later (Knox, 1982). Ninety-four was the average score of 97 students, men and freshmen having more romantic scores and women and seniors having more realistic scores. However, after analyzing the results of a love survey of 12,000 *Psychology Today* respondents, the researcher concluded that "more women than men say that romance is important and men rate their partners as being more romantic" (Rubenstein, 1983, p. 49).

Another study (Knox, 1970a) compared the love attitudes of 50 men and 50 women high school seniors with 50 husbands and 50 wives who had been married more than 20 years. Both the unmarried and married groups re-

My Sexuality

The Love Attitudes Inventory

Directions: Please read each sentence carefully and circle the number which you believe best represents your opinion. Be sure to respond to all statements.

1. Strongly agree (definitely yes)
2. Mildly agree (I believe so)
3. Undecided (not sure)
4. Mildly disagree (probably not)
5. Strongly disagree (definitely not)

	SA	MA	U	MD	SD
1. Love doesn't make sense. It just is.	1	2	3	4	5
2. When you fall head-over-heels-in-love, it's sure to be the real thing.	1	2	3	4	5
3. To be in love with someone you would like to marry but can't, is a tragedy.	1	2	3	4	5
4. When love hits, you know it.	1	2	3	4	5
5. Common interests are really unimportant; as long as each of you is truly in love, you will adjust.	1	2	3	4	5
6. It doesn't matter if you marry after you have known your partner for only a short time as long as you know you are in love.	1	2	3	4	5
7. If you are going to love a person, you will "know" after a short time.	1	2	3	4	5
8. As long as two people love each other, the educational differences they have really do not matter.	1	2	3	4	5

(Continued)

	SA	MA	U	MD	SD
9. You can love someone even though you do not like any of that person's friends.	1	2	3	4	5
10. When you are in love, you are usually in a daze.	1	2	3	4	5
11. Love at first sight is often the deepest and most enduring type of love.	1	2	3	4	5
12. When you are in love, it really does not matter what your partner does since you will love him/her anyway.	1	2	3	4	5
13. As long as you really love a person, you will be able to solve the problems you have with that person.	1	2	3	4	5
14. Usually there are only one or two people in the world whom you could really love and be happy with.	1	2	3	4	5
15. Regardless of other factors, if you truly love another person, that is enough to marry that person.	1	2	3	4	5
16. It is necessary to be in love with the one you marry to be happy.	1	2	3	4	5
17. Love is more of a feeling than a relationship.	1	2	3	4	5
18. People should not get married unless they are in love.	1	2	3	4	5
19. Most people truly love only once during their lives.	1	2	3	4	5
20. Somewhere there is an ideal mate for most people.	1	2	3	4	5
21. In most cases, you will "know it" when you meet the right one.	1	2	3	4	5

(Continued)

	SA	MA	U	MD	SD
22. Jealousy usually varies directly with love; that is, the more you are in love, the greater your tendency to become jealous.	1	2	3	4	5
23. When you are in love, you do things because of what you feel rather than what you think.	1	2	3	4	5
24. Love is best described as an exciting, rather than a calm thing.	1	2	3	4	5
25. Most divorces probably result from falling out of love rather than failing to adjust.	1	2	3	4	5
26. When you are in love, your judgment is usually not too clear.	1	2	3	4	5
27. Love often comes but once in a lifetime.	1	2	3	4	5
28. Love is often a violent and uncontrollable emotion.	1	2	3	4	5
29. Differences in social class and religion are of small importance as compared with love in selecting a marriage partner.	1	2	3	4	5
30. No matter what anyone says, love cannot be understood.	1	2	3	4	5

Source: *The Love Attitudes Inventory,* revised edition, by D. Knox. Saluda, N.C.: Family Life Publications, Inc., 1983. Reprinted by permission.

Unmarried couples tend to be more romantic than married couples.

vealed a romantic attitude toward love. These findings had been expected for the high school seniors but not for the older marrieds. It may be that those who have been married for 20 years adopt attitudes consistent with such a long-term investment of their time and energy; that is, the belief that there is only one person with whom an individual can really fall in love and marry justifies those who have done so.

When the high school seniors and older marrieds were compared with 100 young couples (married less than five years), the latter proved very realistic in their attitudes. For them, moonlight and roses had become daylight and dishes. They had been married too long to believe that "as long as you really love a person, you will be able to solve the problems you have with that person" but not long enough to experience the feeling that "you only really love once."

All of the preceding studies were conducted on white subjects. When 327 black high school and college students completed the Love Attitudes Inventory, the results revealed that black students had more romantic attitudes toward love than white students (Mirchandani, 1973). One explanation suggests that because black students are more likely to come from broken and

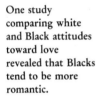

One study comparing white and Black attitudes toward love revealed that Blacks tend to be more romantic.

economically disadvantaged homes, they may seek romantic love relationships as a means of compensation (Larson, Spreitzer, & Snyder, 1976).

Jealousy

Whether a person is a romantic or a realist, feelings of **jealousy** are not uncommon. Jealousy is a set of emotions that occurs when one person perceives the love relationship he or she has is being threatened. The specific feelings are those of fear of loss or abandonment, anxiety, pain, anger, vulnerability, and hopelessness.

"O! beware, my lord, of jealousy; It is the green eyed monster which doth mock The meat it feeds on."

SHAKESPEARE

Incidence

Three-fourths of 103 women and men of varying ages and involvements in relationships reported feeling jealous. One half of the respondents described themselves as "a jealous person" (Pines and Aronson, 1983). Individuals most likely to be jealous are women (they have more reason to be jealous because of the higher infidelity rate among males), those who are not in a monogamous relationship, those who are dissatisfied with the sexual relationship with their partner, and those who are dissatisfied with their relationship in general (Hansen, 1983; Pines and Aronson, 1983).

Causes

Jealousy may be caused by external or internal factors. An external factor is the behavior of the partner, which elicits jealousy. In the study of 103 respondents mentioned above, most said that they became jealous when they were at a party with their partner and their partner spent a great deal of time talking, dancing, and flirting with someone of the opposite gender. "I get to feeling very uncomfortable when I see him enjoying himself and putting his hands all over another woman," remarked one female. Other external behaviors of the partner that create jealousy include the partner expressing appreciation for and interest in someone else, having a close friend of the opposite gender, and being involved in a love or sexual relationship with someone else. Eighty-two percent of the women and 76 percent of the men whose spouses had had an affair reported feeling jealous (Buunk, 1982).

Jealousy may also be triggered by thoughts of the individual who has learned to be distrustful in previous situations. "I know my husband is faithful to me," said one wife, "but my exhusband wasn't and it's hard for me to trust men again."

Jealous feelings may also result from a very low sense of self-esteem. People who feel they cannot get another person to love them and be faithful to them because of their looks or personality are continually jealous of others who, they fear, may take their partner away.

It is not unusual that the interaction of two people in a relationship encourages the development of jealous feelings. Suppose John accuses Mary of being interested in someone else and Mary denies the accusation and responds by saying "I love you" and by being very affectionate. If this pattern continues, Mary will teach John to be even more jealous. From John's point of view he learns that when he is jealous and accuses Mary of her interest in other people, good things happen to him—Mary showers him with love and physical affection. Inadvertently, Mary is reinforcing John for exhibiting jealous behavior. To break the cycle, Mary should tell John of her love for him and be affectionate when he is *not* exhibiting jealous behavior. When he *does* act jealous, she should say that she feels bad when he accuses her of something she isn't doing and to please stop. If he does not stop, she should terminate the interaction until John can be around her and not criticize her.

Consequences

Relationships can tolerate low levels of jealousy, which serves several functions. Not only does it keep the partner aware that they are cared for (the implied message is "I love you and don't want to lose you to someone else") but that the development of romantic and sexual relationships on the side are unacceptable. "When I started spending extra time with this guy at the office," said one wife, "my husband got jealous and told me he thought I was getting in over my head and asked me to cut back on the relationship because it was 'tearing him up' and he couldn't stay married to me with these feelings. I felt really loved when he told me this and drifted out of the relationship I was developing with the guy at the office."

Jealousy may improve a relationship in yet another way. When the partners begin to take each other for granted, involvement of one or both partners outside the relationship can incite the other partner to reevaluate how important the relationship is and stop taking the partner for granted.

However, in its extreme form, jealousy may have devastating consequences, including murder, suicide, spouse-beating, and severe depression. "I turned into an alcoholic overnight," said one male. "I just didn't want to be sober because I would think about her and this other fellow. I almost drank myself into oblivion."

Love and Sex

Diane Keaton: "Sex without love is an empty experience." Woody Allen: "Yes, but as empty experiences go, it's one of the best."

There are both similarities and differences between love and sex. The two experiences are compared here.

Similarities Between Love and Sex

In general, love and sex are more similar than they are different. These similarities include the following.

Both love and sex represent intense feelings. To be involved in a love relationship is one of the most exciting experiences an individual ever has. To know that another person loves us engenders feelings of happiness and joy. "No one ever really loved me until now," remarked one person, "and because of this love I feel filled with life's goodness."

Sex has the same capability to generate intense excitement and happiness. Although sex is more than orgasm, the latter is the epitome of intense pleasure, as we have seen in Chapter 8.

Both love and sex involve physiological changes. When a person is in an intense love relationship, his or her brain produces phenylethylamine, a chemical correlate of amphetamine, which may result in a giddy feeling similar to an amphetamine high (Liebowitz, 1983). When the love affair breaks up, the person seems to crash and go through withdrawal since there is less phenylethylamine in his or her system. Some heartbroken lovers reach for chocolate, which is loaded with phenylethylamine.

Further support for the idea that love has a physiological component has been suggested by Money (1980). He studied patients who had undergone brain surgery or suffered from a pituitary deficiency. Although they were able to experience various emotions, passionate love was not one of them.

The physiological changes the body experiences during sexual excitement have been well documented by Masters & Johnson in their observations of more than 10,000 orgasms. These were discussed in detail in Chapter 8 and included such changes as increased heart rate, blood pressure, and breathing.

Both love and sex have a cognitive component. To experience the maximum pleasure from each, the person must label or interpret what is happening in positive terms. For love to develop, each person in the relationship must define their meetings, glances, talks, and the like as enjoyable. The significance of labeling is illustrated by the experience of two women who dated the same man. Although they spent similar evenings, the first woman said, "I love him—he's great," but the other said, "He is a jerk."

Positive labeling is also important in sex. Since each person's touch, kiss, caress, and body type is different, sexual pleasure depends on labeling sexual interaction with that person as enjoyable. "I can't stand the way he French kisses" and "I love the way he French kisses" are two interpretations of kissing the same person. But only one interpretation will make the event pleasurable.

Both love and sex may be expressed in various ways. The expression of love may include words ("I love you"), gifts (flowers or candy), behaviors (being on time, a surprise phone call or visit), and touch (holding hands, tickling). Similarly, sex as well as love may be expressed through a glance, embracing, kissing, fondling, and intercourse.

The need for love and sex increases with deprivation. The more we get, the less we feel we need; and the less we get, the more we feel we need. The all-consuming passion of Romeo and Juliet, perhaps the most celebrated story of all time, undoubtedly was fed by their enforced separation. The following reflects a similar love-from-afar experience.

● I feel the thing that has affected me the most about love is that we broke up over a year and a half ago and I still think of him every day. I feel that if he walked back in the door tomorrow we would start up where we left off—but that will never happen. A month after we became involved he got a girl pregnant in his hometown and married her. This destroyed me completely and for a long time I wouldn't go out with anyone. The thing that bothered me most was when I saw him recently at a bar he told me that he still loved me but that he had to marry her because his parents found out she was pregnant. ●

Deprivation has the same effect on the need for sex. Statements of people who have been separated from their lover for several weeks may be similar to the following: "I'm horny as a mountain goat," "We're going to spend the weekend in bed," and "The second thing we're going to do when we get together is take a drive out in the country."

Differences Between Love and Sex

There are several differences between love and sex. These include the following.

Love is crucial for human happiness; sex is important but not crucial. After analyzing the data from a study of more than 100,000 people about what makes them happy, one researcher concluded: "Many people are unhappy with their sex lives and many think this is an important lack, but almost no one seems to think that sex alone will bring happiness. Romance and love were often listed as crucial missing ingredients, but not sex; it was simply not mentioned" (Freedman, 1978, p. 56).

Love is pervasive whereas sex tends to be localized. Love is felt all over, but sexual feeling is most often associated with various body parts—lips, breasts, or genitals. People do not say of love, as they do of sex, "It feels good here."

Love tends to be more selective than sex. The standards people have for a love partner are generally higher than those they have for a sex partner. Expressions like "I'll take anything that wears pants," "Just show me a room full of skirts," and "I wouldn't kick him out of bed" reflect the desire to have sex with someone—anyone. Love wants *the* person rather than *a* person.

The standards for a love partner may also be different than those for a sexual partner. For example, some people form love relationships with others to meet emotional intimacy needs not met by their sexual partners. A sexual component need not be a part of the love relationship they have with these people.

Sexual Fantasies

Sexual arousal, with or without a partner, may instigate sexual fantasy, and sexual fantasy may increase sexual arousal. A **sexual fantasy** is a daydream that may be thought of as an erotic movie that you watch in your head. Unlike a real movie, you project yourself into a fantasy and experience the events and sensations as though actually participating in them.

Purposes of Fantasy

Fantasy serves a number of purposes. What you cannot experience in reality at any particular time is immediately available through fantasy. You may be desired by the person of your choice who says and does exactly what you want.

Fantasy also provides variety. There is no limit to the people you have sex with, the sexual behaviors you engage in, or the responsiveness of your partners. Also, partners, scenes, and sexual activities can be switched in an instant. The limits of fantasy are constrained only by one's imagination. Reality is having sex with a few people; fantasy is having sex with anyone, at any time, in any way. One man said:

● My sexual fantasy is for me and a beautiful woman to get on an airplance dressed in nothing but our parachute packs. We jump out of the plane high above the clouds. On the way down, we have intercourse and achieve orgasm. After orgasm, we pull our chutes.   ●

Fantasy is a pleasure in itself. The human mind is the most erogenous organ of the body. Using the mind to create one's own unique fantasy can be highly satisfying. One woman said she always enjoyed a rich fantasy life and many of the best times in her life had happened in her head. "It's the real pleasure that is always yours," she remarked.

Fantasies may heighten sexual arousal. The greater the ability to form clear, vivid images, the greater the sexual arousal (Harris, Yulis, & Lacoste, 1980; Stock & Greer, 1982). Both women and men can achieve an orgasm through fantasy alone. Eleven percent of the women in Clifford's (1978b) study said their fantasy-induced orgasms most often occurred in a state of semisleep or on waking from a sexual dream. Men rarely have ejaculations by fantasy alone. Of the more than 5,000 males in Kinsey's et al. (1948) study, only three or four reported orgasm through fantasy alone. When fantasies are accompanied by masturbation or intercourse, sexual arousal is dramatically increased, as is the chance of orgasm.

Fantasies provide an escape. While walking to class, driving home, or listening to a lecture, you can shift your thoughts to your own world of sexual fantasy. One man said that whenever he gets bored in a class, he switches to his favorite fantasy.

● I am in a big tile room. The floor of the room is covered with warm oil. The room is filled with several beautiful women. Each one of the lovely ladies has "a round" with me, which involves many different positions and oral sex. Each one of them tells me, "You're the biggest and best I've ever had." This ends in a great climax and plenty of sliding around. ●

Finally, sexual fantasies provide excitement with safety. The inside of your head is a safe place to experience whatever sexual activity you want, and you are in control. One woman said:

● Everybody thinks I'm real straight because I dress neatly, make good grades, and take my job seriously. But in my head I have the wildest sexual experiences—one of my favorite is to fantasize that the males in my law study group are all pleasuring me at the same time. With this fantasy in mind I sometimes carry a smile to the study group. ●

Typology of Sexual Fantasies

Mednick (1977) identified the following categories of sexual fantasies.

Fantasizer as Recipient   The fantasizer fantasizes about herself or himself primarily as a recipient of sexual activity from a fantasized sexual object. Martha, a 34-year-old married woman, is the recipient in this sexual fantasy.

● I imagine that I am naked with my lover. Our bodies are close as he kisses me and tells me of his love for me. Then he says to me "hold on" and he begins to kiss down my body until his wet tongue lands on my throbbing clitoris. He licks and nibbles at me tenderly until I feel I can't stand it any more. I orgasm and quiver as he continues to drive me wild. ●

Sexual Object as Recipient   The fantasizer fantasizes about a sexual object as recipient of the fantasizer's sexual attentions within the fantasy. One man reported:

● I imagine being naked with this woman I work with . . . We are on a waterbed in the corner of a room with sunlight coming in through both windows. I am rubbing my hands slowly over all her body. As I reach her soft pubic hair she moans with pleasure. I kiss her breasts and move my mouth slowly down to her vagina. As I slowly suck and nibble at her clitoris she calls my name and jerks with excitement. ●

Fantasizer as Both Recipient and Sexual Object   The fantasizer fantasizes a scene of mutual pleasure in which she or he is both the recipient and the active sexual partner.

● My fantasy starts off by meeting a very handsome young man who shares my interests: he loves acoustic guitar, people, Shakespeare, camping, animals, and nature. We spend most of the afternoon talking and later go to his apartment to burn candles and drink wine in front of the fireplace. We make love on a bearskin rug in front of the fire. We begin by kissing and caressing each other and then perform oral sex until we both reach orgasm. After about 15 minutes of intercourse we both orgasm again. We cuddle and talk before we fall asleep, naked, in each other's arms. ●

Reliving Past Sexual Experiences   The fantasizer fantasizes about past sexual experiences with a former sexual object.

● We used to spend our summers at the beach. We would take a bottle of wine and cheese with us as we walked for miles down the shore until there was just us. Stripped, we would lie in each other's arms as the warm water sparkled around our bodies. For hours it seemed as though we would hold, caress, and talk before having intercourse. Orgasms were always mutual and completely satisfying. It was a time of complete escape from the world. ●

Preferred Sexual Fantasies

What do men and women fantasize about? "New sexual partner" headed the list for men in the Davidson (1982) study. Such a new partner may be an acquaintance or a stranger.

Acquaintance   People who have sexual fantasies about acquaintances may have varying expectations of a future relationship. Whereas some want to become involved in an ongoing relationship with the person being fantasized about, others do not want any real-life interaction. Still others want more of a relationship but feel that it would never happen. One man said there was an attractive woman in his office whom he had been having sex with in his head all year, "but I'd never ask her out."

Stranger Men and women also develop sexual fantasies about strangers. The strangers may be people they see regularly at work but have never spoken to, entertainers, or people seen at a distance. One man said he saw a woman walking across the street and locked a visual image of her in his head, which he used while masturbating that night. Another described sex with a stranger at a laundrymat.

● My fantasy is about washing my clothes at 3:00 A.M. in an empty laundry room. All of a sudden a beautiful woman walks in and uses the machine beside mine. We exchange small talk when she notices my enlarged member about to bust my zipper. She tells me she can relieve the pressure and bends down and unzips my pants. She then takes out my penis and starts to relieve me. I stop her and then proceed to undress her. We are both naked on top of the two machines as it goes from rinse to spin. As the motor increases, my rhythmic stroking increases, and as the machine tops out, I have a tremendous orgasm. I then come back to reality pleased but depressed. My beautiful woman has gone.   ●

A woman described her favorite sexual fantasy as follows.

● My best sexual fantasy involves a total stranger. I think it would be fantastic to be going about my routine business or be on a trip somewhere and look across a room, catch the eye of a complete stranger, and have something "click" between us.

I wouldn't want to meet or talk with him then, but run into him a few more times until the attraction was so strong, we could not resist meeting any more. I would then like to talk, have dinner, go dancing (all this time the attraction is still mounting), and finally end up in bed at his place.

The bedroom encounter is fantastic—we totally enjoy and are uninhibited with each other. This would continue for 3 or 4 days with the attraction still at a peak and then we would part with no regret (except that our time was up), fond memories, and never see each other again.   ●

Current Sex Partner Women most often fantasize about their current sex partner (Davidson, 1982). The fantasy occurs when the sexual partner is away. It may be of past sexual encounters or imagined future ones and may include sexual behaviors the couple have or have not shared before.

Content and Frequency of Sexual Fantasies About 60 percent of both men and women in one study (Sue, 1979) reported fantasizing at least sometimes during intercourse, although most partners are not aware that the other partner is doing so (Davidson & Hoffman, 1980).*

*From "Sexual Fantasies and Sexual Satisfaction: An Empirical Analysis of Erotic Thoughts" by J. Kenneth Davidson, Sr. (University of Wisconsin-Eau Claire) and Linda E. Hoffman (University of Notre Dame). 1980. Reprinted by permission.

The content and frequency of the sexual fantasies of Sue's respondents are listed in Table 9.1. The most frequent reasons for fantasizing were "to facilitate sexual arousal" and "to increase my partner's attractiveness." "Sometimes when we start making love," said one woman, "I can't seem to get aroused until I think of this fantasy of making love to a stranger I saw on a plane. After I get going, I switch back to my partner and it's nothing but glory until the finish."

Are Sexual Fantasies Normal?

Eighty percent of the men and 70 percent of the women in the Kinsey et al. studies (1948, 1953) reported fantasizing about sex. In a more recent study of never-married undergraduates and graduate students at a midwestern community university (Davidson, 1982), 94 percent of 144 men and 95 percent of 166 women reported having experienced a sexual fantasy.* Fantasies may occur anytime, but people most often fantasize during daydreams, masturbation, foreplay, intercourse, and just before orgasm. There does not seem to be a relationship between what people fantasize about and what they actually do or actually want to do (Friday, 1980; Sue, 1979). What they may enjoy in fantasy, they may not want to do in reality. Some individuals have elaborate bondage and discipline fantasies that produce intense erotic arousal. But they are not interested in actually being tied up and whipped. Or a woman

Table 9.1 Fantasies During Intercourse

Theme	Males (%)	Females (%)
Oral–genital sex	61	51
Others finding you sexually irresistible	55	53
An imaginary lover	44	24
A former lover	43	41
Others giving in to you after resisting at first	37	24
Forcing others to have sexual relations with you	24	16
Being forced or overpowered into a sexual relationship	21	36
Group sex	19	14
Observing others engaging in sex	18	13
Others observing you engage in sexual intercourse	15	20
Being rejected or sexually abused	11	13
A member of the same sex	3	9
Animals	1	4

Sue, D. Erotic fantasies of college students during coitus. *Journal of Sex Research*, 1979, 4, 15, 299–305. Reprinted by permission of The Society for the Scientific Study of Sex.

*Reprinted with permission of the author, J. Kenneth Davidson, Sr. from "A comparison of sexual fantasies between sexually experienced never-married males and females: Situational contexts, preferences, and functions." Paper, presented at the Southern Sociological Society's Annual Meeting, 1982.

may have the fantasy of being overpowered by a man who forces her to have sexual relations. But, in reality, the woman is horrified of actually being raped.

Although sexual fantasies are normal in the sense that most of us do fantasize, professional opinion about whether such fantasies are beneficial is divided. Some view sexual fantasies as symptoms of sexual alienation or other sexual problems. They are "pale substitutes for the complexities of joy and pain which are requisites for loving a real person" (Offit, 1977). But others feel that sexual fantasies are healthy and to be enjoyed (Galeman & Bush, 1977). A study of the sexual fantasies of 87 respondents (Zimmer, Borchardt, & Fischle, 1983) revealed a positive relationship between such fantasies and a satisfying sex life. Another study of the fantasy lives of 200 married women (Davidson & Hoffman, 1980) reported that those who incorporate sexual fantasies into their sexual activities were much more likely to report sexual satisfaction in their marriages than those who did not use fantasy.

Should Sexual Fantasies Be Shared?

There is disagreement about whether partners should share their sexual fantasies with each other. Those who feel that fantasy sharing is important point to the increased closeness they feel with their partner as a result of such intimate disclosure. Others say that fantasy sharing is an erotically stimulating experience. "Whether I'm telling Pam of my sexual fantasies or listening to hers, it creates an intense erotic atmosphere which we love. And sometimes we try to make our fantasies come true."

Those who feel negatively about sexual fantasy disclosure emphasize that it may create unnecessary jealousy. "Why should I tell my partner," asked one woman, "that the sexual fantasy that gets me the hottest is the one in which I am getting it on with his best friend? And if he would like to do the same with my best friend, I don't want to know about it." Others feel that sexual fantasies are private and they would not be comfortable sharing them with anyone. "Some of the things I fantasize about, I couldn't and wouldn't want to tell anyone about," commented one man.

In the Davidson and Hoffman study (1980) about 20 percent of the respondents reported that their sex partners were aware of their sexual fantasies. Those who disclosed their sexual fantasies to their partners tended to be as satisfied with their current sex life as those who did not. However, more respondents felt that revealing their personal sexual fantasies would have potentially negative (rather than positive) consequences on their sex partners.

Summary

Love and fantasy are two basic contexts of sexuality. Love is one of the primary emotions in interpersonal sexuality. Psychologists and philosophers have suggested biological, social, psychic, learning, and theological explanations for the origins of love. Although its definition and importance varies from person to person, it can be described on a continuum from romanticism to realism. Unmarried people and older married couples are more likely to be romantic in their attitudes toward love than young marrieds.

The development of love in a particular relationship depends on a number of conditions. Our society fosters the concept of romantic love and socializes its youth to seek it. But various psychological, physiological, and cognitive conditions must be present for "love" to develop.

Love and sex are similar and different. Both love and sex represent intense feelings, involve physiological changes, have a cognitive component, are expressed in various ways, and increase with deprivation. The differences suggest that love but not sex is crucial for happiness, love is pervasive whereas sex is localized, and love tends to be more selective than sex.

Fantasy is another context of sexual expression. Fantasy may function to increase sexual arousal, relieve boredom, provide escape, or permit the individual to enjoy what is not possible in reality. Typologies of sexual fantasies include the fantasizer or the sexual object as the recipient in present or past contexts. A new sexual partner is the most frequent sexual fantasy for males, whereas the current sexual partner is the most frequent for females. Although both genders fantasize most during daydreams, males are more likely to fantasize during masturbation and females during intercourse.

Some experts view sexual fantasies as symptoms of sexual problems; others think such fantasies are healthy. There is also disagreement about whether partners should share their sexual fantasies with each other. It may make the partners feel closer and be erotically stimulating, or it may promote jealousy.

Key Terms

aim-inhibited sex
romantic love
infatuation
limerence

realistic or conjugal love
jealousy
sexual fantasy

Issues in Debate and Future Directions

Sex with or without love: which is better? and How open should you be with your partner? are questions for which there are no clear-cut answers. After looking at the respective viewpoints, we suggest future directions of the love-and-sex relationship.

Sex With and Without Love: Which Is Better?

Some individuals feel that sex is best in the context of a love relationship. This is particularly true of women who have been socialized to equate the two. Men are more likely to compartmentalize sex and love, but there are some who require a love relationship before feeling comfortable about sexual involvement.

Two people expressed their preference for sex with love as follows.

● As a divorced person I have been involved in a number of sexual encounters. I can only say that none have been as fulfilling or pleasurable as the ones in which there was mutual love, understanding, and consideration involved along with it.

Sex is good and beautiful when both parties want it but when one person wants sex only, that's bad. I love sex, but I like to feel that the man cares about me. I can't handle the type of sexual relationship where one night I spend the night with him and the next night he spends the night with someone else. I feel like I am being used. There are still a few women around like me who *need* the commitment before sex means what it should. ●

Others feel that love is not necessary for sexual expression. Indeed, the theme of the book *Sex Without Love* (Vannoy, 1980) is that sex should be enjoyed for its own sake. One person said:

● You choose a lover according to how you wish to be loved, and you choose a sex partner according to how you wish to be laid. There is no guarantee whatever that the person you love and the person whom you find most sexually desirable are one and the same. There are just certain things a lover may not be able to give you, and it may be good sex. (p.24) ●

Vannoy believes the idea that sex with love is wholesome and sex without love is exploitative is a fallacious dualism. Two strangers can meet, share each other sexually, have a deep mutual admiration for each other's sensuous qualities, and go their separate ways in the morning. "Their parting is not evidence that their sexual encounter was exploitation. Rather, it is a sign of their preference for independence and singlehood rather than permanent emotional involvement and marriage" (p. 26). One woman noted:

● I have never had sex with a man I was emotionally involved with or committed to. In fact, I *seek* sex without love or emotional ties. For me, the costs of love (devotion of time and energy, loss of personal space and privacy) far outweigh its benefits. Sex without emotional involvement and commitment is erotic and fulfilling. ●

Each person in a sexual encounter will, undoubtedly, experience different degrees of love feelings, and the experience of each may differ across time. One woman reported that the first time she had intercourse with her future husband was shortly after they had met in a bar. She described their first sexual encounter as "raw, naked sex" with no emotional feelings. But as they continued to see each other over a period of months, an emotional relationship developed and "sex took on a love meaning for us."

Sex with love can also drift into sex without love. One man said that he had been deeply in love with his wife but that he had come to despise her because she was seeing other men. "I used to think of her as a princess but now I think of her as a whore. When we have sex now, there is no love."

It may be helpful to recognize that rarely are sexual encounters with or without love. Rather, they will have varying degrees of emotional involvement. Also, rarely are romantic love relationships with or without sex. Rather, they will have varying degrees of sexual expression. The degree of emotional and sexual involvement will vary from person to person.

How Much Should You Tell?

How much communication is good for your relationship? Does a we-tell-each-other-everything disclosure philosophy have more positive consequences than a discreet disclosure philosophy? One therapist suggested that in spite of all the urging of those who write for the mass media to be open and let it all hang out, to "jump on the bandwagon for fully uncensored communication is a ride couples should not take" (Stuart, 1980, p. 218).

Adopting a "norm of measured honesty" in a relationship may be advisable for two reasons. First, negative information carries more weight than positive information. When a partner discloses negatives, the other partner may have difficulty keeping the disclosure in the context of other positives. One man said that he and his partner had the pattern of being completely open with each other. "One night," he said, "she told me that I really had a short penis. After I knew how she felt, something snapped in me and I didn't want to be near her again. I know she loves me but I couldn't help feeling bad."

Second, all relationships may need some illusions to survive. Falling in love is usually not enough for most of us. We want our relationships, and particularly our new partner, to be perfect (Walster & Walster, 1978). Part of this perfectionist thinking is that our partner loves and is sexually attracted only to us. When our partner tells us that "I am really attracted to this new person at work," we may appreciate the honesty of the statement but feel rejected by the content. The lyrics to an old song, "How many arms have held you but I really don't want to know" aptly describes our ambivalence.

But there are certain items that may be painful to the partner that probably should be disclosed. For example, having a sexual orientation different from what the partner expects is information that could harm the relationship if not told. However, whether this information is disclosed will depend on the nature of the relationship and the goals of the partners.

Future Directions

In the future love will become a more valued context for sex. Impersonal, brief, sex-for-the-sake-of-sex relationships will give way to a new yearning for sex with a loved partner. Of 12,000 respondents in the *Psychology Today* survey, 30 percent of the men and over 40 percent of the women said that sex without love was either unenjoyable or unacceptable. Half of those

(continued)

under the age of 22 felt this way (Rubenstein, 1983). This sex-with-love trend is a side effect of a more general trend—increasingly, Americans have begun to search for more meaningful personal relationships (Yankelovich, 1981a).

But such relationships will not necessarily mean commitment and marriage. Since the proportion of those in our society who are single (through delayed marriage, separation, and divorce) is increasing, a greater proportion of love relationships will occur independently of marriage.

Chapter Ten

Sexual Fulfillment

Too much of a good thing can be wonderful.

MAE WEST

Chapter Ten

"Sexual fulfillment for me," said a 26-year-old woman, "is having sex with someone I love. He accepts my sexuality and is not turned off to my strong responses. In addition he is responsive to my needs and is willing to invest the time it takes to excite me. Good sex takes love, time, patience, caring, and experimentation."

In this chapter we look at the meanings, prerequisites, facts, and myths of sexual fulfillment. Also, since growing older is something we all do, we look at sex in the middle and later years. First, we examine the various meanings of sexual fulfillment.

Meanings of Sexual Fulfillment

Sexual fulfillment means different things to different people—and at different times.

Individual Definitions

Sexual fulfillment may mean

achieving physical pleasure with someone you are emotionally involved with;

letting yourself go from social restrictions and really enjoying sex;

a relationship that releases a need for bodily involvement;

bringing each other to orgasm and sharing the feelings of love and oneness;

a feeling of completeness—mentally and physically;

responsiveness of each partner to the emotional and physical needs of the other;

both partners (not just one) enjoying each other sexually;

having a partner who likes the same things you do during lovemaking;

having all the sex you want with the person you want to have it with;

making love with showers, massages, candlelight, wine, and conversation all night long.

According to the Connecticut Mutual Life Report (1981), people who regard a sexually fulfilling relationship as important are more often male, young, married, and of higher income and education levels (Figure 10.1).

Sexual fulfillment depends in part upon having a good sexual partner. In a survey conducted by the author of this book, 100 respondents were asked to specify the characteristics of a good sexual partner (Table 10.1). The most frequent characteristic mentioned by both genders was being loved or cared for by their sexual partner. "Having sex with someone is easy," said one person. "It's the person behind the genitals who cares about you that makes it special." But other respondents did not mention the emotional relationship with a partner. Rather, they focused on characteristics such as variety, aggressiveness, patience, and endurance. One woman said, "If he can't stay erect for two hours I wouldn't want him."

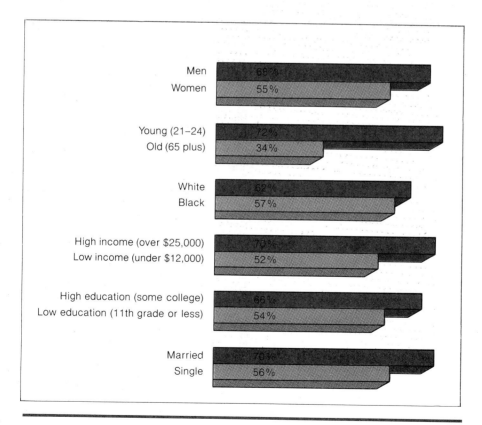

Figure 10.1
Characteristics of People Who Say a Sexually Fulfilling Relationship Is Important

Table 10.1   **What Is a Good Sexual Partner?**

Women say he . . .	Men say she . . .
loves me	loves me
cares about me	cares about me
caresses me gently and tenderly	is aggressive
is patient	likes variety (oral sex, different positions)
is clean; smells good	communicates openly about what she wants
likes variety	
stays erect	is good looking
maintains eye contact	has a trim body
only has sex with me	is more concerned about my satisfaction than hers
is more concerned about my pleasure than his	has good rhythm and duration
has recently shaved or has a soft beard	doesn't cry or feel guilty afterward
holds and cuddles me after he ejaculates rather than going to sleep, to the bathroom, or smoking	plays with my testicles
	talks dirty to me during intercourse
lets me be aggressive without making me feel it is inappropriate	groans or screams at orgasm
doesn't pressure me to do things I don't want to do	

Sexual Fulfillment and Intercourse

The variety of definitions associated with sexual fulfillment make it clear that there is no specific element, including intercourse, in a sexual relationship that must be present in order for sexual fulfillment to exist.

A couple who never has intercourse may also be sexually fulfilled. One couple reported:

● We've been married for 43 years and haven't had intercourse in 10 years or so. The idea that you need to have intercourse with your spouse to be sexually and emotionally happy is nonsense. We love each other, go everywhere together, and have three beautiful grandchildren. There is more to life than intercourse. ●

There are a number of explanations why intercourse is not necessary for some couples who define themselves as sexually fulfilled and happy: (1) There is little peer pressure to have intercourse with one's spouse. (2) Sexual experiences may not have been particularly enjoyable—the man ejaculated prematurely or was impotent or the woman did not climax. (3) Masturbation may be preferred over intercourse. (4) Other shared interests are more enjoyable than sexual involvement. (5) Physical problems (arthritis, slipped disc, or the like) may make sexual participation painful or unpleasant. (6) Definitions such as "we're too old for that" or "that part of our life is over" may be adopted by the couple who feel that sex should diminish with age. (7) Mutual playful physical affection (hugging, holding, kissing) may have become a substitute rather than a prelude to intercourse. (8) One partner may initially be more disinterested in sex than the mate and discourage sexual advances; over time, the mate learns not to expect sex from the partner.

Sexual Fulfillment Over Time

The level of sexual fulfillment also varies with time. Age, career involvements, children, health, and sexual experience all combine to influence the sexual quality of a couple's relationship. As we shall see later in this chapter, while getting older may be associated with decreasing sexual activity, the level of sexual and emotional enjoyment may increase.

Intense career involvement, the presence of children, and poor health also tend to correlate with less frequent sexual activity; but, again, couples do not necessarily define fulfillment in terms of frequency. "It's how you do it when you do it, not how often you do it that matters," said one woman. Change in circumstances (and, sometimes, partners) is inevitable. But the impact of those changes and the definition of them is less certain.

Sexual Fulfillment: Some Prerequisites

Regardless of variations in the definitions of sexual fulfillment, there seem to be several prerequisites for its existence: self-knowledge, a good relationship, open communication, realistic expectations, and a display of sexual interest in the partner.

Self-Knowledge

Being sexually fulfilled implies having knowledge about yourself and your body. To be in touch with yourself and your own body is to know how you can best experience sexual pleasure. "I've read all the books on how to get the most out of sex," said one man, "and I've concluded that the experts know a lot about what some people like sexually, but nothing about what I like. Good sex for me is more related to the context than to the technique. And I'm sure that for the next person it's something else."

A Good Relationship

A rule among counselors who work with couples who have sexual problems is "Treat the relationship before focusing on the sexual problem." The sexual relationship is part of the larger relationship between the partners, and what happens outside the bedroom in day-to-day interaction has a tremendous influence on what happens inside the bedroom. The statement, "I can't fight with you all day and want to have sex with you at night" illustrates the social context of the sexual experience. One woman described this context very clearly.

● I don't understand him. He's ready to go any time. It's always been a big problem with us right from the beginning. If we've hardly seen each other for two or three days and hardly talked to each other, I can't just jump into bed. If we have a fight, I can't just turn it off. He has a hard time understanding that. I have to know I'm needed and wanted for more than just jumping into bed." (Rubin, 1976, p. 50) ●

A good out-of-bed relationship implies spending time together, being affectionate, communicating, and sharing similar values. Also, the nature of a couple's economic relationship can affect their sex life. In a study of dual-career marriages (Johnson, Kaplan, & Tusel, 1979), the researchers reported that the wives became much more assertive and sexually demanding after they became employed. This was viewed as a function of the wife's increased economic power and self-esteem once she began to bring money into the unit. "Many wives seemed less likely to accept the blame for unsatisfactory sexual performance. . . . Some attempted to get their husbands to read sex manuals or were more vocal about the staleness of their sexual relationship" (p. 7).

The type of relationship also may be important. After separate interviews with the spouses of 53 newlywed couples to assess the degree to which their having an equitable relationship contributed to sexual satisfaction (Hatfield et al., 1982), the researchers concluded that equitably treated men and women were more satisfied with their sexual relationships overall than those who felt they were getting more or less out of the relationship than were their partners.

The effects of a couple's overall relationship and their sexual relationship are reciprocal. Someone observed that when sex goes well it's 15 percent of a relationship and when it goes badly it's 85 percent, and undoubtedly many partners would agree. The sexual relationship positively influences the couple's relationship in several ways: (1) as a shared pleasure, a positively reinforcing event; (2) to facilitate intimacy, since many couples will feel closer and share their feelings before or after a sexual experience; and (3) to reduce tension generated by the stresses of everyday living and couple interaction (McCarthy, 1982).

Open Sexual Communication

Sexually fulfilled partners are comfortable expressing what they enjoy and do not enjoy in the sexual experience. Unless both partners communicate their needs, preferences, and expectations to each other, neither is ever sure what the other wants. A classic example of the uncertain lover is the man who picks up a copy of *The Erotic Man* at the bookstore and leafs through the pages until the topic on how to please a woman catches his eye. He reads that women enjoy having their breasts stimulated by their partner's tongue and teeth. Later that night in bed, he rolls over and begins to nibble on his partner's breasts. Meanwhile, she wonders what has possessed him and is unsure what to make of this new (possibly unpleasant) behavior. Sexually fulfilled partners take guesswork out of their relationship by communicating preferences and giving feedback. This means using what some therapists call the touch-and-ask rule. Each touch and caress may include the question "How does that feel?" It is then the partner's responsibility to give feedback. If the caress does not feel good, she or he can say what does feel good. Guiding and moving the partner's hand or body are also ways of giving feedback.

Open sexual communication is more than expressing sexual preferences and giving feedback. Women wish that men were more aware of a number of sexual issues. Some of their comments follow.

- It does not impress women to hear about other women in the man's past.
- If men knew what it is like to be pregnant, they would not be so apathetic about birth control.
- Most women want more caressing, gentleness, kissing, and talking *before* and *after* intercourse.
- The loss of a woman's virginity may have negative psychological effects.
- Sometimes the woman wants sex even if the man does not. Sometimes she wants to be aggressive.
- Intercourse can be enjoyable without a climax.
- Many women do not have an orgasm from penetration only—they need direct stimulation of their clitoris by their partner's tongue or finger. Men should be interested in fulfilling their partner's sexual needs.
- Most women prefer to have sex in a love relationship that is exclusive.
- When a woman says no, she means it. Women do not want men to expect sex every time they are alone with their partner.
- Many women enjoy sex in the morning, not just at night.
- Sex is *not* everything.
- Women need to be lubricated before penetration.
- Many women will wait for a deep love relationship to develop before they have intercourse.
- Men should know more about menstruation.
- Many women are no more inhibited about sex than men.
- Women do not like men to roll over, go to sleep, or leave right after orgasm.
- Intercourse is more of a love relationship than a sex act for some women.
- The man should be concerned about his partner having an orgasm rather than just satisfying himself.
- The woman should not always be expected to supply a method of contraception. It is also the man's responsibility.

- Women tend to like a loving, gentle, patient, tender, and understanding partner. Rough sexual play can hurt and be a turn-off.
- Men should know that all women are not alike. Not all women are ready to jump in bed the same night you meet them, nor are they all as cold as a deep freeze. Each one is different.

Men also have a list of things they wish women knew about sex.

- Men do not always want to be the dominant partner—women should be more aggressive.
- Men want women to enjoy sex totally and not be inhibited.
- Women should learn how to kiss passionately.
- Women need to return love while in bed. They should know how to give pleasurable fellatio.
- Women need to know a man's erogenous zones.
- Oral sex is good and enjoyable—not bad and unpleasant.
- Many men enjoy a lot of romantic foreplay and slow, aggressive sex. One man says, "I hate a dead screw."
- Men cannot keep up intercourse forever. Most men tire more easily than women.
- Looks are not everything.
- Women should know how to enjoy sex in different ways and different positions.
- Women should not expect a man to get a second erection right away.
- Many men enjoy sex in the morning.
- Pulling the hair on a man's body can hurt.
- Many men enjoy sex in a caring, loving, exclusive relationship.
- Men may want either uninvolved or involved sexual experiences.
- It is frustrating to stop sex play once it has started.
- Women should know that all men are not out to have intercourse with them. Some men like to talk and become friends.

Realistic Expectations

To achieve sexual fulfillment, expectations must be realistic. A couple's sexual needs, preferences, and expectations may not coincide. Women and men not only have different biological makeups but they also have been socialized differently. It is unrealistic to assume that your partner will want to have sex with the same frequency and in the same way that you do on all occasions. Sexual fulfillment means not asking things of the sexual relationship that it cannot deliver. Failure to develop realistic expectations will result in frustration and resentment.

Demonstration of Sexual Interest in the Partner

Another prerequisite for sexual fulfillment is for each partner to convey to the other a desire for sexual interaction. The importance of such a demonstration of sexual interest was illustrated in a nationwide survey of 4,000 men, 60 percent of whom reported that the most irritating aspect of sexual intercourse was "when the woman seems cold or disinterested" (Pietropinto & Simenauer, 1977). The need to feel wanted is not unique to men. One woman said, "I like to know that I'm sexually appealing to my partner, otherwise I feel rejected."

Sexual Fulfillment: Some Facts

Sexual fulfillment also requires an awareness of basic facts about human sexuality. In addition to the facts of anatomy and physiology presented in previous chapters, other important facts relate to learned attitudes and behaviors, sex as a natural function, the development of sexual communication, interferences with sexual functioning, and the effects of health on sexual performance.

Sexual Attitudes and Behaviors Are Learned

Whether you believe that "Sex is sinful" or "If it feels good, do it," your sexual attitudes have been learned. Your parents and peers have had a major impact on your sexual attitudes, but there have been other influences as well: school, church or synagogue, and the media. Your attitudes about sex would have been different if the influences you were exposed to had been different.

The same is true of your sexual behavior. The words you say, the sequence of events in lovemaking, the specific behaviors you engage in, and the positions you adopt during intercourse are a product of your and your partner's learning history. Learning accounts for most sexual attitudes and behaviors; and negative patterns can be unlearned and positive ones learned.

Sex Is a Natural Function

Although your sexual attitudes and behaviors are heavily dependent on learning, your genital reflexes are innate. "To define sex as natural means that just as an individual cannot be taught how to sweat or how to digest food, a man cannot be taught to have an erection, nor can a woman be taught how to lubricate vaginally" (Kolodny et al., 1979, p. 479). Sex therapy is often aimed at minimizing the impact of negative learning experiences so that the natural processes can take over (see Chapter 11).

Effective Sexual Communication Takes Time and Effort

Most of us who have been reared in homes in which discussions about sex were infrequent or nonexistent may have developed relatively few skills in talking about sex. Shifting to sex talk with our partner from, say, talking about current events may seem awkward. Overcoming our awkward feelings requires retraining ourselves so that sex becomes as easy for us to talk about as what we had for lunch. Some suggestions that may be helpful in developing effective sexual communication include the following.

Say Sex Words   Develop a list with your partner that contains all of the technical and slang words you can think of about sex. Then alternate with your partner reading one word after the other from the list. Laughter, embarrassed or otherwise, usually accompanies the first few readings, but repeat the readings until each of you is as comfortable with the words on the sex list as with those on a grocery list. It usually takes several readings over a period of weeks before you will develop a neutral reaction to the sex words. This reaction is important for you to feel comfortable talking about sex with your partner.

Read Sexuality Books; See Movies   To give you and your partner a common focus for discussing sexual issues, you might consider reading a chapter or two from one of several books available in your local bookstore. *For Each Other: Sharing Sexual Intimacy* (Barbach, 1982), *How to Make Love to a Woman* (Morgenstern, 1982), and *How to Make Love to a Man* (Penney, 1981) are examples. Or consider seeing a sexually explicit R- or X-rated film. Although some people are offended by such films, others find them exciting. Whatever your reaction, the value of the book or movie will be in its initiating communication about sex.

Ask Open-Ended Questions   To learn more about your partner, ask specific questions that cannot be answered with a yes or no. Examples include "What does orgasm feel like to you?" "Tell me about the sexual activities you like best," and "How often do you feel the need for sex?"

Give Reflective Feedback   When your partner shares a very intimate aspect of her- or himself, it is important to respond in a nonjudgmental way. One way to do this is to reflect back what your partner tells you.

Suppose Mary tells Jim that the best sex for her is when he is holding and caressing her, not when they are actually having intercourse. An inappropriate response by Jim to her disclosure would be "Something must be the matter with you." Such a response would stop any further disclosure of Mary's feelings to Jim. But Jim's reflective statement, "Our being close is what you like best in our relationship," confirms for Mary that he understands how she feels and that her feelings are accepted.

"Spectatoring" Interferes with Sexual Functioning

One of the obstacles to sexual functioning is **spectatoring**. When Masters and Johnson (1970) observed how individuals actually behave during sexual intercourse, they reported a tendency for sexually dysfunctional partners to act as spectators by mentally observing their own and their partners' sexual performance. The man would focus on whether he was having an erection, how complete it was, and whether it would last. He might also watch to see whether his partner was having an orgasm. His partner would ask corresponding questions about herself and him.

Spectatoring as Masters and Johnson conceived it interferes with each partner's sexual enjoyment because it creates anxiety about performance; and anxiety blocks performance. A man who worries about getting an erection reduces his chances of doing so. A woman who is anxious about achieving an orgasm probably will not. The desirable alternative to spectatoring is to relax, focus on and enjoy your own pleasure, and permit your body's natural sexual responsiveness to take over.

Spectatoring is not limited to sexually dysfunctional couples and it is not necessarily associated with psychopathology. Spectatoring is a reaction to our concern that we and our partners are performing consistent with our expectations. We all probably have engaged in spectatoring to some degree. It is when spectatoring is continual that performance is impaired.

Physical and Psychological Health Affects Sexual Performance

Effective sexual functioning requires good physical and mental health. Physically, this means regular exercise, good nutrition, and lack of disease. Regular exercise, whether through walking, jogging, skiing, swimming, or bicycling, is associated with increased sexual activity (Frauman, 1982). Also, as

A healthy body contributes to a good sexual relationship.

might be expected, lack of disease is related to frequent sexual functioning. Sexual behavior is dependent on the proper nerve connections between the brain, spinal cord, and genitals. Any disease that affects neural transmission, such as multiple sclerosis, may result in an impairment in sexual performance.

The genitals also need a rich blood supply, particularly the penis. Diseases like leukemia and sickle cell anemia can cause problems in erection. Hormones released by the endocrine system also play an essential role in sexual functioning. Diseases that affect the endocrine system such as diabetes mellitus and Addison's disease may depress sexual desire and cause difficulties in achieving erection and orgasm (Schiavi, 1979). A large category of people whose sexual functioning may be at least temporarily affected by disease is heart attack victims. The accompanying box "Heart Disease and Sexual Activity" describes their situation.

Physical illness may lead to depression, which may affect a person's sexuality. The ill person may feel emotionally devastated and lose all desire for sex (Mathew & Weinman, 1982). "When I found out that I had cancer, I went numb. And sex seems to have disappeared as a meaningful part of my life," said one man. But there may be other causes for depression than physical illness. Failing in school, at work, or in a love relationship can also trigger feelings of depression and temporarily turn off sexual interest. A husband and wife who are depressed about their marriage have intercourse less frequently and the wife has orgasm less often than spouses in happy marriages (Tamburello & Seppecher, 1977). "Leave me alone is about all I want to say to my husband," expressed one unhappy wife.

Sometimes physical and psychological factors interact to produce a negative effect on sexual functioning. Obesity does not necessarily lead to an undesirable sex life, and when it does it is sometimes related to other medical conditions like diabetes. But more often, the obese person tends to have a poor body image and low self-esteem. "He kept telling me that he wished I was trim and that he didn't enjoy making love to a fat lady," said one woman. Since the tendency to be obese may be genetic or hormonal, obese people often feel helpless to change their condition.

So sexual fulfillment depends on a healthy body, mind, and interpersonal relationship. When all factors are optimum, sexual happiness is more likely to soar. A jogger who is in a loving relationship said, "Our life—both sexual and nonsexual—is tops. We feel in love with life itself as well as each other."

Sexual Fulfillment: Some Myths

Sexual fulfillment also involves recognition that some of the information that passes for fact in our society is actually myth. Let us examine some of the more prevalent myths.

Heart Disease and Sexual Activity

Of the more than 1.5 million Americans who have a heart attack each year, about 950,000 survive (*Heart Facts*, 1983). Although these patients get ample information about eliminating smoking, reducing weight, and getting plenty of exercise, few get advice about their sex lives. Yet sex is one of the primary concerns of the person who has suffered a heart attack. About 30 percent report a decrease in intercourse frequency following a heart attack (Walbrek & Burchell, 1980). A basic question in the mind of the cardiac patient is "How will sexual activity increase my risk of having another heart attack?"

In general, although heart rate and blood pressure do increase during the plateau and orgasmic phases of the sexual response cycle, they return to preexcitement levels within a short time. There is the same stress on the cardiovascular system if the patient climbs two flights of stairs. Physicians usually suggest that their patients can resume intercourse if they have begun an exercise program and can climb two flights of stairs without getting out of breath (Wagner & Sivarajan, 1979).

In addition to the stair test, there are some other conditions the cardiac patient should be alert to before resuming intercourse. These include having intercourse in a room with moderate temperature, waiting at least three hours after a heavy meal or drinking alcohol, and avoiding a new partner, the latter to avoid anxiety. If the partner is an extramarital one, the anxiety might be particularly high.

The cardiac patient should be particularly alert to any of the following conditions and report them to the physician: chest pain during or after intercourse, unusual beating of the heart that continues for 15 minutes or more after intercourse, sleeplessness caused by sexual exertion, and feeling very tired the day after intercourse. Most cardiac patients resume active sex lives. Of 100 couples in which the husband had a heart attack, 76 resumed sexual activity within 3 years (Papadopoulos, 1980). In a study of wives who had a heart attack, their orgasmic responsiveness was not affected (Kolodny, 1981b).

Myth 1: Simultaneous Orgasm Is the Ultimate Sexual Experience

Having an orgasm at the same time as your partner may be an enjoyable experience, but there are two problems in achieving such a goal. First, it is difficult to fully enjoy your own orgasm while trying to do what is necessary to assist your partner in achieving an orgasm. Second, men and women react differently in their bodily movements at the time of orgasm. As McCary (1976) expressed it:

> The man's tendency is to plunge into the vagina as deeply as possible at the moment of his orgasm, to hold this position for a length of time, and to follow, perhaps, with one or two deep deliberate thrusts. The woman's tendency, on the other hand, is to have the same stroking, plunging movements of the earlier stages of intercourse continued during the orgasmic reaction, with perhaps an acceleration of the thrusts and an increase of pressure in the vulva area. These two highly pleasurable patterns of movement are obviously incompatible. Since they cannot both be executed at the same time, whichever pattern is carried out during simultaneous orgasm must perforce detract from the full pleasure of one of the partners. (p.287)

To avoid these incompatibilities and distractions, many couples adopt a "my turn–your turn" pattern in their lovemaking. The man delays his climax until his partner has climaxed (one or more times). In this way the woman can focus on the sexual sensations that are being produced in her body without worrying about whether her partner is climaxing. After she has achieved sexual satisfaction, she can devote her attention to her partner, and he can focus on enjoying his own climax.

Myth 2: Intercourse During Menstruation Is Harmful

Although a woman may prefer not to have intercourse during her period because of an unusually heavy flow or because of cramps, there is no harmful effect on her or on her partner if they do so. Seventy percent of the respondents in one study who were under age 35 reported having intercourse during menstruation (Paige, 1978). Some women report that orgasm helps to relieve menstrual cramps. A couple's doubts about engaging in intercourse during this time may be associated with feelings about menstrual blood, which many people have been taught is "bad."

The taboo against intercourse during menstruation is culturally pervasive and has a long history. Both genders often learn to call menstruation "the curse," "doomsday," or "being sick." The Old Testament warns that anyone lying with a woman within seven days of the onset of her period "shall be unclean seven days and every bed whereon he lieth shall be unclean" (Lev. 15:24). For many, breaking this taboo is difficult.

Myth 3: Sex Equals Intercourse and Orgasm

Once a couple begin kissing, embracing, and taking off their clothes, it is assumed that intercourse and orgasm must follow. This may be the preference of both partners, but it is not always the case. Seven of 10 women in a study of 20,000 women (Sarrel & Sarrel, 1980) said achieving orgasm was not essential for a satisfying sex life. One woman said, "Intercourse is really for him. I'd just as soon cuddle next to him, have him kiss me, play with my face, and curl my hair with his fingers." For these people sexual interaction is pleasure producing though not necessarily orgasm producing.

It is also assumed that to omit intercourse from lovemaking is to leave things incomplete, to be a failure. Since so many values in our culture are encapsulated by ideas like "finish what you start," the person who is not particularly interested in intercourse on a particular occasion nonetheless may feel compelled to have intercourse (Kolodny et al., 1979). This feeling, in turn, may create negative feelings toward the partner and the relationship. Such feelings might be avoided if the partners do not insist on intercourse or orgasm each time they want to enjoy each other sexually.

Myth 4: Sexual Boredom Is Inevitable

Since the frequency of intercourse tends to decrease the longer the partners know each other, it is assumed that sexual boredom is the cause and that such boredom is inevitable. But many partners avoid boredom by introducing variety into their sex lives. Some sex partners vary the time of their sexual encounters (from week nights, to weekend afternoons), place (from bed to bath or shower), and context (from home to motel or friend's apartment). Others use pornography (an X-rated video cassette), devices (vibrators or silk scarves), positions (there are more than 75), and oral sex. Still others play "flip a page" to enhance their sexual relationship. One woman gave her partner a copy of *More Joy of Sex* on their anniversary and said, "You pick a page and let's do it." Sexual boredom is not inevitable.

Sexual Fulfillment Beyond Youth

The assumed focus of our discussion of sexual fulfillment has been on the sexuality of youthful partners. Although the same information is relevant to those in their middle and later years, some people seem reluctant to think about sex among older people. When respondents were asked to complete a questionnaire on their parents' sex lives, one suggested that the only people who think of their parents' sexual relations are "perverts" (Pocs et al., 1977).

Since another view of perversion may be *not* to explore sexuality in the middle and later years, this section will focus on both. These are the periods that your parents are now experiencing, and these are the times through which you will also pass (or are already passing through). The elderly represent the one minority group most of us will join.

Middle Age

When does a person become middle-aged? The U.S. Census Bureau regards you as middle-aged when you reach 45. Family life specialists define middle age as that time when the last child leaves home and continues until retirement or either spouse dies. Humorist Lawrence Peter (1982) has provided a couple of additional definitions: "Middle age is when you can do just as much as you could ever do—but would rather not" and "Middle age is when work is a lot less fun and fun is a lot more work (pp. Oct 9 and May 4)."

Regardless of how middle age is defined, it is a time of transition. Let us examine what happens to women, men, and their sexuality during this period.

Women in Middle Age

Women in middle age undergo a number of social, sexual, and psychological changes. A major social event for most women in middle age is the departure of their children from the home (more than 90 percent of women marry and have children). For 20 to 30 years, the traditional wife and mother has been primarily concerned with cooking meals, washing clothes, and nurturing children. Now her children are gone. Some women become depressed at this time. "I've always been good at taking care of children," a middle-aged mother said. "When my last one leaves for college on Thursday, I don't know what I'll do. I know it's time—and it's best for her to go—but I'll miss her desperately. I almost feel like my life is over." From this woman's perspective, she has lost the social validation of her existence.

But to other women their children's leaving means freedom from the restrictions of the parental role and the beginning of a second life. "I've enjoyed my children, and I love all of them," stated another middle-aged mother, "but I'm very glad it's over. My husband and I are free at last to enjoy ourselves. It's almost like courtship again." Some of these freed mothers seek employment, others return to school, and still others become active in civic affairs. In contrast to the full-time mother, the career woman with children has always lived an active life outside the home. Because her career is firmly established, she is less likely to feel a void when her children move out.

Terms

How do middle-aged women whose children have left home regard their situation? In a national survey (Glenn, 1975), postparental women were asked, "Taken all together, how would you say things are these days—would you say that you are very happy, pretty happy, or not too happy?" Almost half (48.2 percent) reported that they were "very happy." When the responses of these women were compared with those of women of similar age who still had children in the home, the postparental women were happier. Whatever difficulties they experience when their children leave home are short term. Most women regain a sense of equilibrium and view the "present and the future as meaningful extensions of the past" (Barber, 1980, p. 92).

Whereas disengagement from the parental role is the major social event in the life of the middle-aged woman, **menopause** is the primary physical event during this period. Defined as the permanent cessation of menstrua-

The career woman often has an easier adjustment to her children leaving home than the traditional homemaker.

tion, menopause is caused by the gradual decline of estrogen produced by the ovaries. It occurs around age 50 for most women but may begin earlier or later. Signs that the woman may be nearing menopause include decreased menstrual flow and a less predictable cycle. After 12 months with no period, the woman is said to be through menopause.

The term **climacteric** is often used synonymously with menopause. But menopause refers only to the time when the menstrual flow permanently stops, while climacteric refers to the whole process of hormonal change induced by the ovaries, pituitary gland, and hypothalmus.

A typical reaction to such hormonal changes is the "hot flash." The experience is "a sudden rush of fiery heat from the waist up, increased reddening of the skin surface, and a drenching perspiration. Following the hot flash there may be a very cold chill, whitening of the skin surface, and sudden shivers"

(Smallwood & VanDyck, 1979, p. 73). About 4 in 10 menopausal women report hot flashes. Other symptoms experienced, though less often, include heart palpitations, dizziness, irritability, headaches, weight gain, and backache.

Most women do not have these experiences during menopause, but many women report other physiological and behavioral changes as a result of the aging process and of decreasing levels of estrogen: (a) a delay in the reaction of the clitoris to direct stimulation, (b) less lubrication during sexual excitement, (c) a less intense orgasm, (d) a smaller vaginal opening, and (e) perhaps increased sexual interest.

To minimize the effects of decreasing levels of estrogen, some physicians recommend **estrogen replacement therapy** or **ERT**, particularly to control hot flashes during the climacteric. But because the long-range results of ERT are not known and there is some evidence that it contributes to cancer of the uterus, many physicians are cautious about the use of such therapy.

The psychological reaction to menopause is mixed. Some women are elated that they do not have to worry about contraception or contend with the monthly blood flow. "I wish I had gone through menopause 10 years ago," reflected one woman. "My sex life has never been better."

But other women are saddened because they view menopause as the end of their childbearing capacity. At the extreme, some women view it not as the change of life but as the end of life. Their negative feelings about the menopausal years are related partly to the value our society places on the youthful appearance of women. To improve their self-esteem, some menopausal women seek a relationship with a younger man to affirm that they are still sexually desirable (Prosen & Martin, 1979).

A cross-cultural look at menopause suggests that a woman's reaction to this phase of her life may be related to the society in which she lives. For example, among Chinese women, fewer menopausal symptoms have been observed. Researchers have suggested this may be due to the fact that older women in China are highly respected, as are older people generally. Griffin (1977) has hypothesized that the magnitude of the symptoms associated with menopause is correlated with the few roles available to the older woman.

Men in Middle Age

Whereas middle-aged women must adjust to their children leaving home and menopause, many men have to adjust to change—or lack of change—on the job. Most men reach the top level of their earning power during middle age, and some find themselves well short of the peak they had hoped to reach. "A man of 40 may be looking anxiously over his shoulder at the wolf pack yapping and slobbering at his heels as he slips along over competitive ice. At 40, the status of many a man, whether in business or on the assembly line, is frozen, so he feels stuck and fearful" (Henry, 1974, p. 440). One researcher suggested that a principal task for men in the midlife transition is de-illusionment—realistically asking if the goals they have set for themselves are reasonable and attainable (Levinson, 1977).

For many there is the feeling of having reached a dead end. "Had I known that this firm was never going to promote me," one man said, "I would have left 15 years ago. But now it's too late. Who wants to hire a 50-year-old when 30-year-olds are a dime a dozen?" Still others reach the top only to find that "success" is meaningless for them. "I've been with the government since I left school and now I'm the head of my division. But so what? I move papers around on my desk and have conferences that are supposed to mean something but don't. I've always wanted to be a psychologist so I could work with people about something that matters, but now it's too late."

Whether they feel they have failed in the right career or succeeded in a meaningless one, many middle-aged men see their jobs as costing them their health. A man is more likely to develop a heart condition or cancer or to have a stroke between the ages of 45 and 64 than at any other time in his working life.

Some middle-aged men respond to their disappointments and anxieties by having an affair. Love and sex with a young woman is often regarded as the last chance to experience youth.

> For the man who does not find satisfaction in his work, who has done what he had to do, rather than what he wanted to do, or whose life work has turned out to be not quite what he thought it was . . . the cure to his lifelong disorder may seem to be the young and beautiful woman. . . . She gives him a feeling that he is not lost after all, he is not as weak as he thinks. She will, he feels, give him new creative power, because her sex interest proves that he is not dead wood. (Henry, 1974, pp. 440-441)

Physiological changes also accompany middle age in men. The production of testosterone usually begins to decline around age 40 and continues to decrease gradually until age 60 when it levels off. (The decline is not inevitable but is related to general health status.) The consequences of lowered testosterone include (a) more difficulty in getting and maintaining a firm erection, (b) greater ejaculatory control with the possibility of more prolonged erections, (c) less consistency in achieving orgasm, (d) fewer genital spasms during orgasm, (e) a qualitative change from an intense, genitally focused sensation to a more diffused and generalized feeling of pleasure; and (f) an increase in the length of the refractory period, during which time the man is unable to ejaculate or have another erection.

These physiological changes in the middle-aged man, along with psychological changes, have sometimes been referred to as **male menopause**. During this period the man may experience nervousness, hot flashes, insomnia, and no interest in sex. But these changes most often occur over a long period of time, and the anxiety and depression some men experience seem to be as much related to their life situation as to hormonal alterations.

A middle-aged man who is not successful in his career is often forced to recognize that he will never achieve what he had hoped but carry his unfulfilled dreams to the grave. This knowledge may be coupled with his awareness of diminishing sexual vigor. For the man who has been taught that masculinity is measured by career success and sexual prowess, middle age may be particularly traumatic.

But this period in middle age when many men ask themselves "What's the point of it all?" is regarded positively by some. LeShan (1973), who refers to this time as "middle-escence," suggests that it provides an opportunity for continuing the identity crisis of the first adolescence . . . a second chance to find out what it means to 'do your own thing' and to be your own person.

Middle age means different things to different people. It may be either the best or the worst of times. On the positive side, a character in the novel *Anthony Adverse* says, "Grow up as soon as you can. It pays. The only time you really live fully is from 30 to 60. . . . The young are slaves to dreams; the old, servants of regrets. Only the middle-aged have all their five senses in the keeping of their wits." The benefits of middle age may also be stated in negative terms. One middle-aged office worker said, "I wouldn't want to be young, because the hurts are not as sharp now or such a surprise as they used to be" (Frankel & Rathvon, 1980, p. 85).

The Later Years

About 1 in 10 Americans (25 million) is over the age of 65. By the year 2030 they will represent about 20 percent of our population. Because their numbers and visibility is increasing, interest in the elderly is also increasing. College courses on aging are now common, and a current quip is that aging is "in" (Neugarten, 1980).

Before looking at the sex lives of the elderly, let us look at their lives in a larger context—what it means to be old and how people feel about it.

The Meanings of "Old"

"Old" may be defined chronologically, physiologically, psychologically, sociologically, or culturally. Chronologically, an old person is one who has lived a certain number of years, but how many years varies with the perspective. In general a person tends to regard anyone who is 15 years older as "old."

Physiologically, an old person's auditory, visual, and respiratory capabilities are declining. The per capita cost of health care for a person over 65 is three times that for a younger adult. "Sometimes I feel like a young person trapped in an old body," observed one 86-year-old woman. "My wits are as sharp as ever, but my hands tremble and I can't get around like I used to."

Psychologically, a person's self-concept is important in defining how old that person is. Some people over 65 do not view themselves as old. Supreme Court Justice Oliver Wendell Holmes at age 92 reportedly said to a friend as they watched a beautiful woman walk down the street, "Oh, to be 70 again."

Sociologically, people are old if they assume roles that have traditionally been defined as those occupied by old people—grandparent, widow, retiree. "After our daughter had her first child, it occurred to me that I would be sleeping with a grandmother," recalled a retired dentist. "I kidded my wife about that, and she said, 'Yes, grandpa, that's right.' It made me feel old just to know that the word grandparents now meant us."

"You know you're getting older when the candles cost more than the cake."

BOB HOPE

Culturally, the society in which an individual lives defines when a person becomes old and what it means to do so. In many cultures age brings with it prestige and status. The 45-year-old Navajo tribesman, for example, is a revered leader commanding the respect of less experienced members of the tribe (Huyck, 1974).

One researcher has suggested that members of some societies act old—that is, give up almost all productive work—because their society expects them to (Keller, 1977). In societies where the old are expected to be productive, they are. In three cultures in Ecuador, Pakistan, and Russia, for instance, the elderly are expected to weed the fields, milk the cows, do the laundry, and take care of the children on a daily basis (Leaf & Launois, 1973). Kept so busy, they have little time to act old.

Of our society B. F. Skinner (1983) observed, "Our culture does not generously reinforce the behavior of old people. Both affluence and welfare destroy reinforcing contingencies, and so does retirement. Aging scholars," he continues, "lose interest; they find it hard to get to work; they work slowly. It is easy to attribute this to a change in *them* but we should not overlook a change in their world. . . . In old age, behavior is not so strongly reinforced" (pp. 28–29).

A society's view of the elderly is relevant for the expression of their sexuality. Although our society tends to expect people to reduce their sexual activity as they age, this expectation is not characteristic of all societies. In one study (Winn & Newton, 1982), 70 percent of one group of societies had expectations of continued sexual activity for their aging males. Among the Tiv in Africa many older men "remain active and 'hot' for many years after they become gray-haired" (p. 288); and among the Taoist sects of China, there are records of men retaining their sexual desires past 100 years of age. Similar reports of continued sexual activity and interest among aging women were found in 84 percent of societies for which data on this age group were available. The researchers concluded "that cultural as well as biological factors may be key determinants in sexual behavior in the later part of life" (p. 283).

Sample Terms

Feelings about Growing Old

Social class affects how a person views the aging process. While members of the middle class tend to view old age in terms of leisure, relaxation, and security, lower-class people regard old age as a period of progressive physical decline, senility, and full retirement (Huyck, 1974). Our attitudes about aging are also related to our parent's health. If we view their health unfavorably we are more likely to feel anxious about our own aging (Rakowski, Barber, & Seelbach, 1983). Still, most Americans age reluctantly. A woman identified as "Wrinkled in New York" wrote to Dear Abby saying that she was 59 and considering a face lift. She wanted to know if Abby had ever had a face lift. Abby replied, "No, I never have, but when I think I need one, I'll certainly give it serious consideration" (Van Buren, 1977). Most Americans of both genders want to keep a youthful appearance, but doing so seems more important to women. Writer and critic Susan Sontag (1972) believes this is due to the double standard of aging that prevails in our society.

The point for women of dressing up, applying makeup, dying their hair, going on crash diets, and getting face lifts is not just to be attractive. They are ways of defending themselves against a profound level of disapproval directed toward women, a disapproval that can take the form of aversion. The double standard of aging converts the life of women into an inexorable march toward a condition in which they are not just unattractive, but disgusting. . . . Aging in women is a process of becoming obscene sexually, for the flabby bosom, wrinkled neck, spotted hands, thinning white hair, waistless torso, and veined legs of an old woman are felt to be obscene.*

In contrast, the silver hair of aging men (Steve Martin, Johnny Carson, Charlie Rich) is viewed as a mark of distinction, and wrinkles (Willie Nelson, Merle Haggard) are viewed as visible signs of wisdom and kindness. Status and money keep men desirable, not smooth skin. There is the joke of a young woman who said to an old man, "Seventy isn't old for a millionaire."

The fear of becoming useless is also part of a person's negative attitude toward growing old. With no children to look after and no jobs to go to, the elderly are not expected to contribute to our society. And their declining physical capacities have been viewed as synonymous with their potential. As a result, our society has developed the attitude of 'do for' the elderly (Keller, 1977). The message that the elderly receive is, You can't do anything for yourself or for others—you are useless.

Reluctance about growing older is fed by the dread of loneliness. "I could die in my sleep," said an elderly widow, "and rigor mortis would set in before anybody would know or care that I was gone. Being lonely is the hardest part of growing old." Some individuals are unable to cope with the depression that comes with loneliness. Twenty-five percent of all suicides are committed by those over 65 (Butler & Lewis, 1976).

Sexuality of the Elderly: Some Facts

Growing old need not mean an end to a person's sex life. To the contrary, there may be an improvement. In a study of 800 elderly Americans (Starr & Weiner, 1982), three-fourths of those who were sexually active reported that their lovemaking had improved with the years. But let us take a more detailed look at sex among the elderly by reviewing some of the facts.

Data Are Lacking   Since no nationwide random sample of the elderly has been interviewed or completed a questionnaire about their sexual behavior, we have only scattered information based on what some of the elderly tell us in various small-scale studies.

Sexual Behavior among the Elderly Is Variable   As is true of the sexual behavior of other age groups, there are great differences in sexual behavior among the elderly. Whereas some report frequent intercourse, masturbation,

---

*Sontag, S. The double standard of aging. In Sol Gordon and Roger Libby, eds., *Sexuality today—and tomorrow*. Belmont, California: Wadsworth Publishing Co., 1976, p. 362.

Sexuality does not
end with old age.

and oral sex experiences, others are disgusted with the implication that they
would be interested in such activities. These variations are illustrated in the
following conversation between two elderly women. One said, "I think that
sex at my age is a waste of time." Her friend replied, "Speak for yourself."

Frequency of Intercourse Declines with Age   Beginning at age 46, the
frequency of intercourse reported by males decreases every year (Pfeiffer,
Verwoerdt, & David, 1974). Reasons for this decline include societal expectations, physical problems, and satiation. The elderly are forced into manda-
tory retirement from sexual activity. This is most dramatically illustrated in
the segregation of husbands and wives in retirement facilities and nursing
homes (Sviland, 1978). Physical problems also take their toll. In men, diabe-

tes, malfunctions of the thyroid and pituitary glands, and alcoholism may impair the man's ability to get and keep an erection. About half of men 75 and over are impotent (Rossman, 1978). For the elderly man who is not impotent, it is not unusual for him to require 30 to 40 minutes of stimulation before he gets an erection (Runciman, 1978).

Physical changes in women (due to the decrease in estrogen) include diminished vaginal lubrication, shrinkage in the size of the vaginal barrel, and loss of elasticity to the walls of the vagina. However, the primary factor affecting the declining frequency of intercourse in women is the waning interest of her partner or the absence of one. The presence of a culturally approved sexual partner (husband) is often regarded as a prerequisite for heterosexual expression among elderly women.

Masturbation Declines with Age   In a study of 1,000 males aged 51 to 95 (Hegeler & Mortensen, 1977), there was a steady decline of reported masturbation with increasing age. Whereas half of those in their early fifties reported that they masturbated, less than a fourth did so in their early nineties. Masturbation rates also decline with age among females. However, there is an upswing in the rates following separation, divorce, and widowhood.

Lovemaking May Improve with Age   One definition of improvement is what two researchers call the "second language of sex." The first language is "involved largely with physical pleasure . . . but the second language of sex is emotional and communicative as well as physical" (Butler & Lewis, 1976, p. 140). One husband confided:

● At sixty-five I am having the best sex life I have ever had. My wife and I have few inhibitions and try anything we like. I'm usually the aggressor, but she likes to pull me into the bedroom and I don't struggle. We wander around our apartment naked, bathe together, and love each other's body and mind. Our love has been a developing one. First it was more sexual. Now it is that plus many other things (Hite, 1981, p. 860). ●

Lack of anxiety about pregnancy and more time and opportunity help people experience the second language of sex. "When the kids aren't running about the house and you're both home all day, you've got time to do a lot of things including sex," said a 76-year-old man.

Orgasm Remains an Important Experience   Lest we think that sex for the elderly is confined to holding each other, orgasm was viewed by three-fourths of the 800 respondents in the Starr and Weiner (1982) study as important to a good sexual experience. "Orgasm is like eating a Hershey bar—it's good every time," reflected an elderly woman.

Sex, in General, Remains an Important Experience   More important than orgasm is the whole idea of sex. More than 95 percent of the respondents in the previously cited study said they liked sex. This finding contradicts the myth that the elderly never think of sex and certainly do not do anything about it. Indeed, for those who have had an active sex life throughout their youth, there is no time they just stop being interested in sex any more than there is a time they stop being interested in food or music or anything else they have enjoyed.

Continued interest in sex is not unique to heterosexuals. One elderly lesbian said, "My sexual needs increase as I grow older. I think as women grow older we grow more sexual. We are getting in touch with our basic natures" (Raphael & Robinson, 1980).

Sexual Fulfillment among the Elderly

There are several things people can do to achieve sexual fulfillment in the later years: doing what they want to do sexually (including nothing), relabeling their "losses" as "transitions," and adapting as necessary. It is important that the elderly not view the publicity about sex in the later years as an obligation to enjoy an active sex life. Since sexual fulfillment is individually defined, each elderly person should decide what patterns, frequencies, and behaviors she or he feels more comfortable with. There are no right or wrong, normal or abnormal, answers.

Rather than viewing partial erection, impotence, lack of vaginal lubrication, or pain during intercourse as sexual losses, the elderly might see these as inevitable transitions. We expect change in all other areas of life and should not be dismayed to discover that our bodies age, too. Adaptation to change is likely to be a more satisfying response.

Adaptation does not necessarily mean resignation. It may mean finding substitute techniques for sexual expression. For example, for a partial erection or impotence, some couples use the "stuffing technique," manually pushing the penis in the vagina. This often stimulates the penis to erection, which can be followed by intercourse. Another problem that can be helped by a substitute technique is pain during intercourse, which was reported by slightly more than 10 percent of the women in the Starr and Weiner study (1982). Pain may be caused by decreased vaginal lubrication, a smaller vaginal opening, and friction against the thinner walls of the vagina. A liberal use of K-Y jelly, a sterile lubricant, is helpful in minimizing the pain. Applied to both the penis and vagina, it helps the penis slide in and out with less friction.

Sexual fulfillment among elderly women may include another dimension. For some this means breaking through the belief that lovemaking with a husband is the only appropriate way to experience sex. Such a breakthrough may be significant since most women will outlive their husbands by 10 years. One woman who had an active sex life after her husband's death is Mrs. S., who

> was widowed at the age of 56. She is tall, thin, and has a healthy glow about her. Her married sex life had been active and satisfying. In the 23 years since her husband's death, she reports 35 adventures, some lasting the smaller part of an evening, and others going on for as long as 15 years. Her youngest mate was only 15 years old,

while the eldest was 82. Mrs. S. is an intelligent professional woman who spent her professional life in newspaper work, advertising, and public relations. She is the proud mother of living and successful children. (Peterson & Payne, 1975, p. 88)

Other elderly women, both widowed and never married, may go through periods of masturbation, lesbianism, and having young lovers. There is no biological limitation on the sexual capacity of elderly females and their sexual expression may take many forms. Also, there is some indication that our society is becoming more tolerant of the sexual behaviors it regards as appropriate for the elderly (Klemmack & Roff, 1980).

Summary

Sexual fulfillment means different things to different people, and these meanings may vary over time. But there seem to be certain prerequisites for its existence, including self-knowledge, a good relationship, open communication, realistic expectations, and demonstration of sexual interest in the partner.

Sexual fulfillment also requires an awareness of basic facts about human sexuality. These include an awareness that sexual attitudes and behaviors are primarily learned, that sex is a natural function, that sexual communication takes effort, and that spectatoring interferes with sexual functioning. Also interfering with sexual fulfillment are such myths as the belief that simultaneous orgasm is the ultimate experience, that intercourse during menstruation is harmful, and that sexual boredom is inevitable.

Information about facts and myths of sexuality is relevant to all age groups, but certain events seem to be characteristic of the middle and later years. Middle age is a time of transition. Whereas a major social event for most women in middle age is the departure of their children from the home, menopause and the woman's reaction to it are the primary physical and psychological events during this period. Many men in middle age must adjust to change—or lack of change—on the job and reassess their life position. Physiological changes in the middle-aged man are due to the decline in the production of testosterone, which may affect his sexual and psychological functioning.

Old age may be defined chronologically, physiologically, psychologically, sociologically, or culturally. Most Americans age reluctantly because of concern over physical deterioration, a fear of becoming useless, and the dread of being lonely. But these conditions are not inevitable, and growing old need not lead to the end of one's sex life. Although frequency of intercourse declines with age, orgasm and sex, in general remain important. There are several things people can do to achieve sexual fulfillment in the later years: doing what they want to do sexually, relabeling their "losses" as "transitions," and adapting as necessary.

Key Terms

sexual fulfillment
spectatoring
simultaneous orgasm
menopause

climacteric
estrogen replacement therapy (ERT)
male menopause
premenstrual syndrome (PMS)*

*This term is discussed in the "Issues in Debate" section that follows.

Issues in Debate and Future Directions

The existence, nature, and treatment of premenstrual syndrome is an issue over which there is considerable disagreement. After exploring this issue we look at various trends in sexual fulfillment.

Premenstrual Syndrome: Definition, Cause, and Treatment

Also known as **PMS, premenstrual syndrome** refers to the physical and psychological problems a woman experiences from the time of ovulation to the beginning of, and sometimes during, menstruation. There are a number of symptoms, which may include the following.

Psychological	Respiratory
Tension	Asthma
Depression	Rhinitis
Irritability	
Lethargy	Dermatological
Excessive energy	Acne
Altered sex drive	Herpes
Neurological	Orthopedic
Migraine	Joint pains
Epilepsy	Backaches

But it is the experience of the woman that makes the syndrome real.

Alice A., a 35-year-old housewife and mother, is usually a friendly and productive person, but two weeks out of each month she is overwhelmed by extreme irritability, tension, and depression. "It's as if my mind can't keep up with my body. I cook things to put in the freezer, clean, wash windows, work in the yard—anything to keep busy. My mind is saying slow down, but my body won't quit. When I go to bed at night, I'm exhausted, but I can't sleep, and when I do, I have nightmares. And everything gets on my nerves—the phone ringing, birds singing—everything! My skin feels prickly, my back hurts, and my face feels so tight that it's painful. I scream at my husband and son over ridiculous things like asking for a clean pair of socks. I hate myself even when I'm doing it, but I have no control. I can't stand being around people, and the only way I can even be civil at parties is to have several drinks.

"This lasts for about a week, and then I wake up one morning feeling as if the bottom has dropped out of my life. It's as if something awful is going to happen, but I don't know what it is, and don't know how to stop it. I don't even have the energy to make the beds. Every movement is an effort. I burst out crying for no reason at crazy times, like when I'm fixing breakfast or grocery shopping. My husband thinks I'm angry with him, and I can't explain what's wrong because I don't know myself. After about four days of fighting off the depression, I just give up, take the phone off the hook, and stay in bed. It's terrifying. I feel panicky—trapped.

Then one morning I'll wake up and suddenly feel like myself. The sun is shining, and I like life again.*

Between 5 and 10 percent of women experience PMS to the degree that Alice does. Some people have attributed instances of child abuse, alcoholism, divorce, and suicide to PMS. Recently, two British women introduced PMS as part of their legal defense for murder.

Other women experience a milder form of PMS, including different symptoms in varying

*Source: "Premenstrual syndrome: The world's oldest disease?" Copyright © 1981 by Rebecca R. Ball. Reprinted by permission.

degrees. But because more than 150 symptoms have been associated with PMS, there is little agreement about when a person is experiencing the phenomenon. The only agreement on premenstrual syndrome seems to be that the individual's specific symptoms occur together at regular intervals.

There also is no agreement on the causes of PMS and even less agreement on the cure. Hormones, diet, and culture are among the suggested causes. Some physicians treat the woman with PMS as though it is all in her head and will go away in a few days. Others view the problem as an imbalance of hormones and prescribe progesterone (Dalton, 1977). Still others focus on nutrition and exercise. Diet changes include eliminating alcohol, sugar, salt, and caffeine as well as eating several small meals every two to four hours (Harrison, 1982).

But, increasingly, PMS is being recognized as a legitimate set of symptoms requiring treatment. The Premenstrual Syndrome Clinic in Reading, Massachusetts, has treated more than 1,000 women. Their approach to therapy is multidimensional including diet, exercise, vitamins, and progesterone (if necessary). They also assist women in diagnosing PMS and demonstrating its impact on their lives. Such diagnosis is facilitated by getting women to chart their feelings, changes in behavior, and physical reactions consistent with their cycle.

The National PMS Society (P.O. Box 11467, Durham, North Carolina 27703) may be contacted for further information and help. The phone number is 919-489-6577.

Future Directions

Trends in sexual fulfillment include greater access to information about sexual fulfillment, a widening of the range of known conditions for expressing sexual fulfillment, and increased exploration of these alternatives. Magazines like *Cosmopolitan, Redbook, Ladies Home Journal, Readers' Digest* and *Family Circle* regularly feature articles on sexual aspects of the woman–man relationship. Masters and Johnson's research is available to every person who stands in line to pay for groceries. Such visibility of sexual topics is not limited to magazines but includes movies, television, and radio. The openness with which the media treat sex will continue.

One consequence of this visibility is an awareness of the widening range of sexual behaviors expressed by different people. The "Phil Donahue Show" once featured discussions on "safe" topics only, but later programs included such topics as polygamy, bisexual marriage, celibacy, and transsexuality. Exposure to media-mediated sex alerts us to the tremendous variations in sexual experience. Finally, although people do not always try what they see, they are more likely to include new behaviors in their own repertoire than if they were not aware of what others are doing.

These trends will affect both young and old. In time, today's younger generation, socialized exclusively in our sex-conscious society, will become the older generation, and they will carry their socialization with them. Their awareness of alternative ways of sexual fulfillment, including abstinence, will allow them to select from among those behaviors and frequencies the kind of sex life they want.

In the meantime our society will become more encouraging of the elderly to express their sexuality. Physicians will lead this trend by initiating dialogue about sex with elderly patients. The goal is not to exert pressure on older people to engage in sexual activity but to encourage them to feel that such activity is appropriate.

Chapter Eleven

Sexual Therapy

*Therapy is help and we can all
use some of it sometime.*
A THERAPIST

Chapter Eleven

Just as we may consult a physician when we are sick, a dentist when our tooth aches, and a mechanic when our car won't run, we may need to consult a therapist when our sex life is awry. Whereas our understanding of medicine, dentistry, and auto repair is likely to be limited, we may know even less about sex therapy. In this chapter we examine what happens behind those closed doors of sex therapy offices. Included in our discussion is a look at various sexual problems (which may occur regardless of sexual orientation) and their resolutions.

Sex Therapy: Some Questions

Before discussing some facts about sex therapy and the various types, we look at the components of sex therapy and the training of those who provide it.

What Is Sex Therapy?

The term sex therapy is used routinely in popular discourse as though it had a specific meaning like the words watermelon or elephant. But although most people (lay and professional) can probably agree on what a watermelon and elephant are, there is little agreement on what constitutes sex therapy. If a man tells his physician that he ejaculates prematurely and the physician recommends that he try the squeeze technique, has the physician administered sex therapy. If a woman confides in her minister that she has lost interest in sex and he suggests that she read *Recapturing Sexual Desire*, has sex therapy taken place? Or if a couple in marriage counseling are asked to do sensate focus, are they now involved in sex therapy?

Therapists have different answers. Some say that sex therapy is like teaching golf or tennis—the therapist teaches the couple a few basic techniques and encourages them to practice regularly. But other therapists say that such technique training must include attention to personal and interpersonal dynamics. The difference of opinion is really about who can be a sex therapist. If sex therapy is technique teaching, anyone could take a three-hour seminar on sex techniques and be a sex therapist. But if sex therapy includes personal and interpersonal issues, training would need to be more extensive.

Most sex therapists believe that sex therapy is more than teaching techniques. They feel that an effective therapist should be able to deal with the following factors.

Managing Relationships   Since most sexual problems occur in the context of a relationship, either heterosexual or homosexual, it is important to minimize feelings of hostility and encourage a mutually enjoyable out-of-bed relationship. The latter often includes increasing the frequency of love behaviors (verbal expressions of love, affectionate touching, self-disclosure, tolerance for less pleasant aspects of the partner, and so on). In a study of 50 couples in sex therapy (Cookerly & McClaren, 1982), those who focused on their love behaviors reported greater satisfaction with sex therapy and a more satisfactory sex life than those who focused on the sexual aspect of their relationship only.

Changing Attitudes   Negative attitudes about sex interfere with sexual interest and performance. Much of sex therapy consists of exploring more positive ways to look at sex. For example, a therapist may help a couple who think masturbation is sinful and selfish to regard it rather as a means of discovering self-pleasure so as to enhance couple pleasure.

Providing Information   Sex therapy also provides accurate information about human sexuality to replace beliefs that may block sexual expression. For example, one man said he had never had intercourse because he was told that a woman's vagina can act like a vice to squeeze the penis off.

Giving Permission   Because of her or his status as an authority, the sex therapist can suggest that a couple try new things—caressing only, different positions, oral sex, or the like. These suggestions are often regarded as permission to try something new and may encourage a couple to be more innovative.

Reducing Anxiety   Anxiety is disabling to sexual performance. Teaching deep muscle relaxation and eliminating performance expectations are ways in which the therapist might attempt to reduce an individual's anxiety. Unless such anxiety is reduced, success in sex therapy will be limited.

Managing relationships, changing attitudes, providing information, giving permission, and reducing anxiety suggest that sex therapy often has to do with more than sex. Dr. Thomas Szasz (1980), a noted psychiatrist, stated that sex therapists sometimes offer more than they can deliver.

Promising to teach people how to play the sex game well, sexologists seduce them into believing that they can teach them how to play it safely—which, of course, no one can do. Why? Because the dangerousness of *human* sexuality lies in the fact that sexual acts are so very personal. Behaving sexually toward another person is risky because doing so is profoundly self-revealing and because the needs of the participants are constantly changing and are rarely fully complementary. There is simply no way to avoid this. (p. 3)

Because these extrasexual considerations impinge on sexual behavior, sex therapists should proceed with caution.

What Training Should Sex Therapists Have?

There are no laws preventing a person from advertising that she or he is a sex therapist. *Anyone* can legally open an office in your home town and offer sex therapy. Degrees, counseling experience under supervision, and exposure to other aspects of formal training in human sexuality are not necessary. California is the only state that exercises some legal restraint on sex therapy. To be licensed in California as a physician, psychologist, social worker, or marriage, family, or child counselor, the person must have had training in human sexuality.

In the absence of effective legislation, it is not surprising that everyone seems to be doing sex therapy—health educators, sociologists, ministers, psychologists, social workers, marriage counselors, physicians, and psychiatrists. Their training in human sexuality ranges from none or minimal to extensive. It is rare that any one person has all of the skills to provide the basic elements of sex therapy just described. For example, psychologists get a lot of training in helping individuals reduce anxiety but limited training in treating interpersonal relationships. A survey of the American Psychological Association revealed that fewer than 1 percent of the training programs for clinical psychologists approved by the association offer even one course in marital therapy (*Psychology Today*, 1982). Marriage counselors may be expert at resolving interpersonal conflicts but know little about reducing anxiety. Physicians may be authorities on sexual anatomy but have little awareness of, or skill in, anxiety reduction or relationship management. It is doubtful if ministers, social workers, sociologists, and health care professionals have been systematically trained to reduce anxiety, provide sex information, and manage relationships.

The foregoing suggests that extreme care should be taken when selecting a sex therapist. It is estimated that of the 3,500 to 5,000 sex clinics in the United States, only about 100 are operated by trained professionals (Holden, 1976). Similarly, while more than 7,000 health care professionals have attended two-day seminars or five-day workshops at the Masters and Johnson Institute, Masters says they have thoroughly trained only about 30 therapists (Masters & Johnson, 1979b).

To help upgrade the skills of those providing sex therapy, the American Association of Sex Educators, Counselors, and Therapists (AASECT) offers a certificate of Certified Sex Therapist to applicants who have a minimum of a master's degree in a clinical field (psychology, social work, nursing, marriage counseling, or the like), have conducted sex therapy under supervision for a minimum of 100 hours, and have attended a two-day workshop on human sexuality (sponsored by AASECT) to sort out their own attitudes and values about human sexuality. The name of a certified sex therapist in your area can be located by calling 202-462-1171 or by writing to AASECT (11 Dupont Circle, N.W., Suite 220, Washington, D.C. 20036). Knowing that a sex therapist is certified does not guarantee competence, but it reduces the risk of selecting one who knows nothing about sex or therapy.

The 7,000 therapists certified by AASECT are expected to conduct their practice in a manner that reflects the Code of Ethics for Sex Therapists developed by the organization. Beyond being knowledgeable about treating sexual dysfunctions, empathetic, nonevaluative, and a skilled listener, the certified sex therapist is expected to refrain from engaging in sexual activity with clients under the guise of therapy. Although between 5 and 13 percent of physicians and psychologists reported they had had sexual relations with their patients during treatment (Edelwich & Brodsky, 1982), to do so is a blatant exploitation of the client's trust.

Sex Therapy: Some Facts

The practice of sex therapy frequently seems mysterious, implying unknown happenings behind closed doors. What types of clients are offered what types of therapy at what cost are some of the issues dealt with in this section.

Clients in Sex Therapy

Anyone may be a client in sex therapy, although clients are more likely to be of the higher socioeconomic status and to be college educated (Hoch et al., 1980). When compared with those reporting no sexual dysfunctions, people in sex therapy tend to be experiencing more psychological stress, to have greater negative affect (depression, guilt, hostility), and to have less accurate information about sex (Derogatis & Meyer, 1979). One client said that his whole world was caving in since he had been impotent with his partner. "My self-confidence is shaken and I feel I'm losing her." Such anxiety and depression are understandable, since we live in a society that tells us we should be happy in all areas of our life—particularly our sex life.

Types of Sex Therapy

The types of sex therapy are as varied as the problems individuals bring to therapy. Should you consider sex therapy, what are the alternative approaches?

Virginia Johnson
and William E.
Masters

Masters and Johnson Approach

If you were to seek sex therapy at the Masters and Johnson Institute, you would check into a local motel in St. Louis for two weeks, during which you would practice the exercises recommended by the dual sex therapy team who would meet with you and your partner on a daily basis at the institute. The first day would consist of a physical examination and an individual interview of you and your partner by each therapist. This would be followed on the second day by a meeting with the cotherapists in a "roundtable" session "that allows the therapy team to provide their assessment of the situation to the couple, including information related to the origin of the sexual problem(s), the specific pertinent diagnoses, the prognosis, and an overview of the approaches that will be used to solve the difficulty" (Kolodny et al., 1979, pp. 502–503). A beginning exercise you and your partner would be encouraged to try in your motel room is sensate focus. The goal of this exercise is to encourage you and your partner to get and give nongenital pleasure and to increase your nonverbal communication. After you report success in using sensate focus, other procedures would be suggested. (Sensate focus and other techniques are described in a later section of this chapter.)

Hartman and Fithian Approach

A variation of the Masters and Johnson format has been developed by William Hartman and Marilyn Fithian at the Center for Marital and Sexual Studies in Long Beach, California. Here you and your partner would be taken through the 34 steps listed in Table 11.1. A major focus of Hartman and Fithian's (1979) approach is their concern for intimacy.

Table 11.1   Thirty-Four Steps in Hartman and Fithian's Two-Week Therapy Program

1. Initial referral	20. Sexual caress
2. Sociopsychological testing	21. Film: Nondemand techniques—pleasuring/squeeze technique, etc.
3. First sexual history	
4. Second sexual history	22. Assignment: Male active/nondemand technique, female back against male's chest
5. Physical examination	
6. Roundtable discussion	23. Assignment: Female active/nondemand technique, squeeze technique
7. Developing sensuality	
8. Sexological examination	24. Assignment: Male active/nondemand technique, female supine, male pleasuring vagina
9. Kegel film	
10. Body imagery	25. Assignment: The "quiet vagina"
11. Touching and relating (sensitivity)	26. Films of coital positions
12. Assignment: Combing the partner's hair[a]	27. Audiotape: "How to become orgasmic"
13. Hand caress—foot caress	28. Film of coitus
14. Film: Foot, face, body caress, and breathing together	29. Hypnosis when indicated
	30. Film of coitus—romantic
15. Mutual bathing assignment	31. Film of coitus—playful
16. Face caress	32. Assignment: Spontaneity—How do you do your own thing? Write up a contract
17. Assignment: Wash partner's hair	
18. Color film of body caress—body caress	33. Saying goodbye nonverbally
19. Breathing together	34. Follow-up

[a]All assignments are carried out in the privacy of a motel room or in the on site apartment.

From *The Frontiers of Sex Research,* ed. by Vern Bullough. Copyright © 1979 by Prometheus Books. p. 19.

The end-of-the-rainbow which most of them [the clients] were seeking could be summed up in a single word: *Intimacy.* Their cry for help was essentially a plea that they be put in warm and meaningful touch with each other, literally as well as figuratively. Helping a man learn to achieve and maintain an erection, we found, may

Marilyn Fithian and
William Hartman

be a worthwhile immediate goal; but unless he also learns to bring pleasure, satisfaction, and happiness to a partner—and to himself—therapeutic benefits were likely to be shallow and elusive. Precisely the same proved true of women whose presenting symptom was lack of orgasm but whose underlying goal was intimacy and satisfaction within the pair-bond. Very early, accordingly, communication, especially nonverbal communication, became the keystone of our therapeutic approach. (p. 17)

Psychodynamic Approach

Whereas the Masters and Johnson–Hartman and Fithian approaches focus on various exercises to encourage you and your partner to experience new ways of thinking and behaving, therapists of the **psychodynamic** view attempt to uncover unconscious conflicts through detailed exploration of your earlier psychological development. For example, as a man, your impotence might be seen as a symptom of your unconscious hostility toward your mother, which has generalized to all women including your partner. By being impotent, the theory goes, you can frustrate your partner, thereby expressing your unconscious hostility.

Sample

Before 1970 most treatment of sexual dysfunctions was conducted by psychiatrists who had been trained primarily in psychoanalysis. Such treatment took years, was very expensive, and, in general, failed to assist clients in achieving their goals. But the belief that sexual dysfunctions are symptoms of intrapsychic conflicts continues. When 500 physicians were asked, "Do you believe that sexual dysfunction can be treated without dealing with the intrapsychic conflicts or underlying psychopathology?" more than half said "no" (Sexual survey No. 18, 1979).

Rational-Emotive Therapy Approach

Rational-emotive therapy takes as its starting point the words you tell yourself affect how you feel and behave. For example, if you have no interest in sex you may be telling yourself that sex is shameful and sinful and that "good people" regard sex as disgusting. The rational therapist would encourage you to examine the negative consequences of such thoughts and ask you to begin a different vein of "self-talk." By consciously replacing the old, negative thoughts with positive ones like "sex is great, an experience to share, and a fantastic feeling," sexual desire would have a better cognitive context in which to develop.

Kaplan's Approach

Combining the work of Masters and Johnson, Hartman and Fithian, and psychodynamic and rational—emotive therapists, Helen Kaplan (1974) of Cornell Medical Center views sex therapy as a "task-centered form of crisis intervention which presents an opportunity for rapid conflict resolution. Toward this end the various sexual tasks are employed, as well as the methods of insight therapy, supportive therapy, marital therapy, and other psychiatric

Helen Kaplan

techniques as indicated" (p. 199). Although participation of both partners is seen as a crucial ingredient for successful sex therapy, Kaplan does not require that they participate equally in the therapy program. For example, in the case of female orgasmic dysfunction, Kaplan may spend most of her time working with the woman in individual sessions.

Kaplan does not have a rigid two-week format or assume that you would be in therapy for an indeterminate length of time. Her goal would be to assist you and your partner in achieving your sexual goals in as short a time as possible. Sessions are usually held once or twice a week (with an occasional phone call during the week) while you and your partner continue to live at home.

Behavior Therapy Approach

Behavior modification or **behavior therapy** has been used in the treatment of marriage and family problems, weight control, smoking, and phobias. Essentially, a behavioral approach to anything is the systematic application of the principles of learning to the management of human behavior. To some extent, Masters and Johnson, Hartman and Fithian, and Kaplan are behaviorists. In essence, the behavior therapist is more concerned with why a sexual problem continues to occur rather than how it began. If, for example, the problem is lack of orgasm, the behavior therapist identifies the conditions under which the woman will be able to experience an orgasm rather than why she has not been able to do so in the past. Achieving the sexual goals set by the client is a sufficient goal for treatment and examining intrapsychic dynamics is not necessary for successful and permanent change (Fenster-heim & Kanter, 1980).

Aids in Sex Therapy

Therapists may use one or more aids in their therapy program. These include inventories, films, drugs, and surrogates.

Inventories

To gather information, some therapists ask their clients to complete various inventories. The Sex History on pp. 329 and 330 is an example of such an inventory, which gives the therapist an overview of the client's sexual feelings and behaviors. You might explore your own sexual self by completing the Sex History.

Films

Some sex therapists show their clients films. Hartman and Fithian select from among 36 films produced at their center. Whereas clients are often confused by a verbal description of the squeeze technique, sensate focus, or alternative positions in intercourse, there is no misunderstanding when they see two people demonstrate. The film on coital positioning, for example, show a couple in a series of coital positions: scissors, spoon, Persian, male superior, rear entry, and female superior positions (Young, 1980). Unlike X-rated films in adult movie theaters, films used by sex therapists show couples sharing sexual experiences in the context of a caring relationship.

Drugs

Since most sex therapy is not conducted by physicians or in a medical setting, the use of drugs in sex therapy is minimal. But sometimes drugs have been used successfully in the treatment of sexual dysfunctions—testosterone for low sex interest and impotence (Kaplan, 1979), clomipramine for premature ejaculation (Porto, 1980), and amobarbital to aid the patient in relaxation (Myers, 1980).

Surrogates

About one in three adult Americans is single, a group that includes the never married, separated, divorced, and widowed. Because their involvement in

My Sexuality

Sex History*

The purpose of this brief history is to obtain information about your sexual self. By answering these questions as completely and as accurately as you can, you will facilitate your therapeutic program. Please complete this history when you are alone and do not discuss your answers with your partner.

It is understandable that you might be concerned about what happens to this form. Because much or all of this information is highly personal, your history is strictly confidential. No outsider is permitted to see your answers without your written permission.

I. General   Date_____

Name _____

Address _____

Telephone: Office _____
Home _____

Relationship status: Married_____
Divorced_____ Single_____ Separated_____
Living Together_____ Widowed_____

Are you currently living with a partner?_____ How long?_____

How do you feel about the person with whom you are currently having sexual relations or with whom you have been most recently involved?_____

Is your sexual orientation Heterosexual?_____ Homosexual?_____
Bisexual?_____

II. Clinical

Circle the following words that apply to you:

A "nobody," "life is empty," a "somebody," "life is fun"

Stupid, bright, incompetent, competent, naive

Sophisticated, guilty, at peace with self, hostile

Horrible thoughts, pleasant thoughts, kind, relaxed

Full of hate, full of love, anxious, panicky, cowardly

Confident, unassertive, assertive, aggressive, friendly

Ugly, beautiful, deformed, shapely, attractive

Unattractive, pleasant, repulsive, depressed, happy

Lonely, wanted, needed, unloved, loved, misunderstood

Bored, active, restless, confused, worthwhile

Considerate, alcoholic, insomniac, take drugs, fatigued

Suicidal ideas, nightmares

(continued)

III. Background

1. What did you learn about sex from
   your parents?
   your teachers?
   your church?
   your peers?
2. What sexual behaviors, if any,
   make you feel guilty?
3. What level of emotional
   involvement have you had with
   your sexual partners? How have
   you felt about this level?
4. What sexual fantasies do you
   have? How do you feel about your
   fantasies?
5. What is the content of your sexual
   dreams? How do you feel about
   your sexual dreams?
6. How do you feel about your
   mother? Your father?
7. When you use the word "sex,"
   what do you mean? List five
   adjectives for sex.
8. What are your feelings about your
   body? The body of someone of
   the opposite gender? The same
   gender?
9. List the various sexual experiences
   you have had, your age at the time
   of first occurrence, how you felt
   about the experience then, and
   how you feel about having similar
   experiences now.
10. Describe any sexual experiences
    you would regard as negative.
11. Have you or any sexual partner
    ever had a sexually transmitted
    disease? What disease? What was
    the outcome?
12. What are your feelings about oral
    sex?
13. What drugs, if any, do you take?
    How often?
14. When did you first masturbate?
    How often do you masturbate?
    How do you feel about
    masturbation?
15. Describe any specific sexual
    problem you are having. How long
    has this been a problem? What is
    your partner's response to this
    problem?
16. What have you done to try and
    resolve the problem? What was the
    result?
17. Have you consulted a therapist
    before? Who? When?
18. What is the state of your physical
    health? Are your menstrual periods
    regular? Do you have menstrual
    cramps or premenstrual tension?
    How severe are these problems?
19. Have you experienced what you
    define to be an orgasm?
20. On a scale from 0 to 10, how would
    you describe your level of interest
    in sex?

sexual therapy may be limited by not having a partner, some therapists provide a partner, called a **surrogate** or sexual therapy practitioner. The surrogate and the client perform the exercises recommended by the sex therapist in the surrogate's home. Surrogates are not prostitutes. They are better educated, less economically motivated, and establish a warm and loving relationship with their client in the 8 to 10 sessions of therapy (Dauw, 1980). Although most surrogates are women, some are men.

Masters and Johnson no longer use surrogates as part of their sex therapy program because of potential legal problems and a tendency for their surrogates to fall in love with higher-status clients, but other therapists continue to find benefits in the surrogate approach. Sommers (1980) reported 90 percent improvement among 12 sexually dysfunctional men whose sexual therapy included a surrogate.

> It appears quite feasible to treat male sexual dysfunctions in a rapid, effective way with the help of sexual therapy practitioners. The results seem to hold and the patient's whole life changes dramatically. Compared to traditional methods, this therapeutic modality appears to offer hope to many patients unable to bring a partner to therapy, who have had to resign themselves to living socially isolated, constricted lives. Many now plan to marry and start families." (p.598)

In response to the positive benefits of sex therapy with surrogates, the International Professional Surrogates Association has been formed. The accompanying box describes IPSA and its functions.

Inventories, films, drugs, and surrogates are only a few of the aids a sex therapist might use in the treatment of sexual problems. Others include dream analysis (Levay & Weissberg, 1979) and hypnosis (DeShazer, 1978). The latter has been used in treating premature ejaculation and lack of orgasm. Also, therapists often recommend books to their clients, such as *The New Male-Female Relationship* (Goldberg, 1983), *Treat Yourself to a Better Sex Life* (Gochros & Fischer, 1980), *Male Sexuality* (Zilbergeld, 1978), and *For Yourself: the Fulfillment of Female Sexuality* (Barbach, 1975).

Duration and Cost of Sex Therapy

Two primary questions people exploring the possibility of sex therapy have are how long does it take and what does it cost? As of this writing, the program at the Masters and Johnson Institute takes two weeks and costs $5,000 (including a two-year follow-up). But because the institute has a sliding fee scale, many of their clients pay only a small portion of this amount.

The Hartman and Fithian treatment package lasts for 10 days (Friday through the week to the following Sunday) and costs $2,900 (includes follow-up). If additional therapy is needed beyond follow-up, the client can obtain it for $50 per hour.

But since you would be more likely to see a local sex therapist, what can you expect in terms of length of therapy and cost? Although weekend sexual enrichment workshops are available for less than $100 per couple, short-

IPSA Surrogate Training and Therapy Programs

Definition of "Surrogate"

A surrogate is a member of the three-way therapeutic team (supervising therapist, client, surrogate) who acts as partner to a dysfunctional client in the therapy program and participates in experiential exercises involving sensual and sexual touching, as well as social and sexual skills training.

IPSA Code of Ethics

IPSA maintains a Code of Ethics outlining surrogate behavior and responsibility in the three-way therapeutic situation, in order to uphold highest standards of the helping professionals.

IPSA Training Program

IPSA offers a training program for people interested in learning experientially about the surrogate role. IPSA also believes that knowledge of human sexuality is a constantly evolving process and offers an ongoing educational program for its members through lectures and discussions on latest research in the field of human sexual behavior.

IPSA Referral Service

IPSA has a referral service for putting its members and appropriate therapists in contact. IPSA's referral service is also available to clients seeking a surrogate—therapist team for sexual therapy.

Sexual Problems: Therapy Procedures

Types of Sexual Problems Amenable to Surrogate Therapy Sexual problems concerning male clients may involve ejaculation (premature or inhibited

(Continued)

ejaculation) or erection (getting or maintaining an erection). Female sexual problems may concern arousal level, orgasmic response, or vaginismus (tightened vaginal muscle).

Problems for either gender may also result from medical conditions, from negative body image or body disfigurement, physical disability, questions of sexual orientation (hetero- or homosexual identity), sexual self-confidence, or may result from naivete or inexperience.

Gender Combinations of Surrogate–Client   These include female surrogate–male client and male surrogate–female client. Under some circumstances, including gay clients, combinations may be male surrogate–male client or female surrogate–female client.

Surrogate–Client Interaction   When dealing with a person's sexuality, attitudes are often more important than specific behavior. The surrogate role offers an experience in shared physical intimacy, while working with a client's sexual self-concept and body response. The surrogate role-models both sensual closeness and social skills. Often genital-genital contact is a minor part of the therapy program.

Communication Skills   Verbal and nonverbal communication are practiced. Clients also learn to be aware of body language cues and to listen to their own body responses.

Length of Program and Fees

Surrogate sex therapy is short-term, averaging 15 to 20 sessions. Fees vary according to a surrogate's experience. Average range is $50–$100 per session of one to two hours. Some programs are structured as an "intensive," meeting every day for a specific length of time (such as 10 days), in which case the surrogate's fee is a minimum of $800. In each case, the therapist's fee is separate.*

*Source: From IPSA brochure. Reprinted by permission of IPSA, P. O. Box 74156, Los Angeles, CA 90004

A sex therapist can sometimes help us resolve sexual problems when we are unable to do so by ourselves or with our partner.

term, rapid treatment therapy usually lasts three months and costs $50 to $75 for each of the 12 weekly sessions. If you were to see a psychiatrist or a sex therapist with a psychoanalytic orientation, therapy could last for three years, consisting of weekly sessions at $50 to $75 totaling around $10,000.

However, this length and cost is unusual. In general, you can expect to pay $500 or less for 8 to 10 weekly sessions, which is usually sufficient to accomplish most goals in sex therapy. This amount may seem high, but, in perspective, $500 may be a small amount to pay for the relief of anxiety, feelings of inadequacy, or discomfort. Also, the cost of not resolving a sexual problem that strains a committed relationship may result in divorce or break-up, which has its own emotional and economic price tag. Just as we do not hesitate to pay large amounts for needed car or dental repair or surgery, we might also view sexual problems as worth the time and money to resolve.

Effectiveness of Sex Therapy

For your time and money, what degree of success can you expect? The range of successfully reported cases is from 40 to 100 percent; about two-thirds is an overall average (Kaplan, 1979; Nunes & Bandeira, 1980; Schumacher, 1977). Masters and Johnson report a higher success rate—82 percent—for the 1,872 cases they treated at their institute from 1959 through 1977 (Kolodny, 1981a).

Successful sex therapy depends on the person being treated, the problem, and the treatment approach used by the therapist (Springer, 1981). Those who are well motivated and have a minimum of personal and interpersonal difficulties seem to profit the most and the quickest from sex therapy.

Some problems are also easier to treat than others. Premature ejaculation and vaginismus usually respond quickly to therapeutic intervention. Primary impotence, lack of ability to achieve orgasm, and inhibited sexual desire require more time.

Finally, the therapist and her or his treatment recommendations are important to success. Since sexual problems are most often the result of faulty learning, therapists using behaviorally based treatment approaches offer the quickest and most effective resolution of sexual dysfunctions. However, some patients have severe psychopathology that interferes with quick resolution. Kaplan (1979) observed that many patients who have sexual dysfunctions simply are not cured by brief therapies. Combining behavioral and psychodynamic approaches has been effective in treating some of these patients (Obler, 1982).

We now turn to the problems sex therapists treat and the treatment procedures most widely accepted and practiced. In general, sexually dysfunctional partners want something to happen that is not happening (the woman wants to have an orgasm or the man wants to have an erection) or to stop something from happening that currently happens (the woman experiences pain during intercourse or the man ejaculates too soon). First, we look at female sexual dysfunctions.

Female Sexual Dysfunctions

Lack of sexual desire, or **libido**; inability to achieve orgasm; and inability to control constrictions of the vagina (vaginismus) are three main female sexual dysfunctions. The causes and treatment of each follows.

Lack of Sexual Desire

The person who lacks sexual desire, also referred to as inhibited sexual desire, never initiates sexual activity and is rarely receptive to another who does. Sex is a bore and a chore. Although women more frequently experience lack of sexual desire, men, particularly the cold and formal types, may also lack such interest (Goldberg, 1980). Lack of sexual desire may be primary (the person has never been interested in sex) or secondary (in the past the person demonstrated interest in sex with the same or different partner but does not do so presently).

Degree of sexual arousal may be assessed by the Sexual Arousal Inventory on pages 336–337.

Several reasons may account for low libido.

1. *Restrictive child rearing.* The unresponsive woman usually was told as a child that sexual stimulation and sexual pleasure were sinful and dirty. As a result, she has learned to feel guilty and ashamed of her sexual feelings.

My Sexuality

Sexual Arousal Inventory

Answer every item

-1   adversely affects arousal; unthinkable, repulsive, distracting
 0   doesn't affect sexual arousal
 1   possibly causes sexual arousal
 2   sometimes causes sexual arousal; slightly arousing
 3   usually causes sexual arousal; moderately arousing
 4   almost always sexually arousing; very arousing
 5   always causes sexual arousal; extremely arousing

How you feel or think you would feel if you were actually involved in this experience

1. When a loved one stimulates your genitals with mouth and tongue	-1	0	1	2	3	4	5
2. When a loved one fondles your breasts with his/her hands	-1	0	1	2	3	4	5
3. When you see a loved one nude	-1	0	1	2	3	4	5
4. When a loved one caresses you with his/her eyes	-1	0	1	2	3	4	5
5. When a loved one stimulates your genitals with his/her finger	-1	0	1	2	3	4	5
6. When you are touched or kissed on the inner thighs by a loved one	-1	0	1	2	3	4	5
7. When you caress a loved one's genitals with your fingers	-1	0	1	2	3	4	5
8. When you read a pornographic or "dirty" story	-1	0	1	2	3	4	5
9. When a loved one undresses you	-1	0	1	2	3	4	5

(Continued)

10. When you dance with a loved one	− 1	0	1	2	3	4	5
11. When you have intercourse with a loved one	− 1	0	1	2	3	4	5
12. When a loved one touches or kisses your nipples	− 1	0	1	2	3	4	5
13. When you caress a loved one (other than genitals)	− 1	0	1	2	3	4	5
14. When you see pornographic pictures or slides	− 1	0	1	2	3	4	5
15. When you lie in bed with a loved one	− 1	0	1	2	3	4	5
16. When a loved one kisses you passionately	− 1	0	1	2	3	4	5
17. When you hear sounds of pleasure during sex	− 1	0	1	2	3	4	5
18. When a loved one kisses you with an exploring tongue	− 1	0	1	2	3	4	5
19. When you read suggestive or pornographic poetry	− 1	0	1	2	3	4	5
20. When you see a strip show	− 1	0	1	2	3	4	5
21. When you stimulate your partner's genitals with your mouth and tongue	− 1	0	1	2	3	4	5
22. When a loved one caresses you (other than genitals)	− 1	0	1	2	3	4	5
23. When you see a pornographic movie (stag film)	− 1	0	1	2	3	4	5
24. When you undress a loved one	− 1	0	1	2	3	4	5
25. When a loved one fondles your breasts with mouth and tongue	− 1	0	1	2	3	4	5
26. When you make love in a new or unusual place	− 1	0	1	2	3	4	5
27. When you masturbate	− 1	0	1	2	3	4	5
28. When your partner has an orgasm	− 1	0	1	2	3	4	5

To score scale: (1) Add positive scores; (2) add negative scores; (3) subtract the sum of any negative scores from the sum of positive scores. Scores range from − 28 to + 140.

Source: "An Inventory of the Measurement of Female Sexual Arousability" by E. F. Hoon, P. W. Hoon, and J. Wincze, *Archives of Sexual Behavior,* 1976, 5, 4, 291–301. Reprinted by permission of Plenum Publishing Co., 1976.

2. *Passive sexual role.* In addition, the woman with low libido has often been taught to be a passive and dependent sexual partner. The silent message of her socialization has been that it is unfeminine to lose herself in sexual ecstasy. Since such abandonment is incompatible with the passive feminine role, she does not permit herself to become sexually excited.

3. *Psychological factors.* The person who lacks interest in sex may be depressed because of individual or relationship dissatisfaction, may want to avoid sexual involvement because of fear of pregnancy or genital herpes, or may be reacting to previous negative experiences such as incest or rape.

4. *Physical factors.* Disease, drugs, infection, and fatigue may also erase a person's sexual responsiveness. A nurse said, "After I take care of the kids all day and work the night shift at the hospital, sex is the last thing in the world I'm interested in. And when my partner touches me, I just have to tell him the truth—I'm not interested." "Feeling tired" was the reason given by 80% of 1207 married women as the primary reason for their lack of sexual desire (Grosskopf, 1983).

Treatment for sexual unresponsiveness in a woman involves reeducation, the creation of a safe emotional environment, and the use of sensate focus. Reeducation includes a systematic examination of the thoughts, feelings, and attitudes the woman was taught as a child and a reevaluation of them. The goal is to redefine sex so that it is viewed as a positive, desirable, pleasurable experience. Reeducation also means discarding the belief that one must feel interested in sex before one can enjoy it (Kolodny et al., 1979). Rather, the therapist suggests that interest comes after enjoyment and encourages the woman to become involved in sexual activity first.

The woman's relationship with her partner is a central issue in creating a safe emotional environment. Does she love him? Does she trust him? Does she feel emotionally close to him? Most important, does she feel comfortable letting herself go sexually with him? Unless the relationship with her partner is loving and emotionally comfortable, gains in increasing sexual responsiveness may be minimal.

Finally, the woman and her partner are encouraged to participate in sensate focus exercises. Introduced more than 20 years ago by Masters and Johnson, **sensate focus** is the mutual exploration and discovery of the partners through touch, massage, fondling, or tracing. Specific guidelines for the exercises include the following: (1) Both partners are nude. (2) The partners are not to have intercourse or touch each other's genitals, and the man is not to touch the woman's breasts. (3) One partner is to give pleasure by touching and gently massaging the other. (4) The other partner is to pay attention to the pleasurable feelings of being touched and gently massaged and to let the other know when he or she does something that is or is not pleasurable. (5) The partners are to switch roles so that each gives and gets sensual pleasure each session.

Sensate focus creates an environment in which the woman is permitted to explore her sexual feelings without having to perform for her partner. In addition to sensate focus, the woman may be encouraged to masturbate—a suggestion also made to women who have difficulty climaxing. Some physicians recommend testosterone to increase a woman's interest in sex. While unwanted facial hair may occur in 10 to 15 percent of the cases, it may heighten her libido (Greenblatt, 1980).

Inability to Achieve Orgasm

Masters and Johnson characterized women who have never had an orgasm as having **primary orgasmic dysfunction** (also known as primary anorgasmia or preorgasm). Those who have had an orgasm by any means at any time in the past but who are unable to do so currently are regarded as having **secondary orgasmic dysfunction** (also known as secondary anorgasmia). Several studies suggest that between 5 and 10 percent of adult women have not experienced orgasm (see Chapter 8).

More than 95 percent of the orgasmic dysfunction cases seen at the Masters and Johnson Institute are psychogenic in origin (Kolodny et al., 1979). Some of the causes of inability to achieve an orgasm are similar to those for lack of sexual interest (restrictive child rearing, passive sexual role). Other causes include the following.

1. *Focusing on partner.* Many women have been taught to feel it is their duty to satisfy their partners sexually. But having an orgasm requires that a woman focus on the sexual sensations she is experiencing. If a woman is overly intent on pleasing her partner, she may do so at the expense of her own orgasm.
2. *Feelings about the mate.* A woman may feel it is her duty to have sexual relations with her partner, but she may not like him. Masters and Johnson (1970) suggest that negative feelings about the partner are a major explanation for a woman's being preorgasmic. "Does he meet the woman's requirements of character, intelligence, ego strength, drive, physical characteristics, etc. (p. 241)?" If he does not measure up to her criteria of what a man should be, she may be incapable of becoming sexually excited about him or with him. She may also be angry at her partner and refuse to be used by him by not allowing herself to enjoy the sexual experience or to have an orgasm.
3. *Too little stimulation.* The duration of stimulation is associated with whether a woman climaxes. In a study of about 1,000 wives (Brewer, 1981), two-fifths reported climaxing after 1 to 10 minutes of foreplay. When foreplay lasted 21 minutes or more, three-fifths reported climaxing almost every time. Similarly, although foreplay and penetration often blend, the longer her husband's penis stayed erect and inside her, the greater her chance of having an orgasm during intercourse. If penetration was 1 minute, 25 percent reported orgasm; between 1 and 11 minutes, 50 percent reported climax; and if penetration lasted more than 15 minutes, two-thirds reported climax.
4. *Fear of letting go.* Some women feel it would be embarrassing to lose control in an orgasmic experience, so they deliberately block their sexual arousal.

5. *Too much alcohol.* While moderate drinking of alcohol has the effect of inducing relaxation and increasing sexual arousal, heavy drinking has a depressant effect on the woman's orgasmic response (Malatesta et al., 1982).

6. *Too little information.* Some women have not discovered the kinds of touching that produce orgasm either through masturbation or with a partner.

7. *Hooded clitoris.* Some researchers have suggested that the inability to achieve an orgasm may be caused partly by the foreskin of the clitoris covering the glans so as to interfere with adequate stimulation (Hartman & Fithian, 1974). But other researchers in a study of clitoral foreskin adhesions (Graber & Kline-Graber, 1979) showed that 70 percent of those who did and did not have such adhesions could climax during intercourse.

Since the causes of primary and secondary orgasmic dysfunction are extremely variable, the specific treatment procedures must be tailored for the particular woman. We have already discussed sensate focus exercises to encourage a woman to explore her sexual feelings and to increase her comfort with her partner. In addition, the woman may be encouraged to masturbate to orgasm.

> The use of self-stimulation as opposed to partner stimulation as the method of becoming familiar with orgasm is central; having the orgasm under the woman's own control allows her to go at her own pace while eliminating outside distractions provided by the presence of another person. In this manner, the woman can take gradual steps and learn to become familiar with the feelings that accompany sexual excitation rather than having to guard against them for fear they will overwhelm her. She can stop the stimulation if she feels afraid, or continue on as she grows more secure. As the result of growing familiarity and confidence, the woman becomes capable of experiencing an orgasm on her own. (Barbach, 1974, p. 143)

A detailed discussion of using masturbation to encourage orgasm can be found in *Becoming Orgasmic: A Sexual Growth Program for Women* (Heiman et al., 1976). The book deals with all aspects of masturbation, including the feelings of shame and guilt often associated with it. Such feelings must be dealt with for masturbation exercises to be effective (Mosher, 1979).

After the woman has learned how to bring herself to orgasm through masturbation, she is encouraged to teach her partner how to stimulate her manually to orgasm, first while not having intercourse. After a week or two, stimulation during intercourse is begun (Barbach & Flaherty, 1980). Finally, if the partners prefer, the woman is taught how to have an orgasm during intercourse by using the "bridge method."

> The couple make love until the woman is aroused. Then the man penetrates, either in the female superior position or one of the variations of the side-to-side position. Then, with the penis contained, the man (or the woman) stimulates the woman's clitoris. When she nears orgasm, clitoral stimulation ceases at her signal, and the couple commence thrusting actively to bring about her orgasm. (Kaplan, 1974a, p. 138)

Vaginismus

Vaginismus is a less common sexual dysfunction in which the vaginal opening and outer third of the canal constricts involuntarily making penetration impossible. Like anorgasmia, vaginismus may be primary or secondary (Eicher, 1980). Primary vaginismus means that the vaginal muscles have always constricted to prevent penetration of any object, including tampons. Secondary vaginismus, the more usual variety, suggests that the vagina has permitted penetration in the past but currently constricts when penetration is imminent.

A woman with vaginismus does not necessarily have other female sexual dysfunctions. The woman may be sexually aroused, lubricate profusely, and experience orgasm through masturbation. Involuntary vaginal constrictions are most often found in women who have incorporated traditional religious teachings that suggest that intercourse is dirty and shameful.

Other background factors associated with vaginismus include rape, incest, repeated childhood molestation, or organic difficulties. Examples of the latter are a poorly healed episiotomy (an incision in the perineum to prevent injury to the vagina during childbirth), a poorly stretched hymen, infections or sores near the vaginal opening, or a sexually transmitted disease. The woman who fears pain during penetration will try to avoid it, sometimes unconsciously.

The case of Joan and Steve illustrates how vaginismus may be treated. They had been married for three months but had not consummated their marriage. After ruling out any medical causes for Joan's vaginismus, a therapist recommended the following exercises for three independent occasions during each of four weeks.

First week. In Steve's absence, Joan relaxed and inserted her clean index finger (lubricated with K-Y jelly) into her vagina and kept it there for several minutes while she continued to relax. Having successfully accomplished inserting one finger, she inserted two fingers while relaxing.

Second week. With Steve beside her, Joan repeated the procedure for the first week, with the following additions. After she inserted one of her own fingers, she relaxed and then guided one of Steve's fingers into her vagina as she removed hers. Next, she inserted two of her own fingers, relaxed, and inserted two of Steve's fingers after removing hers.

Third Week. The second week's exercises were repeated. But after Steve had inserted two of his fingers into Joan's vagina, he removed them and gently inserted only the head of his penis, keeping it there for several minutes while Joan continued to relax.

Fourth week. Again, the procedure for the third week was repeated. However, instead of inserting just the head of his penis, Steve gradually and gently penetrated deeper, waited a few seconds, and then—just as gradually and gently—partially withdrew. Finally, full penetration was achieved.

It is important to note that the couple had agreed beforehand that Joan could stop at any time if she became overly tense and anxious. Joan was thus assured that at no point would she be pressured into intercourse. The couple's feelings about engaging in these exercises were also dealt with in therapy.

Male Sexual Dysfunctions

Sexual dysfunctions among women are only one side of the bed. Men may be troubled by sexual apathy, inability to achieve and maintain an erection (impotence), inability to delay ejaculation as long as they or their partners would like (premature ejaculation), or inability to ejaculate at all (ejaculatory incompetence).

Sexual Apathy

It is a myth that men are always ready for sex. Some are apathetic or completely uninterested. "I just don't have any desire for sex," said one man. "And if I never have to do it again, I'll feel relieved."

There are many causes of a low sex drive in men: negative feelings about the partner, hormonal insufficiency, restrictive childrearing, career fatigue, fear of parenthood, terror of intimacy, guilt over extrapartner relationships, and drugs. In addition, the cultural expectation that men should always be interested in sex may threaten a man's feelings of masculinity. Treatment for sexual apathy among men may be first to give them permission not to be interested in sex. The therapist tells the male client not to masturbate or have intercourse for one week. Then other contributing factors can be explored.

Impotence

In Alex Haley's *Roots*, Kunte Kinte, a runaway slave, was captured and about to be punished for his attempted escape. His choices were to lose his foot or his genitals. He quickly decided that his foot should go.

His choice illustrates the emotional significance a man attaches to his penis. A male is taught that his penis is his manhood. Lose it and lose everything. Beyond this, a man is concerned about its use. If it will not work—if he cannot get an erection—he feels humiliated and embarrassed. No other problem is as devastating to the male as a penis that will not become and remain erect.

Impotence, also referred to as erectile dysfunction, is the lack or loss of an erection firm enough for intercourse which may occur during foreplay, the moment of penetration, or intercourse. Like some female sexual dysfunctions, impotence may be primary (the man has never been able to have intercourse) or secondary (he is currently unable to have intercourse). Impotence may also be situational—the man can get an erection in one situation (say, through masturbation) but not in another (such as intercourse). Occasional, isolated episodes of inability to get an erection do not warrant the label of impotence, nor is treatment necessary. Such occurrences are often due to alcohol, stress, or acute illness. However, a pattern of nonerection suggests the need for treatment.

Organic Factors

Primary or secondary impotence may be caused by organic or psychosocial (psychogenic) factors. According to various studies, organic causes of impotence account for 10 percent (Kolodny et al., 1979) to 70 percent (Schumacher & Lloyd, 1981) of cases. A urologist should be consulted to rule out potential organic causes, which include endocrine malfunctions (diabetes, hypopituitarism, Addison's disease), neurologic disorders (multiple sclerosis, Parkinsonism), nutritional deficiencies, vascular dysfunctions (sclerosis), cardiorespiratory problems (heart attack, emphysema), and spinal cord injuries. In general, impotence caused by organic factors tends to be progressive. In psychogenic impotence, onset tends to be abrupt and associated with a specific psychological event, such as criticism by the man's partner about his lovemaking ability.

A low testosterone level may also contribute to impotence. An analysis of the levels of serum testosterone of 105 impotent men (ages 18 to 75) revealed that slightly more than one-third had below normal amounts (Spark & White & Connoly, 1980). Although some of the low levels were related to other physiological problems such as pituitary tumors and excessive amounts of thyroid hormone, once these defects were corrected and regular injections of testosterone were begun, more than 90 percent regained potency. Testosterone levels are also susceptible to external factors such as stress. So, while endocrine testing might be indicated to rule out hormonal imbalances, it also may be advisable to examine the degree to which the male is exposed to stress.

In general, if the man is capable of getting and sustaining a firm erection under any condition (masturbation, viewing an X-rated film, sex with a particular partner, fellatio, or the like), it is likely that his impotence is not caused by organic factors. Another indication that rules out organic pathology is the presence of a firm erection at the time of awakening in the morning. Such erections are almost universal in sexually functioning males.

One researcher has noted that healthy males have erections in their sleep (four or five 20-to-40 minute erectile episodes that occur throughout the night) and that failure to do so may suggest an organic basis for impotence (Karacan, 1978). Various muscles play a role in pumping blood into the penis prior to erection. If these muscles are not active during an **NPT** (**nocturnal penile tumescence**) episode, neural damage is indicated.

A **penile implant** may be suggested as treatment for impotence of irreversible organic causes. These implants are of two types. The first type con-

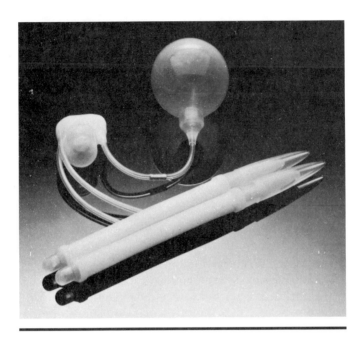

Inflatable penile
prosthesis

sists of semirigid rods made of silicone rubber, acrylic, or polyethylene. The physician surgically places one or two rods inside the penis. The penis stays semierect and intercourse can be accomplished.

The other type of **penile prosthesis** (another word for penile implant) consists of two inflatable cylinders surgically implanted in the penis. These cylinders are connected by a tube to a pumping device placed in the man's scrotum (Figure 11.1). The man uses his fingers to squeeze the device, which pumps fluid stored in a small sack placed behind the abdominal muscles. This fluid goes into the cylinders, which inflate the penis to simulate an erection. After intercourse, the man can return the fluid to the scrotum at will (Sotile, 1979). The implant does not ensure pleasure. For example, the spinal-cord-injured male may not feel genital stimulation. Such a male gets an implant for the benefit of his partner.

Penile implant surgery, which takes about 40 minutes, has been used since 1964; more than 4,000 patients a year have been treated in recent years (Subrini, 1980). Dr. Brantley Scott, a urologist at the Baylor College of Medicine in Houston, Texas, has performed more than 400 such implants. The cost is around $5,000.

Infection is the most often-reported complication of the rodlike device implant. Mechanical failure in the cylinders or tubing system is the most often-reported problem in the hydraulic device implant. But such problems are rare, occurring in only about 5 percent of the cases (Kramarsky-Binkhorst, 1980). The complete failure rate of implant surgery ranges from 3 percent to 1 percent. When 110 patients were asked, "Are you fully satisfied to have been operated on?" 9 in 10 said "yes" (Subrini, 1980). A major benefit appears to be restoration of the male's self-esteem. (Seagraves, Schoenberg, & Zarins, 1982).

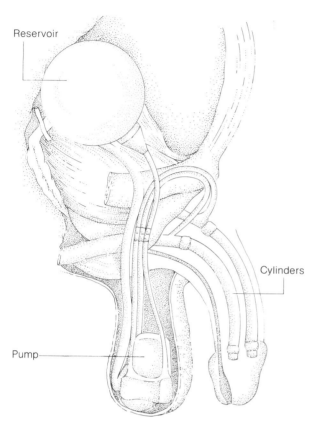

Reservoir

Cylinders

Pump

Reservoir. The reservoir's seamless construction of silicone elastomer makes it an excellent storage compartment for the fluid used in the prosthesis. Implanted under the abdominal muscles, the reservoir is well protected. Radiopaque fluid allows for postoperative inspection of the Inflatable Penile Prosthesis by radiography.

Pump/bulb. The fluid transfer pump/bulb hangs loosely in the scrotum and is connected by silicone elastomer tubing to both the inflatable cylinders and reservoir. Repeated pumping causes the fluid to travel from the reservoir through the tubing, inflating the cylinders and effecting an erection.

Cylinders. The inflatable cylinders are placed in parallel position in the corpora cavernosa of the penis. Surgical placement of the cylinders is accomplished by a small abdominal or scrotal incision rather than an incision in the penis itself. Filled, the inflated cylinders erect the penis; emptied, they do not interfere with urinary function.

Release valve. A pressure release valve in the lower portion of the pump/bulb allows the fluid to leave the penile cylinders and return to the storage reservoir. Because the release valve is small and located with the pump/bulb assembly, the possibility of accidental release and loss of erection is minimal.

Psychosocial Factors

Psychosocial factors are the most frequent cause of impotence, and anxiety heads the list. The anxious male cannot get an erection because an erection depends on a state of relaxation. For example, as a male, assume that you are in a classroom and a platoon of Russian soldiers walks through the door, putting a gun to the head of each student. Their leader announces, "You guys have 30 seconds to get an erection or we'll blow your heads off." The demand for such a performance will create intense anxiety, and no male in the class will be capable of getting an erection.

A similar situation may happen in the bedroom. The woman makes it clear to the man that she expects him to have an erection and to have intercourse with her. Whereas such an expectation is a welcome situation for some men, the man who has been impotent in the past begins to fear that he will not be able to get an erection and satisfy her. His anxiety about performing and fear of her disapproval if he fails, help to ensure that he will not get an erection.

**Figure 11.1
Inflatable Penile
Prosthesis**
The American Medical Systems' Inflatable Penile Prosthesis simulates normal erectile physiology by allowing the patient to transfer fluid from an internal storage reservoir to two inflatable cylinders implanted in the penis.

*U.S. Patent Number 3,954,102.

What follows is a devastating cycle of negative experiences locking the male into impotence at each sexual encounter: anxiety, impotence, embarrassment, followed by anxiety, impotence, and so on.

The man also has his own ideas of how he is supposed to perform as a male. Even if his partner is sympathetic and supportive, it may be his own self-imposed performance demands that create the anxiety. In many cases, this may be the primary source of the anxiety that interferes with achieving an erection.

Anxiety may also be related to alcohol use. After more than the usual number of drinks, the man may initiate sex but fail to achieve an erection. He becomes anxious and struggles even harder to get an erection, ensuring that he will not. Although alcohol may be responsible for his initial failure, his impotence continues because of his anxiety.

Treatment for impotence of psychosocial origin begins with the instruction that the couple not have intercourse. If there is no expectation for intercourse, the associated anxiety is minimized. The therapist then discusses with the couple how anxiety (and alcohol, if this is an issue) inhibits erection. In essence, the partners are given information so they may understand the man's impotence rather than continue to be mystified by its occurrence.

The partners are also instructed to begin sensate focus exercises and the man is encouraged to give up the spectator role—to stop focusing on whether he is getting an erection. Later he is encouraged to give pleasure to his partner through manual or oral stimulation. After several sensate focus sessions, during which there is no pressure to perform and the man learns alternative ways to pleasure his partner, he is more likely to have an erection.

In addition to this basic treatment package, other issues related to impotence may be addressed. For example, the man may feel threatened by his dominating partner, leading to impotence. The antidote is couple counseling in which the power struggle in the relationship is rebalanced (Rosenheim & Neumann, 1981).

Premature Ejaculation

More common than impotence, **premature ejaculation** is the man's inability to control the ejaculatory reflex. Eighty-one percent of 65,381 men in one survey (Petersen et al., 1983a) reported that there are times they ejaculate too quickly (7 percent said it happened frequently). Ten minutes was the average length of time before ejaculation. Whether a man ejaculates too soon is a matter of definition. Some wives are glad their husbands ejaculate quickly ("I'm glad to get it over with").

When ejaculating too soon is defined as a problem, the cause is viewed as more often psychological than physical. Anxiety may trigger the ejaculatory reflex. Masters and Johnson (1970) report that all men experiencing premature ejaculation have the same history. Early attempts at intercourse or orgasm were hurried. The men always felt pressure to ejaculate as soon as they could. One example is the male who had to masturbate quickly before his parents could discover what he was doing; another is the man whose prostitute partners would try to make him climax quickly so they could get to the next customer. These men learned to ejaculate quickly.

Use of the **squeeze technique** (Figure 11.2), developed by Masters and Johnson, is the most effective procedure for treating premature ejaculation. The woman stimulates her partner's penis manually until he signals her that he feels the urge to ejaculate. At his signal she places her thumb on the underside of his penis, her first and second fingers on either side of the ridge formed by the head of his penis, and squeezes hard for 3 to 4 seconds. The man will lose his urge to ejaculate. After 30 seconds she resumes stimulation, applying the squeeze technique again when her partner signals. The important rule to remember is that the woman should apply the squeeze technique whenever the man gives the slightest hint of readiness to ejaculate. (The squeeze technique can also be used by the male during masturbation to teach himself to delay his ejaculation.)

In a variation of the squeeze technique, **Seman's technique**, the woman stimulates her partner's erect penis until he feels he is about to ejaculate (Semans, 1956). At that point he signals her to stop and he relaxes. When he loses his urge to ejaculate, he signals his partner to resume stimulation. After practicing this stop-start method four times, he is allowed to ejaculate at the fifth period of stimulation.

Usually after about five of these training sessions, intercourse is substituted for the woman's hands. After an initial application of the squeeze technique, the woman adopts the female-superior position, stimulates the man with her vagina, and lifts herself off his penis when he signals that he is about to ejaculate. She may then wait until his desire to ejaculate subsides or apply the squeeze technique before resuming stimulation.

Other techniques are sometimes used in treating premature ejaculation but are generally not effective. These include the use of several condoms (one man used six), ointments such as Detane that anaesthetize the head of the penis, and distraction (counting, playing tennis in one's head). Half of the men

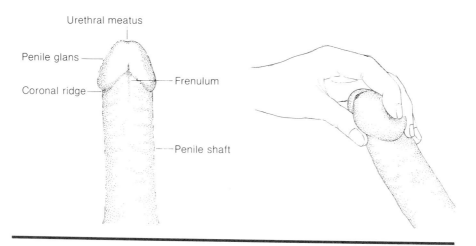

Urethral meatus

Penile glans

Coronal ridge

Frenulum

Penile shaft

**Figure 11.2
The Squeeze
Technique**

From: *Textbook of
Sexual Medicine* by
Robert Kolodny,
William Masters, and
Virginia Johnson.
Published by Little,
Brown and Company,
Boston, Mass.: 1979, p.
526. Reprinted by
permission.

in the *Playboy* survey who reported premature ejaculation said they deal with the problem by stimulating their partner another way (Petersen et al., 1983a). One-fourth said they simply wait and start again.

Ejaculatory Incompetence

In contrast to the man who experiences premature ejaculation, the man who suffers from **ejaculatory incompetence** cannot ejaculate at all, even after prolonged intercourse. Also referred to as retarded ejaculation, absence of ejaculation, ejaculatory impotence, and inhibited ejaculation, ejaculatory incompetence may be primary or secondary. Primary ejaculatory incompetence, describes the man who has never ejaculated inside a woman's vagina. Secondary ejaculatory incompetence, the more common form, refers to current inability to ejaculate inside the woman. It is not unusual for ejaculatory incompetence to be situational—it occurs with one partner but not another or the same partner on one occasion but not on another (Munjack & Kanno, 1979).

Most causes of ejaculatory incompetence are psychological. For example, a 33-year-old husband revealed that he considered his wife's vagina contaminated because she had confessed on their wedding night that she had had intercourse before she met him. "How such a good woman, represented by his wife, could possibly have permitted such a transgression was inexplicable to him" (Masters & Johnson, 1970, p. 120).

In another case a 36-year-old husband at age 13 had been

> surprised in masturbation by his dismayed mother, severely punished by his father, and immediately sent to religious authority for consultation. Subsequent to his lengthy discussion with the religious adviser, the semi-hysterical, terrified boy carried away the concept that to masturbate to ejaculation was indeed an act of personal desecration, totally destructive of any future marital happiness and an open gate to mental illness. He was assured that the worst thing a teenage boy could do was to ejaculate at any time. (Masters & Johnson, 1970, p. 118)

Fear of impregnating the woman, lack of sexual excitement, and efforts to ejaculate too often in too short a time are other causes of ejaculatory incompetence.

Treatment involves discussion of the psychological issues and sensate focus exercises. After these exercises the woman manually helps the man ejaculate. After they are confident that he can be brought to orgasm manually, she stimulates him to a high level of sexual excitement and, at the moment of orgasm, inserts his penis into her vagina so that he ejaculates inside her. After several sessions of first hand, then vagina stimulation, the woman gradually reduces the amount of time she manually manipulates her partner and increases the amount of time she stimulates him with her vagina.

Other Sexual Problems

Both women and men may experience such sexual problems like pain during intercourse, sexual aversion, different desires for frequency of intercourse, and different needs for variety in sexual expression.

Dyspareunia

Dyspareunia is pain during intercourse. Among women it occurs in about 10 percent of gynecological patients and may be caused by vaginal infection, lack of lubrication, a rigid hymen, or an improperly positioned uterus or ovary. Because the causes of dyspareunia are often physical, a physician should be consulted. Sometimes surgery is recommended to remove the hymen.

Dyspareunia also may result from psychological causes. Guilt, anxiety, or unresolved feelings about a previous trauma such as rape or child molestation may be operative. Counseling or psychotherapy may be indicated.

Pain during intercourse is most often associated with women, but dysparenuia also occurs in men. The pain is usually felt in the shaft of the penis, the testes, or lower back and may result from inflammation of the male sex organs, irritation from using a spermacide, a herpes lesion, or a pulled muscle.

Sexual Aversion

Some people have an extreme negative reaction to sexual activity. Unlike the person who is not interested in sex, the person who regards sex as aversive may throw up, start sweating, or get diarrhea when confronted with the expectation of a sexual encounter. "When he reached for my hand," said one woman, "I knew what he wanted and I started to shake and get sick. I just couldn't help myself."

Women are more likely to experience **sexual aversion** than men. The causes of sexual aversion seem multifaceted—negative sexual attitudes acquired in childhood, sexual trauma (rape), and the development of negative sexual patterns, such as promiscuity, that may result in extreme hostility to the other gender.

Treatment for sexual aversion involves providing insight into the possible ways in which the negative attitudes to sexual activity developed, increasing the communication skills of the partners, and sensate focus. Whereas the insight and communication components of the treatment package are cognitive and verbal, sensate focus is experiential. As a result of these procedures, the person unlearns negative associations in reference to sexual stimulation and learns more positive ones.

Frequency of Intercourse

Given different body clocks (some people are "morning people," others are "night people"), different work schedules, and different psychological and physical needs, it is not uncommon for partners to differ in their desire for frequency of intercourse. One woman said that she needed intercourse once a day just like her orange juice but that her partner seemed content to "let it slide" for several weeks.

Differences are managed by compromise or by one partner adapting to the needs of the other. In addition, a partner who wants more frequent intercourse may masturbate or encourage the partner to manipulate him or her to orgasm. Open communication and a concern for each partner's feelings about frequency of intercourse are the keys to successful resolution of differences.

Variety

Partners may also disagree over what sexual behaviors are appropriate before, during, and after intercourse. In general, willingness to include a variety of sexual behaviors in lovemaking is related to age, education, social class, and religious orientation. The younger, better-educated, higher-income individual who does not have a fundamentalist religious orientation is more likely to include manual and oral stimulation in lovemaking and to experiment with a range of coital positions.

Managing differences about sexual variety should be handled like the mating of two porcupines—with great care. Forcing your desires on the partner is never wise. Rather, through involvement in couple therapy (reading and attending lectures or workshops on human sexuality may also be useful) and discussing differences, partners can explore together the basis of their feelings and consider ways in which they might arrive at a compromise acceptable to both. In general, any sexual behaviors both partners consider appropriate for their relationship are appropriate. Getting your partner to engage in a new sexual behavior takes time. Patience is the key. If, say, getting your partner to spend more time kissing and holding prior to intercourse is the goal, you should regard small increases in such time as progress.

Summary

Sex therapy ranges from teaching basic sex techniques (skill training) to examining interpersonal dynamics. The basic elements of sex therapy include managing relationships, changing attitudes, providing information, giving permission, and reducing anxiety. Thus sex therapy is more often concerned with the context of sexual interaction than with the physical aspects of the interaction.

Academic degrees, counseling experience under supervision, and formal training in human sexuality are not necessary to practice sex therapy in most states. Among those practicing sex therapy are health educators, sociologists, ministers, psychologists, social workers, marriage counselors, physicians, and psychiatrists. Their training ranges from none or minimal to extensive. Let the buyer beware!

Anyone may be a client in sex therapy, although such clients are more likely to be of higher socioeconomic status and to be college educated. The sex therapy they become involved in can be extremely varied. Types of treatment include the Masters and Johnson approach, the Hartman and Fithian approach, the psychodynamic approach, the rational-emotive therapy approach, Kaplan's approach, and the behavior therapy approach. But there is considerable overlap of the various approaches to sex therapy. Sex therapists may use one or more aids in their therapy program including inventories, films, drugs, and surrogates.

The duration and cost of sex therapy ranges from weekend sexual enrichment workshops for less than $100 per couple to years of weekly sessions at $50 to $75 totaling around $10,000. In general, $500 or less for 8 to 10 weekly sessions is sufficient to accomplish most goals in sex therapy. Successful sex therapy depends on the person being treated, the problem, and the treatment approach used by the therapist. A reasonable estimate of the percentage of successfully treated cases is about two-thirds.

Sexual problems are a concern in many relationships. Masters and Johnson suggest that at least half of all married couples experience such problems. Lack of sexual responsiveness, failure to achieve orgasm, and inability to control constrictions of the vagina (vaginismus) are the main female sexual dysfunctions. Men may be troubled by an inability to get and maintain an erection (impotence), inability to delay ejaculation (premature ejaculation), or inability to ejaculate at all (ejaculatory incompetence). Sexual problems either partner may experience include pain during intercourse (dyspareunia), sexual aversion, different desires for frequency of intercourse, and different needs for variety in sexual expression.

Key Terms

psychodynamic
rational-emotive therapy
behavior therapy
surrogate
libido
sensate focus
primary orgasmic dysfunction
secondary orgasmic dysfunction
vaginismus
impotence

nocturnal penile tumescence (NPT)
penile implant
penile prosthesis
premature ejaculation
squeeze technique
Seman's technique
ejaculatory incompetence
dyspareunia
sexual aversion

Issues in Debate and Future Directions

Whether one or both partners should attend sex therapy, whether private or group therapy is more effective, and whether one or two therapists as a team should be sought are unsettled issues in sex therapy. After examining these controversies, we look at various trends in sexual therapy.

Is Individual or Couple Therapy More Effective?

Should just the person experiencing the sexual problem or the person and her or his sexual partner become involved in sex therapy? It depends. Some people prefer to see a therapist alone (Zilbergeld, 1980). One woman said, "If I ask him to go to therapy with me, he'll think I'm more emotionally involved than I am. And since I don't want to encourage him, I'll just work out my problems without him." Other reasons for this preference include no available partner, a partner who will not cooperate in therapy, or a feeling of greater comfort in discussing sex in the partner's absence.

But couple therapy has several advantages (Kolodny et al., 1979). It avoids the problem of one partner feeling that she or he is "sick." The presence of both suggests that they view the sexual problem as mutual and seek to resolve it jointly. Also, since many sexual problems are embedded in the relationship, couple therapy affords the therapist the opportunity to assess their communication and interaction patterns. Anger and hostility that might surface during the therapy session can be minimized or eliminated so that the couple may better work on the sexual problem.

Both partners in therapy also permit the therapist to check out unrealistic expectations.

For example, she may expect him to delay ejaculation for two hours and he may expect her to climax every time they have intercourse. Discussing such unrealistic expectations in the presence of both partners is often more beneficial than doing so with just one of them.

While there are exceptions, a greater proportion of sexual problems can probably be more effectively treated by becoming involved in therapy with a partner.

Is Private or Group Therapy Best?

Once the decision to pursue therapy is made, is it best to be seen in private or in groups with other people who are experiencing a similar problem? Such groups are offered for problems ranging from premature ejaculation (Zeiss, Christensen, & Levine, 1978) to lack of orgasm (Barbach, 1980). There are advantages and disadvantages of either treatment pattern. Although being seen privately helps to ensure that therapy will be tailored to fit the specific needs of the client, the cost is considerably higher than if the client is treated in a group setting. Private therapy may cost $75 an hour but only $15 for the same amount of time in a group of five.

But being less expensive is not the only advantage of group therapy. Being surrounded by others who have a similar problem helps to reduce the feeling that "I'm the only one." One woman who had difficulty achieving orgasm said, "When I heard the other women discuss their difficulty with climaxing, I knew I wasn't abnormal." The empathy of a group of peers can be extremely effective in helping a person feel less isolated.

A group setting also furnishes the opportunity

to try new behaviors. For example, some sexual problems may be part of a larger problem, such as the lack of social skills to attract and maintain a partner (Zilbergeld & Ellison, 1979). Fear of rejection can perpetuate being alone. But group members, with the help of their therapist, can practice making requests of each other and getting turned down. Such an exercise helps to develop the social skill of approaching others while learning to deal with rejection. Practicing with other group members is safe and gives a person the necessary confidence to approach someone outside the group setting.

There are at least two disadvantages of group therapy. First is the possibility of not having enough time spent on one's own problem. Second is the risk to the relationship with the partner who may not be involved in the group. In one study of women in group therapy for lack of orgasm (Barbach & Flaherty, 1980), one in four suggested a negative effect on their partner.

Before drawing conclusions about the comparative effectiveness of private versus group therapy, let us examine the types of groups available.

Groups of Individuals   The study just referred to is an example of group therapy for individuals with a common sexual problem. In one such group, five to seven women who lacked the ability to achieve an orgasm in a particular situation met for 10 one-and-a-half-hour weekly sessions. During this time they shared their early sexual learning experiences, their current sexual problems, and their feelings about sexuality. But most of the time they discussed the weekly homework assignments they were to have completed between sessions. These included masturbating, having their partners stimulate them manually or orally to orgasm while not attempting intercourse, and having their partners stimulate them manually during intercourse.

Group therapy is not limited to women with

sexual problems. Impotence has been treated in all-male groups (Lobitz & Baker, 1979). Through a series of homework assignments, the men learned to minimize the anxiety that caused their impotence. These assignments included masturbating to full erection, letting the erection subside, relaxing, and restimulating to full erection. By gaining, deliberately losing, and regaining their erections in private, each man became less fearful of not being able to control loss of erection.

Groups of Couples   As an alternative to group therapy for individuals with specific sexual problems, you and your partner might be seen in group therapy with other couples. Premature ejaculation and orgasmic dysfunction have been treated in group settings of three to four couples (Golden et al., 1978). The format included the discussion of between-session homework assignments. Such assignments included sensate focus for the first several weeks, followed by instructions about the squeeze technique for couples in which the man was a premature ejaculator. Another set of instructions was given to couples working on the woman's orgasmic capacity. These included the woman masturbating to orgasm and teaching her partner how to bring her to orgasm.

What is the comparative effectiveness of couples being treated in a group or in private therapy? In the previously described study, when group couple therapy for premature ejaculation and orgasmic dysfunction was compared with therapy for the same problems treated in private, there were no differences in outcome. Both treatment patterns were effective—males reported satisfaction with their ability to prolong intercourse and females reported satisfaction with their orgasmic ability. Other researchers have found similar results— couples in group therapy are as successful in achieving their goals as couples in private therapy (Duddle & Ingram, 1980).

This suggests that *couples* can be treated effectively in either a private or a group setting. It is, therefore, a matter of preference. But group therapy for individuals may not be as effective as therapy with a partner in private or in a couples group. However, most *individuals* in group sex therapy without a partner do benefit from the experience.

One or Two Therapists?

Is it best to see one therapist or a male–female sex therapy team? Masters and Johnson recommend the latter for couple therapy, suggesting that the man can better relate to the man and the woman to the woman. A dual sex team also provides a model for appropriate male–female interaction.

But although other sex therapists also have adopted the dual sex team approach, there is no evidence that such a team is more effective than individual male or female therapists (Clement & Schmidt, 1983). Rather than how many therapists of what gender are in the therapy setting, the quality of the therapy seems to be the important variable.

Future Directions

Sex therapy of the future will include more sophisticated research, treatment delivered by better-trained therapists, therapy of shorter duration, and therapy that is less expensive. In the past, claims for the effectiveness of various sex therapy procedures, particularly those by Masters and Johnson, have been uncritically accepted (Zilbergeld & Evans, 1980). Sex therapists are now being encouraged to be more critical of new techniques and insistent on solid, replicable data to back up claims for these techniques (Evans & Zilbergeld, 1983).

The movement for better-trained sex therapists is underway. We have already noted California's requirement of training in human sexuality to obtain a license as a psychologist or social worker. In addition, medical schools are continuing to introduce required courses in sexuality into the curriculum. These trends will continue.

However, the licensing of sex therapists will continue to be problematic. Too many groups are involved in the delivery of sex therapy to give the right to practice sex therapy to only one group. For the immediate future, AASECT (American Association of Sex Educators, Counselors, and Therapists) will continue to offer certification for those who volunteer to meet the criteria they have established.

Sex therapy will more often be of the rapid-treatment variety and, hence, will cost comparatively less. Clients will be less willing to spend years and thousands of dollars in sex therapy. Rather, the need to watch expenses will nudge them into seeking therapy that is both efficient and reasonably priced. As a result of the greater demand for rapid treatment, an increasing number of sex therapists will begin to abandon psychodynamic modes of therapy for learning-based models. Psychodynamic treatment procedures will not disappear since some clients may respond best to this form of therapy, but these procedures will more often be supplemented by specific suggestions designed to help the client achieve more effective sexual functioning.

Chapter Twelve

Sexual Health

*I'm not going to get herpes or
any other sexually transmitted
disease.*

ANY OF US

Chapter Twelve

Enjoyable sexual relationships and effective sexual functioning depend on healthy bodies. Although we think of our genitals mostly as sources of pleasure and reproduction, they are also potential sites for disease. Numerous types of sexually transmitted diseases (STDs) and cancers can infect our sex organs. In this chapter we examine some of these threats to our sexual health.

Sexually Transmitted Diseases (STDs)

Sexually transmitted diseases are also known as venereal diseases. Venus was the Roman goddess of love, and since some diseases are transmitted through various acts of love—kissing, cunnilingus, fellatio, intercourse—the term venereal (from Venus) has been used to describe such diseases. They are also referred to as social diseases because they are contracted primarily through sociosexual contact. In effect, any person who has physical or sexual contact with someone who has a sexually transmitted disease may get that disease. The exposure may be through heterosexual or homosexual contacts. Table 12.1 lists a number of myths and facts about STDs.

Contracting a sexually transmitted disease not only affects our body but also our social view of ourselves. Interviews of men and women who had contracted an STD revealed that they acquired an immediate negative social identity (Fox & Edgely, 1983). "I felt plagued" or "I felt as if I had leprosy" were common reactions.

> Our respondents stated that they had always assumed that if a person demonstrated good judgment and common sense, such as the choice of sexual partners or the use of prophylactics, the VD would never have occurred in the first place. Getting the disease, then, was equated with stupidity and the feelings of mortification that are attendant to such a self-identification . . . VD also suggested that the person is a bed-hopper, incapable of forming an enduring relationship and forced to seek sexual gratification through one-night stands. (p. 69)

Table 12.1 Myths and Facts About Sexually Transmitted Diseases (STDs)

Myth	Fact
STDs in the genitals cannot be transmitted to the mouth and vice versa.	Transmission of STD infections from mouth to genitals and vice versa does occur.
If you have syphilis or gonorrhea, you will know it.	Some infected people show no signs of having syphilis or gonorrhea until many years later.
You can avoid having to see a physician by treating your suspected STD infection at home.	Only a physician can recommend a treatment plan for STDs.
You cannot have more than one STD at a time.	More than half of women who visited one STD clinic had two or more STDs.
Birth control pills protect you from STDs.	Birth control pills may increase a woman's chances of contracting various STDs when exposed.
Once you have been cured of an STD, you cannot get it again.	You can get an STD infection any time you come into contact with it whether you have had it or not.
Syphilis and gonorrhea can be contracted by contact with a toilet seat.	The germs of these diseases cannot live in the open air.

Although we comment later in this chapter on other social aspects of contracting sexually transmitted diseases, we begin by reviewing the more common STDs.

Gonorrhea

Known popularly as "the clap," "the whites," and "morning drop," **gonorrhea** is the number two communicable disease in the United States (number one is the cold). "Communicable" means that, like the common cold, the disease is easily caught from someone who has it. About one million cases of gonorrhea are reported every year. The highest percentage of these cases occur in those who are in their teens or early twenties (Zaidi et al., 1983).

Contracting gonorrhea most often occurs through having genital contact with someone who is carrying the gonococcus bacteria. These bacteria live in the urethra and around the cervix of the female and in the urinary tract of the male. During intercourse some of the bacteria are transferred from the mucous membranes inside the urethra of one gender to the other. The bacteria may also enter the throat during oral–genital contact or the rectum during anal intercourse.

Although some infected men show no signs, 80 percent do so between three and eight days after exposure. They begin to discharge a thick, white pus from the penis (thus "the whites" and "morning drop") and feel pain or discomfort during urination. They may also have swollen lymph glands in the groin. Women are more likely to be without symptoms but when they

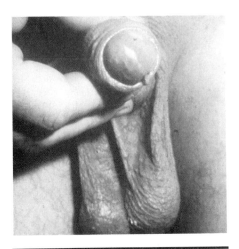

Gonorrhea drip.

have them, they are sometimes in the form of a discharge from the vagina and a burning sensation. More often a woman becomes aware of gonorrhea only after she feels extreme discomfort resulting from the untreated infection traveling into her uterus and Fallopian tubes. Pelvic inflammatory disease (PID) is the term used to describe the inflammation in these areas caused by gonococci or other bacteria. A physician can sometimes verify if a person has gonorrhea by looking at the discharge under a microscope; growing a culture of the discharge and examining it microscopically is an alternative diagnostic procedure. The symptoms of gonorrhea disappear if they are not treated but the bacteria may still be present.

There are a number of negative consequences of undetected and untreated gonorrhea. First is the liklihood that the infected person will pass on the disease to the next partner. Then, the gonococcus bacteria can damage the brain, joints, and reproductive systems. Both men and women can develop meningitis (inflammation of the tissues surrounding the brain and spinal cord), arthritis, and sterility. In men the urethra may become blocked, necessitating frequent visits to a physician to clean the passage for urination. Infected women may have spontaneous abortions and premature or stillborn infants.

To avoid these problems, the person with gonorrhea symptoms should seek immediate medical treatment. Depending on the patient's reaction to various drugs, combinations of penicillin, ampicillin, and other antibiotics are usually prescribed. (In some cases the gonorrhea infection is resistent to penicillin). Within 24 hours the person is usually no longer contagious and the symptoms begin to disappear. The sooner treatment begins, the less the damage. The gonococcus germ can be eliminated but the damage to tissues and organs that has already occurred cannot be repaired. The person who delays treatment by thinking "I hope I don't have the clap" or "I'm too embarrassed to see a physician" only increases the chance of complications.

Nongonococcal Urethritis (NGU)

Nongonococcal urethritis (NGU), thought to be caused by the microorganisms *Chlamydia* and *Mycoplasma*, affects both men and women. NGU causes penile discharge, which is thinner than that of gonorrhea, and causes burning and pain during urination. Infected women may show no symptoms or may have a slight discharge and discomfort when urinating. NGU is suspected when microscopic examination of the penile discharge does not show gonococcus bacteria or when a culture of the discharge from either gender does not grow it.

Once identified NGU is treated with tetracyclines or other antibiotics. If left untreated NGU may be as dangerous as gonorrhea, causing serious problems in both the female and male reproductive tracts. Symptoms may disappear but the person will remain contagious and at risk for internal damage.

Syphilis

Although **syphilis** is less prevalent than gonorrhea or NGU (there are 80,000 new cases annually), the effects of syphilis are more devastating, including mental illness, blindness, heart disease—even death. The spirochete bacteria—the villain germs—enter the body through mucous membranes that line various body openings. With your tongue, feel the inside of your cheek. This is a layer of mucous membrane—the substance in which spirochetes thrive. Similar membranes are in the vagina and urethra of the penis. If you kiss or have genital contact with someone harboring these bacteria, they can be absorbed into your mucous membranes causing syphilitic infection. Your syphilis will then progress through at least three of four stages.

In stage one (primary syphilis), between 10 and 90 days after exposure, a small sore will appear at the site of the infection. The chancre, as it is called, shows up on the tip of the man's penis, in the labia or cervix of the woman, or in either partner's mouth or rectum. The chancre neither hurts nor itches and, if left untreated, will disappear in three to five weeks. The person may believe that she or he is cured, but in reality, the disease is still present and doing great harm even though there are no visible signs.

 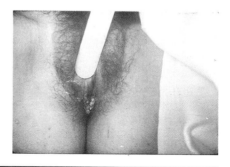

Chancre of primary syphilis as it appears on the penis (*left*) and the labia (*right*).

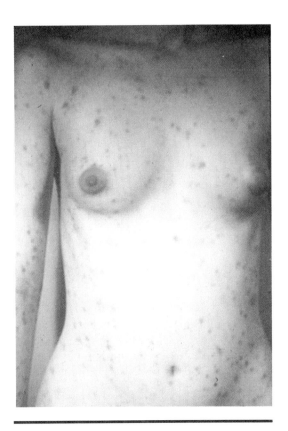

Rash of secondary
syphilis.

During stage two (secondary syphilis), beginning from 2 to 12 weeks after the chancre has disappeared, other signs of syphilis appear. These may include a rash all over the body or just on the hands or feet. The person also may develop welts and sores as well as fever, headaches, sore throat, and hair loss. Syphilis has been called "the great imitator" because it mimics so many other diseases (for example, infectious mononucleosis, cancer, and psoriasis). Whatever the symptoms, they, too, will disappear without treatment. Again, the person may be tricked into believing that nothing is wrong.

For about two-thirds of those with late untreated syphilis (latent syphilis), the disease seems to have gone away with no subsequent effects. However, the spirochetes are still in the body and can attack any organ at any time. For the other third, serious harm results. Tertiary syphilis—the fourth stage— may disable or kill. In addition to heart disease and blindness, mentioned earlier, brain damage, loss of bowel and bladder control, difficulty in walking, and impotence may result.

Aside from avoiding contact with a person infected with syphilis, early detection and treatment are essential. Blood tests and examination of material from the infected site can help verify the existence of syphilis. But such tests are not always accurate. Blood tests reveal the presence of antibodies, which form as a reaction to the infection, not the spirochetes themselves, and it takes up to three months before the body produces detectable antibodies. Sometimes there is no chancre anywhere on the person's body.

Treatment for syphilis is similar to that for gonorrhea. Penicillin or other antibiotics (for those allergic to pennicillin) is effective. Infected persons treated in the early stages can be completely cured, but if the syphilis has progressed into the third or latent stage, any damage that has been done cannot be repaired.

A particularly distressing outcome of syphilis is its effect on the newborn of an infected woman. If the pregnant woman does not receive treatment, her baby is likely to be born deformed or crippled from congenital syphilis. If she is treated by the eighteenth week of pregnancy, the fetus will not be affected.

Genital Herpes

"Herpes" refers to more than 50 viruses related by size, shape, internal composition, and structure. One such herpes is **genital herpes**. Whereas the disease has been known for at least 2,000 years, the media attention to genital herpes is relatively new. Also known as **herpes simplex virus type 2** (HSV-2), genital herpes is a viral infection that is usually transmitted during sexual contact. Symptoms occur in the form of a cluster of small, painful blisters or sores on the penis or around the anus in men. In women, the blisters usually appear around the vagina but may also develop inside the vagina, on the cervix, and sometimes in the anus.

Another type of herpes is labial or lip herpes, which originates in the mouth. **Herpes simplex virus type 1** (HSV-1) is a biologically different herpes virus with which people are familiar as cold sores on the lips. These sores can be transferred to the genitals by the fingers or by oral–genital contact. In the past, genital and lip herpes had site specificity; that is, HSV-1 was

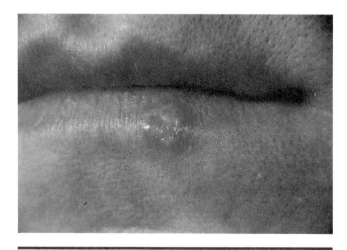

Herpes simplex lesion of the lower lip.

always found on the lips or in the mouth and HSV-2 was always found in the genitals. But because of the increase in fellatio and cunnilingus, HSV-1 herpes may be found in the genitals and anus and HSV-2 may be found on the lips.

The first symptoms of genital herpes appear a couple of days to three weeks after exposure. At first these symptoms may include itching or a burning sensation during urination followed by headache, fever, aches, swollen glands, and, in women, vaginal discharge. The symptoms worsen over about 10 days, during which there is a skin eruption, followed by the appearance of sores that soon break open and become very painful during genital contact or when touched. The acute illness may last from three to six weeks.

As with syphilis, the symptoms of genital herpes subside (the sores dry up, scab over, and disappear) and the person feels good again. But the virus settles in the nerve cells near the spinal column and may cause repeated outbreaks of the physical symptoms in about a third of those infected. The process occurs as follows.

> When a person is first infected, the virus gets into the cells and multiplies rapidly, destroying the cells. The body's defense system moves in and kills the virus. But some invading viruses escape, travel up nerve pathways, and slip into nerve cells, where they remain inactive for a while. Since they don't disturb the nerve cells, the body's defense system doesn't go after them. Then, under a stimulation that isn't yet well understood, the viruses become active again and start the process of infecting cells and multiplying all over again. The body defenses go into action, most of the viruses are destroyed, but some escape and the 'quiet' period starts all over again. (*Straight talk about herpes*, 1982, p. 3)

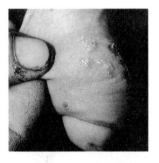 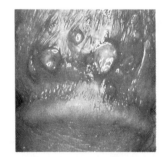

Male genital herpes (*upper left*); herpes corona (*upper right*); primary herpes (*lower left*); female genital herpes (*lower right*).

Stress, menstruation, sunburn, fatigue, and the presence of other infections seem to be related to the reappearance of the virus. Although such recurrences are usually milder and of shorter duration than the initial outbreak, they may occur throughout the person's life. The herpes virus is usually contagious during the time that a person has visible sores but not when the skin is healed. However, the person may have a mild recurrence but be unaware that she or he is contagious. Aside from visible sores, itching, burning, or tingling sensations at the sore site also suggest that the person is contagious.

In general, the problems associated with genital herpes occur less often than those associated with syphilis and gonorrhea. But such problems are serious. In the infected pregnant woman, the fetus may be spontaneously aborted or born prematurely. If the infant passes through the birth canal when the herpes sores are present, he or she may contract a crippling or fatal form of meningitis. To avoid this outcome, babies of infected women who have an active case at term are delivered by caesarean section. An additional complication of herpes in women is the risk of cervical cancer. Women with genital herpes are five to eight times more likely to develop cervical cancer than those who are not infected. Regular Pap tests can help detect the presence of such cancerous cells. Finally, a severe eye infection known as herpes keratitis can result if the genital herpes virus is transferred from the infected site to the eyes. Care should be taken not to touch an infected area and rub one's eyes. It is best to avoid completely touching herpes sores.

At the time of this writing, there is no cure for herpes. The 500,000 new cases of genital herpes reported annually are added to the estimated 20 million who already have herpes. Because it is a virus, it does not respond to antibiotics as do syphilis and gonorrhea. There are a few procedures to help relieve the symptoms and promote healing of the sores. These include treatment of any other genital infections near the herpes sores, keeping the sores clean and dry, taking hot sitz-baths three times a day, and wearing loose-fitting cotton underwear to enhance air circulation. Acyclovir, marketed as Zo-

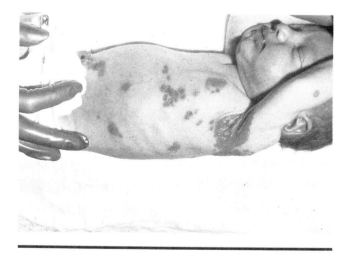

Herpes simplex in a newborn.

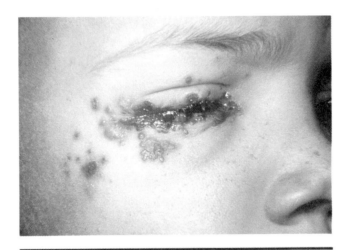

Herpes simplex, showing lesions around the eye.

virax, is an ointment applied on the sores that helps to relieve pain, speed healing, and reduce the amount of time that live viruses are present in the sores. A more effective tablet form of acyclovir is also being developed. While acyclovir seems to help manage the symptoms of first-episode genital herpes, it is less effective with subsequent outbreaks. Proper nutrition, adequate sleep and exercise, and avoiding physical or mental stress helps people to cope better with recurrences. *The Herpes Book* (Hamilton, 1982) is a useful overview of the treatments that are currently available.

A person with genital herpes can prevent infecting someone else by avoiding genital contact until the sores have healed. It is also recommended that the male use a condom and the female use a diaphragm for two weeks after the sores have healed. But using the condom or diaphragm is not completely effective since the herpes virus can pass through these synthetic membranes.

Coping with the psychological effects of genital herpes is often more difficult than coping with the physical aspects of the disease. Herpes victims typically go through a pattern of shock, anger, bitterness, and depression. The latter may result in the person avoiding not only sexual encounters but also social contacts with friends who are not sexual partners. Emotional distress may be lessened by giving herpes sufferers accurate information about the disease, helping them change the negative image they have of themselves, and assisting them in learning how to tell someone with whom they are sexually interested that they have herpes (Greenwood & Bernstein, 1983).

Other Sexually Transmitted Diseases

A number of other diseases may be sexually transmitted, among them LGV, granuloma inguinale, and chancroid. Since these have similar symptoms (sores in the genital area) and treatments (antibiotics), only brief mention will be made of them.

1. *LGV (lymphogranuloma venereum)*   Fever, chills, headaches, and pain in the abdomen often signal LGV. In addition, painful sores that drip pus contribute to the discomfort. As with other genital sores, they are eliminated with antibiotics such as tetracycline.
2. *Granuloma inguinale*   This painful sore tends to spread across the sex organs and may infect the rectum and abdominal wall. Tetracycline and streptomycin are the antibiotics of choice.
3. *Chancroid*   Also known as "soft chancre," one or more usually appear at the site of contact. Although they are painful, they disappear after taking antibiotics.

Other Diseases of the Sex Organs

Some diseases of the sex organs may or may not be transmitted through sexual contact. These include the various forms of vaginitis, pubic lice, scabies, and genital warts.

Vaginitis

The primary symptom of **vaginitis** is itching and burning during urination, which results from acidic urine touching an irritated vulva and vaginal opening. Various types of vaginitis include trichomoniasis, candidiasis, and nonspecific vaginitis. Most women get vaginitis at some time in their lives, and many do not develop it from sexual contact.

Trichomoniasis

Whereas some infected women show no symptoms, others complain of a greenish-yellow vaginal discharge that causes an irritating rash in the vulva. The inner thighs may also become irritated if the discharge is allowed to come in contact with the skin. Left untreated, the irritation continues and causes pain during intercourse. The woman may also infect her male partner who may experience irritation and pain during intercourse. Trichomoniasis, with more than three million new cases annually, is the most common genital disease seen by the family physician (Felman, 1980).

Diagnosis is made by examining mucus from the vagina or penis under a microscope. Since trichomoniasis may occur with syphilis or gonorrhea, a specific diagnosis is essential. Antibiotics such as metronidazole (Flagyl) are usually effective in treating trichomoniasis (caution: Flagyl may be a carcinogen). Because the man may harbor *Trichomonas* organisms without symptoms, both the woman and her sexual partner should be treated.

Candidiasis

Candidiasis, also known as monilia and fungus, is a yeast infection caused by *Candida albicans*. Candidiasis tends to occur in women during pregnancy, when they are on oral contraceptives, or when they have poor resistance to disease. Irritation, itching, discharge, and pain during intercourse typically drive the person to a physician, who most often recommends antifungal suppositories or creams to be inserted into the vagina. Antibiotics are not effective because *Candida* are not bacteria.

Men may also develop candidiasis from their sexual contacts with women. Irritation and redness on the head of the penis and external itching and painful, burning sensations are the typical symptoms. Locally applied antifungal creams are the best antidote.

Nonspecific Vaginitis

Sometimes no cause can be found for vaginitis even though there is itching, pain, and vaginal discharge. When trichomoniasis, candidiasis, and gonorrhea have been ruled out, the diagnosis becomes "nonspecific vaginitis." In some cases, it will disappear only to reappear with complications. Many cases of vaginitis not caused by *Candida* organisms or *Trichomonas* bacteria are believed to be caused by other bacteria. New microscopic and culture methods of diagnosis are being developed. Treatment with antibiotics, especially metronidazole (Flagyl), are effective.

Pubic Lice

Pubic lice, are also called "crabs," attach themselves to the base of coarse pubic hair and suck blood from the victim. Their biting the skin to release the blood causes severe itching. Pubic lice are caught from an infected person, often through sexual contact, and also may be transmitted by contact with toilet seats, old clothing, and bedding that harbor the creatures. Applications of gamma benzene hexachloride, sold under the brand name of Kwell, will kill the lice within 24 hours.

Scabies

As irritating as vaginitis and pubic lice is **scabies** or the "itch." Scabies results from a parasite, *Sarcoptes scabiei*, that penetrates the skin and lays eggs. The larvae of these eggs burrow new tunnels under the skin which causes intense itching. Although genitals are a prime target for the mites, the groin, buttocks, breasts, and knees may also be infested with them. Since the itching is intense, scabies sufferers tend to scratch the affected area, which may not only lead to bleeding and other infections but also spread the scabies to other areas. Treatment includes applying gamma benzene hexachloride (Kwell) or crotamiton (Eurax), and a thorough cleaning of self, clothing, and bedding.

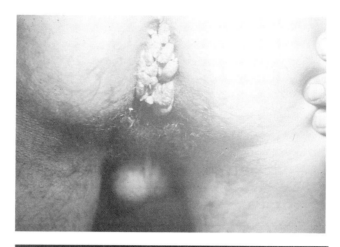

Genital warts.

Genital Warts

Genital warts are lesions caused by a virus, which may appear in the cervix, vulva, urethra, or rectum. Some anal warts may be malignant. Genital warts are usually but not always sexually transmitted. They may be treated by application of liquid nitrogen, which freezes them, by cauterization with an electric needle, by surgical removal, or by podophyllin (a surface application). More recently, interferon has been used successfully to treat genital warts that have not responded to standard treatments.

Acquired Immune Deficiency Syndrome (AIDS)*

Acquired immune deficiency syndrome (AIDS) represents the appearance in previously healthy individuals of various aggressive infections and malignancies. AIDS was first seen among homosexual and bisexual males with multiple sex partners, intravenous drug abusers, hemophiliacs, and Haitian immigrants to the United States. About 95 percent of AIDS victims have been male. More recently, women and heterosexuals have been observed to develop AIDS. The syndrome attacks the immune system of the body and makes it vulnerable to infection. Kaposi's sarcoma (KS), a type of cancer, and Pneumocystis carinii pneumonia (PCP) have been associated with AIDS. Patients often die since their bodies become incapable of combating other diseases and infection. Eighty percent who contract AIDS are dead within three years. At the time of this writing, the cause of AIDS is unknown, although a

*Appreciation is expressed to Elaine Bratic of the Public Health Service, Washington, D.C., for providing information on which this section is based.

virus is suspected, and there is no cure. The incubation period for AIDS ranges from a few months to about two years. Symptoms of AIDS include swollen glands, persistent fever, persistent dry cough, bruiselike markings on the skin, weight loss, night sweats, and persistent diarrhea.

AIDS may be transmitted through sexual intercourse, through contact with infected urine and semen, through blood transfusions, and through the use of unsterilized needles. AIDS cannot be contracted by casual contact with someone who has AIDS. Family members other than sex partners of AIDS victims have not developed AIDS.

Getting Help

If you suspect that you have had contact with someone who has a sexually transmitted disease, or if you have any symptoms of the STDs mentioned in this chapter, call the toll-free national VD hotline at 1-800-227-8922. For specific information about AIDS, call 1-800-342-2437. You will not be asked to identify yourself but you can get information about your symptoms and local STD clinics, which provide confidential, free treatment.

Since no cure is currently available for genital herpes, a newsletter, *The Helper*, is published quarterly to provide the latest information for herpes sufferers. The newsletter can be obtained by writing to HELP (Herpetics Engaged in Living Productively), 260 Sheridan Avenue, Palo Alto, California 94306. Herpes information is also available at 1-415-328-7710. Although no cure is currently available for AIDS, Duke University in Durham, North Carolina, has opened an AIDS clinic to treat AIDS victims (phone 1-919-684-2660).

In addition to getting medical attention or advice for yourself and your sexual partner, sexual contact with others should be avoided until your infection is cured or is no longer contagious. You should also exercise care if you masturbate. For example, if you accidentally touch a herpes sore during masturbation, be careful not to put your finger near your mouth or eye before washing.

Prevention

There are two issues in prevention: avoiding a STD and talking with your partner about prevention.

Avoiding a Sexually Transmitted Disease

The best way to avoid getting a sexually transmitted disease is to avoid sexual contact or to have contact only with those who are not infected. This means restricting your sexual contacts to those who limit their relationships to one person. The person most likely to get a sexually transmitted disease has sexual relations with a number of partners or with a partner who has a variety of partners.

In addition to restricting sexual contacts, a condom put on before the penis touches the other person's body will make it difficult for the STD to pass from one person to the other. However, as noted earlier, a condom is not completely reliable against genital herpes, since the virus may pass through the condom or the genital sores may be on the scrotum, which is not protected by the condom. After genital contact, it is also helpful for the partners to urinate and to wash their genitals with soap and hot water.

Talking with Your Partner about Prevention

It is not very romantic to talk about herpes with a partner you are about to make love with. But not to address the issue one minute is to risk contracting the disease the next; and once you have herpes, you have it forever. Contraception should also be discussed beforehand. Not to do so involves the risk of unwanted pregnancy.

What might you say before engaging in a sexual experience with a new partner about the issues of sexually transmitted diseases and protection from pregnancy? One human sexuality professor asked her students how they would handle the situation if they were on an isolated moonlit beach with a person they wanted to make love with (Hayes, 1983). Some of their responses follow.

● In a situation like this, you have to be open and discuss the consequences. If this "messes up the mood," maybe that's the best thing—better than ending up diseased or pregnant. You can't let your feelings and your hormones (urges) control this situation. (A female)

Even in the heat of passion, one still has to be concerned about herpes and pregnancy. I would first ask if he was going to share something with me that I didn't want to share. I would definitely clarify if necessary. I would also state that I am not ready to be a mother and that some sort of birth control is necessary to continue. (A female)

The discussion of protection against pregnancy could be entwined into the romance of the evening, perhaps even made part of verbiage in sexual play. The discussion would not probably be purely sensual, rather one where feelings of care and/or love are conveyed. The discussion of STD would not be nearly as simple. It would be next to impossible to keep this subject within the mood of the evening. One of the parties will probably be offended. Nonetheless, this topic is of vital importance to discuss, mind you, lightly, but it must be done. Perhaps after putting it into perspective for "our future," not to hurt each other, the ground lost can be recovered later in the evening. (A female)

"Despite a lifetime of service to the cause of sexual liberation, I have never caught venereal disease, which makes me feel rather like an Arctic explorer who has never had frostbite."

GERMAINE GREER

I would just have to come right out and question my partner point blank about the subjects. If she had no protection, I'd make a quick trip to the convenience store to buy a condom if possible or abstain if not. If she had an STD I would take her back to her place and ride off into the sunset as quickly as possible, never to return. (A male)

Bringing up a subject like herpes or contraception would seem to detract from the mood greater than would abstinence. This fact, along with the guilt feelings I would have to deal with after the experience with or without protection, has been enough incentive in this situation in the past to get me to stop short of intercourse so that the beauty of the memory is as great as the beauty of the moment. I'll keep it that way. (A male)

Since this is a new experience for us, we would probably both be more comfortable if we completely leveled with each other about protection. This includes birth control as well as sexually transmitted disease. Is this agreeable with you? If the partner doesn't want to discuss it, I'd be wary of the partner. I'd also be aware that complete honesty is not always forthcoming in such situations. Open communication enhances any relationship—sexual or otherwise. (Gender not specified) ●

In the situations just described, one person is trying to find out from the other if the other has herpes. But suppose the person has herpes and wants to tell the unsuspecting partner who has not brought up the subject. Although such disclosure is never easy, the following is one possible approach.

● What I want to say won't be easy but you know I care for you and I feel it is something you should know and we should deal with. You have heard about genital herpes. Well, I've got it. That means that sometimes I have small sores—like fever blisters—on my genitals. I've got them now which means the virus is in the active stage. They will go away in a few weeks and I won't be contagious. I hate telling you this as much as you hate hearing it but I can't feel the way I do about you and not tell you. ●

But what is it like actually to have herpes and to tell people you are dating that you have it? One woman shared her experience.

● I've had herpes now for almost 2 years and it's been very rough. My herpes is type 1 but in my genital area. I had only 1 breakout, and it was very painful. Since then I've told 4 men; only one reacted harshly. The other three were very understanding.

　　I explained the fact that I wasn't told by my partner of that time (who still denies it, but it could only be him). I also educated the people I've told by explaining that chances are very great that I will never see another breakout, and each year without a breakout, the chances get even better. I told them to ask any questions, and I'll try to answer or find out the answers if I can't. I also explained that I'm not happy about it, and if I could change things, I would. But I can't so I must adapt myself in the best way I can. It's hard at times to talk about the issue but I feel I've done a good job. ●

Cancer of the Sex Organs

Awareness of the forms of cancer that can attack the reproductive system of women and men, their symptoms and treatment, is an important part of maintaining sexual health. In essence, cancer is caused by the abnormal growth of cells. As the cells multiply out of control, they produce a mass, or tumor, pieces of which may break away and travel to other parts of the body, where new growth proliferates. When vital organs are affected, death may ensue.

Cancer is the next-to-leading cause of death in the United States (heart disease is first). Cancer of the breast and uterus for women and cancer of the prostate for men are the most common forms of cancer attacking the reproductive system.

Breast Cancer

Since early detection of breast cancer is essential for effective treatment, women are encouraged to give themselves a breast exam once a month. (Figure 12.1 outlines the recommended procedure.) There are several advantages to the breast self-exam. The woman can provide regular checkups and she is the most familiar with her own breasts. By developing a regular pattern of examining her breasts, she also becomes aware of the normal state of her breasts so that any abnormality will be more easily detected. Even if a lump is discovered, there is only a 20 percent chance that it is cancerous. Finally, the breast-self exam is a way for the woman to get to know her own body better. It is also a way for her to do something positive for herself by taking care of herself.

Breast cancer is the leading cause of death among women in their early forties. If detected early, most can survive it. **Mammography**, an x-ray of the breast, is a diagnostic procedure that may confirm the existence of a breast lump. Some physicians recommend routine mammography for women in their fifties and over, although this is controversial because of the cancer-causing potential of x-rays. Another diagnostic technique is **thermography**, which produces a picture of heat variations over the body. The greater heat given off by rapidly multiplying malignant cells will show up on the thermograph. The most accurate way to find out if a tumor is malignant is to

"Medicine, to produce health, has to examine disease."

PLUTARCH

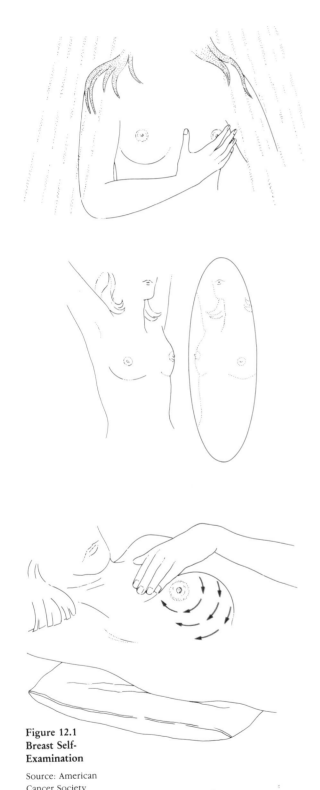

Figure 12.1
Breast Self-
Examination

Source: American
Cancer Society

How to examine your breasts

Regular inspection shows what is normal for you and will give you confidence in your examination.

1

In the shower: Examine your breasts during bath or shower; hands glide easier over wet skin. Fingers flat, move gently over every part of each breast. Use right hand to examine left breast, left hand for right breast. Check for any lump, hard knot or thickening.

2

Before a mirror: Inspect your breasts with arms at your sides. Next, raise your arms high overhead. Look for any changes in contour of each breast, a swelling, dimpling of skin or changes in the nipple.

Then, rest palms on hips and press down firmly to flex your chest muscles. Left and right breast will not exactly match—few women's breasts do.

3

Lying down: To examine your right breast, put a pillow or folded towel under your right shoulder. Place right hand behind your head—this distributes breast tissue more evenly on the chest. With left hand, fingers flat, press gently in small circular motions around an imaginary clock face. Begin at outermost top of your right breast for 12 o'clock, then move to 1 o'clock, and so on around the circle back to 12. A ridge of firm tissue in the lower curve of each breast is normal. Then move in an inch, toward the nipple, keep circling to examine *every part of your breast,* including nipple. This requires at least three more circles. Now slowly repeat procedure on your left breast with a pillow under your left shoulder and left hand behind head. Notice how your breast structure feels.

Finally, squeeze the nipple of each breast gently between thumb and index finger. Any discharge, clear or bloody, should be reported to your doctor immediately.

perform a biopsy in which a portion of the lump is removed and analyzed in the laboratory by a pathologist.

If the analysis reveals that the lump is malignant, one of several surgical procedures may be recommended. A **radical mastectomy** involves the removal of the whole breast, underlying muscle, and lymph nodes. In a **modified radical mastectomy** the breast and lymph nodes are removed but not the muscles. In a **partial mastectomy**, or **lumpectomy** only the lump is removed.

In combination with surgery, radiation therapy or chemotherapy may be used. Eighty-seven percent of those who have localized breast cancer and are treated with these various methods survive at least five years. If the cancer has spread to other parts of the body, the five-year survival rate is 47 percent (American Cancer Society, 1982).

Removal of a breast can be an emotionally traumatic experience. Some women feel they have been mutilated both physically and psychologically. One of their greatest fears is that their partner will cease to love them or view them as attractive. One woman said, "I know having cancer has to do with dying, but my greatest concern is will my partner want to make love with me again."

In a study by Dr. Mildred Hope Witkin (1981) of Cornell Medical Center, 12 women who had had a mastectomy reported going to single bars to test their desirability. After a few hours with a man who then suggested going to bed, they would tell him, "I'd like to go to bed with you but I think you should know that I've had a mastectomy." Only a few men backed away.

Most spouses are very supportive. They are more concerned that the cancer could mean death. Recommendations by Dr. Witkin to spouses or lovers of women who need a mastectomy include the following.

- Get involved with the woman as soon as possible by going with her [to the doctor] after the lump is first discovered.
- Look at the wound. Help the woman change the dressing.
- Have intercourse either on the last night in the hospital or the first or second night home. The point is to communicate to the woman that she is sexually desired by the man significant in her life.
- Recognize that depression over mastectomy is normal. Many women take a year or two to adjust to the event.*

Cervical Cancer

Cancer of the cervix is the second most common type of cancer in women. Although vaginal discharge, pain, and bleeding are the typical symptoms, the cancerous cells can be present for 5 to 10 years before being detected. For early detection, sexually active women taking oral contraceptives and women age 20 and over are encouraged to have an annual Pap test in combination with a pelvic exam for abnormalities of the uterus and ovaries (Figure 12.2).

*From "Recovery From Mastectomy: The Crucial role of the Husband." By Mildred Hope Witkin. Reprinted by permission, 1981.

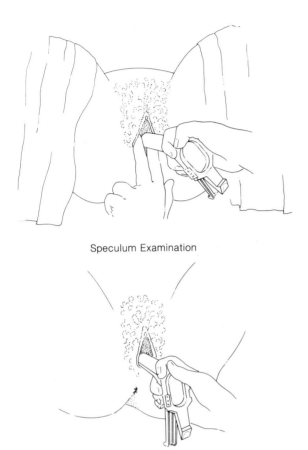

Speculum Examination

Preparation—Usually with the aid of the nurse, your body is draped with a sheet and your feet are placed in stirrups. After routinely examining the breasts, abdomen and groin, your physician inspects the outer genitals. Because good light is important, a lamp may be used during this inspection. Generally, the examiner will place an arm or elbow on your leg or thigh before touching the outer genitals. This is to avoid startling you—in which case your genital muscles might involuntarily contract and interfere with the examination. **Inserting the Speculum**—A speculum is an instrument which enlarges the vaginal opening and spreads the vaginal walls so that your physician can "see what is going on" inside the vagina. Your doctor will carefully insert the speculum into the vaginal entrance with one hand, while using the other hand to gently spread the labia. The type or size of the speculum depends on whether the patient is a virgin, has had children or is post-menopausal. To avoid discomfort, the speculum is inserted slowly and at an angle. But if you feel any distress—which is extremely rare—your doctor will adjust the speculum to make you feel more comfortable.

**Figure 12.2
Pelvic Examination
and Pap Test**

Source: "Reprinted Through the Courtesy of Lederle Laboratories Division, American Cyanamid Company. SERVICE TO LIFE is A Registered Trademark of American Cyanamid Company."

A Pap test is done by a health care professional who uses a speculum (see Figure 12.3) to obtain a sample of cells from the cervix. The cells are examined under a microscope; if they look cancerous, a biopsy is performed—a portion of the cervical tissue is removed and examined to confirm the diagnosis.

Cervical cancer in its early stage may be treated by cyrotherapy—destroying the abnormal tissue by freezing—or by electrocoagulation—using an electric current to destroy the tissue. The advantage of these procedures is to eliminate the cancer without having to remove the uterus. When cervical cancer is in advanced stages, surgery to remove the uterus and cervix may be performed. This is known as a **hysterectomy**. If the ovaries are also removed during hysterectomy, estrogen replacement therapy may be indicated because of the abrupt cessation of the body's ability to produce estrogen. Radiation therapy and chemotherapy also may be used in the treatment of cervical cancer.

The cure rate for cancer of the cervix is about 60 percent. However, if detected in the earliest stages by a routine Pap smear, the cure rate approaches 100 percent. Regular Pap tests are advised for all women, but some women

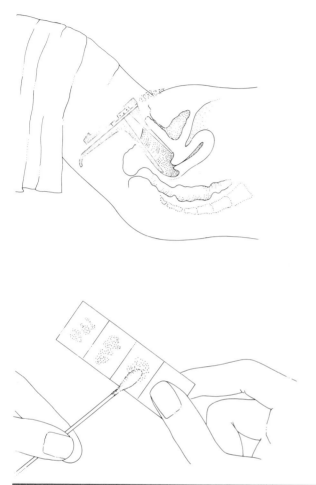

Inspecting the Cervix—As it is gradually rotated, the speculum can be opened to expose the cervix—the "neck" of the lower uterus that connects it with the vagina. Again, this is done with very little discomfort to the patient. By manipulating the speculum, the doctor obtains a clear view of the cervix and can examine it for cysts, tears or other abnormalities. **The Pap Smear**—Named for its developer, Dr. George N. Papanicolau, the Pap test is a simple procedure which detects precancerous cells. In other words, the Pap test can warn of cancer even before clinical signs of disease are apparent.

You've probably been instructed not to use douches, vaginal creams or medications for at least 48 hours prior to your pelvic exam. This is important because these substances can distort the appearance of the cells to be studied in the Pap smear.

While the cervix is still exposed by the speculum, cells are taken from the cervix and vagina with a scraper or cotton-tipped applicator. The cells are then smeared on a glass slide and sent to a laboratory for analysis.

With the speculum still in place, your physician may also take appropriate smears to determine the presence or absence of vaginal infection.

seem particularly vulnerable to cervical cancer, including those who have genital herpes, those who have a variety of sexual partners, and those who began having intercourse at an early age. A woman is most likely to get cervical cancer at age 45 and over.

Figure 12.2
Continued

Testicular Cancer

Cancer of the testicles is the most common cancer in men aged 20–35 and accounts for more than 10 percent of all cancer deaths in this age group. Testicular cancer is more likely to occur in men who were born with an undescended testicle. Even though the cause is unknown, testicular cancer can be cured if detected and treated early.

Because a man can have cancer in his testicles and not feel pain, it is important that he check himself regularly for testicular cancer.

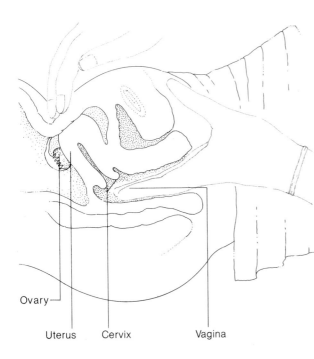

Ovary

Uterus   Cervix   Vagina

Digital Examination

After gradually withdrawing the speculum, the examiner will carry out the digital examination. This is just what it sounds like: an examination with the fingers or "digits." It is also a "bimanual" examination because both hands are used—one internally and one externally on the abdomen.

Wearing a glove, your physician inserts the index and/or middle finger of one hand into the vagina. In this way, the cervix can be palpated or "felt" for consistency, shape and position. The cervix may be moved from side to side to determine if it is tender to the touch. And the upper vagina is explored for masses, tenderness or distortion.

During the digital exam, your physician will also examine the uterus and ovaries. While the finger (or fingers) within the vagina elevate the cervix and uterus, the other hand is gently placed on the abdomen. By "grasping" the upper portion of the uterus between the vaginal fingers and the abdominal hand, the examiner can determine its size, its mobility and the presence or absence of tenderness. The ovaries also can often be located and felt.

Figure 12.2
Continued

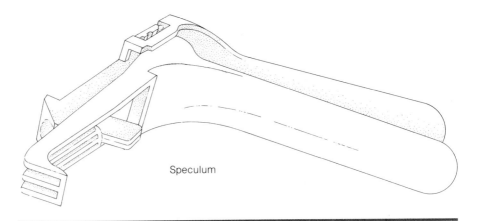

Speculum

Figure 12.3
Speculum

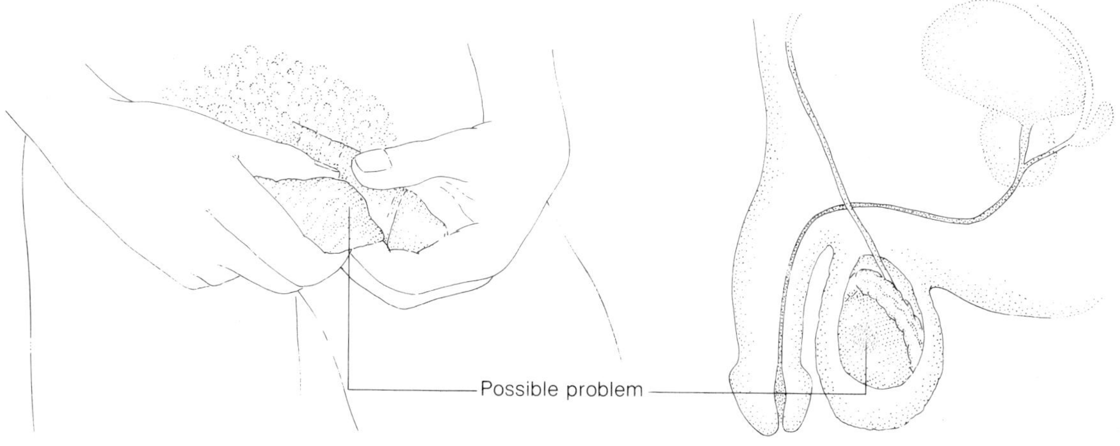

—————— Possible problem ——————

1. Stand in front of a mirror. Look for obvious lumps or swelling of the scrotal sac, or growth of the male breasts.
2. Examine each testicle gently with the fingers of both hands by rolling the testicle between the thumb and the fingers. Feel for any lumps or swelling.
3. Identify the epididymis (the ropelike structure that collects the sperm) on the top and back of each testicle. Don't confuse this structure with an abnormal lump.
4. Repeat the exam on the other testicle.

**Figure 12.4
Testicular Self-
Examination**

Abnormal lumps are often painless, as small as the size of a pea, and usually located in the front part of the testicle.

If you find a lump, contact your doctor or clinic immediately. Remember: not all lumps are cancerous (Cancer Information Service, 1983, pp. 1-3). If the lump is cancer, treatment usually involves surgical removal of the affected testicle, or radiation or chemotherapy.

Prostate Cancer

The prostate is a gland located at the base of the penis just below the bladder and above the rectum. It is about one-and-a-half inches in diameter and secretes one-third of the fluid in semen. Cancer of the prostate is the second most common form of cancer in men (lung cancer is first). The chance of getting prostate cancer increases with age—the typical prostatic cancer patient is 55 or older. Symptoms include difficulty in urinating, frequent urinating, painful urination, and blood in the urine. These symptoms are due to the growth of a tumor that disrupts the surrounding structures of their normal function. Some older men may also experience a nonmalignant enlargement of the prostate. This should be treated as it interferes with urination.

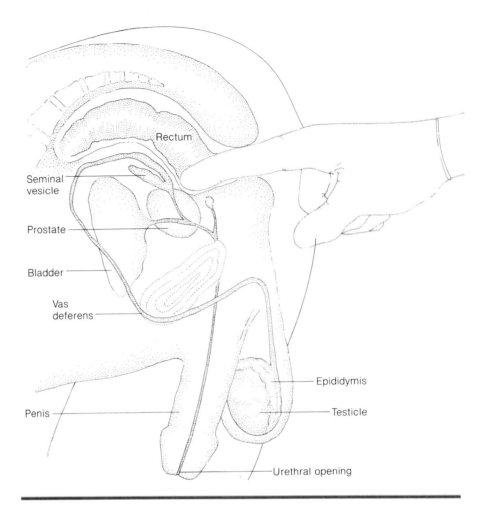

Rectum

Seminal
vesicle

Prostate

Bladder

Vas
deferens

Epididymis

Penis

Testicle

Urethral opening

**Figure 12.5
Digital Examination
of the Prostate**

A physician inserts
an index finger into
the rectum of a male
to assess the
presence of an
enlarged prostate.

Source: American
Cancer Society

A preliminary diagnosis of prostatic cancer is made by rectal digital examination (Figure 12.5) in which the physician can feel the enlarged prostate. Although a history of symptoms is suggestive, an X-ray and other tests (urine and blood analysis and a biopsy) will help to confirm the presence of cancer. Treatment may involve the administration of estrogen to shrink the tumor (there may be side effects such as loss of sex drive or feminization), surgery to remove the prostate gland (total **prostatectomy**), radiation therapy, or chemotherapy. The five-year survival rate of those diagnosed and treated for prostate cancer is about 60 percent. (American Cancer Society, 1982).

Questions about cancer can be answered by calling Cancer Information Service, a national toll-free hotline: 1-800-422-6237.

Summary

Sexual health depends on the absence of disease. Like any other part of the body, the sexual anatomy of both women and men is susceptible to disease. Although not all diseases of the genitals are transmitted sexually, numerous ones are. Among the more devastating sexually transmitted diseases is gonorrhea, which is contracted by more than one million Americans yearly. The consequences of untreated gonorrhea may include meningitis, arthritis, and sterility.

The consequences of syphilis are even more dramatic, including mental illness, blindness, heart disease, and death. But both gonorrhea and syphilis, if detected early, can be eliminated through the systematic use of antibiotics. Genital herpes, on the other hand, is immune to antibiotics. Its consequences include increased risk of cervical cancer and spontaneous abortion and damage to the newborn infant. No cure is currently available.

Many other sexually transmitted diseases (NGU, chancroid, granuloma inguinale) are responsive to appropriate medication. The sooner treatment begins, the quicker the symptoms can be alleviated. While not necessarily transmitted through sexual contact, other diseases of the sex organs include vaginitis, pubic lice, scabies, and genital warts. Help is available for all of these through a national toll-free hotline, local STD clinics, or your own physician.

Acquired immune deficiency syndrome (AIDS), found mostly among homosexual males with multiple sex partners, attacks the body's immune system and makes it vulnerable to infection. AIDS is transmitted primarily through semen, blood, and urine. While there is no cure, help is available for AIDS victims through a national hotline and specialized AIDS clinics.

Cancer is not sexually transmitted, but it may affect the breasts and sex organs. One in 11 women will get breast cancer. Early detection by breast self-examination and appropriate treatment can minimize the negative consequences.

Cervical cancer can be detected through annual Pap tests. Women who have genital herpes or who have a variety of sexual partners should have a Pap smear more often.

Men are not immune to cancer of the sex organs. Testicular cancer accounts for 10 percent of all cancer deaths of men between the ages of 20 and 35. A regular testicle self-exam will help in the early detection of such cancer. Prostate cancer is common among men 55 and over. A digital examination performed by a physician is used to ascertain the presence of prostate cancer.

Key Terms

gonorrhea

nongonococcal urethritis

syphilis

genital herpes

herpes simplex virus type 1

herpes simplex virus type 2

vaginitis
pubic lice
scabies
acquired immune deficiency
    syndrome (AIDS)
mammography
thermography

mastectomy
Pap test
hysterectomy
radical mastectomy
modified radical mastectomy
partial mastectomy, or lumpectomy
prostatectomy

Issues in Debate and Future Directions

The advisability of having a radical mastectomy for breast cancer and whether genital herpes is changing sexual behavior in the United States are among the controversies about sexual health. After examining these issues, we look at some of the trends in this area.

Radical Mastectomy: To Have or Not to Have?

Physicians do not agree on whether a radical mastectomy is the treatment of choice for breast cancer. Since "radical mastectomy" refers to more than one type of operation, it is important to clarify its meanings. A Halsted radical mastectomy, named after surgeon William Halsted, was the most common procedure for treating breast cancer in the United States for 50 years, beginning in the late 1800s. It involves removing the entire breast, skin, pectoral muscles, axillary lymph nodes, and surrounding fat. The physical results of a Halsted mastectomy are a flattened or sunken chest wall and the potential for developing lymphedema (swelling of the arm) and shoulder stiffness.

Beginning in the late 1950s the extended radical mastectomy came into use. In this procedure the same tissue is removed as in the Halsted method plus the internal mammary lymph nodes. It was believed that these nodes must be taken out to prevent subsequent spreading of the cancer. But follow-up studies revealed that spreading occurred even with the removal of the nodes and patient survival rates were no different from those having had the Halsted surgery. About 40 percent of both sets of patients were free of disease after five years.

Studies comparing the Halsted and extended radical mastectomy procedures with modified radical mastectomy in which the chest muscles are left intact have found that survival rates are comparable, and most surgeons now are performing the latter operation (*Breast Cancer Digest,* 1980). Still other comparative studies of these procedures with less extensive procedures (simple mastectomy, simple mastectomy plus radiation, partial mastectomy plus radiation) are helping physicians further evaluate which procedure is best. Although partial mastectomy appears to result in higher local recurrence rates than does more extensive surgery, proponents of this procedure maintain that these rates have little effect on survival rates. "Many radiotherapists believe that the proper dosage of radiation, combined with local excision, is just as effective as mastectomy in eliminating breast cancer recurrence and improving survival. Many other physicians disagree" (*Breast Cancer Digest,* 1980, p. 32). The result of this continuing controversy suggests the need for extreme caution in selecting a treatment procedure or set of procedures for breast cancer. A woman with diagnosed breast cancer should seek several opinions before deciding on a course of treatment.

Is Herpes Changing America's Sexual Behavior?

Has the prevalence and current incurability of genital herpes resulted in a new attitude toward casual sex? Some say yes. In a *Washington Post*–ABC News public opinion poll of 1,505 single people (aged 18 to 37), 22

(continued)

percent agreed with the statement, "I have changed my behavior to avoid the risk of contracting herpes."* Some people are taking no chances. One woman told her new partner that she wouldn't sleep with him until he showed her a statement from a physician that he did not have herpes.

An additional concern is the potential impact of the disease on an existing relationship. In most cases, an individual in a purported exclusive sexual relationship who contracts herpes through an extrapartner encounter will destroy the relationship (Fox & Edgley, 1983). Not only might the partner feel betrayed but also the stigma of the disease is often enough to end the relationship.

Others feel that herpes is something you cannot worry about. When asked about using a condom for protection against sexually transmitted diseases, one man said:

● Personally, I've been through five previous sexual relationships that required this kind of discussion. Sadly, I never dealt with them; I just took a chance. I guess it is basically the trend we have come to, lack of care, lack of concern, my generation doesn't think—they just act. We are impulse oriented. I was lucky, maybe there are others who aren't. Life is something you mess around with. ●

Whether genital herpes will influence sexual behavior may become a moot point. As the vaccine against herpes becomes available, the threat may disappear with technology.

*Copyright © 1983, The Boston Globe Newspaper Company/Washington Post Writer's Group, reprinted with permission.

Future Directions

As more people are sexually active with more partners, the number of people contracting sexually transmitted diseases will continue to increase. Symptoms of sexually-transmitted diseases are a delayed consequence of a sexual encounter. If genital sores appeared immediately upon sexual contact, steps to avoid STDs would be taken more seriously.

Although there is currently no cure for genital herpes, the future may include a vaccine to immunize sexually active individuals against it. Researchers at the University of Washington Medical School are currently working on such a vaccine. Research efforts are also being directed toward finding a cure for AIDS. Interleukin-2, a substance derived from white blood cells that may revive the immune system in AIDS victims, is currently being tested.

In 1984 Genetic Systems Corporation of Seattle, Washington, will make new tests available to the general public that will allow a person to determine in minutes rather than days if he or she has gonorrhea, NGU, or genital herpes. These tests should greatly improve the chances for early diagnosis and treatment.

Cancer research is continuing with resulting advances in diagnosis and treatment. Interferon, a natural body substance known to combat viruses, has shown promise in preliminary research on advanced human cancers of the breast. Early detection of breast cancer may be augmented by the assistance of women's sexual partners. To assist this trend, health care professionals will include men in the discussions of breast cancer with their clients and alert them to their role in early detection (Rose et al., 1980).

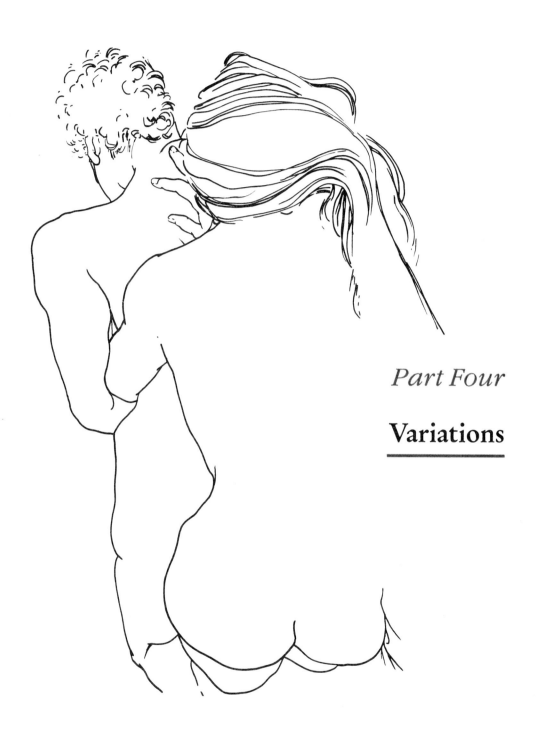

Part Four

Variations

Chapter Thirteen

Sexual Variations

---

*We are preoccupied with what is
normal and what is natural.*

ELIZABETH CANFIELD

Chapter Thirteen

The expression of human sexuality is extremely varied. What some people regard as abnormal and offensive, others think is normal and desirable. In this and the following two chapters, we examine the range of human sexuality. We begin by discussing what is meant by normal sexual behavior.

What Is Normal Sexual Behavior?

When we ask ourselves whether various sexual behaviors are normal, what do we mean by the term *normal*? One meaning is frequency. We assume that if most people engage in a behavior, it is normal. Kissing is a sexual behavior that 9 in 10 people engage in within the first three dates (Knox & Wilson, 1981). So, we conclude, kissing is normal. Defining normal in terms of frequency implies that sexual behaviors that rarely occur are not normal. Since fewer than 1 in 10 people regularly engage in anal intercourse, there is a tendency to assume this sexual behavior is not normal. Sometimes we move from descriptive to value-laden thinking when we assume that frequent behavior is morally correct behavior.

Another criterion for labeling sexual behaviors as normal is whether the behavior is usual to our thinking. We often think of something that is unusual as not normal. For example, some people regard the use of vibrators in sexual play as strange even though it is fairly common.

Sexual behaviors are also considered normal if they are morally right. Penile-vaginal intercourse between husband and wife is the only morally correct form of sexual behavior according to some religions. Homosexuality, masturbation, and oral sex are, therefore, not normal since they are immoral.

Finally, sexual behaviors are viewed as normal if they are natural, that is, if they look natural to the person who is looking. The problem here is one of definition. The person looking at the sexual behavior defines it as natural (normal) in terms of his or her values and attitudes.

However defined, it is assumed that a normal behavior is good and an abnormal one is bad.

Normal Is Learned

Our concepts of what is normal or abnormal, natural or unnatural, legitimate or illegitimate, appropriate or inappropriate are learned. They refer to the value system of the society in which we live. Because most of us have grown up in one society, we assume that our attitudes are natural, or universal. Beef is a staple food in the United States; we do not attach any emotional significance to its consumption. To the people of India, cows are sacred and eating beef is sinful.

We were born into the world without attitudes or values. Our culture taught us its values along with its language through the agencies of family, school, and church. With no standard of comparison and no knowledge of alternatives, as children we accepted as normal the things our society taught us. For example, we were punished for public nudity and learned that wearing clothes in public was normal. But if we had been born into the Chavantez Indian tribe·in Brazil, we would feel that it is normal to walk around without clothes (Smith, 1979).

Normal Is Time Related

We learn what is normal from the society, but our society teaches different values at different times. We preach reverence for life, but during wartime we train our young men to kill. We even give medals to the best killers, whom we call heroes.

As with murder, a society may also have different attitudes about sex at different times. Kissing and intercourse before marriage were viewed differently during the colonial era than today. Kissing in public was considered unacceptable behavior. One historian recorded the event of a Captain Kemble who, returning from a long sea voyage, kissed his lady as he stepped on shore. As a result, he "was promptly lodged in the stocks" (Train, 1931, p. 347).

The penalty for premarital intercourse during the colonial era was more severe. Both men and women were expected to come to the marriage bed as virgins. If they did not, it was evidence that they had succumbed to the temptations of the flesh, which marked them as not being among the "chosen." Once discovered, they had to make a public confession following which they may have been subject to fines, lashes, or more.

In Hartford, Connecticut, in 1739, not only was Aaron Starke pilloried, whipped, and branded on the cheek for seducing Mary Holt, and ordered to pay ten shillings to her father, but he was ordered to marry her when both should be "fit for the condition." (Turner, 1955, p. 74)

Normal Is Society Related

Normality is relative to the society. There are wide variations in sexual preferences and practices in different societies. Whereas having intercourse with one's brother or sister is likely to induce feelings of shame or disgust in our society, the Dahomey of West Africa and the Inca of Peru have viewed such a relationship as natural and desirable (Stephens, 1982). Adolescent sexuality among siblings in our society is severely criticized.

Sexual behavior that is punished in one society may be tolerated in a second and rewarded in a third. In the Gilbert Islands virginity until marriage is an exalted sexual value and violations are not tolerated. Premarital couples who are discovered to have had intercourse before the wedding are put to death. Our society tolerates premarital intercourse, particularly if the partners are "in love." In contrast, the Lepcha people of India believe that intercourse helps young girls to mature. By the age of 12, most Lepcha young women are engaging in regular intercourse.

There are also variations in the frequency of intercourse. Although most couples throughout the world have intercourse between two and five times a week (Gebhard, 1972), the Basongye in the Kasai province of the former Belgian Congo, even in their fifties and sixties, have intercourse every night (Merriam, 1972). In contrast, a Cayapa man may go for several years without having intercourse. Their term for intercourse, *medio trabajo*, means "a little like work."

In summary, what is regarded as normal sexual behavior must be viewed in the context of the society in which the behavior occurs. The following sections discuss some of our different sexual expressions and preferences.

Disability and Sex

The physically disabled (more than 11 million people) are sometimes thought of as unable to engage in "normal" sexual behavior. Among the myths about the disabled are that they are not interested in sex and do not engage in intercourse. Although there are many types of disability (the blind, amputated, deformed, brain damaged), we will examine the sexuality of those whose spinal cords have been injured and who are confined to a wheelchair.

In addition to the war-injured, with the increasing frequency of car and motorcycle crashes, surfboard and skateboard accidents, and gunshot injuries, it is not unusual to be a victim or to know or to have seen someone in a wheelchair who has suffered a spinal cord injury. Parking places with the familiar wheelchair emblem are reminders of the needs of the disabled. But it is difficult for the able-bodied to appreciate the reality of a disability, although, in part, it "can be better appreciated if the reader will imagine that . . . the environment is viewed from about 4 feet above the ground. Conversation is

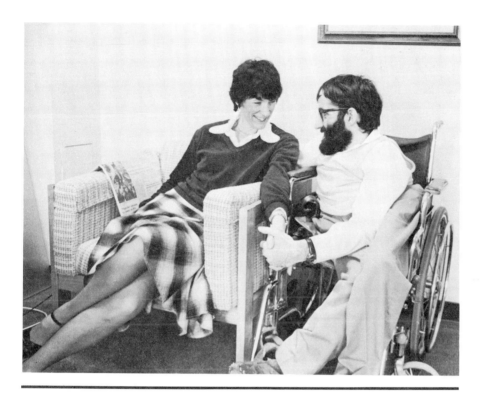

Being in a
wheelchair is not
the end of one's
sexuality.

carried on with erect people by tilting back the head and looking up" (Cole, 1979, p. 252). Also, the impact on an individual's interpersonal life can be dramatic.

Jim L. was a happily married man with two children until his car accident, which left him paralyzed from the waist down. He is also partically paralyzed from his waist up. At the time of the following interview, he was 35 years old and in his senior year at a major state university. His accident had occurred 10 years previously.

● What psychological effect did becoming disabled have on you?

It literally almost drove me crazy. I wanted to die. I was in my own world for six months. But after I accepted the fact that I was paralyzed and would remain that way for the rest of my life, and started thinking positively about it, then I was able to start living again.

Describe your marriage before the accident.

Before my accident I was like any other husband in marriage (I guess). I mean, other than the usual little disagreements that most couples have, we were pretty happy.

What effect did your disability have on your marriage?

It messed it up completely. She stayed with me for five years but only because she felt sorry for me. At least, I think it was because she felt sorry for me. Because as soon as I went to the rehabilitation center and began to manage for myself, she left me.

What type of role changes occurred after your accident?

There were complete changes. Up until the time of my accident, we had a traditional marriage. She was a housewife and I earned the income. After I became disabled, she went to work. I was completely dependent on her.

How did your children feel about what happened?

They were really too young to understand. Now they understand and accept my disability. We get along great.

Would you consider marriage again?

Yes, if the woman was willing and knew completely what she was getting into.

How has your relationship with women changed?

It's very hard to find a woman who doesn't have hang-ups about men in wheelchairs unless they are in one, too. Because I'm not in an environment where there are a lot of disabled people, it's hard to find female companionship.

Have you had any close relationships with anyone since your accident?

Yes, when I was in the rehabilitation center I was dating this nurse for a while. We used to go out a lot. We had a great time together. When I left, we still kept in touch by mail up until a year ago.

What type of sex life do you have now?

I find that women try to pick me up in bars. They are curious about sex with a guy in a wheelchair. What they like me to do is drive them wild orally but after a while they feel it is "nasty" and not the "way you're supposed to have sex." What they want is penis in vagina—missionary style.

Do you believe that love conquers all?

No. I'd say yes for most usual marital problems. But anytime someone [a partner] has been physically impaired, it's not the same. You're just not the same person they married.* ●

---

*Source: Name withheld by request. Used by permission.

The effect of a spinal cord injury on a person's sex life depends on the extent and location of the injury. If the spinal cord was completely severed, the person will not have genital sensation. But if portions of the spinal cord remain intact, sexual sensation—and functioning—can return. In general, the lower the injury on the spinal cord, the greater the damage to sexual functioning. Depending on these factors, the person may regain varying degrees of his or her functioning abilities until approximately two years after the injury (Kenan & Crist, 1981).

To what extent may the person regain sexual functioning? Is erection, intercourse, orgasm, and ejaculation possible? If only the upper part of the spinal cord has been partially severed, the man may have an erection if there is sufficient direct stimulation. It is also possible for the man to get an erection by having erotic thoughts (Higgins, 1979).

Intercourse may take place with the woman sitting down on the erect penis of the spinal cord-injured man. This is usually preceded by a lot of direct stimulation to ensure an erect penis. But intercourse is possible without an erect penis. Some couples use the stuffing technique, in which the partners push the soft penis into the woman's vagina. The woman with strong vaginal muscles can contract them around the penis to hold it inside her. An inflatable penile prosthesis implant (see Chapter 11) is an alternative for some spinal cord-injured men.

Orgasm sometimes occurs as a consequence of the person focusing on physical sensations that can be felt in other areas of the body, such as from stroking the arm, and mentally reassigning these to the genitals (Cole, 1979). The man also may ejaculate, but the aftereffects of orgasm and ejaculation are unpredictable. Although some men report pleasure, sexual excitation, and warm sensations, others report muscular spasticity or a headache (Cole, 1979).

We have been talking about spinal cord injury as it affects men. The effects on women are similar in that complete severance of the spinal cord results in no feeling in the genital area. Where the injury is less complete, sensations at various levels are experienced, including orgasm. The woman also may be able to transfer feelings from body parts not affected by the injury. Spinal cord-injured women may still get pregnant and have children.

But physical concerns may be overshadowed by social concerns. In a study of the sexuality of 68 spinal cord-injured females, only a few noted physical complications (Zwerner, 1982). The more pressing concern was social interaction with men. One woman said:

● My partner resides quite far away and I choose not to become involved in other relationships because opportunities to develop social relationships with men—where they relate to you seriously as a woman and not as a helpless victim or someone to be taken care of—are nonexistent. (p. 165) ●

In summary, spinal cord-injured people will rarely be able to function as they did before their injury. But they may still experience a satisfactory sex life. Indeed, some say their sex lives improved after the injury since they were able to tune in to the sensual aspects of the rest of their bodies. Still other spinal cord-injured people say that they derive immense enjoyment from satisfying their partners by manual, oral, or mechanical stimulation and that this enjoyment is a major source of their own sexual satisfaction. "People in wheelchairs have to stop thinking that their sex life is over," said one spinal cord-injured patient in a rehabilitation center. "While your genitals may be dead, your emotions are very much alive. And you can still express your emotions without your genitals—your eyes, hands, fingers, lips, and tongue still work." Nevertheless, maintaining a healthy self-concept and dealing with the negative stereotypes others have of the sexuality of the physically disabled are recurring concerns.

Celibacy

A **celibate** is a person who does not engage in partner sex activity, although he or she may enjoy an array of sexual fantasies and may masturbate.

Asexuality is sometimes confused with celibacy. But the asexual has no interest in sex and does not engage in any sexual behaviors—masturbation or partner sexual activity. One percent of 12,000 *Psychology Today* respondents said that they were asexual (Rubenstein, 1983).

Sample

Most of us have been asexual at some time in our lives. We were, to some extent, asexual as children. In the preschool years most of us engaged in limited sexual behavior and had infrequent or no erotic thoughts. As we moved from childhood, we became increasingly involved in sexual behaviors and thoughts. Some of us (about 3 percent) become asexual again in our later years (Starr & Weiner, 1982).

Voluntary Celibacy

A person may choose to become a celibate by choice or default. There are a number of reasons why a person might choose to be celibate. Religion is a common reason. Those entering the priesthood are expected to be celibate, which implies being unmarried, so they may have the maximum freedom and energy for the work of the church. Nuns and monks are also expected to be celibate. Other religious people choose celibacy because they want to be spiritually pure and feel that avoiding sexual activity helps to achieve that goal.

Some people who are not religious choose celibacy as a sexual life style. "I haven't had sex with someone in 5 years and that doesn't mean anything is wrong with me," said a computer programmer. "I have a good and happy life; sex just isn't a part of it."

Involvement in work or other activity is another reason some people elect to be celibate. They derive their major satisfaction from these activities. One actress said that being on stage every night took all of her time and energy and that she wanted to give her best to each performance. "It's not that I dislike sex," she said, "on the contrary, I think it's great. But I'm too busy for it now."

Others have periods of celibacy because they want to explore relationships without the sexual dimension and its potential complications (Brown, 1980). "I'm in love with a wonderful person but don't want to change our relationship by introducing sex into it at this time," said one woman. "We both seem to be comfortable with the relationship we have."

For some, "complications" refer to avoiding another failure experience. Impotent or premature ejaculating men and women who are frustrated because they do not achieve orgasm may sometimes prefer celibacy. "It just isn't that important and the bad feelings that follow a sexual experience make it easy for me to avoid the involvement," said one man.

Although celibates avoid partner sex, many enjoy their sexuality by masturbating. Some say that celibacy helps them to concentrate on themselves so that they develop a new sense of freedom, which they regard as valuable in future relationships. Such a "celibacy break" can be a very adaptive and healthy choice (Whelehan & Moynihan, 1982). "It must be emphasized," says one certified sex therapist, "that people can, and many have, lived whole and healthy lives with a minimum of sexual activity" (Baker, 1983, p. 299).

Finally, some decide on temporary celibacy because they are tired of sexual involvement; it has lost its pleasure and meaning. "I've been sexually active since I was 13," said one man, "and I've burned up a lot of energy hunting sexual experiences. I've had it with sex and I'm going to see what else the world has to offer." Some who feel that sex has become an addiction similar to alcohol or nicotine (they are doing it more but enjoying it less) join an organization called Sexaholics Anonymous (P.O. Box 300, Simi Valley, California 93062), which offers a recovery program for those who want to stop their sexually self-destructive ways of thinking and behaving.

Involuntary Celibacy

Some people decide to be celibate, but others feel they have little choice. Hospitals are notorious for encouraging, or enforcing, celibacy. It is assumed that if you are in the hospital you should have no sexual experience of any kind. There is no discussion of sexual activity, no privacy for masturbation (the nurse or doctor can walk in at any time), and no tolerance of your having genital contact, even with your spouse. Your sexuality is supposed to be nonexistent while you are in the hospital.

The lack of an available partner can also result in forced celibacy. This situation is common to many of us at different times in our lives. We may be between relationships, separated from our regular partner, or divorced. Masturbation, bar hopping, asking someone out, going to a party, or just being patient are among the various coping strategies.

While celibates are at one end of the sexual frequency continuum, the nymphomaniac and her male counterpart are at the other end. We examine these behaviors next, followed by a review of other varieties of sexual expression.

Nymphomania and Satyriasis

Nymphomania and **satyriasis** refer to the need to engage in a very high frequency of sexual behavior. In the case of nymphomania the woman seeks almost continual sexual stimulation. Similarly, in satyriasis it is the man who cannot be satisfied. The common belief is that these individuals are always on the lookout for the next sexual partner, that they are highly sexed and have an insatiable sexual appetite. But the meanings of "highly sexed" and "insatiable" vary from person to person. To one who never thinks of sex, a person who wants intercourse three times a week may be viewed as highly sexed.

Greek mythology is the source of the terms nymphomania and satyriasis. The nymphs were young women known for their amorous ways. Their compulsive pursuit of sex was viewed as madness, or mania—hence nymphomania. Their male counterpart, the satyrs, were part human, part animal. They were wine-drinking, libidinous creatures whose devotion to fulfilling their sexual urge was also seen as madness; such sexual compulsion came to be called satyriasis.

Regardless of labels, there are those who seem to have an unusual capacity or demand for sex. Whether their needs are physiological or psychological, their behavior reflects a frequency above the norm. An example is Janice,

> a passionate woman. She averaged forty-five to fifty orgasms per week and, in one week in which a count was kept, reached a hundred and five. Her need was so great that she was largely controlled by her sex desire. These were her natural sexual needs and desires. (Whipple & Whittle, 1976, p. 49)

One man reported having 17 ejaculations within 24 hours. Of the event, he said, "I am 46 years old and feel like I'm 17."

What is viewed as excessive sexual expression depends on who is doing the labeling. Some men use the term nymphomaniac to refer to the woman who wants to have intercourse more often then they do.

Paraphilias

Paraphilia is defined as an erotosexual condition of being recurrently responsive to, and obsessively dependent on, an unusual or unacceptable stimulus, perceptual or in fantasy, in order to have a state of erotic arousal initiated or maintained and in order to achieve or facilitate orgasm (Money & Werlwas, 1982, p. 59). Most paraphilias are believed to occur significantly more frequently in men than in women (Money, 1980). In this section we examine several paraphilias, including exhibitionism, fetishism, transvestism, voyeurism, pedophilia, and sadomasochism.

Exhibitionism

In **exhibitionism** the male exposes his genitals to a strange female without attempting any further sexual activity with her. Exhibitionists expose themselves to more than 40 million women each year (Cox & Maletzky, 1980). The average age of the first-time exhibitionist is 16; the average age of his first arrest for the offense is 22. Most of the victims of exhibitionists are young, attractive women.

There are several reasons why the exhibitionist exposes his genitals to females he does not know. Sexual excitement is a primary one. Hearing a woman yell and watching her horrified face is sexually stimulating for the exhibitionist. Once sexually excited, he may masturbate to orgasm.

Another reason is the desire to shock a female. Exhibiting himself may be a way of directing anger and hostility toward women. Although the woman he exposes himself to has not injured him, other women may have belittled him (or he has perceived it that way); or he has been recently impotent, blames his impotence on women, and exposes himself as a way of getting back at them.

Some exhibitionists expose themselves as a way of relieving stress. When the stress reaches a peak, this behavior followed by masturbation relieves it. Few exhibitionists physically harm the women they expose themselves to. Most do not speak to the women and rarely do they commit rape. They tend to be sexually passive. Their preferred sexual act is exposure, not intercourse (Stoller, 1977). If a woman responds seductively to the exhibitionist, he becomes unsettled because she is not responding as he thinks she should and he runs away.

The laws regarding exhibitionism vary from state to state. Some states view it as a misdemeanor while other states classify it as a felony. The penalty ranges from a fine to a prison term. If the exhibitionist is drunk or mentally retarded, police officers tend to regard his self-exposure differently from those who compulsively and repeatedly are picked up for exhibitionism. But either way, more males are arrested for exhibiting their genitals to females than for any other sexual offense (McWorter, 1977).

Therapeutic approaches to exhibitionism vary. They include **cognitive restructuring**, other behavioral procedures such as learning social skills to interact with women and substituting other behaviors for self-exhibiting when the urge to do so occurs, and psychotherapy. Cognitive restructuring involves having the exhibitionist exhibit himself to someone while an audience observes. Being aware that others are watching him, the exhibitionist often feels guilty, ashamed, and anxious for exhibiting himself to others.

When such feelings are associated with the act of exhibitionism, there is a decreased frequency in the behavior.

In a review of 21 studies that assessed the treatment of exhibitionists (Kilman et al., 1982), the researchers found positive results in all of them. "Although no comparative studies were undertaken, the behavioral procedures seemed to be more effective in a shorter time frame than traditional verbal, insight-oriented psychotherapy." (p. 28)

Fetishism

Fetishism is the use of objects as a repeatedly preferred or exclusive method of achieving sexual excitement when those objects were not designed for the purpose of sexual stimulation, for example, underwear. Although inanimate objects are the primary targets of a fetish, others include sounds (a particular song, the clicking of a train on the tracks), scents (perfume, incense), and textures (satin, leather). Fetish objects are often regarded by the fetishist as a substitute for the person owning them.

Fetish objects are used in masturbation. The person may look, hold, or smell the object while masturbating or use the object to masturbate. A man might wrap his penis with a scarf and stroke it until he ejaculates. A woman with the same fetish might rub the scarf in her vaginal lips until she climaxes.

Fetish objects may also be used to stimulate arousal for intercourse. The person who had a fetish for red hair would select a person with red hair as a sexual partner and would play with the hair before intercourse. The fetish object could also be used to fantasy to orgasm; for example, by holding a bottle of wine that represents the memory of a previous sexual encounter and focusing on that memory. To some degree we all have preferences for conditions of sexual excitement—a particular piece of music, lighting, scent, and so on. A preference becomes a fetish when it becomes a prerequisite for sexual arousal.

Since it is believed that a fetish results from learning to associate a particular object with sexual pleasure, therapy is often designed to recondition the stimulus object by associating an unpleasant experience with it. For example, the person might be given an electric shock or emetic drugs to induce vomiting when in the presence of the fetish object. Eleven case studies have reported successful results with this type of therapy, but, the reviewers say, "the results are only suggestive due to the uncontrolled nature of the research" (Kilmann et al., 1982, p. 212).

Transvestism

Transvestites, also known as cross-dressers, derive emotional, often erotic, satisfaction from dressing in the clothes of the opposite gender. Although most of the estimated two million transvestites in the United States are heterosexual, married men, others are homosexual. Some transvestites may don only one garment, say, a woman's panties; others may dress in full attire including dress, bra, panty hose, and wig. Their reasons for cross-dressing may be emotional ("I like to dress as a woman to express the feminine aspect of myself"), erotic ("I get a sexual charge from wearing a woman's clothes"), or social-psychological ("I like to be somebody else"). Most often the motives are mixed.

The cause of transvestism is unclear, but it is common for a transvestite male to recall dressing up as a girl when he was a child (Bullough, Bullough, & Smith, 1983). He may have been forced to do so, perhaps as punishment or to satisfy his mother's desire. One transvestite recalled, "Mom always wanted a girl, so she dressed me up to be the girl she never had." Or he may have sought the experience. Another man said, "I began putting on my mother's clothes when I was about 12. The first time I did it, I got very excited. When I looked into the mirror I felt as if I was transformed into a woman, and I was in ecstasy. I would do it every week thereafter, when my mother was out" (Talamini, 1981, p.72).

Still other transvestites can point to no specific incident that led to their cross-dressing. "I just don't know how it started but I'm glad it did—it's really fun to dress like a woman."

When a male first identifies himself as a transvestite, he may feel a sense of shame and disgust. But after a while the pleasure and satisfaction associated with the deviance outweighs the negative attitudes society has about his behavior. He begins to rationalize his behavior and to feel good about it: "A lot of men would like to express the feminine aspect of themselves but they're afraid to do it."

Other men excuse their behavior by blaming their heredity. They view transvestism as a biological compulsion: "I can't help the way I am." Some transvestites even feel that the stars and planets are astrologically responsible for their destiny (Talamini, 1981).

Not all societies view transvestism negatively. Among some American Plains Indian tribes, a man who did not choose to play the role of a man could become a transvestite. As such he could have a respected status, wear the clothes of a woman and do a woman's work.

Some transvestites seek therapy to assist them in becoming more accepting and less guilty about their cross-dressing desires and behaviors. In addition, some join Tri-Ess Sorority (P.O. Box 2055, DesPlaines, Illinois 60018), an organization of transvestites. It's purpose is to allow transvestites a forum to discuss the various aspects of their life style with each other.

Other transvestites seek therapy with the goal of wanting to stop their desire to cross-dress. Behavior modification procedures such as electric shock and emetic drugs have been used to assist the transvestite in learning negative associations with cross-dressing desires and behaviors. Each of 13 studies on the treatment of transvestism reported positive results (Kilmann et al., 1982, p. 222). But because cross-dressing occurs in private and the studies were based on the self-reports of the transvestite, the results are inconclusive.

Voyeurism

A voyeur is one who derives sexual pleasure from looking at unsuspecting people who are naked, undressing, or engaging in sexual behavior. The term "peeping Tom," used to describe the voyeur, comes from the legend of Lady Godiva, who, in eleventh-century England rode through the town of Coventry on a horse with only her long hair to cover her naked body (she did so to protest a tax raise). The townspeople, out of respect, stayed in their homes to avoid looking at her—all but Tom the tailor, who became known as Peeping Tom.

It is the rare person who has not done some "peeping," inadvertent or unplanned, for example, scanning the windows of the hotel rooms opposite one's own in the idle hope of seeing something of a sexual nature. But the motive for such behavior is largely curiosity rather than erotic thrill. Most voyeurs (usually men) spend a lot of time planning to peep and will risk a great deal to do so. Climbing over back fences, hiding in bushes, shivering in the cold, the true voyeur regards the trouble as worth it. Peeping is the condition of sexual excitement, which most often results in ejaculation through masturbation then or later. The voyeur's targets are female strangers. Although some voyeurs are married, they do not derive excitement from watching their wives or any familiar female undress.

The treatments for voyeurism are similar to those for transvestism, exhibitionism, and fetishism. The voyeur is asked to think of engaging in the peeping behavior while he is provided a negative association for his thoughts through aversive shock. Voyeurs may also be trained to gain control of their thoughts (thought stoppage) and to assert themselves in more appropriate sexual situations (assertive training), which, it is hoped, will reduce the need to peep. Of four case studies of treatment for voyeurs, all reported successful results (Kilmann et al., 1982).

Pedophilia

The pedophiliac—the child molester—seeks sexual contact with prepubertal children as a repeatedly preferred or exclusive method of achieving sexual gratification. Psycholgists have arbitrarily set the age difference between the adult pedophiliac and the child at 10 years or more. Eighty-five percent of child molestation consists of genital manipulation, indecent exposure, obscene language, and physical advances; 11 percent of the cases involve vaginal intercourse, anal penetration, and rape (Jaffe, 1976).

The pedophiliac is most often an adult relative or family friend. Typically, the family friend visiting the parents of the child may excuse himself as though to go to the bathroom and then sneak into the bedroom of the child for sexual contact; or he may pretend that he is putting the child to bed or saying goodnight when he is actually using the occasion to rub the child's genitals. One woman said that her uncle would regularly come into her bedroom whenever he visited her parents and "look under my pajamas." She only told her parents of this behavior when she became an adolescent. Of almost 800 university students, one of five females and one of seven males reported having had at least one such sexual experience with an adult as a child (Finkelhor, 1979). Sometimes the adolescent is the object of the pedophiliac's behavior.

● Our family was having a family gathering with all the relatives for Thanksgiving. It was held in the back yard of one of my aunt's. I had to go inside the house to get something and while I was inside one of my uncles came in. At that time we were pretty close and so, at first, i didn't think anything of the following events.

My uncle came into the kitchen where I was alone and hugged and kissed me. I kissed him back. Then he kissed me again and because we were close, I didn't think anything about the second kiss. I then moved into the walk-in pantry and my uncle followed me and wanted to hug and kiss me again.

I then realized this was no longer a "friendly kiss." I tried to move from the pantry and he blocked me. I tried not to act scared, even though I was. Trying to dodge him, he moved quickly and knocked a glass jar off the shelf. He told me to get paper towels to clean up the mess. Then my cousin came in the kitchen so I asked her to help me with the broken jar and made an excuse to get outside. That was all that happened. To this day, I get chills when I have to be around my uncle but I'm always careful not to be alone in his presence.

I never told anyone of this event. He is my mother's favorite and closest brother and at the time I decided not to hurt her. ●

The pedophiliac is usually male and may be either heterosexual or homosexual; he is often emotionally disturbed, lacks appropriate sexual alternatives and is under considerable stress (Langevin et al., 1978). As noted earlier, physical harm to the child is rare. In a study of 25 Dutch boys in ongoing relationships with male pedophiles, most viewed the experience in positive terms. They often felt "safe and happy" (Sandfort, 1983, p.180).

Psychological effects depend on parental reaction to the event—a low-key reaction is best. The sexual behaviors of the pedophiliac are most often observation and brief manipulation. However, the pedophiliac may encourage or force the child to stimulate him by hand, mouth, or to have intercourse. Also, he may rape or even murder.

Treatment for pedophilia also involves behaviorally based procedures. Of 11 studies focusing primarily on sex offenders, all reported successful outcomes, although not for all subjects in a particular study (Kilmann et al., 1982).

Sadism and Masochism

Sadism and **masochism** are two sides of the same coin. Both equate sexual pleasure and pain. A sadist becomes sexually aroused while inflicting pain on another. The pain may be only symbolic, as when the sadist "whips" someone with a feather, but more often the pain will be real since the sadist's pleasure comes from the suffering and cries of the partner. In some cases, the sadist may enjoy erotic piercing in which openings in the nipples, scrotum, perineum, and glans and shaft of the partner's penis are made and through which gold, silver, and stainless steel rings are inserted (Buhrich, 1983).

The sexual partner of the sadist is the masochist who derives sexual pleasure from receiving physical pain by being whipped, cut, bitten, spanked, choked, or pricked. The sadist and masochist need each other to live out their sexual scripts. A favorite pattern is bondage and discipline (B and D), where the sadist ties up (bondage) and whips (discipline) the masochist. Often the sadist will act out a scene by telling the masochist of a series of the latter's wrongdoings and the punishment to follow while the masochist screams for mercy. But both delight in the activity.

Some large cities have "clubs" that specialize in sadomasochism. The Chateau in the West Hollywood section of Los Angeles, California, is one. The "staff" consists of 13 women—6 dominants (sadists), 3 submissives (masochists), and 4 "switch hitters." Equipment includes a wide range of racks, cages, chains, wooden crosses, and whipping posts. The price is a dollar a minute (each treatment is 40 minutes) and more than 1,000 customers have been served by being bound, gagged, stretched, and beaten. Similar centers are located in San Francisco, Miami, and Dallas.

Although the sadist and masochist need each other to fulfill their sexual desires, the question of consent and "how much is enough" may arise. If the masochist is too consenting, too eager, his or her agony and suffering may not be sufficient to sexually stimulate the sadist. Also, how tight the ropes

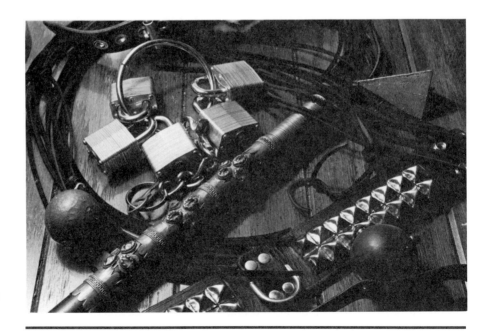

Some of the "hardware" used by a sadist.

should be, how deep the cuts, or how severe the beating must also be managed. The sadist may become excited just as the masochist is terrified and wants to stop. Indeed, both the sadist and masochist may feel frightened, as the case histories in the accompanying box illustrate.

Sadomasochistic sex is rare. Seven percent of over 65,000 men and 8 percent of over 15,000 women reported that they had tried sadomasochism (Lowe et al., 1983). How people learn this variety of sexual expression is unclear. The sadistic tendencies among men may result from typical male socialization, which encourages men to be aggressive, domineering, and controlling. But this explanation is weak, since most men are similarly socialized yet relatively few engage in sadistic behavior.

The development of masochistic behavior is easier to explain. Some masochists report having experienced sexual pleasure while being punished as children; for example, the person who was spanked on a parent's knee may have become sexually excited by having his or her genitals rubbed on the parent's knees. These experiences became linked in the child's mind.

Other Paraphilias

We have discussed the major paraphilias. Others, all of which are rare, include klismaphilia, frottage, bestiality, and necrophilia.

Klismaphilia

A klismaphiliac becomes sexually excited and feels sexual pleasure from an enema. Since the bowels and anus are close to the genitals, it is not surprising that some individuals connect enemas with erotic pleasure. Males often recall having experienced erections when they were administered enemas in their youth.

Frottage

A frotteur derives sexual pleasure from rubbing against another person. The person usually chooses a crowded place for the activity. He presses against the sexually desired person while saying, "Excuse me," then moves to another part of the crowd and presses against someone else. The behavior usually goes unnoticed. But the feelings aroused by pressing against another may be used in a masturbatory fantasy later.

Bestiality

Bestiality refers to sexual contact with animals. Male contact with an animal may involve vaginal penetration, fellatio by the animal (usually licking or mouthing the man's penis), or manual manipulation of the animal's genitals by the man. Female contact with animals most often includes cunnilingus by the animal (usually licking or mouthing the woman's genital area). The animals most frequently used are dogs, calves, sheep, and donkeys.

The Experience of a Sadist

This married man in his 20s requested psychiatric help because he feared he would soon commit murder. Since adolescence, he has been excited by fantasies and pornography depicting women bound and tortured. During courtship of his wife, he introduced mild versions of his fantasy into their sex play, and in this manner only was able to proceed on to intercourse. Now, after 8 years of marriage, they invariably have intercourse by his first binding her tightly with ropes and then, with her still bound, having intercourse. She has noticed that gradually the binding has been less and less symbolic and more and more painful. On two occasions in the last year, binding around her neck choked her into unconsciousness.

It is the nature of his work to enter households of strangers to do repairs. He frequently meets housewives there, and the temptation to bind and torture them is becoming unbearable. So far, he has avoided doing so by going out to his repair truck and masturbating while looking at photographs of bound and tortured women. His fear of killing a strange woman stems not from a belief that such an act would be sexually exciting but rather that, having bound and tortured her, he would have to kill her to remove the witness.

The Experience of a Masochist

The wife of the man described above found, during her courtship, that their first intercourse, under cramped conditions in a car, where her husband fixed her arms and legs so that they could not move, was at first uncomfortable but soon aroused in her a feeling of "interest." In time, this progressed to mild excitement, and now, several years later, she is appalled to find herself greatly excited by being bound. She is frightened by her excitement, and she is frightened by her experience of unconsciousness while being bound. She believes that her husband is dangerous, and at the same time she feels deeply that he loves her.*

*Reprinted with permission of the publisher from "Sexual Deviations" by Robert J. Stoller in Frank A. Beach's (ed.) *Human Sexuality In Four Perspectives*, pp. 204–205. Copyright © 1977 by The Johns Hopkins University Press.

Frottage usually occurs in very crowded places.

Necrophilia

One of the most bizarre forms of the paraphilias is **necrophilia**—looking at or attempting intercourse with a dead person. Necrophilia is particularly dangerous since the necrophiliac may kill in order to have a corpse to interact with. Following sex, the necrophiliac may cut up the limbs and eat them.

Summary

There are many variations of human sexual behavior, some of which we regard as normal and others as abnormal. Our definitions of normal sexual behavior refer to what is frequent, usual or common, moral according to a religious standard, and what appears to be natural. Most people would agree that heterosexual kissing is normal because most people do it, there are no religious injunctions against it, and it looks natural. But cross-dressing is infrequent, unusual, it is considered immoral by some religious leaders, and it may not look natural to some people. Hence cross-dressing, or transvestism, is not viewed as normal.

On closer inspection, sexual behaviors are learned and are time and society related. The degree to which we regard any sexual behavior as normal or abnormal depends on our previous learning experiences and the society in which we are reared.

The physically disabled, especially those who have suffered a spinal cord injury, are sometimes thought of as being involuntarily celibate and unable to engage in "normal" sexual behavior. But they may have a satisfactory sex life by sharing a variety of sexual experiences with their partners.

Celibacy is the absence of partner sex activity in a person's life. A person may be voluntarily celibate for religious or personal reasons or involuntarily celibate because of hospitalization or not having an available partner. Celibacy most often represents a temporary period in a person's life.

Nymphomania and satyriasis are terms that describe a high frequency of sexual behavior by women and men, respectively. But the use of these terms depends, in part, on who is doing the labeling.

An exhibitionist exposes his genitals to a strange female without wanting further sexual activity. Motives for exhibiting oneself include sexual gratification, the desire to shock a female, and the need to relieve stress. Treatment involves the use of a number of behaviorally based procedures.

Fetishism is the use of objects as a repeatedly preferred or exclusive method of achieving sexual excitement when the objects were not designed for the purpose of sexual stimulation. Although we all have preferences for conditions of sexual excitement, a preference becomes a fetish when it is a prerequisite for sexual arousal.

Transvestism, also known as cross-dressing, tends to be characteristic of heterosexual married males. Their motives may be emotional, erotic, or social-psychological. Some societies, such as some American Plains Indian tribes, accord the transvestite a specific feminine role and a respected status.

Although we are all voyeurs to some extent, the term most often applies to a person who derives sexual pleasure from looking at other people undressing or engaging in sexual behavior. Most voyeurs spend a lot of time planning to "peep" and will risk a great deal to do so.

Pedophilia is another term for child molestation and refers to a person who seeks sexual contact with children. Many acts of pedophilia are not physically harmful, but some are violent and all are coercive.

Other paraphilias include sadism/masochism, klismaphilia, frottage, bestiality, and necrophilia. These sexual variations are rare.

Key Terms

celibate	transvestites
asexuality	voyeurism
voluntary celibacy	pedophilia
involuntary celibacy	sadism
nymphomania	masochism
satyriasis	klismaphilia
paraphilia	frottage
exhibitionism	bestiality
cognitive restructuring	necrophilia
fetishism	

Issues in Debate and Future Directions

The behavioral expression of some of the sexual variations discussed in this chapter (exhibitionism, pedophilia, voyeurism) interferes with the rights of others. When people engaging in such behaviors come to the attention of the law, they are often required to enter a treatment program (though some voluntarily seek treatment before being caught.) But the nature and content of treatment programs differ. After reviewing some of these treatment modalities, we look at some trends in sexual variations.

Hormone Therapy for Sex Offenders?

Depo-Provera (medroxyprogesterone acetate or MPA) is a synthetic progestinic hormone that not only lowers the blood level of testosterone but also seems to have a direct pharmacologic effect on brain pathways that mediate sexual behavior. Its effect is to provide some relief from the compulsive need to exhibit, to seek sex with young children, to engage in voyeuristic behavior, and to rape.

Drs. John Money and Richard Bennett (1981) treated 20 adult males with a history of sex-offending behaviors since adolescence with Depo-Provera in doses ranging from 100 mg to 600 mg per week for periods of three months to more than five years. Counseling was also an important part of their program and helped to encourage socially appropriate pair-bonded relationships. "Treatment with MPA does not, per se, bring about pair-bondedness, nor does counseling therapy, per se, though each may enhance the possibility of its occurrence. When pair-bondedness does materialize, the successful rehabilitation of the paraphilic sex offender is greatly enhanced" (p. 129).

Money and Bennett are still evaluating the effectiveness of their treatment program. The 20 men under study have been followed for from 1 to 13 years. The specific effects of hormone and counseling therapy have been obscured by patients leaving the program, varying times between hormonal injections, compliancy (keeping appointments, staying in therapy), use of alcohol, "street" drugs, prescription antiepileptic drugs, and, as noted previously, the establishment of pair-bondedness with an erotosexual partner. However, "for some patients it proved to be the only form of treatment that induced a long-term remission of symptoms and kept them off a treadmill of imprisonment" (p. 132).

Tranquilizers for Sex Offenders?

Mellaril (thioridazine), a major tranquilizer used primarily in the treatment of psychosis, is also sometimes used with sex offenders. Mellaril reduces the probability of erection and, in some cases, sexual desire. Although the drug has been used successfully to treat pedophiliacs, the patient's informed consent is a prerequisite for prescribing the drug. In addition to the effects of erectile dysfunction (loss of ability to get an erection), retarded ejaculation (inability to ejaculate), and decreased libido (loss of sexual desire), a possible long-term side effect is tardive dyskinesia (twitching of the face muscles) (Meador, 1983). As with Depo-Provera, Mellaril is used in conjunction with some form of counseling.

Counseling Only?

Therapists who view pedophilia as a result of inappropriate learning have developed treatment programs to help pedophiliacs learn to feel negatively about their pedophilia and to express their sexuality in more appropriate ways. The types of procedures used by some therapists include aversion therapy, covert sensitization, and social skill training. For the heterosexual pedophiliac, shock aversion therapy is carried out by having the patient look at a series of slides of children and adult females flashed on a wall in the therapist's office. After each picture of a child appears, the therapist administers an aversive electric shock so that the patient associates pain with the visual stimulus of the child. At the moment the shock is turned off, the therapist changes the slide to that of an adult female. In this way the patient associates relief from the pain (and, consequently, a more pleasant feeling) with the visual stimulus of the adult female.

Covert sensitization is a type of aversive conditioning in which the aversive feelings are cognitively induced by the therapist. The therapist might say, "I want you to imagine going into the bedroom of your 7-year-old niece when her parents are in another part of the house. As you open the door you see her asleep in her bed. But as you approach the bed you begin to feel very nauseous and feel that you are going to throw up. You vomit and feel the particles in your mouth and the stench in your nostrils." This scenario is designed to associate negative feelings with the child molestation approach behavior so that the probability of the patient wanting to engage in the behavior is reduced.

Social skill training is more typically a part of therapy for exhibitionists and is based on the premise that the patient does not have the requisite social skills to initiate and maintain appropriate social and sexual relationships with adult females. The training involves systematically identifying the behaviors in courtship and seduction and teaching these to the patient. Social skill training usually takes place in group rather than individual therapy where group members may practice basic social skills with each other.

While there are many ways of treating sex offenders, there is little agreement as to what constitutes the best approach.

Future Directions

Trends in sexual variations include greater acceptance of some of the variations and increased concern among professionals for the sexual adjustment of their disabled patients. While exhibitionists, pedophiliacs, and necrophiliacs will continue to be regarded negatively by most Americans, those who choose to be celibate will be regarded more positively. As our society becomes increasingly sexual and develops an anything goes (pro-choice) posture, tolerance for those who select this variation will increase.

While voluntary celibacy will be increasingly accepted, involuntary celibacy will not. Professionals in charge of rehabilitationg spinal cord injured individuals will increasingly take the initiative in discussing sex among the disabled. This will result from increased training of physicians and rehabilitation counselors regarding the relevance an enjoyable sex life has to the total functioning of the disabled. The title of the book—*The Sensuous Wheeler: Sexual Adjustment for the Spinal Cord Injured* (Rabin, 1980) and the Annual National Symposiums on Sexuality and Disability reflect a new feeling about sexuality and the disabled.

Chapter Fourteen

Homosexuality

Think of us as people, not as gay people.

A GAY PERSON

Chapter Fourteen

Homosexuality is becoming a more acceptable topic of public discussion in our society. Movies and television are taking homosexuality out of the closet and increasing its visibility. Some of us are homosexual individuals or have friends who are. A better understanding of this previously taboo subject is the goal of this chapter. We begin by looking at the definition and incidence of homosexuality.

Definition and Incidence

Homosexuality refers to both emotional attachment and sexual attraction to those of one's own gender. Homosexual people, who are also called "gay" people, may be either men or women. When most people use the term homosexual, they mean a man who has an emotional and sexual preference for other men. The term **lesbian** is used to refer to a woman who has an emotional and sexual preference for other women.

Rarely is anyone entirely homosexual or heterosexual in both attitudes and behavior. Rather, our sexual orientation can be placed on a continuum

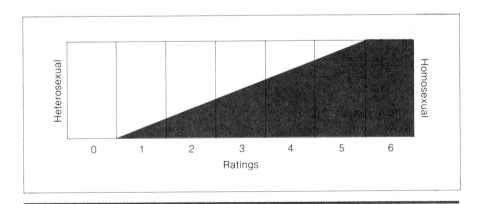

Figure 14.1
The Heterosexual-
Homosexual Rating
Scale

devised by Kinsey et al. (1953) and illustrated in Figure 14.1. Gay people cannot be stereotyped or pigeonholed. They are young and old, white and black, single and married, from all social classes, occupations, and religions. The idea that a homosexual person is instantly recognizable is false. Although some effeminate men are homosexual, others are not.

Thirty-five percent of 65,000 adult males and 20 percent of 15,000 adult females reported having had a homosexual experience during adolescence (Petersen et al., 1983a). Most of these experiences occurred only once or twice with one or two partners. This kind of experience, which may be a part of adolescent sexual exploration, does not mean that an individual is homosexual. Adult men who are predominantly homosexual—that is, who prefer sex with their own gender but may have had incidental heterosexual sexual experiences—represent 5 to 10 percent of all men in Western societies. Adult women who are predominantly homosexual represent 3 to 5 percent of all women (Marmor, 1980). The percentage of people who are exclusively homosexual—who have had no heterosexual experiences—is lower—about 2 percent of men and 1 percent of women.

Figures for the percentage of college students who view themselves as homosexual are also available. About 3 percent of the men and less than 1 percent of the women at one college reported that they were homosexual (Knox &Wilson, 1981). Other studies of college students show similar percentages (Gagnon & Simon, 1973; Huk, 1979). A task group of the American Sociological Association estimated that there are 20 million Americans with a homosexual orientation (Huber et al., 1982). For many, prejudice against homosexuals causes them to conceal their sexual preferences.

Gay females often develop a love relationship before becoming sexually involved.

Most homosexual men are indistinguishable from heterosexual men. This group of homosexual men could, by appearance, be heterosexuals.

Prejudice Against Homosexuals

Like a robin among snakes, gay people live in a hostile environment. They are called pejorative names, ("queers," "dyke," "faggot"), labeled as having negative characteristics ("sick," "dangerous"), and legally prohibited form marrying each other. Many Americans feel that same-gender sexual relations are wrong and that gay people should not be allowed to teach school or hold public office.

Men are less tolerant of gay people than women (Larsen et al., 1980). In addition, those having antiblack attitudes and who are religiously orthodox also tend to view homosexuality more negatively (Larsen, Cate, & Reed, 1983). The Index of Homophobia questionnaire on page 413 may help you to assess your feelings about gay people.

Prejudice against homosexuals has taken the extreme forms of castration, lobotomy, and extermination (the latter by the Nazis in Germany). The more common form of violence is known as "fag bashing." In a study of 1,000 gay men in Chicago (Harry, 1982), one in four said they had been beaten or assaulted by heterosexuals.

The basis for prejudice against homosexual people is religion (primarily traditional religious orientations) and sexism. We noted earlier the religious ban against homosexual relations as nonprocreative sex. Sexist sources of such prejudice lie in the straight man's negative view of another man who is sometimes perceived as being effeminate. The straight man assumes that to be a woman is not as good as to be a man and, therefore, the man who acts like a woman is unworthy.

My Sexuality

Index of Homophobia (IHP)

This questionnaire is designed to measure the way you feel about working or associating with homosexuals. It is not a test, so there are no right or wrong answers. Answer each item as carefully and accurately as you can by placing a number beside each one as follows:

1 Strongly agree
2 Agree
3 Neither agree nor disagree
4 Disagree
5 Strongly disagree

1. I would feel comfortable working closely with a male homosexual. ____

2. I would enjoy attending social functions at which homosexuals were present. ____

3. I would feel uncomfortable if I learned that my neighbor was homosexual. ____

4. If a member of my sex made a sexual advance toward me I would feel angry. ____

5. I would feel comfortable knowing that I was attractive to members of my sex. ____

6. I would feel uncomfortable being seen in a gay bar. ____

7. I would feel comfortable if a member of my sex made an advance toward me. ____

8. I would be comfortable if I found myself attracted to a member of my sex. ____

9. I would feel disappointed if I learned that my child was homosexual. ____

10. I would feel nervous being in a group of homosexuals. ____

11. I would feel comfortable knowing that my clergyman was homosexual. ____

(Continued)

12. I would be upset if I learned that my brother or sister was homosexual. ____

13. I would feel that I had failed as a parent if I learned that my child was gay. ____

14. If I saw two men holding hands in public I would feel disgusted. ____

15. If a member of my sex made an advance toward me I would be offended. ____

16. I would feel comfortable if I learned that my daughter's teacher was a lesbian. ____

17. I would feel uncomfortable if I learned that my spouse or partner was attracted to members of his or her sex. ____

18. I would feel at ease talking with a homosexual at a party. ____

19. I would feel uncomfortable if I learned that my boss was homosexual. ____

20. It would not bother me to walk through a predominantly gay section of town. ____

21. It would disturb me to find out that my doctor was homosexual. ____

22. I would feel comfortable if I learned that my best friend of my sex was homosexual. ____

23. If a member of my sex made an advance toward me I would feel flattered. ____

24. I would feel uncomfortable knowing that my son's male teacher was homosexual. ____

25. I would feel comfortable working closely with a female homosexual. ____

Copyright © Wendell A. Ricketts & Walter W. Hudson, 1978

3, 4, 6, 9, 10, 12, 13, 14, 15, 17, 19, 21, 24

To give yourself a score on the IHP, reverse score the items numbered under the copyright in the following way: 1 = 5, 2 = 4, 4 = 2, 5 = 1. For example, if you wrote a 1 for statement number 3 ("I would feel uncomfortable if I learned that my neighbor was homosexual"), change that number to a 5 for scoring purposes. Reverse score the rest of the items in the same way.

Add up the numbers you assigned to each of the 25 items. Persons who score 0 to 25 have mostly positive feelings about homosexuals; those who score 25 to 50 have positive to neutral feelings about homosexuals; 50 to 75 = neutral to negative feelings; 75 to 100 = mostly negative feelings (Hudson & Ricketts, 1980)

Homophobia involves strong fear and anxiety about homosexuality. In an effort to counter negative feelings toward homosexuality, some communities offer programs entitled "Straight Talk on Homosexuality." These programs are presented to largely heterosexual audiences by heterosexual speakers, often a husband—wife team. "Audiences consistently appreciate the sensitive, informative, and challenging way in which the issues are addressed" (Hoffman, 1982 p. 92). But reversing these attitudes will not be easy. It requires education of the public at all levels and opportunities for such education are limited. For example, only 2 percent of 640 college and university departments of sociology in one survey reported having one or more full courses on homosexuality (Huber et al., 1982).

Causes of Homosexuality

Gay people are often irritated by the concern heterosexual people have for finding the "cause" of homosexuality. Since the same question is never asked of heterosexuality, the concern for homosexual causation implies that something is wrong with homosexuality and that a cure must be found. Nevertheless, scientists continue to look for explanations for differences among members of a population, whatever its composition, and several explanations have been suggested for why some people have a sexual and emotional preference for members of their own gender.

Parent–Child Relationships

One theory of the cause of homosexuality suggests that the relationship an individual has with his or her parents predispose that person toward homosexuality. The family constellation includes a mother with whom he has a close emotional tie and a father who seems emotionally detached from the family unit. The presumed script is as follows: The overprotective mother seeks to establish a binding emotional relationship with her son. But this closeness also elicits strong sexual feelings of the son toward the mother, which are punished by her and blocked by the society through the incest taboo. Fearful of expressing these feelings, he generates fear to other women with the result that they are no longer viewed as sex objects.

While the son's relationship with the mother is contributing to his subsequent rejection of women in general, his distant relationship with his father prevents identification with a male role model. For example, the relationship between playwright Tennessee Williams and his father was one of mutual rejection. The father was contemptuous of his "sissy" son and Tennessee was hostile to his father because of the father's arrogance.

While some studies (Bieber, 1962; Evans, 1969) lend support to the idea of early parent–child relationships as a contributing factor to homosexuality among males, they are not conclusive. Sons with overprotective mothers and rejecting fathers also grow up to be heterosexual, just as those with moderate mothering and warm fathering grow up to be homosexual. Also, two sons growing up in the same type of family may have different sexual orientations. A study of the family backgrounds of 979 homosexual and 477 heterosexual people suggest that parent–child reltaionships as the "cause" for homosexuality is highly questionable and highly suspect (Bell, Weinberg, & Hammersmith, 1981). The researchers concluded that the relationship individuals have with their parents "cannot be said to predict much about sexual orientation." (p. 62)

Other Childhood Experiences

Various childhood experiences are also said to be causes of homosexuality. Money (1980b) suggests that children who are punished for playing heterosexual games and acting out of heterosexual scripts may suppress their heterosexual orientation. Without an outlet for heterosexual expression, they drift toward homosexuality. Since this behavior occurs out of the sight of the parental eye, it goes unpunished and may develop as an alternative to heterosexual expression.

Another explanation of homosexuality is a childhood experience of seduction by an older same-gender adult, which may predispose the child to a homosexual life style. There is no evidence to support this suggested cause since heterosexuals have also been molested as children. The homosexual person who had an early seduction experience may have been already inclined toward homosexuality (Tripp, 1975).

An early homosexual experience may be influential in encouraging a person toward homosexuality if the experience is viewed by the child as "the way I am." Children who have sexual experience with persons of their own gender may see these experiences as evidence of their homosexuality. Unaware that homosexual contacts in childhood and adolescence are not unusual in the process of growing up, the person may become locked into a circular argument and self-fulfilling prophecy. The thinking is, "homosexuals have sex with someone of their own gender. I did this, so I must be one of them." This thinking may further the sexual behavior with the person's gender to complete the prophecy. "Since I am a homosexual, I will act like one and have sex with people like me." Hence, the homosexual orientation does not result from the sexual behavior but from the labeling of that experience (Laury, 1980).

Whether early childhood experiences predispose or predict an adult sexual orientation is unknown. However, different childhood behavioral patterns have been noted between those who later affirmed a homosexual or heterosexual orientation. For example, it is often suggested that gay women were tomboys in childhood and adolescence. Some evidence suggests this is true. When gay women and heterosexual women were compared, 70 percent of the former but only 16 percent of the heterosexuals said they were tomboys when growing up (Saghir & Robins, 1973). "Tomboy" was defined as a preference for male rather than female activities and companions.

A comparison of the backgrounds of gay men and heterosexual men also shows differences (Whitam, 1977). The stronger the man's homosexual orientation (see Figure 14.1), the more likely he was to (a) show interest in dolls, (b) cross-dress, (c) prefer the company of girls rather than boys in childhood games, (d) prefer the company of older women, (e) be regarded by other boys as a sissy, and (f) show a sexual interest in other boys rather than girls in childhood sex play.

In another study that compared the backgrounds of homosexual and heterosexual people, (Bell et al., 1981), the researchers noticed that gay males tended to score higher on "gender nonconformity" than heterosexual males. Specifically, gay males tended to feel sexually different from other boys in childhood and in adolescence, reported being aroused by other males either before or after puberty, and felt sexually indifferent to girls during childhood. Gay females also reported feeling aroused by other females during childhood and to have had homosexual involvements during adolescence. Other research shows that homosexual people have a higher incidence of adolescent homosexual experience than heterosexual people (Cook et al., 1983).

Although some childhood and adolescent experiences may predispose a person to homosexuality, no specific background characteristic causes a person to become homosexual. Some heterosexual males played with dolls and were called sissy by their peers, and some heterosexual women were tomboys.

Age at Puberty

Two researchers have suggested that the timing of sexual maturation is associated with the development of erotic orientation (Storms & Wasserman, 1982). They hypothesized that erotic orientation usually develops in late childhood and early adolescence, at or around the time of puberty, from an interaction among biological factors (onset of puberty), psychological factors (degree of masturbation and erotic fantasizing), and sociological factors (membership in same-gender or opposite-gender groups). In essence, those maturing biologically early but still in same-gender groups would tend to invest their same-gender peers with erotic potential. Their orientation would be homosexual. Those maturing later, when opposite-gender groups are more normative, would tend to invest their opposite-gender peers with erotic potential. Their orientation would be heterosexual. In a study of 97 males, the time of sexual maturation was predictive of their hetero- and homoerotic orientation.

Heredity

"They were born that way" summarizes the explanation of some heterosexuals about the causes of homsexuality. But there is little evidence to support this belief (Money, 1980). A good research design would be a comparison of identical twins who were separated at birth and reared in two different homes. If each sibling were homosexual in spite of being reared by different parents, a good case for a genetic base for homosexuality could be made. The closest to this type of study is one of twins reared in the same home (Kallmann, 1952a, b). The results showed that of 40 identical twins, in 100 percent of the cases where one sibling was a homosexual, so was the twin (Kallmann, 1952a, b). But these twins were not representative of the identical twin population. They were recruited with the aid of psychiatric and penal agencies and more than half were schizoid, schizophrenic, or alcoholic. It is not known to what degree these factors contributed to their homosexuality, and no valid inference can be drawn unless these factors are eliminated. In a more recent study of the siblings of 50 homosexual men and 50 heterosexual men, significantly more (25 percent) of the brothers of homosexual men were also homosexual (Pillard, Roumadere, & Caretta, 1982). This finding only suggests an inherited predisposition toward homosexuality, since the results could be due to similar learning experiences by the twins.

Hormonal Influence

Related to the genetic theory is the hormone-imbalance theory of homosexuality. It has been hypothesized that gay men have a preponderance of estrogen, a female hormone, and gay women an overabundance of androgen, a male hormone. The evidence for a hormonal basis for homosexuality is weak, stated one researcher (Meyer-Bahlburg, 1977). He also examined the hormone levels of gay women and concluded, "The majority of female homosexuals have normal sex hormone levels after puberty. About a third of the lesbian and transsexual women studied have elevated androgen levels but the interpretation of these findings as to a causative role of androgens in female homosexuality is open" (1979, p. 177). Other researchers feel there is increasing evidence for the relationship between hormonal input and sexual preference (Bell et al., 1981). It seems clear although some homosexual people may have more hormones of the opposite gender than most heterosexual people have, this is by itself not sufficient to induce a homosexual orientation.

Homosexuality by Default

Another explanation for homosexuality suggests that this orientation results from a person's lack of acceptance by those of the opposite gender because of his or her presumed unattractiveness. This rejection (the theory goes) caused the person to turn to homosexuality by default. But there is little validity to this hypothesis. Homosexuals are like heterosexuals in terms of attractiveness; some are attractive, some are not.

A related suggestion is that homosexual people have been unable to perform in their sexual relations with the opposite gender and so seek the gay world where there are no heterosexual expectations. The suggestion is not fair. It might equally be suggested that the heterosexual people choose their sexual orientation because it relieves them of the responsibility to perform sexually with homosexuals. The fact that some homosexual people do not want to have sexual relations with someone of the opposite gender does not suggest fear of performance but lack of preference.

What Homosexuals Say about Causation

When a group of gay women were asked the cause of their sexual orientation, 50 percent said it was "free choice"—nothing was predetermined, 20 percent said their homosexuality was "innately determined," and about 14 percent felt their orientation resulted from negative childhood or heterosexual experiences (Ferguson & Finkler, 1978).

Although no comparable study has been conducted on gay men, explanations they give include the following: "I don't know why I am homosexual; I don't care", "I just know that I'm gay and that it feels natural for me", and "I have no explanation; it just feels right to me. I resent the question."

Gay men report that they first discovered an attraction to members of their own gender around age 13, while gay women report such an awareness around age 16 (Bell et al., 1981). The initial attraction of males to other males tends to be sexual, whereas the attraction between gay women is more emotional and relational than sexual.

Living the Gay Life

Certain aspects of the gay life are different from heterosexual life. Some differences are in acknowledging one's sexual preference (referred to as coming out), employment, and relationships.

Coming Out

A major problem for gay people is **coming out**. The term has two meanings. First, to come out is to be aware that one is gay and to acknowledge this to oneself. "The first time I thought to myself, 'I am a homosexual,' it stunned me. I was horrified," recalled one gay man. This initial reaction is typical since the larger heterosexual society holds up social mirrors to the homosexual that reflect disapproval and disdain.

The second meaning is letting others know that one is gay. Elton John, Calvin Klein, Olivia Newton-John, and Dave Kopay (running back of the San Francisco '49ers) are contemporaries who have gone on record as having had sexual involvement with members of their own gender. Coming out may be related to greater personal adjustment. One gay person said, "Coming out

Homosexuals derive social support for their lifestyle from participation in gay political groups.

is something everyone should go through, because if they can handle that, they can handle anything" (Friend, 1980).

But coming out is risky because of the fear of rejection. "If I tell them who I am, will they still accept me?" is the question that nags gay people who resent having to hide who they really are. The following is a letter of a gay woman to her parents and her suggestions to other gay people.

● Dear Mom and Dad,

I love you both very much and would give you the world if I could. You've always given me the best. You've always been there when I needed you. The lessons of love, strength, and wisdom you've taught me are invaluable. Most importantly, you've taught me to take pride and stand up for what I believe. In the past six months I've done some very serious thinking about my goals and outlook on life. It's a tough and unyielding world that caters only to those who do for themselves. Having your help and support seems to make it easier to handle. But I've made a decision that may test your love and support. Mom and Dad, I've decided to live a gay life style.

I'm sure your heads are spinning with confusion and disbelief right now but please try to let me finish. As I said before, I've given this decision much thought. First and foremost, I'd like for you to know that I'm happy. All my life as a sexual being has been spent frustrated in a role I could not fulfill. Emotionally and mentally I'm relieved. Believe me, this was not an easy decision to make. (What made it easier was having the strength to accept myself.) Who I chose to sleep with does not make me more or less of a human being. My need for love and affection is the same as anyone else's; it's just that I fulfill this need in a different way. I'm still the same person I've always been.

It's funny I say I'm still the same person, yet society seems to think I've changed. They seem to think that I don't deserve to be treated as a respectable citizen. Instead, they think I should be treated as a deranged maniac needing constant supervision to prevent me from molesting innocent children. I have the courage and strength to face up to this opposition, but I can't do it alone. Oh, what I would give to have your support! I realize I've thrown everything at you rather quickly. Please take your time. I don't expect a response. And please don't blame yourselves, for there is no one to blame. Please remember that I'm happy and I felt the need to share my happiness with two people I love with all my heart.

Your loving daughter,
Blair ●

Blair's suggestions to other gay people who want to tell their parents include:

1. Avoid speaking from a defensive point of view. Too often gay people are forced to defend their life style as if it is wrong. If you approach your parents with the view that your homosexuality is a positive aspect of your personality, you will have a better chance of evoking a positive response from them.
2. Avoid talking about your current relationship. Homosexuality is often labeled as a phase rather than a permanent facet of one's life. Your parents may feel, as mine did, that your current partner is the cause of your life style. Thus when your relationship ends, so will your homosexuality. Deal with the subject as it affects you as an individual.
3. Try to maintain a constant flow of positive reinforcement toward your parents. Reiterate your love for them as you would like them to do to you.
4. Be confident in your views and outlook on homosexuality. Before you begin to explain your position to anyone else, you must have it clear in your own mind.

It is difficult for many parents to accept the fact that their son or daughter is homosexual. The first reaction is often "What did we do wrong?" One mother "instantly thought of the failure of her first marriage and decided that not having a father around the house explained, at least in part, why Susan had become a lesbian. In seeking the reason for her daughter's homosexuality, she willingly made herself a scapegoat" (Silverstein, 1977, p. 29). Parents also are concerned that their son's or daughter's homosexuality will make it more difficult for him or her to be happy. They fear that society may scorn or mistreat their gay children.

When 20 parents of gay children were asked what advice they would give to children wanting to tell their parents and families of their homosexuality, they mentioned the following points

Tell them! Don't shut parents out, don't withdraw from family.
Be patient with parental evolution of understanding and acceptance.
Let parents know they are needed in life of the child.
Be understanding of parental reactions and feelings—be accepting of their position and ideas, too.

Work with parents or family so that there *is* a family functioning unit. (Schlessinger, 1982, p. 26)

Another source of support is Parents and Friends of Gays and Lesbians (P.O. Box 24265, Los Angeles, California 90025; phone 213–472–8952), a national organization of over 80 local chapters.

About 40 percent of gay people tell their parents about their homosexuality (most already know), and a similar percentage tell their siblings. Gay friends of both genders are the most likely to be told (Jay & Young, 1979). The latter are almost always accepting. Mutual acceptance and support is a factor influencing homosexual people to band together in one area. In San Francisco 20 percent of the population, or 120,000 gay people, have made their home there (Gordon, 1983).

Coming out ranges from disclosure to no one (other than their sexual partners) to disclosure to everyone. "Why should I hide who I am?" reflected one man. This issue divides some gay people. Those who are out of the closet feel that those who stay in are contributing to the repression of other gay people by hiding their homosexuality. If more gay people would come out, they believe, the establishment would learn to accept them. These people also feel that to hide one's homosexuality is to live a two-faced, Dr. Jekyll–Mr. Hyde life. "I get sick when I see gays laughing with straights at queer jokes," said an out-of-the-closet gay person. But others feel that being totally open with straight people is unwise. In particular, they feel that hiding one's homosexuality is important in employment.

Employment

A review of studies on gay people in the work force (Levine, 1979) revealed that one in three have had their careers negatively influenced and one in five have lost or been denied employment as a result of their sexual orientation. The problem occurs not only in gaining employment but also in trying to keep it while under the constant fear of discovery. Discrimination in hiring is illustrated by the experience of a researcher who sent identical resumes except for gender and sexual orientation (indicated by listing participation in Gay People's Alliance under Personal Background) to all Ontario law firms (Adam, 1982). The result—those resumes listing gay interest were least likely to elicit follow-up letters for an interview. Employment agencies may be equally discriminatory. One New York agency used the code H.C.F. (high-class fairy) on the resumes of suspected homosexuals (Zoglin, 1974).

The application form for employment may also pose barriers. There are usually questions about previous arrests and military service. Both are torpedoes for homosexuals. If the reason for the arrest or lack of military service is homosexuality, the person may not be hired. It is a "catch-22 situation." If the person answers honestly, employment may be denied. But if the person hides the facts, dismissal may result if the dishonesty is discovered.

It's very difficult to get a job. I applied for a job at G.E. and told them about my discharge. He said he could have hired me if I had served my time in prison for murder

Some gays are also transvestites.

but not with that discharge. The department store clerk told me, "we're sorry, we don't employ homosexuals." (Williams & Weinberg, 1971, p. 116)

Even though most gay people make it through the hiring phase of the employment barrier, they must then direct their energies to not being found out for fear of losing their job. This means pretending an interest in women (for a gay male) and avoiding the development of friendships with coworkers who might then discover their homosexuality.

> Ken and I have been lovers and living together for two years. Since no one in my company knows I am gay—if they did, they would fire me—I hide our relationship. Ken is not allowed to call me at work. When talking about what I did over the weekend, I change his name to Kate. A girlfriend of mine poses as Kate at all company affairs. I keep her picture on my desk. At work everyone thinks I am a big stud because I constantly flirt with all the secretaries. (Levine, 1979, p. 155)

Frustrated by keeping up this facade, many homosexuals restrict their vocational career goals to work environments accepting of their homosexuality. The result is a disproportionate concentration of gay males in the so-called feminine professions (teaching and library work), lower white-collar jobs (retail sales, office clerk), and service jobs (waiter, hair dresser) (Levine, 1979). Gay people may find it difficult to work in careers of their choice. University sociology departments, which are often thought of as being liberal, are reluctant to hire and promote homosexual people. Six in 10 of 640 chairpersons indicated that hiring a homosexual would produce problems (Huber et al., 1982). Psychologists who are gay are also victims of discrimination in their discipline (Huber et al., 1982).

Not all gay people are discriminated against in the employment arena. Firms that have gone on record forbidding discrimination in hiring or advancement based on affectional or sexual orientation include American Tele-

While homosexuals are often thought of in reference to their sexuality, their role behaviors are similar to those of heterosexuals.

phone and Telegraph (the nation's largest corporate employer); Bank of America; IBM; the radio and television networks ABC, NBC, CBS; and McDonald's. A typical policy statement is the following by AT&T: "An individual's sexual preferences are not criteria either for becoming an employee or remaining an employee of the Bell System. Job retention and promotability are based upon demonstrable job performance and behavior" (Voeller, 1980, p. 248).

Relationships

Just as who to tell and where to work are unique issues for gay people, so are their relationships. Since gay men seem to have different relationships with other gay men than gay women with other gay women, the two groups are discussed separately.

Gay Male Relationships

To put gay male sexuality in perspective, we begin by looking at heterosexual male sexuality. In traditional heterosexual relationships men are more sexually aggressive than women. As we noted earlier, when a man and woman are out for an evening, it is typical that the man will initiate the sexual activity and the woman will act as the gatekeeper controlling the pace of his advances. If this is their first date and she feels no emotional attachment to the man, she is less likely to reward his sexual advances.

When two gay men are out for an evening, who will be the gatekeeper? Who will put the brakes on sexual behavior if they have just met? Generally, neither partner. Of 4,000 gay men who were asked, "How often do you go home to have sex with someone you have just met?" only 7 percent replied "never." Fifty percent said they did so frequently (Jay & Young, 1979). In another study of 574 gay men, 60 percent reported having more than 250 lovers (Bell & Weinberg, 1978). **Cruising** is the term in the gay subculture for going to a bar, bath, or party to pick up a sexual partner. While gay women do cruise, it is much more common among gay men (Sanders, 1980).

The sexual activities of gay male partners, even when they are intensely enjoyable, are usually not enough to keep the couple together. Many of their relationships are short lived. This is not to say that some gays do not establish lasting emotional and sexual relationships. One man said the relationship with his partner had lasted longer and was considerably happier than either of his sisters' marriages. However, although stable relationships based on sexual fidelity and emotional intimacy are desired by most gay men (Harry & Lovely, 1979), such relationships are the exception, not the rule.

Several reasons may account for the transitory nature of gay male relationships. Since men have been socialized to be sexually focused in their relationships, gay men as well as heterosexual ones may prefer the variety that transitory relationships provide. But most (90 percent) heterosexual men marry and make a commitment to their wives that they will be monogamous. Such a wife helps to channel the male's sexual expressions into marriage. Homosexual males do not have a wife expecting them to be faithful and punishing them if they aren't. One gay man said, "If I wanted monogamy I'd get me a wife and stay at home. But being gay means that I can have men, as many as I want, as often as I want with no 'wife' telling me who I can and can't sleep with."

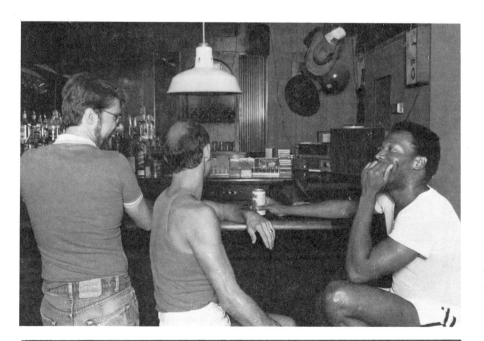

These gay friends enjoy talking together in a bar. (The stereotype of gay men in a bar is that they are always hustling each other sexually.)

Gay relationships also have few social and economic supports. When a heterosexual couple are in love, they can be public about their feelings and expect that others will approve of their relationship. Gay couples must hide their love, their "marriage" is illegal, and their living together is suspect. They cannot file joint tax returns, can't collect social security widowhood benefits (even though they may have lived as a married couple for 50 years), or get favorable insurance rates given to married people. In short, our society does not approve of homosexual relationships and gives the couple no help in establishing or maintaining such a relationship.

Gay relationships are also very intense. Shut off from the rest of the world, gay men try to satisfy all needs for each other. In the midst of a hostile social environment, this goal may be more than either can achieve.

Although many gay male relationships are short lived, they may be very satisfying. In a study of 128 gay men (Peplau, 1981), 80 percent said they were currently in love with their partner and rated their relationship satisfaction 7.7 on a 9-point scale. They described their relationships as "best friendships" with the added component of romantic and erotic attraction. Some gay male relationships are committed. One researcher studied 50 males who had lived with their respective partners an average of 3.7 years (Lewis et al., 1981).

Gay Female Relationships

Some gay women have transitory sexual encounters but this is unusual. When 1,000 gay women were asked how often they had sexual relations with someone they just met, almost 60 percent said they never did and another 35 percent said they rarely did (Jay & Young, 1979). More often, gay women have relationships that last from three to five years; these are based on emotional as well as sexual attraction. About 60 percent of the women in the Jay and Young study noted that they always had sexual relations with someone with whom they were emotionally involved and another 35 percent said this was the case very frequently. Most women, including most gay women, have learned that sexual expression "should" occur in the context of emotional or romantic involvement. Ninety-three percent of 94 gay women in one study said their first homosexual experience was emotional; physical expression came later (Corbett & Morgan, 1983). "Lesbians inflate the traditional female role by becoming even more *romantic* than the norm for women" (Cook et al., 1983, p. 212). So, for gay women the formula is love first; for gay men sex first—just as for their straight counterparts.

While gay female relationships normally last longer than gay male relationships, long-term relationships (20 years or more) are rare. Serial monogamy—one relationship at a time—seems to be the dominant life pattern (Raphael & Robinson, 1980). Loss of romantic love or the inability to sustain the feelings across time seem to be a major reason for the break-up of gay female relationships. Just as strong love feelings brought them together, their absence makes each person in a relationship question why they stay together.

Love relationships between two people of the same gender may be as intense as those between people of the opposite gender.

"I don't know what happened," said one woman. "I just wasn't in love with her anymore. And I couldn't fake my feelings any longer so I left her."

Gay women also are typically denied the experience of rearing children, which can have a stabilizing effect on relationships. Prejudice against their being parents springs from the belief that their children also would become homosexual. But 36 of 37 children reared by lesbian or transsexual parents had heterosexual gender-role preferences (Green, 1978).

Sexual Behavior

Gay people are often perceived solely in terms of their sexual preference. Nongay people may believe they engage in bizarre and unusual sexual activities. However, the sexual behavior of both groups is very similar. Gay people kiss, caress, manually stimulate each other's genitals, orally stimulate each other, and relax after orgasm. But there are some differences in approach to sexual activity. Masters and Johnson (1979), who observed the sexual behavior of committed homosexuals (couples of both genders who had lived together for at least a year), were particularly struck by the amount of time, consideration, and care that gay partners took with each other. Each partner apparently knew how the other wanted to be stimulated and each gave this kind of stimulation to the other. They did not rush to produce an orgasm in their lovers. Rather, they moved slowly from kissing to breast stimulation to genital stroking, holding and caressing each other in loving affection.

The partners also teased each other sexually. Gay men would slowly orchestrate their partner's excitation almost to the point of orgasm but just before ejaculation would stop the stimulation, let the erection subside, and begin again.

Committed partners, both gay men and women, also evidenced more variety in their stimulation. When gay men stimulated their partner's penis, their hands were also manipulating the thighs, anus, scrotum, and lower abdomen. Gay women also were more inventive in providing pleasure for their partners.

> The lesbian approach to cunnilingus started with the breasts, moved to the lower abdomen and thighs, and, in turn, the labia and frequently the vaginal outlet before concentrating on the clitoris. Once focused on the clitoris, the approach varied greatly from forceful stroking to a slow, gentle stimulative technique . . . They inherently knew what pleased and used this knowledge to specific advantage. (Masters & Johnson, 1979, p. 76)

In a study of 127 gay women (Peplau, 1981), 7 in 10 said they almost always experienced climax. In addition, in a study comparing 407 gay with 370 heterosexual women (Coleman, Hoon, & Hoon, 1983), gay women reported having sexual relations more often, more frequent orgasms through masturbation as well as other means of stimulation, more sexual satisfaction and a greater number of partners. The authors believe that gender empathy, women's socialization in self-disclosure and communication, and method of orgasm accounted for the more satisfying sex life reported by gay women.

Although gay men are most likely to engage in fellatio, many also enjoy anal intercourse (77 percent of 1,038 gay men in a study by Spada, 1979). For this activity one of the partners lies face down in a fully prone position or adopts the knee-chest position. After the anal opening and penis are lubricated with saliva or an artificial lubricant like KY jelly, the penis is inserted slowly to keep the anal sphincter relaxed. While the partner receiving the other's penis may experience some discomfort during insertion, it dissipates after full penetration. The other continues thrusting until he ejaculates; rarely does the partner receiving the penis experience ejaculation unless he masturbates while his partner is thrusting.

A less-known and infrequent sexual activity of gay men is **brachioprotic eroticism**, also called "fist fucking" or "handballing," in which one male inserts his hand and forearm in the anus of a partner. While most gay men who participate in this experience enjoy it, there is a considerable risk of puncturing the colon. While unlikely, death can result.

Sexually Transmitted Diseases

Since much of the sexual behavior among gay men is with a variety of partners, the incidence of sexually transmitted diseases is much higher than among heterosexuals. In a study of almost 1,000 gay men (Cook et al., 1983), 30 percent reported having had a sexually transmitted disease in the last five years. Only 1 in 10 of the heterosexual men reported having had an STD. STDs among gays are found in the rectum, penis, and throat.

As discussed in Chapter 12, a new category of diseases, acquired immune deficiency syndrome (AIDS), is more prevalent among homosexuals than among any other category of people. More than 75 percent of AIDS victims have been homosexually active men between 20 and 40 (Mass, 1982). The "acquired" part of the label means that the disease is not inherited; "immune deficiency" means that the body loses its ability to fight infection. The person who contracts AIDS first feels as though he or she might have the flu. But 6 to 18 months later, the person still feels ill. Some AIDS victims develop Kaposi's sarcoma, a cancer of the skin or internal organs. Others may get Pneumocystis carinii pneumonia.

Gay Liberation Movement

As we noted earlier, homosexual people often face severe discrimination and hostility. The **gay liberation movement** provides a way for gay men and women to band together in the hope of changing public attitudes and policy. About 50 percent of gay men and women report that they have worked with other gay people to help the gay cause. About 9,000 are members of the National Gay Task Force (80 Fifth Avenue, Suite 1601, New York 10011, Phone 212-741-5800), the largest organization representing the movement.

Some gay people have organized their own political groups patterning themselves after the Mattachine Society, which is headquartered in New York. Among the services of local chapters are counseling, referral to STD clinics, and the promotion of civil rights legislation for homosexual people. One legislative goal is to remove criminal penalties for private sexual behavior between consenting adults. With the help of other organizations (the American Law Institute, National Committee for Sexual Civil Liberties), some gains are being made. In the early 1980s a New York sodomy law was declared unconstitutional in the case of *People vs. Ronald Onofre*. Mr. Onofre was prosecuted for engaging in consenting sexual conduct with another male in the privacy of his home. He fought the charge and won.

There are many legal issues with which the gay community must deal. Homosexual people are prohibited from immigrating to the United States, kept out of the military (an exception is Sergeant Matlovich who in *Matlovich v. Secretary of the Air Force* was reinstated in the air force by the federal district court in Washington, D.C.), and, in some communities, prohibited from teaching in the public school system. If a teacher's homosexuality becomes public knowledge, the teacher may be dismissed from his or her position on the grounds of "unprofessional conduct" or "moral turpitude."

Gays are taking their dismissals and denials to court. In *Burton v. Cascade School District*, the case of a gay high school teacher was dismissed on the ground of being immoral, the court held that the state statute failed to define immorality and to specify what behavior was prohibited. Another case, *McConnel v. Anderson*, dealt with a suit brought by a gay activist who was rejected for employment as a librarian at the University of Minnesota. The U.S. district court held that to reject an applicant for public employment on the grounds of homosexuality, it must be shown that there is an observable and reasonable relationship between efficiency in the job and homosexuality.

To help ensure against discrimination of homosexuals in employment, housing, and public accommodations, concerned homosexual people launched a Human Rights Campaign to amend the 1964 Civil Rights Act, which guaranteed such rights for blacks, women, and other minorities. While the outcome of this campaign is unknown, it reflects their use of collective action.

Therapy for Homosexuals

Both heterosexuals and homosexual people may seek therapy, but the goals gay people bring to therapy may be different. These goals include developing a heterosexual orientation, feeling good about being homosexual, and improving one's sexual functioning as a gay person.

Goal One: "I Want to Be Heterosexual"

Therapists disagree about whether it is ethical to treat a homosexual who has this goal. Some therapists feel that it is unethical to help a gay person become heterosexual because such help confirms to the gay person that something is wrong with her or him. Since there is evidence to suggest that whatever problems homosexuals experience about their sexual identity are perpetuated by present social structures, some therapists feel that theirm more appropriate concern is the prejudice against homosexuals.

Therapists also feel that the gay person whose goal is to be heterosexual is not free to choose that goal. One therapist suggested that to grow up in a family where the word 'homosexual' was whispered, to play in a playground and hear the words 'faggot' and 'queer,' to go to church and hear of 'sin' and then to college and hear of 'illness,' and finally to the counseling center that promises to 'cure,' is hardly to create an environment of freedom and voluntary choice (Silverstein, 1977). Many therapists believe that gay people who seek to change their sexual orientation are finally accepting society's label that they are abnormal. But other therapists feel that gay people have a right to choose their sexual orientation and that it is the therapist's responsibility to help them achieve their goals. Masters and Johnson (1979) are examples of therapists who accept gay men and women for conversion or reversion to heterosexuality. **Conversion therapy** is for the gay person who has little or no previous heterosexual experience, while **reversion therapy** implies that the person has had previous heterosexual experience and wishes to return to that sexual life style.

The procedures Masters and Johnson use to help gay people become heterosexually oriented include reducing the fear that is associated with heterosexual performance. This is a particular concern for gay men who worry that they will not be able to get an erection with a woman. A major goal is to create conditions of low anxiety. Women partners are instructed not to put pressure on their gay lovers to have an erection. Both partners are taught sensate focus, whereby each partner is expected to give and get pleasure through rubbing, holding, and caressing, which gives the gay man the experience of being close to a woman without feeling pressure to have intercourse. Other procedures include exploration of the person's homosexuality, education about female sexuality, and improvement of the partner's communication.

Over a 10-year period, 9 gay men have been involved in conversion therapy at the Masters and Johnson Institute. Two of these did not convert, giving a failure rate of a little more than 20 percent. Forty-five men have been treated for reversion to heterosexuality with a similar failure rate. Only 3 gay women underwent conversion therapy (zero failure rate) and 10 reversion therapy. Thirty percent of the reversion clients failed to revert (Masters & Johnson, 1979).

Masters and Johnson's work with conversion—reversion clients had two special features. First, they refused about a quarter of those who requested their services. Hence their failure rates were based on working with a very selected population. Second, unlike other therapists, they did not use aversive conditioning procedures. The latter combine electric shock with viewing homosexual-oriented material.

Some homosexual people have completely changed their sexual orientation as a result of participating in a pentecostal church fellowship. "The process of change was not magical, spontaneous, or dramatic," explained the researchers. "Change was embedded in an accepting, evaluative and loving, nonerotic social milieu that provided expectations, ideology, and actual interpersonal experiences and thus promoted what was seen as personal growth into heterosexuality" (Pattison & Pattison, 1980, p. 1559).

Goal Two: "I Want to Feel Better about Being Homosexual"

Most gay people do not want to be heterosexual. But they may come to therapy to improve their self-concept as a homosexual person. Feelings about self may be improved by a combination of procedures. One is to examine the social basis for their negative self-concept—reflection of the attitudes of the heterosexual community, which they are encouraged to reject. Discussing his or her feelings with a therapist (some gay people are more comfortable with a gay therapist) is supplemented by encouraging the gay person to establish close relationships with other gay people who feel good about themselves and who can serve as models.

Systematic desensitization, a procedure used by behavior therapists, is also used to help gay people feel less anxious about the negative attitudes displayed by nongay people. Through simulation the gay learns how to relax (hence how not to be anxious) when in a situation that normally creates anxiety, for example, when someone yells "queer" from a car. After a series of sessions, the gay person is able to stay relaxed when confronted with a number of potentially anxiety-provoking events, such as talking to parents, coworkers, or employers about being gay. He or she learns not to value what others say negatively about gay people.

The gay person also may become involved in a sexual enrichment program "to enhance the self-concept and interpersonal relationships of homosexuals" (Meston, 1979 p. 17). One such program sponsored by the University of Pennsylvania, acknowledges that beyond publications like *The Joy of Gay Sex* and *The Joy of Lesbian Sex* There is little positive nonpornographic information available to gay people. The enrichment program includes 11 hours (Friday evening and all day Saturday) of exercises, films, and small group discussions. An improved self-concept is one of the outcomes. "I learned that there's room for a lot more self-acceptance, that I can actually be gay and still deep down like myself" commented one participant (p. 19).

Goal Three: "I Want to Resolve Some of My Sexual Problems"

Some gay people are committed to the homosexual life style and have positive self-concepts but, nevertheless, are having sexual problems with their lovers. The problems are the same as for their heterosexual counterparts. For gay men this means impotence and premature ejaculation; for women, not being able to have an orgasm. The techniques used to treat gay sex dysfunctions are similar to those used for heterosexual dysfunctions. Although these were discussed in greater detail in Chapter 11, a few comments are relevant here. Masters and Johnson (1979) emphasized the contextual nature of sex and said that many of the successful resolutions of gay sexual problems were due to a loving, patient, cooperative partner. In addition, guilt, fear of performance, and anxiety seem to be common barriers to sexual functioning regardless of sexual orientation. Through cognitive exploration, sensate focus, graduated assignments, and desensitization, most of these barriers can be removed. Of 84 gays treated for sexual dysfunction by Masters and Johnson only 7 percent were not successful in resolving their sexual problems.

Sample

Bisexuality

Kinsey (1953) emphasized that a person's sexual orientation is rarely entirely heterosexual or homosexual but can best be viewed on a continuum as ranging from exclusive heterosexuality, through various degrees of **bisexuality**, to exclusive homosexuality. One researcher estimated that there are 40–50 million bisexual people in the United States, including 30–45 percent of the male population and 15–35 percent of the female population (Klein, 1978).

Bisexuality is a variable phenomenon and, therefore, it is difficult to generalize about people with this sexual orientation. MacDonald (1982) notes some of these variations.

- Bisexual people may have a preference for one gender over the other as indicated on the Kinsey scale—a strong homosexual preference or a strong heterosexual preference.
- Bisexual people may have no preference for one gender over the other (about 22 percent of all bisexual people fall into this category, according to estimates from the available literature). They are referred to as 50:50 bisexuals.
- Bisexual people may prefer a number of different partners, be monogamous (prefer one partner at a time), or be monogamous with one gender and polygamous with the other.

The backgrounds of bisexual people also vary. Some women report that they were exclusively heterosexual before they engaged in homosexual sex (Blumstein & Schwarts, 1976). Others say their first homosexual encounter was a response to a close relationship with a female friend that spilled over into a sexual relationship. "We just cared so much for each other that one night we started holding each other, which led to kissing and the rest. We weren't ashamed, just confused. 'Were we gay?' we wondered." Other women report that their homosexual behavior was situational (it occurred when they were in prison) or it was part of their job (prostitution).

Heterosexual men who try gay sex and find they like it give similar explanations of their behavior. Some men say they always felt they were gay and they had to try it out. Some remain partly in the heterosexual world to keep their employers, partners, or wives from being suspicious. Others who are more ambivalent about their homosexual experiences say they continue their heterosexual relations in the hope that their desire for having sexual relations with their own gender will go away.

Whereas some people drift into bisexuality from a previously heterosexual life style, others come from a homosexual life style. Gay women who have sexual relations with men say they first did so to see what it was like so they would know for themselves. Although the man may have been a pickup, more often it was a male friend with whom sex seemed natural. Gay men report similar motivations—to test out heterosexual sex and as an extension of a friendship they already have with a woman.

Having a liberal, humanistic view of life is a predisposing condition for bisexuality among some people. "They feel that everyone should be free and able to love everyone in a perfect erotic utopia" (Blumstein & Schwartz, 1977, p. 42).

Finally, the life styles that express bisexuality vary. Some bisexual people randomly alternate the gender of their sexual partners. One woman said that when she goes to a bar to pick up a partner, she is not sure when she goes in the door if whe will be walking out with a woman or man. (Woody Allen said that bisexuality doubles a person's chances for a date on Saturday night.)

Another pattern is to have concurrent heterosexual and homosexual relationships such as the gay man who lives with his lover but regularly visits his girlfriend at her apartment where they make love. "I'll admit, it's not easy for me to switch from relating sexually to a man at night and to a woman during the day but it's what I'm into doing for now."

Some bisexuals are married. More than one-third of 3,737 bisexuals in one study were married (Cook et al., 1983). One gay husband said, "Leading a double life adds some drama to my existence. But I should also say that if I didn't have sex with men when I'm away, my marriage wouldn't have lasted. I need to satisfy myself with men. There's no way I could give that up. I knew that when I got married. My family satisfies my emotional needs, but I have to have sex with men (Malone, 1980, p. 144).

Sometimes both spouses are bisexual. One such couple were Barry and Alice who were married for more than six years and had one child (Kohn & Matusow, 1980). Both Barry and Alice agreed that their relationship was primary to their lives but that each needed emotional and sexual contact with members of their own gender.

A less-frequent pattern is to move from one orientation to another and back again. This may be from heterosexual to gay to heterosexual or from gay to heterosexual to gay while spending years in each stage.

Summary

Homosexuality is becoming a more acceptable topic for public discussion in our society. Gay people who represent about twenty million Americans, are often subject to severe social and economic discrimination, informally and by statute. Such discrimination has it basis in traditional religious dogma which views only procreative sex as legitimate. Sexism also contributes to homosexual prejudice by viewing any man who is effeminate as bad.

Answers as to the cause of homosexuality vary. Some researchers say it is the result of negative parent–child relationships in which the mother is overprotective and the father rejecting (such a combination is supposed to be predictive of male homosexuality). Others speak of childhood experiences like being punished for acting heterosexually or seduced by an older, same-gender adult. Still others feel that gayness is the result of genetic factors or hormonal imbalance. Many gay people feel their sexual orientation was freely chosen, but some think it is innate or resulted from negative childhood experiences.

Certain aspects of the gay life are different from heterosexual life. Some differences are in acknowledging one's sexual preference (coming out), employment, and relationships. Coming out risks rejection by family and friends and discrimination in employment. Gay relationships tend to be less stable than heterosexual ones, partly because gay relationships have few social or economic supports and partly because of a desire for sexual freedom. Most gay people engage in the same sexual behaviors enjoyed by heterosexual people. Also, they seem to be better lovers as evidenced by the care, time, and consideration they demonstrate in their lovemaking.

Sexually transmitted diseases are particularly prevalent among gay males with multiple sex partners. AIDS, acquired immune deficiency syndrome, results in the person's body losing its ability to fight infection and disease. The result is death within three years for most AIDS victims. Currently, there is no cure.

The gay liberation movement provides a way for gays to nationalize their influence with the hope of changing discrimination policies and prejudicial attitudes. The most visible organization of the movement is the National Gay Task Force, which consists of about 9,000 members. Local gay political groups offer counseling, referral to STD clinics, and promotion of civil rights legislation for homosexual people.

Homosexual people who seek therapy often have one of three goals: to become heterosexual, to feel better about being homosexual, or to resolve sexual problems. Some therapists will not accept homosexual people for conversion therapy since to do so is to agree that they are abnormal and need curing. Other therapists, such as Masters and Johnson, feel that if the homosexual wants to convert or revert to heterosexuality, it is the responsibility of the therapist to assist in achieving that goal.

About forty to fifty million Americans are bisexual. Bisexuality is a variable phenomenon. Bisexual people differ in gender preference, number of partners, sexual backgrounds, and lifestyle. About a third of the bisexuals in one study were married.

Key Terms

homosexuality	gay liberation movement
lesbian	conversion therapy
homophobia	reversion therapy
coming out	systematic desensitization
cruising	bisexuality
brachioprotic eroticism	

Issues in Debate and Future Directions

Homosexuality is an emotionally laden topic and there are numerous controversies surrounding it. After examining several of them, we look at the future of the gay life style.

Is Homosexuality Natural?

Homosexual sexual behaviors are often viewed as unnatural because they are not procreative. But it should be kept in mind that the vast majority of heterosexual lovemaking acts are not procreative and by this definition are unnatural too. Some heterosexuals also assume that penile-vaginal is natural and any variation in the use of such anatomy borders on the unnatural. Yet studies of animals suggest a need to reexamine beliefs about what is natural. Kinsey et al., as well as other researchers (Gadpaile, 1980), observed that homosexual contacts between lower animals occur among both males and females. Rabbits, rats, cattle, lions, sheep, goats, and monkeys have been observed mounting those of their same sex.

These animal studies suggest that much sexual behavior among humans may be more a result of social learning than biological programming. Our society punishes homosexual interests and behaviors while it rewards heterosexual ones. The result is that people not only engage in the heterosexual life style but also say they prefer it. But suppose our society rewarded us for homosexual interests and punished us for heterosexual ones? Would more people be willing to express the homosexual part of themselves? Open and socially approved homosexuality among *some* Athenians, Spartans, and Romans in previous centuries suggests that the answer is maybe. However, heterosexuality has been the encouraged norm in every society past and present (Diamond & Karlen, 1980).

Do Most Homosexual People Wish They Were Heterosexual?

We might assume that because homosexual people live in a hostile social environment, they would be unhappy with their plight and wish they were straight. They seem to feel otherwise. When 1,000 gay women and more than 4,000 gay men were asked, "If you could take a pill to make you straight, would you do it?" none of the women and only 6 percent of the men answered "yes" (Jay & Young, 1979). Although 5 percent of the women and about 20 percent of the men said they were "not sure," the majority of these gay people enjoyed their lives and did not wish to change them.

One gay male talked about the benefits of his life style.

> . . . it permits you to be a full human. By definition, you do not fit society's picture of the real man or the real woman. Once the program is thus flawed, it makes it much easier to go ahead and explore options supposedly reserved for 'the opposite sex.' As a man you can be tender, intuitive, warm, sensitive, spontaneous, uninhibited, colorful, emotional, or even flirtatious. As a woman you are free to be strong, determined, reliable, forbearing, dependable, tough, smart, and even aggressive . . . And the range of relating is increased for gay people. You are free to relate in depth to anyone, regardless of gender. (Clark, 1977 pp. 49–50.)

Is Homosexuality Pathological?

It is sometimes believed that homosexuality is a disease—that it is a pathological condition. In

1973 the American Psychiatric Association voted to reclassify homosexuality from a psychiatric disorder to a "sexual orientation disturbance." The latter suggests that some homosexuals may have difficulties adjusting to their sexual preference as a result of the prejudice directed toward them by our society. But this is considerably different from suggesting that homosexuality per se is pathological. The American Psychological Association adopted a similar resolution two years later. Subsequent studies continue to confirm the lack of pathological disturbance among homosexuals. When gay men and heterosexual men were compared on a number of psychological characteristics, neither group was more depressed than the other (Siegelman, 1978). However, the gay men were more tender minded (emotionally sensitive), submissive (dependent, suggestible), and anxious (worried, guilty, excitable) than the heterosexual men. The greater tendency on the part of gay men to have these characteristics is probably the result of the prejudice displayed by the majority culture. In another study of 698 individuals from diverse ethnic backgrounds (Nurius, 1983), sexual orientation was not a good predictor or explanation of depression, low self-esteem, marital discord, or sexual discord.

Some evidence suggests that gay men adapt more comfortably to living in a heterosexual world as they get older. One study of 100 older gay men (Berger, 1980) revealed that few experienced serious depression, anxiety, or lack of self-acceptance. Most reported feeling good about themselves and their relationships. The stereotype that old gay men are isolated and unhappy did not hold.

How do gay and heterosexual women compare? Siegelman (1979) noted there were no differences in the tendency of the two groups to be depressed, anxious, alienated, dependent, nurturant, or neurotic. However, gay women were more goal directed and self-accepting. These qualities may be were a result of the unmarried status and greater independence of gay women.

Future Directions

In the future gay men and women will win increased acceptance. There have already been changes in therapeutic attitudes and laws. An increasing number of therapists are assisting homosexuals in enjoying their life styles rather than suggesting that they need to revert or convert to heterosexuality. In addition to viewing homosexuality as an appropriate gender orientation, the American Psychological Association Task Force on Homosexuality recommended that no APA conventions be held in states that had failed to repeal legislation restricting sexual activity between consenting adults or in cities that had not adopted antidiscrimination policies.

Legal decisions favorable to gay people have included the right of a 32-year-old Manhattan man to adopt his 43-year-old homosexual lover with whom he had been living for three years. Although New York does not recognize homosexual marriages, the adoption will facilitate inheritance. Further, a 27-year-old Riverside, California, homosexual male was permitted by the superior court to adopt a 17-year-old boy. Such legal gains will continue and eventually include the right of gay people to marry.

But social acceptance will be slow. Our society is deeply committed to heterosexual monogamy. Most people have been taught to abhor alternatives to woman—man sexuality. Just as resistance to full participation by blacks in society was first muted by legislative changes, followed by a much slower attitudinal change, so will the breakdown of prejudice against gay people follow legal change.

Chapter Fifteen

Abuses of Sexuality

*After I was raped at knifepoint,
I became an anxious, fearful
person. I still wake up at night
with the dream that it is
happening again. I still don't
feel comfortable when my
partner touches me.*

A RAPE VICTIM

Chapter Fifteen

Sex is neither good nor bad. Like alcohol, its appropriateness depends on how it is used, by whom, with whom, in what context, and with what consequences. Sex between two adults who love each other and enjoy sharing sexual pleasures is viewed by most people as an appropriate expression of sexuality. But most people would also agree that rape, incest, sexual harassment, and prostitution are abuses of sexuality. We examine these abuses in this chapter.

Rape

Rape is forced sexual relations against a person's will. Although rape is often thought of as forcing a woman to have sexual intercourse, rape may also involve fellatio, anal intercourse, or penetration of her vagina or anus with an instrument. One rape victim said that her attacker became impotent during the rape so he "shoved a beer bottle up my vagina."

Men are also raped. They may be forced by another man to engage in fellatio as the active or passive partner or in anal sex as the passive partner. However, male rape is less frequent than female rape. The remainder of this discussion focuses on female rape (see Table 15.1).

Rape is an act of violence, in which the man displays his power over a woman and expresses his hostility toward her. It is not an act of passion. Men do not rape to experience sexual pleasure. Little girls as well as great-grandmothers are raped, emphasizing that rape is an act of aggression, not sex.

Rape is the most brutal abuse of sexuality. Part of this abuse may grow out of the exposure—and implicit sanction—sexual violence is given in our society. When two researchers examined all the cartoons and pictures in *Playboy* and *Penthouse* magazines over a five-year period, they found that 10 percent of the cartoons and 5 percent of the pictures depicted sexual violence in the form of rape, sadomasochism, or exploitative, coercive relations (Malamuth & Spinner, 1980). There is some evidence for the negative effects of viewing sexual violence. In one study (Donnerstein, 1980), 120 men who viewed an

Samples
Controls

Table 15.1 Five Rape Myths

Myth 1:	Women secretly want to be raped.
Truth:	Rape is a violent, brutal, degrading act. Women want to be desired, not raped.
Myth 2:	The majority of rapes are committed by black males who don't know their victim.
Truth:	Most rapes are by white males who have a relationship with the woman they rape.
Myth 3:	The primary motive for rape is sexual gratification.
Truth:	Expressing hostility and aggression are the principle motives for rape.
Myth 4:	Most rape events are reported and the rapist is eventually convicted.
Truth:	Only a few rapes are reported and only a small portion of these are convicted.
Myth 5:	Most rapists kill their victims.
Truth:	Only 5 percent of women are killed when they are raped.

aggressive—erotic movie became more aggressive toward women (but not against men) after the film, evidenced by their willingness to give women an electric shock when they had the opportunity to do so. In another study (Zillmann & Bryant, 1982), massive exposure to pornography resulted in a loss of compassion toward women as rape victims and toward women in general.

Rape also has a cultural base. In one study of 95 societies (Sanday, 1981), rape was either absent or rare in almost half (47 percent) of the cases. In these societies, for example, among the Ashanti of West Africa, women tend to have equal status with men. Societies in which the genders are viewed as less equal are more rape prone. Among the Gusii of Kenya, "normal heterosexual intercourse between Gusii males and females is conceived as an act in which a man overcomes the resistance of a woman and causes her pain" (p.10).

Incidence

Although the number of reported rapes in the United States is about 80,000 per year, it is estimated that the number of actual rapes is up to 10 times higher. There are a number of reasons why women may not report rape. Some are in shock. Others may feel ashamed of what has happened. When a woman is raped by her partner, she may relabel the rape event—"He just couldn't help himself"—and deny to herself that she was actually raped. Still other women do not report being raped because they feel the laws do not protect the rape victim. In some states a woman cannot prosecute a man for rape if she dated him in the last year, lives with him, or is married to him. Women also may prefer to avoid the emotional trauma of a court trial.

Rapists: Acquaintance and Stranger

Most unreported rapes are committed by someone the woman knows—her date, boyfriend, fiancee, live-in companion, or husband. Known as "ac-

Most rapes are
committed by
someone the
woman knows.

quaintance rapists," these men rape without detection or prosecution. A college woman reported the following experience of being raped by her boyfriend.

● Last spring, I met this guy and a relationship started which was great. One year later, he raped me. The term was almost over and we would not be able to spend much time together during the summer. Therefore, we planned to go out to eat and spend time together.

After dinner we drove to a park. I did not mind or suspect anything for we had done this many times. Then he asked me into the back seat. I got into the back seat with him because I trusted him and he said he wanted to be close to me as we talked. He began talking. He told me that he was tired of always pleasing me and not getting a reward. Therefore, he was going to "make love to me" whether I wanted to or not. I thought he was joking so I asked him to stop playing. He told me he was serious and after looking at him closely, I knew he was serious. I began to plead with him not to have sex with me. He did not listen. He began to tear my clothes off and confine me so that I could not move. All this time I was fighting him. At one time I managed to open the door, but he threw me back into the seat, hit me, then he got on me and raped me. After he was satisfied, he stopped, told me to get dressed and stop crying. He said he was sorry it had to happen that way.

He brought me back to the dorm and expected me to kiss him good night. He didn't think he had done anything wrong.

Before this happened, I loved this man very much, but afterward I felt great hatred for him and I wished I had the courage to kill him.

My life has not been the same since that night. I do not trust men as I once did, nor do I feel completely comfortable when I'm with my present boyfriend. He wants to know why I back off when he tries to be intimate with me. However, right now I can't tell him, as he knows the guy who raped me. ●

Rapists may also be husbands. One report states that about one in seven husbands have forced their respective wives to have sexual relations with them (Russell, 1982). This may have included not only intercourse but also other types of sexual activities the wife did not want to engage in, most often fellatio and anal intercourse (Groth & Gary, 1981). In most states, the law does not consider a husband forcing his wife to have intercourse as rape. Historically, the penalties for rape were based on property right laws designed to protect a man's property (wife or daughter) from forcible rape by other men. Hence, a husband "taking" his own property was not considered rape. Although most states still do not recognize marital rape, some do. James Creitien of Salem, Massachusetts, was convicted and sentenced to three to five years in prison for raping his wife. Husbands who rape their wives often abuse them in other ways—verbally and physically. Rape is one part of a pattern of violence.

In addition to boyfriends and husbands, rapists may also be strangers—young or old, black or white, single or married. They often have criminal records and have been drinking alcohol at the time of the rape. The stranger as a rapist is the most likely to be arrested.

Other Facts about Rape

Most rapes occur in the individual's home. Some rapes are single incidents; others may be repeated over a period of hours. Some rapists have weapons and threaten the woman with her life if she resists; 5 percent of rape victims are killed. Others do not have weapons but threaten injury or physical beating. Although some rapes are impulsive, most (70 percent) are planned. In the latter case, the rapist usually watches a particular woman over a period of time, learns her schedule, and zeros in on her. Most rapes are intraracial—both parties belong to the same race.

How to Avoid Rape

Not all rape attempts are successful. In about 40 percent of the cases, the woman is able to thwart her attacker (McIntyre, Myint, & Curtis, 1979). What can be learned from these escapes? What works and what does not?

Avoidance

Of course, the best way to prevent a rape is to avoid situations in which it is likely to occur. First, this means not being out alone at night. Also, being with a child is just as bad as being alone, as the rapist may use the child to get compliance from the mother: "If you don't do as I say, I'll kill the baby." Hitchhiking should be avoided. Opening the door to strangers and talking to strangers are also dangerous. If a stranger comes to a woman's door and asks to use the phone to call an ambulance, she should not let him in but offer to call the ambulance for him.

If a strange man calls and asks, "Is your husband there?" the woman should reply, "Yes, he's in the shower. If you leave your name and number, I'll have him return your call when he's through." If she says, "No, I don't have a husband," or "He's not here," she has told the would-be-rapist what he wants to know—she is alone.

Taking these precautions may help to minimize the likelihood of a rape, but rape can still occur. What can a woman do when she is confronted with a rape situation? There are several alternatives, none of which are foolproof but all of which work some of the time.

Words

Trying to talk the rapist out of his plan is one alternative. There are a number of different strategies.

1. "Get the hell away from me." (Attack)
2. "You don't really want to do this. Let's be friends and talk." (Interpersonal liaison)
3. "My boyfriend will be here any moment." (Distraction)
4. "Please don't. I've got cancer (I've got a tumor, I'm pregnant)." (Disease, illness)
5. "I'll kill myself if you do this; I won't be able to live with myself." (Self-punitiveness)

6. "I'm going to be married Saturday. I've never had sex before. Please don't do this to me." (Virginity)

7. "It's wrong to do this. You'll go to hell if you do this." (Moral appeal)*

Which of these tactics have the highest chance of success? Convicted rapists were asked to select from the preceding statements those they felt would reduce the chance of their raping a woman (Brodsky, 1976). Verbal attack and outright refusal were the tactics most often chosen. "In my case," said one rapist, "It could have been stopped if the woman would have put up a little more struggle . . . I was just as scared as she was" (p. 86). Other rapists said that the woman's attempt to talk them out of it would have helped "by talking to me and telling me I did not want to really do this and by showing no fear . . . (p. 86).

But other rapists said verbal attack would only make them more violent, and some said listening to a woman plead would intensify their excitement.

Physical Resistance

Fighting, screaming, and running might reduce the chance of being raped. They may also increase the chance of injury (McIntyre et al., 1979). A woman who screams, kicks, and bites may, indeed, discourage a rapist since the encounter may be more trouble than he anticipated. But her screaming may also frighten him and cause him to knock her unconscious to stop her from screaming.

The combination of physical resistance, trying to flee, and screaming was the most frequent strategy of 51 women who reported that they had been attacked but had avoided being raped (Bart & O'Brien, in press). In contrast, 43 other women (who were attacked but who were unable to avoid being raped) said they used pleading as their primary strategy. The researchers, who interviewed both sets of women, designated one woman who had successfully avoided being raped as "Queen of the Negotiators." Her experience follows.

● She awoke to find herself effectively pinned beneath the covers of her bed by a naked armed man who was straddling her. She made an attempt to reach the phone, but agreed to give up this bid for assistance in return for his removing his knife from her throat. She told the assailant she was menstruating and feigned embarrassment at the thought of removing her tampon in his presence. He agreed to allow her to go to the bathroom. However, once there, he would not allow her to close the door completely, which thwarted her plan to close the door and scream for help.

*Reprinted by permission of the publisher, from *Sexual Assault*, edited by Marcia J. Walker and Stanley L. Brodsky (Lexington, Mass.: Lexington Books, D. C. Heath and Company, Copyright 1976, D. C. Heath and Company).

Returning to the bedroom, he began to fondle her breasts and perform digital penetration of her vagina. In response to this act, she feigned the beginnings of hysteria in an effort to make him think she was going "crazy." Finding this strategy unsuccessful, she asked him if she could smoke some hash in an effort to relax. The hash pipe was described as being "big and heavy" and initially she planned on using it as a weapon; however, she was unable to work up "enough nerve." After pretending to smoke for awhile, she asked if it would be all right if she went to the kitchen for a beer, as the "hash" had not had the desired effect. He refused and at this time shoved her on her back on the bed.

She responded by jumping and throwing him on his back, grabbing his hair and yanking his head as hard as she could over the footboard of the bed. At this point, the assailant began to whimper. She reprimanded him for being "pushy" and for hurting her, and once again made her request for a beer and cigarette. The assailant complied, but retrieved his knife and followed her to the kitchen, pressing the knife to her back. . . . As they were returning to the bedroom with the requested items, she feigned anger at their return to the initial scenario—being in the bedroom with an armed man. In order to appease her, he placed the knife on a bookcase in the living room . . .

After smoking her cigarette . . . she clutched her stomach and feigned nausea and ran out of the room. When he realized that she wasn't heading for the bathroom, he began to pursue her, but by this time she had reached the knife. He reached for a nearby lamp, which he intended to use as a weapon, but discovered that it was far too light to be useful. At this point, she was moving toward the door and he said, "All right, that's it, I'm leaving. I was gonna try and be nice, but I'm just leaving. Forget it." She ran out the back door and screamed for help. He made a couple of attempts to run out after her, but every time he did, she'd raise the knife to threaten him. Finally, he made a dash out the door, still naked from the waist down, carrying his pants. Less than a week after the attack, he parked his car behind her building after following her home from work. At this time, she flagged down a police car and he was apprehended.* ●

———————————————

As this woman's experience indicates, strategies to avoid rape depend on the situation. In general, if the attacker is a stranger with no weapon, a combination of words and physical resistance may be effective. If the attacker has a weapon (as he does in 60 percent of reported rape cases), physical resistance should be used with caution, if at all. If the person is an acquaintance, the woman should demand that the person leave her alone and physically resist any advance. The chance of an acquaintance physically harming a woman is much less than that of a stranger.

Most rape events are sudden and the woman often does not have the time to think out strategies of avoidance. Doing whatever she can may include doing nothing since the goal is to survive the event.

*Pauline B. Bart and Patricia O'Brien. "Women Who Stopped Their Rapes" *Signs* (in press).

Effects of Rape on the Woman

Rape is a traumatic experience. The most devastating aspect of rape is not genital contact but the woman's sense of mental violation. The woman who felt that her environment was safe and predictable, other people were trustworthy, and she was competent and autonomous is transformed into someone who is fearful of her surroundings, suspicious of other people, and lacks confidence in her ability to control her life. She is vulnerable.

After the initial shock, the victim may be plagued with concerns. Could she have prevented the rape? Is she in some way responsible for it? Is she pregnant? Will she get a sexually transmitted disease? How will her boyfriend or husband react? Should she tell the police? If she does, will the rapist kill her? Her sleep is affected. She has recurrent flashbacks of the event and recreates it repeatedly in her mind.

Rape trauma is the term for the acute disorganization a woman feels after she has been raped (Burgess & Holmstrom, 1976). Some are immobilized from the physical beating they sustained. They may be extremely fearful of a repeated attack and as a consequence change their job or living situation. Most women eventually adjust to having been raped, but adjustment takes time. In a study of 20 rape victims, follow-ups at 1 month, 6 months, and 12 months revealed that they were more anxious, fearful, suspicious, and confused than nonvictims, although there was a steady improvement over the 12-month span (Kilpatrick, Resick, & Veronen, 1981).

Rape victims need not suffer their experience alone but can contact a rape crisis center immediately.

Many communities have rape crisis centers that offer counseling to the victim. Such counseling seems particularly helpful to the woman who feels shocked, humiliated, and guilty. Anonymity is assured and contacting the police is at the victim's option. "We try to let the person know we care about her and that she isn't responsible for what happened," said one rape counselor. "If the victim wants to contact the police we will go with her but we don't encourage her to do anything she's uncomfortable doing."

Sometimes it is necessary to counsel the boyfriend, husband, father, or brother of the victim to help them cope with their own guilt and anger. "If they don't blame the victim, they want to beat somebody up. These are feelings that must be dealt with," said one rape counselor.

Consequences of Rape for the Rapist

In most cases, the rapist is neither caught nor convicted. Most often he is not caught because the rape is not reported. But of those rapes that are reported and where the alleged rapist is apprehended, few cases come to trial. Of nearly 1,000 rapes·that were reported to the Denver police, less than 5 percent of the accused were brought to trial and only a few were convicted (Sheppard, Giacinti, & Tjaden, 1976). In *Against Our Will*, Susan Brownmiller (1975) says that men rape because they can get away with it. Rapists often escape conviction with the help of a lawyer who contends that the rape complaint is "unfounded" and requests that the police stop prosecution procedures. A rape complaint may be unfounded if the woman has a weak case, for example, if she was intoxicated at the time, delayed reporting the alleged attack, refused to submit to a medical examination, had a previous relationship with the rapist, and if there is a lack of physical evidence to document that the rape occurred (LeGrand, 1977).

Evidence that helps to ensure a conviction includes proof of penetration (vaginal tears, sperm), force (body bruises, a weapon, torn clothing), or an eyewitness to the rape.

Convicted rapists may be sentenced to prison and/or required to submit to some form of treatment designed to "reduce, inhibit, or eliminate the sexual assaultiveness of the offender" (Groth, 1979 p. 215). Treatment may include psychotherapy, education, and chemotherapy. Psychotherapy is the most common and involves individual and group therapy to assist the offender in exploring his psychological makeup. He is also encouraged to learn more appropriate social skills in relating to women.

Education includes providing basic information in human sexuality, female—male relationships, and, where necessary, sex therapy with the offender's wife or partner.

Another alternative is chemotherapy. Depo-Provera, an antiandrogen hormone, reduces interest in sexual behavior. With weekly injections the offender loses any desire to commit sexual assault (Groth, 1979). Treatment through hormones, tranquilizers, and counseling were discussed in the Issues in Debate section of Chapter 13.

Incest

Incest is defined as sexual relations between close relatives such as father—daughter, mother—son, and brother—sister. "Sexual relations" usually implies intercourse, but it may also refer to genital stimulation by hand or mouth, and "close relations" may also include stepparents and stepsiblings.

Incest, particularly parent—child incest, is an abuse of sexuality in that it is an abuse of power and authority. A child is not in a position to consent to a sex act instigated by an adult. The following describes the experience of a woman who as a child was forced to have sexual relations with her father.

● I was around 6 years old when I was sexually abused by my father. He was not drinking at that time; therefore, he had a clear mind as to what he was doing. On looking back, it seemed so well planned. For some reason, my father wanted me to go with him to the woods behind our house to help him saw wood for the night. I went without any question. Once we got there, he looked around for a place to sit and wanted me to sit down with him. In doing so, he said, "Susan, I want you to do something for daddy." I said, "What's that daddy?" He went on to explain that "I want you to lie down and we are going to play mama and daddy." Being a child, I said "OK" thinking it was going to be fun. I don't know what happened because I can't remember if there was any pain or whatever. I was threatened not to tell and in remembering how he beat my mother, I didn't want the same treatment. It happened approximately two other times. I remember not liking this at all. Since I couldn't tell mama, I came to the conclusion it was wrong and I was not going to let it happen again.

But what could I do? Until age 18, I was constantly on the run, hiding from him when I had to stay home by myself with him, staying out of his way so he wouldn't touch me by hiding in the corn fields all day long, under the house, in the barns, and so on until my mother got back home, then getting punished by her for not doing the tasks she had assigned to me that day. It was a miserable life growing up in that environment. ●

Incidence

Of nearly 800 respondents in one study (Finkelhor, 1979), almost 15 percent of the women and 10 percent of the men reported that they had had sexual contact with a parent or sibling. When uncles, aunts, grandparents, and cousins were included, about 25 percent of both sexes reported some contact. These sexual experiences may have occurred only once or many times over a period of years.

Studies on larger populations indicate that about 4 percent of Americans have experienced incest (Gebhard et al., 1965), mostly between siblings (Finkelhor, 1980), with petting the typical behavior. Incest occurs in all social classes and at all economic levels (Forward & Buck, 1980). Rarely is incest reported to the police.

The Incest Taboo

The **incest taboo** which apparently is universal, prohibits sexual interaction between related individuals. In many countries, and in all states of the United States, this social prohibition is backed by legal sanctions.

Several reasons for this taboo have been advanced. As we noted, in societies like ours that are concerned with the protection of children, parent—child sexual contact is strongly condemned. The possibility of hereditary defects in the offspring of incestuous unions is another reason. The incidence of mortality and physical and mental handicaps are significantly higher in these children (Renvoize, 1978). If a father with a mental handicap sires a child with his daughter, their offspring is much more likely to have a mental handicap than if either the daughter or the father had a child with someone else. The prohibition of incest also has an economic basis. If family members are allowed to mate and marry, their resources are kept among themselves and no new resources are brought into the family unit. When a person marries outside the family, he or she brings to the marriage the resources of their respective families, generating new resources.

The incest taboo may serve to buttress parental authority. If parents have intercourse with their offspring, their authority may be weakened, and parental authority is necessary for family order. Sexual relations among family members might also result in sexual competition for partners. The ensuing jealousy and guilt could create discord within the family unit and disrupt family functioning.

Why do people sometimes break the incest taboo? Internalized social constraints are supposed to operate, but sometimes they do not. Several factors may contribute to a breakdown in such constraints—alcoholism, an unhappy marriage, or overcrowded living conditions. A history of aggressive behavior or a sociopathic personality may also characterize those engaging in incest. The sociopath has been referred to as a person without a conscience. Whereas the typical person would feel overwhelmed with guilt at having sex with a child, the sociopath has no such reaction.

Who Has Incest?

The most frequent combinations of incestuous relations are brother–sister and father–daughter. Mother–son incest is less common.

Brother–Sister

This is the most common form of incest (Finkelhor, 1979). It also has been the least visible. Siblings are peers. Their incest may seem natural to them and they may wonder why there is a taboo against it.

Whether brother–sister incest is a problem for siblings depends on a number of factors. If the siblings are young, of the same age, have an isolated sexual episode, engage only in exploratory, nonintercourse behavior, and both consent to the behavior, there may be only limited harm. But a change in any of these factors increases the chance that such incest will have negative consequences for future heterosexual relationships.

If the siblings are young (4 to 8), they will have had less exposure to the idea that sexual behavior among siblings is inappropriate. Although they may have vague feelings that their parents would not approve of their sexual behavior, they will probably not feel the guilt usually associated with such behavior. As they grow older, they may relabel their former behavior as "child's play," thus minimizing its impact.

Being of the same age will minimize the negative consequences of sibling incest. Although in most cases the siblings are of the same age, it is not uncommon for an older brother to seduce his younger sister into having intercourse with him. It is less common for an older sister to become sexually involved with a younger brother. A difference in age increases the chance that the sexual relationship will be exploitative.

A childhood sexual experience with a sibling that occurs once or twice is also less devastating than a series of such experiences that occur over a number of years. Most such experiences are limited, but some develop into a pattern and continue for years.

The nature of the sexual behavior is also important. Playing doctor or strip poker or "you show me, I'll show you" probably has minimal impact on siblings. Siblings learn that these are common childhood experiences. Intercourse may increase the potential for negative effects. In one study (Finkelhor, 1980), 18 percent of brother–sister incest experiences in which the siblings were both over the age of 13 involved intercourse. Half of the reactions to the experiences were positive, half were negative.

Consent is important if the negative consequences are to be minimal. Particularly when one sibling is older than the other, a brother or sister may use blackmail, bribery, or force to get the sibling to comply, as in the case of Tom, 14, and his sister Lisa, age 11.

● Tom pushed her down on the floor, hitting her, tearing her clothes, and trying to rape her. She prevented penetration, but Tom masturbated while he pressed against her thighs. Even though she could keep him from having intercourse, he continued to feel her up and masturbate against her several times over the next few years. The storm in Tom seemed to pass as he got older and he never mentioned what he had done to Lisa. She did not mention it either, although lasting emotional scars were left. (Justice & Justice, 1979, p. 105) ●

Father–Daughter

Father–daughter incest is second in frequency, but it has received the most attention. Irate mothers and guilt-ridden children make such incest visible by alerting professionals at mental health centers, various "hotline" services, or the police. Incest may begin by affectionate cuddling between father and daughter, which is often enjoyable for both. Over time the cuddling may involve more extended bodily contact, stroking of the genitals, or intercourse. Both father and daughter usually give each other mixed signals. Both may enjoy the physical contact but feel that it is wrong. One woman wrote of the ambivalence she experienced as a child:

● Why I did it I'm not sure. I think partly because there was still that need for affection or whatever. Partly because it felt good. Usually I would just lie there and accept his advances and feel bad about it. (Finkelhor, 1979, p. 66) ●

As with this woman, ambivalence may result in the daughter continuing to participate in sexual activity with her father. Not only may she derive attention and affection from the relationship but also she may develop a sense of power over her father. She may even demand gifts as the price for her silence. If her parents have an unhappy relationship (this is usually the case), she may enjoy her role as the "little wife."

Father–daughter incest may begin by force. There are a few cases of fathers having raped their daughters when they were very small—even babies—injuring them badly (Renvoize, 1978). Baby incest is difficult for the wife to overlook, but she may sanction the sexual relations of her husband and daughter in her to desire to preserve the family unit. One woman said that her "nerves" were about to "snap" because her husband and daughter were sexually involved. But she did not say anything about it because if she did, her husband, on whom she depended economically, might leave her alone with the children. "At least," she said, "his playing around is kept in the family."

Of all father–daughter incest, that among stepparents and stepchildren is the most common (Finkelhor, 1979), probably because of a weaker taboo against social than biological incest. Also, stepfathers may not have seen their daughters as infants and may have less paternal feeling toward them. A stepfather may view his stepdaughter as a desirable woman rather than as his little girl grown up.

Mother–Son

The least frequent variety of incest is between mother and son. This rarely involves intercourse, but is usually confined to various stimulating behaviors. The mother may continue to bathe her son long after he is capable of caring for himself, during which she stimulates him sexually. Later she may masturbate her son to ejaculation (Renvoize, 1978).

The mother may also sleep with her son. Although no specific sexual contact may occur, she may sleep in the nude—sexually provocative behavior that is also stimulating. In some cases, there is sexual contact.

● Mrs. M. and her 15-year-old son had slept together since the father left home seven years earlier. Under the guise of "teaching" [the boy] sex education, Mrs. M. masturbated her son and asked that he in turn do the same for her. She had sex relations with him a number of times, and was reported by an uncle in whom the boy had confided. (Justice and Justice, 1979, p. 103) ●

In another case, a mother had intercourse with her son two to three times a week from the time he was 13 until he left for college (Sarrel & Masters, 1982).

Consequences and Prevention of Incest

Father–daughter and mother–son incest usually have the most undesirable consequences. Masters and Johnson (1976) report that the daughters of such incest relationships usually develop one of two behavior patterns. One is to become promiscuous, having sexual relations with anyone; the other is to become fearful of sex, avoiding men. Although a negative attitude toward sex can be unlearned and a more positive attitude learned, it takes time and the direction of a skilled therapist.

Men may become impotent as a consequence of intimate, quasi-sexual relationships with their mothers. In essence, they were confronted with a sexually inappropriate stimulus and had to learn to turn themselves off sexually. Such negative learning can usually be reversed in therapy.

Not all who have incestuous sexual encounters with parents or siblings have sexual difficulties as adults. Indeed, many learn to relabel what happened when they were younger so that there is minimal guilt or concern. Subsequent sexual relationships not only provide pleasurable experiences but also help to temper the effects of the earlier sexual encounters.

In her book, *Kiss Daddy Goodnight*, Louise Armstrong (1979) suggests two ways parents can help to prevent sexual abuse of their children. "One is to tell kids that nobody has the right to touch you in ways that you don't like—even people we know and love. And two, support kids in refusing to have others touch them in ways they don't like—such as being continually hugged and grabbed by adults" (p. 241). These statements let children know that they have control over their own bodies.

Sexual Harassment

Another abuse of sexuality is **sexual harassment**, defined as any act by persons of either gender that uses the sex or sexuality of the other to impose restrictions on that person. Although this implies male domination of females, it may also include gay people being sexually harassed by their straight employers. Also, it is not uncommon to find cases where young men are harassed by their female supervisors. Sexual harassment also can occur between coworkers, for example, when one coworker habitually uses abusive language, or touches, pats, or pinches another so that the latter is made uncomfortable.

However, the most common form of sexual harassment is the abuse of sexuality by a male employer on a female employee (MacKinnon, 1979). This often means the imposition of a requirement by men in their role of employer that women provide sexual favors as a condition of being hired, retained, or promoted. The victim of sexual harassment may be a woman of any age, occupation, or social class, but she is often a woman in her twenties and thirties who is married (Safran, 1976). Black women are particularly vulnerable because they are considered more sexually accessible and economically at risk—they are the least likely to protest because if they lose their job they may have greater difficulty finding another job than if they were white.

Types and Impact of Sexual Harassment

Women report various types of sexual harassment on the job. The first is verbal abuse. Their employer sees them primarily in terms of their sexual characteristics. References to "big breasts," "nice fanny," and "sexy legs," may be made on a regular basis. Although some women may be flattered and sometimes enjoy the attention, the comments rarely stop there. Women are asked about their sex life, whether they "cheat" on their husbands or "fool around," their preferences for intercourse positions and pornography. They may be drawn into sexual conversations they do not choose to be involved in, yet they may feel forced to participate for fear they will be negatively labeled, discriminated against, or fired. Such "uncooperativeness" may appear

It is sometimes hard to define what is sexual harassment and what is looking.

in an evaluation as "an office worker who lacks effective interpersonal skills," placed in her personnel file, and used against her.

Another type of harassment is physical abuse. The woman is not raped but kissed, felt, stroked, and pressed against. She resents these unwanted behaviors yet feels powerless to control the situation.

> Mary "X" is a clerk who was employed by General Electric in Lynn, Massachusetts. She filed a grievance against two supervisors whom she said insisted that she accompany them to a party in celebration of National Secretary's Week. Mary recalls, "I didn't want to go. I told them if they wanted to be nice to me they should send flowers."
>
> In her grievance she stated that "on the way to the restaurant they were fooling around, grabbing my legs and trying to hug me. They said they were glad to get me alone . . . In the lobby one of them grabbed my rear. In the car they made me sit between them. One of them put his arms around me and got me in a bear hug trying to give me a kiss, feeling my legs, biting on parts of my body. One said, 'I want the top half,' the other, 'the bottom half.' "(Elliot, 1982, p. 15)

Finally, the woman may be directly threatened that if she does not have intercourse, she will not be hired or promoted. Rarely is the threat explicit but the message is clear—"I hope you will be cooperative," "I know that taking the occasional trip with me won't be a problem for you," and "If you play along, you'll get along."

In 1981 the U.S. Merit Systems Protection Board conducted a study of sexual harassment of all federal employees. One in four reported being sexually harassed. Figure 15.1 shows the percentage who reported various forms of harassment. Examples of sexual harassment given by these federal employees include the following.

● A woman whose only access to a telephone is in her superintendent's office says that whenever she (or other women) use the phone, "the superintendent persists in putting his arm around me, kissing me, making obscene suggestions about what I should do with him, suggesting I go away for long weekends with him and his buddies so they can show me a really "good time."

The male supervisor of a sandblaster grabs him while he's working on a scaffold.

A secretary says her district director "practically sits on my lap when I ask a question, embarrassing me with his constant twisting of every word I say into some sexual connotation." (p. 36) ●

College women also experience sexual harassment. In a random sample of 77 students, 8 percent reported that their teachers had "touched, patted, or pinched them to the point that they were uncomfortable" (Kraus & Wilson, 1980, p. 4) and 3 percent said that a "male instructor suggested or demanded that they engage in sexual relations for a higher grade or a letter of recommendation" (p. 4).

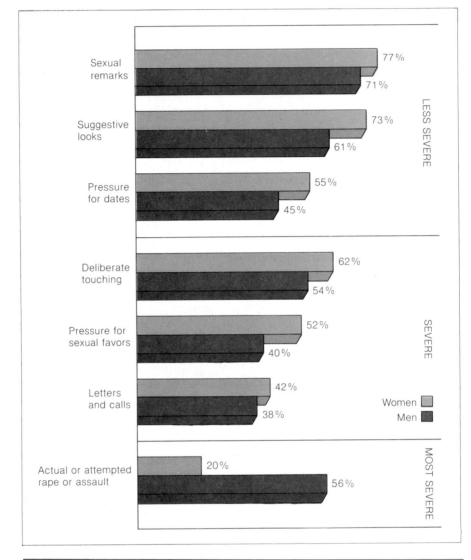

Figure 15.1
Frequency of Sexual Harassment Incidents
Percentage of Female and Male Victims of Each Form of Harassment Who Experienced That Form of Sexual Harassment More Than Once[a] (Question 17)

[a]Once a month or less, 2–4 times a month, or once a week or more

Source: *"Sexual Harassment in the Federal Workplace: Is it a Problem?" A report of the U.S. Merit Systems Protection Board, Office of Merit Systems Review and Studies. U.S. Government Printing Office, Washington, D.C. 1981, p. 39.*

These instructors were a varied lot—married and single, young and old—and were in all departments on campus. But the female students being harassed had a more specific profile—they were bright (had high grade-point averages) attractive, and well liked.

Kraus (1981) reported what it was like for 24 students who had been sexually harassed.

Such harassment included stares and leers, sexual comments ("You have nice breasts"), subtle pressure ("Get a coke with me"), touching, dates, propositions, bribes, threats ("If you don't sleep with me, I'll ruin your career"), and physical assaults. While the duration of harassment ranged from 20 minutes to five years, the average length of harassment lasted two semesters. Strategies to cope with the harassment included joking ("Get back in your cage"), ignoring, refusing ("I'm offended—stop it"), complaints to the administration, avoiding class, and collusion with a male friend. The latter involved a male friend saying to the teacher, "Hey, keep your hands off," and was the most effective strategy a woman employed in coping with sexual harassment.

The impact of sexual harassment on each student was generally negative. Most said that they found it difficult to study and ended up making a lower grade (some got a higher grade for not complaining to the administration). Most said that they were angry, hurt, and fearful over the incident(s) and sometimes these feelings lasted for years. Some generalized their negative feelings to other teachers, the department, and the university. The result of such generalizations, for some, was to lose interest in their career goals.

In essence, most felt in conflict. They resented their professor's inappropriate sexual advances. But because they were dependent on their teachers for grades, they needed to avoid retaliating.*

Like women who have been raped, sexually harassed women feel humiliated, ashamed, and cheap. They also feel angry, nervous, fearful, and helpless. Women have made the following comments about their experiences of harassment.

● As I remember all the sexual abuse and negative work experience I am left feeling sick and helpless and upset instead of angry . . . Reinforced feelings of no control—sense of doom . . . I have difficulty dropping the emotion barrier I work behind when I come home from work. My husband turns into just another man . . . Kept me in a constant state of emotional agitation and frustration; I drank a lot . . . soured the essential delight in the work . . . Stomachache, migraines, cried every night, no appetite. (Silverman, 1977) ●

What is supposed to be an environment where women earn money for performing a job is sometimes an arena where they feel like blind Pygmies being tormented by gladiators.

Dealing with Sexual Harassment

Although there is legal recourse for people subjected to sexual harassment, it is expensive, time consuming, and often unproductive. Students rarely file a complaint against their teachers. About half of all sexual harassment claims made to the Equal Employment Opportunity Commission are withdrawn and those that are followed through are rarely successful (MacKinnon, 1979). In a survey of 2,000 business executives who had observed various out-

*From "A Situational Analysis of Sexual Harassment in Academia" by Linda A. Kraus. Master's thesis, Department of Sociology and Anthropology, East Carolina University, 1981. Reprinted by permission of Linda Kraus.

comes (Safran, 1981), most said that either nothing happened or the woman in the case quit her job or was fired.

Proving sexual harassment is difficult. One judge noted that before an employer can be held liable, there must be evidence of the sexual advance, retaliation by the maker of the advance, and that "other agents of the employer with knowledge of her charge assisted the retaliation or impeded the complaint" (MacKinnon, 1979, p. 68). In addition, a judge or hearing board may feel that women's judgment of what constitutes sexual harassment varies; what some women view as harassment, others may view as desirable attention or be indifferent toward.

Some women do win claims. In Tomkins v. Public Service Electric & Gas Co., Ms. Tomkins, a secretary, was offered a promotion in exchange for sexual relations with her boss. She refused and asked for a transfer to a comparable position in the company.

> When one was not forthcoming, afraid to return to her previous job, she temporarily took an inferior position. Over a period of months, her new superior threatened demotions, charged that she was incapable of holding the position, pressured her to take a salary cut, and solicited and gathered unfavorable material about her and had it placed in her personnel file. She was twice put on disciplinary layoff without just cause and was finally terminated. (MacKinnon, 1979, p. 70)

Ms. Tomkins' lawyer argued that her employers were expecting something from her (sex) that they would not expect from a man in the same position. Hence, they were discriminating against her on the basis of her gender. She was granted $20,000 as a settlement.

In addition to seeking legal redress for sexual harassment, women have been active in promoting a positive, formal organizational policy toward the issue. The official policy on sexual harassment of employees and students at one univeristy begins by defining such harassment. Its key provisions are as follows:

1. It is illegal and against the policies of East Carolina University for any employee to sexually harass another employee by (a) making unwelcomed sexual advances or requests for sexual favors or other verbal or physical conduct of a sexual nature a condition of an employee's continued employment or, (b) making submissions to or rejections of such conduct the basis for employment decisions affecting the employee or, (c) creating an intimidating, hostile or offensive working environment by such conduct.
2. It is against the policies of East Carolina University for any employee to sexually harass a student by (a) making unwelcomed sexual advances or requests for sexual favors or other verbal or physical conduct of a sexual nature a condition of a student's grade, progress, or recommendation or, (b) creating an intimidating, hostile or offensive learning environment by such conduct.

Before taking formal action, the offended person might take the intermediate step of writing a letter to the offender. Mary Rowe (1981), who works as a mediator in sexual harassment cases, suggests the following as a model.

> The letter I recommend has three parts. The first part should be a detailed statement of facts as the writer sees them: "This is what I think is happening . . ." I en-

courage a precise rendition of all facts and dates relevant to the alleged harassment. This section is sometimes very long.

In the second part of the letter, writers should describe their feelings and what damage they think has been done. This is where opinions belong. "Your action made me feel terrible"; "I am deeply embarrassed and worried that my parents will hear about this"; "You have caused me to ask for a transfer (change my career objectives; drop out of the training course; take excessive time off; or whatever)." The writer should mention any perceived or actual costs and damages, along with feelings of dismay, distrust, revulsion, misery, and so on.

Finally, I recommend a short statement of what the accuser would like to happen next. Since most persons only want the embarrassment to end, the letter might finish by saying so: "I ask that our relationship from now on be on a purely professional basis."

Someone who knows that he or she contributed to the problem does well to say so: "Although we once were happy dating, it is important to me that we now establish a formal and professional relationship, and I ask you to do so."

If the letter writer believes some remedy or recompense is in order, this is the place to say so: "Please withdraw my last evaluation until we can work out a fair one"; "I will need a written answer as to the reference you will provide from now on"; and statements of this type. *

A letter of this nature is an attempt to stop the harassment peaceably. It should be sent when the person first begins to feel sexually harassed. If the desired behavior change is not forthcoming, the offended person can use the letter as evidence of intent to alert the offending person of the problem. If appropriate action is not taken within the organization, legal assistance may be indicated.

Prostitution

Whereas most people would agree that rape, incest, and sexual harassment are abuses of sexuality, opinion is divided on the issue of prostitution. Proponents of the prostitution-as-abuse idea state that prostitutes are physically and morally exploited. In opposition, many prostitutes say that theirs is an occupation like any other and that they are abused by the courts and the police who harass them. To answer those who believe that prostitution is immoral, COYOTE, an acronym for Call Off Your Old Tired Ethics, was formed in San Francisco by an ex-prostitute, Margo St. James. COYOTE has promoted the idea of a prostitutes' union to change the public image of prostitutes and the moral and legal discrimination they are subject to.

Prostitution is the exchange of sexual services for money. "It is 'cash on the barrelhead' that distinguishes prostitution from other forms of heterosexual relations" (Gagnon, 1977, p. 278). Prostitution is big business. It is es-

*From "Dealing with sexual harassment," by Mary P. Rowe, *Harvard Business Review*, May-June, 1981, p. 43. Reprinted by permission of Mary P. Rowe © 1983.

timated that American men spend close to $10 billion for the sexual favors of prostitutes each year (Surawicz & Winick, 1979). Although sexual favors may include any sexual activity the client wants, oral sex and intercourse are the most frequent services.

Types of Prostitutes

Some prostitutes are men but most are women. Some typical categories of women prostitutes include streetwalker, house prostitute, massage parlor prostitute, and call girl.

Streetwalker

As late afternoon arrives, this woman dresses in provocative attire and goes to that part of the city where men will be looking for prostitutes. As she walks the streets, she will try to catch the eye of a male coming toward her. If he looks back she will slow her pace and say something like "You looking for a date?" "Hi, lonesome," "What's happening?" or any such phrase to catch his attention and engage him in conversation. If he stops she immediately tries to establish his identity. Is he a cop? Talking prices to a stranger can mean jail, so she must be careful. After she is convinced that he is not "the man" (an undercover police officer), she finds out what he wants (straight intercourse, fellatio, anal intercourse, and so on), they negotiate a price, and discuss where the contact is to take place. It is usually in her apartment or a motel room set up for her clients.

Upon reaching the room and before sexual contact, she receives the money. Gagnon (1977) observed that the act of paying money defines the actors in the sexual script to follow. He is the "john," "the trick," "the square." (Table 15.2 defines terms used by prostitutes.) By taking the money, she is the

---

Table 15.2 Terms Used by Prostitutes

The man   The police or an undercover cop.

John   A customer of a prostitute.

Mark   Another word for john.

Trick   Sexual act performed with a john; also, another name for john.

Pimp   A man who finds johns for a prostitute. He also has a relationship with the prostitute and protects her from the police while exploiting her economically.

Madam   A woman who owns and manages a brothel, whorehouse, cathouse.

Hooker   Female prostitute.

Jane   A lesbian customer of a prostitute.

Stable   A number of prostitutes controlled by one pimp.

To get burned   To give service without getting paid.

Quota   The number of johns (or amount of money) a prostitute must see (or earn) each day to keep her pimp happy.

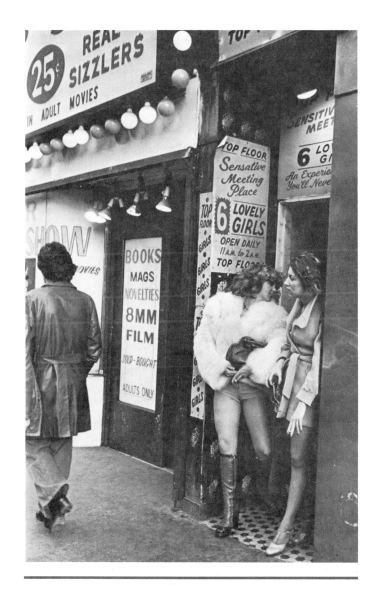

Streetwalkers are the most common type of prostitute.

"whore," "the hooker," "the slut." "The symbolic mediation of mutual degradation, a degradation that must be kept secret while the act is going on, is
critical to the maintenance of the ephemeral good will that allows the sex to
occur" (p. 290).

Of all prostitutes the streetwalker is usually the least educated and sophisticated and her services are the least expensive. She is more likely to have sexually transmitted diseases and to have been arrested and jailed. Since her social world consists almost entirely of other prostitutes, and pimps, it is easier
for her to become involved in the criminal subculture of drugs, shoplifting,
and stealing from clients.

A variation of the streetwalker is the CB (citizen's band) prostitute, who has been described as follows.

> She talks to male truck drivers on channel 19 of her CB radio as they move on interstate highways within range of her shortwave radio.
>
> To attract them, one prostitute was heard to say—"Mr. 18-wheeler going down the highway? Would you like to have some fun? . . . Come on, talk to me. Come on, one of you horny truck drivers out there." (p. 62)

Sociologists Lloyd Klein and Joan Ingle listened to similar conversations and observed prostitutes climbing into the truck cabs to service their customers. The prostitutes would stay about 10 minutes and visit up to 30 truck cabs an evening. These cabs were parked at an interstate rest stop in Oklahoma known as "Good Buddy Park."

The customers sought by the CB prostitutes were males who drove the 18-wheel vehicles. They represented a group whose "occupational loneliness, boredom, and isolation from sexual companionship intensifies preoccupation with sexual desires."* (p. 63)

House Prostitute

Also referred to as a brothel, whorehouse, cathouse, bordello, parlor house or just "house," this is a place where several prostitutes see men in their respective rooms. A madam oversees the house by paying for the electricity and police protection and seeing that the women get regular medical checkups. Being a brothel prostitute is a step up from being a streetwalker. She does not have to find her own customers, has health care, and avoids harassment from the police and her pimp, who may beat her if she does not make her quota.

Brothel houses such as Mustang Ranch, Miss Kitty's, and the Pink Pussycat are legal in rural counties of Nevada that have populations under 300,000. The women are fingerprinted, carry prostitute identification cards, and are checked weekly by public health officials. Although brothel houses exist in other places in the United States, they are illegal.

Massage Parlor Prostitutes

There are some legitimate massage parlors complete with trained masseurs (or masseuses if the clientele is female), sauna baths, and suntanning rooms, but others are little more than disguised brothels. Intercourse and manual or oral sex are among the services offered. Some give massage and masturbation (M and M) only. (Massage parlor prostitutes are also known as "hand whores.")

The women are young, often transient, and work in a parlor because it is the best job they can find for the pay. Their services and fees are usually specified in advance: $15 for a massage; for an extra $5 the woman wears no

*Reprinted with permission of the publisher from "Sex Solicitation by Short Wave Radio: The CB Prostitute" in *Free Inquiry in Creative Sociology*, 1981, 9, 1 pp. 61–64.

top; another $10 no bottom, and so on. Their weekly income ranges from $125 to $600, for which they may serve forty or so clients. The object is to "get 'em in, get 'em up, get 'em off, and get 'em out" (Bryant & Palmer, 1977, p. 137).

Call Girl

A call girl makes appointments over the telephone with male clients for sexual entertainment at her apartment or that of the client. Call girls are usually the most attractive, educated, and socially skilled of all prostitutes. Some work for themselves; others have pimps or madams who refer clients to them. One prostitute who was shy in approaching men had an older woman accompany her to the bars in expensive hotels. This woman would sit down next to the potential john, ask him if he "wanted some company" and point to the beautiful woman sitting alone in a booth. If he was interested he would go to the booth (after paying the madam) and arrange with the woman to go to her apartment.

Becoming a Prostitute

Unlike setting out to be a schoolteacher or physician, few women grow up with the goal of becoming a prostitute. Rather, they drift into the role and become locked into the occupation. Several factors, when combined, seem to contribute to becoming a prostitute.

Early Sexual Activity

The average age of first intercourse for the 30 prostitutes in one study was 13.5 (Davis, 1978). This is about four years earlier than is usual for nonstudent females (DeLamater & MacCorquodale, 1979). Early intercourse is significant because it usually occurs with a male five or six years older, which suggests lack of parental control.

Lack of Family Ties

High rates of divorce, separation, desertion, and alcoholism also seem to characterize the background of prostitutes. Many report having been brought up in foster homes or shuffled from home to home. Strong parental relationships seem to be lacking. The girl often views home as a place to escape from. Being a runaway is strongly associated with prostitution.

Peer Influence

Escaping from home means going somewhere, usually with friends. These friends are also escaping from an unhappy home environment, have dropped out of school, and have no job and no source of income. One woman explained that her boyfriend encouraged her to turn her first trick.

● I was on the run . . . I didn't get up until 3 P.M. I was staying with my boyfriend. He was planning to set me up [for prostitution] . . . it was kind of like prearranged for me. Crazy! We were staying in a hotel with lots of pimps, prostitutes, and faggots living there. The first time was at the World's Series. I was dressed like a normal teenager.* (p. 204) ●

Quick Money

After the first experience, sometimes just for fun, to please her boyfriend, or because "everyone else is doing it," the woman continues to turn tricks and the connection between the behavior and the money is made. Sex for fun becomes sex for quick money. Since no other job is available to the woman in which she can earn so much so quickly, she finds it easy to continue.

● My boyfriend worked in the ——— Hotel. He called me up to say that he had a man who had fifty dollars to get a girl, and so there it was. I got forty-five dollars the first night—for four men. Everyone was doing it, anyway. Then I walked back downtown, and had three more, and then went back to my apartment.* (p.206) ●

The Pimp Connection

A **pimp** finds men for a prostitute, pays off the police, provides companionship for the woman, and, in general, looks after her. In exchange, he demands that she turn over the majority of her earnings to him each night. A relationship with a pimp is usually a sign that the woman has "arrived" at being a prostitute. The boyfriends referred to by the prostitutes are often pimps who have several women working for them. Their techniques for getting their women to hustle tricks vary. Some feign love for them; others beat them when they fail to meet their quotas. The woman stays with the pimp partly because she is lonely and he is the one stable figure in her environment. The johns come and go but the pimp is there. He is not only her manager and protector but her lover and companion. In some cases, he may be her husband and the father of her children.

The Life of a Prostitute

Most prostitutes are trapped in a life style that is dangerous and unrewarding. The prostitute is victimized by her clients (they degrade her), her pimp (he

*Reprinted by permission of Schocken Books from an article entitled "Prostitution: Identity, Career, and Legal Enterprise" by Nanette Davis in *The Sociology of Sex* edited by James Henslin and Edward Sagarin. Copyright © 1978 by James M. Henslin and Edward Sagarin.

beats her), and the police (they jail her). Many become alcohol or chemical dependent to dissociate themselves from their work. The stereotype of the glamorous call girl fits only a few of all prostitutes.

> Many of the prostitutes reported suffering feelings of degradation which made them the willing victims for the dope salesman, the beatings of a pimp, for the sadistic practices of a client, and even for suicide . . . prostitution turns out to be hard work, and while some women demand extremely high fees, very few manage to hold on to the money they earn. (Bullough, 1979, p. 92)

In one case, a young prostitute earned $100,000 for her pimp, but she ended up with only $800 (Geiser, 1979). Most prostitutes earn about what a secretary might make. But while the secretary might look forward to improving her skills and moving up in terms of status and income, the prostitute is in a downwardly mobile profession. When her looks are gone, so are her clients and pimp. She is left with no marketable skill and may have nothing to show for her years in the profession.

Exit from the profession is through marriage, lower-paying jobs, or suicide. Most do manage to find alternative ways of living. Some call girls, because of their appearance and social skills, launch themselves into a satisfactory alternative life style with minimal repercussions from their earlier years as a prostitute. Even the streetwalker with no skills can prostitute herself for a few years, create a dowry, and settle into monogamous matrimony (Surawicz & Winick, 1979). Some prostitutes receive direct help. Family Services of Minneapolis offers a therapy program for prostitutes who want another life style. The therapist for the program is herself a former prostitute.

Customers of Prostitutes

In a study of men who went to massage parlors, the researchers reported that the typical customer was 35 to 40 years old, temporarily separated from his spouse or female companion, and away from home (Bryant & Palmer, 1977). They were businessmen or traveling salesmen and clearly middle class.

Men who seek a prostitute may do so for a number of reasons, including the desire for a new experience, curiosity about what a sexual experience with a prostitute is like, the desire for a sexual companion who will engage in sexual behavior that the client's usual sexual partner is unwilling to do, and as an antidote to boredom. Still other men cannot attract a woman because of their age, physical impairment, or lack of social skills.

Male Prostitutes

Although the term "prostitute" is most often thought of as referring to females, some men also provide sex for money. Those serving male customers are known as **hustlers**. They frequent gay bars, homosexual baths, and walk the streets in large cities searching for business. Others may be a "kept boy" (supported by a wealthy male), a "call boy" (similar to a call girl), or one who works in a homosexual brothel disguised as a massage parlor.

Gigolos are male prostitutes for women. They are usually attractive young men who serve as companions, escorts, or sex partners to the women who hire them. They operate out of escort agencies, dance studios, and massage parlors. Some gigolos are "kept men" (put on full salary) by wealthy middle-aged and upper-class women.

Summary

Abuses of sexuality include rape, incest, sexual harassment, and prostitution. Rape is forced sexual relations against a person's will. Both women and men may be victims, but male rape is much less frequent. Rape is an act of aggression, not of passion.

Although most reported and convicted rapists are strangers, rape more frequently occurs between a woman and someone she knows—a boyfriend, or husband. Women usually do not report acquaintance rapes out of shame, fear, or concern that they may have led the partner on.

Avoiding the situation is the best defense against rape. But once a man threatens a woman with rape, she can decide to try and talk him out of it, fight back, or both. If the attacker has a weapon, physical resistance should be used with caution, if at all.

"Rape trauma" is the term used to describe the acute disorganization a woman feels after she has been raped. Anxiety, fear, and mistrust of men and her environment are frequent reactions to rape. Most rapes are not reported and for those that are, few cases come to trial. Convictions are difficult to obtain because of evidence requirements. Convicted rapists may be required to submit to some form of treatment, including psychotherapy, education, and chemotherapy.

Incest is defined as sexual relations between close relatives such as father-daughter, mother-son, and brother-sister. Parent-child incest is the ultimate abuse of power and authority since the child is not in a position of being able to consent to the sexual acts. The incest taboo is universal and exists in reference to potential heredity defects, economic resources, and parental authority.

Sexual harassment is defined as any act by persons of either gender that uses the sex or sexuality of the other to impose restrictions on that person. Sexual harassment is becoming visible as a sexual abuse. Women are often required to provide sexual favors in exchange for being hired, retained, or promoted. Women are increasingly seeking legal redress for sexual harassment. They may attempt to solve the harassment problem peaceably by writing a letter outlining the grievance and requesting a remedy.

Prostitution is the exchange of sexual services for money. There is disagreement about whether prostitution is an abuse of sexuality. Some prostitutes are men but most are women. Some categories of prostitutes are streetwalker, house prostitute, massage parlor prostitute, and call girl. Most prostitutes drift into the occupation. A combination of factors seems to contribute to becoming a prostitute: early sexual activity, lack of family ties, peer influence, and the association of money and sexual behavior.

Males may also be prostitutes. Hustlers are male prostitutes serving other males. They typically go to gay bars, gay baths, or walk the streets in large cities looking for male clients. Some may be "kept" by a wealthy male. Gigolos are male prostitutes who service females. They operate out of escort agencies or dance studios and offer companionship and sex for a price. Some are "kept" by wealthy women.

Key Terms

rape

rape trauma

incest

incest taboo

sexual harassment

prostitution

pimp

hustler

gigolo

Issues in Debate and Future Directions

Whether prostitution should be legalized or decriminalized is an unresolved issue among researchers, law enforcement officials, politicians, and prostitutes. After examining both sides of the issue, we look at trends regarding rape legislation, assistance for incest victims, and sexual harassment.

Should Prostitution Be Legalized or Decriminalized?

Legalization of prostitution would involve legalizing the profession and subjecting it to government control. Prostitutes would be required to meet certain age requirements, register with local officials, take weekly STD tests, pay taxes, and work only in licensed brothels. Arguments for legalization are that it would permit taxation of the billions of currently untaxed dollars spent on prostitution, help control and regulate the criminal activity associated with prostitution, prevent teenage prostitution, eliminate the abusive pimp, and get prostitutes off the street so that others will not be offended by their presence.

The argument against legalization of prostitution is essentially a moral one: The exchange of sexual favors for money is wrong. Prostitution is an attack on the sanctity of the family and, therefore, on the society. If prostitution were legalized, the argument goes, there would be a flood of women from low-paying jobs into the profession.

Prostitution has been legalized in Germany. The women work in large dormitories and are checked regularly by a physician for sexually transmitted diseases. Clients make their selection by observing the available women on closed circuit TV monitors. But many German men avoid the large government brothels, which they regard as too obvious for married men. Illegal prostitution still exists.

In Nevada, legal prostitutes cannot choose their customers but must service whomever comes in the door. They also feel that the law interferes with their private lives. For example, they can go to town only during certain hours and cannot appear in the company of a man in a restaurant. The stigmatization of the profession through fingerprinting and registration makes it difficult for them to leave prostitution and enter another profession.

Short of legalization is decriminalization, which would remove criminal penalties for involvement in prostitution. The basic argument for decriminalization is that since sexual behavior is the outcome of a private agreement between both the client and the prostitute, what consenting adults do should not be against the law. While prostitutes would not be prosecuted for prostitution, they would need to meet minimum age requirements, pay taxes, and have regular STD checkups.

The British have essentially decriminalized prostitution. No fines or jail terms are given for solicitation, although streetwalkers might be issued a citation if they interfere with the rights of pedestrians. Other European cities such as Amsterdam set up areas in the city where streetwalking is permitted.

One researcher (James, 1976) observed that although reducing the abuses of prostitution can begin by a change in our laws, change is also dependent on equality in social and economic relationships. "It is critical that males reject the attitude that sex is purchasable and that society provide women with viable alternatives. Both the clientele and the occupation are dependent upon existing, economic, social, and sexual values in our society (p. 122).

Future Directions

Trends in the area of sexual abuses include greater legal protection for wives raped by their husbands. But such legal changes will occur slowly since the courts are reluctant to legislate sexual relations in the marital bedroom.

Rape reform laws will also concern rape outside the marriage relationship. Passage of the criminal sexual conduct bill in Michigan makes past sexual conduct of the victim irrelevant as evidence in determining if a woman consented to the rape and in establishing her credibility. A raped prostitute would have as much legal protection as a raped nun. Other states will follow Michigan's lead in legal protection of the rape victim.

Incest will continue to have low visibility, although some assistance will continue to be offered to those who seek help. Some rape crisis centers currently provide help for daughters sexually molested by their father or stepfather.

As the rights of sexually harassed women become more visible, women will file an increasing number of claims to the Equal Employment Opportunity Commission. To alert employers to the issue, the commission has published new regulations stating that federal, state, and local companies with 15 or more employees have an "affirmative duty" to prevent and eliminate sexual harassment (both physical and verbal).

Our society will continue to have mixed feelings about prostitution. It is not likely to be legalized, but neither will it be targeted for elimination. The inequities of the social, sexual, and economic order that perpetuate prostitution will continue.

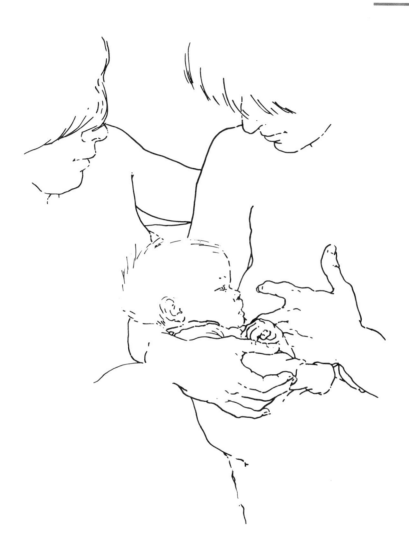

Chapter Sixteen

Planning Children

Love is a fourteen letter word—
family planning.

PLANNED PARENTHOOD FEDERATION*

Chapter Sixteen

This final section of the text is about procreation. Since the overwhelming majority of us (more than 90 percent) express a desire for children, procreation is an important part of our sexuality; and parenthood is perhaps the most crucial aspect of procreation.

Parenthood should begin with planning. As a student, before each academic term you decide how many courses you want to take and when you want to take them. You probably try to avoid an overload and feel pleased when you get the schedule you want. Successful family planning means having the number of children you want, if any, at the times you want to have them. Although this seems a sensible and practical way to approach parenthood, many couples leave having children to chance.

Family planning has benefits for the mother and child. Since having several children at short intervals increases the chances of premature birth, infectious disease, and death for the mother or baby, parents can minimize such risks by planning fewer children at longer intervals. Before the middle of the nineteenth century, the average woman became pregnant every other year during her reproductive life (between 15 and 45 years of age) (Bullough, 1980). Fathers may also benefit from family planning by pacing financial demands.

Conscientious family planning may also reduce the number of children born to parents who do not want them. Although most unplanned births are failures in timing, in one year eight million children were born to women who did not want them (U.S. HEW, 1980). A child born to rejecting parents is tragic and unnecessary.

Society also benefits from family planning by enabling people to avoid having children they cannot feed and clothe adequately—children whose rearing may have to be subsidized by the taxpayer. Finally, family planning is essential to halting the continuing expansion of the world population and its consequent drain on limited environmental resources. There are currently more than 4.5 billion people on this planet and the population has been increasing at a rate of more than 78 million a year.

*The chapter opening quote is printed by permission of Planned Parenthood Federation of America, Inc.

In this chapter you are encouraged to consider four basic questions: Do you want to be a parent? If so, how many children do you want? When is the best time to begin your family? Do you want to be a single parent?

Do You Want to Have Children?

Most young adults say they want to have children "some day." In this section we examine the social influences on the decision to have children, the reasons people give for wanting children, and the child free alternative to parenthood.

Social Influences on Having Children

Unless the members of a society have children, the society will cease to exist. In general, our society encourages childbearing, an attitude known as **pronatalism**. Our family, friends, religion, government, and schools help to develop positive attitudes toward parenthood. Cultural observances reinforce these attitudes.

Family

The fact that we are reared in families encourages us to have families of our own. Our parents are our models. They married, we marry; they had children, we have children. Some parents exert a much more active influence. "I'm 67 and don't have much time. Will I ever see a grandchild?" asked the mother of an only child. Other remarks parents may make include: "If you don't hurry up, your younger sister is going to have a baby before you do," "We're setting up a trust fund for your brother's child, and we'll do the same for yours," "Did you know that Nash and Marilyn [The child's contemporaries] just had a daughter?" "I think you'll regret not having children when you're old," and "Don't you want a son to carry on your name?"

Friends

Our friends who have children influence us to do likewise. After sharing an enjoyable weekend with friends who had a little girl, one husband wrote to the host and hostess, "Lucy and I are always affected by Karen—she is such a good child to be around. We haven't made up our minds yet, but our desire to have a child of our own always increases after we leave your home." This couple became parents 16 months later.

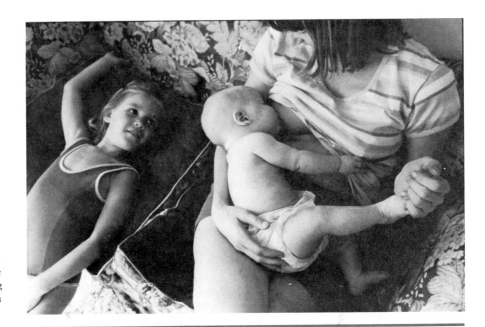

Having been reared in a family is a subtle influence in creating the desire to have a child of one's own.

Religion

Religion may be a powerful influence on having children. Catholics are taught that having children is the basic purpose of marriage and gives meaning to the union. While many Catholics use contraception and reject their church's emphasis on procreation, some internalize the church's message. One Catholic woman said, "My body was made by God and I should use it to produce children for Him. Other people may not understand it, but that's how I feel." Judaism also has a strong family orientation. Couples who choose to be child free are less likely than couples with children to adhere to any set of religious beliefs.

Government

The tax structure imposed by our federal and state governments support parenthood. Married couples without children pay higher taxes than couples with children, although the reduction in taxes is not large enough to be a primary inducement to have children.

Governments in other countries may promote different family-planning policies. Beginning in 1979 in China, one-child families have been strongly encouraged. Couples who have only one child are given a "one-child glory certificate," which entitles them to special priority housing, better salaries, a 5-percent supplementary pension, free medical care for the child, and an assured place for the child in school. If the couple has more than one child, they may lose their jobs, be assigned to less desirable housing, and be required to pay the government back for the benefits they have received.

The Schools and Special Observances

One-third of 29 current high school family studies texts have a pronatalism bias (Patterson & DeFrain, 1981). Early reading material, such as The Dick and Jane series, also emphasizes the family context.

In addition, our society reaffirms its approval of parents every year by allocating a special day for mom and dad. Each year on Mother's Day and Father's Day parenthood is celebrated across the nation with gifts and embraces.

Personal Reasons for Having Children

The influence of pronatalism is reflected in the reasons people give for having children. Some of these reasons follow.

Social Expectations

A psychologist and father of two daughters said, "Having children was never a conscious decision. It was more of a feeling that one ought to have a family." A mother of two expressed a similar feeling: "All my friends were having babies, and I never questioned whether I would, too." Our society expects its members to conform to certain conventions, not the least important of which is having children. Conforming to society's expectations assures a degree of acceptance from peers and places us in the mainstream of American life.

Personal Fulfillment

Some parents encourage their daughters to anticipate having children of their own. Dolls and a dollhouse reinforce this. In some cases the socialization is so strong that womanhood is equated with motherhood. "I suppose I felt I had to get pregnant to verify that I was a real woman," a young mother said.

Men also derive personal fulfillment from children. Paternalism—pride and affection for their offspring—is a strong motive for some men. Men may also affirm their masculinity by proving that they can conceive children.

Personal Identity

Related to the quest for personal fulfillment is the feeling that a baby provides a specific identity for the parent. As one woman explained, "Before my son, Benny, I was nothing. I was bored, I hated my job, and I didn't have any goals or focus to my life. Now I know who I am—a mother—and feel that I am needed." Some fathers express the same feeling. "Having my child is the meaning of life," remarked the father of a newborn. "I am a lousy employee, but I'm a great father. For the first time in my life, I really feel like somebody."

Influence of Spouse

Some spouses have children primarily to please their mates. "I wasn't wild about the idea of having children but decided to go along with it because my husband wanted one. As it turns out, I'm glad we did," one mother said. When husband and wife feel differently about having children, the disagreement is not always resolved in favor of having them. However, since the woman bears the child, her preferences are usually given more weight.

Accident

A good many couples have children without intending to. "I was out of pills and we didn't have any condoms," recalled a young wife, "but we wanted to have intercourse and decided to take a chance. An 8-pound baby was the result." Such accidents are not unusual. About one-third of all conceptions in the United States are not planned.

Immortality

Some people have children to ensure a kind of immortality. They view parenthood as a way of making a lasting mark on the world. "If you have kids, and they have kids, there will always be a part of you around," said one parent. In one study (Englund, 1983), men were more concerned about the biological and lineage aspects of parenthood than women. Having a son to continue the family line is an important issue for some men. After his fourth daughter was born, one father said, "I always wanted a son to carry on the family name, but it looks like I'll fill up the back yard with girls before I get one."

Close Parent–Child Relationship

The most frequent reason given by 700 adolescent boys and girls for wanting children was the opportunity of experiencing a close affiliative relationship (Townes et al., 1979). "You're closest to your own people," said one 15-year-old. "And I want a close relationship with kids that are mine".

Whatever the reasons parents give for having children, the rewards of parenthood are basically intangible. Parents often speak of the delight of seeing children discover their world for the first time, the joy of holding a baby in their arms and realizing that it is a part of them and their partner, and the pleasure of following the development of children through the years and of relating to them as adults. A clinical psychologist, the father of three children, said, "The real problem with children is not their coming but their going. My first daughter will soon be married and move six states away. I used to feel that babies were not worth the trouble, but now I know the joy of an adult parent–child relationship."

The Child-free Alternative

For all the happiness they may provide, children also cause problems. They tend to interfere with the marriage relationship, disrupt careers (particularly the mother's), cost money, and make noise. In addition, parenthood is a demanding role that not all people feel qualified to assume. For these and other reasons, some couples choose to remain child-free.

What are the reasons couples actually give for remaining child-free? When 55 couples who chose not to have children were asked about their reasons, the wives gave as the most important reasons their desire for more personal freedom, greater time and intimacy with their spouses, and career demands (Cooper, Cumber, & Hartner, 1978). The most important reasons for husbands included the desire not to take on increased responsibilities. Less frequently, the couples mentioned financial reasons, concern with overpopulation, and dislike of children.

Other couples do not initially decide to be child-free. They put off having children—"We'll wait till we're out of school . . . until we get a house . . . until we get some money . . . until we feel like we're ready"–become satisfied with the child-free life style, and decide to continue it. But those who never have children voluntarily are a minority. Of a representative national sample of 17,000 married women (ages 15–44), about 2 percent chose not to have children (Mosher & Bachrach, 1982).

Is the child-free life style for you? If you get your primary satisfactions from interacting with adults and from your career and if you require an atmosphere of freedom and privacy, perhaps the answer is yes. But if your desire for a child is at least equal to your desire for a satisfying adult relationship, career, and freedom, the answer is probably no. A specialist in voluntary childlessness observed that the child-free alternative is particularly valuable for some persons who would find the demands of parenthood an unnecessary burden and strain (Veevers, 1983). *A Child: To Have or Have Not?* (Elvenstar, 1982) is a good resource on this issue. Also, asking yourself the questions on p. 480 might help you to define your attitudes toward having children.

How Many Children Do You Want?

If you decide to have children, how many do you want? Most couples want two children, but an increasing number want just one. Family size has an impact on the entire family constellation as well as on the individual child.

An Only Child

Many people who are hesitant about having an only child make statements like "It's not fair to the child," "Only children are lonely," "Only children are spoiled," and "One child doesn't make a real family."

Are these beliefs justified? Is the one-child family bad for the child and the parents? To find out, Hawke and Knox (1977) surveyed 105 only children

My Sexuality

Some Questions to Ask Yourself Before Deciding to Have Children

1. Do you like children—not just cuddly infants but also cranky 2-year-olds, curious 8-year-olds, and anxious teenagers?
2. Do you view parenthood as a burden or as an enriching experience?
3. Do you feel your marriage is strong enough for you to take on the responsibility of nurturing another person?
4. Are you willing to let go of your childhood and really become an adult?
5. Can you give love without needing an equal amount in return?
6. Do you respond well to helplessness?
7. Do you have unrealistic expectations about parenthood; do you believe, for example, that having a child will automatically ensure solace in your old age?
8. Are you prepared for the profound changes parenthood will bring to your life style—in terms of money, time, and professional goals?
9. Are you prepared to work out the necessary compromises regarding child care (a particularly critical issue for dual-career couples)?
10. Are you prepared to let a child develop according to his or her bent, rather than as an exact replica of you or your spouse?
11. Are you prepared to depend more heavily on family and friends, as is usually necessary when a couple has a child?
12. Most important, can you accept the fact that you'll feel some ambivalence, regardless of your decision?

Excerpted material from "Parenthood By Choice" by Constance Rosenblum, January, 1979, Copyright © 1978 *Human Behavior* Magazine. Reprinted by Permission.

and 168 parents of only children. Table 16.1 indicates what these only children and their parents saw as the advantages and disadvantages to the one-child family pattern.

When the parents of only children were asked how many children they would have if they were starting over, 23 percent said they would wish to have an only child, 40 percent would like to have two, and another 21 percent would like to have more than two. Although only children have often been maligned, they are brighter, more career oriented, and have higher self-esteem than children with siblings (Pines, 1981).

Two Children

The most preferred family size in the United States is the the two-child family. How does having two children differ from having one? One hundred and forty-four mothers who had two children and whose second child was less than 5 years old revealed their motivations for having a second and the consequences of doing so (Knox & Wilson, 1978). About half of the mothers said they enjoyed their first child and wanted to repeat the experience. More than one-quarter stated they wanted a companion for the first child. Other rea-

Table 16.1   Advantages and Disadvantages of a One-Child Family as Reported by Only Children and Their Parents

Only Children (N = 105)		Parents of Only Children (N = 168)	
Advantages	*Percent*	*Advantages*	*Percent*
More possessions, opportunities	34	Financial	35
More parental attention	30	Child gets more attention, experience, time	28
Better for personal development	16	Less demanding for parents	13
No sibling problems	20	Closer parent–child relationship	8
		Freedom of career for mother	5
		Other (no estate problems, no sibling comparisons, parents have more time for each other)	11
Disadvantages	*Percent*	*Disadvantages*	*Percent*
Lack of companionship	58	Too much attention, protection, focus, etc.	28
Parents overfocus, -protect, -expect, etc.	27	Child lonely	24
Personal development retarded	10	Child misses sibling experience	22
Other (no motherhood preparation, holidays lonely, no excitement, etc.)	5	Parents have to entertain child	5
		Other (parent criticized for having one child, parent feels child is deprived, etc.)	21

SOURCE: From the book, *One Child by Choice* by Sharryl Hawke and David Knox, pp. 188–89 and 198–99. © 1977 by Prentice-Hall, Inc. Published by Prentice-Hall, Inc., Englewood Cliffs, N.J. 07632.

The two-child family is the most desirable family size in America.

Sample Deceptive

One mother was asked the difference between having one and two children. She said that when her first child swallowed a quarter, they took him to the hospital to have his stomach pumped out. When her second child swallowed a coin, he was told, "It will come out of your allowance."

sons included the husband wanting another child, personal fulfillment, and wanting a child of the opposite gender.

These mothers also commented on the consequences of having a second child. Almost half (49 percent) said the first child had made a greater personal impact than the second child. Specific comments included "I lost my freedom to truly enjoy life and do what I wanted with the first child. Once I began forgetting self, my second child had little effect"; "Childbirth and responsibility for a baby were new experiences with the first child. I felt more confident with the second child"; and "I got used to never being alone after my first child was born" (p. 24)

Although the second child had a minimal personal impact relative to the first, the mothers reported that their marriages were more affected by their second child than by their first. Specific statements included "The main difference I noticed with the second child was that I was more tired more of the time since I had to relate emotionally to two children throughout the day." Another woman said, "After I had listened to incessant pleadings such as 'I need a fork,' 'Can I have some more grape juice?' and 'I don't like oatmeal,' there was little left of me for my husband. And when the children were finally in bed, I needed to use the rest of the evening to catch up on the housework I was unable to do during the day because of the constant interruptions" (p. 15)

Three Children

Some couples want three children, and wanting to have a third child is related to the perceived consequences of doing so. For example, 59 married women with two children were asked whether they intended to have another (Werner, Middlestadt-Carter, & Crawford, 1975). Those who wanted a third child felt that the child would further their self-development, help fulfill them as wives and mothers, and strengthen the relationship with their husbands. Those not desiring another child felt that the opposite consequences would occur.

Having a third child creates a "middle child." Some researchers feel the middle child may be neglected (Forer & Still, 1976). Parents of three children, they contend, tend to focus on "the baby" and the "first born" and rarely on the one in between.

But some middle children see their position in the family in positive terms.

● I feel that being a middle child has turned out to be a great advantage for me. I received the love, but not the overattention that was given my older brother and younger sister. Although I have at times been envious of my siblings, I am very close to them (even though they cannot get along with each other). I feel that I am capable of taking care of myself, and also capable of being responsive and caring for others when they need someone. All things considered, it's *great* to be a middle child!!

I have one older brother and one younger sister and they are loved very much along with myself. However I am the one to be spoiled out of the three of us. I get whatever I want, not only from my parents, but also from my grandparents (my grandparents gave me a new Ford Mustang for graduation). At Christmas I get very unhappy because I can see that my brother and sister resent me very much, and I have been told by their best friends that they resent me. But what can I do? ●

Four or More Children

Larger families have complex interactional patterns and different values. The addition of each subsequent child dramatically increases the possible relationships in the family. For example, in the one-child family, 4 interpersonal relationships are possible—mother–father, mother–child, father–child, and father–mother–child. In a family of four, 11 relationships are possible; in a family of five, 26; and in a family of six, 57 (Henry & Warson, 1951).

In addition to relationships, values change as families get larger. Whereas members of a small family tend to value independence and personal development, large-family members necessarily value cooperation, harmony, and sharing. A parent of nine children said, "Meals around our house are a cooperative endeavor. One child prepares the drinks, another the bread, and still another sets the table. You have to develop cooperation or nobody gets fed."

Table 16.2 Ideal Family Size

Number of Children Wanted	Percent
None	2
One	2
Two	55
Three	20
Four or more	12
No opinion	9

SOURCE: The Gallup Report, Report No. 185, Princeton, N.J., 1981.

Issues to Consider

Table 16.2 indicates the number of children Americans say they want. The percentages are almost identical to those found by the National Opinion Research Center (Davis, 1982). Before deciding on the ideal family size for you and your partner, keep two issues in mind. First, each child will be different. One couple had decided to have an only child but because their daughter was beautiful, cooperative, and happy, they decided to have another. Their second child was born with a disfiguring birthmark on his face and was demanding and withdrawn. "We should have stopped while we were ahead," the mother said. Genetic differences, birth order, family economic situation, and parental experience ensure that each child will be different—often radically different.

Second, every family size has advantages and disadvantages. Only children may have more possessions, opportunities, and parental attention, but they may be lonely. Two or more children provide companionship for each other, but such interaction may turn into intense sibling rivalry or the middle child may be neglected, or the parental resources of time and money may be spread thin. In a large family the individual needs of each child may be neglected.

Married women preferring smaller families tend to be from a small family and a higher social class, be currently employed, enjoy a high-status career, earn a good income, and perceive themselves as an equal partner with their husbands. Those preferring larger families tend to have the opposite characteristics.

Recent Demographics

In 1982 American women gave birth to about 3.7 million babies. This represented an increase of about 2 percent over 1981. According to projections of the U.S. Bureau of the Census, between 1982 and 1985 there will be only small increases in the annual number of births.

The birthrate (number of live births per 1,000 population) in 1982 was 15.9; no significant change was predicted for 1983. The fertility rate (number of live births per 1,000 women aged 15–44) for 1982 was 67.8, which was slightly above the rate for 1981 (67.6) (National Center for Health Statistics, 1983).

Individuals have typically chosen to have children while in their twenties, but increasingly they are having children at later ages, especially women between the ages of 30 and 34. These numbers, rates, and percentages mean that having children is still very much a part of our personal and couple choices.

Gender Selection

In addition to wanting a certain number of children, some couples are concerned about the gender of their children. In his desire to have a male heir, King Henry VIII discarded several wives because they delivered only female children. The hapless Anne Boleyn was beheaded. But only the third of his six wives gave him a son, who died in childhood. Although few American men and women feel the same desperation to have a son, most express a slight preference for a male child.

Enter **gametrics**—the application of biological–mathematical theory to gamete separation. The biological part is the knowledge that Y chromosomes determine a male child and X chromosomes a female child. The mathematical part is increasing the probability of a male child by isolating the sperm carrying Y chromosomes, putting them together, and artificially inseminating the female.

The Y sperm are isolated by putting all the sperm from an ejacultaion on top of a thick substance in a test tube. Since Y sperm are stronger and swim faster, those sperm going through the substance and swimming to the bottom first are more often male sperm. These are collected from several ejaculations and are used to artificially inseminate the female. The probability of conceiving a male child using the procedure is 75 percent. If left to chance, the probability is 50 percent. A list of Centers for Gender Selection in your area can be obtained from Gametrics Limited, 475 Gate Five Road, Sausalito, California 94965; phone 415-332-3141.

Although very controversial, the method of **amniocentesis** and abortion may be used in gender selection. Fluid from the uterus in which the fetus floats contains fetal cells. These cells can be analyzed by withdrawing a sample of the fluid with a needle inserted into the pregnant woman's abdomen to see if the cells carry XX (female) or XY (male) chromosomes. (The same procedure can be used to test for certain genetic defects like Down's syndrome and sickle-cell anemia.) If the fetus is the gender desired by the parents, it is allowed to develop. Otherwise, it may be aborted. Examples of the use of amniocentesis in baby gender selection include a couple who wanted a male child to carry on the family name and to satisfy the condition of a relative's will stating they would inherit a million dollars if they had a male child. In another case, amniocentesis was used to preclude the possibility of a male birth since a lethal inherited disease was characteristic of male babies in that family. However, use of amniocentesis for the purpose of having a baby of the desired gender is unlikely to become routine.

Timing Your Children

Having decided how many children, if any, you want to have, when is the best time to have them? We now consider the various issues.

The First Child

Since most couples (85 percent) are fertile, many young couples are not concerned about their capacity to have children. Rather, the timing of the pregnancy becomes the central issue. There are at least four considerations in planning the first pregnancy.

Mother's Age

Medically, the best time for a woman to have her family is in the prime of her reproductive life—between ages 25 and 35. Although the chance of dying in childbirth is extremely low (9.2 deaths occur per 100,000 live births), the risks increase with age.

Risks to the baby's life also increase with age. The chance of a chromosomal abnormality is 1 percent if the woman is in her early twenties, 2 percent at ages 35–39, 3 percent at 40, and 10 percent at 45 (Seashore, 1980). A higher proportion die or have **Down's syndrome** (sometimes improperly called mongolism). This is a genetic defect caused by an extra chromosome. A Down's syndrome baby is physically deformed, mentally retarded, and will have a shorter life span.

Having a Down's syndrome baby is a particular fear of women who become pregnant after age 40. Many physicians recommend amniocentesis, described earlier, to determine the presence of this and other chromosomal abnormalities.

Amniocentesis is not without risks. In rare cases (about 2 percent of the time), the fetus may be damaged by the needle. Congenital orthopedic defects, such as clubfoot, and premature birth have been associated with amniocentesis. Also, if no abnormality is detected, this does not guarantee that the baby will be normal and healthy (Powledge, 1983).

An alternative to amniocentesis is **chorion biopsy**. This procedure involves placing a tube into the vagina to the uterus. Chorionic tissue, which

While more women are having their babies later in life, additional risks are involved.

surrounds the developing embryo, is removed and analyzed in the laboratory to assess the presence of genetic defects. The procedure can be performed in a physician's office as early as the eighth week of pregnancy, and results are available within 24 hours. (Amniocentesis is not performed until the sixteenth week and results are not known for four weeks.)

There are also risks if the mother is too young. Studies have shown that mothers 17 or younger are more likely to give birth to babies who are premature, have birth defects, and die before they are a year old. Teenage mothers are also likely to be less psychologically competent than older ones. A nationwide study of 5,000 women aged 14 to 24 (McLaughlin & Micklin, 1983) noted that women who have their first child before age 19 seem to have reduced personal efficacy; that is, they are more likely to feel they are not in control of their environment.

Most women have their first child in their early to mid-twenties. This age has positive consequences for the mother and child and permits ample time for subsequent births. A woman who wants to become established in a career and waits until she is in her mid-thirties to become pregnant will have less time to work out fertility problems if they develop. However, as we noted earlier, increasing numbers of women are choosing to wait until their thirties to have children, and for these women the risks they take by delaying conception may be insignificant compared with the joy they derive from motherhood. (Bongaarts, 1982)

Father's Age

The father's age is also a consideration in deciding when to have the first child. Down's syndrome is associated with increased paternal as well as maternal age. Other abnormalities that may be related to the age of the father include achondroplasia (a type of dwarfism), Marfan syndrome (height, vision, and heart abnormalities), Apert syndrome (facial and limb deformities), and fibrodysplasia ossificans progressiva (bony growths).

Since between 2 and 4 percent of newborn infants have a significant birth defect of genetic origin, older couples and those whose family histories show evidence of hereditary defect or disease might consider genetic counseling. Such counseling helps the potential parents to be aware of the chance of having a defective child.

Number of Years Married

Although most spouses are confident in their decision to have children when in their twenties or early thirties, they are somewhat ambivalent about how long it is best to be married before having a baby. In one study 54 couples waited an average of 39 months between their marriage and the birth of their first child (Steffensmeier, 1982). One viewpoint suggests that newlyweds need time to adjust to each other as spouses before becoming parents. If the marriage is dissolved, at least there would not be problems of child custody, child-support payments, and the single-parent status.

But if couples wait several years to have a baby, they may become so adjusted and so content with their child-free life style that parenthood is an unwelcome change. "We were married for seven wonderful years before Helen was born," recalled one mother. "The adjustment hasn't been easy. We resented her intrusion into our relationship."

The results of one study of more than 5,000 parents on the effect of delaying children versus having them soon after the marriage indicated that marital satisfaction after children was about the same regardless of length of time before having children (Marini, 1980).

However, being pregnant before marriage and having the first child within a few months after the marriage did have a significant negative effect on the marriage.

Timing Subsequent Births

Assuming you decide to have more than one child, what is the best interval between children? Most couples space their children within three years of each other. This interval allows parents to avoid being overwhelmed with the care of two infants yet is short enough so that children can be companions. In general, the smaller the family, the longer the interval between the children and vice versa (National Center for Health Statistics, 1982).

A family's economic situation may influence the spacing of children, and also the economic situation of the family may be influenced by child spacing. In one study (Reimer & Maiolo, 1977), the slower the rate of family growth, the better the financial position of the family and the greater the likelihood of home ownership.

Career Commitment

How committed you are to your career is an issue to consider in timing your first child. Although agreements regarding child care vary by couple, most couples prefer for the wife to be primarily responsible for child care. Such allocation of responsibility will be a major barrier to the woman who wants to pursue a full-time career with the demands of training, commitment, mobility, and continuity. Career-oriented women often decide to get their career going before beginning their family or to have their children first and then launch a career. Unless the partners opt to truly coparent or for the wife to have a job rather than a career, having a child while pursuing a career will be difficult.

Single Parenthood

Each year more than 600,000 children are born to unmarried women (National Center for Health Statistics, 1982). Although most are born to women between the ages of 18 and 24, an increasing number are being conceived by women aged 30 and over. Many of these women are single or divorced. They want the experience of motherhood yet feel they cannot delay having a baby indefinitely. Rather than wait for a hypothetical marriage, they choose to get pregnant without marriage. Artificial insemination is one alternative. Other women may seek impregnation from a man on the understanding that he will have no financial or other obligation for the child.

Some single and divorced men also want to be fathers but, like the women just discussed, are not in a socially legitimate sexual relationship (heterosexual marriage). Some may advertise for a woman who is willing to become impregnated and to give up the child at birth. We discuss the issues of artificial insemination and surrogate motherhood in the Chapter 17.

What Is Single Parenting Like?

More than 5,600,000 parents are rearing their children alone. Five million of these are mothers; 600,000 are fathers (Jones, 1981). Most of these mothers and fathers became single parents when their marriages ended in divorce. Since single parenthood is the role some unmarried people are seeking, let us examine what it is like for those already in the role of single parent.

Single parents are often stigmatized. Their families are often described as "broken," "disorganized," or "disintegrated," and the terms motherless and fatherless clearly imply that something is missing. But many single parents choose to ignore these labels. "My child and I have a tremendous relationship," said one single mother. "I can't imagine how a man around the house could improve our family life."

Nevertheless there are certain problems with which single-parent families must cope. These include the following.

1. *Satisfaction of emotional needs of children.* Perhaps the greatest challenge for single parents is to satisfy the emotional needs of their children—alone. Children need love, which a parent may express in a hundred ways—from hugs and kisses to help with homework. But the single parent who is tired from working all day and has no one with whom to share parenting at night may be unable fully to express her or his love.

2. *Satisfaction of adult emotional needs.* Single parents have emotional needs of their own that children are often incapable of satisfying. The unmet need to share an emotional relationship with an adult can weigh heavily on the single parent. Most single parents seek such a relationship. All 71 of the divorced single parents in one study were extremely interested in dating and 80 percent were doing so (DeFrain & Eirick, 1981).

3. *Satisfaction of adult sexual needs.* Most single parents regard their role as interfering with their sexual relationships. They may be concerned that their children will find out if they have a sexual encounter at home and frustrated if they have to go away from home to enjoy a sexual relationship. They may have to deal with questions like "Do I wait until my children are asleep and then ask my lover to leave before morning?" "Do I openly acknowledge my lover's presence in my life to my children and ask them not to tell anybody?" and "Suppose my kids get attached to my lover who may not be a permanent part of our lives?" (Most single parents hide their sexual relationships from their children and make them aware of another person in their life only if the other person is of significant emotional importance to the single parent.)

4. *Child care and supervision.* Since the single parent is likely to be employed, adequate child-care arrangements must be made. Using a relative or a hired sitter is the most frequent arrangement for the preschool child. There are also commercial day-care centers. But when child-care services must be paid for, it may take a large slice out of the single parent's usually modest income.

5. *Money.* Lack of money may be one of the most difficult aspects of single parenthood. The problem may be particularly acute when the single parent is a woman. The mean income for female-headed single-parent families is less than half the mean income for two-parent families.

None of these concerns imply that the single-parent family is inferior or abnormal. Also, not all single-parent families have the problems just described. "Children in such families often do not suffer from economic or psychological deprivation. Whether or not the single-parent household becomes a personal or social disaster depends upon the availability of sufficient material resources, supportive social networks, and the tenor of culturally structured attitudes toward it" (Bilge & Kaufman, 1983, p. 59).

Is Single Parenthood for You?

In deciding to become a single parent, each of these problems should be considered. Do you have the financial resources to pay for the cost of rearing a child? Who will take care of the child while you are working? Can you view the stigma attached to the unmarried single parent as somebody else's problem and not be bothered by what other people think or say? Do you have family and friends whom you can call on to help you in times of crisis? Do you want to allocate a major part of your life to rearing a child alone? Women contemplating single parenthood might want to contact Single Mothers by Choice (501 12th Street, Brooklyn, NY 11215; phone 212-965-2184).

Summary

The decision whether to become a parent is one of the most important you will ever make. Unlike marriage, parenthood is a role from which there is no easy withdrawal. "We can have ex-spouses and ex-jobs but not ex-children" (Rossi, 1968, p.32). Spouses, children, and society all benefit from family planning. These benefits include less health risk to mother and child, fewer unwanted children, decreased economic burden for individuals and society, and population control.

But your decision to become a parent is less than free. Parenthood is encouraged by family, peers, religion, government, education, and cultural observances. The reasons people give for having children include social expectations, influence of spouse, accident, the desire for immortality, personal fulfillment, and the desire for a close affiliative relationship.

Some couples opt for the child-free life style. Reasons wives give for wanting to be child-free include more personal freedom, greater time and intimacy with their spouses, and career demands. Husbands also are motivated by the desire for more personal freedom. They mentioned disinterest in being a parent and the desire to avoid the responsibilities that parenthood would involve.

The most preferred family size in the United States is the two-child family. Some of the factors in couples' decisions to have more than one child are desire to repeat a good experience, for companionship for their child or children, for a child of a different gender, and to strengthen the marriage relationship.

Every family size has inherent advantages and disadvantages. Only children may have more possessions, opportunities, and parental attention, but they may be lonely. Two children may be competitive, the middle child of three may be relatively neglected, and four or more children may be handicapped by parental resources being spread thin.

The timing of birth of the first child and the interval between children are important. Issues to consider in planning your first child include the ages of both spouses, the number of years you have been married, your career commitment, and your financial situation. The desire to have children far enough apart in age to ease the burden of infant care but close enough together to ensure that they can become playmates and the family's economic situation usually influence the spacing of children. Typical American couples have their first child about three years after their marriage and subsequent children at three-year intervals. The greater the number of children, the shorter the interval.

Some individuals choose single parenthood. But the role is demanding and several issues should be considered before taking this step. Some of the potential problems are satisfaction of the emotional needs of the child, satisfaction of the adult's emotional and sexual needs, child care and supervision, and money.

Key Terms

pronatalism
gametrics
amniocentesis

Down's syndrome
chorion biopsy

Issues in Debate and Future Directions

People disagree over the relative benefits and costs of parenthood; some actively seek the role while others actively avoid it. After examining the positive and negative aspects of parenthood, we look at trends in family planning.

Parenthood: A Role to Seek?

In their book *Parents in Contemporary America,* researchers LeMasters and DeFrain (1983) write that "rearing children is probably the hardest, and most thankless, job in the world" (p. 22). Yet, as mentioned earlier, more than 90 percent of Americans express a desire to have this experience. In addition to the reasons parents give for having children discussed earlier are the following presumed benefits.

Play   Children give you an excuse to express the child in you that society assumes you have outgrown. One parent said, "I like to ride an inner tube down a river with my kids in the summer and swing off a rope into the water as I did when I was a kid. I can't ask my friends to play like that; they'd think I was nuts. With your own kids, you've got the chance to play, really play, again." It is also fun to observe and participate in the spontaneity that children bring to their activities. Children have no internal schedule that tells them what they should do next. Being tickled, playing hide and seek, and flying a kite always have the potential of leading to something else, which may be a surprise.

Honesty   Children are honest. Unburdened by years of social programming, children express exactly what they feel. "When your 5-year-old wraps her or his arms around you and says 'I love you,' you know the feelings are real," one parent said.

Companionship   A mother of three children remarked, "After you finish school, all your friends scatter. The only relationships that really last are family relationships. Having children lets you become intimately involved in family over a long period of time."

Parental Pride   "I can't describe the pleasure it gave me to see my daughter ride a horse for the first time," said a rancher. Pride in one's children is a major reward of parenthood, and it is not dependent on the child's potential for becoming president. Parents feel pride when their children first walk, talk, ride a bike, and swim.

Spouse–Child Relationship   An additional delight for parents is to observe the interaction between their child and their spouse. A young father said, "Amy asks when she awakens from her nap, 'When's Mama coming home?' and when 'Mama' gets home, she lifts Amy in the air and they begin laughing with each other. As a result of watching them play together, I've developed a special love for my wife."

Parenthood: A Role to Avoid?

These positive aspects of parenthood have a flip side. The spontaneity children exhibit may erupt at the wrong time—when the parents are making love, reading, watching the evening news, talking on the telephone or to each other. The honesty of children may also include telling a neighbor that mommy said daddy was a

(continued)

"pompous ass" or telling grandma that the oil painting she gave the family is only hung up on the occasion of her annual visit. Parent–child companionship may also leave one spouse feeling excluded. Finally, parental pride can become parental grief when the child fails a grade, shoplifts, gets pregnant at 15, or takes drugs.

One woman who does not want children said, "They take the best years of your life and turn them into the best years of their life." Some additional negative aspects of parenthood include the following.

Increased Expenses Since the wife may drop out of the work force when she becomes a mother (less than 40 percent of young mothers are employed), having a baby may mean that a couple's income is cut drastically. But whether or not she stops working, expenses will climb. Costs for the first year (prenatal, delivery, and postnatal care) are around $3,000. It is estimated that the direct out-of-pocket cost to a middle-class family of rearing a son from conception through four years of college, is $215,000, or 23% of the family's total income. The cost of a daughter is an average of $900 more per year (Olson, 1983).

Restricted Social Life In a study of 102 first-time fathers (Gilman & Knox, 1976), the respondents were asked how often then went out with their wives to eat, see a movie, or take a drive before and after the baby was born. Half of the fathers said they spent less time sharing these events with their wives after the baby came. "Before you have a baby," said one father, "you assume that you can always get a sitter when you want and that your social life won't change. The reality is that when you spontaneously decide to go out, it's too late to find a sitter. You have to plan every social event at least three days ahead. The result—you go less often."

Another father who had been married 10 years before his child arrived expressed bitter resentment about the baby's interference with the sailing weekends he and his wife had enjoyed from April through late fall. "You can't take a baby on a sailboat, and being with Carol was part of the fun. We fought it for three months but finally sold the boat. If we had known that a baby equals a blackout on our sailing together, we would have reconsidered having a child."

New Routines   Children influence the total life style of the couple, who must adjust to new routines. These include more frequent visits by and to parents and in-laws, less sleep (sometimes chronic exhaustion), family-focused entertainment (G or PG movies) and lovemaking only when the children are asleep.

Parents experience these aspects of parenthood in different degrees at different times throughout the family life cycle. Parenthood is neither positive nor negative all the time but involves a mixture of experiences over the years.

Future Directions

The future of family planning will include increased tolerance for the child-free alternative. Couples who decide not to have children will be viewed less often as selfish and immature and not having children recognized as a viable option. "You're no longer a sickie if you don't have kids," said one woman.

The one-child family will become more prevalent as current concerns about inflation, personal freedom and growth, and the woman's career influence young couples to limit family size. Also, as more parents become aware that only children tend to be bright, career-oriented, and to have high self-esteem, fewer will have a second child out of obligation to the first.

More single people will want to have babies without the entanglements of marriage. Three in four Americans now consider it morally acceptable to be single and have children (Yankelovich, 1981a).

Finally, a greater number of women will delay childbearing until their thirties because of later age at marriage and a desire to pursue their careers. As the risks to the baby increase as the mother gets older, amniocentesis and chorion biopsy will be used more often to diagnose genetic abnormalities.

Chapter Seventeen

Fertilization and Contraception

We have both the technology to increase or decrease the probability of fertilization. But whether people use it or not is up to them.

A UNIVERSITY HEALTH SERVICE

PHYSICIAN

Chapter Seventeen

When a couple or individual decides to have a baby, getting pregnant becomes a goal. Recently, the natural way of pregnancy through sexual intercourse has been supplemented by the methods of artificial insemination, test-tube fertilization, and ovum transfer. If people decide to remain child free or to delay having children, effective contraception is important. In this chapter we review the methods of fertilization and contraception and also examine sterilization and abortion. We conclude by looking at the prochoice and prolife views on abortion.

Fertilization

Fertilization takes place when the female's egg, or ovum, unites with the male's sperm. This may occur through sexual intercourse, or artificial insemination, or, most recently, through the laboratory method called test-tube fertilization.

Sexual Intercourse

At orgasm in sexual intercourse the man ejaculates a thick white substance called semen, which contains from two to five million sperm cells. Once the semen is deposited in the vagina, the sperm begin to travel up the vagina, through the opening of the cervix, up the uterus, and into the Fallopian tubes. If the woman has ovulated (released a mature egg from an ovary into a Fallopian tube) within eight hours, or if she ovulates during the two or three days the sperm may remain alive, a sperm may penetrate and fertilize the egg. About 30 percent of fertilized eggs die. **Conception** refers to a fertilized egg that survives through implantation in the uterine wall.

If the goal is to get pregnant, it is important to be aware of the probability of conception, keep anxiety about getting pregnant at a minimum, time intercourse to coincide with ovulation, and use the most efficient position dur-

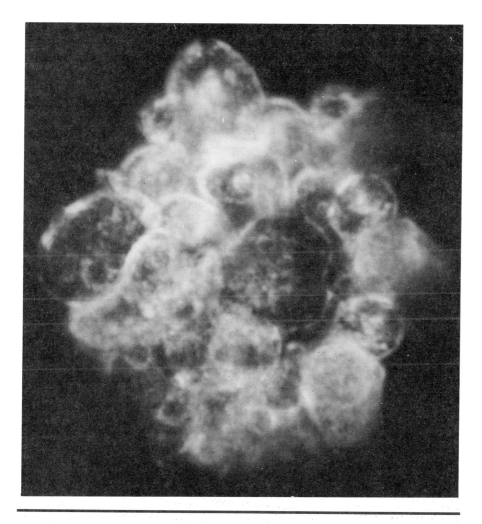

Human embryo
three days old.

ing intercourse. Table 17.1 shows the chances of a fertile woman getting pregnant. Notice that the younger the woman, the greater her chance of conceiving in a fewer number of months. But regardless of age, it takes most women several months to conceive. Hence there should be no cause for alarm if pregnancy does not occur as soon as desired.

A woman who gives herself time to get pregnant will be less anxious about doing so. This is important since anxiety may affect ovulation. Social workers in adoption agencies have noted that women, frustrated and despairing over their attempts to get pregnant and seeking to adopt a child, frequently become pregnant soon after they obtain a child and their anxiety over pregnancy disappears. Stress may affect male fertility, too. Testicle biopsies performed on men awaiting execution revealed a progressive negative effect on sperm production. Although this is an extreme example of a stressful situation, other types of stress may have the same effect (Silber, 1980).

Table 17.1   Likelihood of Pregnancy in Fertile Women

Age	Probability of Conception per Month	Average Time to Conception (Months)	Probability of Conception Within a Year
Late 30s	8.3–10%	12–10	65–72%
Early 30s	10–15%	10–6.7	72–86%
Late 20s	15–20%	6.7–5	86–93%
Early 20s	20–25%	5–4	93–97%

SOURCE: Sherman J. Silber, Table from *How to Get Pregnant.* Copyright © 1980 by Sherman J. Silber. Reprinted by permission of Charles Scribner's Sons.

When is the best time to have intercourse to maximize the chance of pregnancy? Since a woman is fertile for only about 48 hours each month, the timing of sexual intercourse is important. In general, 24 hours before ovulation is the best time. There are several ways to predict ovulation. Many women have breast tenderness and some experience a "pinging" sensation at the time of ovulation. Also, a woman may keep a record of her basal body temperature and examine her cervical mucus. These latter two methods are discussed in detail later in this chapter, but we briefly describe the cervical mucus timing method here. After menstruation the vagina of most women is without noticeable discharge because the mucus is thick. As the time of ovulation nears, the mucus thins to the consistency of egg white, which may be experienced by the woman as increased vaginal discharge. Intercourse should occur during this time.

During intercourse the woman should be on her back and a pillow placed under her buttocks after receiving the sperm so a pool of semen will collect near her cervix. She should remain in this position for about 30 minutes to allow the sperm to reach the Fallopian tubes.

Getting pregnant is easier for some than for others. Between 10 and 15 percent of couples who have regular intercourse for a year or more and who do not use contraception are infertile. Forty percent of the time the male is infertile; forty percent of the time the female is infertile; ten percent of the time both partners are infertile; and ten percent of the time neither partner is determined to be infertile but the woman of the couple still cannot get pregnant. Some of the more common causes of infertility in men include low sperm production, poor sperm motility, effects of sexually transmitted diseases such as gonorrhea and syphilis, and interference with the passage of sperm through the genital ducts due to an enlarged prostate. The causes of infertility in women include blocked Fallopian tubes, endocrine imbalances that prevent ovulation, dysfunctional ovaries, chemically hostile cervical mucus that may kill sperm, and the effects of sexually transmitted diseases. About half of all infertility problems can be successfully treated so that a baby will result. Couples not successful in becoming pregnant after trying to correct infertility sometimes opt for artificial insemination, test-tube fertilization, or ovum transfer.

Artificial Insemination of Wife

When the sperm of the husband is low in number or motility, it sometimes helps to pool the sperm from several ejaculations and artificially inseminate the wife (called **AIH—artificial insemination by husband**). In other cases, sperm from an unknown donor (**AID—artificial insemination by donor**) is used. Sometimes the donor's and husband's sperm are mixed so that the couple may have the psychological benefit of knowing that the husband may be the biological father. Another situation in which AID may be sought is when the husband is the carrier of a genetic disease, such as Tay-Sachs disease.

Some couples have sought sperm from the Repository for Germinal Choice. This controversial sperm bank in Escondido, California, specializes in providing sperm from men who are known for their intellectual achievements. Among their donors have been three Nobel prize winners.

In the procedure of artificial insemination, a physician, or the husband who has been trained by the physician, deposits the sperm through a syringe in the wife's cervix and places a cervical cap over her cervix, which remains in place for 24 hours (see Figure 17.1). On the average, it takes about three such inseminations before fertilization occurs. One couple's experience with AID follows.

● Because of my need to get pregnant, my husband and I decided after long, hard thinking and sleepless nights to try artificial insemination. But I wasn't sure if that was what I wanted. I was very afraid that after the baby was born my husband

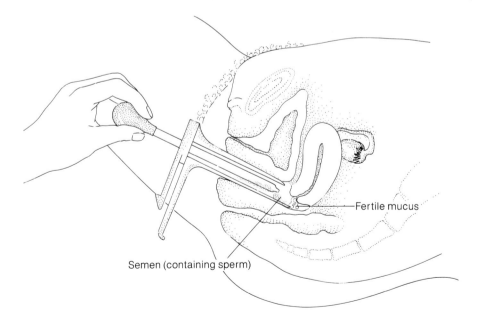

Fertile mucus

Semen (containing sperm)

**Figure 17.1
Artificial
Insemination**
The physician deposits sperm through a syringe into the woman's cervix.

would resent the child because it would be from another man's sperm. He tried to assure me that he would not feel that way. He wanted a baby almost as much as I did. So we began the procedures.

The first thing that we had to do was to turn in my basal body temperature chart so that the physicians could determine the exact time that I ovulated. Then we had to give them a picture of my husband and his personal and biological traits (they also categorize donors according to these characteristics). Then they tried to find a donor with the characteristics that matched those of my husband.

The injections of the donor semen cost $25 and were done the day before and morning of ovulation. The actual procedure was very humiliating. I had to lay on the examination table after I received the injection with my feet up in the air at a 90-degree angle for 30 minutes.

I became pregnant after the first set of injections. It was really hard to believe that we were finally going to have a child. My husband was as excited as I was.

I carried the child full term and had no complications. It was hard to believe that after all those years of failing, some other man's sperm got me pregnant. Actually, I don't think about that now. We have a beautiful boy named Mark who is the joy of our lives. He is named after my husband, is very healthy, and we feel lucky to have him. As long as both parents agree, I feel that artificial insemination with donor sperm is the best answer to the problem of sterility. At least our son is a part of one of us in flesh and bone! Our marriage is closer than ever now. ●

Like this couple, most of the 62 AID couples who participated in a follow-up study reported having a positive experience (Czba & Chevret, 1979). Although couples recalled feeling severe emotional pain when they learned of the husband's inability to impregnate the wife, they decided on AID because, as the wife in the preceding narrative noted, it would allow at least one-half of them as a couple to be biologically related to the prospective child. The fact of AID was usually kept a secret and neither their friends nor the child was told.

About 20,000 babies are born from both types of artificial insemination every year. Before AID is carried out, the parents-to-be agree that any child produced by this procedure will be regarded as their own and their legitimate heirs.

The potential legal problems with AID have not been worked out. Only 18 states have laws pertaining to this procedure. One researcher observed, "A doctor could be charged with criminal conspiracy for producing an illegitimate child, and in the event the child were to be born with a severe defect, the parents or child could take legal action against the physician on grounds of negligence" (Zimmerman, 1982, p. 236).

Artificial Insemination of Surrogate Mother

Sometimes artificial insemination does not help a woman to get pregnant (for example, her Fallopian tubes may be blocked or her cervical mucus may be hostile to sperm). The couple who still want a child and who have decided against adoption may consider parenthood through a **surrogate mother**— a woman who is impregnated with the husband's sperm and carries the child to term. As with AID, the motivation of the prospective parents is to have a child that is genetically related to at least one of them. For the surrogate mother, the apparent motivation is to help involuntary childless couples achieve their aspirations of parenthood.

The concept of surrogate pregnancy is not new. The Bible reports that Abraham and his wife Sarah could not conceive a child. Their solution was for Abraham to have intercourse with Sarah's Egyptian maid, Hagar, who bore a child for them.

In 1980 Elizabeth Kane (a fictitious name) gave birth to a healthy baby boy for a couple in which the wife could not get pregnant. Elizabeth Kane was artificially inseminated with the husband's sperm through Surrogate Parenting Associates, Inc., of Louisville, Kentucky (see Resources & Organizations in Appendix D for address), and gave up her legal right to the baby. Mrs. Kane, a 38-year-old mother of three, indicated it was a fulfilling experience. In a study of 125 women who had applied for surrogate motherhood (Parker, 1983), more than 100 had already had children and described their pregnancies in glowing terms, saying they felt "more complete" or "more feminine and attractive." Although 9 in 10 said they would require a fee for their service, in no case was money the primary motivating factor.

Legally, there are few guidelines to protect involuntary childless couples who engage a surrogate mother for procreative services. She could change her mind and decide to keep the child, leaving the childless couple little recourse even if they had a contract (Zimmerman, 1982). Some states require that the social parents adopt the baby whose birth they have arranged. Engaging a surrogate mother is expensive. Total costs in 1983 through the Louisville organization (excluding the cost for travel and board) began at approximately $25,000.

Test-Tube Fertilization

About two million couples cannot have a baby because the woman's Fallopian tubes are blocked or damaged, preventing the passage of the eggs to the uterus. **Test-tube** or **in-vitro fertilization** is an additional option to parenthood by a surrogate mother for such couples.

Using a laparoscope (a narrow telescopelike instrument inserted through an incision just below the woman's navel to view the tubes and ovaries), the physician is able to see a mature egg as it is released from the woman's ovary. The time of release can be predicted accurately to within two hours. When the egg emerges, the physician uses an aspirator to remove the egg, placing it in a small tube containing a stabilizing fluid. The egg is taken to the laboratory, put in a culture dish, kept at a certain temperature–acidity level, and surrounded by sperm from the husband. After one of these sperm fertilizes the egg, it divides and is implanted by the physician in the wall of the woman's uterus (Edwards & Steptoe, 1980). Usually, several fertilized eggs are implanted in the hope that one will survive.

Louise Brown of Oldham, England, was the first baby to be born by in-vitro fertilization. Since her birth in 1978, the first test-tube clinic in the United States opened at the Eastern Virginia Medical School in Norfolk, Virginia. Only women less than 35 years of age whose reproductive functions are normal (except for malfunctioning Fallopian tubes) are accepted. The procedure costs from $3,000 to $5,000, excluding hospitalization.

Other U.S. in-vitro fertilization clinics include those at the University of Texas, Duke University, and the University of North Carolina at Chapel Hill. As of this writing, eight test-tube babies have been born in the United States. Although the number will undoubtedly increase, public opinion on the appropriateness of test-tube conception is divided. The readers of *Good Housekeeping* split 50–50 on the issue (*Good Housekeeping Poll*, 1980). Those approving felt that every couple should have the opportunity to have a child and viewed test-tube conception as helping to provide that opportunity. Those who disapproved did so for religious reasons ("It's against God's plan") or fear that a baby so conceived would be deformed.

Ovum Transfer

An alternative to test-tube fertilization for the infertile couple in which the woman's Fallopian tubes are blocked or damaged is **ovum transfer**. The man allows his sperm to be artificially inseminated in a surrogate woman. After about five days her uterus is flushed out (endometrial lavage) and the contents analyzed under a microscope to identify the presence of a fertilized ovum, which is then inserted into the uterus of the otherwise infertile woman.

Infertile couples opt for ovum transfer, also called embryo transplant, because the baby will be half theirs (the man is the biological father) and the woman will have the experience of pregnancy and childbirth. The surrogate woman participates out of her desire to help an infertile couple.

Ovum transfers are being conducted at Harbor-UCLA Medical Center, 1000 W. Carson Street, Torrence, California 90509. Information about this and other fertility procedures may be obtained by calling the Endocrinology Department at 213-533-3869.

Contraception

Most people have no problem getting pregnant. But many get pregnant when they do not want to. **Contraception**, the prevention of pregnancy by one of a number of methods, has been used throughout history by men and women.

All contraceptive practices have a common purpose—to prevent the male sperm from fertilizing the female egg or to keep the egg from implanting in the uterus. In performing these functions, contraception permits couples to make love without making babies. If no method of contraception is used, the chance that a sexually active woman will get pregnant is 90 percent during a one-year period. With contraception the risk of becoming pregnant can be reduced to almost zero depending on the method and how systematically it is used.

Unmarried individuals most likely to use contraception consistently have positive feelings about their sexuality, are involved in serious heterosexual relationships, are not guilty about having intercourse, and have partners who encourage contraceptive use (Herold & Goodwin, 1981; Herold & McNamee, 1982); but resistance to contraception on first intercourse among young unmarried people may be strong. In a random sample of university women, only 30 percent said they used contraception the first time they had intercourse (Huk, 1979). Reasons typically given for not using contraception include "I didn't want it to look like I was planning to have intercourse," "I thought I would be lucky and not get pregnant," "Sex should be spontaneous," and "It's against my religion to use birth control."

Even those who say they intend to use contraception, do not always do so. In a study of 71 unmarried undergraduate women, 40 percent of those who said they intended to use birth control pills had not done so at the time of follow-up (McCammon & Cafferty, 1982).

Married couples are the most likely to consistently use some form of contraception. Table 17.2 shows the percentage of wives between the ages of 15 and 44 using various contraceptives. Each of these contraceptives is discussed in the following pages.

Table 17.2 Percentage of U.S. Wives Using Various Nonsurgical Contraceptives

Type of Contraceptive	Percent
Pill	46
Condom	15
IUD	13
Rhythm	7
Diaphragm	6
Foam	6
Withdrawal	4
Douche	1
Other	2

SOURCE: U.S. Department of Health and Human Services, Public Health Service, "Contraceptive Utilization: United States 1976," Office of Health Research, Statistics, and Technology. National Center for Health Statistics, Hyattsville, Maryland, Publication No. 81–1983. p. 6 March, 1981.

Oral Contraceptives

Birth control pills are the preferred contraceptive by most women, married and unmarried. Although there are over 40 brands available in North America, there are basically two types of pills—the combination pill and the minipill.

The **combination pill** contains the hormones estrogen and progesterone (also known as progestin), which act to prevent ovulation and implantation. The estrogen inhibits release of the follicle-stimulating hormone (FSH) and the luteinizing hormone (LH) from the pituitary gland so that no egg will develop. The progesterone serves as secondary protection by causing a change in the composition of the cervical mucus. It becomes both thick and acidic, creating a hostile environment for the sperm. So even if an egg were to mature and ovulation were to occur, the progesterone would ward off or destroy sperm. Another function of progesterone is to affect the lining of the uterus, making it unsuitable for implantation.

The combination pill is taken for 21 days, beginning on the fifth day after the start of the menstrual flow (see discussion of menstruation in Chapter 3). Three or four days after the last pill is taken, menstruation occurs and the 28-day cycle begins again. To eliminate the problem of remembering when to begin taking the pill every month, some physicians prescribe a low-dose combination pill for the first 21 days and a placebo (sugar pill) or iron pill for the next seven days. In this way, the woman takes a pill every day.

The second type of oral contraceptive is the **minipill**, which contains the same progesterone found in the combination pill but at much lower doses. The minipill contains no estrogen. As in the combination pill, progesterone

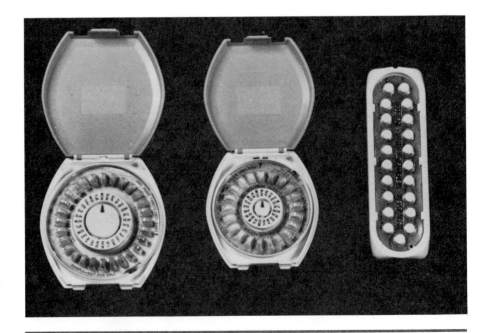

Birth control pills are the most widely used contraceptive in America.

provides a hostile environment for sperm and inhibits implantation of a fertilized egg in the uterus.

Either the combination or minipill should be taken only when prescribed by a physician who has detailed information about the woman's previous medical history. Contraindications, or reasons for not prescribing birth control pills, include hypertension, impaired liver function, known or suspected tumors that are estrogen dependent, undiagnosed abnormal genital bleeding, pregnancy at the time of the examination, and a history of poor blood circulation. The major complications associated with taking oral contraceptives are blood clots and high blood pressure. Also, the risk of heart attack is increased in women over age 30, particularly those who smoke or have other risk factors. Women over 40 should generally use other forms of contraception as side effects of contraceptive pills increase with the age of the user. Infertility problems also have been noted in women who have used the combination pill for several years without the breaks in pill use recommended by most physicians.

While the long-term consequences of taking birth control pills are still the subject of research, short-term effects are experienced by 25 percent of women. These mild side effects include increased susceptibility to vaginal infections, nausea, slight weight gain, vaginal bleeding between periods, breast tenderness, mild headaches, and mood changes (some women become depressed and experience a loss of sexual desire). Nevertheless, numerous studies involving hundreds of thousands of women show that the overall risk of pill use is less than that of full-term pregnancy and giving birth (Ory, Rosenfeld, & Landman, 1980).

There are also immediate health benefits from taking birth control pills. Oral contraceptives tend to protect the woman against breast tumors, ovarian cycts, rheumatoid arthritis, and pelvic inflammatory disease. They also regularize her menstrual cycle, reduce premenstrual tension, and may reduce menstrual cramps and blood loss during menstruation. Finally, oral contraceptives are convenient, do not interfere with intercourse, and, most important, provide highly effective protection against pregnancy.

Condom

Also referred to as a "rubber," "safe," or prophylactic, the condom is currently the only form of male contraception. The **condom** is a thin sheath, usually made of synthetic material or lamb intestine, which is rolled over and down the shaft of the erect penis before intercourse. When the man ejaculates, the sperm are caught inside the condom. When used in combination with a spermicidal, or sperm-killing, agent, which the woman inserts in her vagina, the condom is a highly effective contraceptive and is the only contraceptive that provides some protection against sexually transmitted diseases. Although some men say they do not like to use a condom because it decreases sensation, others say that having the woman put the condom on their penis is an erotic experience and that the condom actually enhances the pleasurable feelings during intercourse.

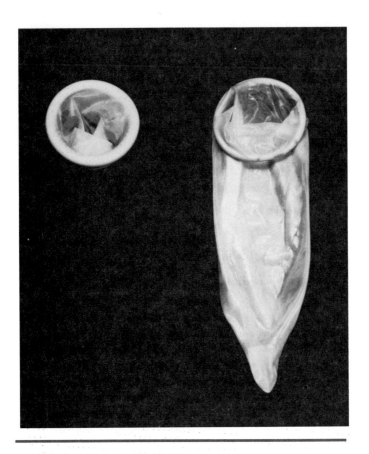

Condoms are currently the only form of male contraception.

Like any contraceptive, the condom is effective only when properly used. A space should be left at the top of the condom (some condoms already have a recessed tip) when it is rolled onto the penis to provide room for the semen to collect. Otherwise the condom may break. In addition, the penis should be withdrawn from the vagina soon after ejaculation. If the penis is not withdrawn and the erection subsides, the semen will leak from the base of the condom into the vaginal lips. The sperm can then travel up the vagina into the uterus and fertilize the egg.

In addition to furnishing extra protection, spermicides also provide lubrication, which permits easy entrance of the condom-covered penis into the vagina. If no spermicide is used and the condom is not of the prelubricated variety, K-Y jelly, a sterile lubricant, may be needed. Vaseline or other kinds of petroleum jelly should not be used because they may increase the risk of vaginal infection.

Condoms can be purchased in drugstores and most conveneince stores. Among the brand names are Trojan, Rameses, Naturalamb and Fourex. The latter two are made from lamb intestine and are considerably more expensive than those made from synthetic material.

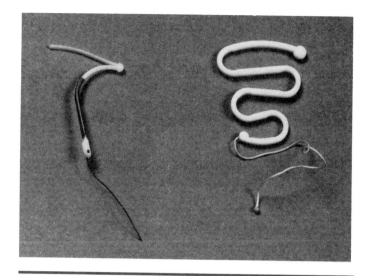

Two types of
IUDs—Copper 7
and Lippes loop.

Intrauterine Device (IUD)

The **intrauterine device**, or **IUD**, is a small plastic object that is inserted by a physician into the woman's uterus through the vagina and cervix. Most IUDs have two plastic threads attached to them that hang down into the vagina so the woman can feel them and check regularly that the device is in place. The four most commonly used IUDs are the Lippes loop, Saf-T-Coil, Copper-7, and Progestasert T. The latter contains a slow-releasing progesterone and must be replaced every year. The IUD should stay inside the uterus until it is removed by a physician. Although used most frequently by women who have had a child, some women who have never been pregnant may also use the IUD.

The IUD works by preventing implantation of the fertilized egg on the uterine wall. The exact chemistry is unknown, but one theory suggests that the IUD stimulates the entry of white blood cells into the uterus, which attack and destroy "invading" cells, in this case, the fertilized egg. Implantation may also be prevented by the IUD mechanically dislodging the fertilized egg from the uterine wall.

Side effects of the IUD may include cramps, excessive menstrual bleeding, and irregular bleeding, or spotting, between menstrual periods. These effects may disappear after the first two months of use. Infection and perforation are more serious side effects. Users of the IUD have a higher incidence of pelvic inflammatory disease, which infects the uterus and Fallopian tubes and may lead to sterility. In addition, the IUD may cut or perforate the uterine walls or cervix, resulting in bleeding and pain. Women who plan to have children should consider using another method of contraception.

Some women are unable to retain the IUD; it irritates the muscles of the uterus causing them to contract and expel the IUD. About 10 percent of all women who begin to use an IUD expel the device within the first year. Once this happens there is only a 50 percent chance that she will be able to retain another one. To make sure that the IUD remains in place, a woman should check at least once a month just after her period.

The fact that the IUD does not prevent conception is both its greatest advantage and disadvantage. The advantage is that the IUD does not interfere with the body's normal hormonal and physiological responses. The disadvantage is that it permits conception and then destroys the fertilized egg, which is morally repugnant to some people. Also, women who do get pregnant while using the IUD must make a decision about whether to leave it in or remove it. There is a 50 percent chance for miscarriage if the IUD is left in and a 25 percent chance for miscarriage if the IUD is removed. However, there are no reports of birth defects if the IUD is left in and the baby is carried to term delivery.

Diaphragm

The **diaphragm** is a shallow rubber dome attached to a flexible, circular steel spring. Varying in diameter from 2 to 4 inches, the diaphragm covers the cervix and prevents sperm from moving beyond the vagina into the uterus. It should always be used with a spermicidal jelly or cream.

To obtain a diaphragm, the woman must have an internal pelvic examination by a physician or nurse practitioner who will select the appropriate size of diaphragm and instruct the woman how to insert it. She will be told to apply the spermicidal cream or jelly on the inside of the diaphragm and to insert it at least two hours before intercourse. The diaphragm must be left in place after intercourse for at least six hours to permit any lingering sperm to be killed by the spermicidal cream. Figure 17.2 illustrates the diaphragm's use.

After the birth of a child, a miscarriage, abdominal surgery, or the gain or loss of 10 pounds, a woman who uses a diaphragm should consult her physician or health practitioner to ensure a continued good fit. In any case, the diaphragm should be checked every two years for fit.

A major advantage of the diaphragm is that is does not interfere with the woman's hormonal system and has few, if any, side effects. Also, for those couples who feel that menstruation diminishes their capacity to enjoy intercourse, the diaphragm may be used to catch the menstrual flow.

Figure 17.2 Diaphragm: Insertion, Check, and Removal

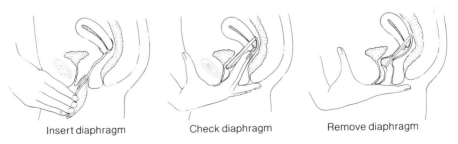

Insert diaphragm   Check diaphragm   Remove diaphragm

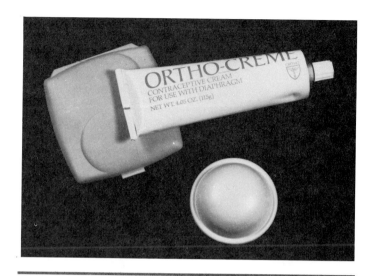

Diaphragm and contraceptive cream.

On the negative side, some women feel that use of the diaphragm with the spermicidal gel is messy and a nuisance. In addition, for some the use of the gel may produce an allergic reaction. Furthermore, some partners feel that the gel makes oral–genital contact less enjoyable. Finally, if the diaphragm does not fit properly, pregnancy can result.

Cervical Cap

Not to be confused with the diaphragm, the **cervical cap** is a small rubber or plastic cap that fits snugly over the cervix and is held in place by suction. It blocks sperm from entering the cervix but (the newer models) have a one-way valve that permits menstrual material and cervical secretions to flow outward. Unlike the diaphragm, the cervical cap can be left in place for a week.

Cervical caps are currently being tested in the United States for FDA approval. Of 550 women who requested the cap, about one-fourth could not be fitted with one of the four sizes available (Koch, 1982a). Those who were able to obtain a proper fit were instructed to fill the cap completely with spermicide before inserting it, to leave it in place for no longer than seven days, and to avoid using it during menstruation. In a two-year follow-up, 30 percent reported that the cap had become dislodged during intercourse and 4 in 10 said that the most objectionable feature of the cap was a noticeable odor during use.

Vaginal Spermicides

Spermicidal foam contains chemicals that kill sperm. The foam must be applied near the cervix (appropriate applicators are included when the product

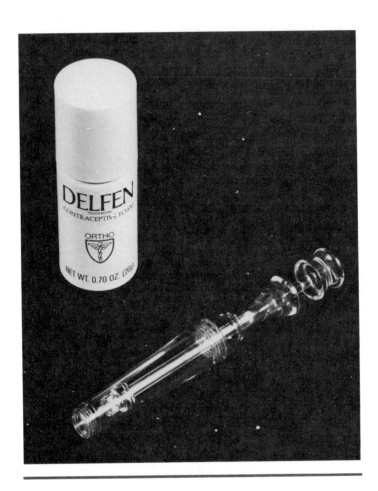

Spermicidal foam
with applicator.

is purchased) no more than 20 minutes before intercourse; and each time intercourse is repeated, more foam must be applied. Foams such as Delfen and Emko should not be confused with vaginal deodorants like Summers' Eve. The latter have no contraceptive value.

Spermicidal foams also should not be confused with spermicidal gels that are used in conjunction with a diaphragm. These gels should never be used alone since they do not stick to the cervix as well as foam.

Foams are advantageous because they do not manipulate the woman's hormonal system and they have few side effects. These include allergic reactions in some men and women (their genitals may become irritated by the chemicals in the foam). The main disadvantage is that some regard its use as messy and its taste may be unpleasant if oral–genital contact is enjoyed.

Vaginal suppositories also contain spermacide and are inserted about thirty minutes before intercourse. Also known as pessaries, vaginal supppositories provide protection by killing sperm and weakening sperm motility.

The sponge.

Vaginal Sponge

One of the newest contraceptives to win approval by the FDA is the vaginal **sponge**. The sponge is 2 inches in diameter, 1 ¼ inches thick, and contains spermicide that is activated when the sponge is immersed in water before insertion into the vagina. A small loop allows for easy removal of the sponge. Like condoms and spermicidal foams, the sponge is available in drugstores without a prescription. The brand name for the sponge is Today and it sells for about $1. It prevents fertilization not only by releasing spermicide to kill sperm but by blocking the cervix to prevent entrance by sperm and by absorbing sperm into the sponge.

A major advantage of the sponge is that it allows for spontaneity since it can be inserted early in the day, may be worn for up to 24 hours, and may be used for more than one act of intercourse without requiring additional applications of spermicide. According to FDA tests on 1,582 sponge users, the sponge is comparable to the diaphragm in effectiveness. The disadvantage of the sponge is that there is some possibility that it may cause toxic shock syndrome. Because of this possibility, the sponge should "not be used during the menstrual period" (Kafka & Gold, 1983, p. 146)

Rhythm Method

The rhythm method is based on the premise that fertilization cannot occur unless live sperm are present when the egg is in the Fallopian tubes. Sperm usually live two to three days while an egg lives 24 hours. Women who use the rhythm method must know their time of ovulation and avoid intercourse just before, during, and after that time. There are three ways of predicting the presumed safe period: the calendar method, the basal body temperature method, and the cervical mucus method.

Calendar Method

When using the **calendar method** to predict when the egg is ready to be fertilized, the woman keeps a record of the length of her menstrual cycles for eight months. The menstrual cycle is counted from day one of a menstrual period through the last day before the onset of the next period. She then calculates her fertile period by subtracting 18 days from the shortest cycle and 11 days from the longest. The resulting figures indicate the range of her fertility period. It is during this time that she must avoid intercourse.

For example, suppose that during an eight-month period, a woman had cycle lengths of 26, 32, 27, 30, 28, 27, 28, and 29 days. Subtracting 18 from her shortest cycle (26) and 11 from her longest cycle (32), she knows the days the egg is likely to be in the Fallopian tubes. To avoid getting pregnant, she must avoid intercourse on days 8 through 21 of her cycle.

The calendar method of predicting the safe period is unreliable for two reasons. First, the next month the woman may ovulate at a different time from any of the previous eight months. Second, how long sperm live may vary; they may live long enough to meet the next egg in the Fallopian tubes.

Basal Body Temperature (BBT) Method

The **basal body temperature (BBT) method** is based upon temperature changes that occur in the woman's body shortly after ovulation. The basal body temperature is the temperature of the body at rest upon waking in the morning. To establish her BBT, the woman must take her temperature (for 3 months) at this time before she gets out of bed. Just before ovulation, her temperature will drop about 0.2° F. Between 24 and 72 hours later, there will be a rise in temperature of about 0.6° F–0.8° F above her normal BBT, signaling the time of ovulation. Intercourse must be avoided from the time the woman's temperature drops until her temperature has remained elevated for three consecutive days. Beginning on the night of the third day after the temperature shift is observed, she may resume having intercourse.

Cervical Mucus Method

The **cervical mucus method** is based on observations of changes in the mucus cycle from no perceptible mucus for several days after menstruation to sticky to very slippery during ovulation to a cloudy discharge after ovulation ends. The mucus becomes thin and slippery, similar to raw egg white, during ovulation to create a favorable environment for sperm. The woman should abstain from intercourse as soon as mucus appears before ovulation and continue to do so for four complete days after the peak of cervical mu-

Basal Body Temperature By Computer

A new computer device, recently approved by the FDA, can assist a woman in identifying her basal body temperature. Similar in size to a pocket calculator, the "personal rhythm clock" contains a microprocessor and comes with a temperature–sensitive probe that the woman puts under her tongue for about three minutes upon awakening. When the probe signals the microprocessor what her temperature is, it beeps to let her know.

After 10 days of the routine, a lined pattern appears on the display window. On fertile days the display window is blank. Developed and first tested in England, the device adjusts for menstrual cycles that are shorter or longer than usual. The device costs $100, is not available in stores, but can be obtained from Rite-Time Corporation, 200 N. Sutton St., North Andover, MA 01845. Effectiveness of the computer–assisted Basal Body Temperature Method on a large sample awaits empirical verification.

cus. A woman can check her cervical mucus by wiping herself with toilet paper several times a day before she urinates and observing the changes. This method requires the woman to distinguish between mucus and semen, spermicidal agents, lubrication, and discharges by infection. Also, she must not douche since douching will wash away what she is trying to observe.

Other labels for the cervical mucus method are natural family planning and the Billings method (named after Evelyn and John Billings) (Billings et al., 1974). Associated with the Billings method is observation of the Mittelschmerz—the midcycle abdominal pain or "ping" sometimes associated with ovulation.

Other Methods

Some people erroneously regard withdrawal and douching as effective methods of contraception. They are not.

Withdrawal

Withdrawal, also known as coitus interruptus, is the practice of the man taking his penis out of the vagina before he ejaculates. Not only does this technique interrupt sexual pleasure, it is an unreliable means of contraception. Even before ejaculation, the man may, without his awareness, emit a small amount of fluid from the Cowper's gland, which may contain sperm. In addition, the man may delay his withdrawal too long and inadvertently ejaculate some semen near the vaginal opening of his partner. Sperm deposited here can live in the moist vaginal lips and make their way up the vagina to the uterus.

Douching

Douching refers to rinsing or cleansing of the vaginal canal. After intercourse the woman fills a syringe with water or a spermicidal agent and flushes (so she assumes) the sperm from her vagina. But in some cases, the fluid will actually force sperm up through the cervix. In other cases, a large number of sperm may already have passed through the cervix to the uterus so that the douche may do little good. In effect, a douche does little to deter conception and may encourage it. Also, most physicians question the advisability of douching as it may create a chemical imbalance in the vagina leading to infection.

Postcoital Contraception

Some women who have engaged in unprotected intercourse in the middle of their cycle elect to take a **morning-after pill**, which contains high levels of estrogen to prevent implantation of the fertilized egg on the uterine wall.

This is an emergency form of birth control, is potentially dangerous, and is available only by prescription from a physician.

Diethylstilbestrol (DES) is the most commonly used morning-after pill. The first of 10 25 mg doses must be taken within 72 hours after intercourse and preferably within 12 to 24 hours. Normally, the pills are taken twice a day for five days. Of 5,593 woman treated with DES, only 26 became pregnant (Hatcher et al., 1978). Side effects of nausea, vomiting, bleeding abnormalities, and blood clots make routine use of this durg undesirable. In addition, studies indicate that the offspring of women who took DES during pregnancy are more likely to have birth defects and have an increased risk of vaginal cancer and infertility. If the woman remains pregnant after taking DES, she might consider a therapeutic abortion.

Contraception: A Personal Decision

With the array of contraceptive methods available (and more being developed), you might ask, "Which one is best for me?" Issues to consider in selecting a contraceptive include personal values, health, reliability of the contraceptive procedure, sexual fulfillment, psychological contentment, and age. Do your personal values permit you to use one of the more reliable forms of contraception? "It's a sin to use anything but the rhythm method," one woman said. "I would feel immoral putting any of those devices in my body or contaminating my system with birth control pills." But others feel it is immoral *not* to use one of several birth control methods.

Another major concern is your health. Some women are at risk using the pill or IUD. If safety is the major concern, barrier methods such as the condom plus spermicide or diaphragm plus spermicide offer the greatest protection with the least risk to the woman's health. Some women, whose values permit abortion, choose one of these methods for health reasons and consider abortion as a backup.

Reliability of the contraceptive chosen is another crucial concern. Abstinence is, of course, the ultimate contraceptive, but the various nonsurgical contraceptives have varying rates of effectiveness. Table 17.3 indicates the failure rate of different contraceptive methods among one group of women. Other studies show that the pill and IUD are identical in effectiveness and that the condom with spermicidal agent and diaphragm with spermicidal agent approximate the effectiveness of birth control pills. The least effective method in all studies is the rhythm method.

Sexual fulfillment and psychological contentment are other issues. "It's important to me to have a good sex life," said one woman, "and fooling with a diaphragm every night is no fun. Yet, I don't take the pill because I think it will harm my body." Her feelings emphasize that any decision about which contraceptive method to use will involve some trade-offs.

Your choice of a contraceptive may also depend on your age and whether you have already had the number of children you want. One pattern for the young woman is to use birth control pills until the desired family size is

Table 17.3   Contraceptive Failure Experienced by U.S. Wives Who Wanted to Have Children in the Future

Contraceptive Method	Failure Rate (%)
Pill	2.5
IUD	7.1
Condom	12.3
Diaphragm	17.2
Foam, cream, jelly, suppository	18.4
Other (withdrawal, douche, abstinence)	18.9
Rhythm	25.0

Adapted with the permission of the Population Council from William R. Grady, Marilyn B. Hirsch, Nelma Keen, and Barbara Vaughn's, "Contraceptive Failure and Continuation Among Married Women in the United States, 1970–1975." *Studies in Family Planning,* 14, No. 1 (January 1983): Table 1.

achieved and then for either the husband or wife to be sterilized. Sterilization is the most frequently used method of birth control for those over 30. Sterilization is considered in the next section.

It should be kept in mind that any contraceptive measure has a lower death risk than childbirth itself. Summarizing his findings on this issue, one researcher said:

> . . . levels of mortality associated with all major methods of fertility control (tubal sterilization, the pill, IUD, condom, diaphragm, spermicides, rhythm, and abortion) are low in comparison with the risk of death associated with childbirth and ectopic pregnancy when no fertility control method is used. The exceptions are the risks associated with pill use after the age of 40 for women who do not smoke, and with pill use after the age of 35 for smokers. The safest approach to fertility control is to use the condom and to back it up by abortion in case of method failure. (Ory, 1983, p. 62)

Sterilization

Unlike the temporary and reversible methods of contraception just discussed, sterilization is a surgical procedure that permanently prevents the capacity of either gender to reproduce. Sterilization is losing its stigma as an extreme and undesirable method of birth control (U.S. HHS, 1981). It may be a method of choice for reasons of health (the woman should not have more children or cannot use other contraceptives), a desire to have no more children, or a desire to remain child-free. Most couples complete their intended childbearing in their late twenties or early thirties. This leaves more than 15 years of continued risk of unwanted pregnancy. Because of the risk of pill use at older ages and the lower reliability of alternative methods, sterilization is being increasingly chosen as the primary method of fertility control (Forrest and Henshaw, 1983). Only about 1 percent of women and men who have been sterilized change their mind and want a reversal (Riggall, 1980; Sibler, 1980).

About 20 percent of married couples use sterilization as a means of contraception (Lederer, 1983). Fifty-two percent of the 888,000 sterilizations performed in 1981 were on women. Although male sterilization is easier and safer than female sterilization, women feel more certain they will not get pregnant if they are sterilized. This fact may explain the higher rate of female sterilizations (AVS, 1982).

Female Sterilization

Although a woman may be sterilized by removal of her ovaries or uterus (**hysterectomy**), these operations are not normally undertaken for the sole purpose of sterilization. The ovaries produce important hormones as well as eggs. Also, while a hysterectomy (see Figure 17–3) may be necessary because of disease, it is major surgery that involves significant risks not associated with the usual procedures of female sterilization—salpingectomy, including laparoscopy.

Salpingectomy, also known as tubal ligation or "tying the tubes," is often performed under a general anesthetic while the woman is in the hospital just after she has delivered a baby (Figure 17.4). An incision is made in the lower abdomen, just above the pubic hair line, and the Fallopian tubes are brought into view one at a time. A part of each tube is cut out, and the ends are tied, clamped, or cauterized. The operation takes about 30 minutes. About 700,000 such procedures are performed annually.

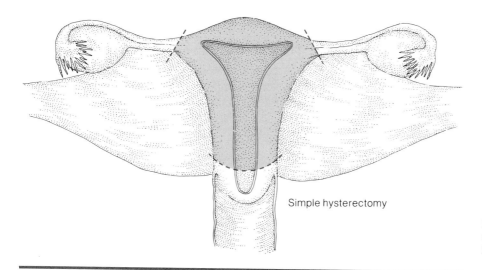

Simple hysterectomy

Figure 17.3a
Simple
Hysterectomy

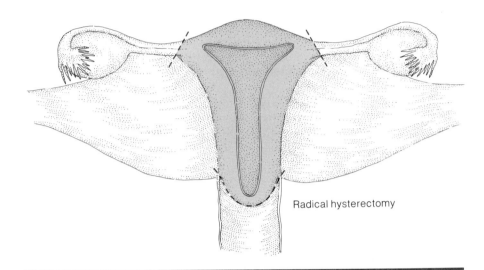

Radical hysterectomy

**Figure 17.3b
Radical
Hysterectomy**

A less expensive and quicker form of salpingectomy, which is performed on an outpatient basis, is **laparoscopy**. Often using local anesthesia, the surgeon inserts a small, lighted viewing instrument (laparoscope) through her abdominal wall just below the navel through which the uterus and the Fallopian tubes can be seen. The surgeon then makes another small incision in the lower abdomen and inserts a special pair of forceps that carry electricity to cauterize the tubes. The laparoscope and forceps are then withdrawn, the small wounds are closed with a single stitch, and small bandages are placed over the closed incisions (laparoscopy is also known as "the band-aid operation").

As an alternative to reaching the tubes through an opening below the navel, the surgeon may make a small incision in the back of the vaginal barrel (vaginal tubal ligation).

**Figure 17.4
Laparoscopy**
The physician inserts the laparoscope just below the naval to see where the Fallopian tubes are. Through an incision just above the pubic hair, the tubes are then cut, tied, or cauterized.

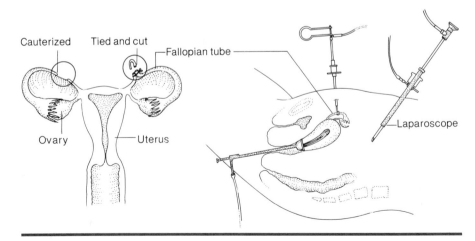

Cauterized   Tied and cut
Fallopian tube
Ovary   Uterus
Laparoscope

These procedures for female sterilization are highly effective. But sometimes there are complications. In rare cases, a blood vessel in the abdomen is torn open during the sterilization and bleeds into the abdominal cavity. When this happens, another operation is necessary to find the bleeding vessel and tie it closed. Occasionally, there is injury to the small or large intestine, which may cause nausea, vomiting, and loss of appetite. The fact that death may result, if only rarely, is a reminder that female sterilization is surgery and, like all surgery, involves some risks.

Male Sterilization

The most frequent form of male sterilization is **vasectomy**. About half a million vasectomies are done annually. The operation is usually performed in the physician's office under local anesthetic. It involves making two small incisions in the scrotum so that a small portion of each vas deferens (the sperm-carrying ducts) can be cut out and tied closed (Figure 17.5). Sperm are still produced in the testicles, but since there is no longer a conduit to the penis, they remain in the testicles and eventually dissolve. The operation takes about 15 minutes, costs about $200, and the man can leave the physician's office within a short time.

Since sperm do not disappear from the ejaculate immediately after a vasectomy, another method of contraception should be used until the man has had about 20 ejaculations. He is then asked to bring a sample of his ejaculate to the physician's office so that it can be examined under a microscope to see if the sperm are still present. In about 1 percent of cases, the vas deferens grow back and the man becomes fertile again.

A vasectomy does not affect the man's desire for sex, ability to have an erection, orgasm, or the amount of ejaculate (sperm comprise only a minute portion of the seminal fluid). In a follow-up study of 1,012 men who had had vasectomies, 98 percent reported that their sex life had improved or was unchanged. Two percent said their sex life had become worse (Simon Popula-

Control

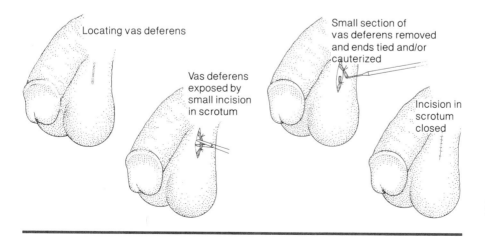

Locating vas deferens

Vas deferens exposed by small incision in scrotum

Small section of vas deferens removed and ends tied and/or cauterized

Incision in scrotum closed

Figure 17.5
Vasectomy

tion Trust, 1973). In another study husbands reported an increase in intercourse of 2.5 times per month following their vasectomies (Maschoff, Fashier, & Hansen, 1976).

In contrast to mostly positive evaluations of vasectomy, there are some suspected long-term negative side effects. In some men, some of the trapped sperm escape into the circulatory system with the result that the body produces antibodies against the sperm. Some physicians are concerned that this may lead to a breakdown in the body's immune system.

But these concerns are speculative. In a comparison of 4,385 vasectomized and 13,155 nonvasectomized men (matched by age and race), one researcher found no significant difference for a large number of symptoms and diseases, including those of the cardiovascular system (Petitti, 1983). Her conclusion was that vasectomy does not lead to disease in humans.

Sterilization: A Personal Decision

Mumford (1983) studied 235 couples and single men seeking a vasectomy and observed that there were seven basic stages in the decision-making process: becoming aware of vasectomy, discussing the procedure with a man who has had a vasectomy, deciding to have no children, beginning seriously to consider vasectomy, deciding that temporary contraceptive methods are no longer acceptable, deciding vasectomy is the best method, and having a scare (for example, the man's partner misses her period or has severe side effects from the pill).

Among the issues to be considered in sterilization for either the man or woman are the following.

1. *Permanence.* Sterilization should be considered permanent. Although microsurgery techniques do permit reversal of tubal ligations and vasectomies, there are only a few physicians who have the skill and technology to perform reversal operations, and the percentage of successful reversals is less than half.
2. *Self-image.* How do you predict you will feel about yourself following sterilization? As a woman, will you feel less feminine knowing that you are no longer capable of conceiving a child? As a man, will you feel less masculine because you can no longer father a child?
3. *Effect on Relationship.* How do you think sterilization will influence the relationship with your partner? Are you considering sterilization as a means of improving this relationship? In one follow-up study of vasectomy (Maschoff et al., 1976), both husbands and wives reported that they received somewhat less affection from their spouses. But there were reported increases in the amount of communication and a marked decrease in the number of men who considered separation or divorce.
4. *The Future.* There are a number of questions you might ask yourself about the future. Are you certain that you will never want another child under any conditions? If you are child-free, is it possible that you will change

your mind and decide you want to have a baby? If you have children, suppose they are killed by disease or accident? Would you then want to have another child? Suppose you were to get divorced (half of all married spouses do)? Might you want to have children with a new spouse?

There is also the possiblity that your present spouse will die while you are still young enough to have children. One woman said, "I was 29 and had my tubes tied after my second child was born. Brock and I had the boy and girl we wanted and saw no more reason for me to continue with birth control pills. But only a month after my laparoscopy, Brock had a heart attack. I'm now remarried and my new husband and I want a child of our own."

To keep their options open, some men who decide to get a vasectomy deposit some of their sperm in a sperm vault. The largest sperm banks are Xytex in Augusta, Georgia; the Infertility–Sperm Bank Service at the University of Oregon Medical School, Portland; and Idant Corporation in New York City. Sperm storage the first year at Idant Corporation is $300. Subsequent years, the cost is $135. The probability of frozen sperm fertilizing an egg is somewhat less than that of fresh sperm.

In deciding about sterilization, it is important to balance considerations of its effect on you, your relationships, and the future against the costs and benefits associated with less permanent forms of contraception. Because of the significance of the sterilization procedure, a consent form must be signed (see Figure 17.6).

Abortion

What if an unwanted pregnancy occurs? One alternative is an **abortion**—the removal of the fetus from the woman's uterus early in pregnancy before it can survive on its own (90 percent of abortions are obtained within the first 12 weeks of gestation). Of the 1.5 million abortions performed annually in the United States, most are obtained by young (18–19-year-olds), white (70 percent of abortions), and unmarried (80 percent of abortions) women, including the never married, separated, divorced, and widowed (Henshaw & O'Reilly, 1983). Reasons for getting an abortion are related to age (Lewis, 1980). Unmarried women 18 and over state, "I wasn't ready to take care of a child," "I couldn't stay home and take care of a baby," and "I didn't have the money to support a child." (p. 450) In contrast, those less than 18 often have an abortion because of social shame or parental pressure. "My folks told me I would have to get an abortion," said one 16-year-old.

The woman with an unwanted pregnancy may be beset by a number of strong feelings: fear ("What will I do now?"), self-anger ("How could I let this happen?"), guilt ("What would my parents think if they knew I was pregnant?"), ambivalence ("Will I be sorry if I have an abortion?) and, sometimes, desperation ("Maybe suicide is the only way out").

CONSENT FORM

NOTICE: YOUR DECISION AT ANY TIME NOT TO BE STERILIZED WILL NOT RESULT IN THE WITHDRAWAL OR WITHHOLDING OF ANY BENEFITS PROVIDED BY PROGRAMS OR PROJECTS RECEIVING FEDERAL FUNDS.

■ CONSENT TO STERILIZATION ■

I have asked for and received information about sterilization from _____. When I first asked for
(doctor or clinic)
the information, I was told that the decision to be sterilized is completely up to me. I was told that I could decide not to be sterilized. If I decide not to be sterilized, my decision will not affect my right to future care or treatment. I will not lose any help or benefits from programs receiving Federal funds, such as A.F.D.C. or Medicaid that I am now getting or for which I may become eligible.

I UNDERSTAND THAT THE STERILIZATION MUST BE CONSIDERED **PERMANENT** AND **NOT REVERSIBLE**. I HAVE DECIDED THAT I DO NOT WANT TO BECOME PREGNANT, BEAR CHILDREN OR FATHER CHILDREN.

I was told about those temporary methods of birth control that are available and could be provided to me which will allow me to bear or father a child in the future. I have rejected these alternatives and chosen to be sterilized.

I understand that I will be sterilized by an operation known as a _____. The discomforts, risks and benefits associated with the operation have been explained to me. All my questions have been answered to my satisfaction.

I understand that the operation will not be done until at least thirty days after I sign this form. I understand that I can change my mind at any time and that my decision at any time not to be sterilized will not result in the withholding of any benefits or medical services provided by federally funded programs.

I am at least 21 years of age and was born on _____.
Month   Day   Year

I, _____, hereby consent

of my own free will to be sterilized by _____
(doctor)

by a method called _____. My consent expires 180 days from the date of my signature below.

I also consent to the release of this form and other medical records about the operation to:
Representatives of the Department of Health, Education, and Welfare or
Employees of programs or projects funded by that Department but only for determining if Federal laws were observed.
I have received a copy of this form.

_____ Date: _____
Signature   Month   Day   Year

You are requested to supply the following information, but it is not required:

Race and ethnicity designation(please check)

☐ American Indian or   ☐ Black (not of Hispanic origin)
   Alaska Native   ☐ Hispanic
☐ Asian or Pacific Islander ☐ White (not of Hispanic origin)

■ INTERPRETER'S STATEMENT ■

If an interpreter is provided to assist the individual to be sterilized:

I have translated the information and advice presented orally to the individual to be sterilized by the person obtaining this consent. I have also read him/her the consent form in _____ language and explained its contents to him/her. To the best of my knowledge and belief he/she understood this explanation.

_____ _____
Interpreter   Date

■ STATEMENT OF PERSON OBTAINING CONSENT ■

Before _____ signed the
name of individual
consent form, I explained to him/her the nature of the sterilization operation _____ , the fact that it is intended to be a final and irreversible procedure and the discomforts, risks and benefits associated with it.

I counseled the individual to be sterilized that alternative methods of birth control are available which are temporary. I explained that sterilization is different because it is permanent.

I informed the individual to be sterilized that his/her consent can be withdrawn at any time and that he/she will not lose any health services or any benefits provided by Federal funds.

To the best of my knowledge and belief the individual to be sterilized is at least 21 years old and appears mentally competent. He/She knowingly and voluntarily requested to be sterilized and appears to understand the nature and consequence of the procedure.

_____
Signature of person obtaining consent   Date

_____
Facility

_____
Address

■ PHYSICIAN'S STATEMENT ■

Shortly before I performed a sterilization operation upon
_____ on _____ ,
Name: individual to be sterilized   Date: sterilization operation
I explained to him/her the nature of the sterilization operation _____ , the fact that
specify type of operation
it is intended to be a final and irreversible procedure and the discomforts, risks and benefits associated with it.

I counseled the individual to be sterilized that alternative methods of birth control are available which are temporary. I explained that sterilization is different because it is permanent.

I informed the individual to be sterilized that his/her consent can be withdrawn at any time and that he/she will not lose any health services or benefits provided by Federal funds.

To the best of my knowledge and belief the individual to be sterilized is at least 21 years old and appears mentally competent. He/She knowingly and voluntarily requested to be sterilized and appeared to understand the nature and consequences of the procedure.

(Instructions for use of alternative final paragraphs: Use the first paragraph below except in the case of premature delivery or emergency abdominal surgery where the sterilization is performed less than 30 days after the date of the individual's signature on the consent form. In those cases, the second paragraph below must be used. Cross out the paragraph which is not used.)

(1) At least thirty days have passed between the date of the individual's signature on this consent form and the date the sterilization was performed.

(2) This sterilization was performed less than 30 days but more than 72 hours after the date of the individual's signature on this consent form because of the following circumstances (check applicable box and fill in information requested):
☐ Premature delivery
Individual's expected date of delivery: _____
☐ Emergency abdominal surgery:
(describe circumstances):

_____
Physician
Date _____

**Figure 17.6
Sterilization
Consent Form**

One of the best decisions during this period of crisis is to talk with an abortion counselor or a counselor at a local mental health center. These professionals are trained to help women look at alternatives and decide what is best. Perhaps most important, they can help the pregnant woman to make her decision with care and deliberation rather than acting under pressure.

Methods of Induced Abortion

An abortion may be spontaneous (miscarriage) or induced. Methods of inducing an abortion include the following.

Vacuum Curettage

In **vacuum curettage** a hollow plastic rod attached to a vacuum aspirator is inserted into a woman's uterus through the cervix. The device draws the fetal tissue and surrounding matter out of the uterus (see Figure 17.7). The woman's cervix is anesthetized and a speculum is inserted to widen or dilate the cervical opening. Vacuum curettage can be performed in a physician's office and takes about 10 minutes. If done within eight weeks of the last menstrual period, the dilation and anesthesia may not be necessary and the procedure is referred to a menstrual extraction.

Dilation and Curettage (D and C)

In place of the vacuum curettage, a sharp metal surgical instrument is used to scrape the fetal tissue and placenta from the walls of the uterus (Figure 17.8). A general anesthetic is usually administered. This more traditional procedure is regarded as inferior to the vacuum curettage method.

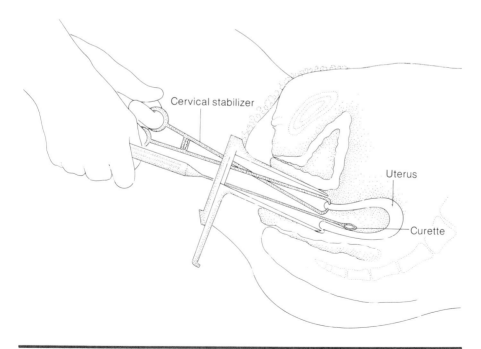

Cervical stabilizer

Uterus

Curette

**Figure 17.7
Vacuum Curettage**

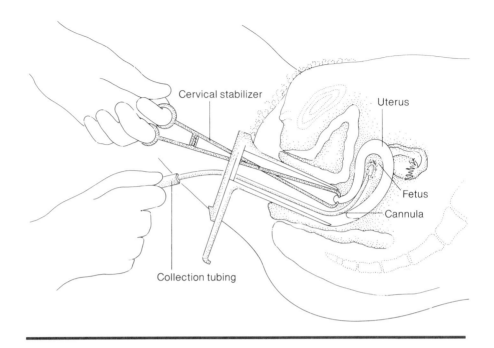

Cervical stabilizer

Uterus

Fetus

Cannula

Collection tubing

Figure 17.8
Dilation and
Curettage

Dilation and Evacuation (D and E)

Used early in the second trimester, **D and E** is a combination of vacuum curettage and **D and C**. But more dilation of the cervical opening is required. More than 95 percent of all abortion procedures involve vacuum curettage, D and C, and D and E (Morbidity and Mortality Report, 1983).

Saline Injection

As pregnancy progresses, the fetus becomes too large to be removed safely by any of the preceding methods. Abortion by saline may be performed by inserting a long needle containing a concentrated salt solution through the abdominal and uterine walls into the amniotic cavity (Figure 17.9). This kills the fetus. From 6 to 48 hours later, the uterus contracts until the fetus is pushed out into the vagina. Because **saline injection** is a major surgical procedure, earlier termination of pregnancy is desirable.

A variation of the saline method of abortion is the use of prostaglandins—hormonelike substances that cause the uterus to contract. When introduced into the vagina as a suppository or injected into the amniotic sac, they induce labor and the fetus is aborted.

Hysterotomy

Hysterotomy is abdominal surgery through a caesarean section in which the surgeon cuts through the uterine wall and takes out the fetus. Because it is major surgery and expensive, it is used when the pregnancy is between 16

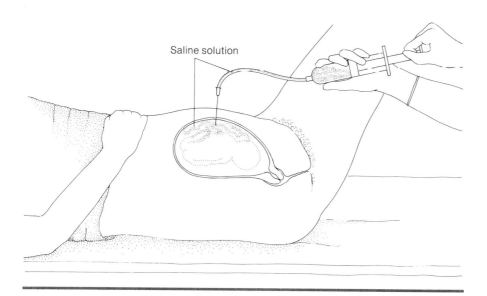

Saline solution

Figure 17.9
Saline Injection

and 24 weeks and when the mother's health precludes the use of induction methods. Less than 4 percent of abortions are of the saline, prostaglandin, or hysterotomy variety (Morbidity and Mortality Report, 1983).

Abortion Legislation

In 1973 the US Supreme Court ruled that during the first three months of pregnancy, a woman has the right to obtain an abortion from a licensed physician without interference by the state. From the fourth through the sixth month, the decision to have an abortion belongs to the woman and her physician, but because an abortion at this later stage of pregnancy is more dangerous, the state may require that the abortion be performed in a hospital. During the last three months of pregnancy, the state may prohibit abortion except in those cases where the life or health of the mother is in danger. Neither a woman's husband nor her parents may veto her decision. In effect, the Supreme Court ruled that the fetus is a *potential* life and not a "person." Since the Supreme Court ruling, the number of legal abortions has increased and the number of abortion-related deaths has vastly decreased (Binkin et al., 1982).

In 1980 the Supreme Court ruled that federal funds could not be used to pay for abortions. This ruling upheld the Hyde Amendment (sponsored by Representative Henry Hyde), which restricted congressional spending of Medicaid funds for abortions where the mother's life was not in danger or in cases where she was not impregnated through rape or incest. Although the decision has little effect on abortion among affluent women, a woman with limited income who has an unwanted pregnancy—about half a million women per year—is seriously affected. Many of these women carry their pregnancies to term rather than resort to nonmedical abortions that are likely to be unsafe.

In 1981 Senator Jesse Helms sponsored the Human Life Amendment to the Constitution, which would define life as beginning at conception. Passage of the amendment would mean that the developing embryo would have a right to life and that those terminating a pregnancy by abortion could be prosecuted for murder.

In 1983 another constitutional amendment was suggested that would give the states the power to ban abortion. This amendment sidesteps the issue of when life begins but permits a mechanism to outlaw abortion.

But in 1983 the Supreme Court reaffirmed its position on abortion and struck down several state and local regulations that had been designed to make obtaining an abortion more difficult. The court declared unconstitutional regulations requiring that:

- All abortions for women more than three months pregnant be performed in hospitals rather than clinics.
- Physicians tell women seeking abortions about possible birth-giving alternatives, abortion risks, and that the fetus is a human life.
- There be at least a 24-hour waiting period between the time a woman signs a consent form and the abortion is performed.
- All pregnant, unwed girls under 15, no matter how "mature," must obtain a parent's consent or have a judge's approval before having an abortion.

Summary

Fertilization is the result of the union of egg and sperm. This may occur through sexual intercourse, artificial insemination of the wife by husband or donor (AIH or AID), artificial insemination of a surrogate mother by the husband, or test-tube fertilization. Artificial methods of conception are being used increasingly by couples of which one of the pair cannot or should not conceive.

The primary methods of birth control are contraception, sterilization, and abortion. With contraception, the risk of becoming pregnant can be reduced to almost zero depending on the method and how systematically it is used. Contraception includes birth control pills, which prevent ovulation; IUDs, which prevent implantation of the fertilized egg; condoms, diaphragms, and the cervical cap, which are barrier methods; vaginal spermacides and sponge, the rhythm method, withdrawal, and douching. These methods vary in effectiveness and safety. Issues to consider in choosing a contraceptive are personal values, health, reliability, sexual fulfillment, psychological contentment, and age.

Sterilization is a surgical procedure that prevents fertilization, usually by blocking the passage of eggs or sperm through the Fallopian tubes or vas deferens, respectively. This procedure for female sterilization is called salpingectomy, or tubal ligation. Laparoscopy is one method of tubal ligation. The most frequent form of male sterilization is vasectomy. Since sterilization should be regarded as permanent, the decision to become sterilized should include a consideration of the individuals, their relationship, and the future balanced against the costs and benefits associated with less permanent forms of contraception.

Abortion is one alternative if an unwanted pregnancy occurs. Methods of inducing abortion include vacuum curettage, dilation and curettage (D and C), dilation and evacuation (D and E), all used in the earlier stages of pregnancy, and hysterotomy, and saline and prostaglandin injection, used when the pregnancy is more advanced. In 1973, the U.S. Supreme Court ruled that the abortion decision rests with the woman and her physician. While the right to abortion has come under increasing legislative attack, the Supreme Court in 1983 struck down a number of state and local regulations which were designed to restrict abortions.

Key Terms

fertilization
conception
artificial insemination husband (AIH)
artificial insemination donor (AID)
surrogate mother
test-tube (in vitro) fertilization
ovum transfer
contraception
combination pill
minipill
condom
intrauterine device (IUD)
diaphragm
cervical cap
spermacidal foam
sponge

calendar method
Basal body temperature (BBT)
    method
cervical mucus method
morning-after pill
hysterectomy
salpingectomy
laparoscopy
vasectomy
abortion
vacuum curettage
D and C
D and E
saline injection
hysterotomy

Issues in Debate and Future Directions

The political and social issue of abortion has become highly polarized between so-called prolife, or right-to-life, advocates, who are against abortion, and prochoice advocates, who believe that the decision to have an abortion should rest with the woman. After reviewing both perspectives of the abortion issue, we look at trends in fertilization and contraception.

Prochoice Views on Abortion

Prochoice advocates believe that legislation prohibiting abortion is governmental intrusion into what should be a woman's personal, private decision "Keep your laws and your morality off my body" is the message many women have conveyed to legislators who want to pass laws that, in essence, would require women to continue with a pregnancy whether they choose to or not. The slogan "A woman's life is a human life" is a vivid reminder that Senator Jesse Helms's Human Life Amendment would inflict tragedy and suffering upon millions of women who would be forced to choose between having babies they did not want or seeking an illegal abortion with the possibility of infection, permanent damage to the reproductive system, and even death. The prochoice proponents are

a majority. Two-thirds of American women, with few differences among subgroups, believe that abortion should be legal (Henshaw & Martire, 1982).

Prolife Views on Abortion

Those against abortion are just as adamant in their feelings as those who want the decision about abortion left up to the woman. Prolife advocates feel that the unborn are defenseless human beings and that abortion is murder. "Choose life for your baby" and "Abortion is America's Holocaust" are two of the slogans on placards frequently carried by prolife advocates. They feel that legislation for the protection of the unborn is essential to prevent "helpless babies" being killed without caution. Prolife proponents are not without supporters. Twenty-six thousand people demonstrated on the tenth anniversary of the 1973 Supreme Court decision legalizing abortion and vowed to restore protection for all innocent persons. About one-third of American woman would favor a law that viewed abortion as a serious crime such as murder (Henshaw & Martire, 1982). The controversy between prochoice and prolife groups is represented by the different labels they use for the same concept, for example, an IUD becomes a "Concealed weapon" in prolife terminology.

The use of biased terminology by both prochoice and prolife groups may be effective in changing peoples' attitudes. After viewing a debate between prochoice and prolife representatives, 35 percent of 115 respondents changed their views regarding abortion on demand. Twenty percent became less approving of the idea and 15 percent became more approving. The researchers concluded that "college students attitudes toward abortion on demand are far from stable, but rather, susceptible to change form external influences" (Dunn & Ryan, 1982a, p. 8).

Future Directions

Artificial insemination, in vitro fertilization, an ovum transfer will be used by an increasing number of people who cannot or should not conceive a child through sexual intercourse. Technological reproductive innovations will also occur. The development of cryogen will allow the storage of human embryos for later implantation in the womb so that couples may have children at the desired intervals. Embryos will also be screened for desired gender and genetic and developmental defects. Also, before the twenty-first century, it may be possible to develop embryos in artificial wombs.

The legal issues raised by these developments will be numerous. Does a surrogate mother have a right to her baby if she changes her mind after delivery? If a deformed child results from an artificial insemination in a surrogate mother, do the parents who paid for the child have a right to reject it? What are the responsibilities of a sperm bank to provide sperm that is free of defects and diseases?

Regarding the future of contraception, there will be continued difficulty in reaching sexually active adolescents, more people who choose sterilization, continued controversy about abortion, and new contraceptives. The latter include a subdermal implant of levonorgestrel (a synthetic progestin) under the skin of the woman's arm. The procedure takes about five minutes and provides protection against pregnancy for five years or more. A long-lasting (three months) injection of 150 mg. of the progestin Depo Provera is also being tested for FDA approval.

For men, hormonal contraceptives such as MPA (medroxyprogesterone acetate) and TO (testosterone oenanthate) have been tested in Toronto, London, and Santiago, but have not received FDA approval for use in the United States. Gossypol, and extract of cottonseed oil, has also been tested in China as an oral contraceptive. U.S. research firms are now testing the long-term safety of gossypol. Some form of male contraceptive in the form of a pill, nasal spray, or injection is expected to be on the market by 1990 (Lederer, 1983).

Chapter Eighteen

Having Children

*Before I got married I had six
theories about bringing up
children; now I have six
children and no theories.*

JOHN WILMOT, EARL OF ROCHESTER

(1647–1680)

Chapter Eighteen

"We were both child development majors in college, had taken a preparation for parenthood class, and had been involved six weeks in a Lamaze course in anticipation of our baby. While we thought that we were prepared for the experience, we weren't. We're happy that we have Jennifer but we're still adjusting to her," said a new parent. Such an experience is not unique. Since the reality of parenthood is often different from the dreams and thoughts we have about it, it remains a mystery until we experience it. In this chapter we look at parenthood from conception through pregnancy, childbirth, and the establishment of the new family unit.

When a Woman Becomes a Mother

"I had been married several years when my baby was born," recalled one mother. "Before her birth I had an interesting job and a good marriage and had seriously considered remaining a child-free wife. But despite my hesitations, I think down deep I always expected that someday I'd become a mother."

Such feelings are not uncommon. Although many women are aware of the potential problems of motherhood, most want to have a baby of their own. Whether instinctive or learned, this desire cuts across racial, religious, and social class lines.

Because having children is such a common experience, society tends to overlook the profound effect that becoming a mother has on the individual woman. In the following section we explore what that effect is and how it changes the life of a woman from the time she conceives.*

*Appreciation is expressed to Sharryl Hawke for her assistance in the development of the following section.

Pregnancy

Motherhood begins not with childbirth but with conception. Immediately after the egg is fertilized by the sperm in the Fallopian tube, it begins to divide and is pushed by hairlike cilia down the Fallopian tube into the uterus where it attaches itself to the inner wall of the uterus. Furnished with a rich supply of blood and nutrients, the developing organism is called an embryo the first three months and a fetus thereafter.

Signs of Pregnancy

Although a missed period, morning sickness, enlarged and tender breasts, more frequent urination, and excessive fatigue are indications of pregnancy, the condition is best confirmed by laboratory tests and a physical examination.

There are several laboratory tests of pregnancy that have a high degree of accuracy. All of them depend upon the presence of a hormone produced by the developing embyro, **human chorionic gonadotropin (HCG)**, which appears in the pregnant woman's urine. One procedure, formally known as the **lutex agglutination** inhibition immunologic slide test, detects HCG in about 2 ½ hours and can reveal if the woman is pregnant within 14 days after the first missed menstrual period. Whereas all commercially available pregnancy tests use the lutex agglutination principle, they are not as accurate as the slide tests conducted in the laboratory.

HCG also appears in the bloodstream of the pregnant woman. A **radioimmunoassay** test, a laboratory examination of the blood, can suggest if the woman is pregnant within 8 days of conception. A new test, **radioreceptorassay,** also analyzes the blood and is 100 percent accurate on the first day after the first missed period.

Pregnancy tests in which urine of the presumed pregnant woman is injected into a mouse, rabbit, or frog have been replaced by these tests (Green, 1977).

If the laboratory test indicates pregnancy, the physician usually conducts a pelvic examination to find out if the woman's uterus has enlarged or changed color. These changes take place around the sixth week of pregnancy. Confirmation of the pregnancy is dependent on hearing and counting the fetal heart pulsations (to differentiate them from the mother's heartbeat). This occurs between the sixteenth and twentieth week.

On rare occasions women have a **false pregnancy.** All the usual signs of early pregnancy (morning sickness, cessation of menstrual period, and so on) are present but there is no developing embryo inside the woman's uterus. Such false pregnancies are usually the result of an intense desire to get pregnant. The mind induces what the body fails to provide. The woman is usually emotionally devastated when she learns that she is not pregnant.

Table 18.1 Side Effects of Pregnancy

	Trimester		
	First: Week 0–14	Second: Week 15–26	Third: Week 27–40
Nausea	*		
Vomiting	*		
Frequent urination	*		*
Leg cramps	*		
Vaginal discharge	*	*	*
Fatigue	*	*	*
Constipation	*	*	*
Swelling		*	*
Varicose veins		*	*
Backache		*	*
Heartburn		*	
Shortness of breath		*	

Side Effects of Pregnancy

Pregnancy is divided into trimesters, or three-month periods, during which the woman may experience some minor discomforts due to physical changes (Table 18.1).

One of the first discomforts the newly pregnant woman may experience is a feeling of nausea that may be accompanied by vomiting. The nauseous feeling occurs sometime after the first missed menstrual period and may be triggered by the odor of particular foods. Other women feel nauseated early in the morning or if they go too long without food. The specific cause of **morning sickness** is unknown, but hormonal and metabolic changes are the likely causes. Although the ultimate remedy is time (the nausea usually disappears by the fourth month), some women find that eating dry crackers or toast before getting out of the bed each morning helps to prevent the onset of nausea. One woman said that "popcorn was the only thing I could eat without throwing up." Many physicians feel that medication should be avoided because of possible negative effects on the developing embryo.

Frequent urination is also characteristic of the first trimester. The enlarging uterus presses against the bladder and causes the urgent feeling to urinate. When the uterus moves out of the pelvic area into the abdominal cavity, the urge to urinate lessens until the third trimester when the fetus presses against the bladder again. While sometimes inconvenient, frequent urination is regarded as a normal part of pregnancy.

Vaginal discharge increases in the first trimester of pregnancy and continues until delivery. Known as leukorrhea, the discharge is a whitish mucus, and although not harmful, should be kept from accumulating by daily bathing. Wearing cotton underpants is also recommended as nylon retains heat and moisture, encouraging infection. If there are significant changes in the vaginal discharge, a physician should be consulted.

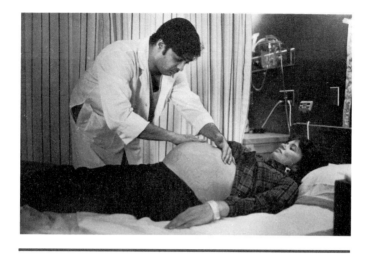

A woman experiences a number of physical changes during pregnancy.

Leg cramps, particularly in the calf, may also be experienced during pregnancy. Such discomfort results from pressure on the nerves that supply the legs. Some physicians recommend calcium to reduce these cramps.

Other side effects are more likely to occur in the second and third trimesters. These include heartburn, constipation, backache, varicose veins, and ankle swelling. Each of these conditions tends to be temporary and the discomfort can be ameliorated. For example, aching varicose veins and ankle swelling can be reduced by lying on the floor and elevating the legs so that they rest on the seat of a sofa or chair. In this way, the blood can more easily flow from the legs. Heartburn can be reduced by avoiding greasy foods and eating smaller, more frequent meals. Constipation can be helped by drinking more water and eating more roughage (like celery, apples, and lettuce.) Backache can be eased by pelvic tilt exercises.

Nutrition During Pregnancy

Ensuring a healthy baby depends on adequate nutrition, controlled weight gain, and avoidance of substances like alcohol and nicotine that are harmful to the fetus. A national Healthy Mothers, Healthy Babies Campaign has been established to improve maternal and infant health (Bratic, 1982).

Ideally, women should attend to their nutrition before becoming pregnant. Not only should they eat the proper type and quantity of foods but also they should avoid foods high in sugar and fat. Table 18.2 details the foods by number of servings nonpregnant, pregnant, and lactating, or breastfeeding women need for the proper development of their infants.

Ideally, too, underweight women should gain weight and overweight women should lose weight before becoming pregnant. If the woman begins her pregnancy at her ideal weight, she should gain about 20 to 24 pounds during pregnancy. But even if she is obese, she should still gain about 24

Table 18.2 Daily Food Guide for Pregnant Women

Food	Number of Servings		
	Nonpregnant Woman	Pregnant Woman	Lactating Woman
Protein foods			
Animal (2 oz. serving)	2	2	2
Vegetable (at least one serving of legumes)	2	2	2
Milk and milk products	2	4	5
Enriched or whole-grain breads and cereals	4	4	4
Vitamin C-rich fruits and vegetables	1	1	1
Dark-green vegetables	1	1	1
Other fruits and vegetables	1	1	1

SOURCE: Reprinted by permission from *Nutrition: Concepts and Controversies,* Second Edition by Eva May Nunnelley Hamilton and Eleanor Noss Whitney, Copyright © 1978, 1982 by West Publishing Company. All rights reserved.

pounds to ensure adequate development of the fetus. If the mother does not gain enough weight, she may give birth to an underweight baby. A low-birth-weight baby is defined as one that weighs less than 5½ pounds. Birthweight is the single most potent indicator of the infant's future health status. Low birthweight is associated with a higher incidence of disease and early mortality (Hamilton & Whitney, 1982).

Pregnant women should also monitor their alcohol intake to avoid fetal alcohol syndrome, which refers to the negative consequences for the fetus and infant of the mother who drinks alcohol at the level of a social drinker. These include increased risk of low birthweight, low birth length, smaller head circumference, distorted facial features, and intellectual retardation. Likewise, smoking during pregnancy is associated with lower birthweight babies, premature babies, spontaneous abortions, and fetal deaths.

Concerned about the health of their babies, some pregnant women avoid not only alcohol but also over-the-counter drugs like aspirin and antihistamines, prescription drugs like amphetamines and tranquilizers and illegal drugs like marijuana. Still others avoid caffeine since its use has been associated with birth defects.

Emotions During Pregnancy

Emotional reactions to pregnancy may be varied. A woman may react to pregnancy with excitement, viewing her morning sickness, growing belly, and enlarging breasts as confirmation of her ability to create and sustain life. Her protruding abdomen announces to the world that her role in life is soon to change. Her husband, parents, and friends help to define her movement toward motherhood in positive terms.

But pregnancy may also trigger feelings of ambivalence. While the woman is developing an emotional attachment to her fetus (Valentine, 1982), incompatible thoughts may flash through her mind. She may be excited about having a baby but apprehensive about its impact on her career and marriage. How can she balance career and family needs? Also, her husband may share her excitement about their baby, but will he still view her as sexually desirable after the baby is born?

Anxiety and fear also are not uncommon. One concern is that the baby will not be "perfect." "My closest friend was born with a birthmark that covered her right leg below the knee. I always avoid looking at her leg and hope it won't happen to my baby," remarked a woman in her seventh month. Other women are anxious about the gender of their baby. "Both of us want a boy," said one wife. "We tried the recommended procedure for having a boy and hope that it works. But my brother says you grow to love either sex child you have so I guess it doesn't really matter."

Near the end of pregnancy, a more serious concern may arise—fear of childbirth, or parturiphobia. Common fears are of pain during delivery, the unknown ("What will it really be like?"), and losing emotional control during delivery. Some women fear death.* Various techniques of childbirth (Dick-Read, Lamaze, LeBoyer), discussed later in this chapter, are designed to help the woman work through her fear and to give her needed emotional support.

Labor and Delivery

Whatever emotions a woman experiences during pregnancy, they are likely to intensify as she nears the birth of her baby. Labor occurs in three stages and, although there are great variations, it lasts an average of 13 hours for the woman having her first baby (she is referred to as a **primigravida**) and about 8 hours if the woman has given birth before (**multigravida**). It is not known what causes the onset of labor, which is marked by uterine contractions. But there are distinctions between the contractions of true and **false labor**. These include the following.

Contractions of true labor	*Contractions of false labor*
Occur at regular intervals	Occur at irregular intervals
Intervals gradually shorten	Intervals remain long
Intensity gradually increases	Intensity remains the same
Discomfort in back and abdomen	Discomfort chiefly in lower
Cervix dilates	abdomen
Not affected by sedation	Cervix does not dilate
	Usually relieved by sedation

First Stage of Labor

Figure 18.1 illustrates the stages of labor. Labor begins with regular uterine contractions at 15- to 20-minute intervals, which last from 10 to 30 seconds. The first stage of labor lasts for about nine hours if it is the first baby and

---

*Maternal death is rare. In the United States in 1982, 8 of 100,000 deaths resulted from complications of pregnancy and childbirth (U.S. HHS, 1982).

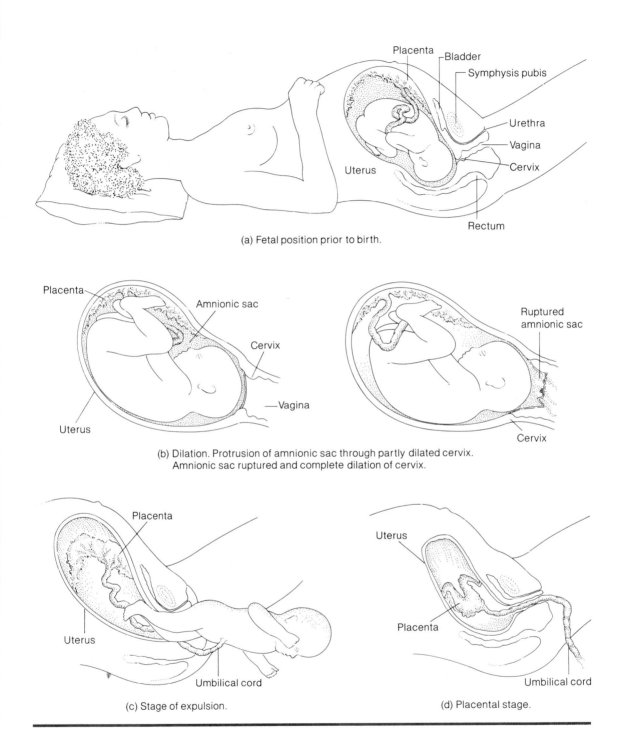

(a) Fetal position prior to birth.

(b) Dilation. Protrusion of amnionic sac through partly dilated cervix.
Amnionic sac ruptured and complete dilation of cervix.

(c) Stage of expulsion.

(d) Placental stage.

Figure 18.1 The Birth Process

about five hours in subsequent deliveries. During this time the woman often has cramps and backache. The membranes of the amniotic sac may rupture, spilling the amniotic fluid.

Throughout the first stage, the uterine contractions become stronger, lasting for 30 to 45 seconds, and more frequent (every 3 to 5 minutes). These contractions result in effacement and dilation of the cervix. With **effacement** the cervix flattens out and gets longer; with **dilation** the cervical opening through which the baby will pass gets larger. At the end of the first stage, the cervix is dilated 3 ½ to 4 inches; contractions occur every 1 to 2 minutes and last up to a minute.

During this stage, the fetal heart rate is monitored continually by stethoscope or ultrasound and the woman's temperature and blood pressure are checked. She may experience leg cramps, nausea, irritability, or panic during this transitional phase of labor when the baby is getting into position to be born. Medication or anesthesia may be used at some point during this stage (see box on page 542).

Second Stage of Labor

Also known as the expulsive stage of labor, the second stage begins when the cervix is completely dilated and ends when the baby is born. It lasts about 50 minutes if it is the woman's first baby, 20 minutes if a later baby. Uterine contractions may last 1 ½ minutes and be 1 to 2 minutes apart. These contractions move the baby further into the vaginal birth canal. The woman may help this process by pushing movements. The head of the baby emerges first followed by the shoulders and trunk. While most babies are born head first, some are born breech. This means that the baby's feet or buttocks come out the vagina first. Such deliveries are much more complicated.

To ease the birth the physician may perform an episiotomy. This involves cutting the perineum, the area between the vagina and the anus, to make a larger opening for the baby and to prevent uncontrolled tearing.

Immediately after the baby is born, the nostrils are cleared of mucus using a small suction bulb. The umbilical cord is then clamped twice—about 1 and 2 inches from the infant's abdomen—and cut between the clamps. The baby is cleaned of placental matter and put in a temperature-controlled bassinet.

Third Stage of Labor

After the baby is born, the placenta, or afterbirth, is delivered. Usually within five minutes, the placenta separates itself from the uterine wall and is expelled from the vagina. If it does not disengage easily and by itself, the physician will manually remove it. After the placenta is delivered, the physician will repair the episiotomy by stitching up the incision.

The time from 1 to 4 hours after delivery is regarded by some physicians as a fourth stage of labor. During this time, the mother's uterus relaxes and returns to a more normal state and bleeding of the cervix, resulting from the detachment of the placenta from the uterine wall, stops.

Medication During Childbirth

More than 90 percent of women take some type of medication to relieve the anxiety or pain of childbirth.

The four types of drugs used include the following.

1. Tranquilizers, such as promethazine, to reduce anxiety during labor.

2. Analgesics, like meperidine, to relieve pain.

3. General anesthesia, such as nitrous oxide or cyclopropane, which makes the women unconscious during delivery.

4. Regional anesthesia, which blocks out pain in the vaginal area while the woman remains awake. An epidural is the most common form of regional anesthesia. Using a needle, the physician injects medication into the outer space around the spinal column, causing loss of sensation from the waist down.

There is professional disagreement on the possibility of harm to the baby from drugs. Some physicians feel that risk is minimal and that judicious use of drugs helps to avoid a negative birth experience. Other physicians feel that the infant is at risk when drugs are introduced into the mother's body as they may depress the infant's breathing ability.

Although labor is often thought of as a painful ordeal, some women describe the birthing experience as "fantastic," "joyful," and "unsurpassed." One woman said, "I would rather give birth every day than any other thing I can think of. Having that baby come out of me was literally the grandest experience I have ever had."

Methods of Childbirth

Around 1900 all but 5 percent of babies were born at home. Because there were few physicians and fewer hospitals, a midwife was usually summoned to assist the laboring mother-to-be with her delivery. Birthing was a family event with father, mother, and children competing to hold the new infant.

But because of infant mortality, the developing political strength of the medical profession, and the development of hospital facilities to handle difficult deliveries, home births became less common. Today more than 95 percent of all births take place in a hospital. When the woman experiences uterine contractions that are regular and intense, she is encouraged to check in the hospital, be prepped (have her pubic hair shaved, and an enema, and her vaginal area cleaned.), and complete labor in a special room near the delivery room. Her husband may or may not be allowed to remain with her during labor and delivery.

Some expectant parents are concerned that hospital childbirth procedures are too impersonal, autocratic, and rigid. They want more control over how their children are born. Among the alternatives to traditional childbirth preparation practices and hospital-managed deliveries are various childbirth methods, including the Lamaze, Dick-Read, Bradley, and LeBoyer methods. Home births are also being considered as an alternative to hospital births.

Lamaze Method of Childbirth

Preferred by an increasing number of couples, the **Lamaze method** of childbirth, often called natural childbirth, was developed by a French obstetrician, Dr. Fernand Lamaze. The method is essentially a preparation for childbirth, in which the woman and her partner take six 1 ½ -hour classes during the last trimester of pregnancy, usually with several other couples. The goal of the sessions is to reduce the anxiety and pain of childbirth by viewing it as a natural process, by educating the couple about the labor and delivery process, and by giving them specific instructions to aid in the birth of their baby. (See Appendix D on Resources and Organizations for the address of the American Society of Psychoprophylaxis in Obstetrics, which certifies Lamaze instructors.)

There are several aspects of the Lamaze method.

1. *Education about childbirth.* The instructor explains the physiology of pregnancy, stages of labor, and delivery.
2. *Timed breathing exercises.* Specific breathing exercises are recommended for each stage of labor to help with the contractions by refocusing the

The Lamaze method allows both parents to share in the birth of their baby.

laboring woman's attention and keeping the pressure of the diaphragm off the uterus. These exercises are practiced between sessions so that the couple will know when and how to use them when labor actually begins.

3. *Pain control exercises.* The woman is taught selectively to tense and relax various muscle groups of her body, for example, her arm muscles. She then learns how to tense these muscle groups while relaxing the rest of her body so that during labor she can relax the rest of her body while her uterus is contracting involuntarily.

4. *Husband's involvement.* A major advantage of the Lamaze method is the active involvement of the husband in the birthing event. His role (or that of a coach substitute if the father is not available) is to tell his wife when to stop and start the various breathing exercises, give her psychological support throughout labor, and, in general, take care of her (get ice, keep her warm, and so on). Most husbands and wives report that the sharing of the labor and delivery is one of the most significant and memorable events of their lives. When the couple does not share the birth experience, the husband sits in the waiting room while his wife is in the labor room alone. One woman said, "The nurses were playing cards and between hands would come to check on me. I felt like a pig in the woods having her litter for all the help I got."

One woman described her Lamaze experiences as follows.

● *Interviewer:*   Tell me what it was like.
Jane: It went very fast. The contractions were coming faster and faster and stronger and stronger. In between I started shaking from nerves, uncontrollable shaking, so I had a shot of Valium to calm that. I was going through natural

childbirth and the nurse was very helpful. You could study and practice for 90 years, but you need someone right there. I guess I was ready before they thought. The next thing I knew, my husband was in a yellow suit and everyone was wearing masks and garments. They put me into the delivery room and moved me onto the table. Sometimes I'd push well and other times I wasn't prepared enough. Finally she came and it was such a relief to have her out. It was a "zippo" compared to the first one. (Laugh.)

Interviewer: What's the baby like?

Jane: She seems like a good baby. She doesn't cry much. She's a hungry baby, I guess, because of her size—she really gobbles the formula. When I heard she was a girl, I was delighted. I was just delighted in general—that it was finished, that she was a girl, that she was healthy.

Interviewer: What was your husband's role during labor and delivery?"

Jane: Just having him in the room was very comforting. He held my hand and he brought ice chips, which was very helpful. In the delivery room, he helped with the breathing and he told me to look when the baby was actually being born so I wouldn't miss it. He was very supportive. I think I would have panicked if he wasn't there. When I needed him, he was able to do whatever crazy thing I needed him to do. He understood my gestures to do this or not do that without my telling.* ●

Dick-Read Method

Grantly Dick-Read introduced his concept of natural childbirth to the United States in the 1930s, about a decade before Lamaze. He felt it was a woman's fear of childbirth that produced the physical pain during delivery and that pain could be avoided by teaching the woman to relax. Similar to the Lamaze method, Dick-Read classes emphasize breathing and relaxation exercises, basic information about the birth event, and the husband' support. In addition, they focus on preparation for parenthood.

Bradley Method of Childbirth

Another method of childbirth less well known than the Lamaze method is one developed by a Denver obstetrician Robert Bradley. Also known as "husband-coached childbirth," the **Bradley method** focuses on the couple—their marital communication, sexual relationship, and parental roles as well as on relaxation exercises and proper nutrition during pregnancy. An important aspect of the Bradley method is the couple's relationship with their physician. They are encouraged to deal with issues like the kind of delivery they want (hospital or home birth) and breast feeding well in advance. The Bradley method emphasizes the freedom to choose the type of birth experience.

*Frances K. Grossman, Lois S. Eichler, and Susan A. Winickoff, *Pregnancy, Birth, and Parenthood.* San Francisco, California: Jossey-Bass, Inc., Publishers, 1980, p. 75, reprinted by permission.

If the physician is reluctant to cooperate, the couple is encouraged to seek another physician.

LeBoyer Method of Childbirth

The **LeBoyer method** of childbirth is named after its French founder, Frederick LeBoyer, who has delivered more than 10,000 babies in the manner he has made famous. The goal of a LeBoyer birth experience is to make the infant's transition to the outer world as nontraumatic as possible. The delivery room into which the baby is born is quiet and dimly lit. After emerging from its mother, the baby is placed on the mother's abdomen where she gently strokes and rubs her child. The umbilical cord is cut only after it stops throbbing. This is thought to help the newborn's respiratory system adjust to its new environment.

After a few moments, the baby is immersed in water approximately the temperature of the amniotic sac in which she or he has been floating for the past nine months. The infant is allowed to relax and enjoy the bath. Then the baby is wrapped in layers of cotton and wool and placed on her or his side next to the mother. Placing the child on its back is avoided since it is felt that the spine should not be stressed this soon after birth.

To what degree is the LeBoyer method of childbirth beneficial to infants and mothers? A study comparing babies born LeBoyer style with babies born by conventional hospital procedures revealed no differences in responsiveness or irritability during the first three days of life (Nelson, 1979). Mothers delivered by the LeBoyer method did not see the experience any differently or make a different postnatal adjustment than those delivered by a conventional method.

Home Births

Increasingly, couples are demonstrating an interest in having their baby at home. Safety is a primary concern in home births. However, it is usually possible to predict a dangerous delivery since high risk mothers (such as those with hypertension or diabetes) can be identified early in the pregnancy. Some proponents of the home birth movement feel that, for the mother without prenatal complications, there is greater risk in having a baby in the hospital than at home.

The nurse-midwife is most often asked to assist in home births. Some are certified members of the American College of Nurse-Midwives and have successfully completed a one-year midwifery course such as those offered at Georgetown University and the University of Miami.

Two organizations—ACAH (Association for Childbirth at Home) and HOME (Home Oriented Maternity Experience)—help couples prepare for home births. Couples may attend several classes during which the following issues are discussed.

Home births, properly screened and supervised, provide a viable alternative to hospital births.

1. *Advantages of home births.* These include the birthing of a child in a familiar environment with the woman's spouse and children involved in the birthing process.
2. *Screening for home birth.* Home birth advocates recognize that some women should deliver their babies in the hospital. Such women with high-risk pregnancies are identified and encouraged not to have a home birth.
3. *Practical aspects of home birth.* Finding a midwife-nurse or obstetrician, proper nutrition, gathering necessary supplies, and developing a backup plan if the need for hospital assistance arises are among the practical concerns of a home birth.
4. *Psychological issues.* Attitudes of parents, friends, and medical professionals toward home births, the emotional aspects of birthing, parenthood, and so on are discussed.
5. *Labor management.* This includes information about stages of labor, breathing exercises, and pain control.

What is the relative safety of home versus hospital births? A research study that attempts to answer this question must control for the screening of home birth choosers, who are for the most part women who are healthy and who have few risk factors. Also, since those choosing home birth have been educated in the techniques of prepared childbirth in some form, home birthers must be compared with prepared hospital birthers.

A study that meets these criteria involved a sample of 1,146 pairs of home and hospital births matched on the basis of obstetrical history, general health, socioeconomic status, risk factors, and childbirth preparation (Melh, 1976). Home birthers were all those who planned to birth at home, even if, for whatever reason, the actual birth took place in the hospital (88 percent of births begun at home were completed at home).

There were no differences in infant mortality rates between the home and hospital birth groups. However, infant and maternal morbidity (disease) rates were lower in the home birth group. Birth injuries, maternal high blood pressure, and episiotomies were also less frequent in the home births. Additional evidence comes from a review of studies of doctor- and midwife-attended home births, in which it was noted that such births were as safe or safer than hospital births (Tew, 1978).

Table 18.3 summarizes the range of birthing alternatives and notes their suitability for different groups of women.

Caesarean Births

Most babies are born by passage through the vaginal canal. But about one in five babies are delivered by **Caesarean section**, in which an incision is made in the woman's abdomen and uterus and the baby removed (see Figure 18.2). The woman is put to sleep with general anesthesia or given a spinal injection, enabling her to remain awake and aware of the delivery. Caesarean deliveries are most often performed when there would be risk to the mother or baby through normal delivery; for example, the fetus may be positioned abnormally, the head may be too large for the mother's pelvis, or the mother may have diabetes or develop toxemia during pregnancy.

For most women, the knowledge that they will have a C-Section is a surprise. In one study women reported that they knew they were to deliver by Caesarean less than two hours before the surgery was performed (Affonso & Stichler, 1980). Some women became anxious or upset at not being able to

**Figure 18.2
Childbirth by
Caesarean Section**

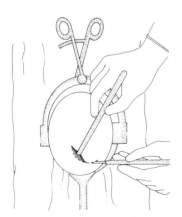
(a) A curved incision is made in the lower uterus.

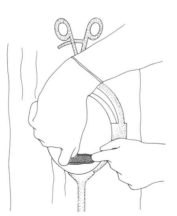
(b) Incision is stretched.

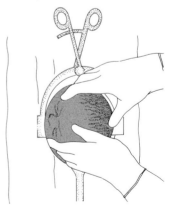
(c) Baby's head is gently lifted out of the opening.

Table 18.3 Birthing Alternatives

Type of Birth	Suitability	Description
Nonprofessionally supervised home birth	Questionably suitable	Includes do-it-yourself and unprepared or informally apprenticed lay-midwifery care. Prenatal care may or may not be carried out, and a backup with the hospital system may or may not be available.
Professionally supervised home birth	Suitable for normal or low-risk births	Includes care supervised by a formally prepared practitioner duly licensed to provide maternity services, i.e., a physician (specialist or nonspecialist), nurse-midwife, or in some states lay-midwife. Prenatal care and postpartum follow-up are provided by the practitioner, and there are appropriate links to consultation and care within the hospital system.
Birth and childbearing centers	Suitable for normal or low-risk births	Includes independent and system-sponsored homelike settings away from, near, or within hospital, but with autonomous policies. Aspects of home birth are included, such as presence of family members, flexible routines, nonseparation of infant and parents, inclusion of family in decision making, and early discharge with follow-up. Care is provided by all levels of licensed practitioners with some technological supports available in the event of emergency. Effective linkage to the system and specialist consultation are available. Home visiting also included in follow-up. Consumer voice in policy making is an essential.
Humanized hospital birth	Suitable for "at-risk" or "complicated" births. May or may not be satisfactory for normal and uncomplicated births.	Includes birth rooms within labor-delivery suites, childbirth education, and rooming-in. Somewhat flexible care dominated by obstetrical practitioners with nurse support. May, but usually does not, include nurse-midwives or nonspecialist physicians. Priorities generally those of staff, based on institutional needs and student physician teaching requirements rather than consumers' requests. Technology in selective, rather than generalized, use.
Conventional hospital birth	Considered suitable for "at-risk" or "complicated" births. Low or no priority given to satisfaction.	Specialist-dominated birth with routine interventions such as amniotomy, use of ultrasound and electronic monitors, pitocin induction of labor, analgesia, regional and general anesthesia, lithotomy position for birth, separation of family members, deemphasis of childbirth education and breastfeeding. High value placed on "benefits" of caesarean section and emphasis on consumer "inability" and "lack of desire" to participate in decision making. Neonatal period also liable to be technologically conducted.

SOURCE: Reprinted with permission of the publisher from "Alternative Maternity Care: Resistance and Change," by Ruth Watson Lubic in *Childbirth: Alternatives to Medical Control* by Shelly Romalis (ed.), pp. 220–221. Copyright © 1981 by University of Texas Press, Austin, Texas.

have a normal delivery; others were relieved since the Caesarean meant the end to a long and agonizing labor.

Although Caesareans are major surgery, the risk of death to the mother is less than 2 percent. When death occurs it is usually the result of a pre-existing condition such as severe toxemia or heart disease, not of the surgery itself. The Caesarean section is regarded as one of the safest of all abdominal surgeries and has the record for the fewest postoperative problems (Stichler & Affonso, 1980).

However, in recent years there has been considerable criticism of physicians who routinely perform Caesarean surgery even when it is not medically indicated. As until recently a woman who had a C section had to have all subsequent births by C-section, these physicians were accused of creating a market for Caesarean surgery. But in 1982 the American College of Obstetricans and Gynecologists reversed its 75-year-old policy and said that some women who had a Caesarean delivery for their first child could have subsequent vaginal deliveries. More than 28,000 such cases have occurred.

Reactions to Childbirth

More than 3,682,000 babies are born annually in the United States (U.S.HHS, 1983). But these numbers do not reflect the individual experiences of the mother. Once her baby is born, she often feels an enormous sense of pride. This pride is heightened as parents and friends come to view the baby, give gifts, and assure the new mother that she has accomplished a miracle. A mother of three days explained, "I love to hear people tell me how beautiful my baby is. I immediately project into the future and count them lucky to have seen a baby who is destined for greatness."

The emotional bond between mother and baby is strong and develops early so that mother and infant resist separation. Some researchers feel that there is a biologic base for the mother-infant bond (Marano, 1981). Studies of female rats suggest that oxytocin, a hormone of the pituitary gland released during the expulsive stage of labor, induces maternal behavior (Pederson & Prange, 1979).

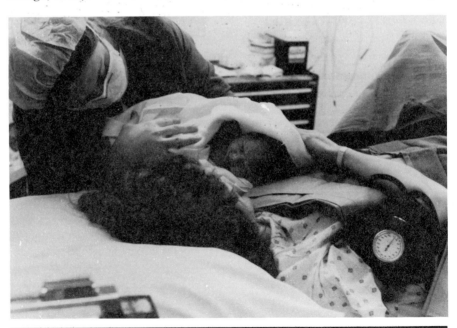

A mother in the recovery room experiences the first hour of life with her baby.

How's the Baby: The Apgar Score

Regardless of method, after the baby emerges from the woman's body, a physician (in hospital deliveries) evaluates the physical condition of the infant at one and five minutes after birth. An Apgar score (developed by Virginia Apgar) is provided as a way of predicting the infant's survival. The score is a result of assigning scores of 0, 1, or 2 to each of several physical signs—heart rate, respiratory effort, muscle tone, reflex irritability, and color. The top score is 10 and suggests that all is well with the infant. The following is a list of how babies in the United States scored in 1978 (Querec, 1981).

- Only 5.3% of the infants had perfect scores of 10.
- 91% scored 7 or above at one minute. 98% scored 7 or above at five minutes.
- Higher scores were associated with the infant weighing between 5 lbs. 8 oz. and 9 lbs. 14 oz.
- Higher scores were associated with those infants whose mothers were between the ages of 20 and 34.
- Higher scores were also seen for infants of mothers who had high educational attainment, were married, and who had prenatal care.

Since 1978 there has been a decline in the proportion of births with high (9 or 10) scores at both 1 and 5 minutes after birth (Vital Statistics, 1983).

But not all mothers feel immediate joy, and emotional bonding may be temporarily impeded by a mild depression characterized by irritability, crying, loss of appetite, and difficulty in sleeping. About 50 percent of mothers experience what is known as postpartum depression, or "the blues." The feeling is thought to be the result of the numerous physiological and psychological changes of pregnancy, labor, and delivery. Although the woman may become depressed in the hospital, she more often experiences these feelings after returning home with her baby. Most women recover within a few days. About 5 percent require some form of counseling.

Postpartum depression reaction may occur two, three, or even four weeks after the mother is home. A study by Richard and Katherine Gordon at the Englewood Hospital in New Jersey (see Newton, 1976) revealed that adopting the following behavior patterns before and during pregnancy helped women avoid the blues: (1) getting advice about parenthood, (2) making friends with couples who had young children, (3) continuing outside interests, (4) having the husband rearrange his schedule to be home more, and (5) having a relative or private nurse help with the baby soon after the arrival from the hospital.

Adjusting to Motherhood

"You can read about motherhood, watch your friends as they become mothers, and fantasize about having your own baby, but until you've done it, you can't really evaluate how you will feel about motherhood," reflected a young mother. Whereas people can try out living together, they cannot try out parental roles.

Since every woman goes into motherhood naively, it is not surprising that women have widely differing experiences in managing the role. For some women motherhood is the ultimate fulfillment; for others, the ultimate frustration. Most women experience mixed emotions during their mothering experience. Whatever a woman's attitude before the birth of her baby, she is not likely to take her role lightly. From the time she knows she is pregnant (or about to become an adoptive mother), no woman's life is ever the same.

Motherhood brings with it changes in a woman's daily routine, an increased feeling of responsibility, worry and often a need to balance the demands of job or career and family. The extent of these changes will be influenced by her partner's participation in child rearing, but the woman is usually more involved in the parenting role. Whereas it is rare to find a father who stays home and takes care of a preschool child everyday, about 60 percent of mothers do so.

Work

The new mother finds herself with a new set of tasks. Feeding, diapering, and bathing the infant are added to the responsibilities she already has. "Extra work to care for the baby" and "loss of sleep" were the two most common problems mentioned by mothers of two-month-old infants (Kach & McGhee, 1982). The new mother's own mother often helps when the mother and baby come home from the hospital (Broschart, 1979), but she soon finds herself alone with her infant, and although her husband may help when he is home, she ends up with 75 to 85 percent of the child-care tasks (Grossman, Eichler, & Winickoff, 1980).

Responsibility

Most mothers contend that the actual day-to-day (and night-to-night) work of child care is not the factor that makes motherhood difficult, but it is, rather the incessant and unrelenting responsibility. "The new mother starts out immediately on 24-hour duty, with responsibility for a fragile and mysterious infant totally dependent on her care. It is as if the woman shifted from a graduate student to a full professor with little intervening apprenticeship experience of slowly increasing responsibility" (Rossi, 1968, p. 35). Even in those relationships where the husband and wife say they share the responsibility for child care, the final responsibility more often falls to the wife.

The responsibility of motherhood is long term. A middle-class woman with two children observed, "People tend to think of having children only in terms of the baby period. While it may seem like an eternity, the baby–toddler stage of a child is short compared with the 12 or 16 years of the school-age child. Parents may not be legally responsible for a child beyond age 21 but morally and emotionally, once a parent, always a parent."

Worry

"You can lock them in their room but not out of your mind," said the mother of three daughters. Her observation reflects that children are an emotional as well as a physical drain. First, a child's safety is a major concern. "I look at the clock at three and know that my child will soon be crossing the street from school," one mother said, "and although there is a policewoman there, I don't relax until I hear, 'I'm home, Mom.' " When mothers do not worry about busy streets, it is money (Will there be enough for them to complete college?) or peer persecution (Will they make fun of her because she has one crossed eye?) or health (Does a sore throat warrant a trip to the doctor?) or her own employment (Will my children become delinquents because I am too involved in my career?).

The Career Woman as Mother

For the traditional housewife who stays at home, adding the role of mother may be relatively easy. She will have the time and resources (with her husband's economic support) to cope with her infant's demands. Indeed, being at home with her own baby is her dream come true.

But increasingly, more women (more than 50 percent) are working outside the home and drop out of the labor force only long enough to have their children. To the demanding roles of employee and wife, she must add that of mother. Even with her husband's support, the career woman must find ways to fit the demands of motherhood into her busy schedule. Priorities must be established. When forced to choose between career and family responsibilities (the baby sitter does not show up, the child is sick or hurt, or the like), the career woman and mother generally responds to the latter role first. "Sarah, my 2-year-old, fell and cut her lip as I was about to leave for the office," remarked a young lawyer. "Instead of dropping her at the day-care center, I took her to the doctor, who stitched her up. I didn't have to think about whether I was going to be late to the office. My child is more important to me." Many employed women use their own sick leave when their child is sick.

But other career women decide other priorities at the time of crisis. The managing editor for a national magazine said, "My work comes first. I will see that my child is taken care of, but I'm not playing the role of the resident nurse. Last week, my son got sick, but I took him to the sitter anyway. Of course, there are occasions I will let my job go, but they are rare."

Some career women give up their work completely. "No job is so fulfilling, no experience so rich as that of being with my baby," said one woman. 'And your employed friends with children don't like it. They think you are a traitor. But many of them feel guilty about not being with their children."

When a Man Becomes a Father

Whereas the woman may have dreamed of being a mother since early childhood and nourished the dream during pregnancy, her partner often has not fully considered the implications of fatherhood. The impact of becoming a parent is sometimes more profound for the man than for the woman. In this section we examine how men view parenthood, their transition to fatherhood and their reactions to their new role.

How Men View Fatherhood

Most fathers are guided by certain impressions they have of what a father is and does. They may variously view their role as provider, teacher, companion, and caretaker.

Provider

Most fathers feel that one of their primary responsibilities is making money for their family. But this need to be the main economic provider, which many men have been taught to see as part of their masculine role, may conflict with other needs.

Earning money to support a family often makes it necessary to be responsible to an employer. A salesman must face his field manager periodically with a report on the number of items he has sold. If he has performed poorly, he loses his job. The employer is not interested in knowing if the employee goes camping with his children or eats lunch with them or picks them up after school. "How many did you sell?" is the only question.

The conflict between family and career is particularly acute if the father chooses to climb the executive ladder in a large company. This requires taking work home at night, traveling extensively, and working more than the standard 40-hour week—all of which may interfere with spending time with children and relaxing as a family together. For the man whose family comes first, there will be fewer promotions, smaller raises, and generally less in the way of career rewards of all types.

Because men are rewarded for putting their career above their family, they often justify their minimal parenthood contribution in economic terms. "I've given them everything they ever wanted," said one father. But fathers are often criticized because making money is all they do. One 27-year-old graduate student said, "My dad put me through school and bought me a car, but he is a stranger to me. I'll never get over his not spending time with me when I was younger."

Teacher

Some fathers believe it is their responsibility to make their child ready for life by teaching him or her to be independent, self-sufficient, and self-reliant. "I taught all my kids," said one father of three, "that there is always room at the top and the only way to get there is good morals and discipline."

Companion

"Regardless of how busy my dad was, he always spent some time with me in the evening and on weekends. We would talk about everything from football to what really matters in life. I've always felt my dad cared about me, and I've tried to be the same kind of father to my children," said the father of two youngsters.

A father often likes to think of himself as a friend and companion to his offspring, though the relationship varies with the age and gender of the children. For example, a father may relate quite differently to his son and daughter during their childhood and adolescence. "I've always been closer to my son, even when he was a kid," observed one father. "We just had more in common. When he was an adolescent, we worked on cars together and did some hunting. Now we're in business together. I love my daughter but have never had much in common with her."

But a father of two daughters said, "I can't imagine what it would be like to have a son because I've always related to my two children as people, not girls. I have enjoyed them since they were babies, and while we had our differences when they were teenagers, we are friends."

Caretaker

The traditional father participated only minimally in the physical care of his children but his modern counterpart, especially one with a working wife, more often views child care as a shared responsibility. Putting them to bed, helping with homework, and playing with them are common behaviors of a father in two-income families (Kamerman, 1980). Some fathers do it all. "I enjoy taking care—feeding, bathing, singing to the baby—more than my wife," stated one husband. Beatle John Lennon provided all the child care for his son for two years and noted that he was proud of it. The father's participation in child care is discussed in more detail later.

Transition to Fatherhood

The fatherhood role begins with the woman's pregnancy and the husband relating to his wife as mother-to-be. This means sharing her excitement about the pregnancy with parents and close friends. "It was like telling people that we were getting married," said one father. "We delighted in breaking the news to people who were as excited as we were."

Beyond this, husbands do very little to prepare for fatherhood. In a study of 102 first-time fathers (Knox & Gilman, 1974), only one-third attended parenthood classes offered by a local university, while one-fourth attended Lamaze classes. (Most fathers who do attend these classes are white and middle class [Block, 1981]). It would be inaccurate to assume that the fathers-to-be already knew what to expect from the fatherhood role. In fact, only 25 percent of them had discussed fatherhood with another male on several occasions and more than 40 percent had never fed a baby or changed a baby's diapers.

In another study (Price-Bonham & Skeen, 1979), 160 fathers (black and white) reported that "trial and error" was their first source of help with fatherhood.

Thirty men whose wives were in their last month of pregnancy said that while they were mostly concerned about what labor and delivery would be like, they were also worried about how to care for a baby and how to parent (Fein, 1976). Some men mentioned that their fathers had been emotionally distant from them when they had been growing up and that they (the fathers-to-be) did not want to repeat that pattern.

Participation in Child Care

After the mother and baby are home from the hospital, one of the discoveries of the new father is that a baby requires an enormous amount of physical care. To assess the degree to which fathers actually participate in child care, the 102 first-time fathers in the Knox and Gilman (1974) study, who had been parents for an average of slightly more than six months, were asked, "How

Fathers are becoming closer to their children during the first weeks and months.

many times have you fed your baby in the last week?" Five was the average number reported by those fathers whose babies were bottle fed. When asked how often they had changed their babies' diapers during the last week, the fathers reported an average of six times. A 6-month-old baby requires feeding and changing about 4 and 12 times a day respectively.

Those who advocate equal sharing in child-care responsibilities suggest that as men become increasingly involved in parenting, they will experience more of the emotional rewards of parenthood. In a review of several studies of the degree to which fathers participate in child care, two researchers concluded that (a) fathers are interested in newborns and, if given the opportunity, do become involved; (b) fathers are just as nurturant as a mother in their interactions with newborns; (c) fathers do apparently engage in less caretaking; but, (d) fathers can be competent in the execution of caretaking activities (Parke & Sawin, 1976). Fathers may also bond with their newborns as mothers do.

For fathers to participate more actively in child care, they need to be encouraged by their wives. However, some women who desire more egalitarian relationships with their husbands may still feel conflict about giving up control of the house and child care and about their husband becoming less competitive and more family oriented (Bear, Berger, & Wright, 1979).

Reactions to Fatherhood

Since there is considerable social pressure to make only positive remarks about being a new parent, it is difficult to find out how fathers really feel about it. However, 25 percent of Knox and Gilman's (1974) sample agreed with the statement, "Sometimes I wish my wife and I could return to the time before my baby was born."

Men differ in the degree to which they are bothered by the irritations of early fatherhood. These differential reactions are related to the wife's feelings about motherhood, the effect of the baby on the marriage, and various characteristics of the father and the baby.

Effect of Wife's Attitude

A wife who responds favorably to her role as parent influences her husband to react in the same way. "To be honest, I could have gone either way," one father said. "After several nights of lost sleep, the sound of a crying baby during meals, and a drawer full of baby bills, I was ready to admit that we had made a big mistake. But Connie was excited about Pam and encouraged me to bathe her, feed her, and get involved. As a result, I began to enjoy the delight of fatherhood. Had it not been for Connie, my attitude would have been pretty negative."

Effect of Baby on Marriage

Related to the wife's reaction is the way the husband perceives the effect of the baby on his marriage. In the Knox and Gilman (1974) study, if the marriage improved after the baby was born, the father reported a very favorable reaction to the baby. "Our baby gave us a common goal, a purpose," said the manager of a grocery store. "Since she was born, we have been much closer. She's the best thing that every happened to our marriage."

In another study, husbands who perceived the baby as having had a disruptive effect on the relationship with their wives reported more difficulty in adjusting to fatherhood (Wente & Crockenberg, 1976). "No baby is worth my marriage," said a computer programmer for IBM. "I wish the baby had never been born. My wife feels differently and it has cost us our relationship. We are getting together with our lawyers on Thursday to sign separation papers."

Childfree spouses have more time for each other and their interaction is not interrupted by children.

Other Factors

Fathers who are in their twenties are more likely to report a favorable reaction to parenthood than fathers who are in their thirties when their first child is born (Russell, 1974). In addition, fathers report a more favorable adjustment if the baby is quiet (Russell, 1974) and healthy (Hobbs & Cole, 1976). Indeed, the birth of an abnormal baby may induce severe strain in the marriage and increase the chance of divorce (Tew et al., 1977).

It is not clear whether taking classes in preparation for parenthood is effective in easing the transition to fatherhood. For example, in two studies fathers who attended parenthood classes reported more satisfaction with the infants than fathers who did not attend such classes (Beebe, 1978; Russell,

1974). But another study that compared fathers who attended Lamaze classes with those who did not found that adjustment was unrelated to Lamaze preparation (Wente & Crockenberg, 1976). This latter finding may be related to the fact that, traditionally, Lamaze classes have concentrated more on preparation for childbirth than on parenting.

When a Couple Becomes a Family

How does the prospect of having a child affect a couple's relationship, and what happens to that relationship after the baby is born?

The Couple During Pregnancy

"Children brighten up a home—because they leave the lights on all over the house."

LAWRENCE PETER

As soon as the woman becomes aware that she is pregnant, the future infant begins to influence the couple's relationship. In anticipating the baby, the couple will deal with matters that are entirely new to them—telling parents and friends about the pregnancy, allocating existing space for the baby (or getting a larger house or apartment), furnishing a nursery, choosing names for the child, and deciding on whether to attend parenthood classes.

Pregnancy also affects the couple's sexual behavior. One husband said, "Sex has been a sticky subject lately. Linda's stomach has been so upset that just the thought of sex turns her off. The few times we have made love since we knew she was pregnant have been a little different for me, too. Not negatively though. Something about a child growing inside makes me think about families, children, and reproduction rather than just love and pleasure" (Cass & Cass, 1980, pp. 62–63).

In a study of 43 women in their first pregnancies, 33 reported losing interest in lovemaking during the first three months (Masters & Johnson, 1966). Chronic fatigue, sleepiness, and contending with nausea were the primary reasons. Reduced interest also characterized the third but not the second trimester. During these middle three months, "sexual patterns generally reflected a marked increase in eroticism and effectiveness of performance" (Masters and Johnson, 1966, p. 158). This finding should be viewed cautiously. At least six other studies failed to find evidence for an increase in sexual interest during the second trimester (Calhoun et al., 1981).

Samples
Terms
Deceptive

In another study of 260 pregnant women (98 percent were married), the average frequency of intercourse before getting pregnant was 17 times per month (Solberg, 1973). This frequency steadily decreased throughout pregnancy to less than three times per month during the ninth month. Reasons for decreased intercourse given by another group of wives included not feeling attractive and fear of hurting the baby (LaRossa, 1979).

Does having intercourse during pregnancy involve a risk to the baby? Generally not. Women who have had a previous miscarriage or who are experiencing vaginal bleeding, ruptured membranes, or threatened premature labor should consult their physician about intercourse during pregnancy. In the absence of these complications, most couples can continue intercourse as late in pregnancy as they desire. The resumption of intercourse usually occurs about six weeks after delivery.

The Baby Comes Home

After the initial excitement of the birth of their child and sharing this experience with parents and friends and when the help that parents may give during the first few weeks has ended, the spouses are alone with their baby. Theirs is now a different marriage. The prebaby days are gone forever. The box on page 562 describes the author's conclusion of a study of pregnancy, birth, and parenthood of 84 married couples (Grossman et al, 1980).

Summary

The reality of parenthood is often different from the thoughts we have about it. Motherhood begins not with childbirth but with conception. During each trimester of pregnancy, the woman may experience some minor discomforts. Adequate nutrition to ensure a healthy baby is an important concern. The pregnant woman also has an array of emotional reactions to her pregnancy and impending delivery. Labor occurs in three stages and is sometimes thought of as a painful ordeal, but some women describe the experience as "joyful." Some expectant parents, dissatisfied with traditional, hospital-managed deliveries, are choosing alternative childbirth methods, including the Lamaze, Dick-Read, Bradley, and LeBoyer methods, and an increasing number of couples are choosing home birth. When there is a risk to the mother or baby through vaginal delivery, a Caesarean section may be performed.

A woman's reactions to childbirth may include temporary feelings of depression as well as a developing emotional bond with her infant. Motherhood brings with it changes in a woman's daily routine, and an increased feeling of responsibility, worry, and often the need to balance the demands of job or career and family. For some women, motherhood is the ultimate fulfillment; for others, the ultimate frustration. Most women experience mixed emotions during their mothering experience.

The impact of becoming a parent is sometimes more profound for the man than for the woman since he often has not fully considered the implications of fatherhood. Most men are guided by certain impressions they have of what a father is and does. They tend to view the father as provider, teacher, companion, and caretaker. Although fathers participate less in child care than

The Myth and Reality of Parenthood

Finally, a few words need to be said about what we have come to call the myth of parenthood, our culture's idealized image of pregnancy, childbirth, and parenthood. According to this image, childbearing is undertaken out of the love between husband and wife and their desire to expand and enrich their relationship by having a child to share it with. The myth holds that such a wanted pregnancy is undertaken joyfully, that it unites a couple more strongly during the nine months of gestation which culminates in an uncomplicated delivery. The postpartum period, according to this story, requires a few, and only a very few, moments of adjustment to the new baby and then becomes a time when both parents feel comfortable and natural in their unambiguous roles. Of course, as an ideal image, this is an oversimplification and most parents today do not have such rosy expectations. However, sophisticated as we may be, the myth of parenthood still survives, and, to a certain extent, tyrannizes most new parents in their efforts to at least approximate the idealized image.

Our data certainly confirms our sense that pregnancy and early parenthood, while usually full of joy and rich in meaning, also entail major adjustments and inevitable strains. Ours was a very favored group of people. All were married; most were relatively happy and reasonably comfortable; and most had undertaken their pregnancies in a positive and planned manner. And yet, even this group of fortunate individuals found aspects of the undertaking difficult and stressful. Most reported unpleasant physical symptoms during the pregnancy and the majority of the women had some complications of labor and delivery. Most couples experienced strain in their marriages, especially immediately after childbirth. Almost all the parents described the considerable psychological work entailed in adjusting to the new baby and including it in the newly changed family structure. Although many of the couples were able to describe some of these difficulties, we sensed that their reports were self-censored, that the crisis they were experiencing was even more difficult than they were willing to describe, that even these generally privileged couples were at least somewhat tyrannized by the myths of parenthood.*

*Frances K. Grossman, Lois S. Eichler, and Susan A. Winickoff and Associates. *Pregnancy, Birth, and Parenthood.* San Francisco, California: Jossey-Bass, Inc., Publishers, 1980, pp. 254–255. Reprinted by permission.

mothers, they are interested and capable and, if given the opportunity and encouragement, do become involved. Their reactions to fatherhood are related to the wife's feelings about her role as parent, the effect of the baby on the marriage, and various characteristics of the father and the baby.

Having a baby affects the marriage relationship during pregnancy as well as after. During pregnancy the couple may have to adjust to a new division of labor and an altered sexual relationship. After the baby is born, according to one study, the rosy expectations of parenthood give way to inevitable strains as the couple tries to adjust to the new family constellation.

Key Terms

human chorionic gonadotropin
  (HCG)
lutex agglutination
radioimmunoassay
radioreceptorassay
false pregnancy
morning sickness
primigravida
multigravida
false labor

effacement
dilation
Lamaze method
Dick-Read method
Bradley method
LeBoyer method
Caesarean section
Apgar score

Issues in Debate and Future Directions

Researchers differ on the degree to which children have a positive or negative impact on a couple's relationship. After reviewing the data, we look at the future of parenthood.

Children Increase Marital Happiness

In several studies parents reported that having a baby improved the relationship with their spouses. Sixty percent of the men and women in a national sample said their children had brought them closer together (Hoffman & Manis, 1978). In another study only 6 percent of the husbands and 8 percent of the wives said their marriages had deteriorated since the baby's birth (Russell, 1974). Further, after an intensive study of 84 married couples who had had a baby, the researchers concluded, "Overall, our couples seem to feel that, in general, the baby had enhanced their marital relationship even though it created more stresses on it" (Grossman et al., 1980). Spouses also reported a very positive and surprising impact of their baby on them individually. "Feeling love and attachment" for the baby was the biggest surprise for mothers and among the biggest for fathers in a study of couples who had just had their baby (Kach & McGhee, 1982, p. 382). These spouses reported that they were glad they had children, that their marriages had improved since the baby, and they looked forward to having more children.

Children Decrease Marital Happiness

But other parents seem to feel just the opposite. In one study 83 percent of the respondents said the birth of their first child represented a "crisis" event for the marriage (LeMasters, 1957). Other researchers have found similar negative effects of children on the marriage relationship. In a study of 850 married couples, Feldman and Feldman (1977) compared the marriages of those who had an infant with those who had been married the same length of time but were child-free and found that lower marital satisfaction was characteristic of the couples with children. This remained true even in the middle and later years of marriage. Another researcher compared couples with and without children and concluded, "Those without children appear to be the most happily married" (Nock, 1979, p. 22).

Whereas all of these studies had relatively small samples, a more recent study included more than 9,000 respondents in six national surveys over a six-year period (Glenn & McLanahan, 1982). Regarding the relationship between having children and marital happiness, the researchers said of their data:

They do indicate that the negative effects are quite pervasive, very likely outweighing positive effects among spouses in the United States of both sexes and of all races, major religious preferences, educational levels, and employment status . . . Children tend to interfere with marital companionship and to lessen the spontaneity of sexual relations and their presence in the family creates the potential for jealousy and competition for affection, time, and attention. (p. 69)

Factors Affecting the Relationship of Marital Satisfaction and Children

Why children enhance satisfaction in some marriages but not in others may lie in the different way spouses cope with having a new baby. Fantasy (thinking back to prebaby times when things were less hectic) and going out together without the baby are two means some couples use to adapt to the strains of parenthood. In a study focusing on how fathers coped with a new baby, only the second coping mechanism worked (Gilman & Knox, 1976). Staying at home thinking about how things used to be was not only unhelpful but also it made things worse. Getting a babysitter and going out alone helped the couple to renew their relationship.

Couples also differ in their ability to reduce role strain. When the husband expects his wife, who is now a new mother, to give him the same time and attention that she did before the baby, it is unlikely that she will be able to meet his expectations. The strain of managing the wife and mother roles if the husband does not alter his expectations of the former may be particularly difficult for the woman.

Future Directions

The future of parenthood will see a greater awareness of what the role involves, increased sharing by both spouses in the birth and rearing of their child or children, and a questioning of traditional delivery procedures. Proponents of the child-free alternative will sensitize would-be parents to the realities of parenthood. As a result, although most couples will continue to opt for having children, they are likely to enter parenthood with a more realistic awareness of the positive and negative aspects of that role. Also, the increased availability of and enrollment in preparation-for-parenthood classes suggest that spouses will be better informed about parenthood when their children are born.

The number of couples who want to share the birth of their babies through some form of prepared, natural childbirth will also increase. In the past the mother was the only parent present at the birth of a couple's baby. Now the father may be part of the experience. This trend, coupled with more mothers working outside the home will help the father assume a more active role in parenting.

Finally, traditional delivery procedures will be increasingly questioned. Physicians will be asked to justify to couples who want natural childbirth the rationale for various delivery procedures: shaving pubic hair, enema, labor induction, episiotomy, forceps, delivery in the supine position, and anesthesia. Although the physician will continue to be in control of the delivery process, the couple's wishes will be taken into account. In one case, a physician decided to have his partner deliver a baby rather than induce labor before his vacation because the couple questioned—and protested—his original decision.

Abramson, P. R., & Mechanic, M. B. (1983). Sex and the media: Three decades of best-selling books and major motion pictures. *Archives of Sexual Behavior, 12,* 185–206.

Adam, B. D. (1982). Stigma and employability: Discrimination by sex and sexual orientation in the Ontario legal profession. *Canadian Review of Sociology and Anthropology, 18,* 216–221.

Affonso, D. D., & Stichler, J. F. (1980). Cesarean birth: Women's reactions. *American Journal of Nursing, 80,* 468–470.

Allen, D. M. (1980). Young male prostitutes: A psychosocial study. *Archives of Sexual Behavior, 9,* 399–426.

Allen, G. (1972). Sex study: Problems, propaganda, and pornography. In S. E. Fraser (Ed.), *Sex, schools, and society,* (pp. 201–224). Nashville: Aurora.

Allen, H. (1933). *Anthony adverse.* New York: Farrar & Rinehart.

American Cancer Society. (1982). *Cancer facts and figures: 1983.*

Armstrong, L. (1979). *Kiss Daddy goodnight: A speakout on incest.* New York: Hawthorne.

Association for Voluntary Sterilization. (1982). U.S. sterilizations near 14 million. *AVS News 20* (4), 1.

Atwater, L. (1979). Getting involved: Women's transition to first extramarital sex. *Alternative Lifestyles, 2,* 33–68.

Atwater, L. (1982). *The extramarital connection: Sex, intimacy, identity.* New York: Irvington.

Auerback, A. (1980). Quality of man's first sexual experience. *Medical Aspects of Human Sexuality, 14* (12), 6.

Ayalah, D., & Weinstock, I. J. (1979). *Breasts: Women speak about their breasts and their lives.* New York: Summit Books.

Baker, L. G. (1983). In my opinion: The sexual revolution in perspective. *Family Relations, 32,* 297–300.

Ball, R. R. (1981). *Premenstrual syndrome: The world's oldest disease?* Unpublished manuscript, Ayden, NC. Reprinted by permission.

Balswick, J. (1980). Explaining inexpressive males: A reply to L'Abate. *Family Relations, 29,* 231–233.

Bancroft, J. (1983). *Human sexuality and its problems.* New York: Churchill.

Barbach, L. G. (1974). Group treatment of preorgasmic women. *Journal of Sex and Marital Therapy, 1,* 139–145.

Barbach, L. G. (1975). *For yourself: The fulfillment of female sexuality.* New York: Doubleday.

Barbach, L. G. (1980). *Women discover orgasm.* Riverside, NJ: Free Press.

Barbach, L. G. (1982). *For each other: Sharing sexual intimacy.* New York: Doubleday.

Barbach, L. G. & Flaherty, M.(1980). Group treatment of situationally orgasmic women. *Journal of Sex and Marital Therapy, 6,* 19–29.

Barber, C. E. (1980). Gender differences in experiencing the transition to the empty nest: Reports of middle-aged and older women and men. *Family Perspective, 14,* 87–95.

Barnes v. Costle, 561 F.2d 983, 999–1000 (D.C. Cir. 1977).

Barrett, F. M. (1980). Sexual experience, birth control usage, and sex education of unmarried Canadian university students: Changes between 1968 and 1978. *Archives of Sexual Behavior, 9,* 367–390.

Bart, P. B., & O'Brien, P. (in press). Women who stopped their rapes. *Signs.*

Bartell, G. (1972). *Group Sex.* New York: Wyden.

Bates, J. A., & Martin, M. (1980). The thematic content of graffiti as a nonreactive indicator of male and female attitudes. *Journal of Sex Research, 16,* 300–315.

Beach, F. A. (1977). Cross-species comparisons and the human heritage. In F. A. Beach (Ed.), *Human sexuality in four perspectives* (pp. 296–316). Baltimore: Johns Hopkins University Press.

Bear, S., Berger, M., & Wright, L. (1979). Even cowboys sing the blues: Difficulties experienced by men trying to adopt nontraditional sex roles and how clinicians can be helpful to them. *Sex Roles, 5,* 191–198.

Beebe, E. R. (1978). Expectant parent classes: A case study. *Family Coordinator, 27,* 55–58.

Bell, A. P., & Weinberg, M. S. (1978). *Homosexualities: A study of diversity among men and women.* New York: Simon and Schuster.

Bell, A. P., Weinberg, M. S., & Hammersmith, S. K. (1981). *Sexual preference.* Bloomington: Indiana University Press.

Bell, R. R., & Coughey, K. (1980). Premarital sexual experience among college females, 1958, 1968, 1978. *Family Relations, 29,* 353–357.

Belzer, E. G. (1981). Orgasmic expulsions of women: A review and heuristic inquiry. *Journal of Sex Research, 17,* 1–12.

Bennett, S. M., & Dickinson, W. B. (1980). Student-parent rapport and parent involvement in sex, birth control, and venereal disease education. *Journal of Sex Research, 16,* 114–130.

Berger, R. M. (1980). Psychological adaptation of the older homosexual male. *Journal of Homosexuality, 5,* 161–175.

Bermant, G. (1976). Sexual behavior: Hard times with the Coolidge Effect. In M. H. Siegel & H. P. Zeigler (Eds.), *Psychological research: The inside story* (pp. 76–103). New York: Harper & Row.

Bernard, J. (1972). *The future of marriage.* New York: Bantam.

Berscheid, E., Walster, E. & Bohrnstedt, G. (1973, November). Body image—The happy American body: A survey report. *Psychology Today,* pp. 119–131.

Better Homes and Gardens survey: (1983). *What's happening to American families?* Des Moines: Meredith.

Bieber, I., et al. (1962). *Homosexuality: A psychoanalytical study.* New York: Random House.

Bilge, B., & Kaufman, G. (1983). Children of divorce and one-parent families: Cross-cultural perspectives. *Family Relations, 32,* 59–71.

Billings, E. L., Billings, J. J., & Catarinch, M. (1974). *Atlas of the ovulation method.* Collegeville, MN: Liturgical Press.

Binkin, N., Gold, J. & Cates, W. Jr., (1982). Illegal-abortion deaths in the United States: Why are they still occurring? *Family Planning Perspectives, 14* (3), 163–167.

Bixler, R. H. (1983). The multiple meanings of "incest." *Journal of Sex Research, 19,* 197–201.

Blank, J., & Cottrell, H. L. (1978). *I am my lover.* Burlingame, CA: Down There Press.

Block, C. R., Norr, K. L., Meyering, S., Norr, J. L., & Charles, A. G. (1981). Husband gatekeeping in childbirth. *Family Relations, 30,* 197–204.

Blumstein, P. W., & Schwartz, P. (1976). Bisexuality in women. *Archives of Sexual Behavior, 5,* 171–181.

Blumstein, P. W., & Schwartz, P. (1977). Bisexuality: Some social and psychological issues. *Journal of Social Issues, 33,* 30–45.

Bobys, R. S. (1983). Research fraud factors and effects. *Free Inquiry in Creative Sociology, 11,* 44–48.

Bohlen, J. G., Held, J. P., & Sanderson, M. O. (1980). The male orgasm: Pelvic contractions measured by anal probe. *Archives of Sexual Behavior, 9,* 503–521.

Bohlen, J. G., Held, J. P., Sanderson, M. O., & Boyer, C. M. (1982). Development of a woman's multiple orgasm pattern: A research case report. *Journal of Sex Research, 18,* 130–145.

Bongaarts, J. (1982). Infertility after age 30: A false alarm. *Family Planning Perspectives, 14* (2), 75–78.

Boston Women's Health Book Collective. (1976). *Our bodies, ourselves* (2nd ed.). New York: Simon and Schuster.

Bouchard, T. J., Eckert, E., Resnick, S., & Keys, M. (1980). *The Minnesota study of twins reared apart: Project description and sample results.* Reprinted by permission.

Bragonier, J. R., & Bragonier, B. J. (1979). The physiology of sexual function. In V. L. Bullough (Ed.), *The frontiers of sex research* (pp. 5–12). Buffalo, NY: Prometheus Books.

Bratic, E. B. (1982). Healthy mothers, healthy babies coalition. *Prevention, 97,* 503–509.

Breast cancer digest (NIH Publication No. 80–1691). (1980, May). Bethesda, MD: National Cancer Institute.

Bremer, J. (1959). *Asexualization: A follow-up study of 244 cases.* New York: Macmillan.

Bremer, T. H., & Wittig, M. A. (1980). Fear of success: A personality trait or a response to occupational deviance and role overload? *Sex Roles, 6,* 27–46.

Brewer, J. S. (1981). Duration of intromission and female orgasm rates. *Medical Aspects of Human Sexuality, 15,* (4) 70–71.

Britton, T. (1982). Personal communication, Lenoir Community College, Kinston, NC.

Brodsky, S. L. (1976). Prevention of rape: Deterrence by the potential victim. In M. J. Walker & S. L. Brodsky (Eds.), *Sexual assault* (pp. 75–90). Lexington, MA: Lexington Books.

Brooks-Gunn, J., & Matthews, W. S. (1979). *He and she: How children develop their sex role identity.* Englewood Cliffs, NJ: Prentice-Hall.

Broschart, K. R. (1979). Learning family roles: A study of the use of help following childbirth. *Family Perspective, 13,* 131–135.

Brown, G. (1980). *The new celibacy.* New York: McGraw-Hill.

Brown, I. S. & Pollack, R. H. (1982). *Sex knowledge, sex guilt, and sexual behavior among university students.* Paper presented at the annual meeting of the American Psychological Association, Washington, D.C. Used by permission.

Brown, W. B., Monti, P. M., & Corriveau, D. P. (1978). Serum testosterone and sexual activity and interest in men. *Archives of Sexual Behavior, 7,* 97–103.

Brownmiller, S. (1975). *Against our will: Men, women, and rape.* New York: Simon and Schuster.

Bryant, C. D., & Palmer, C. E. (1977). Tense muscles and the tender touch: Massage parlors, "hand whores," and the subversion of service. In C. D. Bryant (Ed.), *Sexual deviancy in social context* (pp. 131–145). New York: New Viewpoints.

Budoff, P. W. (1983). *No more hot flashes and other good news.* New York: Putnam.

Buhrich, N. (1983). The association of erotic piercing with homosexuality, sadomasochism, bondage, fetishism, and tattoos. *Archives of Sexual Behavior, 12,* 167–171.

Bullough, V. (1979). Prostitution, psychiatry and history. In V. L. Bullough (Ed.), *The frontiers of sex research* (pp. 87–96). Buffalo, NY: Prometheus Books.

Bullough, V. (1980). Technology and female sexuality and physiology: Some implications. *Journal of Sex Research, 16,* 59–71.

Bullough, V., Bullough, B., & Smith, R. (1983). A comparative study of male transvestites, male to female transsexuals, and male homosexuals. *Journal of Sex Research, 19,* 238–257.

Burchardt, C. J., & Serbin, L. A. (1982). Psychological androgyny and personality adjustment in college and psychiatric populations. *Sex Roles, 8,* 835–851.

Burgess, A. W., & Holmstrom, L. L. (1976). Rape: Its effect on task performance at varying stages in the life cycle. In M. J. Walker & S. L. Brodsky (Eds.), *Sexual assault* (pp. 23–33). Lexington, MA: Lexington Books.

Burgoyne, D. (1980). Women's interest in fellatio. *Medical Aspects of Human Sexuality, 14* (7), 15.

Bussey, K., & Perry, D. G. (1982). Same-sex imitation: The avoidance of cross-sex models or the acceptance of same-sex models? *Sex Roles, 8,* 773–784.

Butler, R. N., & Lewis, M. I. (1976). *Sex after sixty.* New York: Harper & Row.

Buunk, B. (1980). Sexually open marriage. *Alternative Lifestyles, 3,* 312–328.

Buunk, B. (1982), Strategies of jealousy: Styles of coping with extramarital involvement of the spouse. *Family Relations,* 31, 13–18.

Calderone, M. S. (1980). Ethical and moral issues in sex education. In R. Forleo & W. Pasini (Eds.), *Medical sexology* (pp. 462–466). Littleton, MA: PSG Publishing.

Calderone, M. S. (1983). Fetal erection and its meaning to us. *SIECUS Report, 11* (5/6), 9–10.

Caldwell, M. A., & Peplau, L. A. (1982). Sex differences in same-sex friendship. *Sex Roles, 8,* 721–732.

Calhoun, A. (1960). *A social history of the American family.* New York: Barnes and Noble.

Calhoun, L. G., Selby, J. W. & King, H. E. (1981). The influence of pregnancy on sexuality: A review of current evidence. *Journal of Sex Research, 17,* 139–151.

Cancer Information Service, Duke University. (1983). *Men: How to examine your testicles.* Durham, NC.

Carns, D. E. (1973). Talking about sex: Notes on first coitus and the double standard. *Journal of Marriage and the Family, 35,* 677–688.

Cass, L., & Cass, R. (1980, May). Pregnancy diary: The first months. *Parents,* pp. 59–65.

Cassell, C. (1983). A perspective on the great sex education debate. In C. Davis (Ed.), *Challenges in sexual science* (pp. 85–108). Philadelphia: Society for the Scientific Study of Sex.

Catania, J. A., & White, C. B. (1982). Sexuality in an aged sample: Cognitive determinants of masturbation. *Archives of Sexual Behavior, 11,* 237–245.

Census Bureau. (1980). *Statistical abstract of the United States: 1980* (101st ed., Washington, DC: U.S. Government Printing Office.

Census Bureau. (1983). *Current population reports: Lifetime earnings for men and women in the United States: 1979* (Series P–60, No. 139). Washington, DC: U.S. Government Printing Office.

Chasen, B. (1977). Toward eliminating sex role stereotyping in early childhood classes. *Child Care Quarterly, 6,* 30–41.

Cherry, L., & Lewis, M. (1976). Mothers and two-year-olds: A study of sex-differentiated aspects of verbal interaction. *Developmental Psychology, 12,* 278–282.

Clark, D. (1977). *Loving someone gay.* New York: New American Library.

Clark, L. (1970). Is there a difference between a clitoral and vaginal orgasm? *Journal of Sex Research, 6,* 25–28.

Clement, U., & Schmidt, G. (1983). The outcome of couple therapy for sexual dysfunctions using three different formats. *Journal of Sex and Marital Therapy, 9,* 67–78.

Clifford, R. E. (1978a). Subjective sexual experience in college women. *Archives of Sexual Behavior, 7,* 183–197.

Clifford, R. E. (1978b). Development of masturbation in college women. *Archives of Sexual Behavior, 7,* 559–573.

Cole, T. M. (1979). Sexuality and the spinal cord injured. In R. Green (Ed.), *Human sexuality: A health practitioner's text* (2nd ed., pp. 243–263). Baltimore: Williams and Wilkins.

Coleman, E. M., Hoon, P. W., & Hoon, E. F. (1983). Arousability and sexual satisfaction in lesbian and heterosexual women. *Journal of Sex Research, 19,* 58–73.

Coleman, T. F. (1979). Sex and the law. In V. Bullough (ed.), *The frontiers of sex research* (pp. 141–149). Buffalo, NY: Prometheus Books.

Connecticut mutual life report on american values in the 1980s: The impact of belief (1981). Hartford CT: Connecticut Mutual Life Insurance Company. Copyright © 1981 Connecticut Mutual Life Insurance Company, Hartford, CT.

Cook, K., Kretchmer, A., Nellis, B., Lever, J., & Hertz, R. (1983, May). The *Playboy* readers' sex survey (Part 3). *Playboy,* p. 126.

Cook, K., Kretchmer, A., Nellis, B., Petersen, J. R., Lever, J. & Hertz, R. (1983, October). The *Playboy* readers' sex survey (Part 5). *Playboy,* p. 92.

Cookerly, J. R., & McClaren, K. A. (1982), Sex therapy with and without love: An empirical investigation. *Journal of Sex Education and Therapy, 8*(2), 35–38.

Cooper, P. E., Cumber, B., & Hartner, R. (1978). Decision-making patterns and post-decision adjustment of childfree husbands and wives. *Alternative Lifestyles, 1,* 71–94.

Corbett, S. L., & Morgan, K. D. (1983). The process of lesbian identification. *Free Inquiry in Creative Sociology, 11,* 81–83.

Coutts, R. L. (1973). *Love and intimacy: A psychological approach.* San Ramon, CA: Consensus.

Cox, D. J., & Maletzky, B. M. (1980). Victims of exhibitionism. In D. J. Cox & R. J. Daitzman (Eds.), *Exhibitionism* (pp. 289–293). New York: Garland STPM Press.

Crain, I. J. (1978). Afterplay. *Medical Aspects of Human Sexuality,* 72–85.

Cuber, J. F. (1969). The sexless marriage. *Medical Aspects of Human Sexuality, 3*(11), 19–33.

Czba, J. C., & Chevret, M. (1979). Psychological reactions of couples to artificial insemination with donor sperm. *International Journal of Fertility, 24,* 240–245.

Dalton, K. (1977). *The premenstrual syndrome and progesterone therapy.* Chicago: Year Book Medical.

Dauw, D. C. (1980). *The stranger in your bed.* Chicago: Nelson-Hall.

Davidson, J. K., Sr. (1982). *A comparison of sexual fantasies between sexually experienced never-married males and females: Situational contexts, preferences, and functions.* Paper presented at the annual meeting of the Southern Sociological Society. Memphis, Tennessee. Used with permission.

Davidson, J. K., Sr., & Hoffman, L. E. (1980). *Sexual fantasies and sexual satisfaction: An empirical analysis of erotic thoughts.* Unpublished paper, University of Wisconsin–Eau Claire and University of Notre Dame, Notre Dame, IN. Used with permission.

Davis, J. A. (1972–1982). *General social surveys* [Machine-readable data file]. James A. Davis (Principal investigator); Tom W. Smith (Senior study director. Chicago: National Opinion Research Center (Producer). Storrs, CT: University of Connecticut, Roper Public Opinion Research Center (Distributor).

Davis, N. (1978). Prostitution: Identity, career, and legal-economic enterprise. In J. M. Henslin & E. Sagarin (Eds.), *The sociology of sex* (rev. ed., pp. 195–222). New York: Schocken Books.

Davis, S. M., & Harris, M. B. (1982). Sexual knowledge, sexual interests, and sources of sexual information of rural and urban adolescents from three cultures. *Adolescence, 17,* 471–492.

Dean, S. A., & Hrnyak, J. M. (1982). Are parent educators and trainers helping parents to become "askable"? *Journal of Sex Education and Therapy, 8*(1), 41–43.

Deaux, K. (1976). *The behavior of women and men.* Monterey, CA: Brooks-Cole.

DeFrain, J., & Eirick, R. (1981). Coping as divorced single parents: A comparative study of fathers and mothers. *Family Relations, 30,* 265–274.

DeLamater, J., & MacCorquodale, P. (1979). *Premarital sexuality: Attitudes, relationships, behavior.* Madison: University of Wisconsin Press.

DeLaney, J., Lupton, M. J., & Toth, E. (1977). *The curse: A cultural history of menstruation.* New York: New American Library.

Denfeld, D. (1974). Dropouts from swinging. *Family Coordinator, 23,* 45–50.

Derogatis, L. R., & Meyer, J. K. (1979). A psychological profile of the sexual dysfunctions. *Archives of Sexual Behavior, 8,* 201–223.

DeShazer, S. (1978). Brief hypnotherapy of two sexual dysfunctions: The crystal ball technique. *American Journal of Clinical Hypnosis, 20,* 203–208.

Diamond, M. (1982). Sexual identity, monozygotic twins reared in discordant sex roles and BBC follow-up. *Archives of Sexual Behavior, 11,* 181–185.

Diamond, M., & Karlen, A. (1980). *Sexual decisions.* Boston: Little, Brown.

Dickman, I. R. (1982). *Winning the battle for sex education.* New York: Sex Information and Education Council of the U.S., Washington, D.C.

Diederen, I., & Rorer, L. (1982). *Do attitudes and background influence college students' sexual behavior?* Paper presented at the annual meeting of the American Psychological Association. Used with permission.

Dodson, B. (1974). *Liberating masturbation.* New York: Bodysex Designs.

Donnerstein, E. (1980). Aggressive erotica and violence against women. *Journal of Personality and Social Psychology, 29,* 269–277.

Douglas, J. D., Rasmussen, P. H., & Flanagan, C. A. (1977). *The nude beach.* Beverly Hills, CA: Sage.

Duckworth, J., & Levitt, E. E. (1982). *A personality analysis of a "swinger" club.* Unpublished manuscript, Ball State University, Counseling Psychology and Guidance Services, Muncie, IN; and Indiana University School of Medicine, Indianapolis, IN. Department of Psychiatry. Used with permission.

Duddle, C. M., & Ingram, A. (1980). Treating sexual dysfunction in couple's groups. In R. Forleo & W. Pasini (Eds.), *Medical sexology* (pp. 598–605). Littleton, MA: PSG Publishing.

Dunn, P. C., & Ryan, I. J. (1982a). *Effects of a video-taped debate between pro-life and pro-choice representatives on college students.* Paper presented at the annual meeting of the Society for the Scientific Study of Sex. San Francisco, CA. Used with permission.

Dunn, P. C ., & Ryan, I. J. (1982b, December). Reduction of teenage pregnancy as a rationale for sex education: A position paper. *Journal of School Health,* p. 611–613.

Edelwich, J., & Brodsky, A. (1982). *Sexual dilemmas for the helping professional.* New York: Brunner-Mazel.

Edwards, J. N. (1973). Extramarital involvement: Fact and theory. *Journal of Sex Research, 9,* 210–224.

Edwards, R., & Steptoe, P. (1980). *A matter of life.* New York: Morrow.

Eicher, W. (1980). The treatment of vaginismus. In R. Forleo & W. Pasini (Eds.), *Medical sexology* (pp. 584–590). Littleton, MA: PSG Publishing.

Eicher, W. (1983). German surgeon discusses positive impact of transsexual surgery. *Sexuality Today, 6* (34), 3–4.

Eichler, M. (1980). *The double standard.* New York: St. Martin's Press.

Elliot, C. (1982). Sexual harassment on the job. *Political Affairs, 61*(3), 5–18.

Ellis, H. (1931). *Studies in the psychology of sex: Vol. 6. Sex in relation to society.* Philadelphia: F. A. Davis. (Original work published 1910)

Ellison, C. R. (1980). *A critique of the clitoral model of female sexuality.* Paper presented at the annual meeting of the American Psychological Association. Montreal, Quebec. Used with permission.

Elvenstar, D. (1982). *Children: To have or have not?* San Francisco: Harbor.

Englund, C. L. (1983). Parenting and parentage: Distinct aspects of children's importance. *Family Relations, 32,* 21–28.

Evans, J. G. (1980). Involving parents in sex education. *SIECUS Report, 8*(4), 4–5.

Evans, M. D., & Zilbergeld, B. (1983). Evaluating sex therapy: A reply to Kolodny. *Journal of Sex Research, 19,* 302–306.

Evans, R. B. (1969). Childhood parental relationships of homosexual men. *Journal of Consulting and Clinical Psychology, 33,* 129–135.

Fein, R. A. (1976). Men's entrance into parenthood. *Family Coordinator, 25,* 341–348.

Feldman, H., & Feldman, M. (1977). *Effect of parenthood at three points in marriage.* Unpublished manuscript, Cornell University, Ithaca, NY. Used with permission.

Feldstein, J. H., & Feldstein, S. (1982). Sex differences on televised toy commercials. *Sex Roles, 8,* 581–587.

Felman, Y. M. (1980). Complications of some "minor" sexually transmitted diseases. *Medical Aspects of Human Sexuality, 14*(9), 61–74.

Fensterheim, H., & Kanter, J. S. (1980). The behavioral approach to sexual disorders. In B. B. Wolman & J. Money (Eds.), *Handbook of human sexuality* (pp. 314–324). Englewood Cliffs, NJ: Prentice-Hall.

Ferguson, K. D., & Finkler, D.C. (1978). An involvement and overtness measure for lesbians: Its development and relation to anxiety and social zeitgeist. *Archives of Sexual Behavior, 7,* 211–227.

Finkelhor, D. (1979). *Sexually victimized children.* New York: Free Press.

Finkelhor, D. (1980). Sex among siblings: A survey on prevalence, variety and effects. *Archives of Sexual Behavior, 9,* 171–194.

Fisher, C., Cohen, H. D., Schiavi, R. C., Davis, D., Furman, B., Ward, K., Edwards, A., & Cunningham, J. (1983). Patterns of female sexual arousal during sleep and waking: Vaginal thermo-conductance studies. *Archives of Sexual Behavior, 12,* 97–122.

Fisher, S. (1973). *The female orgasm.* New York: Basic.

Fisher, S. (1980). Personality correlates of sexual behavior in black women. *Archives of Sexual Behavior, 9,* 27–35.

FitzGerald, F. (1981, May 18). A reporter at large [Interview with the Reverend Jerry Falwell]. *New Yorker,* p. 53.

Frankel, F., & Rathvon, S. (1980). *Whatever happened to Cinderella?* New York: St. Martin's Press.

Frauman, D. C. (1982). The relationship between physical exercise, sexual activity, and desire for sexual activity. *Journal of Sex Research, 18,* 14–46.

Freedman, J. L. (1978). *Happy people.* New York: Harcourt Brace Jovanovich.

Freeman, D. (1983). *Margarert Mead and Samoa: The making and unmaking of an anthropological myth.* Cambridge, MA: Harvard University Press.

Freese, M. P., & Levitt, E. E. (in press). Relationships among intravaginal pressure, orgasmic function, parity factors, and urinary leakage. *Archives of Sexual Behavior.*

Freud, S. (1960). *Group psychotherapy and analysis of the ego* (J. Strachey, Trans.). New York: Bantam. (Original work published 1922)

Freud, S. (1965). *New introductory lectures in psychoanalysis* (J. Strachey, Ed. & Trans.). New York: Norton. (Original work published 1933)

Freud, S. (1974). Some physical consequences of an anatomical distinction between the sexes. In J. Strouse (Ed.), *Women and analysis.* New York: Grossman. (Original work published 1925)

Friday, N. (1975). *Forbidden flowers.* New York: Pocket Books.

Friday, N. (1980). *Men in love: Men's sexual fantasies: The triumph of love over rage.* New York: Delacorte.

Friedman, M. (1978). Men who fake orgasms. *Medical Aspects of Human Sexuality, 12* (6), 33.

Friend, R. A. (1980). Gaying: Adjustment and the older gay male. *Alternate Lifestyles, 3,* 231–248.

Frieze, I. H., Parsons, J. E., Johnson, P. B., Ruble, D. N., & Zellman, G. L. (1978). *Women and sex roles.* New York: Norton.

Fromm, E. (1956). *The art of loving.* New York: Harper & Row.

Gadpaille, W. J. (1980). Cross-species and cross-cultural contributions to understanding homosexual activity. *Archives of General Psychiatry, 37,* 349–356.

Gagnon, J. H. (1977). *Human sexualities.* Glenview, IL: Scott, Foresman.

Gagnon, J. H. (1983). Modern sexual theory and sexual reform: Emergence, transformation, and criticism. In C. Davis (Ed.), *Challenges in sexual science* (pp. 32–41). Philadelphia: Society for the Scientific Study of Sex.

Gagnon, J. H. & Simon, W. (1973). *Sexual conduct: The social sources of human sexuality.* Chicago: Aldine.

Galeman, D., & Bush, S. (1977, May). The liberation of sexual fantasy. *Psychology Today,* p. 48.

Flake-Hobson, C., Skeen, P., & Robinson, B. E. (1980). Review of theories and research concerning sex-role development and androgyny with suggestions for teachers. *Family Relations, 29,* 155–162.

Fletcher, J. (1966). *Situation ethics: The new morality.* Philadelphia: Westminister.

Folsom, J. K. (1948). Love and courtship. In R. Hill & H. Becker (Eds.), *Marriage and the Family.* Boston: Heath.

Ford, C. S., & Beach, F. A. (1951). *Patterns of sexual behavior.* New York: Harper & Row.

Forer, L. K., & Still, H. (1976). *The birth order factor: How your personality is influenced by your place in the family.* New York: McKay.

Forrest, J. D. & Henshaw, S. K. (1983). What H. S. woman think and do about contraception. *Family Planning Perspectives, 15,* 157–166.

Forward, S., & Buck, C. (1980). *Betrayal of innocence: Incest and its devastation.* New York: Penguin.

Fox, E., & Edgley, C. (1983). Effects of non-physical stigma in venereal disease. *Free Inquiry in Creative Sociology, 11,* 68–72.

Fox, G. L., & Inazu, J. K. (1980). Mother-daughter communication about sex. *Family Relations, 29,* 347–352.

Fox, L. H. (1981). *The problem of women and mathematics.* New York: Ford Foundation.

Foxman, S. (1982). *Classified love.* New York: McGraw-Hill.

Frank, E., & Enos, S. F. (1983, February). The lovelife of the American wife. *Ladies Home Journal,* p. 71.

Gallup report. (1981, February). *Moral majority* (Rep. No. 185, p. 38). Princeton, NJ: Gallup Organization.

Gebhard, P. H. (1972). Human sexual behavior: A summary statement. In D. S. Marshall & R. C. Suggs (Eds.), *Human sexual behavior* (pp. 206–217). Englewood Cliffs, NJ: Prentice-Hall.

Gebhard, P. H., Gagnon, J. H., Pomeroy, W. B., & Christenson, C. W. (1965). *Sex offenders: An analysis of types.* New York: Harper & Row.

Geiser, R. L. (1979). *Hidden victims.* Boston: Beacon Press.

Geller, A., & Geller, D. (1979). *Living longer and loving it.* Maplewood, NJ: Hammond.

Gilbert, F. S., & Bailis, K. L. (1980). Sex education in the home: An empirical task analysis. *Journal of Sex Research, 16,* 148–161.

Gilbert, L. A., Holahan, C. K., Manning, L. (1981). Coping with conflict between professional and maternal roles. *Family Relations, 30,* 419–426.

Gilman, R. C., & Knox, D. (1976). Coping with fatherhood: The first year. *Child Psychiatry and Human Development, 6,* 134–148.

Gilmartin, B. G. (1974). Sexual deviance and social networks: A study of social, family, and marital interaction patterns among co-marital sex participants. In J. Smith & L. Smith (Eds.), *Beyond monogamy* (pp. 291–323). Baltimore: Johns Hopkins University Press.

Glenn, N. D. (1975). Psychological well-being and the postparental stage: Some evidence from national surveys. *Journal of Marriage and the Family, 35,* 105–110.

Glenn, N. D., & McLanahan, S. (1982). Children and marital happiness: A further specification of the relationship. *Journal of Marriage and the Family, 44,* 63–72.

Gochros, H. L., & Fisher, J. (1980). *Treat yourself to a better sex life.* Englewood Cliffs, NJ: Spectrum, Prentice-Hall.

Goldberg, D. C., Whipple, B., Fishkin, R. E., Waxman, H., & Fuk, P. J. (1983). The Grafenberg spot and female ejaculation: A review of initial hypotheses. *Journal of Sex and Marital Therapy, 9,* 27–39.

Goldberg, H. (1983). *The new male-female relationship.* New York: Morrow.

Goldberg, M. (1980). Frigidity in men. *Medical Aspects of Human Sexuality, 14* (8), 32.

Golden, J. S., Price, S., Heinrich, A. G., & Lobitz, W. C. (1978). Group versus couple treatment of sexual dysfunctions. *Archives of Sexual Behavior, 7,* 359–602.

Goldman, R., & Goldman, J. (1982). *Children's sexual thinking.* New York: Routledge and Kegan.

Good Housekeeping poll: Test tube babies. (1980, November). *Good Housekeeping,* pp. 58–60.

Gordon, K. (1983). Homosexuality and social justice: Report of the task force on gay/lesbian issues commission on social justice, Archdiocese of San Francisco. *SIECUS Report, 11*(3), 1–4.

Gordon, S. (1977). *Community family life education programs for parents.* Charlottesville, VA: Ed-U Press.

Gordon, S. (1982). Sexuality education in the 1980s: No more retreats. *Journal of Sex Education and Therapy, 8*(2), 6–8.

Gordon, S., & Dickman, I. R. (1980). *Schools and parents: Partners in sex education* (Public Affairs Pamphlet No. 581). New York, Public Affairs Committee.

Gordon, S., & Dickman, I. R. (1981). *Sex education: The parents' role.* (Public Affairs Pamphlet No. 549). New York, Public Affairs Committee.

Graber, B., & Kline-Graber, G. (1979). Clitoral foreskin adhesions and female sexual function. *Journal of Sex Research, 15,* 205–212.

Grady, W. R., Hirsch, M. B., Keen, N., & Vaughan, B. (1983). Contraceptive failure and continuation among married women in the United States, 1970–1975. *Studies in Family Planning, 14*(1), 9–19.

Graham, S. (1848). *Lecture to young men, on chastity, intended also for the serious consideration of parents and guardians* (10th ed.). Boston: C. H. Pierce.

Green, R. (1978). Sexual identity of 37 children raised by homosexual or transsexual parents. *Ameican Journal of Psychiatry, 135,* 692–697.

Green, T. H. (1977). *Gynecology: Essentials of clinical practice.* Boston: Little, Brown.

Greenblatt, C. S. (1983). The salience of sexuality in the early years of marriage. *Journal of Marriage and the Family, 45,* 289–299.

Greenblatt, R. B. (1980). Hormones to increase libido in women. *Medical Aspects of Human Sexuality, 14*(11), 107.

Greenwood, V. B., & Bernstein, R. (1982). *Coping with herpes: The emotional problems.* Washington, DC: WCCT. (Available from Washington Center for Cognitive Therapy, P.O. Box 39119, Washington, DC 20013)

Gregg, C. H. (1982). Sexuality education: Who should be teaching the children? *SIECUS Report, 11*(1), 1–5.

Griffin, J. A. (1977). Cross-cultural investigation of behavioral changes at menopause. *Social Science Journal, 14,* 49–55.

Griffith, G. C. (1973). Sexuality and the cardiac patient. *Heart Lung, 2,* 70.

Gross, A. (1981). Sex through the ages in China. *SIECUS Report, 10*(2), 1–2.

Grosskopf, D. (1983). *Sex and the married woman.* New York: Wallaby.

Grossman, F. K., Eichler, L. S., & Winickoff, S. A. (1980). *Pregnancy, birth, and parenthood.* San Francisco: Jossey-Bass.

Groth, A. N. (1979). *Men who rape: The psychology of the offender.* New York: Plenum Press.

Groth, N., & Gary, T. S. (1981). Marital rape. *Medical Aspects of Human Sexuality, 15*(3), 122–132.

Gunderson, M. P., & McCary, J. L. (1980). Effects of sex education on sex information and sexual guilt, attitudes, and behaviors. *Family Relations, 29,* 375–379.

Haber, S. (1980). Cognitive support for the career choices of college women. *Sex Roles, 6,* 129–138.

Haeberle, E. J. (1982). The Jewish contribution to the development of sexology. *Journal of Sex Research, 18,* 305–323.

Haeberle, E. J. (1983). The future of sexology: A radical view. In C. Davis (Ed.), *Challenges in sexual science* (pp. 141–160). Philadelphia: Society for the Scientific Study of Sex.

Hamilton, E. (1978). *Sex with love.* Boston: Beacon Press.

Hamilton, E. M. N., & Whitney, E. N. (1982). *Nutrition: Concepts and controversies* (2nd ed.). St. Paul: West Publishing.

Hamilton, R. (1982). *The herpes book.* Los Angeles: J. P. Tarcher.

Hansen, G. L. (1983). Marital satisfaction and jealousy among men. *Psychological Reports, 52,* 363–366.

Harris, R., Yulis, S., & Lacoste, D. (1980). Relationships among sexual arousability, imagery ability, and introversion-extraversion. *Journal of Sex Research, 16,* 72–86.

Harrison, M. (1982). *Self-help for premenstrual syndrome.* New York: St. Martin's Press.

Harry, J. (1982). Derivative deviance: The cases of extortion, fag-bashing, and shakedown of gay men. *Criminology, 19,* 546–564.

Harry, J., & Lovely, R. (1979). Gay marriages and communities of sexual orientation. *Alternative Lifestyles, 2,* 177–200.

Hartman, W. E., & Fithian, M. A. (1974). *Treatment of sexual dysfunction.* New York: Jason Aaronson.

Hartman, W. E. & Fithian, M. A. (1979). The development of a treatment program for sexual dysfunction at the Center for Marital and Sexual Studies. In V. L. Bullough (Ed.), *The frontiers of sex research* (pp. 13–27). Buffalo, NY: Prometheus Books.

Hassett, J. (1978, March). Sex and smell. *Psychology Today,* pp. 40–45.

Hassett, J. (1981, December). But that would be wrong. *Psychology Today,* pp. 34–53.

Hastings, D., & Markland, C. (1978). Post-surgical adjustment of twenty-five transsexuals (male to female) in the University of Minnesota study. *Archives of Sexual Behavior, 7,* 327–336.

Hatcher, R. A., Stewart, G. K., Stewart, F., Guest, F., Stratton, P., & Wright, A. H. (1978). *Contraceptive technology* (9th rev. ed.). New York: Irvington.

Hatfield, E., Greenberger, D., Traupmann, J., & Lambert, P. (1982). Equity and sexual satisfaction in recently married couples. *Journal of Sex Research, 18,* 18–32.

Hawke, S., & Knox, D. (1977). *One child by choice.* Englewood Cliffs, NJ: Prentice-Hall.

Hayes, M. (1983). Personal communication, University of Oklahoma, School of Human Development.

Hearnshaw, L. S. (1979). *Cyril Burt: Psychologist.* Ithaca, NY: Cornell University Press.

Heart facts. (1983). Dallas: American Heart Association.

Heath, D. (1983). G Spot/female ejaculation researchers vindicated by new research. *Sexuality Today,* 6(29), 1.

Hedahl, K. J. (1980). Caesarean birth: A real family affair. *American Journal of Nursing, 80,* 466–468.

Hegeler, S., & Mortensen, M. (1977). Sexual behavior in elderly Danish males. In R. Gemme & C. Wheeler (Eds.), *Progress in sexology* (pp. 285-292). New York: Plenum Press.

Heiman, J., LoPiccolo, L., & LoPiccolo, J. (1976). *Becoming orgasmic: A sexual growth program for women.* Englewood Cliffs, NJ: Prentice-Hall.

Henry, J. (1974). Forty-year-old jitters in married urban women. In C. Perrucci & D. Tary (Eds.), *Marriage and the family* (pp. 440–448). New York: McKay.

Henry J., & Warson, S. (1951). Family structure and psychic development. *American Journal of Orthopsychiatry, 21,* 59–73.

Henshaw, S. K., & Martire, G. (1982). Abortion and the public opinion polls: Morality and legality. *Family Planning Perspectives, 14,* 53–60.

Henshaw, S. K. & O'Reilly, K. (1983). Characteristics of abortion patients in the United States, 1970 and 1980. *Family Planning Perspectives, 15,* 5–16.

Herold, E. S., & Benson, R. M. (1978). Problems of teaching sex education: Survey of Ontario secondary schools. *Family Life Educator, 9*(2), 12.

Herold, E. S., & Goodwin, M. S. (1981). Premarital sexual guilt and contraceptive attitudes and behavior. *Family Relations, 30,* 247–253.

Herold, E. S., & McNamee, J. E. (1982). An explanatory model of contraceptive use among young single women. *Journal of Sex Research, 18,* 289–304.

Hessellund, H. (1976). Masturbation and sexual fantasies in married couples. *Archives of Sexual Behavior, 5,* 133–147.

Higgins, G. E., Jr. (1979). Sexual response in spinal cord injured adults: A review of the literature. *Archives of Sexual Behavior, 8,* 173–196.

Hill, C. T., Rubin, Z., & Peplau, L. A. (1976). Breakups before marriage: The end of 103 affairs. *Journal of Social Issues, 32,* 147–168.

Hite, S. (1977). *The Hite report: A nationwide study of female sexuality.* New York: Dell.

Hite, S. (1981). *The Hite report on male sexuality.* New York: Knopf.

Hobbs, D. F., Jr., & Cole, S. P. (1976). Transition to parenthood: A decade replication. *Journal of Marriage and the Family, 38,* 723–731.

Hock, Z. (1980). The sensory arm of the female orgasmic reflex. *Journal of Sex Education and Therapy, 6*(1), 4–7.

Hock, Z. (1983). The G spot. *Journal of Sex and Marital Therapy, 9,* 166–167.

Hock, Z., Safir, M. P., Shepher, J., & Peras, J. Y. (1980). An interdisciplinary approach to the study of sexual dysfunction in couples: Preliminary findings. In R. Forleo & W. Pasini (Eds.), *Medical sexology* (pp. 553–558). Littleton, MA: PSG Publishing.

Hoelter, J. W. (1983). Factorial invariance and self-esteem: Reassessing race and sex differences. *Social Forces, 61,* 834–846.

Hoffman, A. L. (1982). Straight talk on homosexuality. *Journal of Sex Education and Therapy, 8*(2), 42–44.

Hoffman, L. W. & Manis, J. D. (1978). Influences of children on marital interaction and parental satisfactions and dissatisfactions. In R. M. Lerner & G. B. Spanier (Eds.), *Child influences on marital and family interaction* (pp. 165–213). New York: Academic Press.

Holden, C. (1976). Sex therapy: Making it as a science and an industry. In A. Kilbride (Ed.), *Focus: Human sexuality* (pp. 98–101). Guilford, CT: Dushkin.

Hoon, E. F., Hoon, P. W., & Wincze, J. P. (1976). An inventory for the measurement of female sexual arousability: The SAI. *Archives of Sexual Behavior, 5,* 291–301.

Hopson, J. L. (1979). *Scent signals: The silent language of sex.* New York: Morrow.

Houge, D. R. (1981). Long-term effects of a medical school sexuality course. *Journal of Sex Education and Therapy, 7*(2), 15–19.

Huber, J., Gagnon, J., Keller, S., Lawson, R., Miller, P. & Simon, W. (1982). Report of the American Sociological Association's Task Group on Homosexuality. *American Sociologist, 17,* 164–180.

Hudson, W. W., Murphy, G. J. & Nurius, P. S. (1983). A short-form to measure liberal versus conservative orientations towards human sexual expression. *Journal of Sex Research, 19,* 258–272.

Hudson, W. W. , & Ricketts, W. A. (1980). A strategy for the measurement of homophobia. *Journal of Homosexuality, 5,* 361.

Huk, Z. B. (1979). *Sexual attitudes and behavior of East Carolina University coeds.* Unpublished master's thesis, East Carolina University, Department of Psychology, Greenville, NC. Used with permission.

Humphrey, F. G., and Strong L. D. (1978). *A comparison of the effects of husband's versus wife's extramarital relationships upon the process and outcome of marital therapy.* Unpublished manuscript, University of Connecticut, Storrs. Used with permission.

Hunt, M. M. (1959). *The natural history of love.* New York: Knopf.

Hunt, M. M. (1974). *Sexual behavior in the 1970s.* New York: Dell.

Hunt, M. M., & Hunt, B. (1977). *The divorce experience.* New York: McGraw-Hill.

Huyck, M. H. (1974). *Growing older.* Englewood Cliffs, NJ: Prentice-Hall.

Imperato-McGinley, J., Guerrero, L., Gautier, T., & Peterson, R. E. (1974). Steroid 5 and reductase deficiency in men: An inherited form of male pseudo hermaphroditism. *Science, 186,* 1213–1215.

Inazu, J. K., & Fox, G. L. (1980). Maternal influence on the sexual behavior of teenage daughters: Direct and indirect sources. *Journal of Family Issues, 1*(1), 81–102.

Istvan, J., & Griffitt, W. (1980). Effects of sexual experience on dating desirability and marriage desirability: An experimental study. *Journal of Marriage and the Family, 42,* 377–385.

Jaffe, A. C. (1976). Child molestation. *Medical Aspects of Human Sexuality, 10*(4), 73.

James, B. E. (1979). Viewpoint: Should a man ask his sex partner if she had an orgasm? *Medical Aspects of Human Sexuality, 13*(5), 126.

James, B. E. (1980). Marriages in which the wife is the sexual initiator. *Medical Aspects of Human Sexuality, 14*(17), 16–28.

James, J. (1976). Prostitution: Arguments for change. In S. Gordon & R. W. Libby (Eds.), *Sexuality today and tomorrow* (pp. 110–123). North Scituate, MA: Duxbury.

James, W. H. (1981). The honeymoon effect on marital coitus. *Journal of Sex Research, 17,* 114–123.

Jay, K., & Young, A. (1979). *The gay report.* New York: Summit Books.

Jayaram, B. N., Stuteville, O. H., & Bush, I. M. (1978). Complications and undesirable results of sex-reassignment surgery in male to female transsexuals. *Archives of Sexual Behavior, 7,* 337–341.

Jensen, G. D. (1978). Repeated orgasm in men. *Medical Aspects of Human Sexuality, 12*(1), 139.

Jessor, C. J. (1978). Male responses to direct verbal sexual initiatives of females. *Journal of Sex Research, 14,* 118–128.

Jessor, S. L., & Jessor, R. (1975). Transition from virginity to nonvirginity among youth: A social-psychological study over time. *Developmental Psychology, 11,* 473–484.

Johnson, F. A., Kaplan, E. A., & Tusel, D. J. (1979). Sexual dysfunction in the "two-career" family. *Medical Aspects of Human Sexuality, 13*(1), 7–17.

Johnson, V. E. (1976, March). What's good—and bad—about the vibrator. *Redbook,* p. 85.

Johnson, W. S. (1979). *Living in sin: The Victorian sexual revolution.* Chicago: Nelson-Hall.

Jones, S. Y. (1981). Single parenthood. *SIECUS Report, 10*(1), 1.

Jourard, S. M. (1964). *The transparent self.* Princeton, NJ: Van Nostrand.

Juhasz, A. M. (1981). Interpersonal relationships in primative society. *Journal of Sex Education and Therapy, 7*(2), 24–31.

Justice, B., & Justice, R. (1979). *The broken taboo: Sex in the family.* New York: Human Sciences Press.

Kach, J. A., & McGee, P. E. (1982). Adjustment of early parenthood: The role of accuracy of pre-parenthood expectations. *Journal of Family Issues, 3,* 375–388.

Kafka, D., & Gold, R. B. (1983). Food and drug administration approves vaginal sponge. *Family Planning Perspectives, 15,* 146–148.

Kahn, S. S. (1983). *The Kahn report on sexual preferences: What the opposite sex likes and dislikes—and why.* New York: St. Martin's Press.

Kallman, F. J. (1952a). Comparative twin study in the genetic aspects of male homosexuality. *Journal of Nervous and Mental Disease, 115,* 283–298.

Kallman, F. J. (1952b). Twin and subship study of overt male homosexuality. *American Journal of Human Genetics, 4,* 136–146.

Kamerman, S. B. (1980). *Parenting in an unresponsive society.* New York: Free Press.

Kaplan, H. (1974a). The classification of the female sexual dysfunctions. *Journal of Sex and Marital Therapy, 1*(2), 124–138.

Kaplan, H. (1974b). *The new sex therapy.* New York: Brunner-Mazel.

Kaplan, H. (1979). *Disorders of sexual desire.* New York: Brunner-Mazel.

Karacan, I. (1978). Advances in the advancement of erectile impotence. *Medical Aspects of Human Sexuality, 12*(5), 85–97.

Katz, P. (1979). The development of female identity. *Sex Roles, 5,* 155–178.

Keating, K. (1983, July). What's happening to American families? (Part 2). *Better Homes and Gardens,* p. 15.

Keller, J. F. (1977). *The gray revolution: The life and times of the elderly.* Paper presented at the Seventeenth Annual Family Life Conference, East Carolina University, Greenville, NC. Used with permission.

Keller, J. F., Elliott, S. S., & Gunberg, E. (1982). Premarital sexual intercourse among single college students: A discriminant analysis. *Sex Roles, 8,* 21–32.

Kemper, T. D., & Bologh, R. W. (1981). What do you get when you fall in love? Some health status effects. *Sociology of Health and Illness, 3,* 72–88.

Kenan, E. H., & Crist, T. (1981). Counseling the spinal cord injured female and female partner of a spinal cord injured male. *Journal of Sex Education and Therapy, 7*(1), 29–32.

Kenkel, W. F., & Gage, B. A. (1983). The restricted and gender-typed occupational aspirations of young women: Can they be modified? *Family Relations, 32,* 129–138.

Khattab, A. A. (1983). Anti-female circumcision stance. *Sexuality Today, 6*(33) 1–3.

Kilmann, P. R., Sabalis, R. F., Gearing, M. L., Bukstel, L. H. & Scovein, A. W. (1982). The treatment of sexual paraphilias: A review of the outcome research. *Journal of Sex Research, 18,* 193–252.

Kilmann, P. R., Mills, K. H., Bella, B., Caid, C., Davidson, E., Drose, G. & Wanlass, R. (1983). The effects of sex education on women with secondary orgasmic dysfunction. *Journal of Sex and Marital Therapy, 9,* 79–87.

Kilpatrick, D. G., Resick, P. A., & Veronen, L. J. (1981). Effects of a rape experience: A longitudinal study. *Journal of Social Issues, 37,* 105–122.

King, K., Balswick, J., & Robinson, I. (1979). The continuing premarital sexual revolution among college females. *Journal of Marriage and the Family, 39,* 455–459.

Kinsey, A. C., Pomeroy, W. B., & Martin, C. E. (1948). *Sexual behavior in the human male.* Philadelphia: Saunders.

Kinsey, A. C., Pomeroy, W. B., Martin, C. E. & Gebhard, P. H. (1970). *Sexual behavior in the human female.* New York: Pocket Books. (Original work published 1953)

Kirby, D., Alter, J., & Scales, P. (1979). *An analysis of the U.S. sex education programs and evaluation methods.* Bethesda, MD: Mathtech.

Klein, F. (1978). *The bisexual option: A concept of one hundred percent intimacy.* New York: Arbor House.

Klein, L., & Ingle, J. (1981). Sex solicitation by short wave radio: The CB prostitute. *Free Inquiry in Creative Sociology, 9,* 61–71.

Klemmack, D. L., & Roff, L. L. (1980), Heterosexual alternatives to marriage. *Alternative Lifestyles, 3,* 137–148.

Knapp, J. J. (1976). An exploratory study of seventeen sexually open marriages. *Journal of Sex Research, 12,* 206–219.

Knoepfler, P. (1981). Transition: A prephase of the human sexual response cycle. *Journal of Sex Education and Therapy, 7*(1), 15–17.

Knox, D. (1970a). Conceptions of love at three developmental levels. *Family Life Coordinator, 19,* 151–157.

Knox, D. (1970b). *Conceptions of love of older married adults.* Unpublished manuscript, East Carolina University, Department of Sociology, Greenville, NC.

Knox, D. (1982). *What kind of love is yours?* Unpublished manuscript, East Carolina University, Department of Sociology, Anthropology, and Economics, Greenville, NC.

Knox, D. (1983). *Discussion guide to accompany the love attitudes inventory* (rev. ed.). Saluda, NC: Family Life Publications.

Knox, D., & Gilman, R. C. (1974). The first year of fatherhood. *Family Perspective, 9,* 31–34.

Knox, D., & Sporakowski, M. J. (1968). Attitudes of college students toward love. *Journal of Marriage and the Family, 30,* 638–642.

Knox, D., & Wilson, K. (1978). The differences between having one and two children. *Family Coordinator, 27,* 23–25.

Knox, D., & Wilson, K. (1981). Dating behaviors of university students. *Family Relations, 30,* 83–86.

Knox, D., & Wilson, K. (in press). Dating problems of university students. *College Student Journal.*

Koch, J. P. (1982a). The Prentif contraceptive cervical cap: A contemporary study of its clinical safety and effectiveness. *Contraception, 25,* 135.

Koch, J. P. (1982b). The Prentif contraceptive cervical cap: Acceptability aspects and their implications for future cap design. *Contraception, 25,* 161.

Kohn, B., & Matusow, A. (1980). *Barry and Alice: Portrait of a bisexual marriage.* Englewood Cliffs, NJ: Prentice-Hall.

Kolberg, L. (1966). A cognitive-development analysis of children's sex-role concepts and attitudes. In E. E. Maccoby (Ed.), *The development of sex differences.* Stanford, CA: Stanford University Press, pp. 82–193.

Kolberg, L. (1969). State and sequence: The cognitive-developmental approach to socialization. In D. A. Goslin (Ed.),. *Handbook of socialization theory and research* (pp. 347–480). Chicago: Rand McNally.

Kolodny, R. C. (1981a). Evaluating sex therapy: Process and outcome at the Masters and Johnson Institute. *Journal of Sex Research, 17,* 301–318.

Kolodny, R. C. (1981b). Female sexuality after myocardial infarction. *Medical Aspects of Human Sexuality, 15*(1), 156.

Kolodny, R. C., Masters, W. H., & Johnson, V. E. (1979). *Textbook of sexual medicine.* Boston: Little, Brown.

Komarovsky, M. (1950). Functional analysis of sex roles. *American Sociological Review, 15,* 508–516.

Koos, E. L. (1953). *Marriage.* New York: Holt.

Kramarae, C. (1981). *Women and men speaking.* New York: Newbury House.

Kramarsky-Binkhorst, S. (1980). Counseling couples regarding partner's penile prosthesis. *Medical Aspects of Human Sexuality, 14*(8), 73–74.

Kraus, L. A. (1981). *A situational analysis of sexual harassment in academia.* Unpublished master's thesis, East Carolina University, Department of Sociology, Anthropology, and Economics, Greenville, NC.

Kraus, L. A., & Wilson, K. R. (1980). *Coercion in the college classroom: A study of sexual harassment.* Paper presented at the annual meeting of the Southern Sociological Society, Louisville, KY. Used by permission.

Ladas, A. K., Whipple, B., & Perry, J. D. (1982). *The G. spot.* New York: Holt, Rinehart and Winston.

Lance, L. M. (1979). The traditional American value of equality and the reverse double standard. *Journal of Sex Education and Therapy, 1,* 29–34.

Langevin, R., Paitich, D., Freeman, R., Mann, K., & Handy, L. (1978). Personality characteristics and sexual anomalies in males. *Canadian Journal of Behavioral Science, 10,* 222–238.

Lanson, L. (1983). Endometriosis. *Family Life Educator. 1*(4), 8–9.

LaPlante, M. M., McCormick, N., & Brannigan, G. G. (1980). Living the sexual script: College students' views of influence in sexual encounters. *Journal of Sex Research, 16,* 338–355.

LaRossa, R. (1979). Sex during pregnancy: A symbolic interactionist analysis. *Journal of Sex Research, 15,* 119–128.

Larsen, K. S., Cate, R., & Reed, M. (1983). Anti-black attitudes, religious orthodoxy, permissiveness, and sexual information: A study of the attitudes of heterosexuals toward homosexuality. *Journal of Sex Research, 19,* 105–118.

Larsen, K. S., Reed, M., & Hoffman, S. (1980). Attitudes of heterosexuals toward homosexuality: A Likert-type scale and construct validity. *Journal of Sex Research, 16,* 245–257.

Larson, D. L., Spreitzer, E. A., & Snyder, E. E. (1976). Social factors in the frequency of romantic involvement among adolescents. *Adolescence, 11*(41), 7–12.

Latham, A., & Grenadier, A. (1982, October). The ordeal of Walter/Susan Cannon. *Psychology Today,* pp. 64–70.

Laury, G. V. (1980). My most unusual sexual case: Heterosexual youth "persuaded" he is a homosexual. *Medical Aspects of Human Sexuality, 14*(2), 113.

Laws, J. L., & Schwartz, P. (1977). *Sexual scripts: The social construction of female sexuality.* Hinsdale, IL: Dryden Press.

Leaf, A., & Launois, J. (1973). Search for the oldest people. *National Geographic, 143,* 93–118.

Lederer, J. (1983, June). Birth-control decisions. *Psychology Today,* pp. 32–38.

Lee, R. V. (1980). The case for chastity. *Medical Aspects of Human Sexuality, 14*(12), 57–58.

LeGrand, C. E. (1977). Rape and rape laws: Sexism in society and law. In D. Chappell, R. Geis, & G. Geis (Eds.), *Forcible rape: The crime, the victim, and the offender* (pp. 67–86). New York: Columbia University Press.

LeMasters, E. E. (1957). Parenthood as crisis. *Marriage and Family Living, 19,* 352–355.

LeMasters, E. E., & DeFrain, J. (1983). *Parents in contemporary America.* Homewood, IL: Dorsey.

Lennon, (1981, January). [Interview with John Lennon and Yoko Ono]. *Playboy,* p. 75.

LeShan, E. J. (1973). *The wonderful crisis of middle age,* New York: McKay.

Lester, D. (1972). Incest. *Journal of Sex Research, 8,* 268–285.

Levay, A. N., & Weissberg, J. (1979). The role of dreams in sex therapy. *Journal of Sex and Marital Therapy, 5,* 334–339.

Levine, M. P. (1979). Employment discrimination against gay men. *International Review of Modern Sociology, 9,* 151–163.

Levinson, D. J. (1977). The mid-life transition: A period in adult psychosocial development. *Psychiatry, 40,* 99–112.

Lewin, B. (1982). The adolescent boy and girl: First and other early experiences with intercourse from a representative sample of Swedish school adolescents. *Archives of Sexual Behavior, 11,* 417–428.

Lewis, C. C. (1980). Abortion decisions of adult and minor women. *American Journal of Orthopsychiatry, 50,* 446–453.

Lewis, H. R., & Lewis, M. E. (1981). *The parents' guide to teenage sex and pregnancy.* New York: Atlantic Institute, Division of Atcom.

Lewis, R. A., Kosac, E. B., Milardo, R. M., & Grosnick, W. A. (1981). Commitment in same-sex love relationships. *Alternative Lifestyles, 4,* 22–42.

Liebowitz, M. (1983). *The chemistry of love.* Boston: Little, Brown.

Liljestrand, P., Gerling, E., & Saliba, P. A. (1978). The effects of social sex-role stereotypes and sexual orientation on psychotherapeutic outcomes. *Journal of Homosexuality. 3,* 361–373.

Lobitz, W. C., & Baker, E. L. (1979). Group treatment of single males with erectile dysfunction. *Archives of Sexual Behavior, 8,* 127–138.

Lowe, W., Kretchmer, A., Petersen, J. R., Nellis, B., Lever, J., & Hertz, R. (1983, July). The *Playboy* readers' sex survey (Part 4). *Playboy,* p. 130.

Lowry, T. P. (1979). The volatile nitrates as sexual drugs: A user survey. *Journal of Sex Education and Therapy, 1*(5), 8–10.

Lubic, R. W. (1981). Alternative maternity care: Resistance and change. In S. Romalis (Ed.), *Childbirth, Alternatives to medical control* (pp. 216–249). Austin: University of Texas Press.

Lynch, J. J. (1977). *The broken heart: The medical consequences of loneliness in America.* New York: Basic.

Maccoby, E., & Jacklin, C. N. (1974). *The psychology of sex differences.* Stanford, CA: Stanford University Press.

MacDonald, A. P. (1982). Research on sexual orientation: A bridge that touches both shores but doesn't meet in the middle. *Journal of Sex Education and Therapy, 8*(1), 9–13.

MacKinnon, C. A. (1979). *Sexual harassment of working women: A case of sex discrimination.* New Haven, CT: Yale University Press.

Macklin, E. D. (1978). Review of research on nonmarital cohabitation in the United States. In B. I. Murstein (Ed.), *Exploring intimate lifestyles* (pp. 197–243). New York: Springer Publishing.

Magoun, F. A. (1948). *Love and marriage.* New York: Harper & Row.

Mahoney, E. R. (1979). Sex education in the public schools: A discriminant analysis of characteristics of pro and anti individuals. *Journal of Sex Research, 15,* 264–275.

Malamuth, N. M., & Spinner, B. A. (1980). A longitudinal content analysis of sexual violence in the best selling erotic magazines. *Journal of Sex Research, 16,* 226–237.

Malatesta, V. J., Pollack, R. H., Crotty, T. D., & Peacock, L. J. (1982). Acute alcohol intoxication and female orgasmic response. *Journal of Sex Research, 18,* 1–17.

Malone, J. (1980). *Straight women/gay men: A special relationship.* New York: Dial.

Mancini, J. A., & Orthner, D. K. (1978). Recreational sexuality preferences among middle-class husbands and wives. *Journal of Sex Research, 14,* 96–106.

Marano, H. E. (1981, December). Biology is one key to the bonding of mothers and babies. *Smithsonian,* pp. 60–69.

Marini, M. M. (1980). Effects of the number and spacing of children on marital and parental satisfaction. *Demography, 17,* 225–242.

Marmor, J. (1980). The multiple roots of homosexual behavior. In J. Marmor (Ed.), *Homosexual behavior: A modern reappraisal,* (pp. 3–22). New York: Basic.

Marshall, D. S. (1972). Sexual behavior on Mangaia. In D. S. Marshall & R. C. Suggs (Eds.), *Human sexual behavior* (pp. 103–162). Englewood Cliffs, NJ: Prentice-Hall.

Maschoff, T., Fashier, H., & Hansen, D. (1976). Vasectomy: Effect upon marital stability. *Journal of Sex Research, 12,* 295–314.

Mass, L. (1982). What does AIDS mean? *SIECUS Report, 11*(2), 4.

Masters, W. H., & Johnson, V. E. (1966). *Human sexual response.* Boston: Little, Brown.

Masters, W. H., & Johnson, V. E. (1970). *Human sexual inadequacy.* Boston: Little, Brown.

Masters, W. H., & Johnson, V. E. (1976). *The pleasure bond.* New York: Bantam.

Masters, W. H., & Johnson, V. E. (1979a). *Homosexuality in perspective.* Boston: Little, Brown.

Masters, W. H., & Johnson, V. E. (1979b, November). *Playboy* interview: Masters and Johnson. *Playboy,* p. 87.

Masters, W. H., & Johnson, V. E., & Kolodny, R. C. (1982). *Human sexuality.* Boston: Little, Brown.

Mathew, R. J., & Weinman, M. L. (1982). Sexual dysfunctions in depression. *Archives in Sexual Behavior, 11,* 323–328.

Mazur, R. (1973). *The new intimacy.* Boston: Beacon Press.

McCammon, S., & Cafferty, T. (1982). *The theory of reasoned action applied to birth control pill use by college women.* Paper presented at the annual meeting of the Southeastern Psychological Association, New Orleans, LA. Used with permission.

McCance, A. A., Luff, M. C., & Widdowson, E. C. (1952). Distribution of coitus during the menstrual cycle. *Journal of Hygiene, 37,* 571–611.

McCarthy, B. W. (1982). Sexual dysfunctions and dissatisfactions among middle-years couples. *Journal of Sex Education and Therapy, 8*(2), 9–12.

McCary, J. L. (1976). Sexual myths and fallacies. In J. L. McCary & D. Copeland (Eds.), *Modern views of human sexual behavior* (pp. 286–312). Palo Alto, CA: Science Research Associates.

McEwen, B. (1981). Neural gonadal steroid actions. *Science, 211,* 1303–1311.

McGhee, P. E., and Frueh, T. (1980). Television viewing and the learning of sex-role stereotypes. *Sex Roles, 6,* 179–188.

McIntyre, J. J., Myint, T., & Curtis, L. (National Institute of Mental Health, 1979). *Sexual assault outcomes: Completed and attempted rapes.* Washington, DC: U.S. Government Printing Office.

McLaughlin, S. D., & Micklin, M. (1983). The timing of the first birth and changes in personal efficacy. *Journal of Marriage and the Family, 45,* 47–55.

McMahan, I. D. (1982). Expectancy of success on sex-linked tasks. *Sex Roles, 8,* 949–958.

McWorter, W. L. (1977). Flashing and dashing: Notes and comments on the etiology of exhibitionism. In C. D. Bryant (Ed.), *Sexual deviancy in social context* (pp. 101–110). New York: New Viewpoints.

Mead, M. (1928). *Coming of age in Samoa.* New York: Morrow.

Mead, M. (1967). *Male and female.* New York: New American Library.

Meador, L. (1983). *Tranquilizer use with sex offenders.* Paper, Unpublished manuscript, East Carolina University, Greenville, NC. Used with permission.

Mednick, R. A. (1977). Gender specific variances in sexual fantasy. *Journal of Personality Assessment, 41,* 248–254.

Mehl, L. (1976) Statistical outcomes of home birth in the United States: Current status. In D. Stewart and L. Stewart (Eds.), *Safe alternatives in childbirth* (2nd ed.). Chapel Hill, NC: National Association of Parents and Professionals for Safe Alternatives in Childbirth (NAPSAC) Press, pp. 73–100.

Mercer, G. W., & Kohn, P. M. (1979). Gender differences in the integration of conservatism, sex urge, and sexual behaviors among college students. *Journal of Sex Research, 15,* 129–142.

Merriam, A. P. (1972). Aspects of sexual behavior among the Bala (Basongye). In D. S. Marshall & R. C. Suggs (Eds.), *Human sexual behavior* (pp. 71–102). Englewood Cliffs, NJ: Prentice-Hall.

Messinger, J. C. (1972). Sex and repression in an Irish folk community. In D. S. Marshall & R. C. Suggs (Eds.), *Human sexual behavior* (pp. 3–38). Englewood Cliffs, NJ: Prentice-Hall.

Meston, J. T. (1979). The use of a sexual enrichment program to enhance self-concept and interpersonal relationships of homosexuals. *Journal of Sex Education and Therapy, 91*(6), 17–20.

Meyer, J. K., & Reter, D. J. (1979). Sex reassignment. *Archives of General Psychiatry, 36,* 1010–1015.

Meyer-Bahlburg, H. F. L. (1977). Sex hormones and male homosexuality in comparative perspective. *Archives of Sexual Behavior, 8,* 101–119.

Meyer-Bahlburg, H. F. L. (1979). Sex hormones and female homosexuality: A critical examination. *Archives of Sexual Behavior, 8,* 101–119.

Miller, H. L., & Seigel, P. S. (1972). *Loving: A psychological approach.* New York: Wiley.

Miller, W. R., & Lief, H. I. (1976). Masturbatory attitudes, knowledge, and experience: Data from the sex knowledge and attitude test (SKAT). *Archives of Sexual Behavior, 5,* 447–467.

Mirchandani, V. K. (1973). Attitudes toward love among blacks. Unpublished master's thesis, East Carolina University, Department of Sociology, Greenville, NC.

Money, J. (1980). *Love and love sickness.* Baltimore: Johns Hopkins University Press.

Money, J. (1982). Sexosophy: A new concept. *Journal of Sex Research, 18,* 364–366.

Money, J., & Alexander, D. (1967). Eroticism and sexual function in developmental anorchia and hyporchia with pubertial failure. *Journal of Sex Research, 3,* 31–47.

Money, J., & Bennett, R. G. (1981). Postadolescent paraphilic sex offenders: Antiandrogenic and counseling therapy follow-up. *International Jouranl of Mental Health, 10,* 122–133.

Money, J., & Tucker, P. (1975). *Sexual signatures: On being a man or a woman.* Boston: Little, Brown.

Money, J., & Werlwas, J. (1982). Paraphilic sexuality and child abuse: The parents. *Journal of Sex and Marital Therapy, 8,* 57–64.

Montagu, A., & Matson, F. (1979). *The human connection.* New York: McGraw-Hill.

Morbidity and mortality weekly report (Vol. 32, No. 5). (1983, February 11). Atlanta:U.S. Center for Disease Control.

Morgan, A. J. (1978). Psychotherapy for transsexual candidates screened out of surgery. *Archives of Sexual Behavior, 7,* 273–283.

Morgenstern, M. (1982). *How to make love to a woman.* New York: Crown.

Morin, J. (1981). *Anal pleasure and health.* Burlingame, CA: Down There Press.

Morris, J. (1975). *Conundrum.* New York: New American Library.

Mosher, D. L. (1979). Sex guilt and sex myths in college men and women. *Journal of Sex Research, 15,* 224–234.

Mosher, D. L. (1980). Three dimensions of depth of involvement in human sexual response. *Journal of Sex Research, 16,* 1–42.

Mosher, W. D., & Bachrach, C. A. (1982). Childlessness in the United States. *Journal of Family Issues, 3,* 517–543.

Mugford, S., & Lally, J. (1981). Sex, reported happiness, and the well-being of married individuals: A test of Bernard's hypothesis in an Australian sample. *Journal of Marriage and the Family, 43,* 969–975.

Mumford, S. D. (1983). The vasectomy decision-making process. *Studies in Family Planning, 14,* 83–88.

Munjack, D. J., & Kanno, P. H. (1979). Retarded ejaculation: A review. *Archives of Sexual Behavior, 8,* 139–150.

Murstein, B. I. (1978). Swinging. In B. I. Murstein (Ed.), *Exploring intimate lifestyles* (pp. 109–130). New York: Springer Publishing.

Myers, D., Jr., Kilmann, P. R., Warlass, R. L., & Stout, A. (1983). Dimensions of female sexuality: A factor analysis. *Archives of Sexual Behavior, 12,* 159–166.

Myers, L. (1976). Orgasm: An evaluation. In S. Gordon & R. W. Libby (Eds.), *Sexuality today and tomorrow* (pp. 281–286). North Scituate, MA: Duxbury.

Myers, L. (1981). Sex researchers and sex myths: A challenge to activism. *Journal of Sex Research, 17,* 84–89.

Myers, R. G. (1980). Sub-abreactive and abreactive intravenous amobarbital in the management of sexual dysfunction. In R. Forleo & W. Pasini (Eds.), *Medical sexology* (pp. 590–593). Littleton, MA: PSG Publishing.

National Center for Health Statistics. (1982, November). Advance report of final natality statistics, 1980. In *Monthly vital statistics report* (Vol. 31, No. 8, Suppl. DHHS Pub. No. PHS 83–1120). Hyattsville, MD: Public Health Service.

National Center for Health Statistics. (1983, March). Births, marriages, divorces, and deaths, United States, 1982. In *Monthly vital statistics report* (Vol. 31, No. 12, DHHS Pub. No. PHS 83–1120). Hyattsville, MD: Public Health Service.

Negri, M. (1981). Moral majority versus humanism. *Humanist, 41*(2), 4–5.

Nelson, N. M. (1979). A randomized controlled trial of the LeBoyer approach to childbirth. Paper presented at the *Birth and Family Journal* Conference on Technological Approaches to Obstetrics.

Neubeck, G. (1974). The myriad motives for sex. In L. Gross (Ed.), *Sexual behavior* (pp. 89–100). Flushing, NY: Spectrum.

Neugarten, B. (1980, April). Acting one's age: New rules for the Old. *Psychology Today,* pp. 66–80.

Newton, M. (1976). New baby! Why so sad? *Family Health, 8*(5) 17.

Nock, S. L. (1979). The family life cycle: Empirical or conceptual tool. *Journal of Marriage and the Family, 41,* 15–26.

Notman, M. (1977). Is there a male menopause? In L. Rose (Ed.), *The menopause book* (pp. 130–143). New York: Hawthorn.

Nunes, J. S., & Bandeira, C. S. (1980). A sex therapy clinic in Portugal: Some results and a few questions. In R. Forleo & W. Pasini (Eds.), *Medical sexology* (p. 605–608). Littleton, MA: PSG Publlishing.

Nurius, P. S., & Hudson, W. H. (1982). A sexual profile of social groups. *Journal of Sex Education and Therapy, 8*(2), 15–30.

Nurius, P. S., & Hudson, W. H. (1983). Mental health implications of sexual orientation. *Journal of Sex Research, 19,* 119–136.

Obler, M. (1982). A comparison of a hypnoanalytic/behavior modification technique and a cotherapist-type treatment with primary orgasmic dysfunctional females: Some preliminary results. *Journal of Sex Research, 18,* 331–345.

Offit, A. (1977). *The sexual self.* New York: Ballantine.

Ohanneson, J. (1983). *And they felt no shame: Christians reclaim their sexuality.* Minneapolis: Winston Press.

O'Kelly, C. (1980). Sex-role imagery in modern art: An empirical examination. *Sex Roles, 6,* 99–111.

Olson, L. (1983). *Costs of children.* Lexington, MA: Lexington Books.

Orr, M. T. (1982). Sex education and contraceptive education in U.S. public schools. *Family Planning Perspectives, 14,* 304–313.

Ory, H. W., Rosenfeld, A., & Landman, L. C. (1983). Mortality associated with fertility and fertility control: 1983. *Family Planning Perspectives, 15,* 57–63.

Ory, H. W., Rosenfeld, A., & Landman, L. C. (1980). The pill at 20: An assessment. *Family Planning Perspectives, 12,* 278–283.

Paige, K. E. (1978, July). The declining taboo against menstrual sex. *Psychology Today,* pp. 50–51.

Papadopoulos, C. (1980). How wives feel about coitus after husband's heart attack. *Medical Aspects of Human Sexuality, 14*(8), 57.

Parke, R. D., & Sawin, D. B. (1976). The father's role in infancy: A reevaluation. *Family Coordinator, 25,* 365–371.

Parker, P. J. (1983). Motivation of surrogate mothers: Initial findings. *American Journal of Psychiatry, 140,* 117–118.

Patterson, L. A., & DeFrain, J. (1981). Pronatalism in high school family studies texts. *Family Relations, 30,* 211–217.

Pattison, E. M., & Pattison, M. L. (1980). "Ex-Gays": Religiously mediated change in homosexuals. *American Journal of Psychiatry, 137,* 1553–1562.

Patton, R. D., & Wallace, B. C. (1979). Sexual attitudes and behaviors of single parents. *Journal of Sex Education and Therapoy, 1*(5), 39–41.

Pedersen, C. A., & Prange, A. J., Jr. (1979). Induction of maternal behavior in virgin rats after intracerebroventricular administration of oxytocin. *Neurobiology, 76,* 6661–6665.

Peele, S., & Brodsky, A. (1976). *Love and addiction.* New York: New American Library.

Penney, A. (1981). *How to make love to a man.* New York: Clarkson Potter.

Peplau, L. A. (1981, March). What homosexuals want in relationships. *Psychology Today,* pp. 28–38.

Perry, J. D., & Whipple, B. (1981a). Pelvic muscle strength of female ejaculation: Evidence in support of a new theory of orgasm. *Journal of Sex Research, 17,* 22–39.

Perry, J. D., & Whipple, B. (1981b, April). How to find your own Grafenberg spot. *Forum,* pp. 54–58.

Persky, H., Lief, H. I., Strauss, D., Miller, W. R. & O'Brien, C. P. (1978). Plasma testosterone level and sexual behavior of couples. *Archives of Sexual Behavior, 7,* 157–173.

Peter, L. J. (1982). *Peter's almanac.* New York: Morrow.

Petersen, D. M., & Dressel, P. L. (1982). Equal time for women: Social notes on the male strip show. *Urban Life, 11,* 185–208.

Petersen, J. R., Kretchmer, A., Nellis, B., Lever, J., & Hertz, R. (1983a, January). The *Playboy* readers' sex survey, (Part 1). *Playboy,* p. 108.

Petersen, J. R., Kretchmer, A., Nellis, B., Lever, J., & Hertz, R. (1983b, March). The *Playboy* readers' sex survey, (Part 2). *Playboy,* p. 90.

Peterson, J. A., & Payne, B. (1975). *Love in the later years.* New York: Association Press.

Petitti, D. (1983). *Longitudinal study on safety of vasectomy.* Unpublished manuscript, Kaiser-Permantente Medical Care Program, Oakland, CA. Used with permission.

Petras, J. W. (1978). *The social meanings of human sexuality.* Boston: Allyn and Bacon.

Pfeiffer, E., Verwoerdt, A., & David, G. (1974). Sexual behavior in middle life. In E. Palmore (Ed.), *Normal aging II* (pp. 243–251). Durham, NC: Duke University Press.

Pietropinto, A., & Simenauer, J. (1977). *Beyond the male myth.* New York: Quadrangle.

Pillard, R. C., Roumadere, J., & Caretta, R. A. (1982). A family study of sexual orientation. *Archives of Sexual Behavior, 11,* 511–520.

Pines, A. & Aronson, E. (1983). Antecedents, correlates, and consequences of sexual jealousy. *Journal of Personality, 51,* 108–136.

Pines, M. (1981, March). Only isn't lonely (or spoiled or selfish). *Psychology Today,* pp. 15–19.

Pleck, J. H. (1981, September). Prisoners of manliness. *Psychology Today,* pp. 69–83.

Pocs, O., Godow, A., Tolone, W. L., & Walsh, R. H. (1977, January). Is there sex after 40? *Psychology Today,* pp. 54–57.

Pomeroy, W. (1976, April). The male orgasm: What every girl should know. *Cosmopolitan,* p. 203.

Porto, R. (1980). Double-blind study of clomipramine in premature ejaculation. In R. Forleo & W. Pasini (Eds.), *Medical sexology* (pp. 624–628). Littleton, MA: PSG Publishing.

Powledge, T. M. (1983, March). Windows on the womb. *Psychology Today,* pp. 37–42.

Price-Bonham, S., & Skeen, P. (1979). A comparison of black and white fathers with implications for parent education. *Family Coordinator, 28,* 53–59.

Prince, V. (1978). Transsexuals and pseudotranssexuals. *Archives of Sexual Behavior, 7,* 263–272.

Procci, W. R. (1981). Benefits of nonorgasmic sex. *Medical Aspects of Human Sexuality, 15*(4), 90–103.

Prosen, H., & Martin, R. (1979). Postmenopausal promiscuity. *Medical Aspects of Human Sexuality, 13*(6), 26–34.

Psychology Today. (1982, December). Embarrasing fact, p. 84.

Querec, L. J. (1981, May 6). Apgar score in the United States, 1978. In *Monthly vital statistics report (Vol. 30, No. 1).* Hyattsville, MD: Public Health Service, National Center for Health Statistics.

Rabin, B. J. (1980). *The sensuous wheeler: Sexual adjustment for the spinal cord injured.* San Francisco: Multi Media Resource Center.

Rakowski, W., Barber, C. E., & Seelbach, W. C. (1983). Perceptions of parental health status and attitudes toward aging. *Family Relations, 32,* 93–99.

Raphael, S. M., & Robinson, M. K. (1980). The older lesbian: Love relationships and friendship patterns. *Alternative Lifestyles, 3,* 207–229.

Ratcliff, B., & Knox, D. (1982). University students' motivations for intercourse. Paper presented at the annual meeting of the Southern Sociological Society, Memphis, TN. Used with permission.

Reik, T. (1949). *Of love and lust.* New York: Farrar, Straus, and Cudahy.

Reimer, R. J., & Maiolo, J. (1977). *Family growth and socioeconomic status among poor blacks.* Unpublished manuscript, used with the permission of John Maiolo. East Carolina University, Greenville, NC.

Reiss, I. L. (1976). The effect of changing trends, attitudes, and values on premarital sexual behavior in the United States. In S. Gordon & R. Libby (Eds.), *Sexuality today and tomorrow* (pp. 190–203). North Scituate, MA: Duxbury.

Reiss, I. L. (1981). Some observations on ideology and sexuality in America. *Journal of Marriage and the Family, 43,* 271–283.

Reiss, I. L. (1982). Trouble in paradise: The current status of sexual science. *Journal of Sex Research, 18,* 97–113.

Renvoize, J. (1978). *Web of violence.* London: Routledge and Kegan Paul.

Restak, R. M. (1979, December). The sex-change conspiracy *Psychology Today, 20*–25.

Richardson, L. W. (1979). The "other woman": The end of the long affair. *Alternative Lifestyles, 2,* 397–415.

Ridley, C. A., Lamke, L. K. Avery, A. W., & Harrell, J. E. (1982). The effects of interpersonal skills training on sex-role identity of premarital dating partners. *Journal of Research in Personality, 16,* 335–342.

Riemer, J. W., & Bridwell, L. M. (1982). How women survive in nontraditional occupations. *Free Inquity in Creative Sociology, 10,* 153–158.

Riggall, F. C. (1980). Reversing female sterilization. *Medical Aspects of Human Sexuality, 14*(7), 107.

Riisna, E. (1983, July). My C-R group 10 years later: Our most unforgettable character. *Ms.,* pp. 69–69.

Robbins, M. B., & Jensen, G. D. (1977). Multiple orgasm in males. In R. Gemme & C. Wheeler (Eds.), *Progress in sexology* (pp. 323–328). New York: Plenum Press.

Roberts, E. J., & Holt, S. A. (1980). Parent-child communication about sexuality. *SIECUS Report, 8*(4), 1.

Robinson, I. E., & Jedlicka, D. (1982). Change in sexual attitudes and behavior of college students from 1965 to 1980: A research note. *Journal of Marriage and the Family, 44,* 237–240.

Rockwell, W. J. K., Ellinwood, E. H., & O'Hare, T. H. (1977). Sex on campus: Changing attitudes towards the double standard. *Journal of the American College Health Association, 25,* 314–316.

Romer, N., & Cherry, D. (1980). Ethnic and social class differences in children's sex-role concepts. *Sex Roles, 6,* 245–263.

Roper Organization. (1980). *The 1980 Virginia Slims American women's opinion poll: A survey of contemporary attitudes.* Storrs: University of Connecticut, The Roper Center.

Rose, M. A., Fore, V., & Rachide, M. (1980). Husbands as health educators for their wives: A plot study in breast cancer education. *Oncology Nursing Forum, 7,* 18–20.

Rosenblum, C. (1979, January). Parenthood by choice. *Human Behavior,* pp. 58–59.

Rosenheim, E., & Neumann, M. (1981). Personality characteristics of sexually dysfunctioning males and their wives. *Journal of Sex Research, 17,* 124–138.

Ross, L., Anderson, D. R., & Wisocki, P. A. (1982). Television viewing and adult sex-role attitudes. *Sex Roles, 8,* 589–592.

Rossi, A. S. (1968). Transition to parenthood. *Journal of Marriage and the Family, 30,* 26–39.

Rossman, I. (1978). Sexuality and aging: An internist's perspective. In R. L. Solnick (Ed.), *Sexuality and aging* (pp. 67–77). Los Angeles: University of Southern California, Ethel Percy Andus Gerontology Center.

Rowe, M. P. (1981, May–June). Dealing with sexual harassment. *Harvard Business Review,* pp. 42–47.

Rubenstein, C. (1982, October). Wellness is all. *Psychology Today,* pp. 27–37.

Rubenstein, C. (1983, July). The modern art of courtly love. *Psychology Today,* pp. 40–49.

Rubin, A. M. (1982). Sexually open versus sexually exclusive marriage: A comparison of dyadic adjustment. *Alternative Lifestyles, 5,* 101–108.

Rubin, J. Z., Provenzano, F. J., & Luria, Z. (1974). The eye of the beholder: Parents' views on sex of newborns. *American Journal of Orthopsychiatry, 44,* 512–519.

Rubin, L. B. (1976, August). The marriage bed. *Psychology Today,* p. 44.

Rubinson, L., Ory, J., & Marmatu, J. (1981). Differentiation between actual and perceived sexual behaviors amongst male and female college students. *Journal of Sex Education and Therapy, 7*(1), 33–36.

Runciman, A. P. (1978). Sexual problems in the senior world. In R. L. Solnick (Ed.), *Sexuality and aging* (pp. 78–95). Los Angeles: University of Southern California, Ethel Percy Andus Gerontology Center.

Russell, C. S. (1974). Transition to parenthood: Problems and gratifications. *Journal of Marriage and the Family, 36,* 294–303.

Russell, D. (1982). *Rape in marriage.* New York: Macmillan.

Safilios-Rothchild, C. (1977). *Love, sex, and sex roles.* Englewood Cliffs, NJ: Prentice-Hall.

Safran, C. (1976, November). Sexual harassment. *Redbook,* p. 149.

Safran, C. (1981, March). Sexual harassment: The view from the top. *Redbook,* p. 45.

Saghir, M. T., & Robins, E. (1973). *Male and female homosexuality: A comprehensive investigation.* Baltimore: Williams and Wilkins.

Sanday, P. R. (1981). The socio-cultural context of rape: A cross-cultural study. *Journal of Social Issues, 37*(4), 5–27.

Sanders, G. (1980). Homosexualities in the Netherlands. *Alternative Lifestyles, 3,* 279–311.

Sandfort, T. (1983). Pedophile relationships in the Netherlands: Alternative lifestyle for children? *Alternative Lifestyles, 5,* 164–183.

Sarrel, P., & Masters, W. (1982). Sexual molestation of men by women. *Archives of Sexual Behavior, 11,* 117–131.

Sarrel, P. & Sarrel, L. (1980, October). The *Redbook* report on sexual relationships. *Redbook,* pp. 73–80.

Scales, P. (1982). Sex education update: Community action that works. *Journal of Sex Education and Therapy, 8*(2), 17–20.

Scarf, M. (1980, July). The promiscuous woman. *Psychology Today,* pp. 78–87.

Schacter, S. (1964). The interaction of cognitive and physiological determinants of emotional state. In L. Berkowitz (Ed.), *Advances in experimental social psychology* (pp. 49–80). New York: Academic Press.

Schaefer, L. (1981). Women and extramarital affairs. *Sexuality Today, 4*(13), 3.

Schiavi, R. C. (1979). Sexuality and medical illness: Specific reference to diabetes mellitus. In R. Green (Ed.), *Human sexuality: A health practitioner's text* (2nd ed. pp. 203–212). Baltimore: Williams and Wilkins.

Schiller, P. (1977). *Creative approach to sex education and counseling* (2nd Ed.). Chicago: Follet.

Schiller, P. (1980). New advances in sex education. In R. Forleo & W. Pasini (Eds.) *Medical sexology* (p. 466–476). Littleton, MA: PSG Publishing.

Schlessinger, L. C. (1982). Counseling families with homosexual children. *Journal of Sex Education and Therapy, 8*(1), 25–28.

Schmidt, G. (1982). Sex and society in the eighties. *Archives of Sexual Behavior, 11*, 91–97.

Schofield, A. T., & Jackson, P. (1913). *What a boy should know.* New York: Casswell.

Schumacher, S. (1977). Effectiveness of sex therapy. In R. Gemme & C. C. Wheeler (Eds.), *Progress in Sexology* (pp. 141–151). New York: Plenum Press.

Schumacher, S. & Lloyd, C. W. (1981). Physiological and psychological factors in impotence. *Journal of Sex Research, 17*, 40–50.

Schwartz, M. F., Kolodny, R. C., & Masters, W. H. (1980). Plasma testosterone levels of sexually functional and dysfunctional men. *Archives of Sexual Behavior, 9*, 355–366.

Seashore, M. R. (1980). Counseling prospective parents about possible genetic disorders in offspring. *Medical Aspects of Human Sexuality, 14*(11), 97–98.

Seeley, T. T., Abramson, P. R., Perry, L. B., Rothblatt, A. B., & Seeley, D. M. (1980). Thermographic measurement of sexual arousal: A methodological note. *Archives of Sexual Behavior, 9*, 77–85.

Segraves, R. T. (1981). Psycholophramacological agents associated with sexual dysfunction. *Journal of Sex Education and Therapy, 7*(1), 43–45.

Seagraves, R. T., Schoenberg, H. W., & Zarins, C. K. (1982). Psychosexual adjustment after penile prosthesis surgery. *Sexuality and Disability, 5*, 222–229.

Seagraves, R. T., Schoenberg, H. W., & Ivanoff, J. (1983). Serum testosterone and prolactin levels. *Journal of Sex and Marital Therapy, 9*, 19–26.

Seidenberg, R. (1974). Is sex without sexism possible? In L. Gross (Ed.), *Sexual behavior: Current issues* (pp. 59–72). Flushing, NY: Spectrum Publications.

Semans, J. H. (1956). Premature ejaculation: A new approach. *Southern Medical Journal, 49*, 353–362.

Serbin, L. A. & O'Leary, K. D. (1975, December). How nursery schools teach girls to shut up. *Psychology Today*, p. 56.

Serdahley, W. J. (1982). One approach to personalizing a college human sexuality course. *Journal of Sex Education and Therapy, 7*(1), 33–35.

Sexual harassment in the federal work place: Is it a problem? (1981). A report of the U.S. Merit System Protection Board, Office of Merit Systems Review and Studies. Washington, DC: U.S. Government Printing Office.

Sexual survey #18: Current thinking on sexual inadequacy. (1979). *Medical Aspects of Human Sexuality, 13*(1), 130.

Sexual survey #43: Current thinking on counseling couples after infidelity. (1981). *Medical Aspects of Human Sexuality, 15*(3), 33.

Shanor, K. (1978). *The Shanor study: The sexual sensitivity of the American male.* New York: Dial.

Shaver, P., & Freedman, J. (1976, August). Your pursuit of happiness. *Psychology Today*, pp. 26–32.

Shea, R. (1980, February). Women at war. *Playboy*, p. 86.

Sheppard, D. I., Giacinti, T., & Tjaden, C. (1976). Rape reduction: A citywide program. In M. J. Walker & S. L. Brodsky (Eds.), *Sexual assault* (pp. 169–173). Lexington, MA: Lexington Books.

Shornack, L. L., & Shornack, E. M. (1982). The new sex education and the sexual revolution: A critical view. *Family Relations, 31*, 531–544.

Siegelman, M. (1978). Psychological adjustment of homosexual and heterosexual men: A cross-national replication. *Archives of Sexual Behavior, 7*, 1–11.

Siegelman, M. (1979). Adjustment of homosexual and heterosexual women: A cross-national replication. *Archives of Sexual Behavior, 8*, 121–125.

Silber, S. J. (1980). *How to get pregnant.* New York: Scribner.

Silverman, D. (1976–1977). Sexual harassment: Working women's dilemma. *Quest, 3*, 15–24.

Silverstein, C. (1977). *A family matter: A parents' guide to homosexuality.* New York: McGraw-Hill.

Silverstein, C. & White, E. (1977). *The joy of gay sex.* New York: Simon and Schuster.

Simkins, L., & Rinck, C. (1982). Male and female sexual vocabulary in different interpersonal contexts. *Sex Roles, 18,* 160–172.

Simon Population Trust. (1973). Vasectomy: Follow-up of a thousand cases. In L. Lader (Ed.), *Foolproof birth control: Male and female sterilization* (pp. 131–140). Boston: Beacon Press.

Simpson, I. H., & England, P. (1981). Conjugal work roles and marital solidarity. *Journal of Family Issues, 2,* 180–204.

Singer, B. (1982). Conversation with Robert McGinley. *Alternative Lifestyles, 5,* 69–77.

Skeen, D. (1981, March). Academic affairs. *Psychology Today,* p. 100.

Skinner, B. F., (1983, September). Origins of a behaviorist. *Psychology Today,* p. 22.

Smallwood, K. B., & VanDyck, D. G. (1979). Menopause counseling: Coping with realities. *Journal of Sex Education and Therapy, 1*(6), 72–76.

Smith, P. B., Flaherty, C., & Webb, L. J. (1982). Human sexuality training programs for public school teachers: An evaluation. *Journal of Sex Education and Therapy, 8*(1), 14–17.

Smith, R. D. (1979). What kind of sex is natural? In V. Bullough (Ed.), *The frontiers of sex research* (p. 103–112). Buffalo, NY. Prometheus Books.

Snyder, D. K., & Berg, P. (1983). Determinants of sexual dissatisfaction in sexually distressed couples. *Archives of Sexual Behavior, 12,* 237–246.

Solberg, D. A., Butler, J., & Wagner, N. W. (1973). Sexual behavior during pregnancy. *New England Journal of Medicine, 288,* 1098–1103.

Solomon, R. C. (1981). *Love: Emotion, myth, and metaphor.* New York: Anchor Press.

Sommers, F. G. (1980). Treatment of male sexual dysfunction in a psychiatric practice integrating the sexual therapy practitioner (surrogate). In R. Forleo & W. Pasini (Eds.), *Medical sexology* (pp. 593–598). Littleton, MA: PSG Publishing.

Sontag, S. (1972). *The double standard of aging.* New York: Farrer, Straus and Girou.

Sorensen, T., & Hertoft, P. (1982). Male and female transsexualism: The Danish experience with 37 patients. *Archives of Sexual Behavior, 11,* 133–155.

Sorenson, R. (1973). *Adolescent sexuality in contemporary America.* New York: World.

Sorokin, P. (1956). *The American sexual revolution.* Boston: Porter Sargent.

Sotile, W. M. (1979). The penile prosthesis: A review: *Journal of Sex and Marital Therapy, 5,* 90–102.

Spada, J. (1979). *The Spada Report: The newest survey of gay male sexuality.* New York: Signet.

Spanier, G. B. (1979). Mate swapping: Marital enrichment or sexual experimentation? In G. B. Spanier (Ed.), *Human sexuality in a changing society* (pp. 198–203). Minneapolis: Burgess.

Spanier, G. B. and Margolis, R. L. (1983). Marital separation and extramarital sexual behavior. *Journal of Sex Research, 19,* 23–48.

Spark, R. F., White, R. A., & Connoly, P. B. (1980). Impotence is not always psychogenic. *Journal of the American Medical Association, 243,* 750–755.

Springer, K. J. (1981). Effectiveness of treatment of sexual dysfunction: Review and evaluation. *Journal of Sex Education and Therapy, 7*(1), 18–22.

Starr, B. D., & Weiner, M. B. (1982). *The Starr-Weiner report on sex and sexuality in the mature years.* New York: McGraw-Hill.

Steffensmeier, R. H. (1982). A role model of the transition to parenthood. *Journal of Marriage and the Family, 44,* 319–334.

Stein, P. J. (1981). *Single life: Unmarried adults in social context.* New York: St. Martin's Press.

Stephen, W., Berscheid, E., & Walster, E. (1971). Sexual arousal and heterosexual perception. *Journal of Personality and Social Psychology, 20,* 93–101.

Stephens, W. N. (1982). *The family in cross-cultural perspective.* Washington, DC: University Press of America.

Stevens, G., & Boyd, M. (1980). The importance of mother: Labor force participation and intergenerational mobility of women: *Social Forces, 59,* 186–199.

Stichler, J. P., & Affonso, D. D. (1980). Caesarean birth. *American Journal of Nursing, 80,* 466–468.

Stock, W. E., & Greer, J. H. (1982). A study of fantasy-based sexual arousal in women. *Archives of Sexual Behavior, 11,* 33–47.

Stroller, R. J. (1977). Sexual deviations. In F. A . Beach (Ed.), *Human sexuality in four perspectives* (pp. 190–214). Baltimore: Johns Hopkins University Press.

Storms, M. D., & Wasserman, E. (1982). *Toward better theories of sexual orientation.* Paper presented at the annual meeting of the American Psychological Association, Washington, D.C. Used with permission.

Straight talk about herpes. (1982). Burroughs Wellcome: Research Triangle Park, N.C.

Stuart, R. R. (1980). *Helping couples change.* New York: Guilford Press.

Subrini, L. P. (1980). Treatment of impotence using penile implants: Surgical, sexual, and psychological follow-up. In R. Forleo & W. Pasini (Eds.), *Medical sexology* (pp. 629–636). Littleton, MA: PSG Publishing.

Sue, D. (1979). Erotic fantasies of college students during coitus. *Journal of Sex Research, 15,* 229–305.

Sullivan, H. S. (1947). *Conceptions of modern psychiatry.* Washington, D.C.: Alanson White Psychiatric Foundation.

Surzwicz, F., & Winick, C. (1979). Debate: Should prostitution be legalized? *Medical Aspects of Human Sexuality, 13*(9), 120–129.

Suttie, I. D. (1952). *The origins of love and hate.* New York: Julian Press.

Sviland, M. A. (1978). A program of sexual liberation and growth in the elderly. In R. L. Solnick (Ed.), *Sexuality and aging* (pp. 96–114). Los Angeles: University of Southern California, Ethel Percy Andus Gerontology Center.

Swieczkowski, J. B., & Walker, C. E. (1978). Sexual behavior correlates of female orgasm and marital happiness. *Journal of Nervous and Mental Disease, 166,* 335–342.

Symons, D. (1979). *The evolution of human sexuality.* New York: Oxford University Press.

Szasz, J. T. (1980). *Sex by prescription.* New York: Doubleday.

Talamini, J. T. (1981). Transvestism: Expression of a second self. *Free Inquiry in Creative Sociology, 9,* 72–74.

Talese, G. (1980). *Thy neighbor's wife.* New York: Doubleday.

Tamburello, A., & Seppecher, M. F. (1977). The effects of depression on sexual behavior. In R. Gemme & C. C. Wheeler (Eds.), *Progress in sexology,* New York: Plenum Press, (pp. 107–128).

Tatum, M. L. (1980). Schools: An essential component in good sex education. *SIECUS Report, 4,* 3.

Tavris, C., & Offir, C. (1977). *The longest war: Sex differences in perspective.* New York: Harcourt Brace Jovanovich.

Tavris, C., & Sadd, S. (1977). *The Redbook report on female sexuality.* New York: Delacorte.

Tennov, D. (1979). *Love and limerence.* New York: Stein and Day.

Tew, B. J., Lawrence, K. M., Payne, H., & Rawnsley, K. (1977). Marital stability following the birth of a child with spina bifida. *British Journal of Psychiatry, 131,* 79–82.

Tew, M. (1978). The case against hospital deliveries: The statistical evidence. In S. Kitzinger & J. A. Davis (Eds.), *The place of birth* (pp. 56–65). New York: Oxford University Press.

Thompson, A. P. (1983). Extramarital sex: A review of the research literature. *Journal of Sex Research, 19,* 1–22.

Thornton, A. (1977). Children and marital stability. *Journal of Marriage and the Family, 39,* 531–540.

Tillich, P. (1960). *Love, power, and justice.* New York: Oxford University Press.

Tissot, S. A. (1766). *Onania, or a treatise upon the disorders produced by masturbation.* (A. Hume, Trans.) London: J. Pridden. (Original work published 1758)

Tobias, S. (1976, September). Math anxiety: Why is a smart girl like you counting on your fingers? *Ms.,* pp. 56–59.

Townes, B. D., Wood, R. J., Beach, L. R., & Campbell, F. L. (1979). Adolescent values for childbearing. *Journal of Sex Research, 15,* 21–26.

Train, A. (1931). *Puritan's progress.* New York: Scribner.

Tripp, C. A. (1975). *The homosexual matrix.* New York: McGraw-Hill.

Trussell, J., & Westoff, C. F. (1980). Contraceptive practice and trends in coital frequency. *Family Planning Perspectives, 12,* 246–249.

Turner, E. S. (1955). *A history of courtship.* New York: Dutton.

U.S. Census Bureau. (1980). *Statistical abstract of the United States: 1980.* (101st edition). Washington, DC: U.S. Government Printing Office.

U.S. Department of Health, Education and Welfare. (1980). *Wanted and unwanted births reported by mothers 15–44 years of age: United States, 1976.* (Vital & Health Statistics, No. 56). Hyattsville, Md.: Public Health Service.

U.S. Department of Health and Human Services. (1981). Annual summary of births, marriages, and divorces: United States, 1981. In *Monthly vital statistics report, 1981* (Vol. 29, No. 13). Hyattsville, Md.: Public Health Service.

U.S. Department of Health and Human Services. (1982). Annual summary of births, deaths, marriages, and divorces: United States, 1981. In *Vital statistics report* (Vol. 30, No. 13). Hyattsville, Md.: Public Health Service.

U.S. Department of Health and Human Services. (1983, January 17). Births, marriage, divorces, and deaths for October 1982. (1983, January 17). *Monthly vital statistics report,* (Vol. 31, No. 10).

Valentine, D. P. (1982). The experience of pregnancy: A developmental process. *Family Relations, 31*(2), 243–248.

Van Buren, A. (1977, May 1). Face lifts can be deducted. *The Daily Reflector* (Greenville, NC.)

Vance, E. B., & Wagner, N. N. (1976). Written description of orgasm: A study of sex differences. *Archives of Sexual Behavior, 5,* 87–98.

Van de Velde, T. H. (1968). *Ideal marriage.* New York: Random. (Original work published 1926).

Van Emde Boas, M. C. (1980). Ten commandments for parents providing sex education. *Journal of Sex Education and Therapy, 6*(1), 19.

Vannoy, R. (1980). *Sex without love: A philosophical exploration.* Buffalo, NY: Prometheus Books.

Vaughn, J., & Vaughn, P. (1980). *Beyond affairs.* Hilton Head, SC: Dialog Press.

Veevers, J. E. (1983). Researching voluntary childlessness: A critical assessment of current strategies and findings. In E. Macklin & R. Rubin (Eds.), *Contemporary families and alternative lifestyles.* Beverly Hills, CA: Sage, pp. 75–96.

Voeller, B. (1980). Society and the gay movement. In J. Marmor (Ed.), *Homosexual behavior: A modern reappraisal* (pp. 232–252). New York: Basic Books.

Voss, J. R. (1980). Sex education: Evaluation and recommendations for future study. *Archives of Sexual Behavior, 9,* 37–59.

Wagner, N. N., & Sivarajan, E. S. (1979). Sexual activity and the cardiac patient. In R. Green (Ed.), *Human sexuality: A health practitioner's text* (2nd ed., pp. 193–199). Baltimore: Williams and Wilkins.

Walbrek, A. J., & Burchell, R. C. (1980). Male and sexual dysfunction associated with coronary heart disease. *Archives of Sexual Behavior, 9,* 69–75.

Walster, E., & Walster, G. W. (1978). *A new look at love.* Reading, MA: Addison-Wesley.

Waltner, R. H. (1981). Masturbation and body integration in the postorgasmic female. *Journal of Sex Education and Therapy, 7*(2), 40–43.

Walum, L. R. (1977). *The dynamics of sex and gender: A sociological perspective.* Chicago: Rand McNally.

Washington Post. (1982, October). [Reference to study in article by Ellen Goodman]. Used with permission.

Wasow, M. (1976). *Sexuality and aging.* Saluda, NC: Family Life Publications.

Waterman, C. K., & Chiauzzi, E. J. (1982). The role of orgasm in male and female sexual enjoyment. *Journal of Sex Research, 18,* 146–159.

Watson, M. A. (1981). Sexually open marriage: Three perspectives. *Alternative Lifestyels, 4,* 3–21.

Waxenberg, S. E. (1969). Psychotherapeutic and dynamic implications of recent research on female sexual functioning. In G. D. Goldman & D. S. Milman (Eds.), *Modern woman: Her psychology and sexuality* (pp. 3–24). Springfield, IL: Charles C Thomas.

Weisberg, M. (1981). A note on female ejaculation. *Journal of Sex Research, 17,* 90–91.

Weiss, D. L., & Slosnerick, M. (1981). Attitudes toward sexual and nonsexual extramarital involvements among a sample of college students. *Journal of Marriage and the Family, 43,* 349–358.

Weisstein, N. (1982, May). Tired of arguing about biological inferiority? *Ms.,* p. 42.

Wente, A. S., & Crockenberg, S. B. (1976). Transition to fatherhood: Lamaze preparation, adjustment difficulty and the husband-wife relationship. *Family Coordinator, 25,* 351–357.

Werner, P. D., Middlestadt-Carter, S. E., & Crawford, T. J. (1975). Having a third child: Predicting behavioral intentions. *Journal of Marriage and the Family, 37,* 348-358.

Westheimer, R. (1983). *Dr. Ruth's guide to good sex.* New York: Warner Books.

Westoff, C. F. (1976). Trends in contraceptive practice: 1965–1973. *Family Planning Perspectives, 8,* 54–57.

Westoff, C. F., & McCarthy, J. (1979). Sterilization in the United States. *Family Planning Perspectives, 11,* 147–152.

Westoff, L. A. (1977). *The second time around.* New York: Viking Press.

Whelehan, P. E. & Moynihan, F. J. (1981). Secular celebacy as a reaction to sexual burnout. *Journal of Sex Education and Therapy, 8*(2), 13–15.

Whipple, C. M., Jr., & Whittle, D. (1976). *The compatibility test.* Englewood Cliffs, NJ: Prentice-Hall.

Whitam, F. L. (1977). Childhood indicators of male homosexuality. *Archives of Sexual Behavior, 6,* 89–96.

Whitam, F. L. (1983). Culturally invariable properties of male homosexuality: Tentative conclusions from cross-cultural research. *Archives of Sexual Behavior, 12,* 207–226.

White, C. B. (1982). Sexual interest, attitudes, knowledge, and sexual history in relation to sexual behavior in the institutionalized age. *Archives of Sexual Behavior, 11,* 11–21.

Whitehurst, C. A. (1977). *Women in America: The oppressed majority.* Santa Monica, CA: Goodyear.

Whiting, B., & Edwards, C. P. (1973). A cross-cultural analysis of sex differences in the behavior of children aged three though 11. *Journal of Social Psychology, 91,* 171–188.

Wilcox, D., & Hager, R. (1980). Toward realistic expectations for orgasmic response in women. *Journal of Sex Research, 16,* 162–179.

Williams, C. J., & Weinberg, M. S. (1971). *Homosexuals and the military.* New York: Harper & Row.

Williams, J. E., & Best, D. L. (1982). *Measuring sex stereotypes: A thirty-nation study.* Beverly Hills, CA: Sage.

Willson, R. J., Beecham, C. T., & Carrington, E. R. (1975). *Obstetrics and Gynecology,* St. Louis: Mosby.

Wilson, K., Faison, R., & Britton, G. M. (in press). Cultural aspects of male sex aggression. *Deviant Behavior.*

Wilson, K., & Knox, D. (1981). *Sex role identity and dating appeal.* Paper presented at the annual meeting of the National Council on Family Relations, Milwaukee, Wis. Used with permission.

Winn, R. L., & Newton, N. (1982). Sexuality in aging: A study of 106 cultures. *Archives of Sexual Behavior, 11,* 283–298.

Wise, T. N. (1979). Viewpoint: Should a man ask his sex partner if she had an orgasm? *Medical Aspects of Human Sexuality, 13*(5), 126–127.

Witkin, M. H. (1981). *Recovery from mastectomy: The crucial role of the husband.* Unpublished manuscript. Used with permission.

Wolfe, L. (1980, September). The sexual profile of that *Cosmopolitan* girl. *Cosmopolitan,* p. 254.

Wolfe, L. (1982). *The Cosmo Report.* New York: Bantam.

Wyatt, J., & Stewart-Newman, C. (1982). The sexually oriented adult: Attitudes toward sex education. *Journal of Sex Education and Therapy, 8*(1), 22–24.

Yablonsky, L. (1979). *The extra-sex factor: Why over half of America's married men play around.* New York: Times Books.

Yankelovich, D. (1981a) *New rules: Searching for self-fulfillment in a world turned upside down.* New York: Random.

Yankelovich, D. (1981, November). The publilc mind/stepchildren of the moral majority. *Psychology Today,* pp. 5–10.

Young, M. (1980). Attitudes and behavior of college students relative to oral genital sexuality. *Archives of Sexual Behavior, 9,* 61–67.

Zablocki, B. (1977). *Alienation and investment in the urban commune.* New York: Center for Policy Research.

Zaidi, A. A., Aral, S. O., Reynolds, G. H., Blount, J. H., Jones, O. G., & Fichtner, R. R. (1983). Gonorrhea in the United States: 1967–1979. *Sexually Transmitted Diseases, 10*(2), 72–76.

Zeiss, R. A., Christensen, A., & Levine, A. G. (1978). Treatment for premature ejaculation though male only groups. *Journal of Sex and Marital Therapy, 4,* 139–143.

Zelnik, M., & Kantner, J. F. (1977). Sexual and contraceptive experience of young unmarried women in the United States, 1976 and 1971. *Family Planning Perspectives, 9,* 55–71.

Zelnik, M., & Kantner, J. F. (1980). Sexual activity, contraceptive use and pregnancy among metropolitan-area teenagers: 1971–1979. *Family Planning Perspectives, 12,* 230–237.

Zelnik, M., Kim, Y. J., & Kantner, J. F. (1979). Probabilities of intercourse and conception among U. S. teenage women, 1971 and 1976. *Family Planning Perspectives, 11,* 177–183.

Zelnik, M., & Kim, Y. J. (1982). Sex education and its association with teenage sexual activity, pregnancy and contraception use. *Family Planning Perspectives, 14,* 117–126.

Zelnik, M., & Shah, F. K. (1983). First intercourse among young Americans. *Family Planning Perspectives, 15,* 64–70.

Zilbergeld, B. (1978). *Male sexuality.* New York: Bantam.

Zilbergeld, B. (1980). Alternative to couples counseling for sex problems: Group and individual therapy. *Journal of Sex and Marital Therapy, 6,* 3–18.

Zilbergeld, B., & Ellison, C. R. (1979). Social skills training as an adjunct to sex therapy. *Journal of Sex and Marital Therapy, 5,* 340–350.

Zilbergeld, B., & Evans, M. (1980, August). The inadequacy of Masters and Johnson. *Psychology Today,* pp. 29–43.

Zillmann, D., & Bryant, J. (1982). Pornography, sexual callousness, and the trivialization of rape. *Journal of Communication, 32,* 10–21.

Zimmer, D., Borchardt, E., & Fischle, C. (1983). Sexual fantasies of sexually distressed and non-distressed men and women: An empirical comparison. *Journal of Sex and Marital Therapy, 9,* 38–50.

Zimmerman, S. L. (1982). Alternatives in human reproduction for involuntary childless couples. *Family Relations, 31,* 233–242.

Zoglin, R. (1974, July–August). The homosexual executive. *MBA,* pp. 26–31.

Zuckerman, D. M., & Sayre, D. H. (1982). Cultural sex-role expectations and children's sex-role concepts. *Sex Roles, 8,* 853–862.

Zuckerman, M. (1979). *Sensation seeking: Beyond the optimal level of arousal.* Hillsdale, NJ: Lawrence Erlbaum.

Zwerner, J. (1982). Yes we have troubles but nobody's listening: Sexual issues of women with spinal cord injury. *Sexuality and Disability, 5,* 158–171.

A

Abortion (uh-BOR-shun)—the ending of a pregnancy through miscarriage or medical inducement.

Acyclovir (uh-sihk-loh-veer)—an ointment applied to herpes sores or a tablet to relieve pain, speed healing, and reduce the amount of time live viruses are present in the sores.

Adrenal (uh-DREE-nuhl) glands—endocrine glands located on each kidney. These glands produce small amounts of estrogen, progesterone, and androgen.

Adrenalectomy (uh-DREE-nuhl-ehk-toh-mee)—surgical removal of the adrenal glands.

Adultery (uh-DUL-tuh-ree)—sexual intercourse by a married person with someone other than that person's spouse.

Agape (AG-uh-pee)—unselfish love which is concerned only with the welfare of the beloved.

AIDS—acquired immune deficiency syndrome, in which the immune system of a person's body is weakened so that it becomes vulnerable to disease and infection.

Aim-inhibited sex—Freud's term for love, by which he meant that love is sexual lust that cannot be expressed physically.

Amenorrhea (ay-mehn-uh-REE-uh)—the absence of menstruation for three or more months when the woman is not pregnant, through menopause, nor breast feeding.

Amniocentesis (am-nee-oh-sehn-TEE-sihs)—procedure whereby cells from the developing fetus are extracted from the amniotic sac and tested for genetic disorders.

Ampulla (am-PUHL-uh)—enlarged area of the vas deferens used to store the sperm. Also, the middle part of the Fallopian tubes.

Anal stage—according to Freud, the second psychosexual stage in which sexual pleasure is derived from the organs and activities of elimination.

Anaphrodisiacs (an-AF-roh-DIHZ-ee-ak)—those substances thought to decrease sexual desire.

Androgen (AN-droh-juhn)—the general class of male sex hormones. Testosterone is one example of an androgen.

Androgen-insensitivity syndrome—see *testicular feminization syndrome.*

Androgenital syndrome—Condition in which the external genitals of an individual appear to be male but the internal organs are those of a female.

Androgyny (an-DRAH-juh-nee)—the state of having a blend of feminine and masculine traits.

Annular hymen—hymen that has a singular opening.

Anorgasmia (an-or-GAZ-mee-uh)—see *primary orgasmic dysfunction* and *secondary orgasmic dysfunction.*

Anus—the opening of the rectum located between the buttocks.

Apgar (AP-gahr) score—a physician's rating of a newly born infant's heart rate, breathing, color, muscle tone, and reflex irritability.

Aphrodisiacs (AF-roh-DIHZ-ee-ak)—substances that are thought to stimulate sexual desire.

Areola (uh-ree-OH-lah)—the darkened area around the nipple.

Artificial insemination—the introduction of sperm into a woman's vagina or cervix by means of a syringe rather than a penis. The sperm may be from the husband (AIH) or a donor (AID).

Artificial insemination donor (AID)—see *artificial insemination.*

Artificial insemination husband (AIH)—see *artificial insemination.*

Asecticism (uh- SEHT-uh-sihzm)—doctrine that self-denial and avoidance of pleasure is the most desirable life style.

Asexual (a-sehk-shoo-uhl)—a person who has no interest in sex and who does not engage in any form of sexual activity.

Autoeroticism—see *masturbation.*

Aversion (uh-VER-zhun) therapy—type of behavior therapy in which the person learns to associate the undesirable behavior (for example, sex with children) with a painful consequence (such as electric shock) with the goal of decreasing the desire to engage in the undesirable behavior.

B

Bartholin's (BAR-toh-lihnz) glands—two small glands just inside the vaginal opening, which secrete a small amount of fluid during sexual arousal.

Basal body temperature method—basal body temperature is the temperature of a woman recorded immediately upon awakening before any activity of any kind. The temperature is taken orally or rectally and recorded on a graph. Observation of the temperatures on the graph during a menstrual cycle provide some evidence of ovulation.

Behavior sex therapy approach—assumes that sexual dysfunctions have been learned and focuses on teaching the individual or couple new ways of behaving and relating sexually.

Bestiality (behs-chee-AL-uh-tee)—sexual relations between a human being and an animal.

Billings method—see *cervical mucus method.*

Biopsy (BIGH-ahp-see)—removal of a small piece of tissue from the body for analysis in the laboratory by a pathologist.

Bisexual (bigh-SEHK-shoo-uhl)—persons who have emotional and sexual attractions to members of their own and opposite gender.

Body image—the way an individual perceives his or her own body.

Brachioprotic (BRAY-kee-oh-proh-tihc) eroticism—aspect of gay sexual behavior whereby one male inserts his hand and forearm in the anus of a partner.

Bradley method of childbirth—also known as husband-coached childbirth, this method emphasizes marital communication, the couple's sexual relationship, and parental roles.

Bulbocavernosus (buhl-boh-kav-er-NOH-suhs) muscle—the ring of sphincter muscles surrounding the opening to the vagina.

Bundling—also called tarrying; a courtship custom among the Puritans in which the would-be groom slept in the girl's bed in her parents' home. Both were fully clothed and a wooden bar was placed between them.

C

Calendar method—birth control procedure whereby the time of greatest fertility is determined by careful observation of the woman's menstrual cycle over an eight-month period and intercourse is avoided during this time.

Candidiasis (kan-dih-DIGH-uh-sihs)—yeast infection that may infect either gender.

Case study research—studying in detail one individual or situation rather than numerous individuals or situations.

Castration (kas-TRAY-shun)—surgical removal of the testes (orchiectomy) or ovaries (ovariectomy) or inactivation of their function by radiation, drugs, or disease.

Causal analysis—ascertaining if one variable (for example, heat) is the cause of another variable (such as boiling water).

Celibate (SEHL-ih-buht)—person who does not engage in sexual behavior with other people. Celibacy may be voluntary (as with priests) or involuntary (as with a person who is in hospital).

Cervical (SER-vih-kuhl) cap—a birth control device whereby a small rubber or plastic cap fits snugly over the cervix to prevent sperm from entering the uterus.

Cervical mucus—a thin, watery lubricative secretion produced by the cervix that aids sperm migration from the vagina to the egg in the Fallopian tubes.

Cervical mucus method—also known as the Billings method and the natural family planning method, this rhythm method of birth control is based on a careful monitoring of the cervical mucus to detect when ovulation occurs and an avoidance of intercourse after ovulation.

Cervix (SER-vihks)—the narrow portion of the uterus that projects into the vagina.

Cesarean (suh-ZAIR-ee-uhn)—delivery of a baby by cutting open the woman's abdomen and uterus rather than delivery through the vaginal canal.

Chancre (SHAN-ker)—small sore that appears on the genitals of either gender, which indicates the presence of a viral infection.

Chancroid (SHAN-kroyd)—sexually transmitted disease that may be successfully treated with antibiotics.

Change of life—see *menopause.*

Chastity—abstaining from sexual activities.

Chicken porn—child pornography.

Child-free marriage—alternative term for childless marriages, implying that a couple chooses not to have children.

Chorion biopsy—an alternative to amniocentesis that involves placing a tube into the vagina to the uterus. Chorionic tissue, which surrounds the embryo, is removed and analyzed for genetic defects.

Chromosomes (KROH-moh-sohmz)—thin, threadlike structures carrying genes, which are located within the nucleus of every cell.

Circumcision (ser-kuhm-SIHZ-uhn)—surgical removal of the foreskin of the penis. See also *clitoral circumcision*.

Climacteric (kligh-MAK-tuh-rihk)—aging process of the reproductive system in females, occurring between ages 45 and 60, which involves hormonal changes in the ovaries, pituitary gland, and hypothalmus. The term may also refer to the aging process of the male reproductive system.

Clitoral circumcision—surgical removal of the clitoral hood.

Clitoral orgasm—an orgasm resulting from stimulation of the clitoris. Freud viewed such an orgasm as a sign of immaturity and/or fixation in early psychosexual development.

Clitoridectomy (klit-uhr-ih-DEK-toh-mee)—surgical removal of the clitoris.

Clitoris (KLIHT-uh-ruhs)—A small, erectile structure embedded in the tissues of the vulva at the junction of the minor labia. Its primary function is pleasure.

Cognitive restructuring—also known as shame aversion therapy; negative consequences are associated with a particular behavior by viewing another person engaging in the behavior so that the first person will want to engage in it less often.

Cohabitation (coh-hab-uh-TAY-shun)—two people of the opposite gender living together and sharing a common bed without being legally married.

Coitus (KO-ih-tuhs)—see *sexual intercourse*.

Combination pill—oral contraceptive containing both estrogen and progesterone, which act to prevent ovulation and implantation.

Coming out—term used to describe homosexuals who acknowledge their sexual preference to themselves and others.

Communard—member of a commune.

Commune—three or more individuals who live together for the purpose of sharing their life style, who are not bound together by blood, marriage, or legal ties.

Conception (kahn-SEP-shun)—also known as the biological beginning of pregnancy; a fertilized egg that has implanted on the wall of the uterus.

Condom (kahn-duhm)—also referred to as "rubber," "safe," and "prophylactic," it is a thin sheath, usually made of synthetic material, which is rolled over and down the erect penis before intercourse to provide a barrier to the sperm entering the vagina.

Contraception (kahn-truh-SEP-shun)—using artifical means to prevent sperm from fertilizing an egg or to prevent the egg from implanting on the uterine wall.

Control group—see *experimental method*.

Convenience sample—a sample that is not representative of the population about which inferences will be made.

Conversion therapy—therapy for homosexuals who want to become heterosexual.

Coolidge effect—the availability of a new sexual partner stimulates the male's desire to have intercourse with the new partner.

Corona (kohr-OH-nuh)—raised rim above the body of the penis that begins the glans of the penis.

Corpora cavernosa (KOR-por-uh kav-er-NO-suh)—twin cylinders of spongy tissue in the penis that become engorged with blood, resulting in an erection. Also present in the clitoris.

Corpora spongiosum (KOR-por-uh spun-jee-OH-suhm)—a cylinder of spongy tissue in the penis that becomes engorged with blood during an erection.

Corpus luteum (KOR-puhs LOO-tee-uhm)—a yellow structure that forms on the surface of the ovary at the site of ovulation. It produces the progesterone characteristic of the second half of the menstrual cycle and is necessary to prepare the uterine lining for implantation by the fertilized egg.

Correlational analysis—ascertaining if a relationship exists between variable X and variable Y.

Covert sensitization—behavior therapy technique whereby the person learns to associate negative feelings with the undesirable behavior by thinking of negative associations.

Cowper's (KAH-perz) glands—also known as bulbourethal glands; they are two pea-sized glands located below the prostate, which act to neutralize the natural acidic environment of the uretha. The small amount of clear, sticky fluid that is visible at the urethral opening prior to ejaculation is from these glands.

Cribriform (KRIHB-ruh-form) hymen—hymen in which there are three or more openings.

Cruising—term used in the homosexual community that refers to a gay person going to a bar, bath, or party to pick up a sexual partner.

Crura (CROO-ruh)—two structures linking the top of the shaft of the clitoris to the pubic bone. Similar structures also link the penis to the pubic bone.

Cryotherapy (KRIGH-uh-THEH-uh-pee)—procedure whereby cancerous growth is killed by freezing it.

Cryptorchidism (Krihp-TOR-kuh-dizm)—failure of the testes to descend into the scrotum.

Cunnilingus (kuhn-ee-LIHN-guhs)—stimulation of the vulva area by the partner's mouth.

Cystitis (sihs-TIGH-tuhs)—inflammation and infection of the bladder.

D

Decriminalization—the elimination of legal penalties for an act previously considered illegal.

Depo-Provera (DEPH-oh-proh-VAIR-uh)—also known as medroxyprogesterone acetate or MPA; a synthetic progestinic hormone that is being tested as a method of contraception. In sufficient doses, it protects the woman against conceiving for a three-month period following an injection. The hormone has also been associated with decreased libido.

DES [Diethylstilbestrol] (digh-EHTH-yl-stihl-BEHS-trohl)—commonly referred to as the morning-after pill, it contains high levels of estrogen to prevent implantation of the fertilized egg on the uterine wall.

Descriptive analysis—describing the phenomenon being observed in contrast to conducting statistical tests.

Desire prephase—the second of two prephases to the sexual response cycle, during which the individual develops a desire for sexual involvement.

Detane—commercial ointment placed on the glans of the penis to delay ejaculation. No studies have been conducted to verify that such ointments are effective in delaying ejaculation.

Diaphragm (DIGH-uh-fram)—a circular rubber dome between two and four inches in diameter that covers the cervix and prevents sperm from entering the uterus.

Dick-Read childbirth method—named after Grantley Dick-Read, a method of natural childbirth.

Dilatation (digh-luh-TAY-shun)—a widening of the cervical opening. Prior to delivery the cervix dilates from 3 1/2 to 4 inches.

Dilation (digh-LAY-shun) and curettage (kyoor-uh-tahj)—also known as a D and C; a form of abortion whereby the physician dilates the cervix and scrapes the embryo and placenta from the walls of the uterus with a curette.

Dilation and evacuation—also known as a D and E; an abortion procedure used in the second trimester that is a combination of the vacuum curettage and D and C methods.

Dildo (DIHL-doh)—artificial penis substitute.

Dimorphism (digh-mor-fihzm)—the condition of a species having two different forms, as animals that show marked differences between female and male genders.

Double standard—condition in which one behavior standard is applied to males and another to females.

Douching (DOOSH-ihng)—term used to describe the process of rinsing and cleaning the vaginal canal.

Down's syndrome—genetic defect resulting in a baby who is physically deformed, mentally retarded, and has a shorter life span.

Duct system—canals or tubular passages.

Dysmenorrhea (dihs-mehn-uh-REE-uh)—painful menstruation.

Dyspareunia (dihs-puh-roo-NEE-uh)—pain experienced during intercourse.

E

Ectopic (ehk-TAHP-ihk) pregnancy—a pregnancy in which implantation takes place outside the uterine cavity, usually in one of the Fallopian tubes.

Effacement—a flattening and extension of the cervix.

Ejaculation (ih-jak-yoo-LAY-shun)—expulsion of semen from the penis. See also *female ejaculation*.

Ejaculatory duct—short canal at the end of the vas deferens that empties into the urethra.

Ejaculatory incompetence—also referred to as retarded ejaculation, absence of ejaculation, ejaculatory impotence, and inhibited ejaculation; the inability to ejaculate even after substained stimulation through intercourse. Primary ejaculatory incompetence refers to never having ejaculated inside a woman's vagina; secondary ejaculatory incompetence involves having been able to do so in the past but not currently.

Electra (ih-LEHK-truh) complex—according to Freudian theory, the young girl (at about age four) recognizes she has no penis, wishes she did (penis envy), and blames her mother for its absence.

Electrocoagulation (ih-lehk-troh-coh-ag-yoo-LAY-shun)—killing cancerous tissue through extreme heat and electric current.

Embryo (EHM-bree-oh)—term used to refer to the human organism from the time of conception until the end of the eighth week.

Endocrine (EHN-doh-krihn) system—a system of ductless glands producing hormones, including the pituitary, parathyroid, thyroid, and adrenal glands and the testes and ovaries.

Endocrinologist (ehn-doh-krihn-ahl-uh-jihst)—a physician who specializes in the diagnosis and treatment of diseases of the hormone systems.

Endometriosis (ehn-doh-mee-tree-OH-sihs)—a condition where endometrium, the tissue that is normally found lining the uterine cavity, grows on other surfaces such as the Fallopian tubes and ovaries. Pain during intercourse, bowel elimination, and menstruation may result.

Endometrium (ehn-doh-MEE-tree-uhm)—inner layer of the uterine wall where the fertilized egg implants.

Epididymus (ehp-uh-DIHD-uh-muhz)—tubes running from the testes to the vas deferens.

Episiotomy (ih-pee-zee-AHT-uh-mee)—incision of the vaginal opening made during childbirth to make it easier for the baby to be born without tearing the vagina.

Erectile dysfunction—also known as impotence, the term refers to an inability of the male to create and maintain an erection sufficient for intercourse. The condition may be primary, in which the person has never been able to have intercourse, or secondary, in which the person has been but is no longer able to have an erection sufficient for intercourse.

Estrogen (EHS-truh-jehn)—Hormone produced primarily by the ovaries to stimulate the development of cervical mucus and ovulation and to help prepare the uterine lining for possible implantation after fertilization. Estrogen also stimulates the development of female secondary sex characteristics, such as breasts.

Estrogen replacement therapy (ERT)—Treatment sometimes recommended for women in the climacteric who experience severe symptoms. ERT reduces or completely alleviates hot flashes. Some evidence suggests that ERT may increase the risk of uterine cancer.

Ethics—moral codes that guide decisions and behaviors.

Eunuch (YOO-nuhk)—a person who has been castrated.

Excitement phase—the first of four stages of the sexual response cycle described by Masters and Johnson. Vaginal lubrication and penile erection are the primary responses of females and males during this phase.

Exhibitionist—person (usually a male) who is sexually aroused by exposing his genitals to strange females.

Experimental group—see *experimental method.*

Experimental method—conducting an experiment in which something is done in situation X that is not done in situation Y. The former would be the experimental group; the latter, the control group.

Extinction—terminating the reinforcement of a behavior, which results in the behavior eventually stopping.

Extramarital intercourse—sexual intercourse by a married person with someone other than that person's spouse.

F

Fallopian (fuh-LOH-pee-uhn) tubes—tubes leading from each ovary to the uterus; also known as oviducts (egg tubes).

False labor—irregular contractions of the undilated uterus that mimic true labor.

False pregnancy—the symptoms of early pregnancy (morning sickness, cessation of menstrual period) without the presence of a fetus in the woman's uterus.

Fantasy—see *sexual fantasy.*

Fantasy phone mate—individuals who engage in sexually stimulating talk on the phone to a customer for a fee.

Fantasy typologies—ways of categorizing sexual fantasies, such as fantasizer as recipient or sexual object as recipient.

Fellatio (fuh-LAH-shee-oh)—stimulation of the penis by the partner's mouth.

Female ejaculation—the emission of a fluid described as "watered down fat-free milk" from the Skene's glans just inside the urethral opening, in about 10 percent of women. Other researchers say the fluid is primarily urine.

Fertilization (fuhr-tih-lih-ZAY-shun)—union of a sperm and an egg resulting in the development of an embryo.

Fetishism (FEHT-ihsh-ihzm)—the use of inanimate objects (such as panties) or part of the body (like a foot) as a repeatedly preferred or exclusive method of achieving sexual excitement.

Fetus—term given to the developing human organism from the third month of conception until delivery.

Fimbriae (FIHM-bree-ee)—hairlike fibers in the Fallopian tube that pick up the egg from the ovary as it is released.

Follicle (FAHL-ih-kl)—the structure in the ovary that has nurtured the ripening egg and from which the egg is released.

Follicle-stimulating hormone (FSH)—a hormone produced and released by the pituitary gland. In the female it stimulates estrogen production and the development of follicles in the ovary. In males, FSH stimulates sperm production.

Follicular phase—see *preovulatory phase.*

Foreskin—see *prepuce.*

French kissing—style of kissing in which the respective partners' tongues caress each other's; also known as deep, soul, and tongue kissing.

Frenulum (FREHN-yoo-luhm)—thin strip of skin that connects the glans of the penis with the shaft of the penis.

Frottage (Fruh-TAHJ)—term used to describe the behavior of a froteur who derives sexual pleasure from rubbing against other people in a crowded place.

Fructose (FRUHK-tohz)—chemical substance responsible for making sperm mobile.

Fundus (FUHN-duhs)—the broad, rounded part of the uterus.

G

G spot—abbreviation for Grafenberg spot; an extremely sensitive area on the front wall of the vagina about 1 or 2 inches into the opening. Not all women can locate the presence of a G spot and scientists do not agree on its existence.

Gamete (GAM-eet)—mature reproductive cells; sperm in men and eggs in women.

Gametrics—the application of biological and mathematical theory to gamete separation. The procedure involves identification, selection, and separation of Y and X sperm, which are artificially inseminated in the female to produce a baby of the desired gender.

Gay—see *homosexuality.*

Gay liberation movement—an informal association of thousands of gay people banding together to further the rights of gay individuals.

Gender—the biological distinction of being female or male.

Gender identity—the psychological state of viewing oneself as a woman or a man.

Gender role—the socially accepted characteristics and behaviors typically associated with one's gender identity.

Gene (jeen)—that part of a chromosome that transmits a particular heredity characteristic (for example, left-handedness).

Genital apposition—form of petting in which the partners rub their genitals together while laying close together with or without having their clothes on and without having intercourse.

Genital herpes—also known as herpes simplex type 2; a sexually transmitted viral infection that affects the genitals of either gender.

Genital stage—according to Freud, the final stage of psychosexual development in which sexual pleasure shifts from self-pleasure through masturbation to interpersonal sexual pleasure.

Genital warts—sexually transmitted lesions that may appear in the cervix, vulva, urethra, or rectum.

Gestation (jehs-TAY-shun)—the time from conception to delivery.

Gigolo (jihg-uh-loh)—male prostitute who services women.

Glans (glanz)—head of the penis or clitoris.

Gonads (GOH-nadz)—testes in the male and ovaries in the female, which produce sperm and eggs, respectively.

Gonorrhea (Gahn-uh-REE-uh)—also known as "the clap," "the whites," and "morning drop," gonorrhea is the most common sexually transmitted disease.

Granuloma inguinale (gran-yuh-LOH-muh ihn-gwih-NAH-lee)—sexually transmitted disease that may be successfully treated with antibiotics.

H

Halsted radical mastectomy—a method for treating breast cancer in which the entire breast, skin, muscles, lymph nodes, and fat are removed. The result is a flattened or sunken chest. This method has not been proven to be the most effective.

Hartman and Fithian sex therapy approach—William Hartman and Marilyn Fithian at the Center for Marital and Sexual Studies (Long Beach, California) combine many of the procedures developed by Masters and Johnson with an array of their own exercises to assist sexually dysfunctional individuals learn more positive sexual behaviors.

Hedonism (HEE-duh-nihzm)—the doctrine that pleasure is good and should be the aim of action.

Hermaphrodite (her-MAF-ruh-dight)—condition in which an individual has both ovarian and testicular tissue. In some cases, the individual has one ovary and one testicle.

Heterosexual (het-er-uh-SEK-shoo-uhl)—persons who have an emotional and sexual attraction to those of the opposite gender; also referred to as straight.

Homophobia—fear of homosexuals or being homosexual.

Homosexual (hoh-moh-SEHK-shoo-uhl)—persons who have an emotional and sexual attraction to those of their own gender; also referred to as gay.

Hooded clitoris—also known as clitoral foreskin adhesions; the condition in which the foreskin of the clitoris covers the glans of the clitoris to the extent that it interferes to some degree with adequate stimulation.

Hormone (HOR-mohn)—a chemical substance produced by various endocrine glands that enters the bloodstream and influences physiological functioning.

Human chorionic gonadotropin (koh-ree-AHN-ihk goh-nad-uh-TROH-pihn)—referred to as HCG; a hormone produced by the human placenta, which can be detected in the pregnant woman's urine.

Human sexuality—a broad concept including relationships, anatomy, behaviors, thoughts and feelings, values, and variability.

Hustler—male prostitute who serves other males seeking homosexual relations.

Hymen (HIGH-muhn)—thin membrane that covers the vaginal opening in most virgin females. However, some virgins do not have a hymen.

Hyperventilation—excessive rapid and deep breathing.

Hypothalamus (high-poh-THAL-uh-muhs)—the region of the brain just above the pituitary gland that controls the hormone production of the pituitary gland. The hypothalamus also produces releasing factors (RF) for hormones produced by the pituitary gland.

Hysterectomy (hihs-tuh-REHK-tuh-mee)—surgical removal of the uterus and cervix.

Hysterotomy (hihs-tuh-RAH-tuh-mee)—method of abortion in which the fetus is removed by means of a cesarean section.

I

Identification—in reference to gender-role learning, identification occurs when the child takes on the demeanor, behaviors, and personality of the same-gender parent.

Imperforate (ihm-PER-for-uht) hymen—hymen with no openings. Surgical incision at the time of first menstruation is indicated.

Impotence—see *erectile dysfunction.*

Incest (IHN-sehst)—sexual relations between close relatives such as father–daughter, mother–son, and brother–sister. Sexual relations may include intercourse, oral sex, and genital manipulation.

Incest taboo—strong social norms against sexual relations between members of the same family (other than spouses).

Infertility—the inability of a heterosexual couple to conceive a pregnancy after one year of regular unprotected intercourse.

Infundibulum (ihn-fuhn-DIHB-yuh-lum)—the funnel-shaped end of the Fallopian tube leading to the ovary.

Inhibited sexual desire—also known as sexual apathy; the condition in which the person lacks sexual desire, never initiates sexual activity, and is rarely receptive to one who does. The condition may be primary, in which the person is never interested in sex, or secondary in which the person has been interested in sex in the past but is not currently.

Intercourse—see *sexual intercourse.*

Internal sex organs—Fallopian tubes, uterus, and vagina in females; epididymus, vas deferens, seminal vesicles, and prostate in males.

Intrauterine (ihn-truh-yoot-uh-rihn) device—also known as the IUD; a small object placed in the uterus to prevent the fertilized egg from implanting on the uterine wall or to dislodge the fertilized egg if it has already implanted.

Introitus (ihn-TROH-ih-tuhs)—the opening to the vagina.

Ischiocavernosus (ihs-kee-oh-kav-er-NOH-suhs) muscle—muscle extending from the hip bone to the penis or clitoris.

Isthmus (ISH-muhs)—the narrow end of the Fallopian tubes leading to the uterus.

K

Kaplan's sex therapy approach—developed by Helen Kaplan of Cornell Medical Center; a blend of psychodynamic and behavioral approaches.

Kaposi's (kuh-POH-see) sarcoma—referred to as KS; a type of skin cancer that tends to develop in a person who contracts AIDS.

Kegel exercises—repeated contractions of the pubococcygeal muscles designed to strengthen them. Researchers disagree on the benefits of such exercises.

Klinefelter's (KLIGHN-fehl-terz)—syndrome—sex chromosome pattern of XXY or XXXY. The result is a male child with abnormal testicular development, infertility, low libido, and sometimes mental retardation.

Klismaphilia (klihz-muh-FIHL-ee-uh)—person who derives sexual pleasure from an enema.

L

Labia majora (LAY-bee-uh muh-JOR-uh)—outer lips of the vulva.

Labia minora (LAY-bee-uh muh-NOR-uh)—inner lips of the vulva.

Lamaze (lah-mahz) childbirth—developed by Dr. Fernand Lamaze, a method of childbirth whereby the couple take a series of classes to educate them about childbirth and to prepare them for the experience.

Laparoscopy (lap-uh-RAHS-koh-pee)—a tubal ligation performed with the use of a laparoscope, a small telescopelike instrument that allows the physician to see into the abdominal cavity.

Legalism—adherence to a strict set of laws or code of conduct as a guide to decision making.

Legalization—passage of a law to make an activity legal.

Lesbian—female homosexual. See *homosexual*.

Leydig (ligh-dihg) cells—cells, found in the seminiferous tubules, that secrete the male hormone testosterone.

Libido (lih-BEE-doh)—Freud's term for sexual drive.

Limerence—see *romantic love.*

Locus of control—the degree to which an individual views outcomes (events and rewards) as happening because of her or his own ability (internal control) or because of chance, fate, or powerful others (external control).

Lumpectomy—removal of only the malignant mass from the breast.

Luteal (LOOT-ee-uhl) phase—last 14 days of the ovulatory cycle in which the corpus luteum is formed and the uterus is prepared to nourish a fertilized egg.

Luteinizing (LOOT-ee-ihn-eye-zihng) hormone—also known as LH; it is produced and released by the pituitary gland and is responsible for ovulation and the maintenance of the corpus luteum for progesterone production. In the male it stimulates testosterone production and the production of sperm cells.

Lymphogranuloma venereum (lihm-foh-gran-yuh-LOH-muh vuh-NIHR-ee-uhm)—also known as LGV; a sexually transmitted disease that may be successfully treated with antibiotics.

M

Male menopause—time during middle age when the male begins to respond to lowered testosterone production. Although men react similarly to menopausal women, anxiety and depression during this time seem more related to the male's life situation than to hormonal changes.

Mammography (muh-MAH-gruh-fee)—an X-ray of the breast that identifies the location and extent of any suspicious growth.

Manual stimulation—a sexual activity in which the genitals of one partner are caressed, manipulated, and stimulated by the hands of the other.

Marital intercourse—sexual intercourse between partners who are legally married to each other.

Masochism (MAS-uh-kihzm)—person who derives sexual pleasure from physical pain.

Mastalgia (mas-tahl-juh)—painful swelling of the breasts.

Mastectomy (mas-TEHK-toh-mee)—surgical removal of the cancerous tissue and the surrounding tissue of the breast.

Masters and Johnson sex therapy approach—William Masters and Virginia Johnson of the Masters and Johnson Institute in St. Louis focus on exercises for sexually dysfunctional individuals to help them learn new ways of relating sexually.

Masturbation (mas-tuhr-BAY-shun)—stimulating one's own genitals for pleasure.

Meatus (mee-AY-tuhs)—opening at the top of the penis through which urine and semen are expelled.

Meiosis (migh-oh-suhs)—process by which each new cell contains only half the normal number of chromosomes (one from each of the 23 pairs of chromosomes).

Menarche (muh-NAHR-kee)—first menstrual period in a woman's life.

Menorrhagia (mehn-or-ah-jee-uh)—prolonged menstruation.

Menopause (MEHN-oh-pawz)—the cessation of the menstrual cycle. Physiologic menopause is when the event occurs naturally (around age 50); surgical menopause occurs when the ovaries are removed surgically.

Menses (MEHN-seez)—another term for menstruation of menstrual flow.

Menstruation (mehn-stroo-WAY-shun)—the regular shedding of the uterine lining, resulting in cyclic vaginal bleeding approximately two weeks after an egg is released from an ovary that is not fertilized.

Minipill—oral contraceptive containing low dose of progesterone and no estrogen.

Mittleschmerz (MIHT-tl-shmehrtz)—pain felt by some women at midcycle during ovulation.

Modeling—learning through observation.

Modified radical mastectomy—removal of the breast and lymph nodes but not the underlying muscles.

Mongolism (MAHN-guh-lihzm)—term sometimes used to describe Down's syndrome. See *Down's syndrome.*

Mons veneris (mahns vuh-NAIR-ihs)—the soft cushion of fatty tissue overlaying the pubic bone.

Moral Majority—those who have a conservative, religiously oriented view of life.

Morning sickness—often a sign of early pregnancy; symptoms involve feeling nauseous and vomiting in the morning.

Müllerian (myoo-LEER-ee-uhn) ducts—the duct system in the female embryo that later develops into the Fallopian tubes, uterus, and vagina in the adult female.

Multigravida (muhl-tee-GRAV-ihd-uh)—the condition of having had given birth before.

Multiple orgasm—the ability to have several orgasms in succession with no refractory period and no break in stimulation. Both women and men are capable of multiple orgasms.

Mutual masturbation—masturbation as a couple activity in which each person stimulates himself or herself while the partner does the same or just observes.

Myometrium (migh-uh-MEE-tree-uhm)—strong uterine muscles that contract and aid in delivery during childbirth.

Myotonia (migh-uh-TOH-nee-uh)—increased muscular tension sometimes resulting in muscle contractions and spasms.

N

Natural childbirth—term used to describe various methods of childbirth (LeBoyer, Lamaze, and so on) emphasizing preparation of the couple for delivery.

Necrophilia (nek-ruh-FIHL-ee-uh)—deriving sexual pleasure from looking at or having intercourse with a corpse.

Negative reinforcement—increasing the frequency of a behavior by associating it with the removal of something aversive.

Nocturnal emission—male ejaculation during sleep while having an erotic dream; also known as a "wet dream."

Nocturnal orgasm—female vaginal vascular engorgement during sleep while having an erotic dream.

Nocturnal penile tumescence—erection during sleep.

Nongonococcal urethritis (nahn-gahn-uh-KAHK-uhl yoor-ee-THRIGHT-uhs)—also known as NGU; an inflammation of the urethra in either gender that results from microorganisms other than the gonococcus germ.

Nonprocreative sex—sexual activity that does not result in producing children.

Nonspecific vaginitis (vaj-uh-NIGHT-uhs)—classification used when all the symptoms of vaginitis are present but no cause can be found. Antibiotics are used as treatment.

Nymphomania (nihm-foh-MAY-nee-uh)—an extremely high need in a female for continuous sexual stimulation.

O

Oedipal (ED-uh-puhl) complex—according to Freudian theory, the male child views his father as a rival for his mother's attention, fears that his father wants to castrate him, and wants to kill his father.

Oligogmenorrhea (ahl-ee-goh-mehn-uh-REE-uh)—unpredictable, irregular menstrual periods.

Operant learning—learning that occurs as the result of the consequences of a behavior. Positive consequences increase the frequency of behavior; negative consequences decrease it.

Oral sex—see *fellatio* and *cunnilingus*.

Oral stage—according to Freud, the first of four psychosexual stages in which sexual pleasure is derived through stimulation of the lips and mouth.

Orgasm (OR-gaz-uhm)—third phase of the sexual response cycle, which is intensely pleasurable and involves a number of physiological changes (such as vasocongestion and myotonia).

Ovary—the primary female sex gland, which produces ova (eggs) and hormones such as estrogens, progesterone, and androgen. There are two ovaries, one on each side of the uterus.

Ovulation (ahv-yoo-LAY-shun)—release of a mature egg from a follicle in an ovary.

Ovum—female reproductive cell; egg.

P

Pap smear—procedure in which surface cells are scraped from the vaginal walls and cervix to detect the presence of cancer.

Paraphilia (pair-uh-FIHL-ee-uh)—heterosexual condition in which the person is dependent on an unusual or unacceptable stimulus for sexual excitement and orgasm.

Participant observation—the collection of data while being involved in the phenomenon being studied.

Pedophilia (peh-doh-FIHL-ee-uh)—term used to describe an adult (usually a man) who seeks contact with young children as a repeatedly preferred or exclusive method of achieving sexual excitement and gratification.

Pelvic examination—an external and internal visual and manual examination whereby the physician evaluates the health of a woman's reproductive organs.

Pelvic inflammatory disease (PID)—infection and inflammation of the uterus and Fallopian tubes.

Penile prosthesis (prahs-THEE-sihz)—penile implant. Inflatable cylinders surgically placed inside the penis and attached to a pumping device placed in the man's scrotum. Used in those cases in which the erectile dysfunction is physiologically based.

Penis (PEE-nihs)—the male sexual organ used for sexual intercourse and urination.

Perimetrium (pair-uh-MEE-tree-uhm)—the external cover of the uterus.

Perineum (pair-uh-NEE-uhm)—the sensitive area of skin between the vaginal opening and the anus.

Petting—any interpersonal physical stimulation that does not include intercourse.

Phallic (FAL-ihk)—according to Freud, the third psychosexual stage in which sexual pleasure is derived primarily from the genitals.

Phenylethylamine (fehn-nihl-EHTH-uhl-meen)—a chemical found in chocolate that is similar to an amphetamine. A person romantically in love is said to have an increased amount of phenylethylamine in the bloodstream.

Pheromones (fear-oh-mohz)—odor signals that attract sex partners.

Pituitary (pih-TOO-uh-tair-ee) gland—known as the "master gland," the pituitary gland is located at the base of the brain and secretes several hormones that stimulate the production of other hormones (such as testosterone, estrogen, progesterone) important in sexual and reproductive functioning.

Plateau phase—second of four stages of the sexual response cycle described by Masters and Johnson. During this phase the outer third of the vagina tightens and the clitoris withdraws behind the clitoral hood in females. In males the diameter of the penis may increase slightly and the size of the testicles may increase considerably. In both genders there is myotonia, hyperventilation, and tachycardia.

Pornography—any photograph, movie, or book designed to arouse or excite a person sexually.

Positive reinforcement—something positive that happens after a behavior has occurred. The result is to increase the frequency of the behavior.

Postmarital intercourse—sexual intercourse by a formerly married person (a divorced person or a widow or widower).

Postovulatory phase—third stage of the menstrual cycle in which the corpus luteum of the ovary secretes hormones (estrogen and progesterone) that prepare the uterus for a fertilized egg to implant.

Premature ejaculation—the male's inability to control the ejaculatory reflex as long as he or his partner wishes.

Premarital intercourse—sexual intercourse before the person is married.

Premenstrual syndrome (PMS)—term referring to the physical and psychological problems a woman experiences from the time of ovulation to the beginning of, and sometimes during, menstruation.

Preorgasm—see *primary orgasmic dysfunction.*

Preovulatory phase—stage of the menstrual cycle that begins with the release of follicle-stimulating hormone (FSH) from the pituitary, which stimulates the growth of a follicle in the ovary.

Prepuce (pree-pyoos)—layer of skin that covers the glans of the penis in males and the clitoris in females.

Primary orgasmic dysfunction—also known as primary anorgasmia or preorgasm; refers to never having had an orgasm.

Primary sex characteristics—biologicial characteristics such as genitalia, gonads, chromosomes, and hormones that differentiate females from males.

Primigravida (pree-mih-GRAV-ih-duh)—a woman who is pregnant for the first time.

Prochoice—proabortion philosophy in which the person supports the right of a woman to choose whether she will have a baby.

Procreation—creating or producing offspring.

Progesterone (proh-JEHS-tuh-rohn)—a hormone produced and released by the corpus luteum of the ovary during the second half of the ovulatory cycle. It is necessary for the preparation of the lining of the uterus for the implantation of the fertilized egg. Progesterone is also produced by the placenta during pregnancy.

Progestin—synthetic progesterone.

Prolife—antiabortion philosophy in which the person supports the right of a fetus to live.

Proliferative (proh-LIHF-er-uh-tihv) phase—see *preovulatory phase.*

Promiscuity (prah-mihs-KYOO-uh-tee)—indiscriminate sexual involvement with a large number of partners.

Pronatalism (proh-NAYT-uhl-ihzm)—social bias that having children is good; social influences designed to encourage procreation.

Prophylactic (proh-fuh-LAK-tihk)—condom.

Prostaglandins (prahs-tuh-GLAN-dihnz)—fatty acids that promote the onset of labor.

Prostate (PRAHS-tayt)—gland that surrounds the male urethra at its exit from the bladder and contributes secretions to the seminal fluid. Some evidence also suggests that some females have a form of prostate gland responsible for their "ejaculation" at orgasm.

Prostatectomy (prahs-tuh-TEK-tuh-mee)—surgical removal of the prostate gland.

Prostatic urethra (prah-STAT-ik yoo-REE-thruh)—that portion of the urethra that passes through the prostate.

Prosthesis (prahs-THEE-sihs)—an artificial substitute for a missing part.

Prostitute—person who performs sexually activity for another in exchange for money.

Pseudohermophrodism (soo-doh-her-MAF-ruh-dight-ihzm)—condition in which an individual has the gonads of one gender and the external genitals of another. See *androgenital* and *testicular feminization syndromes.*

Psychoanalysis—type of therapy developed by Sigmund Freud which assumes that all problems are the result of improper psychosexual development and can be solved only by exploring one's unconscious past.

Puberty (pyoo-ber-tee)—the age at which the testes of the male and the ovaries of the female begin to function and the person becomes capable of reproduction, usually around age 12 or 13. At this time secondary sex characteristics also appear.

Public lice—also known as "the crabs," they are blood suckers that attach themselves to the base of coarse hair.

Pubococcygeal (pyoo-boh-kahk-sih-jee-uhl) muscles—muscles surrounding the outer third of the vaginal barrel.

Pudendum (pyoo-DEHN-duhm)—another term for vulva.

Punishment—a negative experience following a behavior; the result is that the behavior will occur less often.

R

Radical mastectomy (mas-TEHK-toh-mee)—removal of the entire breast, all underlying tissue, and lymph nodes.

Radioimmunoassay (RAY-dee-oh-ih-myoon-oh-AS-ay)—a test whereby the blood of a woman is analyzed to determine if she is pregnant.

Random sample—a sample in which every item in the population being studied has an equal chance of being selected.

Rape—forced sexual relations against a person's will; may include intercourse, oral sex, anal sex, and insertion of an object into the person's vagina or anus.

Rape trauma—acute mental disorientation after rape.

Rational-emotive therapy approach—assumes that people think irrationally and this leads to irrational behavior. By encouraging more rational thinking, depression and anxiety can be minimized.

Realistic love—also known as conjugal love; a type of love that is calm and based on information and interaction with the partner over a number of years. The opposite end of the continuum from romantic love.

Reflex—automatic, unlearned response that occurs without conscious effort.

Refractory (ree-FRAK-tuh-ree) period—a temporary state of not wanting additional stimulation immediately following an orgasmic experience.

Representative sample—see *random sample*.

Resolution phase—the last of four stages of the sexual response cycle described by Masters and Johnson. During this stage the body returns to its preexcitement-orgasm condition.

Retarded ejaculation—see *ejaculatory incompetence*.

Reversion therapy—see *conversion therapy*.

Rhythm—also known as the rhythm method; a procedure whereby the woman has intercourse at times she feels she is least likely to get pregnant. This time is determined by carefully monitering her menstrual cycle.

Rimming—manual or oral stimulation of the anus and surrounding area.

Romantic love—intense emotional feelings for another person that are based on self-constructed illusions about that person. Also known as limerence, romantic love involves drastic mood swings, palpitations of the heart, and intrusive thinking about the partner.

S

Sacred ideology—a religious, spiritual view.

Sadism (SAY-dihsm)—person who becomes sexually aroused and who derives pleasure from inflicting pain on another.

Saline—method of abortion in which the amniotic sac is filled with a saline solution that kills the fetus.

Salpingectomy (sal-pihn-GEHK-toh-mee)—also known as tubal ligation or "tying the tubes;" a sterilization procedure in which a section of the woman's Fallopian tubes are cut out and the ends are tied, clamped, or cauterized so that eggs cannot pass down the Fallopian tubes to be fertilized.

Satyriasis (sat-uh-RIGH-uh-sihs)—an extremely high need in a male for continuous sexual stimulation.

Scabies (SKAY-beez)—condition in which a parasite penetrates the skin and lays eggs. The larvae make tunnels in the skin and cause intense itching.

Scientific ideology—view of sexual phenomena from a scientific, clinical viewpoint.

Scrotum (SCROH-tuhm)—pouch beneath the penis containing the testes.

Secondary anorgasmia—see *secondary orgasmic dysfunction.*

Secondary orgasmic dysfunction—describes a woman who has been orgasmic in the past but is not currently.

Secondary sex characteristics—physical changes that occur during puberty, which include the development of larger breasts in females, the development of different patterns of facial and body hair in females and males, and the development of a deeper voice in males.

Secretory phase—see *postovulatory phase.*

Secular ideology—worldly view of sexual phenomena.

SEICUS—Sec Education and Information Council of the United States; an organization dedicated to improving sex education.

Self-fulfilling prophecy—behaving to make the expectations come true. A person who is expected to engage in a particular behavior (be faithful, be unfaithful) will tend to behave consistyently with those expectations.

Semen (SEE-muhn)—also known as seminal fluid; a thick mixture emitted from the penis during intense sexual arousal, which contains sperm from the testes and fluids from the prostate, seminal vesicles, and Cowper's glands.

Seminal vesicles (SEHM-uh-nl VEHS-ih-klz)—twin glands on either side of the male prostate that secrete fluid into the vas deferens to enhance sperm motility.

Seminiferous tubules (sehm-uh-NINF-er-uhs TOOB-yoolz)—structures in the testes that produce the sperm.

Semen's technique—a technique developed by James Semens for treating premature ejaculation. The male signals his partner to stop stimulation when he feels the urge to ejaculate and signals it is time to resume when the feeling of impending ejaculation goes away.

Sensate focus—sex exercise for couples in which the partners engage in non-genital touching. The goal is to permit the partners an environment to explore their sexual feelings without feeling pressure to perform sexually.

Septate (sehp-tayt) hymen—hymen with two or more openings.

Sex education—the formal and informal learning about the biological, sociological, psychological, and interpersonal aspects of human sexuality.

Sex flush—vasocongestive skin response to increasing sexual tensions.

Sex science—the scientific approach to sex.

Sex steroids— a group name for compounds including sex hormones with estrogenic and androgenic properties.

Sexism—the systematic degradation and domination of women based on the belief that being male is superior to being female.

Sexology—body of knowledge concerned with the differentiation and dimorphism of sex and the erotosexual pair bonding of partners.

Sexosophy—philosophy, principles, and knowledge that people have about their own personally experienced erotosexuality and that of other people, singly and collectively.

Sexual apathy—see *inhibited sexual desire.*

Sexual aversion—extreme negative reaction to sexual activity.

Sexual dysfunction—inability to engage in or enjoy sexual encounters.

Sexual fantasy—erotic thoughts that produce sexual arousal.

Sexual fulfillment—the state of being satisfied with one's sex life and sexual relationships.

Sexual harassment—any act by a person of either gender that involves the use of sex or sexuality of the other to impose restrictions on that person.

Sexual intercourse—insertion of the male penis into the female vagina.

Sexual response cycle—the four stages through which an individual passes when responding to sexual stimulation: excitement, plateau, orgasm, resolution.

Sexual script—shared interpretations and expected behaviors in a social situation. Scripts define situations, name actors, and plot behaviors.

Sexually open relationship—see *swinging*.

Sexually transmitted diseases (STDs)—diseases that are transmitted primarily through sociosexual contact; formerly known as venereal or social diseases.

Shaping—rewarding small approximations to the desired goal.

Simultaneous orgasm—two partners engaging in sexual activity and reaching orgasm at the same time.

Singlehood—state of not being married.

Situationism—decision making on the basis of the context of a particular situation, not on the basis of a prescribed set of laws or codes of action.

Sixty-nine—simultaneous cunnilingus and fellatio.

Skene's glands—small glands located just inside the urethral opening in females, believed to develop from the same embryonic tissue as the male prostate gland and responsible for emitting fluid (in about 10 percent of women) from the urethra during orgasm.

Smegma (SMEHG-muh)—foul-smelling secretions beneath the clitoral hood and the foreskin of the uncircumcised penis.

Social skill training—used in the treatment of sex offenders, this procedure teaches the person how to initiate and maintain socially appropriate relationships as an alternative to the undesirable behavior (such as pedophilia).

Sodomy—anal intercourse between two males.

Sonogram (SAH-nuh-gram)—a live video image of the fetus resulting from an ultrasound scan that is used to position the needle during amniocentesis.

Spectatoring—self-awareness during sexual relations that interferes with sexual response.

Spermicidal (sper-muh-SIGHD-uhl) foam—birth control substance containing chemicals lethal to sperm. When applied around the cervix, sperm are killed before entering the uterus.

Spermicidal gel—sperm-killing substance that is applied to the diaphragm before it is inserted.

Spermatozoa (sper-maht-uh-ZO-uh)—mature sperm cells.

Spirochete (SPIGH-roh-keet)—bacteria that causes syphylis.

Sponge—a soft pliable plastic device containing spermacides that is inserted into the vagina before intercourse to prevent sperm from entering the uterus.

Squeeze technique—used in the treatment of premature ejaculation, the procedure involves squeezing the penis below the coronal ridge just before the male ejaculates so that he will lose his urge to ejaculate.

Sterilization—surgical procedure designed to permanently prevent the capacity of either gender to reproduce.

Straight—see *heterosexual*.

Stuffing technique—procedure whereby the partners literally stuff the penis in the vagina. Used by elderly men who have soft erections and by spinal cord-injured males.

Sublimation—according to Freud, redirection of sexual energy.

Surrogate (SER-oh-gayt) sex partner—also known as a sex therapy practitioner, this person provides sexual experiences with the client that are recommended by the therapist so that the client learns new ways of relating sexually in a controlled environment. Most sexual surrogates are women.

Surrogate mother—a woman who voluntarily agrees to be artificially inseminated, carry a baby to term, and give up the legal right to the baby at birth to a couple or individual desiring such baby.

Survey research—collecting data by interviewing people or giving them a questionnaire.

Swinging—spouses of one marriage or pair-bonded relationship having sexual intercourse with the spouse or partners of another relationship.

Syphilis (SIHF-uh-lihs)—sexually transmitted disease caused by spirochete entering the mucous membranes that line various body openings.

Systematic desensitization—a procedure whereby the person learns to become more relaxed and at ease when in the presence of the stimulus that previously caused anxiety. For the gay person in therapy, it means learning how not to become angry when being called names by homophobic heterosexuals.

T

Tachycardia (tak-ih-KAR-dee-uh)—excessive heart rate or activity.

Test tube fertilization—also known as in vitro fertilization; a procedure in which an egg is removed from a ripe follicle and fertilized by a sperm cell in a culture dish. The fertilized egg is allowed to divide for about two days and then inserted into the woman's uterus where it implants.

Testes (TEHS-teez)—also known as testicles; the male gonads located inside the scrotum, which produce sperm and male hormones (androgen and testosterone).

Testicular (tehs-TIHK-yoo-ler) feminization syndrome—condition in which an individual has the external genitals of a female but the internal organs (testes embedded in abdomen) of a male. TFS is also known as androgen-insensitivity syndrome.

Testosterone (tehs-TAHS-tuh-rohn)—the principal androgen or male sex hormone produced by the testes, which is responsible for the development of male secondary sex characteristics and for the sex drive in both males and females. Testosterone is also produced by the adrenal cortex and the ovaries.

Thermography—a picture showing heat variations in the body.

Tissot—French physician who believed that semen was a vital body fluid and should not be carelessly depleted.

Toxic shock syndrome—condition in which the bacteria *Staphylococcus aureus* produces a poison that is released into the bloodstream. Larger, absorbent tampons are thought to produce a favorable environment for the growth of such bacteria.

Transition prephrase—the first of two prephases to the sexual response cycle, during which the individual makes the transition from a nonsexual to a sexual physiologic state.

Transsexual (trans-SEHK-shoo-uhl)—an individual who has the external genitals of one gender, the self-concept of the other gender, and the desire to have his or her genitals altered to fit the gender of the self-concept.

Transvestite (trans-VEHS-tight)—a person of one gender who dresses in the clothing of the opposite gender for sexual pleasure and emotional gratification. Transvestites are usually male heterosexuals who do not desire sex reassignment as a female.

Trichomoniasis (trihk-oh-moh-NIGH-uh-sihs)—vaginal infection that results in vulvar burning and itching; usually, but not always, sexually transmitted.

Turner's syndrome—condition in which a female has only one sex chromosome (XO) rather than two (XX). The result is abnormal development of the ovaries, failure to menstruate, and infertility.

U

Ultrasound scan—procedure whereby sound waves are used to project an image on a video screen to help the physician identify where to place the needle during amniocentesis.

Urethra (yoo-REE-thruh)—in females, a short tube connecting the bladder to the urethral opening; in males, the tube connecting the bladder to the end of the penis where urine is discharged.

Urethral (yoo-REE-thuhl) opening—opening to the female urethra located below the clitoris and above the vaginal opening.

Urethritis (yoor-ih-THRIGHT-uhs)—inflammation of the urethra and bladder in males.

Urologist—a physician who specializes in diseases of the urinary and reproductive systems of the body.

Uterus (YOOT-uh-ruhs)—pear-shaped, hollow organ in which the fertilized egg implants and develops into a fetus.

V

Vacuum currettage (kyoor-uh-TAHJ)—abortion method whereby a hollow plastic rod is inserted into the woman's uterus to suck out the embryo and placenta.

Vagina (vuh-JIGH-nuh)—elastic canal from the cervix to the vulva. Provides a place for the penis during intercourse and serves as a passageway for the fetus at birth.

Vaginal lip stimulation—method of stimulating the penis and vulva by rubbing the penis up and down the vaginal lips of the female.

Vaginal opening—see *introitus*.

Vaginal orgasm—an orgasm that results from intercourse without direct clitoral stimulation.

Vaginismus (vaj-uh-NIHZ-muhs)—involuntary, spasmodic contraction of the vaginal muscles making penetration during sexual intercourse difficult or impossible.

Vaginitis (vaj-uh-NIGHT-uhs)—bacterial infection of the vagina.

Vas deferens (vas DEF-uh-renz)—ducts in the male which carry sperm from the epididymes to the ejaculatory duct.

Vasectomy (vas-EHK-toh-mee)—minor surgical procedure whereby the vas deferens are cut so as to prevent sperm from entering the penis; the primary method of male sterilization.

Vasocongestion (vays-oh-kahn-JEHS-chuhn)—congestion of the blood vessels; a primary physiologic response to sexual stimulation.

Venereal disease—see *sexually transmitted diseases*.

Vestibular bulbs—muscles located beneath the bulbocavernosus muscles on both sides of the vaginal opening that help to grip the penis.

Vestibule—the area between the labia minora that includes the urethral and vaginal openings.

Vibrator—a device that produces pleasurable sensations (and often an orgasm) when placed in the clitoral region of the female and on the glans of the male.

Voyeurism (vwah-YUHR-ihzm)—state in which the person (usually a man) becomes sexually excited and derives sexual pleasure from watching unsuspecting people who are naked, undressing, or engaging in sexual activity.

Vulva (VUHL-vuh)—the external genital region of the female.

W

Wolffian (WUHL-fee-uhn) ducts—the duct system in the male embryo that later develops in the epididymes, vas deferens, ejaculatory ducts, and urethra in the adult male.

Womb—see *uterus*.

X

X Chromosome—the sex chromosome that produces a female baby.

Xeroradiography (zihr-oh-ray-dee-AHG-ruh-fee)—an X-ray examination in which the results are recorded in the form of a picture on paper.

Y

Y Chromosome—the sex chromosome that produces a male baby.

Z

Zygote (ZIGH-goht)—a fertilized egg resulting from the union of a sperm and an egg. Represents the first cell in the development of a human being.

Appendix C

Sexual Autobiography Outline

To further explore your sexuality, you might consider developing a sexual autobiography with particular emphasis on your feelings about your experiences. The outline below may help to organize your thinking, but your essay need not be limited to it. If some of the items are not part of your experience, you might examine why you have not engaged in this behavior and what feelings the mention of this activity generates in you.

I. Earliest Sex Education
   A. First information about intercourse, pregnancy, etc.
   B. False information: type and source.
   C. First experimentation
      1. Solitary
      2. With playmate ("doctor", "show and tell", etc.)

II. Masturbation
   A. Age
   B. How learned? Who taught?
   C. Feelings then? Feelings now?
   D. Current frequency
   E. Techniques: where, when, how?
   F. Aids, fantasies

III. Sex Dreams
   A. Reaction to first
   B. Current frequency
   C. Dream content

IV. Heterosexuality
   A. Preadolescent sex play
   B. Semisexual games ("spin the bottle," etc.)
   C. First "sexual" experience (self-defined); Emotional reaction to first experience
   D. First intercourse
      1. Age, circumstances
      2. Emotional reaction to first intercourse

*Reprinted with the permission of Richard Hartley, 1983.

3. Any problems?
4. How soon repeated? Same person? Different person?

E. Current heterosexuality (past year or so)
1. How active? How many partners?
2. Preferred activities in necking, petting, or foreplay
3. How do you feel about the status of your current sex life?

F. Oral–genital sex experience and feelings
1. As giver
2. As receiver

V. Homosexual experiences

A. During childhood
B. Preadolescent and early adolescent
C. Current
D. Fantasies and temptations

VI. Traumatic sexual experiences

A. Molestation, indecent exposure
B. Rape or near rape
C. Relationship, if any, to offender
D. Discovered by parents in sexual activity?

VII. Describe your erotic response, if any, to such phenomena as sights, sounds, smells, fantasies, alcohol, marijuana, X-rated or R-rated films

VIII. Describe your favorite sexual fantasy

IX. What was your most unusual sexual experience? How did you feel about it then? Now?

Appendix D

Resources and Organizations

Abortion

Pro Choice

National Abortion Rights Action
League
1424 K St., N.W.
Washington, DC 20005

Pro Life

National Right to Life
Committee
419 7th St., N.W.
Washington, DC 20045

Birth Alternatives

American Society for
Psychoprophylaxis in
Obstetrics
1523 L St., N.W.
Washington, DC 20005

Nurse-Midwives
American College of Nurse-
Midwives
1522 K St., N.W. Suite 1120
Washington, DC 20005

Breastfeeding

LaLeche International, Inc.
9616 Minneapolis Ave.
Franklin Park, IL 60123

Cancer

American Cancer Society
777 Third Ave.
New York, NY 10017

Disability

Sex and Disability Unit
Human Sexuality Program
University of California
814 Mission St., 2nd Floor
San Francisco, CA 94103

Family Planning

Planned Parenthood
1220 19th St., N.W.
Washington, DC 20036

Zero Population Growth
1346 Connecticut Ave., N.W.
Washington, DC 20036

Fertility

American Fertility Foundation
1608 13th Ave., S.
Suite 101
Birmingham, AL 35205

Genetic Counseling

National Genetics Foundation
555 W. 57th St.
New York, NY 10019

Journals

Journal of Sex Research
P.O. Box 29795
Philadelphia, PA 19117

Archives of Sexual Behavior
Plenum Publishing Corp.
233 Spring St.
New York, NY 10013

Journal of Sex Education and
    Therapy
American Association of Sex
    Educators, Counselors, and
    Therapists
2000 N. St., NW, Suite 110
Washington, D.C. 20036

Journal of Sex and Marital
    Therapy
Brunner/Mazel Inc.
19 Union Square West
New York, NY 10003

Journal of Social Work and Human
    Sexuality
Haworth Press
28 East 22nd St.
New York, NY 10010

Sexuality and Disability
Human Sciences Press
72 Fifth Ave.
New York, NY 10011

Journal of Homosexuality
Haworth Press
28 East 22nd St.
New York, NY 10010

Medical Aspects of Human
    Sexuality
Hospital Publications, Inc.
360 Lexington Avenue
New York, NY 10017

Sexuality and Disability
Human Sciences Press
72 Fifth Ave.
New York, NY 10011

Journals (continued)

Family Relations
National Council on Family
    Relations
1219 University Ave., SE
Minneapolis, MN 55414

Journal of Marriage and the Family
National Council on Family
    Relations
1219 University Ave., SE
Minneapolis, MN 55414

Alternative Lifestyles
Human Sciences Press
72 Fifth Ave.
New York, NY 10011

Sexuality Today
published weekly at ATCOM, Inc.
2315 Broadway
New York, NY 10024

SEICUS Report
published bimonthly by Sex
    Information and Education
    Council of the U.S.
80 Fifth Ave., Suite 801
New York, NY 10011

Emphasis Subscriber Service
Planned Parenthood Federation of
    America, Inc.
810 Seventh Ave.
New York, NY 10019

Moral Majority

Moral Majority, Inc.
Jerry Falwell
Thomas Road Baptist Church
305 6th St.
Lynchburg, VA 24502

Rape

National Rape Information
    Clearing House

Rape (continued)

National Center for Prevention
and Control of Rape
5600 Fishers Land
Rockville, MD 20857

Relationship Counseling

American Association for Marriage
and Family Therapy
1717 K St., N.W.
Suite 407
Washington, DC 20006

Sex Education

Sex Information and Education
Council of the United States
(SIECUS)
80 Fifth Ave.
New York, NY 10011

Sex Research

Institute for Sex Research, Inc.
Room 416, Morrison Hall
Indiana University
Bloomington, IN 47401

Society for the Scientific Study of
Sex
P.O. Box 29795
Philadelphia, PA 19117

Sexual Life Styles

National Gay Task Force
80 Fifth Ave., Suit 1601
New York, NY 10011

Parents and Friends of Gays and
Lesbians
P.O. Box 24565
Los Angeles, CA 90025

or

5715 16th St., N.W.
Washington, DC 20011

Sexual Life Styles (continued)

Tri-Ess Sorority
P.O. Box 2055
Des Plaines, IL 60018

Sexaholics Anonymous
P.O. Box 300
Simi Valley, CA 93062

Sex Selection

Gametrics Limited
180 Harbor Dr.
Sausalito, CA 94965

Sexual Aids

Adam and Eve
One Apple Court
Box 800
Carrboro, NC 27510

Eve's Garden
104 Greene St.
New York, NY 10012

Sexual Equality

National Organization for
Women
425 13th St., N.W.
Washington, DC 20004

Sexual Harassment

Working Women's Institute
593 Park Ave.
New York, NY 10021

Sexual Health

National Premenstrual Syndrome
Society
P.O. Box 11467
Durham, NC 27703

Sexual Therapy

American Association of Sex
Educators, Counselors, and
Therapists (AASECT)

Sexual Therapy (continued)

11 Dupont Circle, Suite 220
Washington, DC 20036

Center for Marital and Sexual
    Studies
5199 East Pacific Coast Hy.
Long Beach, CA 90804

Masters and Johnson Institute
24 South Kings Highway
St. Louis, MO 63108

Loyola Sexual Dysfunction Clinic
Loyola University Hospital
2160 S. lst Ave.
Maywood, IL 60153

Society for Sex Therapy
c/o Barry McCarthy, Ph.D.
Department of Psychology
The American University
Washington, DC 20016

Sexually Transmitted Diseases

American Social Health
    Association
260 Sheridan Rd.
Palo Alto, CA 94306

Center for Disease Control
Technical Information Services
Bureau of State Services
Atlanta, GA 30333

Herpes Resource Information
Box 100
Palo Alto, CA 94302

National VD Hotline
1–800–227–8922
(in California: 1–800–982–5883)

National AIDS Hotline
1–800–342–2437

Single Parenthood

Parents Without Partners
7910 Woodmont Ave.
Washington, DC 20014

Single Mothers by Choice
501 12th St.
Brooklyn, NY 11215

Sterilization

Asssociation for Voluntary
    Sterilization, Inc.
708 Third Ave.
New York, NY 10164

Surrogate Parenting

Surrogate Parenting Associates,
    Inc.
Suite 222, Doctor's Office
    Building
250 E. Liberty St.
Louisville, KY 40205

Test-tube Fertilization

Eastern Virginia Medical School
Norfolk General Hospital
The Howard and Georgeanna
    Jones Institute for
    Reproductive Medicine
304 Medical Tower
Norfolk, VA 23507

Transsexual Counseling

The Janus Information Facility
c/o Paul A. Walker
1952 Union St.
San Francisco, CA 94123

CONFIDE
Personal Counseling Services, Inc.
Box 56
Tappan, NY 10983

Index